Aspects of the Third Reich

EDITED BY
H. W. KOCH

M

MACMILLAN

First published 1985

Published by
Higher and Further Education Division
MACMILLAN PUBLISHERS LTD
Houndmills, Basingstoke, Hampshire
RG21 2XS
and London
Companies and representatives
throughout the world

Typeset by
Wessex Typesetters Ltd
Frome, Somerset

Printed in Hong Kong

British Library Cataloguing in Publication Data
Aspects of the Third Reich.
1. Germany—History—1933–1945
I. Koch, H. W.
943.086   DD256.5
ISBN 0–333–35272–6
ISBN 0–333–35273–4 Pbk

Contents

Preface

This volume of essays on the Third Reich does not claim to cover it in anything like its entirety. As the title says only certain 'Aspects' have been selected which stand and will continue to stand for decades in the centre of historical debate.

The individual contributions are placed within the brackets, so to speak, of the contributions by Ernst Nolte at the beginning and Thomas Nipperdey at the end. Within these brackets five main areas are covered: first, the assumption and early consolidation of Hitler's power as well as the emerging conservative opposition. Secondly, aspects of National Socialist (NS) Germany's foreign policy. Thirdly, economic policy with regard to foreign trade with south-eastern Europe, German rearmament and German economic policy during the Second World War. Fourthly, the subject of genocide will be re-examined and in connection with it Himmler's *SS* empire. The fifth and final part deals with the problem of examining the Third Reich by concentrating on Hitler himself.

Instead of a general introduction the editor has preferred to write for each section a linking commentary in which not only is the reader's attention drawn to further literature on the subject, but also, wherever necessary, points raised in the individual essays are further amplified or additional debatable points discussed. Thus it is hoped an element of continuity will be given to the volume.

My thanks are obviously due to the contributors who have made their essays available for reprinting in this volume or who have written original contributions specifically for it. I am also indebted to Harvard University Press for permission to reprint excerpts from Burton H. Klein's *Germany's Economic Preparations for War*.

Last, but by no means least, I must express my gratitude to my colleague W. J. D. Trythall whose critical comments on the linking commentary were extremely valuable as were his suggestions for stylistic improvements. However, the responsibility for their content is my own as is the selection of the individual essays from a virtually countless multitude on the subject. Within this volume there are unavoidable gaps, but if they did not exist this book would be a history of the Third Reich and not a consideration of certain of its aspects.

H. W. KOCH
Spring 1985

PART I

Introduction

Although there are many volumes on 'theories of Fascism' and comparative analyses of Italian Fascism and German National Socialism, the term 'Fascism' has become a synonym covering both; an undefined slogan bandied about in day-to-day politics, and also undefined by many historians. With such usage scholarly discussion unwittingly follows a Comintern ruling of the late 1920s endeavouring to eliminate the use of Socialism in any other but a purely Communist context. Thus members of Social Democratic parties became *Sozialfaschisten* and the National Socialists *Radikalfaschisten*, both in essence the tools of the international forces of reaction, capitalism and imperialism.

It is not the task of this volume to provide yet another comparative analysis since it is concerned only with Hitler's Third Reich. Hence a few marginal remarks on the meaning of Fascism must suffice. As early as 1921 Mussolini was claiming a universalist role for Fascism with the aim of uniting Europe, failing which Europe as a power would be relegated to the second rank while the 'axis of world history' would shift beyond the Atlantic to the United States. He elaborated on this idea well into the 1930s. For these sentiments Mussolini found receptive ears, especially among the intelligentsia of the 'homeless right' in Europe who lived in fear of Europe's becoming ultimately the battleground of the superpowers such as the United States and nascent Asiatic Bolshevik Russia. Indeed, if we follow the development of Fascist movements in western and northern Europe we find that their early example and model is Fascist Italy rather than National Socialist Germany. In many sectors, especially the creative arts, Fascist Italy was certainly more open than Hitler's Germany. The 'Futurist' school of painting flourished, while in Germany it was dismissed and forbidden as 'degenerate art', *entartete Kunst*, a phrase coined not by the National Socialists, but by the early Zionist Max Nordau.

Bt comparison German National Socialism was the progeny of defeat, political instability and economic misery. Anti-semitism was to become the only internationalist aspect of its ideology, from which Italian Fascism was free until 1938. National Socialism was saddled with the inferiority complex brought about by defeat and lacked a truly European dimension until late in the Second World War. Not without misgivings on Hitler's part, such a dimension emerged only with the beginning of the 'Crusade against Bolshevism', though it culminated by the end of 1944 in almost a quarter of a million western and northern Europeans fighting in the ranks of the *Waffen-SS* against the Russians. However, this does not indicate a change of heart on Hitler's part, for in common with his opponents he looked at this volunteer movement with disdain, suspicion and even contempt. It is a bitter irony that in the last days of April 1945 the Reich chancellory in Berlin, and with it Hitler's bunker, were defended by a mixed bunch of Frenchmen, Spaniards and Scandinavians, that the last successful counter-attack in Berlin was carried out by a French contingent of the 'Charlemagne' division across Berlin's *Belle Alliance Platz* (the German name for Waterloo), and that the last Knight's Cross to be awarded in Berlin went to a Frenchman.

Between 1933 and 1945 the turning of Fascist movements to Germany was entirely the result of the apparent stability Hitler achieved within Germany, and, even more, of his successes in foreign policy and ultimately his military successes. Victory in the West was regarded by many members of the defeated nations not only as a defeat on the battlefield, but as the collapse of the rotten and corrupt structure of their respective societies. In the summer months of 1940 it was in Hitler's power to impose a 'New Order' on most of Europe, but in Germany there was neither a concept of such a new order nor any planning for one. The relationship was simply one between victors and vanquished. Laval's admonition that 'you want to win the war in order to create Europe – you have to create Europe to win the war' was ignored by Hitler. His philosophy was not that of a European, but of a radical German nationalist. In 1944 the French writer and collaborator with the Germans, Pierre Drieu la Rochelle, drew up a frank balance sheet:

1. There should have been no infringement of the autonomy of the conquered European peoples. Annexations and levies should have been avoided.
2. Peace treaties should have been concluded with the nations defeated, freeing their prisoners of war and providing for the elimination of customs barriers, followed by the establishment of a European customs union.
3. If the governments of the occupied countries had opposed a policy of European understanding, referenda and elections should have been conducted to create a European parliament and to prepare the Europeanisation of strategically important territories. This internationalisation should have included the Baltic straits, the harbours of northern Norway and Finland, the Calais–Boulogne–St. Omer triangle and the Channel Islands.
4. The German army should have been restructured into a European army and the *Waffen-SS* should have become the core and meeting point of European youth.
5. In all European countries Fascist unity parties should have been created whose task it would have been to proclaim in Brussels or Strasbourg a Fascist International.
6. The European political measures should then have been secured by far-reaching social reforms.

A year before, Drieu had already conceded the point that 'the French who looked for support in Germany were ill-advised'; or, as one former member of the French *Waffen-SS* was to put it years later, 'We have sacrificed nationalism for a united socialist Europe. Confronted by Germany's silence and the intentional obscurity in which Hitler shrouded his phrases we did not sense that we contributed to a new nationalist hegemony'.

Hitler deliberately refrained from making any commitments to his collaborators, let alone concluding peace treaties until 'final victory' occurred; then, that peace was to be a German, not a European one. Indeed, National Socialism was not, to use Hitler's phrase, 'an article for export'. From late 1943 onwards Mussolini's Fascism rediscovered its 'Europeanism', but at a time when the Duce and his regime existed merely by Hitler's grace; this fact and the change in the fortunes of war meant that Italian Fascism could no longer exercise the influence it possessed in the 1920s and early 1930s. To all intents and purposes Italian Fascism was dead while German National Socialism struggled on to its final defeat.

Hence this volume concentrates on German National Socialism rather than on the ambivalent term 'Fascism'. Much of the discussion on NS Germany has been and still is overshadowed by an excessively personalised biographical approach, notably in the two outstanding Hitler biographies by Alan Bullock and Joachim Fest. A structural analysis of the Third Reich has made headway only during the last decade and a half, but not as yet with sufficient impact to gain access into general textbooks. To a large extent this is the fault of some of the historians themselves, among whom little consensus exists on issues such as the social composition of the Nationalsozialistische Deutsche Arbeiterpartei (NSDAP) and on 'who voted for Hitler?' For example a study by Michael Kater on the social composition of the early NSDAP points to its being essentially petit bourgeois in character with few workers in its ranks. He arrives at this conclusion by counting as workers only unskilled labourers, while skilled workers are defined as lower middle class. Much the same crude approach is applied in Kater's *The Nazi Party. A Social Profile of Members and Leaders, 1919–1945* where his definition of 'elite' includes the entrepreneur, the *Unternehmer*, an activity which could include almost anything. Certainly, for example, a rag and bone merchant would have described himself as an *Unternehmer*, though he would hardly have been a member of the elite. The American historian Max Kele on the other hand has convincingly demonstrated that National Socialism held a not inconsiderable appeal for the German workers. By 1933 approximately one-third of the members of the NSDAP were workers and the same applies to those who voted for Hitler. In the 1932 elections as well as that of March 1933 one-third of the NSDAP vote came from workers. H. A. Winkler, too, sees the electoral support of the NSDAP coming primarily from the lower middle class, a result strongly qualified by the recent empirical findings by R. F. Hamilton which demonstrate that strong NSDAP support came equally from upper-class urbanised centres. However, what most of these class-based studies tend to ignore is that the very strength of National Socialism was its theoretical imprecision which, for a time at least, allowed it to be all things to all men, a 'collective basin' which contained all sorts of groups, even those with mutually exclusive aims. A class-based, or more specifically, a Marxist approach to National Socialism is bound to produce a distorted picture. T. W. Mason's assertion that the Third Reich was marked by the continuance of working-class struggle is contradicted by many of the documents which he has appended to his study. The idea of the *Volksgemeinschaft*, the classless national community, did exercise a wide general appeal, so much so that even the conspirators against Hitler who were responsible for the bomb plot of 20 July 1944 thought they could not do without it. Indeed if one reads their plans carefully, it emerges that they envisaged a National Socialist state minus Hitler and his satraps.

Another issue which tends to confuse the debate is the question of what National Socialism promised in the social sphere and what it actually achieved. It seems an artificial question because in spite of the vast transformations which took place on the international and the domestic scene, the Third Reich lasted little more than twelve years, half of which were wartime. This short time-span appears to make any comparisons between claims and reality unreal. Another closely associated issue is whether National Socialism was a force for the modernisation of German society, or whether it was anti-modern; whether it was an ideology based on an agrarian 'blood-and-soil' anti-industrial movement, or one favouring industrialism and the society associated with it. Again the dichotomy between the two appears purely artificial. Assuming that Hitler could have realised his aims, there was room for both: for the one in the need to conquer additional living space, for the other in the forces needed for opening it up. Hitler's interest in technical and industrial developments, ranging from autobahns to the technical intricacies of armaments, is amply documented, as is his insistence on careers that were open to all talents, providing they were German or 'Germanic'. Even Himmler, notorious, among other things, for his romantic notions of the peasant-soldier, had to yield to those intellectuals within his own *SS* empire who were making a late bid for the *SS* to take over the German economy. On the whole, the forces favouring industrialisation seem to have carried the day; whether intentionally or not, the traditional elites had been destroyed by the end of the Third Reich and the way to modernity was not only open but had already been entered, albeit at a terrifying cost. In the light of this is the history of the Third Reich in need of revision?

Ernst Nolte poses this question by placing National Socialism firmly in its general historical context and in that of the industrial revolution in particular, showing that with the onset of class conflict the notion of physically annihilating one's opponents did have some quite 'respectable' antecedents, even among the early socialists in Europe. Nolte argues that this concept has a more or less rational character. Yet the question may be raised here whether, given Hitler's racial and biopolitical beliefs, his actions were not terrifyingly logical and consistent. Or is mass murder, to call it by its proper name, more or less rational in the name of an economic determinism than when committed in the name of a biological determinism? According to the most recent biography of Stalin by Anton Antonov-Ovseenko – himself the son of one of Lenin's closest associates and living in Russia – the commissions called into being by Khrushchev during the thaw to investigate Stalin's crimes emerged with the staggering total of 41 million Russians killed during the Stalin era, not counting Russian losses during the Second World War. True enough, the schemes of the early propagators of mass murder remained on paper; it was left to Lenin and Stalin on the one hand, to Hitler on the other, to transform theory into practice.

Nolte's contribution, in placing the fact of extermination at the centre of his analysis, raises the problem to which the German historian Hans Buchheim had already drawn attention just under twenty years ago. To those for whom Hitler was the inevitable product of the German historical process, it may appear logical that once he had come to power genocide was inevitable. Yet, as will be seen in another section below, the road to Auschwitz was a very twisted one; the 'inevitability' argument represents a short-circuit in the historian's thinking, because it tempts him to neglect the detailed study of viable alternatives. As Buchheim puts it: 'All in all one must unfortunately note that with increasing distance from the Third Reich, the picture of it becomes not more faithful, but rather more distorted'. A speculative view is rampant 'which uses history only as the material from which to demonstrate a principle'.

According to Buchheim a speculative trend of thought dominates the writing of German contemporary history. Among the older generation, in so far as it concerns itself with the Third Reich at all, an unreflective attitude dominates, determined mainly by personal experience. In contrast, among the younger generation, the speculative trend dominates and they 'consider any differentiating view as apologetic and immoral, because within their conceptions the morality of judgment increases in the measure with which all aspects of a problem are concentrated upon one aspect alone'. That aspect is genocide, which throws its broad shadow over the interpretation of German history as far back as the Bismarckian empire.

The first of the editor's two essays examines the legality of Hitler's assumption of power and affirms it, emphasising moreover that none of the German parliamentarians could have been in any doubt as to what would happen to German democracy and to German political parties once he obtained power. In contrast to his public statements on German foreign policy or the Jewish question, at no time

did Hitler, even in court, take refuge in ambiguity or veil
his aims, but categorically stated what he would do, even
prior to the March election of 1933. The assertion that he
'was jobbed into office by a backstairs intrigue' (Alan
Bullock) is simply untenable, ignoring the constitutional
process and reality of the Weimar Republic. But Hitler's
entente – not alliance – with the conservatives and the
army took on a different complexion once he was in power.
Even then, as Hans Mommsen brilliantly demonstrates, the
legislation that followed the Reichstag fire shows the degree
of unpreparedness and improvisation on the part of Hitler
and his associates, quite unlike a coup prepared in advance.
The first part of Mommsen's essay has been omitted since it
deals exclusively with the Reichstag fire and the controversy
surrounding it, which is easily accessible to any reader.

The events leading up to the 'Röhm purge' of 30 June
1934 need further investigation. In view of Röhm's ambitions
in the military sphere, Hitler came under considerable
pressure from the army on the one hand and from his
stormtroopers on the other, the latter considering themselves
the force that had actually secured Hitler's victory but had
then been left empty-handed, in contrast to the leaders of
the NSDAP or the conservatives who represented the
majority in cabinet. In the view of many of the Stormtroopers
(*SA*) Hitler had sold out to these groups. Hitler made
numerous attempts to contain the unrest and to conciliate,
but there is incontrovertible evidence that the army
leadership under General von Blomberg and his *chef de
cabinet*, the then Colonel von Reichenau, deliberately
escalated the conflict to eliminate the threat from the *SA*
once and for all. In so doing they, and particularly
Reichenau, did not shrink from manufacturing alarming
news and submitting it regularly to Hitler. Even among the
army district commanders doubts arose. When one such
commander, together with a local *SA* commander, visited
Reichenau late in June 1934, they said it seemed as though
some unknown third force was setting the army and *SA*
against one another. Reichenau placidly replied that that
might well be so, but now it was too late anyway. The news
which caused Hitler to fly to Munich stemmed from a

misunderstanding. Röhm had agreed with the local *Reichswehr* commander in Munich to surrender his arms to the *Landespolizei*. *SA* formations armed specifically to fulfil that agreement did not escape the notice of the *SS* security service, the *Sicherheitsdienst* (*SD*), which reported to Berlin, and Berlin to Hitler. The *SD* knew nothing of the local agreement and nor did Hitler, hence his conviction that he was facing an armed rebellion seems genuine enough. Though *SS* units carried out the executions, they were equipped and transported by the *Reichswehr*, and army units were at full alert just in case Hitler could not handle the situation. In Berlin Göring and Himmler, *together* with Blomberg and Reichenau, decided upon the liquidations. When they met in Berlin it took the combined pressure of Göring and Himmler to persuade a very reluctant Hitler to have Röhm shot.

The *Reichswehr* seemed to have won the day. Its position as the second pillar, next to the NSDAP, of the German state appeared to have been further consolidated. To maintain its monopoly of arms and in order to increase its influence in the political decision-making process the *Reichswehr* leadership had already made very important concessions to Hitler and the NSDAP, such as the application of the 'Aryan paragraph', which excluded certain categories of Jews from holding public office, in the main civil servants, within the *Reichswehr* and the adoption of NS symbols on uniforms and flags, concessions made by Blomberg and Reichenau without their actually having been demanded by Hitler and the NSDAP. Little more than a month after the 'Röhm-purge' the Reich President von Hindenburg died. By unanimous cabinet decision the offices of the chancellor and the president were combined. Again on Blomberg's and Reichenau's initiative and not as the result of a demand made by Hitler, Germany's armed forces were sworn in personally by Hitler. To Blomberg, romantically inclined as he was, the relationship between the head of state and the armed forces seemed to have been re-established as in the days of the Kaiser.

In assessing the 'Röhm-purge', a few thoughtful people apart, the consensus in Germany as well as among foreign diplomats appears to have been that while it was an ugly business, on the other hand the 'radical forces' seemed to have been eliminated. The way was now open for the 'moderate Hitler'. Few if any took note of the precedent set by Hitler in justifying the murders before the Reichstag. He claimed for himself in this emergency situation the role of the supreme judge in Germany, a function he was formally to usurp eight years later, on 26 April 1942.

After Hindenburg's death the *Führer* cult could really begin and did so successfully almost to the end of the Third Reich. However much they might deplore the behaviour of some of the NS functionaries, the bulk of the population accepted Hitler and 'If only the *Führer* knew' became a well-worn phrase. Hitler was not only the *Führer*, he also acted as the major integrating factor in NS Germany, a theme which Lothar Kettenacker explores, along with the way this role was instrumentalised by NS propaganda. In common with many other historians, Kettenacker sees Hitler primarily as the product and the reflection of the collective mentality of the German petit bourgeoisie. However, at least since Speer's memoirs, quite apart from other empirical studies already mentioned, it is known that he appealed just as much to the haute bourgeoisie. By narrowing down Hitler's appeal as well as his tastes exclusively to the lower middle class we run the risk of ignoring the other sectors of German society. Hitler's taste for the adventure stories of Karl May was shared by Germans of all social classes and still is – even in East Germany! If we consider personalities such as Friedrich Naumann and his personal assistant, Theodor Heuss, the first President of the Federal Republic, and their pre-1914 involvement in attempting to create a *Volksgemeinschaft*, and also the historian Friedrich Meinecke, it may be too simple to reduce this concept to a product of the lower middle-class mentality. This also applies to the firmly held belief in the stab-in-the-back-legend after 1918. Hitler's chief of the general staff until 1938 and later his opponent, Col. General Ludwig Beck, wrote on 28 November 1918: 'In the most difficult moment of the war – and about this I do not have a moment's doubt – revolution, prepared long in advance, fell on us from behind', Where does this place Beck on the social scale? It was a sentiment shared by many if not most Germans irrespective of class. It was not only the lower middle class that felt the deep emotional impact of the Nuremberg party rallies; they left their imprint equally strongly even upon foreign ambassadors as is documented by their memoirs, for example, those of Nevile Henderson and André François-Poncet.

Certainly, Hitler's taste in painting was very conventional, but explicable as a reaction to much of what masqueraded as art in the Weimar Republic, about which Ernst Nolte has already made some pertinent remarks in his essay. However, in architecture, in so far as Hitler's plans were realised, he differed very little in his preference for the gigantic from predominant tastes in the USA and the USSR, a valid point already made by Speer. However, this does not alter the fact that the cult of the *Führer* fell on the fertile soil of a nation deeply insulted and humiliated after 1918. Even as level-headed a man as Chancellor Heinrich Brüning condemned the Young Plan of 1928 as a 'Diktat'. As for the middle class, it was the sector of German society most severely hit by inflation, which completely eroded its economic base from 1916 to 1923. In the light of events as they unfolded between 1919 and 1933 the middle class was *perhaps* most prone to see Hitler not merely as the *Führer* but also as the saviour of the German nation. Goebbels required only a small effort to elicit the required tune from chords already well prepared.

Lothar Kettenacker is the first of the contributors to this volume to make use of Hermann Rauschning's *Hitler Speaks* (*Gespräche mit Hitler*), a source about whose original value some other historians have already expressed reservations. Ernst Nolte, for instance, once remarked that in no document, neither in *Mein Kampf* nor in his speeches nor in his table talk was Hitler as literate as in Rauschning's conversations with him. In 1983 the Swiss historian Wolfgang Hänel in a piece of highly detailed research concluded that Rauschning's work was a collaboration with a British and French journalists, backed by an American publishing house in 1939. Rauschning, by then a poor émigré in Paris, got to work and by using his own *The*

Revolution of Nihilism plus ample quotations from Ernst Jünger as well as from Nietzsche turned this amalgam into Hitler's own words. Rauschning met Hitler on five occasions at most, and then always in the company of others.

In the final essay in this section Klaus-Jürgen Müller discusses the opposition that emerged against Hitler from conservative sources which had been part of the 'entente' of 1933. Müller argues that only with their aid could Hitler achieve power, but the converse is equally true: only with the mass base which Hitler commanded in membership and voting terms could they hope to exercise power again, or for that matter retain it. In contrast to the hagiography, produced not only by German historians, Müller subjects the conservative opposition to close scrutiny and concludes that in most cases they did not disagree with Hitler over ends in the realm of foreign policy but over means. They all shared the conviction that Germany would have to regain its great power status, that Czechoslovakia would have to be eliminated or at least neutralised, that Danzig and the Polish corridor would have to return to Germany and that Germany would have to build up a colonial empire.

Indeed, the head of the civilian section of the opposition, the former Lord Mayor of Leipzig, Carl Goerdeler, raised demands on his first visit to Britain in 1937 which even Hitler had not raised at that time. When Hitler began to move against Czechoslovakia, he encountered the opposition of Beck who was convinced that this would embroil Germany in a war with the western powers for which the German forces were not sufficiently armed. Beck resigned over this issue but, unfortunately, Hitler was to be proved right yet again, as he had been over the public renunciation of the military clauses of the Versailles treaty in 1935, the reoccupation of the demilitarised zone of the Rhineland a year later and the *Anschluss* of Austria in March 1938. The opposition within the German foreign office centred on Ribbentrop's secretary of state, von Weizsäcker, who wanted colonies and a free hand in the East. This seems to accord with Hitler's aims, except that Hitler wanted the former as a bargaining counter to obtain the latter, that is, a free hand in the East and British toleration. However, Ribbentrop was more realistic than his secretary of state. In his final report on his period as ambassador in London he assessed British attitudes more accurately, in that he stated to Hitler that Britain would oppose, if necessary by force, any German attempt to make a drastic revision of the status quo in eastern central Europe.

Given the problem of space in a volume such as this, Müller could not carry his analysis beyond 1940. However, anyone examining the genesis of the bomb plot of 1944 can only reach the depressing conclusion that for most participants it had nothing to do with a 'rising of conscience' but rather more with the fact that Germany was losing the war. Where was the conscience of Generals Hoepner and Heinrich von Stülpnagel when, in 1941, well beyond the call of their duties, they collaborated with the *SD* extermination squads? Where was the conscience of *SS-Gruppenführer* Arthur Nebe, who as head of an *Einsatzgruppe* had already liquidated 40,000 Jews? And of all the *Einsatzgruppen* leaders in the East, Nebe was the only one who had volunteered for this task. His colleague Ohlendorf, in contrast, had refused twice, until ordered to take charge of such a group. Even according to the evidence of his brother, the two principles of National Socialism which were whole-heartedly endorsed by Colonel Claus von Stauffenberg were the concept of the *Volksgemeinschaft* and the emphasis on 'racial purity'.

One blind spot in our knowledge of the German resistance in the events leading up to 1939 remains: what role, if any, did the resistance play in the Allies' decision to honour their obligations towards Poland, at least in so far as they declared war on Germany? The evidence is contradictory and far from complete; not all British cabinet files on this period are accessible to the historian. But the following remarks give food for thought: Neville Chamberlain on 10 September 1939 wrote: 'But what I hope for is not a military victory – I very much doubt the feasibility of that – but a collapse of the German home front'. As late as 31 August 1939 the Polish ambassador in Berlin staked his reputation that German morale was breaking 'and that the present regime would soon crack'. And during the same month the French chief of the general staff, General Gamelin, declared that to him it was a matter of indifference whether the *Wehrmacht* had 100 or 200 Panzer divisions, he would probably never have anything to do with the German army because 'on the day of our declaration of war to Germany Hitler will be overthrown! Unrest will break out in Berlin. Instead of defending the frontiers of the Reich, the German army will flood back into the capital to restore order. The forces stationed on her western defence will offer little resistance. Then we shall easily and quickly penetrate into Germany, like a knife cutting through butter.' The French foreign minister in 1939, Georges Bonnet, wrote in his memoirs after the war that in August 1939 'one hoped for a quick and easy victory in the hope of an imminent assassination, which was prepared and which was to bring National Socialism's fall. . . . As in 1938, so in the last week before the war, we were continuously being told and begged: Hold out and the German generals will overthrow Hitler!' No wonder Bonnet remarks: 'They [the German generals] described in the Nuremberg trials their immense detailed efforts of what they had prepared against the *Führer*, and one asks oneself why they did not carry it out. . . . In the same way before and after our defeat we were told about military conspiracies against the *Führer*. Nevertheless Hitler lived until 1945!'

1. Between Myth and Revisionism? The Third Reich in the Perspective of the 1980s

ERNST NOLTE

If the inhabitants of a distant star could come to earth now to gather information about the history of mankind, and especially about the Third Reich, they would probably come to the following conclusion: the Third Reich is still alive 40 years after its downfall. Not that countless people remember it longingly, or that memorial festivals attract great masses; neither does any influential political party want to restore it – quite the contrary. The feeble attempts to restore a National Socialist Party merely provide the raw material for sensational news items; and the 'Hitler waves' about which we read from time to time do not serve to glorify the *Führer*. Indeed, a film [*Holocaust Ed.*] whose subject was the worst outrages of the Third Reich considerably moved many people both in the USA and in Germany.

For many years the best known school of social analysis has based its research on constant references to the Third Reich, and prominent politicians in the Federal Republic of

Original contribution to this volume.

Germany have had to resign or fear for their positions if the slightest, relatively harmless, connection with the Third Reich has been proved. Statements denying that many who were *SA* men around 1933 had criminal intentions, despite their bloodthirsty songs, are considered dangerous minimisations, and in numerous popular publications in the USA *SA* and *SS* men are constantly depicted as plundering houses, torturing prisoners and raping women.

Nothing in the least comparable could be observed 40 years after the downfall of the Second French Empire. The rule of Napoleon III had long since become a merely historical subject despite the vehement denunciations of it during the early 1870s. It was quite different, however, 40 years after the collapse of the First Empire: by 1850 the Napoleonic legend had long been established, and the memory of the emperor had become the positive weapon of a strong party, although in the first few years after 1815 opinions about the Corsican from nearly all sides had been hardly less negative than those about Hitler after 1945. In fact, this legend had already made his nephew president of the French Republic, and a little later it was to become the state legend of the Second Empire. In sharp contrast to this the present memory of the Third Reich is – except for the views espoused by some of the lunatic fringe – thoroughly negative, and there are a number of reasons for this.

The first and most compelling reason, which is barely contested, is that the Third Reich caused the greatest and bloodiest war yet known to mankind. By his refusal to enter into negotiations in time, to resign or to capitulate, Hitler brought the war to such a catastrophic end that the memory of it is, especially for the Germans, inextinguishable. Hitler's moral condemnation of all survivors encourages the negative response in Germany.

Secondly, seen from the perspective of what is now called 'the Western Welfare State' the Third Reich appears grotesquely old-fashioned and reactionary. It enshrined the motto 'blood and soil'; the concept of the farmers being the 'first estate'; the degradation of non-Aryan races; the glorification of hierarchy and discipline; and the subordinate role of women, who never doubted that their sphere of life was the home, and that on the 'battlefield of birth' they shared in the nation's fight for eternity. When democracy was mentioned, it was not a participatory or even a direct democracy that was implied, but a 'Germanic' democracy, the mere assent to autocratic leadership.

Thirdly, the outrages perpetrated under the Third Reich were considerable. It is true that there are precedents for and parallels to the concentration camps, and even to the destruction of the workers' movement, but the annihilation of several million European Jews, many Slavs, the mentally insane and gypsies is without precedent in its motivation and execution. The cold, inhuman, technical precision of the quasi-industrial machinery of the gas chambers especially created an unparalleled sense of horror. This has for some time been suppressed or ignored by many Germans, but it has always been prominent in published literature, so that in retrospect only the voice of the victims was audible. Not even a rudimentary justification has ever been attempted.

Finally, the Third Reich lends itself to caricature. Hitler was the ideal creation for Chaplin. The 'Reichs-drunkard' Ley [Dr Robert Ley, leader of the *Deutscher Arbeitsfront*, the German Labour Front which replaced the German trade union movement in 1933. *Ed.*], the agitating pornographer Streicher [Dr Julius Streicher, *Gauleiter* and editor of the radically anti-semitic paper *Der Stürmer*. *Ed.*], the bull-necked Bormann, the vain failure Göring, the bespectacled *Reichsheini* Himmler, who believed himself to be the reincarnation of the first Saxon king – all these are caricatures in themselves.

The continued existence of the Third Reich is therefore thoroughly negative. The literature about the Third Reich is at the same time a symptom and a cause of this, for it is basically a literature of catastrophe and accusation. Titles such as *The German Catastrophe* or *The Way into Catastrophe* were characteristic immediately after the war. A title like *Deutsche Daseinsverfehlung* ('Germany's Failure to Exist') turned the accusation into rejection. The accusation was directed above all against specific traditions or strata of society: against the *Junkers* as well as against the *Preussentum* (Prussians), who were said to be responsible for Germany's disastrous dissociation from West European development and thus for the German *Sonderweg* (special way); and against the capitalists as the most important promoters, indeed the foster fathers, of the NSDAP (the National Socialist Party). These tendencies did not appear only in literature: the Prussian state was liquidated by a unanimous decision of the four occupying powers, and the Nuremberg trials were not only instituted against the 'Major War Criminals' but also against diplomats, and chiefly against industrial magnates such as Friedrich Flick and Gustav Krupp von Bohlen und Halbach. It is true that differences of opinion were already noticeable at an early stage. At the beginning of the 1950s the Americans and British released a considerable number of those prisoners sentenced for 'war crimes', and the literature of accusation was joined by a literature of apology in which, for example, Gerhard Ritter solicited some understanding for Prussia, or Louis P. Lochner advocated the case of the capitalists. However, these were only adjustments of details and did not alter the basic picture. Not only did the literature, influenced by the concept of 'Totalitarianism', not give rise to major changes, it merely extended the negativity so that the Russians too were included, or, to put it more precisely, it re-established the older and more comprehensive negativity which can easily be deduced from the positive concept of the liberal democratic society. Moreover, this literature is basically confined to a comparison of the structures of the Third Reich and the Stalinist Soviet Union, and its scholarly monographs could make only vague general assumptions beyond their immediate object of research, the Third Reich. Even in 1960 William Shirer's trivial anti-German book *The Rise and Fall of the Third Reich* could become a bestseller [Shirer had tried unsuccessfully for five years to place his manuscript, when Eichmann was kidnapped and taken to Israel. This reawakened public interest in the Third Reich and Shirer's work was published, though even in 1960 it was some ten years behind the current state of research. *Ed.*], and the gradually emerging neo-Marxist literature resumed, with considerable effect, the Nuremberg trials against the industrial leaders in order to construct a more comprehensive accusation against the 'capitalist system'. The so-called bourgeois literature on the 'fascist movements' or 'regimes' in Europe conformed to the same pattern, even though it tried to conceive of European history since 1917 as a whole. It had to conform to the pattern since the catastrophe had indeed taken place, since finding out the causes is an essential element for the historian as well as for the political and social scientist.

In spite of this it cannot be denied that the continuing negative existence of such a historical phenomenon represents a great, even deadly, danger for the historian. A continuing negative or positive existence tends to assume the character of a myth, which is especially dangerous because it can become a founding or supporting state ideology. We need only imagine, for example, what would happen if the Palestine Liberation Organisation, assisted by its allies, succeeded in annihilating the state of Israel. Then the historical accounts in the books, lecture halls and schoolrooms of Palestine would doubtless dwell only on the negative traits of Israel; the victory over the racist, oppressive and even Fascist Zionism would become a state-supporting myth. For decades and possibly centuries nobody would dare to trace the moving origins of Zionism to the spirit of resistance against European anti-semitism, or to describe its extraordinary civilising achievements before and after the founding of the state, to show the clear differences from Italian Fascism. In the German Democratic Republic for example, the 'victory over Fascism' has indeed become something of a state-supporting myth. For the western historian, on the contrary, 'revision' is absolutely fundamental: the ever-renewed criticism not only of single conclusions but of prevailing basic assumptions. Every successful revision itself becomes an assertion, and in due time the object of a new revision. For example, the history of the American Civil War was at first exclusively written by the victors. But relatively soon a better understanding developed in the North of the motives and way of life of the defeated southern states. Although this tendency never prevailed, it was strong enough to give rise, in other circumstances, to a new revisionism. The same is true of German historiography, which prepared and later described the foundation of the Bismarck Reich; its spectrum was always broad enough to prevent the establishment of an imperturbable state myth.

The fundamental question must therefore be: is the history of the Third Reich, 40 years after the end of the war, in need of revision, and if so, what form should this take? From the beginning any possibility must be ruled out that revision could consist of a mere reversion of the negative basic tendency of the literature, that is, be an apology. In that case, it would either have to deny incontestable facts, or even imply the renewal of the National Socialist ethos and its main postulates, such as the vindication of the demand for absolute sovereignty of an all-German state, or, to take the extreme case, the resumption of the theory about the fatal influence of the Jews. The one is as impossible as the other. The innermost core of the negative picture of the Third Reich needs no revision. But perhaps contemporary events suggest that it is possible to place the Third Reich as a whole in a new perspective and to extend the negativity in a different direction from the classical theory of 'Totalitarianism' of the 1950s. Very instructive in this respect is the renaissance of anarchist historiography in which each organised and hierarchical society bears an essentially negative (repressive) character, no matter whether it deals with the *polis* of antiquity, which was based on slave labour, or with the contemporary states of the 'real socialism', so that the Third Reich can only maintain with some difficulty a prominent place in the universal history of repression.

At the beginning of the 1960s there were two books above all which established historiography regarded as revisionist and therefore a challenge: A. J. P. Taylor's *The Origins of the Second World War* and David L. Hoggan's *Der erzwungene Krieg*. Both were, however, narrowly limited in their revisions. Taylor presented basically only a variation on the anti-German literature of accusation [Taylor's basic thesis, overlooked by many of his critics at the time, was that Hitler was as normal a German as Germans usually are; therefore beware of them! *Ed.*]; Hoggan, by confining himself to the question of the outbreak of the war, did not touch

upon the really decisive questions [see p. 186 below *Ed.*].
Nevertheless one book underlined the problem of continuity
and the other raised some useful questions on the rather too
simplistic thesis of the 'unleashing of the Second World
War' by Hitler. Both books were therefore symptomatic of
the end of the second phase of the post-war period.

At the end of the 1960s an entirely new situation had
been created by the war in Vietnam. It is true that it had a
direct and comprehensive effect only on the historiography
of the Cold War, but indirectly it contributed to a
considerable strengthening of the neo-Marxist thesis of the
final causality of the capitalist system. At the same time,
due to the detente in the East–West conflict, the concept of
'Totalitarianism' lost much of its persuasiveness, so that,
seen in another way, only the western capitalist system
seemed to remain as the object of accusation.

At the end of the 1970s the situation had changed
fundamentally. The end of the American 'intervention' in
Vietnam had brought no peace, but the alleged victims of
genocide, the reunited Vietnamese, proved to be strong
enough to wage a war of aggression against Cambodia, and
they in turn became the victims of a 'punitive expedition'
by the Peoples' Republic of China. At the same time they
started a mainly ethnically oriented mass flight which has
been described as the 'holocaust on the water' to epitomise
the painful mass death of countless refugees. The weakness
and fragility of so-called western imperialism could no
longer remain unnoticed while the Soviet Union was
continuously strengthening its military power and supporting,
with great success, 'liberation movements' in Africa and
elsewhere (the latest in Afghanistan) which in their turn
had, and have, to fight against other 'liberation movements';
while an astonished world watched a remarkable revolution
in Iran which, according to widespread opinion, must be
called both 'progressive' because it eliminated American
influence, and thoroughly 'reactionary' because it established
the rule of a high priest. Does this situation not again, and
this time in a less partial and isolated way, call for a
revision of the history of the Third Reich?

Before I try to give an answer to this question I shall sketch briefly the basic assumptions or main conclusions of three books which, each in a different way, have to be regarded as the latest revisionist approaches, although the situation described above has not yet been incorporated. Two books by Englishmen deal with aspects or periods of the Third Reich: the third is an overall interpretation of Italian Fascism by an Italian author. This interpretation, however, can be used directly as regards the question of the necessity of revision of the history of the Third Reich.

Domenico Settembrini has given his book, which appeared in 1978, the provocative title *Fascismo Controrivoluzione imperfetta* ('Fascism, the imperfect counter-revolution'). He starts with firmness from the thesis which Piero Gobetti expressed in the title of his review 'Rivoluzione liberale', namely that the real and modernising revolution is that of liberal capitalism or of economic freedom, which began 200 years ago in England and which was first completed in the USA. This revolution of individualism was challenged at an early date by the so-called revolutionary socialism, whose guideline was the archaic community, with its transparency of social conditions, as the most comprehensive counter-revolution, namely as the tendency for totalitarian collectivism. Due to very special circumstances, and not just by chance, this counter-revolution came to power in Russia in 1917, and very soon disclosed its nature: the establishment of an omnipotent centre and the subjection of the individual under an economic plan which solved the most pressing problems of development but which proved totally unworkable in meeting the needs of individuals. Whether Russia was to become the model for Italy, who despite all her backwardness was much more differentiated and much more closely connected with the history of western civilisation, was the great question with which Italy saw herself confronted in 1918–19. In the controversy with socialist maximalism, Mussolini, formerly the first man of the Socialist Party in Italy, initially stood almost alone, and Settembrini maintains that he was completely right in this struggle with his former comrades. The Fascism which Mussolini founded was a double-faced phenomenon, at the same time negative and positive, anti-revolutionary and revolutionary. It was negative in so far as it deviated from the western model by the suspension of political freedom and by the corporate regulation of the economy; it was positive in so far as it did not completely eliminate economic freedom and the market. Thus Mussolini spared the Italian people Stalin's perfect totalitarianism, and he was right again when he later turned against the left wing of his own party, which wanted to see in the Duce's compromise a preliminary stage of the transition to a complete collectivism, and whose representatives, incidentally, converted to Communism in great numbers after the war. Today, however, according to Settembrini, the decisive question is whether the Italian Communists consider the 'historic compromise' to which they are aspiring, after the model of Fascism, merely as a tactical instrument to reach their old goals, or whether they are following Mussolini's change of 1919 towards the right-wing assessment of the liberal democratic and capitalist system. In this way, Mussolini and Fascism have again been fully integrated in the national history, and they have become a point of orientation for the most up-to-date of all contemporary questions, not through uncritical glorification but from a point of view which is explicitly non-Fascist. If this interpretation found recognition it would be the model of a successful revision. However, to extend it to Germany would obviously not be possible. The German Social Democrats of 1918–19 were not maximalists; Hitler's decision for war was not an 'unfortunate' decision taken under foreign influence; his totalitarianism, at least after the outbreak of the war, very well matched that of Stalin; and his will for annihilation was not merely political, like Mussolini's, but biological. Even a successful revision of the assessment of Italian Fascism in the framework of Italian history would not be transferable to National Socialism and to Germany.

A revision of a completely different nature was undertaken by Timothy W. Mason in 1975 in his extensive investigation of *Arbeiterklasse und Volksgemeinschaft*. After 1945 it had been more or less taken for granted that no stratum of the German people could be acquitted of a share of guilt for the

National Socialist regime, and shortly after the war even
the Communists had made confessions of guilt. The petit
bourgeois thesis of many theories of Fascism had already
shifted the emphasis considerably, but Mason is probably
the first who saw one main reason for Hitler's defeat in the
class struggle for the working class, which, he says, sabotaged
the war preparations of the National Socialist regime with
that energy which would have 'objectively' been possible
and which (one has to add) would have led to Hitler's
victory over the Allies. Mason can in fact present various
cases when the regime had to take into consideration the
morale of the workers, and he thinks himself justified in
speaking of the powerlessness of the totalitarian dictatorship
in that respect. One could say perhaps that Mason's revision
consists of the fact that he proclaims the German working
class as the real victors over National Socialism. However, a
closer look at his enormous documentation reveals more
and more discordant traits: the important role of the
organisational imperialism of the German Labour Front
which in the internal fight for power successfully made itself
the speaker of the wishes of the masses; the almost complete
absence of any genuine resistance and in its place a clever
taking of advantage of the conditions caused by shortage of
labour which led only to secondary difficulties; the
consequences arising out of the improved standard of living
whose existence Mason does not deny; the ruthless
competition of the industrial managers for the sparse labour
force, and so on. What Mason does not say directly but
which emerges from his material is the picture of a hard-
pressed economy demanding considerable sacrifices from all
strata of the population, not least from the shareholders,
which found itself largely confronted with the population's
egoistic skill at dodging and taking advantage of the
situation. What is completely lacking is an account of
Hitler's *Weltanschauung*, which more than anything else was
responsible for the fact that the reservoir of female labour
was not exploited nearly as well as, for example, in England,
and that in the midst of the war vast means were dissipated
in those annihilating measures which, seen solely from the
standpoint of the war effort, were completely irrational and

even counter-productive. Therefore, despite Mason, we still have to maintain that Hitler's war was waged by 'the German people', although certain losses by friction or individual acts of resistance cannot be denied.

A completely different motive is at the basis of the attempt at revision by another Englishman: David Irving's 1975 book *Hitler und seine Feldherren* whose English version appeared only two years later under the title *Hitler's War*. Irving's goal is undisguisedly a vindication of Hitler who, according to him, 'alone did not have any voice after 1945' whereas his friends and foes alike, through one-sided descriptions and genuine errors, gave an untrue picture of the war. It was characteristic that the German publisher refused to incorporate in the German edition the most controversial assertion by the author, that Hitler had not known anything about the 'Final Solution'. This is said to come from a telegram discovered by Irving in which, so he says, Hitler forbade the liquidation of the Jews. [Irving reprints Himmler's notes of a telephone conversation with Hitler on 30 November 1941, in which Hitler ordered a particular transport of Berlin Jews *not* to be liquidated. *Ed.*] But in reality this is the weakest point of the whole book since, seen in the true perspective, this telegram expresses the exact contrary, because it presupposes the fact of the widespread liquidations. However, not all of Irving's theses and references can be set aside so easily. What Irving suggests as a general impression is certainly more than questionable, namely that Hitler could have won the war if those surrounding him had better grasped his strategic ideas and had turned them into reality without hesitation and attempts at sabotage. But it can hardly be denied that Hitler had good reasons to be convinced of his enemies' determination to annihilate him much earlier than when the first information about Auschwitz came to the knowledge of the world. The 1940 pamphlet 'Germany must perish' by Theodore N. Kaufmann has often been mentioned in the literature, but I do not remember seeing it in any of the more important German books I have read about Chaim Weizmann's official declaration in the first days of September 1939, according to which Jews in the whole world would

fight on the side of England [see p. 378 below. *Ed.*].
Anyway, I have to reproach myself for not knowing of this
statement in 1963 and not having made use of it, although
it can be found in the *Archiv der Gegenwart* of 1939, and it
might justify the consequential thesis that Hitler was allowed
to treat the German Jews as prisoners of war and by this
means to intern them. Equally Irving's *a priori* thesis that
the bomb attack on Hamburg in July 1943 bore witness to
the Allies' will to destroy the German civilian population,
and that this could not have its origin in any knowledge of
the 'Final Solution', cannot be refuted. Irving's tendency to
place Auschwitz as well into a more comprehensive
perspective would be remarkable even if the counter-thesis
were acknowledged as convincing, namely that not even the
President of the Jewish Agency had the right to pronounce
something like a declaration of war, and that the attack on
Coventry preceded the one on Hamburg by three years.
[However, there is now a general consensus that, apart
from several specific 'retaliation' raids, of which Coventry
was one, the *Luftwaffe*'s attacks were restricted to military
and industrial targets. For the fact that Hitler opposed the
attacks on civilian targets as late as August 1940, see p. 306
below. *Ed.*]

This indeed would seem to me the most necessary and
the most difficult task if the Third Reich is to receive a new
and revisionary interpretation as seen from the perspective
of the 1980s. This interpretation should not start with the
Weimar Republic or even with the European situation of
1919. As a point of departure we could perhaps take the
announcement of the so-called 'National Unity Front' in
Cambodia, which was reprinted in the official East German
daily *Neues Deutschland* in December 1978 and therefore can
in no way be regarded as 'anti-communist propaganda'.
From there on it would have to go back to the beginnings
of the industrial revolution in England and France. The
announcement reads:

> The reactionary Pol Pot/Ieng Sary Clique has usurped all
> powers. It undertook everything possible to betray the
> country and to do harm to the people. It caused immense

pains and misery for our compatriots and threatened to exterminate our people, and the Chinese authorities have encouraged and supported these traitors and tyrants to the last. Only a few days after the liberation, under the etiquette of 'radical social revolution in all fields' and of 'purity of the society' they have extinguished the cities and they have forced whole communities to leave their houses as well as their belongings and to go to the countryside. There they lived in poverty and under a forced labour regime. They were doomed to slow extinction. The traitors cut through all holy emotional ties of men with their parents, wives and husbands, brothers and sisters and even with their neighbours. Indeed, they destroyed the villages and parts of the country in which our people has lived for thousands of years and with which its feelings are connected. They proclaimed a 'forced collectivization', the 'abolition of money and the market' and they forced the people to eat and sleep in communities. In reality, however, they imprisoned our citizens in camouflaged concentration camps, they requisitioned all means of production, forced our people to endless work while they gave them only a minimum of food and clothing. They forced all strata of the population to live in poverty and pushed them back into slavery. They divided the people into various categories in order to facilitate their suppression and make them kill each other. The crimes of the Pol/Ieng Sary Clique certainly can no longer be counted.

This text arouses numerous reminiscences. It reminds us of 'Rob what has been robbed', a motto to which the Russian Revolution in its beginnings in 1917 and 1918 owed much of its success; it leads our thoughts back to the 'war Communism' of those years when the Communists boasted that money had been abolished and men had again been made completely collective beings; it brings before our eyes the picture of the forced collectivisation of 1929/30 when millions of 'kulaks' were driven not from the cities to the villages but from the villages into the tundra in order to 'trickle away' there, as Solzhenytsin puts it; i.e., to die. It

revives the atrocious years from 1936 to 1938 of which
Moshe Pijade, in 1951, said in retrospect: 'In the years
1936, 1937 and 1938 more than three million people were
killed in the Soviet Union. They did not belong to the
bourgeoisie, because in that country it had been liquidated
for a long time'. But the text also stirs up memories of
much older times and much more harmless occurrences
which existed only in ideas and projects, and even in well-
meant and for many sympathetic or understandable ideas
and projects which cannot be removed from history and
which have undoubtedly played a positive role in more than
one respect.

There was Thomas Spence, the English 'agrarian reformer'
who looked upon a society as being 'unhealthy' in which
the 'commons', i.e. the common land and the privileges
connected with it, were taken away from the parish in
favour of the class of property owners and a distant central
bureau. He therefore, again and again, and finally in his
newspaper *The Giant Killer*, called for the elimination of the
class of landlords and for the re-establishment of a far-
reaching sovereignty of the parishes. Before him we have
Morelly, the early French socialist, as he is sometimes
called, but who was rather a kind of village-collectivist who
wanted to re-establish, either without limitation or with
improvements, the consensus of all villagers who had been
injured by the progress and differentiation in agriculture.
Then we have John Gray who, certainly with philanthropic
motives, in his important 1825 lecture 'On Human
Happiness' investigated all classes and strata of society with
respect to their 'usefulness', by which, for example, the
'freeholders of the better sort' were completely excluded
from the productive sphere, though he did consider at least
half of the 'lesser freeholders and farmers' as necessary.
Then we have William Benbow, who in 1832 developed the
concept of the 'sacred month' in the course of which the
great majority of the poor would take away from the
rapacious rich and the state functionaries the expropriated
surplus of their labour. But men like Fourier and Owen
also have a place in that picture, because they were led by
the ideal of a simple, comprehensible community of men

who are self-sufficient and lead a life without a fixed division of labour, a life unendangered by crises, independent of events in foreign countries, undisturbed by the noise of factories. And Babeuf had wanted to lead the population of the large cities back to the country and to found an 'agricultural republic without money' and without 'artificial needs'.

All these projects can, as to their point of departure, be characterised as communalistic diagnoses, that is to say, as an interpretation of the social development which, taken from an imagined perspective and yet based on the real circumstances of a small and hardly differentiated welfare society, saw a mortal disease of the social body in the beginning of a money – and communications – economy with its accumulation of capital, with its irregular and painful replacement of manual work by machines, with its more and more involved credit operations and their worldwide and not completely reciprocal dependencies and the crises resulting therefrom. Tories such as Robert Southey and Samuel Taylor Coleridge differed only very little from those who are considered to have been their strongest political opponents. They, however, did not make any far-reaching suggestions for therapy. Their suggestions can be divided into two main groups, the peaceful or *evolutionary* on the one side and the *annihilating* on the other, so that Fourier and Owen are to be found on the one side, while Spence, Babeuf, Benbow and Bronterre O'Brien stand on the other.

In view of the widespread misery and the extraordinary differences in income, especially in early nineteenth-century England, and also because the new element of individualistic money economy was closely connected with the old, corporative noble society, and finally in view of the fact that, for example, the new Poor Laws of 1834 were often regarded as the 'Poor Man's Destruction Bill', all these diagnoses and suggestions for therapy were very understandable. As a precondition for the formation of a new consciousness they had a positive significance. It was to be expected, however, that only the attempt to realise the *annihilation* therapy would be the criterion for the correctness or falsity of the analysis, and that this might possibly lead to unexpected and very grave consequences. If the 'ruling classes' constituted more than a tiny minority in society, if they were convinced that they were in no way just 'idle' but that they had to fulfil an indispensable and progressive function, if considerable parts of the 'oppressed population were loyal towards them, it, to put it shortly, the society had already become much too complex and too mobile to be adequately described by the simple and static dichotomies of 'rich and poor', 'ruling and ruled', 'oppressors and oppressed', then the annihilation therapy would fail, and in periods of crisis it could possibly hit back at its protagonists, or at those who were held to be its protagonists.

In fact, serious differences very soon became apparent in the various states. The French Revolution, for the first time in modern European history, made the concept of class and group *annihilation* a reality, but in view of its final result, it too must be counted among the 'unfinished' or synthetising revolutions in the same way as the American Revolution of 1776, the English Reform Bill of 1832, and the German Revolution of 1918. [It is doubtful whether the American Revolution can be grouped together with the French Revolution. If we divide the concept of revolution into *horizontal* and *vertical* revolution, then the American Revolution, i.e. the separation of the colonies from the mother country, belongs to the former, the French Revolution with its profound changes in the social structure and so on, to the latter. *Ed.*] The Russian Revolution of 1917–18 was of an entirely different character. Here the annihilation therapy, which was more Babouvistic-Spencean than Marxist, was successful. This was partly due to the weakness of the bourgeoisie, which existed only in an embryonic state, and partly because of the particular war conditions. This occurrence was so novel, so monstrous and so upsetting that especially grave reactions were to be expected.

Even so, it would be a gross simplification if in the National Socialist will for annihilation one wanted to see nothing more than a reaction to the Bolshevik actions of annihilation. It also had autonomous roots which reached far back into history, namely:

1. The theories of annihilation of the very early Right which, as a reaction to the terror, and still more to the programmatical declarations of the French Revolution, were hinted at in the books of men such as Joseph de Maistre, the abbé Barruel or the Scottish natural philosopher John Robison, in which terms like 'worms' and 'vermin' began to play a role, just as in the utterances of their opponents. These postulates of counter-annihilation rarely had an anti-Jewish tinge before the Dreyfus affair, but Metternich had already occasionally tended to establish a close relationship between liberalism and the Jews.
2. The annihilation therapy of the radical wing of Malthusianism, which sprang from the fear of the unprecedented increase of population, and which in some cases led to the proposal to eliminate surplus children painlessly by gas.
3. The Prussian version of Napoleon's military annihilation strategy which could easily lose the restrictions imposed by adhering to the Clausewitz theory of military strategy, and indeed finally did lose them during the First World War.

Now the following objection could be raised: the will to annihilate unbelievers and heretics was a quite natural thing during the Middle Ages and still in early modern times – one need only remember the Spanish Inquisition or the revocation of the Edict of Nantes – but starting with the Enlightenment, liberal progressive optimism prevailed, so that the facts mentioned could be regarded merely as corollaries and the National Socialist measures of annihilation had to be regarded simply as an inconceivable relapse into barbarism. To me, however, it seems that a completely new situation arose through the fact that in the wake of Enlightenment and its successful polemics against the religious wars of the past, a society had emerged for which 'tolerance' seemed to be the basis, and in which for that reason especially the unprecedented process of the Industrial Revolution could take place. By this time, however, the stage had been erected on which statements could be made, questions asked, threats uttered and fears experienced in such a manner as had not been possible in more closed societies, no matter how violent and obvious the hatred against deviation in those societies. When we speak of the victory of the light over darkness, this may not be understood in a naïvely optimistic way: only in the light can the light appear light and the dark dark; only in the light can there be a fight; only in the light does the wound appear as what it is. The light (the keener and more comprehensive consciousness) is not in itself good, but it is as much the precondition for good as for evil, and what appear in it are mostly mixtures of both. Therefore I will summarise and continue this train of thought.

The far-reaching and disturbing process of the Industrial Revolution called forth among the most concerned or the most sensitive strata an interpretation which understood this process as one of disease. Among the suggestions for therapy they took a prominent, although not exclusive, place which postulated a cure by annihilating whole groups. Depending on the social structure, this therapy has a more or less rational character; it need not aim from the very beginning at the extermination of individuals, and it can in any case be guided by moral and highly respectable motives. In an advanced country with a broad and complex middle class its archaic nature soon becomes apparent, but in a backward country the elimination of a small and mainly parasitic ruling group can become the elementary precondition for modernisation, even when the original motive is a radically reactionary one, namely the establishment of a 'pure' society. But even here it may lead to extraordinary sufferings for large parts of the population. And if this process takes extraordinary dimensions due to the size and importance of the country involved, then it can call forth extremely violent and possibly totally irrational reactions in neighbouring countries. This was exactly the situation in the relationship between Soviet Russia and Germany after the First World War. It is true that the Red terror, in the number of its victims, was hardly much worse than the White terror. It had, however, a basically different dimension.

When membership of a class as such was a reason for deserving death, when Lenin demanded the clearing of Russian soil from the 'dogs and pigs of the dying bourgeoisie' and Zinoviev cold-bloodedly considered the extermination of ten million people, when, according to widespread reports, sailors in Sevastopol and Odessa shot everybody who had clean fingernails, then this had to give rise to a much deeper horror than the mass executions of prisoners of war on the part of the Whites. Although detailed investigations do not exist as far as I know [In 1955 Nikita Khrushchev established a 'Commission for Research into Violations of Socialist Justice' headed by Anastas Mikoyan. It consisted of 83 subgroups which produced results of which Khrushchev's revelations at the XXth and XXIInd Party Congresses were only the tip of an iceberg. The Commission continued its work until 1964. In other words, detailed investigations do exist. *Ed.*], we may yet be permitted to state that the terror of the civil war and the annihilation of the kulaks did not produce especially severe reactions in the more distant and more consolidated western countries such as England, France and the USA. But in more closely situated Germany, which was more deeply and more intensely shaken by the economic and spiritual crisis, it was and had to be different, although at the beginning it was not predictable what form the reaction would take.

The annihilation of entire classes in Soviet-occupied eastern Europe after 1945 contributed to the genesis of the Cold War mentality in the West, but it was often, and not totally without reason, understood as the elimination of regimes and conditions that were corrupt and much too oriented towards the past. Khrushchev's acknowledgment in 1956 of Stalin's terror and its many million victims paradoxically marked the beginning of the detente. But events in Indo-China should by now have made clear what was the original and what the copy in the sphere of class, peoples or group annihilation. He who does not want to see Hitler's annihilation of the Jews in this context is possibly led by very noble motives, but he falsifies history. In his legitimate search for the direct causes he overlooks the main precondition without which all those causes would have remained without effect. Auschwitz is not primarily a result of traditional anti-semitism. It was in its core not merely a 'genocide' but was above all a reaction born out of the anxiety of the annihilating occurrences of the Russian Revolution. This copy was far more irrational than the original because it was simply absurd to imagine that 'the Jews' had ever wanted to annihilate the German bourgeoisie or even the German people, and it is very hard to admit even a perverted ethos. It was more horrifying than the original because the annihilation of men was conducted in a quasi-industrial manner. It was more repulsive than the original because it was based on mere assumptions, and almost free from that mass hatred which, in the framework of horror, is nevertheless an understandable and as far as it goes a reconciling element. All this constitutes singularity but it does not alter the fact that the so-called annihilation of the Jews during the Third Reich was a reaction or a distorted copy and not a first act or an original.

Out of this understanding the following three postulates for the historiography of the Third Reich should be deduced:

1. The Third Reich should be taken out of the isolation in which it still finds itself even when it is seen within the framework of the 'Epoch of Fascism'. Above all, it has to be placed in relation to the changes, crises, fears, diagnoses and therapies produced by the Industrial Revolution, and thus has to be investigated historico-genetically instead of only by a comparison of structures; it has to be seen particularly in relation to the Russian Revolution as its most important precondition; its future-oriented aspects should be reworked on the analysis of those 'liberation movements' to which it belonged to a certain degree, and which in their turn have to be brought into connection with the peculiar 'nationalisation' of the 'Communist World Movement'.

2. The instrumentalisation of the Third Reich, to which it owes a good deal of its continued existence, should not be accepted. He who criticises the Third Reich because he really wants to attack the Federal Republic

of Germany or the capitalist system must appear as the fool he is. It is indeed true that the liberal system is the root of Fascism, because without the freedom of the individual and the ensuing limitation of state power no Fascism can arise. But without this freedom and without this limitation there is also no criticism, no protest, no anarchism and no socialism. Many things can be criticised in the Federal Republic, for example that the artistic and spiritual life of this successful economic society consists mainly of clowning of an intricate or provocative nature. One could add with more justification that western society is much too complex and too abstract for a kind of 'common spirit' to be created, even through classes. But one should not overlook the fact that next to the 'Bolshevik chaos' Adolf Hitler hated no sort of society as much as the one which had already emerged in the Weimar Republic of Germany.

3. The demonisation of the Third Reich should be opposed. We must speak of demonisation when the Third Reich is denied any humaneness, which means that everything human is finite and thus can be neither completely good nor completely bad, neither completely light nor completely dark. A thorough investigation and penetrating comparison will not eliminate the singularity of the Third Reich, but they will make it appear nevertheless as a part of the history of mankind which not only reproduced traits of the past in a very concentrated form, but which at the same time anticipated future developments and tangled manifest problems of the present. The Third Reich, too, can and must be an object of historical investigation, investigation which is not beyond politics but which is yet not merely the servant of politics.

Certainly the Third Reich is of the material out of which legends are made. Therefore its challenge will be the greater for a society whose nature does not tolerate legends or historical myths, because in this society free historical investigation is possible. This implies continued revision.

But revision is not irreconcilable with permanent insight, and from the history of the Third Reich there must result the fundamental insight that the absence of *annihilating* measures towards political, economic, social or biological groups is the great distinction of that society which, with all its weaknesses, we call the liberal one. And revision must not be revisionism in a narrow sense, that is, an attempt at continuing reinterpretation based on explicit or underlying intentions. Neither historical myth nor revisionism, but good revision emanating from the changed historical situation should, so it seems to me, be the postulate of the historiography of the Third Reich as seen from the perspective of the 1980s, of a science which tries to free itself from limitations arising from specific circumstances.

2. 1933: The Legality of Hitler's Assumption of Power

H. W. KOCH

Historians are the greatest enemies of conspiracy theories, but paradoxically they also invent them. This applies with a vengeance to the events leading to Hitler's appointment as German chancellor by Reich president von Hindenburg on 30 January 1933, which, especially in Germany's contemporary historiography, is often described as the result of a conspiracy between Hindenburg, his advisers, the conservatives, the army and German industrialists.[1]

Before addressing the question of the legality of the National Socialist (NS) assumption of power, we must question the constitutionality of this event. This in turn requires an examination of the politics of the Weimar Republic in its last phase; without that the unfolding of events in 1932 is hard to understand.

The last 'great coalition' from May 1928 until March 1930 did not dissolve because of the attitude adopted by the German People's Party (DVP), one of the coalition partners, over the question of financing unemployment benefits. It disintegrated because of the attitude of the Social Democrats (SPD) whose party provided the chancellor of the great coalition, Hermann Müller, and several other ministers.

Original contribution to this volume.

Hostility to the great coalition emanated from the party base, not from the government ministers. In the election campaign of 1928 the SPD had fought primarily against the 'Bourgois Bloc Governments' which had run German politics between 1924 and 1928.[2] Hence disappointment among the SPD rank and file was great when in 1928 it was the SPD which headed just another bourgeois bloc government. The SPD's left wing, especially, tended towards the Communists, a tendency which was articulated vociferously at the SPD party rally in Magdeburg in 1929. For example, the delegate Wendt insisted that he was opposed to 'our party comrades in the government enjoying special rights. The attitude of "standing above parties" is a throw-back to the bourgeois-liberal mentality.'[3] Rudolf Breitscheid, leader of the SPD's left wing, spoke out explicitly in favour of breaking the great coalition. With considerable insight he sketched the scenario of what was to follow; however, he believed the SPD would have nothing to fear from it. After the collapse of the great coalition a dissolution of the Reichstag would change very little because without the SPD no majority government could be created. He then pointed to the consequences:

> Then we really will have a genuine crisis of parliamentarianism, the exploitation of certain paragraphs of the Constitution which do not accord with the spirit of democracy but which are nevertheless contained in the Constitution. These could give the Reich president rights under certain circumstances which basically are not in keeping with democratic principles. We would then have a kind of civil service cabinet which would probably already be a veiled form of dictatorship.[4]

A clear-headed prophecy indeed! In spite of this Breitscheid did not intend that the SPD should save the parliamentary system 'at any price', should make 'any sacrifice' for it. In those circumstances the organised workers outside parliament would have to save democracy. In other words: a general strike and a resumption of the battle in the streets of Germany. These quotations are just a few of many, which serve to illustrate how passionately the break-up of the great coalition was desired by the SPD's left wing, in contrast to the party leadership, which like Stresemann *vis-à-vis* the DVP still believed they had a general responsibility to the German people and not only to their own electorate.[5] The time of the nineteenth-century liberal conception of parliamentarianism was past, however; Weimar politicians lived in the age of mass democracy, though many of them realised it too late. In the end the SPD cabinet members had to vote against legislation which they themselves had introduced in the Reichstag. The great coalition had collapsed, and with it more than most contemporaries realised. On the appointment of Heinrich Brüning, himself a member of the Catholic Centre Party, as chancellor many hoped that this party, in the past always the linch-pin of coalition governments, could produce another coalition, supported by a parliamentary majority. This proved an illusion; for Brüning there was nothing else but to request Hindenburg to invoke Article 48 of the Constitution.[6] This Hindenburg did with the utmost reluctance, in the end persuaded only by being made aware that his predecessor Friedrich Ebert had also made use of it. From that moment Hindenburg strove continuously to get away from government by Article 48 and to return to a government supported by a parliamentary majority, though given his own inclinations he wanted its orientation to be centre-right rather than centre-left.

Article 48 of the Weimar Constitution had been framed by the republic's founding fathers under the impact of the internal upheaval in Germany 1918/19 and it gave the president the right to apply it in cases of emergency throughout Germany or in any of its *Länder*. The article was intended to be followed up by detailed implementing legislation, which for reasons unknown was never drafted, let alone submitted to the Reichstag.[7] Throughout the duration of the republic, not once was there any demand for its scope to be clearly specified. As it stood it was extremely flexible and even Germany's foremost legal brain, Carl Schmitt, warned that the article as it stood could open the way to a dictatorship.[8] Nevertheless without its use it is doubtful whether the republic would have survived its early years. With its aid the German currency was stabilised in 1923/4 and an end put to the inflation that had begun in 1916 and had by 1923 reached grotesque proportions. With its aid attempts at internal revolution were suppressed. What the constitutional provisional National Assembly failed to foresee was that the Reichstag, through excessive party pluralism, to mention only one factor, would deprive itself of the role of national legislator and integrator of the national will, condemn itself to impotence, and thus cause a power vacuum which was filled in the end only by the bureaucracy and presidential cabinets.

Initially Brüning, too, was reluctant to govern by Article 48; when he used the rejection of his emergency legislation by the Reichstag to have the president dissolve it and call premature elections, the Reichstag still had two years to run. He hoped either to gain a majority or to secure toleration, especially from the right. The successes achieved by Stresemann in 1929, such as the evacuation of Allied occupation forces in the Rhineland by 1930, were something which Brüning hoped the German voter would reward. For Brüning himself the election campaign was also a decisive struggle between self-emasculating parliamentarianism and stable democracy.[9]

The elections of 14 September 1930 brought Brüning's hopes to an end. The NSDAP, represented in the Reichstag since 1928 by 12 deputies, gained a sensational 107 seats and became the second strongest party in the Reichstag. The Communists increased their number of seats from 54 to 77, while the SPD was reduced from 152 to 143 seats. Hugenberg's German National People's Party (DNVP) showed losses, as did the Liberals. Of the other parties only the Centre and its Bavarian offshoot, the Bavarian People's Party (BVP) could register minor gains. The various right-wing splinter groups, upon which Brüning had placed his hopes, did not obtain enough votes to allow him to build a coalition with them.

The parties of the old great coalition now had a total of 280 seats; they had lost their majority, they could not have formed a coalition even if they had wished to do so, but that wish was not present, certainly not among the SPD. NSDAP and Communists (KPD) together possessed 184 seats and thus were a blocking minority, because at best the SPD was able to extend the coalition only as far as the DVP.

Among contemporaries as well as historians there is a widespread view that the NSDAP had the Depression to thank for its breakthrough, but this is a completely erroneous opinion.[10] First of all Germany only fully became a victim of the Depression towards the end of 1930. Secondly, if the election returns are analysed it is immediately clear that the votes gained by the NSDAP did not come from primarily industrial regions, but in the main from agrarian regions and areas in which cottage industries predominated, for instance Schleswig-Holstein and the Erzgebirge regions. This is not to say that economic factors played no role. The so-called 'golden twenties' may have been golden for a few, but less so for the majority. A Holstein dairy farmer, for example, had his livestock confiscated because he was unable to sustain the crippling tax-burden.[11] Even without the Depression, unemployment was never lower than 800,000 and by 1929/30 had exceeded the 2 million mark.

A third factor often overlooked is that the Reich organisation leader of the NSDAP, Gregor Strasser, had already devised a new election strategy, which came too late to have any effect in May 1928, but had since then proved effective in *Land* and communal elections. Up to 1928 the NSDAP had concentrated equally on all constituencies and thus dissipated much of its strength. Strasser changed all that, placing the *Schwerpunkt*, the main weight of the NSDAP's election effort, in constituencies where the outcome was finely balanced, where by special effort a gain of a few per cent could decide the contest in favour of the NSDAP. This strategy proved very successful in *Land* and communal elections between 1928 and 1930.[12] The national elections of 1930 simply confirmed the trend which had already been in operation for the best part of two years. Consequently the events of 1930 are not the sensation which they seemed to many at the time and to many historians since.

To describe the NSDAP after its refoundation in 1925 as a stagnating body simply contradicts the facts. Certainly it was not a party which enjoyed mass-membership but it experienced a period of slow but steady growth.[13] At no time did the NSDAP perceive itself as a political party within the generally accepted meaning of the term, but saw itself as a movement, with the primary aim of removing the class and party political barriers which had characterised not only the republic but also the empire before it.

By creating the racially homogenous *Volksgemeinschaft*, the national community, it was believed that the NSDAP would succeed in bringing about a fundamental reconstruction, a new order, and so give Germany the chance to become a world power again. By the early 1930s sociologists of New York's Columbia University had carried out research among the NSDAP's 'old fighters' about their motivation for joining Hitler. Among the criteria listed by the sociologists, the *Volksgemeinschaft* took first place,[14] while anti-semitism for instance is to be found on the lower end of the motivation scale. In other words, it was not the obscene anti-semitism *à la* Streicher, nor the pseudo-scientific racisms of Hitler, Rosenberg and Himmler which determined entry into the NSDAP, but the belief that the creation of the *Volksgemeinschaft* would provide the panacea for all the problems confronting the Reich as well as the individual.

Until 1923 the NSDAP had been a purely revolutionary party which refrained from participating in elections. The disaster of the Beer Hall putsch of 9 November 1923 caused a radical *volte face* in Hitler. Correctly assessing the existing power relationships, especially the position of the *Reichswehr*, Hitler when refounding the party in 1925 decided in favour of the path of legality.[15] He set out on the so-called 'march through the institutions', without, however, ever attempting to veil his aims by affirming the principle of parliamentarianism. When in 1930 three *Reichswehr* lieutenants were accused of high treason because they had carried out NS propaganda among their comrades, the investigations showed that they had not enjoyed the slightest support from the NSDAP leadership. One of the defence counsel had the brilliant idea of calling Hitler to give evidence.[16] Questioned closely,

Hitler openly declared that the Constitution dictated to him the path by which he might obtain power but not the aims which he should pursue once he had the majority. Asked by one of the judges whether he had once said that after a NS assumption of power 'heads would roll in the sand', Hitler confirmed this, stating that once the NSDAP was in power with the necessary majority, it would call into being a state court to judge the 'November criminals'. And then, of course, 'heads would roll'.[17] Only a few days before the 1930 Reichstag elections Hitler publicly declared:

> We National Socialists have never claimed to be representatives of a democratic point of view, we have openly declared that we would deploy democratic means only to attain power, and after our assumption of power we would deny our enemies all those means which are allowed to us while in opposition. . . . For us parliament is not an end in itself, but a means to an end. We are not a parliamentary party as a matter of principle; that would be a contradiction of our entire conception. We are a parliamentary party under duress, and what constrains us is the Constitution.[18]

As late as 27 July 1932 Hitler made a speech in Eberswalde in Brandenburg which was filmed by the NSDAP and widely used after Hitler had become chancellor in the election campaign of February and March 1933. In this speech Hitler warned his opponents against comparing him with themselves; the NSDAP was not a parliamentary party and would never be one. On the contrary, he saw it as his main task to sweep out of Germany the 34 or so parties then existing in the country.[19] Nor was there anything unconstitutional about this aim. The Weimar Constitution had made no provisions for political parties and they were not anchored in the constitution.

None of Hitler's opponents could therefore have any doubts as to their party's future if and when the NSDAP gained power, or about the aim of the NSDAP to create a one-party state, unless, of course, they were naïve enough to believe the old German proverb that 'no soup is as hot in the eating as it is in the cooking'.

The simple question may be raised why a party like the NSDAP was not forbidden as unconstitutional? The answer to this lies in the Weimar Constitution itself. As mentioned above the Constitution did not contain a single article providing parties with a constitutional anchor. That was by no means novel. The US Constitution does not possess such a provision either – and nothing was more suspect to the Founding Fathers than political parties. They originated in Washington's second term as President, when conflicting opinions in his cabinet, particularly between Hamilton and Jefferson, polarised themselves to the extent that two political parties were the end product; the first party political elections in the history of the United States were those of 1796. Washington left the presidency a deeply disappointed man, warning explicitly in his 'Farewell Message' that the dangers arising from the emergence of political parties would endanger the existence of the young republic.

More important, the Weimar Constitution contained no article making it illegal to attack the republican form of state, or even to abolish it, as long as the aim was pursued legally, within the framework of the Constitution. In terms of actual political practice there was no violation of the Constitution in aiming at a one-party state, provided that a two-thirds majority of the Reichstag, necessary to change the Constitution, could be obtained in accordance with Article 76 of the Constitution. That the founders of the Weimar Constitution did not draft an article outlawing that is explained by the limited horizon of their political experience. No one foresaw the possibility of a political party arising whose aim it was to overthrow the republic by *constitutional means*. Even after the election results of 1930 this idea occurred to very few.[20] Quite apart from that, the blocking minority in the hands of the NSDAP and KPD would not then have allowed constitutional legislation to protect the Constitution to be passed by the Reichstag. In view of Hitler's openly declared aims it came as no surprise that he refused to cooperate with the parties represented in

the Reichstag, and that in 1930 as well as in 1932 he
rejected mere participation in coalition governments which
inevitably would have associated the NSDAP with a policy
of failure.

Brüning's economic policies led to disaster, but for reasons
which even today are hardly understood. The key to his
economic policy is the problem of reparations.[21] Since the
Dawes Plan of 1924 German governments had paid
reparations, but with money borrowed mainly from abroad,
notably the USA. This and other factors led to Germany's
almost irretrievable indebtedness. Brüning's policy was one
of 'fulfilment' in the same sense as Rathenau's, namely to
demonstrate by punctual reparations payments that even
with the best of good will Germany was in the long term
unable to meet these payments, and that the one-sided flow
of capital across the Atlantic would eventually destabilise
not only Germany's economy, but the world's.[22]

The realisation of this fact should have compelled
Germany's former enemies to cancel reparation payments
completely. Brüning achieved his objective, but without
being able to reap the fruit of the seed he had sown. Nor
was he willing to finance German reparation payments by
taking up new loans. He financed them through increased
and cheap exports and a drastic reduction of imports.[23] Export
increases were brought about by a drastic rationalisation
of Germany's industries which reduced price levels of
manufactured goods and increased their output, while
German agricultural output was maximised to reduce foreign
imports to an absolute minimum. One aspect of Brüning's
agrarian policy was the *Osthilfe* (Eastern Aid) designed to
help the estate owners east of the Elbe river to consolidate
their economic position.[24] At the same time Brüning's policy
called for drastic cuts in public expenditure, which
particularly hit the civil service with 25 per cent salary cuts,
and entailed wage cuts in industry which hit blue- and
white-collar workers alike, and of course led to further
unemployment.[25]

Brüning actually succeeded in achieving a balanced
budget in 1930/31, while at the same time raising sufficient
funds from Germany's own resources to meet reparation

payments.[26] The lessons of Brüning's policy were quickly
recognised in France and Britain: that, as a British
Commission of Investigation noted, this policy was bound
to lead to an all-out economic war, a realisation which
ultimately led to the cancellation of German reparation
payments in the latter half of 1932.[27]

In Germany the consequences of this policy were
catastrophic. Unemployment reached hitherto unprecedented
levels,[28] and the government, in view of the impotence of the
Reichstag, had to continue to govern with the aid of Article
48 by means of emergency legislation. In spite of Hindenburg's
pressure on Brüning to obtain parliamentary backing, Brüning
could find no majority. The fact that Hitler was his opponent
in the run-off of the two presidential polls of 1932 turned
Hindenburg into a candidate of the centre to moderate left,
an uncomfortable position for the old president, who always
considered himself as the representative of the entire German
people and not of party political groupings.[29]

Hindenburg's re-election was followed by the Reichstag
elections of July and November 1932. Brüning, in no
position to muster a parliamentary majority, was compelled
to resign at the end of May 1932.[30] Into his place stepped
Franz von Papen, a figure largely unknown to the German
public, who had been recommended not by the *Reichswehr*,
but by General Kurt von Schleicher, a close friend of
Hindenburg's son. Schleicher hoped to hold the reins of
government via Papen, while Papen hoped to find at least
toleration from the DNVP and the NSDAP in the Reichstag.
Schleicher, however, even before Papen knew he was to
become chancellor, had committed the future government
to rescinding the ban which Groener as minister of the
interior had imposed upon the para-military formations of
the NSDAP.[31] By doing so he hoped to draw Hitler into the
government in a subordinate position, or at least to get the
NSDAP's support in parliament. Schleicher had also received
news from Paris of the opinion of leading French politicians
that the NSDAP's participation in the government of Prussia
as well as the Reich was inevitable, even welcome, 'because
everyone who must carry the burden of responsibility pours
water into his own wine'.[32] Hence upon his appointment

Papen had the Reichstag dissolved and called for new elections. These were held on 31 July 1932 and yielded a result unexpected by Papen. The NSDAP gained 230 seats and thus became the strongest single party in parliament. Papen could choose between a coalition with the National Socialists or forming a minority government backed by the president and Article 48, but the former foundered on Hitler's excessive demands, so the latter was the only choice.

Contrary to Schleicher's expectations, Papen now began to play politics himself. He considered implementing a profound change in the German Constitution, which would ultimately result in a two-party system according to the Westminster model, possibly with a monarch at the head. The extremes of left and right were to be forcibly suppressed with the aid of the army.[33] Since, however, the NSDAP and KPD – the latter had increased its number of seats from 78 to 89 – possessed a total of 319 seats, this would have meant a confrontation with more than 60 per cent of the German voters; it would possibly have meant civil war. A war game conducted by the army demonstrated its inability to conduct a war on such a scale while at the same time protecting Germany's eastern frontier, where it was feared that any sign of German weakness would be exploited, leading to further Polish territorial aggrandisement.[34]

In this hopeless atmosphere Papen once again took refuge in national elections to obtain a majority in the Reichstag, or at least a party political constellation which would tolerate his cabinet. In the elections of 6 November 1932 the NSDAP lost over 2 million votes, but remained the strongest single party. The Communists now held an alarming 100 seats, close on the heels of the SPD with 124 seats.

It is often argued that in these elections the electoral reservoir of the NSDAP had been exhausted and that from now on its path could lead only downhill.[35] This argument remains an unsubstantiated hypothesis. With equal validity it can be argued by comparing the trends of all the Reichstag elections of the Weimar Republic that the support for the NSDAP was levelling out and would in future elections have remained very high, though not overwhelming.

This argument of the inevitable decline of the voters' support is frequently linked with the other argument that once Hitler had become chancellor Germany had already overcome the depths of the recession and Hitler benefited from the general upturn of the world economy, an argument equally devoid of any basis in fact.[36] While never cutting as deep as in Germany, in Britain the recession on the whole continued almost until the Second World War. In the USA Roosevelt's 'New Deal' temporarily alleviated the situation in some sectors, but the recession continued with great severity until the Second World War.[37]

The November elections did not produce the result for which Papen had hoped and much against the will and the inclination of Hindenburg, he had to resign. Nor, as will be seen, was the loss of 2 million votes without its impact on Hitler. In Papen's place Schleicher became chancellor while also holding on to the office of Reichswehr minister which he had held in Papen's cabinet. He believed he had two options: an opening to the left and an opening to the right. By continuing Papen's campaign of slowly abandoning Brüning's deflationary policy he hoped to obtain the support of the trade unions and through them the toleration of the SPD. It proved a vain hope, for the left wing of the SPD opposed any support of Schleicher: anti-militaristic sentiment was too great.[38] There remained the opening to the right by way of splitting the NSDAP. Objectively the conditions for this seemed favourable. Since 1930 the NSDAP had stood on the threshold of power without being able to cross it; in some quarters of the storm-troopers there were signs of disquiet.[39] Schleicher established contact with Gregor Strasser and Strasser appeared to be receptive to Schleicher's arguments for the NSDAP joining the government, but without Hitler. Strasser put this idea to Hitler who rejected it outright. Strasser resigned his party offices forthwith and went on holiday, but without leaving the NSDAP.[40] But for Schleicher both openings were now closed. He was in the same position as his predecessor. And Hindenburg, now as before, was not prepared to hold on to a chancellor who failed to obtain majority support in the Reichstag. He wanted to see an end to presidential cabinets, the use of Article 48 and emergency decrees.

What were the alternatives? In the 14 years of its existence the Weimar Republic had had 19 governments and political talent was squandered. There was a small circle centred on the journal *Die Tat*, the 'Tat-circle', to which renowned publicists such as Ernst Jünger, Hans Zehrer and Ernst von Salomon belonged. They believed that Schleicher actually had a political concept: that of a military dictatorship. For this elitist group the NSDAP was a product of liberal democracy, and of the revolution of the masses. A dictatorship under Schleicher was to give the German Reich a new spiritual, political and military elite.[41] Whether Schleicher agreed with these ideas is more than doubtful, since after all this group was in touch with Schleicher only via one of its members, who was Schleicher's dentist.[42] The picture of Schleicher in the dentist's chair, being acquainted with the ideas of the 'conservative revolution' while the dentist drilled away at his teeth is not without grotesque comedy. Nevertheless during Schleicher's chancellorship rumours never ceased about an impending army putsch.

Three factors now began to determine future events, firstly Hindenburg's insistence on a cabinet backed by a majority in the Reichstag, secondly Schleicher's failure to exploit the opening either to the left or to the right, and thirdly the increase in the Communist vote. Hindenburg, always insistent on acting within the Constitution, would never have sanctioned a military *coup d'état*. But the Reichstag was in no condition to offer advice. Schleicher's approaches to the left alarmed the conservatives, an alarm reinforced by the third factor, the increase in the Communist vote. This increase was considered even more alarming in view of the fact that a few days prior to the November election the NSDAP and KPD had joined hands in supporting the Berlin transport strike.

Hindenburg was left to his own devices and could rely only on the advice given to him by his immediate entourage. To seek counsel where he could find it was not foreseen in the Constitution, neither had it been declared unconstitutional: for Hindenburg there was no other way. Now as ever Papen remained his favourite, but Papen lacked majority support. Six million unemployed, economic chaos, the increase in the extreme left-wing vote, all that called for a solution that could only be obtained by gaining the support of the mass base of the NSDAP. An opening to the left, that is, a coalition between the SPD and KPD, was also theoretically impossible because together they would have been in a minority *vis-à-vis* the NSDAP, DNVP and Centre.

It is against this background that we must view the negotiations of January 1933 which were conducted between the banker Baron von Schröder, Papen, Hugenberg, Joachim von Ribbentrop, Oskar von Hindenburg (Hindenburg's son) and Hitler. They have nothing to do with a conspiracy, but represent the last attempt to form a functioning government within the framework of the Constitution. Nevertheless the strongest opposition to Hitler's appointment as chancellor came from none other than Hindenburg himself. Indeed the initial negotiations centred on a Papen government in which the NSDAP was represented. Hitler would have none of it, but the loss of votes had not left him untouched. Although he demanded the chancellorship for himself, his other demands were extremely modest when compared with those of the summer of 1932. Papen realised that Hitler would not budge and was prepared to accept the vice-chancellorship but in the hope that he, and not Hitler, would dictate policies. If there was a deception, then Papen's failure to communicate the reality of the situation to Hindenburg from mid-January 1933 to 26 January was the only one.

Pressure also increased on Hindenburg, especially from the Centre Party which demanded a return to constitutional government, even if it meant Hitler's chancellorship.[43] Members of the Reichswehr leadership also intervened. On 28 January 1933 Hindenburg received the army chief, General von Hammerstein-Equord. Hindenburg gave him a rap across the knuckles for interfering in politics, but Hammerstein simply pleaded that Hindenburg should not appoint Papen again because this would result in civil war, and that he should not appoint Hitler because this would lead to National Socialist influence in the army. Hindenburg exclaimed that Hammerstein should never believe that he would appoint this Bohemian corporal as chancellor.[44]

What then caused Hindenburg to change his mind within three days? He would have been prepared to appoint a Papen cabinet, provided it was backed by a majority. Without the NSDAP and the DNVP no such majority could be obtained. Hence, whether he liked it or not – and Papen also pointed this out to him on 26 January – he was compelled to accept a Hitler cabinet, which in view of Hitler's moderate demands no longer seemed an insurmountable obstacle; apart from Hitler there were only two other National Socialist ministers, Frick and Göring, all three surrounded by a solid phalanx of dyed-in-the-wool conservatives. Moreover, Hitler was to have access to the president only in company with his vice-chancellor von Papen. There was still one problem: to keep the army out of Hitler's reach and that of Schleicher, surrounded as he was by rumours of a military putsch. This required the appointment of a new Reichswehr minister. General Werner von Blomberg was suggested as replacement by Hindenburg's son, one of the experts advising the German delegation at the Disarmament Conference in Geneva. What neither Hindenburg nor his son knew was that Blomberg had come via his chief of staff, the then Colonel von Reichenau, to sympathise with National Socialism.[45]

Hindenburg's and Papen's objective was basically a Papen cabinet whose chancellor, Hitler, was to serve as a figurehead. What was important was that the number of NSDAP parliamentary seats, when allied with those of Hugenberg's DNVP and tolerated by the Centre Party, would provide the government with a clear majority in the Reichstag. The 'entente' of the conservatives with the NSDAP was intended not so much to put Hitler in the saddle but to provide the mass support for a conservative government which the conservatives so sadly lacked. Consequently, on 29 January 1933, Hindenburg with heavy heart decided in favour of Hitler's appointment. But to make quite sure, he had Blomberg immediately recalled to Berlin, where he was met in the early hours of 30 January and was sworn in by the president as Reichswehr minister several hours before the new cabinet.

The Reichswehr seemed to have been removed from Hitler's influence and the danger of any army putsch eliminated as well. But much loose talk about an impending putsch circulated in Berlin during the last days of January 1933, rumours not entirely devoid of substance. On 28 January Schleicher's secretary of state, Planck, Colonel von Bredow, Lt Colonel Ott and Major Marcks agreed with the chief of the army, General von Hammerstein, that Hindenburg should be presented with an ultimatum not to appoint Hitler as chancellor. If he refused, then Hammerstein would proclaim a state of military emergency. But the ultimate decision to take this course was left in Schleicher's hands and Schleicher would not take it. He knew that the fate of his cabinet was sealed but hoped that he would serve as Reichswehr minister under Hitler, and at first Hitler does not seem to have been averse to including Schleicher in his cabinet. But as late as 29 January Hammerstein again took the initiative, telephoning Hitler to inform him that the Reichswehr would not tolerate his appointment as chancellor.[46]

Thus, irrespective of the hostility shown him by the army leadership, Hitler achieved power by perfectly legal means. That members of the the Reichstag had not been consulted was not unconstitutional; rather, this omission was the Reichstag's own fault, for its impotence left Hindenburg with no other choice. Hindenburg has often been accused of making concessions to Hitler which he denied to Schleicher, such as the dissolution of the Reichstag, a presidential government based on Article 48, new elections and an Enabling Law. The crucial difference is that these concessions if made to Schleicher would not in the end have produced a government backed by a parliamentary majority, whereas a Hitler cabinet would have that majority. However, everyone had underestimated Hitler. They acknowledged his great talent for public oratory, but they assumed that once burdened with governmental responsibility he would quickly burn himself out and become Papen's willing follower. Hitler's postulated aims were the subject of derision. 'We have got him boxed in', Hugenberg said.[47] Who in January 1933 could anticipate the road Germany was to take up to May 1945?

The Marxist 'agent theory' which to this day sees Hitler as the tool of Germany's industry, the agrarians and the army is devoid of any factual substance. The attitudes adopted by the army leadership have already been mentioned. The *Reichslandbund*, the association in which the big estate owners east of the Elbe were organised, was one of the first organisations infiltrated by the NSDAP, but there is no evidence of its having decisively influenced Hindenburg's decision. And what do we mean by 'Industry'? Definition is necessary here. To the iron, coal and steel industry Hitler's autarchy programme may have been welcome but not to Germany's export-orientated industry, especially the chemical and electrical industries. The American historian Henry Ashby Jr, who had access to West and East German archives as well as to the archives of individual industrial combines, has discovered that Hitler received financial contributions from industries from late 1930 onwards, but only token amounts, a kind of 'reinsurance' much less than the Centre Party or other right-wing parties received, for example. And if Hitler was the product of big business, how was it that he and not the industrial magnate Hugenberg became chancellor? The financial sacrifices which were demanded from the individual NSDAP members, even when they were unemployed, are not generally known, but they enabled the NSDAP to be largely self-financing.[48] Ironically, that sector which could expect the greatest benefits from Hitler's policy, German heavy industry, notably Krupp, did not open their coffers for Hitler until after 30 January 1933. By the end of 1932 the treasury of the NSDAP was almost exhausted, as Goebbels' diaries show.[49] The standard source book of the Marxist interpretation, Thyssen's *I paid Hitler*, has been shown by Turner to be the fabrication of the British journalist of Hungarian origin, Emery Reeves (the very man who was to assist Rauschning in the fabrication of his *Hitler Speaks*). It was not Thyssen's work.[50]

Hitler had achieved his aim, but was far from sure that his position remained uncontested. At any moment, the new government expected militant action either from the SPD, the KPD or both.[51] Therefore it is not surprising that emergency legislation was passed, through which any repetition during the election campaign of the excesses of 1932 could be prevented and public order maintained. This of course favoured the NSDAP, but no more so than previous legislation had favoured its opponents.[52]

It should not be surprising that Göring in his role as Deputy Reich Commissioner for Prussia used the *SA* and *SS* as an 'auxiliary police force'. Prussia had been one of the bulwarks of Germany's Social Democracy. Between 1920 and 1932 the Prussian government under the Social Democrat Otto Braun had purged the civil service and the police.[53] The SPD membership card reigned supreme down to the lowest levels of the civil service and the police force. And at a national level Groener in April 1932 had already created a precedent by prohibiting the uniformed formations of the NSDAP. That after Hitler's appointment a good many storm-troopers took their revenge is regrettable, but the fact remains that of all political parties in the Weimar Republic the NSDAP had paid the highest toll of blood.[54] That the elections of 5 March 1933 took place nonetheless in a free atmosphere is confirmed by the election results themselves, for the NSDAP failed to obtain the absolute majority it had aimed for.

Less than a week before the elections, an event took place which seemed to confirm Hitler's worst fears of a Communist rising. The Reichstag was set ablaze. Hans Mommsen (see below, p. 62), in a study of the political consequences of the Reichstag fire, has demonstrated in great detail that the emergency legislation which followed, like the suspension of all civil rights under the Constitution, had not been planned long beforehand, but was the product of improvisation, arrived at as the Reichstag burned, in Frick's Ministry of the Interior and in the Berlin offices of the NS paper, the *Völkischer Beobachter*. At various cabinet meetings prior to 28 February Hitler had opposed Hugenberg's demand for the prohibition of the KPD; underground they were more dangerous than on the surface.

Now the signal for the rising seemed to have been given, but it did not take place. The NSDAP and KPD were united in their opinion that the pitiful figure arrested, the Dutchman Marinus van der Lubbe, could not have set fire to the building himself. Each suspected the other. Only the painstaking research of Fritz Tobias,[55] himself a victim, along with his father, of National Socialist persecution, has confirmed that van der Lubbe was the sole culprit; nothing of hard and irrefutable substance has yet been produced to contradict his conclusions.

Nevertheless, improvised or not, the emergency legislation following the Reichstag fire opened unexpected new horizons and possibilities for Hitler to consolidate his own and his party's position, one more reason to ask why the Reichstag passed the Enabling Bill with much more than the necessary two-thirds majority. Only the SPD voted against it *en bloc*.

Enabling laws, by which Parliament gives the government the right to legislate for a period of time, were nothing new in Germany's constitutional history. After the outbreak of the First World War the Reichstag had enabled the *Bundesrat* to legislate in the economic sphere for the duration of the war. The first great coalition under Stresemann as well as his successor passed Enabling Laws on 13 October and on 8 December 1923, to stabilise Germany economically, that is to end inflation. *In practice* all presidential cabinets between 1930 and 1932 acted on the basis of enabling laws, that is, emergency decrees. While in 1930 a total of 98 laws were enacted, in 1931 the number of laws had been reduced to 34 compared with 42 emergency decrees. In 1932, 5 laws were passed, and 60 emergency decrees enacted. Hitler had made an Enabling Law one of the conditions of his chancellorship.

Much has been written of how Hitler had allegedly tricked the Centre Party into voting for the Bill.[56] No trickery was needed. Article 76 of the Weimar Constitution states that laws changing the Constitution require the assent of two-thirds of the legally stipulated quorum for that purpose, two-thirds of the members of the Reichstag. In other words Hitler did not need the entire Centre Party vote at all. Due to an above-average electoral turnout in the elections 647 deputies had been returned. Had all been present on 23 March, 431 would have had to vote for the Bill; in fact 444 votes were cast in favour of it. On 23 March, not 647 but 538 deputies were present (due to the Reichstag fire 81 KPD deputies were temporarily under lock and key, as well as 39 SPD members, though a number of them had already sought exile abroad), in other words a number considerably in excess of the two-thirds figure called for by the Constitution. If only 432 deputies had turned up the necessary two-thirds quorum would have been achieved and Hitler with his 288 seats would have had a two-thirds majority. But Hitler also had the votes of his DNVP coalition allies which increased his vote to 341. If Hitler had wanted to make absolutely sure that his Enabling Bill passed he could have reduced the attendance figure to 511 by taking into 'protective custody' another 27 deputies. However, he did not do this because he was confident of victory. With 538 deputies present, 359 represented two-thirds. He could be sure of the support of the smaller splinter parties and so all he needed were five votes from the Centre Party, of which he could equally be sure. Yet, as has already been said, Hitler did not receive only the required 359 votes, but 444. Even had all the Reichstag deputies been present, Hitler would still have had his two-thirds majority by 13 votes, though in this case the complete support of the Centre Party would have been necessary, which he could take for granted. The Centre Party under the ultra-conservative Prelate Kaas was unlikely to join the KPD or the SPD, which had torpedoed the great coalition of 1930 and whose increasing drift to the radical left since then could not be ignored. Nor would a combined vote of SPD and KPD have created a blocking minority.

It is none the less surprising that Hitler received this overwhelming vote. After all, in introducing the Bill he clearly stated that some of his envisaged measures would require laws changing the Constitution. Article 2 of the Enabling Bill was to empower the government to pass legislation *deviating* from the constitution 'in so far as their subject is not the institution of the Reichstag and Reichsrat as such. The rights of the Reich President remain unimpaired'. So that there could be no doubts or confusion about his intentions, Hitler stated:

> It would contradict the spirit of the national rising and would not suffice for the intended purposes if the Government in each case had to request or bargain with the Reichstag for every piece of legislation. The Government is not driven to give up the Reichstag as such. On the contrary, it preserves for itself the right to call the Reichstag from time to time to inform it about the Government's measures or to ask for its assent.
>
> Its authority and the fulfilment of its task would suffer heavily if doubts should arise among the people concerning the stability of the new regime. The Reich Government considers a further session of the Reichstag in the present condition of deep emotional upheaval of the nation as impossible.[57]

It cannot be said that Hitler did not keep his word. He did not permanently dissolve the Reichstag, but called it from time to time to inform it about measures taken. Having been granted powers to enact laws deviating from the Constitution, he did so by abolishing all parties other than the NSDAP. But then the Constitution contained nothing which placed political parties under any constitutional protection. The institution of the Reichstag *as such* was not affected and the question of the *Reichsrat* had already become irrelevant when the Enabling Bill was introduced because the process of *Gleichschaltung* was already in full swing.[58] Nor were the rights of the Reich President, whose death was expected at any time, impaired. When Hindenburg died on 2 August 1934, Hitler, on the basis of a unanimous cabinet decision taken the day before, fused the offices of chancellor and president and had it sanctioned by a plebiscite.[59] Without pressing need Hitler had the Enabling Act prolonged three times, in 1937, in 1939 and again in 1942. He changed its 'present condition' into one of plebiscitary acclamation. He swept the political parties out of the country as he had promised for years.

Those deputies at the debate who might have nodded off were certainly made aware of the consequences of the Enabling Bill by the SDP's spokesman, Otto Wels. Not only did the Centre Party give its support to the Bill but also liberal and other groupings. Also it was agreed the Enabling Act was to expire 'when the present government is replaced by another'. But it was never replaced until 1945, though additional ministers were added or replaced. The first such replacement was the sacking of the 'economic dictator' Hugenberg because of his performance at the World Economic Conference in London in the summer of 1933, where he aggressively raised demands which, as yet, Hitler had not made and which in Hitler's view were bound to alienate his potential ally, Britain.

More than 82 per cent of the professional politicians in the Reichstag had given Hitler powers, the purpose of which he had never left in doubt. Much is made in post-1945 historiography of the 'reign of terror' by the *SA* and *SS* outside the Reichstag. But how was it that all 94 Social Democrats present voted against the Bill, without being molested afterwards? Were they the only heroes and the others cowards? This is an unlikely explanation. Certainly *SS* and *SA* men were posted in the corridors of *Kroll-Oper* which served as the new forum for the Reichstag, understandably in view of the Reichstag fire, but not one of them molested the dissenters.

Hitler – and about this he had never left any doubt – wanted agreement on the Enabling Law in order to dissolve the multi-party state, and this he received. Hence the Weimar Republic was not removed by a conspiracy, 'by a backstairs intrigue' (Alan Bullock), or by lies and tricks; it was simply removed by the greater proportion of its own politicians. The republic gave up. It was the self-emasculation of the republic, the final confirmation of a process already set in motion at the founding of the republic, a republic that could always be sure of its opponents even among parties, which, so to speak, carried the republic. The manner in which the political process operated in the republic convinced even democrats that the liberal principle of the Weimar vintage no longer had any future. In the end even the Social Democrats succumbed when in the Reichstag session of 17 May 1933 they unanimously endorsed Hitler's foreign policy resolution and together with the NSDAP deputies gave Hitler a standing ovation and joined in singing the German national anthem. Hitler was allegedly moved to tears by this spectacle.[60] But already, just over a fortnight before, trade unions had been forbidden, and property confiscated by what was to call itself the German Labour Front. The last 'patriotic' gesture of the SPD had become superfluous before it had even been made.

3. The Reichstag Fire and Its Political Consequences

HANS MOMMSEN

Their [Hitler's and Göring's] surprise was genuine. When Hanfstaengl phoned him the news, Goebbels thought it was a bad joke.[1] Göring seems to have been utterly thunderstruck; he went at once to the burning building. His first thought was to save the tapestries and the library.[2] He arrived at about 9.30 p.m., shortly after the main hall had gone up in flames and the fire had reached ten-alarm proportions. It cannot be inferred from Göring's behaviour that he welcomed the fire.[3] He gave the necessary instructions, spoke chiefly with Fire Chief Gempp, and inquired after Councillor Galle, the president of the Reichstag. Assistant Secretary Grauert, who was with him, inquired at once into the origin of the fire, learned of the grounds for suspecting Ernst Torgler and Wilhelm Koenen [Ernst Torgler, chairman of the parliamentary party of the KPD, Koenen a KPD deputy Ed.], and was convinced from that moment on that the Communists were behind the fire.[4]

Göring later said that the moment he heard the word 'incendiary' the idea that the Communist Party was to blame had come to him spontaneously.[5] But it seems more likely that the idea was first suggested by the information he obtained from Grauert. A little later Rudolf Diels [chief of the Gestapo Ed.] arrived, accompanied by Assessor Schnitzler, learned that van der Lubbe had been arrested, and took part in the first hearings.[6] At the same time Göring seems to have been told that the only one of the

From *Vierteljahrshefte für Zeitgeschichte* (Munich, 1971).

incendiaries to be apprehended was a Dutch Communist –
it was assumed from the first that van der Lubbe was a
Communist. Göring did not question the generally prevailing
view that the fire had been organised on a large scale by a
considerable number of incendiaries. He ordered a search of
the pipe tunnel, which was carried out without results by
his bodyguard, the SS man Walter Weber, and three
policemen.[7]

Sommerfeldt tells how he was awakened at about 11.00
p.m. and taken to the Reichstag building in a car. This,
however, must have occurred considerably earlier, at about
10.15, for he met Göring before Göring, as Goebbels reports,
'got all steamed up'.[8] According to Sommerfeldt, Göring
was perfectly calm and gave the impression 'of being
somewhat affected by this incendiary act, but of not
attaching too much importance to it'. Göring had calmly
instructed him to draw up the above-mentioned report.[9]
Shortly after ten o'clock Göring, in his capacity as Prussian
Minister of the Interior, must have ordered the first security
measures. When Hitler arrived, Göring reported that he
had mobilised the entire police force and placed all public
buildings under police protection. The other security
measures are reported in the WTB for 28 February.[10]

In all probability Hitler, Goebbels and their retinues did
not arrive at the scene of the fire before 10.20 p.m. Delmer
[Sefton Delmer, Berlin correspondent of the *Daily Express*
Ed.] informs us that Goebbels first sent Gauleiter Hanke to
find out what was actually going on.[11] Göring received
Hitler at the entrance to the lobby adjoining Portal 2.
According to Delmer, Göring explained that it was
undoubtedly the work of the Communists, that an incendiary
had been arrested, and that several Communist Reichstag
members had been in the building twenty minutes before
the outbreak of the fire. Papen had arrived earlier; Göring
had greeted him with the remark: 'This can only be a plot
against the new government!'[12] Papen expressed no doubts.

Thus it is clear that, on the basis of rumours that had
come to his ears, Göring hit on the idea that the Reichstag
fire was connected with a projected Communist uprising.
This accounts for the elaborate security measures which he

spontaneously ordered and which Sir Horace Rumbold
[British ambassador in Berlin *Ed.*] termed a manifestation
of 'hysteria'.[13] Delmer comments: 'I am convinced that he
took it seriously and was not play-acting'.[14] After Göring's
report the VIPs made a tour of the building while the
firemen were trying to contain the terrible fire in the main
hall. The main hall served to illustrate the danger that
Göring had conjured. Delmer, the only journalist who
succeeded in entering the building and in speaking to Hitler
in the course of his tour, reported the following utterances:
' "I hope to God," he said to me, "that this is the work of
the Communists. You are now witnessing the outbreak of a
great epoch in German history." ' And Delmer quotes Hitler
as saying a little later to Papen: 'This is a signal sent by
God, Herr Vice Chancellor. If, as I believe, the fire is the
work of the Communists, then we must crush the murdering
monster with an iron fist.' From these utterances Delmer
inferred that Hitler was not quite sure. That night, he
writes, the Chancellor was 'not yet fully convinced that this
was a Communist plot'.[15] But beyond a doubt Hitler soon
became convinced. Did he believe in the plot, or was he
putting on an act?

Rudolf Diels speaks of Hitler's reaction in his memoirs.
He writes that he met Hitler and his entourage on a
platform opening out on the main hall. Hitler had been
extremely agitated when Göring came up to him and said,
with the emotion of a man conscious of his historic mission:
'This is the beginning of the Communist uprising. They are
about to strike. There is not a moment to lose!'[16] The VIPs
gathered in the room of the president of the Reichstag.
Diels tried to tell Hitler about the hearing on van der
Lubbe. Hitler was completely out of control, demanding
that every Communist functionary should be shot on the
spot and that the Communist members of the Reichstag
should be hanged that same night; it was also high time, he
said, to stop handling the Social Democrats and the
Reichsbanner with kid gloves. Under these circumstances
Diels's efforts to convince Hitler that van der Lubbe had set
the fire by himself were hopeless.[17]

Diels's story is corroborated by Schnitzler's [Police Inspector Heinrich Schnitzler *Ed.*] notes that were drawn up independently of Diels.[18]

Diels characterised the National Socialist conference in the burning Reichstag, at which the first political measures were decided upon, or rather ordered on the spur of the moment without being clearly thought out, as 'agitated' and 'wild'. After Hitler had recovered from a kind of epileptic trance, he had, still according to Diels, flown into an interminable outburst of rage and vilified the Communist 'subhumans'. He no longer required any semblance of proof to be convinced that the Communists by 'shamefully setting fire to a German palladium had wished to give the signal for their loudly heralded mass action'. Hitler had seriously given the order to hang all Communist Reichstag members.[19]

Was Hitler's customary monomaniacal rage still rationally controlled at this point? Was this the feigned agitation which led Hitler, while speaking, to believe in the truth of his words? Undoubtedly the following entry in Goebbels' diary is more than suspect: 'The decisive moment has come. Not for one moment does the Führer lose his calm; it is admirable to see him giving his orders, the same man who only half an hour ago was still having a carefree chat with us at dinner.'[20]

This conference in the Reichstag president's room lasted little more than half an hour. In addition to Göring, Hitler and Goebbels, Minister of the Interior Frick, Police President von Levetzow, whom Göring had sent for, and probably Count Helldorf[21] [Wolf Heinrich Count von Helldorf, leader of the SA in Berlin-Brandenburg and Police President of Potsdam] and Mayor Sahm were present, whereas Papen had left the building to notify President Hindenburg.[22] The conference was taken up mainly by Hitler's tirades; calm not to say lucid discussion was out of the question. Hitler seems to have confined himself mainly to ordering measures of terror and violence against the Communists. In all probability he was thinking chiefly of the elections. A later press report[23] contains the information:

> As previously noted, Adolf Hitler announced while still at the scene of the fire that, come what might, the elections would take place on March 5. He declared that the Reich government would take the measures necessary to crush and exterminate this dire threat not only to Germany but to Europe as well.

Nonetheless, it was not Hitler who issued orders, but Göring; Hitler's outpourings of hatred had given him the green light. This was Göring's great hour. Diels tells us that Göring subjected him to a flood of rather confused instructions, including 'police on an emergency footing, shoot to kill, mass arrests of Communists and Social Democrats'.[24] 'During the conference,' Schnitzler recalled,[25] 'Diels noted the various points on a sheet of paper, and afterward worried whether he had carried out the orders given in their frenzy by the agitated members of the new government, untroubled by the slightest knowledge of the instrument of power and law which they claimed to be able to play.' Without a doubt Göring had also demanded the arrest of all Social Democratic functionaries, and not only a two weeks' suspension of the Social Democratic press in Prussia. This can be inferred from the fact that the parallel action of Helldorf, who was either present at the conference or received orders from Göring a little later, included the Social Democrats. It was presumably with Diels's approval that Schnitzler issued instructions to all police radio stations to send out a call for the arrest of all Communist members of the Reichstag, of the provincial diets and of the town councils as well as of all Communist functionaries, and for the suppression of all Communist newspapers.[25]

What chiefly struck Diels and Schnitzler in connection with this episode was that far-reaching political decisions were made by men who had lost all self-control and gave no thought to the political consequences. The National Socialist leaders were among themselves; hence there was no reason to engage in theatricals for propaganda purposes.

These were not cynically calculating politicians putting on a show for the public. Thus the theory that they had a clear grasp of the situation and exploited it with virtuosity for their purposes is without foundation. Manifestly Hitler and Göring were in such a state that they could not listen to the real facts about the fire, and it would even be misleading to say that they did not wish to do so. They reacted on a subrational level, dominated by instinct and vanity. Hitler's outbursts of rage and hatred, culminating in the absurd demand that the Communist Reichstag members be hanged immediately, cannot be viewed in a rational light. Nor were Göring's reactions feigned; under normal circumstances he was capable of giving clear, intelligible orders. Undoubtedly the desire to put himself, as Prussian Minister of Police, in the limelight had a good deal to do with it, especially in view of the keen rivalry between himself and Goebbels.

Under these circumstances it is not irrelevant to ask whether Göring's orders to Diels were motivated by the situation or based on fantasy. Göring's belief in a Communist uprising was not merely an emanation of his overheated imagination. It was encouraged by reports from police headquarters. Police Inspector Heisig questioned the incendiary at police headquarters. On the witness stand he stated once again that van der Lubbe had used the words 'signal' and 'flare' (*Fanal*) and had said it was time to 'strike' to do away with a system that was hostile to the working class.[27] At the same time this was interpreted by him and the observers present at the interview, including Police President von Levetzow, as pointing to a Communist uprising. In the hectic, unreal atmosphere of that night, these words sufficed to transform suspicion into certainty. Only a few remained free from this psychosis, which developed spontaneously and which there was no need to foster artificially. It is adequately accounted for by the tense political situation. There is no reason to believe that the National Socialist leadership did not take the spectre of a Communist uprising seriously, especially as they had been expecting something of the sort. On 31 January Goebbels had written in his diary: 'The attempt at Bolshevist revolution must first flare up. Then, at the right moment, we will strike.'[28] Concerning the conference in the burning Reichstag building he noted: 'There is no doubt that the Communists are here making a last attempt to create confusion by arson and terror, in order to seize power amid the general panic.'[29] What danger if any the National Socialist leadership in their calmer moments really feared from their Communist adversaries is a question that can be left open for the moment. All indications are that the orders for the arrest of Communists were a spontaneous reaction to the key words 'Communist uprising' as they fell on the avid, overheated imaginations of the National Socialists.

The inclusion of the Social Democrats in these measures was connected with van der Lubbe's statements under questioning, from which it was inferred that the SDP as well as the KPD was behind the supposed plot, though the examining magistrate was obliged to deny that this was so in a statement to the press of 22 March.[30] This grotesque inference was made possible by the weird, unreal atmosphere, in which the most absurd rumours were believed, and by the propaganda and mentality of the National Socialists, who consciously and unconsciously lumped the Communists and Social Democrats together. Moreover, the threat of a general strike called by both parties was still taken seriously by the government, as Article 6 of the 28 February Decree to Combat Treason Against the German Nation bears witness.[31] It is hard to imagine what would have happened if Diels had taken seriously the order to arrest the Social Democrats, disband the Reichsbanner, and so on. If there was any calculation behind this order, it was only the idea of making a clean sweep in a situation of civil war.

The conference in the office of the Reichstag president ended at about eleven o'clock and brought no further results. But the idea of proclaiming a state of emergency seems already to have been brought up at this time. According to a press report, the cabinet 'was to meet again during the night in special session' to deliberate 'on the political consequences of the Reichstag fire.'[32]

At about 11.15 Hitler and Göring left the still smouldering Reichstag building and went to the Prussian Ministry of the

Interior. There a conference was held which seems to have been what the above-mentioned press report refers to erroneously as a cabinet meeting. It was attended by Vice Chancellor von Papen, Police President von Levetzow, Assistant Secretary Grauert, State Secretary von Bismarck, and Councillor Diels. Frick, who had attended the previous meeting, was absent, perhaps merely because the competence of this body extended only to Prussia. The composition of the meeting indicates that it was called chiefly to discuss security measures and arrests. Concerning this meeting Göring had the following to say in his testimony before the Reich Court: 'We again discussed the whole situation. It was decided at the very start that I should immediately cancel ... my election rallies ... scheduled for the next few days. Because in such an atmosphere I could obviously not leave Berlin.' He went on to say that he had been authorised to take all necessary measures, and that a cabinet meeting had been called for the following day.[33] As can be gathered from the above-mentioned press report on Hitler's remarks at the scene of the fire, his chief concern was that the elections should be held 'under any circumstances', and one wonders what led him to make this strange statement. According to the testimony of Detective Superintendent Heller, the arrest orders previously given in feverish haste were repeated and made official at this session, and a list of the persons to be arrested may have been drawn up.[34] The much discussed 'Reichstag fire decree' was not at the centre of the discussion. Probably with a view to the fact that nothing had been done to legalise the arrests, the German Nationalist Grauert suggested an 'emergency decree against arson and terrorist acts'. Thus Grauert, who was firmly convinced that the Communists were responsible for the fire, suggested what was to be a decisive step toward Hitler's unlimited dictatorship.[35]

The emergency decree proposed by Grauert was undoubtedly very different from the draft submitted to the Reichstag the following day. The original plan seems to have been a decree applicable only to Prussia, and it is possible that this accounts in part for Frick's reference to the Prussian decree of 20 July. For otherwise we should be at a loss to explain

Blomberg's remark at the 1 March meeting of the High Command:[36] [General Werner von. Blomberg, Reichswehrminister 1933–8 *Ed.*] 'Thanks to Hitler's foresight, the new emergency decree was extended to the entire Reich.' In this view, Hitler accepted Grauert's suggestion, but decided that it should be discussed at next day's cabinet meeting. This fits in with Grauert's statement that the matter had been taken out of the hands of the Prussian Ministry of the Interior.[37]

After the meeting at the Prussian Ministry of the Interior Hitler and Goebbels went to the offices of the *Völkischer Beobachter*; they stopped the presses and had a new front page written.[38] The South German edition had already appeared and contained not a word about the Reichstag fire. Goebbels launched a wild press campaign. That same night he wrote an inflammatory editorial, painting the horror of a successful Communist campaign of terror and stating that the Communists were planning to seize power in the midst of the 'general panic'.[39] In the dispatches of the Official Prussian Press Bureau, which the WTB published in the second edition of 28 February, the Reichstag fire was characterised as a 'signal for bloody revolution and civil war'; it was declared that 'the first assault of the criminal forces has been beaten off',[40] a statement inspired by Göring's bluster, for at the time the report was sent out the police action had barely begun.[41] The police, the report went on, had been put on a top emergency footing and two thousand members of the SA auxiliary police had been called in to defend the capital. On 1 March the *Völkischer Beobachter* spoke of a projected 'Saint Bartholomew' in Berlin, and disclosed Communist plans for insurrection which Göring had borrowed from obsolete directives for civil war.[42]

Despite all its efforts, as Tobias has shown, Goebbels' press bureau blundered, and not only in connection with the reporting of the fire and its causes. Amid the general confusion, even the *Völkischer Beobachter* reported that Torgler had given himself up voluntarily and was obliged to change its story the following day.[43] But it is understandable that on the night after the fire Göring should have termed

Sommerfeldt's communiqué 'crap', 'a police report from Alexanderplatz' [police presidium] which he could have no use for at a time when he was preparing to strike a crushing counterblow against the Communists.[44] Sommerfeldt believed that Goebbels was behind this change of heart on Göring's part, but the truth was much simpler; even if Göring had believed that van der Lubbe had acted alone, it was too late to retract the 'political signal' theory without making himself – and his police measures – look ridiculous.

That was the situation on the night of 27 February. It raises a number of questions. As we have seen, the National Socialist leadership was taken by surprise and acted in a state of excitement. Were the National Socialist leaders really convinced that the Reichstag fire was an act of Communist terror? At first, as we have seen, Hitler was not quite sure; but this does not mean that he did not immediately swing over to Göring's view, especially as the results of the investigation, including the misstatements about Torgler, confirmed his suspicions and as a political exploitation of the fire was in the air in any case. Thus it may be presumed that the National Socialists were convinced that the Communists were behind the fire. A much more difficult question to answer is whether, and if so in what degree, they believed in a Communist uprising or a planned series of terrorist acts, and at what moment they recognised this to be a mistake. It is hard to answer this question because we possess virtually no statements on the subject that do not admit of, or indeed call for, a tactical interpretation, and because the essential character of National Socialist thinking, even in the consciousness of its proponents, was to substitute resentment for the experience of reality. Goebbels' expectation of a 'Communist attempt at revolution' fits in with a good deal of indirect testimony[45] to the effect that the National Socialists did not believe the Communists would let them come to power without putting up a fight. Our present knowledge of the situation and policy of the KPD in the weeks after the seizure of power[46] permits us to infer that the National Socialists had overestimated their adversary. Undoubtedly Hitler's conviction that it was politically inexpedient to outlaw the KPD, as his German National partners wished, was not motivated solely by the tactical consideration that this would have added appreciably to the Social Democratic vote.[47] The history of his own movement taught him that there was very little to be gained by outlawing a political party.[48]

At the same time, however, the National Socialists derived an appealing campaign promise from their undertaking to combat Communism successfully, and there is no doubt that the bourgeoisie's fear of Communism, fanned by the propaganda of all the right-wing parties and also by the actual situation of civil war between the KPD and the NSDAP, contributed very considerably to the rise of National Socialism. Thus for tactical reasons it was to the advantage of the National Socialists not to eliminate this adversary until they themselves were firmly in the saddle. Nevertheless it seems probable that the National Socialist leadership were increasingly alarmed at the question of why, generally speaking, the KPD took the increasing provocations of the SA lying down and failed to strike the counterblow that would release Hitler from the shackles imposed on him by the German National cabinet members and the independent position of the Reichswehr. The extraordinary agitation into which Hitler worked himself on the night of the fire suggests that he really thought the great conflict was at hand, that he regarded a Communist putsch as imminent. This would account for the hasty reaction of the National Socialists, the immediate measures for the security of public buildings, museums, castles, bridges, and railroads. Because, if that were the case, it became essential to get the jump on the Communists.

In order to appraise this hypothesis we must first determine whether the situation gave the government cause to believe that the Communists were planning an armed uprising. True, the memory of Communist uprisings under the Weimar Republic was still fresh. The actual situation, however, was much more complicated. The tactics of the KPD in those weeks were vacillating and inconsistent. While in the Central Committee plans for an active struggle of the working class against Hitler were postponed indefinitely, the Communist organisations were provided with literature calling indirectly or often directly for armed resistance.[49] Large amounts of such material reached the news bureau of the Ministry of the Interior, and at the same time large stores of weapons were found.[50] The nature of the material found in the second search of the Karl-Liebknecht House, which Göring cited as the main justification of his measures, remains unknown.[51] These finds along with the rumours then circulating increased the general nervousness and fear of a Communist uprising. On 27 February, the Berlin Criminal Investigation Department (*Landeskriminalpolizeiamt*) broadcast a report to the effect that the KPD was planning systematic armed attacks on police patrols and 'national' organisations on the day of the Reichstag elections, or shortly before or after, and recommended that 'suitable countermeasures be taken immediately and that Communist functionaries should perhaps be taken into protective custody'.[52] This information was more than dubious, but should not be interpreted as a deliberate propagandist invention; rather, it indicates the general overestimation of Communist activity, and shows that the idea of Communist responsibility for the fire was in the air. A great mass of material has been assembled in connection with the Reichstag fire and the propagandist use to which it was put. This material confirms the fact that despite acts of individual terror the Communist Party leadership remained passive.

In the light of what we now know of Communist revolutionary strategy, the evidence that the Communists were planning an uprising was meagre. But in the then prevailing atmosphere, propaganda pamphlets like Sommerfeldt's *Die Kommune* were taken at face value. Even the high police officials concerned with the case, who at that time had by no means been 'Nazified' (*gleichgeschaltet*), tended to overemphasise the activity of the Communists. In a report of 14 March the view was expressed 'that not only does the organisation of an armed uprising for the overthrow of the government figure in the Communist program; they are determined to carry out their programmatic demands and principles in practice.'[53] Before the Reich Court, Detective Superintendent Heller, testifying as an expert, submitted material to prove that the Communists were planning an uprising, but then denied that they were preparing for action.[54] Nevertheless, Heller continued to believe that his exposé justified the assertion that the Communists had been planning an uprising.

As for Göring, it seems certain that at least on the night of the fire he believed in the spectre of a Communist uprising. Ever since he had become Prussian Minister of the Interior it had been his dream to crush such an uprising.[55] As he stressed at the cabinet meeting of 2 March, he did not expect one before the elections. The cynical frankness and tactical ineptitude of Göring's testimony before the Reich Court make it seem likely that he was telling the truth, and it is no doubt for this reason that his remarks were sharply criticised by Goebbels. The Reichstag fire, Göring declared, had come as a surprise to him and had not fitted in with his plan of action. True, he had been resolved from the start to strike a counterblow against the Communists, but the police apparatus he had taken over was still deficient; in particular, it lacked the determination to strike with the necessary ruthlessness. Göring expressly claimed authorship of the 'shoot-to-kill' order, as it came to be called. He had considered carrying on the fight with the SA and SS alone, but had deliberately discarded this idea:

In the first place, there was the newly created state with its whole civil service corps which I wished to rebuild, to transform, and to imbue with the new spirit – I could not totally exclude it from this task which offered an opportunity to employ it for the first time as a state organ for the preservation of the new state. That would have shaken the confidence of the civil service corps in the new state from the very start.[56]

It is certain that at the time of the Reichstag fire, the Prussian police had not yet been transformed into a reliable instrument of National Socialism. The SA auxiliary police established by the decree of 22 February was still in process of organisation; in Berlin it took no appreciable part in the campaign of arrest.[57] And the changes of personnel at the Berlin Police Presidium were only in their beginnings.

If the improvised campaign of arrests nevertheless brought appreciable results, it was primarily because the old Political Police apparatus was still intact; the old officials from Severing's [Carl Severing, former SPD Minister of the Interior of Prussia *Ed.*] day were still on the job. The arrests were carried out on the basis of lists that had been drawn up by the democratic government for the eventuality that the Communist Party would be suppressed; Göring had had these lists completed and brought up to date.[58] Despite the official statements that four thousand Communists were arrested in the weeks after the Reichstag fire, there can be no doubt that the action was improvised and premature, a stroke in the dark, which induced the KPD to build up its underground organisation. Sir Horace Rumbold reported on 2 March: 'Though Communist leaders have been arrested, I am told on reliable authority that organisation has gone to ground and is intact, but that no instructions for armed resistance have been issued to the party members.'[59] Although the KPD was taken by surprise – at the time of the fire the Central Committee was in session and even party functionaries were unable to reach it[60] – numerous Communists evaded arrest.

Thus the action was by no means the brilliant success that the National Socialist press claimed. Indirectly Göring admitted as much when he remarked that he had felt the Reichstag fire to have 'interfered completely' with his 'beautifully laid plans'; he had found it 'inconvenient, extremely inconvenient'; he had been in the situation of 'a general, who wants to carry out a great battle plan and is then compelled by an impulsive action of the enemy to proceed in an entirely different way, to move his troops in haste and take up battle positions'. He had expected the Communist counter-offensive later, during the three or four weeks between the Reichstag fire and the meeting of the Reichstag, 'that is, at a time when the Communist mandates had been annulled but of course no Communist leaders were yet under arrest'. He had wanted the enemy to open hostilities, but not until he had completed his deployment.

'The elections were to be the climax, if only because they would provide a rough idea of the strength of the Communist following. After the elections,' Göring went on, 'the Communist mandates were of course to be annulled.' It was not likely, in his opinion, that the party would accept this measure without a struggle, for then it would have lost face in the eyes of its adherents. In either case the party could easily have been crushed, and a part of the leadership would not have been able to save themselves as they had after 27 February.[61]

This statement made under the eyes of world opinion is typical of the cynical frankness with which the National Socialist leadership revealed the motives of their actions. It shows not only that the National Socialists wished to provoke a Communist uprising, but also that the government planned to annul the Communist mandates in case it should prove impossible to gain a two-thirds majority for the Enabling Act by quasi-legal methods.[62] It would not have been to the interest of the National Socialists, Göring explained, to outlaw the Communist Party, because then the Communist electorate would have voted for the SPD or the Centre Party.[63] Göring now admitted that the first search of the Karl-Liebknecht House had been undertaken chiefly for propaganda reasons and had not brought very impressive results, and that only consideration for the prevailing mood of the people had led him to attack during the night of the fire.

Was this an admission that Göring had decided on arrests and the measures of violence against the KPD for electoral reasons, in consideration of 'the prevailing mood of the people'? Göring's statement fits in with Hitler's remark at the cabinet meeting of 28 February, to the effect that the 'psychological moment' had come for dealing with the Communists.[64] A number of considerations argue against such an oversimplification. Göring's remarks were made at a time when the passivity of the KPD had rendered the idea of a large-scale revolutionary plan absurd. That, precisely, is what made the suspicion vented in the world press that Göring was the actual incendiary seem so plausible. Exactly like the police investigators, Göring tried to represent the Reichstag fire as a link in a chain of terrorist acts leading to revolution, since it was no longer possible to uphold the original contention that the fire was to be the immediate signal for an uprising. Göring clung tenaciously to his over-all suspicion and described the events as though the measures taken on the night of the fire had got the jump on the Communists. In response to Torgler's objections, he asked with none too convincing irony why the Communists had issued instructions for civil war if they had no intention of carrying them out.[65] It was the same Göring who had heedlessly, without regard for Diels's warnings, initiated the preparations for the monster trial for high treason.

From all this it follows that the National Socialist leadership were indeed expecting a Communist counteraction, but only at a later date. Our fragmentary sources enable us to give only a partial answer to the questions of how Hitler and his followers judged the political situation on the night of the fire and what political measures they were considering. It is conceivable, however, that Hitler became more and more obsessed with the idea, noted in Goebbels' diary, that the Communists wished to provoke a general panic. His first reactions, such as demanding that all the Communists be hanged, were absurd. It was perfectly possible to quench Communist agitation effectively by suppressing their newspapers, meetings and demonstrations, and this had largely been done. Undoubtedly Hitler, with his keen instinct for the mood of the population, thought of using the 'Communist bugaboo' for purposes of electoral propaganda. This may have been the motivation for the security measures which Rumbold calls 'hysterical',[66] and which were not suspended after the elections but remained in force for two weeks. But the inclusion of the Social Democrats in these arrests would largely have deprived them of their effect and above all constituted a break with the tactical line that Hitler followed in the weeks before the Enabling Act, to wit, emphasis on the legal methods of the new government.

In this context the statement that the elections must take place on 5 March 'under any circumstances' takes on a particular weight. The main topic discussed at the conference at the Prussian Ministry of the Interior was the continuation of the election campaign. The following morning at the cabinet meeting Hitler took up the matter again: 'The attack on the Reichstag building must have no effect on the date of the elections or the reconvening of the Reichstag'. At the same time he suggested the chateau of Potsdam as a meeting place for the Reichstag.[67] From this it may be inferred that Hitler looked on the fire as a primitive attempt to prevent the Reichstag from meeting. It is not clear, on the other hand, why, even before the meeting at the Prussian Ministry of the Interior, Hitler should have come out against a change in the date of the elections. Had Papen suggested that under the circumstances it might be expedient to postpone them? This is unlikely, because in this case Hitler would not have bothered the cabinet with the question. What was the meaning of 'under any circumstances'? It can only have meant that the elections must take place even in an exceptional situation, perhaps a state of emergency. Neither his spontaneous belief in a Communist *putsch* nor his insistence that the elections should not be postponed can have resulted from propagandist designs.

In view of the hysteria that had gripped the National Socialist members of the government in the burning Reichstag, one inclines to infer that in this 'crime against the new government' Hitler saw an attempt to deprive him of the weapon of legality, to force the NSDAP into a civil war, and above all to prevent it from carrying through the elections. In this connection Hitler's introductory remarks at the cabinet meeting of 28 February are significant:

The Chancellor declared that a ruthless confrontation with the KPD had now become indispensable, that the psychological moment for this confrontation had come, that there was no point in waiting any longer, that the action against [the KPD] must not be subordinated to juridical considerations. Since the Reichstag fire, he said, he no longer doubted that the government would obtain 51 per cent at the elections.[68]

From this it follows, first of all, that the National Socialist leadership had decided that the showdown must take place sooner than they had expected. For this there were two reasons: as usual with Hitler, the propagandist necessity and the practical necessity of the confrontation went hand in hand. It is true that since the night of the fire, when Communist actions were felt to be imminent, the situation had grown calmer. No one could claim that a *putsch* was in the offing. Still, it can hardly have been a purely propagandist exaggeration when Hitler said that the KPD had decided to stop at nothing. It could still not be foreseen that the KPD would be crushed without a struggle. Hitler's remark that this action must not be 'subordinated to juridical considerations' referred not so much to the methods of the SA auxiliary police as to the fact that the arrest of the Communist Reichstag members would transgress the principle of parliamentary immunity.[69] Hitler's saying that he no longer doubted that the government would obtain a majority implies that on 27 February the National Socialist leadership was not yet sure the elections would bring the desired results; the frequent statements that they would remain in power in any case point in the same direction. In the given context Hitler's remark was probably an argument against postponing the elections because of a potential or actual civil war situation.

Interestingly enough, the Chancellor attached relatively little importance to the emergency decree, the last point on the agenda of the conference, perhaps, for one thing, because he had little knowledge of it. In any case, he still spoke of it as a merely defensive measure, remarking for example on the necessity of 'special measures to safeguard all the cultural documents of the German people'. Grauert's [Ludwig Grauert, head of the Berlin police department, Göring's comrade in the First World War *Ed.*] proposal had been along these lines. But meanwhile Frick had taken the matter in hand and probably in the morning hours had prepared his draft which differed radically from all previous emergency decrees. Characteristically, it did not occur to the author of the new decree to modify the Decree to Combat Treason Against the German Nation[70] which had been voted by the cabinet on the morning of 27 February and submitted to the president for his signature on the following day, although it partly covered the situation created (in the National Socialist view) by the Communist act of incendiarism. This indicates the spontaneity with which the Reichstag fire decree came into being and is presumably also explained by the fact that the initiators of the first decree knew nothing about the drafting of the second.

The genesis of the Reichstag fire decree, which Helmut Krausnick calls the 'Fundamental Law of the Third Reich'[71] and whose crucial importance for the stabilisation of the National Socialist system has been demonstrated by Karl Dietrich Bracher,[72] is obscure. What we know for sure is that it came into being spontaneously and that there had been no plans in this direction before the Reichstag fire. At the cabinet meeting Frick observed 'that he had originally intended, because of the fire in the Reichstag building, to modify the Decree for the Defence of the German Nation of February 4 of this year'.[73] The February decree placed the first serious restrictions on the parties competing with the NSDAP in the elections. Frick may have thought of increasing and extending the penal provisions; in particular, he may have considered a new version of Article 22, so as to remove all limitations on the use of protective custody against the Communists.[74] A contributory factor may have been that in view of the urgency of the situation it seemed too complicated to modify the February decree, which was rather unclear to begin with; in any case Frick made it known that he then decided to use the Prussian decree of 20 July as a basis for the new decree.

With this the decree took on a fundamentally different character. The originally intended version was reflected only in the harsh penal provisions of Article 5 against high treason and a number of criminal acts imputed to the Communists. Some of these provisions go back to the modifications desired by Gürtner [Dr Franz Gürtner, Minister of Justice *Ed.*], which incidentally show that he was not present when the decree was drafted.[75] As for the genesis of the two decisive provisions of the decree, the suspension of constitutional rights and the infringement embodied in Article 2, on the sovereignty of the *Länder*, we can only resort to conjecture. Undoubtedly there is a direct connection between Article 2 and Göring's statement at the cabinet meeting of the previous day to the effect that by 6 March at the latest, that is, the day after the elections, he would request authorisation to place the Hamburg police under the Reich Minister of the Interior.[76] A little later Göring spoke of Hamburg as a 'rallying point for Communism', and even earlier pressure had been put on the Senate to replace the Socialist chief of the Hamburg police by a National Socialist.[77]

To strike a nation-wide 'counterblow' at the Communists, it was necessary to simplify the complicated mechanism governing the cooperation of the police in the various *Länder* with the central government. In its struggle against the extremes of right and left the Weimar Republic had been seriously hampered by the absence of any central police authority: the Reich Public Prosecutor could take action only through the public prosecutors of the *Länder* and their subsidiary organs.[72] On 1 March Frick, invoking the decree, called on the governments of the *Länder* to suppress all Communist publications and meetings; formally, the ministers of the interior of the *Länder* decided in what degree to accept the measures demanded by Berlin.[79] Article 2 of the new decree went much further, however, and for that reason Papen objected to it at once. This article had been inspired by Frick's interests as Reich Minister of the Interior. Already on 20 and 21 February, when Württemberg had complained that the Reich government was overstepping its prerogatives, Frick had responded by threatening to appoint a Reich commissioner in accordance with Article 48, Paragraph 2; on 24 February, in a public speech, he addressed the same threat to Bavaria and Hamburg.[80] By 27 February it was rumoured that Reich commissioners were about to be appointed in the *Länder*.[81] Beyond any doubt Frick intended to press the *Gleichschaltung* of the *Länder* with the help of Article 2. The changes in the decree obtained by Popitz [Johannes Popitz, Reich Minister without Portfolio and Reich Commissar in charge of the Prussian

Finance Ministry in 1932; Prussian State and Finance Minister, 1933–44] and Papen proved ineffectual.[82] At first, to be sure, Frick denied the intention attributed to him and on 1 March assured the Württemberg ambassador that the decree was aimed primarily at the Hanseatic cities, since the government did not wish the *Länder* governed by 'Marxists' to obtain the powers conferred by Article 1.[83] This statement accurately reflects the original intention of the decree; but it is obvious that he was acting in the interest of his ministry.

But whose idea was it to abrogate the basic civil rights rather than curtail them as was usually done? This remains an open question. Possibly this idea also originated in the Reich Ministry of the Interior, though probably it did not occur to Frick at the time that this was the most effective way in which to legalise the ruthless persecution of the Communists.[84] As the *Frankfurter Zeitung* commented on 1 March,[85] the new situation created by Article 1 came very close to a proclamation of martial law. This meant a considerable deviation from the political line followed since 30 January. The emergency decree cannot be regarded as an organic preliminary phase of the Enabling Act which the National Socialist leadership had been striving for from the start; though formally it remained within the framework of the president's right to issue emergency decrees, it was actually a kind of *coup d'état*, anticipating the Enabling Act. This is also shown by a comparison of its style with that of earlier decrees. Whereas the earlier decrees, that of 4 February for example, formally retained certain legal guarantees – such as the principle that the acts of government agencies were subject to review by the courts; the right, in practice ineffectual to be sure, to register complaints with higher authorities; and an exact definition of the situations to which the decree was applicable – the Reichstag fire decree simply abrogated the principle of constitutional rights. It gave the government a blank cheque, subject only to a fictitious time limit.[86] The motivation cited in the preamble – 'defence against Communist acts of violence' – did not in any way limit its sphere of application. It was no accident that Frick invoked the model of Papen's Prussian decree. The crucial difference between the Prussian decree and the present one was that not the President but the Reich government decided when Article 2 was to be applied. Consequently Papen suggested feebly in the afternoon session of 28 February that it would be better to let the president decide whether Reich commissioners should be appointed in the *Länder*.[87]

Up to now the Reichstag fire decree has been attributed largely to electoral motives. But why was it needed? True, it created a 'better' legal basis for measures directed against the press and freedom of speech and assembly, for breaking up election meetings and demonstrations, confiscating leaflets and propaganda material, searching party offices, and arresting Socialist and Communist leaders. The February decree was invoked in justification of the arrests on the night of the fire. A large part of the opposition press had already been suppressed on the basis of existing decrees, and where the legal basis was insufficient, that did not greatly trouble the authorities. An analysis of the repressive practice in force before the Reichstag fire shows that the change occurring in the days after 8 February was not so much qualitative as purely quantitative. In the non-Prussian *Länder* the Reich Minister of the Interior had been able even before the decree to put through far-reaching repressive measures against the Centre press and other newspapers.[88]

The implementation order of the Prussian Minister of the Interior of 3 March 1933, points in the same direction. It states 'that the Decree for the Defence of Nation and State of February 28, 1933 is to be invoked for measures which become necessary against members or institutions of other than Communist, Anarchist, or Social Democratic parties or organizations, only when these measures serve to combat Communist efforts in the broadest sense.' In other cases the decree of 4 February was to be invoked.[89] Göring demanded frequent and detailed reports from the various government agencies,

informing him how often and under what circumstances
the Reichstag fire decree had been applied. These reports
and the résumés drawn up at the ministry show clearly
that the decree was seldom used against the bourgeois
parties, that at first the overwhelming majority of the
measures taken were directed against the KPD, and that
the persecution of the SPD did not take on importance
until April.[90] It seems likely that Göring's purpose in
limiting the application of the decree was to counter the
accusation that the decree had been issued solely to help
the National Socialists in their election campaign.

If the emergency decree was created with a view to
electoral considerations, it was a means of further
terrorising the voters. But the relative success of the
NSDAP concealed the fact that such a measure cut both
ways. The sharply critical attitude of the *Frankfurter
Zeitung*, which pointed out that elections in Germany had
never before been held in a state of emergency,[92] indicates
that this obvious break with the constitutional order, for
which *provocateurs* or undisciplined subordinates could no
longer be blamed, alienated the sympathies of certain
sections of the electorate. After the elections, moreover,
the Enabling Act would have been passed in any case,
and the full powers anticipated by the emergency decree
would have fallen into the government's lap.

There are a number of indications that on the night of
the fire and the following day the leading National
Socialists, with their utter inability to distinguish between
reality and imagination, were misled by Hitler's visions of
Communist terror and revolution. After the conference at
the Prussian Ministry of the Interior it was rumoured
that a state of emergency would be declared. All
indications are that on the night of the fire such a
measure, limited to Prussia, was considered, and that
Ebert's decree of 26 September 1923, was taken as a
model. According to press reports, it was decided at the
cabinet meeting of 28 February not to proclaim martial
law.[93] The idea did actually come up. At the High
Command meeting recorded in Liebmann's [General Kurt
Liebmann] notes, Blomberg discussed the emergency

decree and the question of the relationship between the Reichswehr and the nationalist paramilitary organisations. In the present context the following note is significant: 'Significant that Army has been left out (military support at first intended. But this would have meant martial law). Not likely that Army will be drawn in.'[94]

As we have seen, it is difficult to draw a clear dividing line between the statements Hitler made for tactical reasons and his real estimate of the situation, and this in turn makes it difficult to interpret the negotiations between the party leadership and the Reichswehr that must have taken place after the Reichstag fire. The High Command meeting itself had been scheduled before the fire and took place on the morning of 1 March. The topics under discussion were the emergency decree and, in view of the projected actions against the KPD, the relations between the Reichswehr and the SA auxiliary police. The probability of serious clashes on election night between the nationalist organisations and the KPD was discussed. And the question of proclaiming a 'state of revolution' was raised.[95] On 3 March Liebmann issued an order implementing Blomberg's instructions that all passes should be cancelled on election night from 8.00 p.m. to 6 a.m., that all troops should be confined to their barracks and those living off post should stay at home during this period, that the telephone switchboards should be kept in operation, that the commanding officers and post commanders were to remain within reach, and that on the night of 5 March no military personnel of any description should appear on the street in uniform.[96]

These instructions permit of various interpretations. First of all, they fit in with Göring's statement at next day's cabinet meeting that the Communist leadership had originally intended to strike in the evening and night of election day.[97] This would lead us to presume that the National Socialist leadership were really counting on a Communist counter-blow, and that since it had not occurred at the time of the Reichstag fire, they assumed it would take place at a later date. At the time when the emergency decree was framed, it was thought that the

Communists would definitely strike on election night, but on 2 March Göring expressed the belief that they had postponed their action until 15 March. From the High Command meeting it can be inferred that the National Socialist leadership had been impelled to revise their views concerning the nature of the Communist counter-blow. The terse utterances of Goebbels, Göring and Hitler give the impression that at first a regular uprising, an attempt at revolution, had been expected. For such an action the republic provided precedents. A general strike and military engagements would have led to an overt test of strength, in which the government could have obtained the support of the Reichswehr. A feverish study of the available material relating to Communist activity – it would seem that at the time of the fire the documents confiscated on 26 March at the Karl-Liebknecht House had scarcely been looked at – and the total absence of revolutionary action despite the provocative arrests showed these suppositions to be unfounded. Nevertheless it is conceivable that the National Socialists at first considered calling on the Reichswehr but immediately dropped the idea, because a declaration of martial law would have meant postponing the elections and would have strengthened the German National element in the government coalition.

It is certain that Hitler wished to avoid involving the Reichswehr in the political conflict. The correspondent of the *Frankfurter Zeitung* reported that the government did not intend to call on the Reichswehr.[98] Still, it is interesting to note that the idea did arise. Conservative circles may have suggested it on the night of the fire, which would explain why Hitler insisted on going through with the elections and why he insisted on 28 February that the government would gain an absolute majority. That the idea was in the air is confirmed by Dertinger [Georg Dertinger, a former editor of the *Stahlhelm* and a German Nationalist who first became press officer, then general secretary of the Christian Democratic Union in the Soviet Zone, was Foreign Minister of the German Democratic Republic from 1949 to 1953. Arrested for espionage and treason in 1953 and sentenced to 15 years, he was amnestied in 1964.] (a none too reliable witness, to be sure), who noted under 7 March that Blomberg had asked the president to declare martial law, arguing that this solution would make it possible 'to maintain order in the contested capitals of certain *Länder*'. On 9 March Dertinger notes: 'To preserve the relation of forces in the cabinet, the idea was put forward of entrusting the executive power in the entire Reich to a Reich commissioner or of declaring martial law.'[99] This reflects the conservatives' utopian hopes of checking the consolidation of Hitler's power at the last moment. But it permits the supposition that the application of martial law was demanded in connection with the Reichstag fire and the civil war situation invoked by Goebbels and Göring.

All this may have led Hitler to conclude that everything must be done to avoid a situation into which the Reichswehr would have to be drawn. This consideration would account for the marked haste of the National Socialist leadership and also for the change in their view (apparent from Blomberg's speech) of the Communists' aims. Now they spoke of the 'new tactics' adopted by the KPD, which had realised that it could not overthrow the government by gaining control over the 'larger centres of power' (that is, presumably, by seizing the big cities with the help of a general strike) and had consequently shifted over to guerrilla warfare that could be combated by military means. Consequently the Reichswehr should remain neutral, 'benevolently' so of course, while the fight was carried on by the 'people', that is, by the SA shock troops. True, the emergency decree enabled the government to employ all organs of state power against the Communists, but the legal military power – the Reichswehr – would not be adequate.[100]

In the High Command meeting Blomberg had the greatest difficulty in overcoming the generals' attitude of scepticism toward the 'national revolution' and the National Socialist army of civil war. He himself characterised the actions of the SA as 'expeditions of vengeance', but excused them by saying that as in Italy they were unavoidable. Inconsistently he on the one hand demanded benevolent support, 'in order that the SA should not be impeded in its struggle against the Communists', and on the other hand made it clear that a 'soldier must stand apart and not involve himself in the "acts of vengeance" of the SA and the police'. The divided attitude of the Reichswehr is made evident by Blomberg's speech, in which he largely deferred to the wishes of the National Socialists. The Reichswehr Ministry, as Rumbold reported on 2 March,[101] feared a National Socialist coup on election night. In deciding to take the offensive against the Communists, Hitler may consequently have aimed not only to terrorise the parties of the left, but also to secure his power in case he were defeated at the polls.

The 'Emergency Decree for the Defence of Nation and State', decided by the cabinet on 28 February and immediately submitted to Hindenburg for signature, substituted a civil state of emergency for the military state of emergency (martial law) desired by the conservatives. It entrusted the Reich cabinet with all the powers which in case of military dictatorship are normally conferred on the commander in chief; indeed, it fell short of military dictatorship only in one point, namely, that the appointment of Reich commissioners in the *Länder* was made subject to certain conditions (though, to be sure, these were fictitious). This explains its deviation in form from all comparable emergency decrees, including the Decree to Combat Treason Against the German Nation. There is good reason to believe that the president's agreement to sign it at once was obtained in part by the argument that this was a lesser evil than martial law – a parallel to the situation at the fall of Schleicher.

The decree was drawn up *ad hoc*. By setting aside constitutional guarantees it played an important psychological role in the elections. Hitler deliberately disregarded the plea to nullify the decree as soon as possible.[102] Nevertheless the National Socialists did not

make use of the power conferred by the decree to
'integrate' the *Länder* until after the elections. There is
reason to believe that Hitler expected greater resistance.
At the scene of the fire he obviously believed that it
would be necessary to strike ruthlessly, to employ all
legal and semi-legal means in order to put through the
elections and to win them. This does not mean that
Hitler was panicstricken; his reaction was not, as Tobias
supposes,[103] a 'reaction of terror', Hitler was too much of
a monomaniac for that; it was not fear but autosuggestive
faith in his mission that made him a power-intoxicated
dictator, and this was nothing new. On the other hand,
the campaign of arrests and the actions that followed it
were not the outcome of clear and purposive decisions.
Nor was it 'adroit' manipulation that led to the
emergency decree of 28 February, but a kind of 'flight
forward'. This is especially true of Göring, who became
so obsessed with the idea of a political signal on the part
of the Communists that from the standpoint of propaganda
he made considerable mistakes.

Goebbels' reaction to the absence of Communist action
was characteristic. 'Resistance nowhere in sight. The
enemy camp *seem* to be so bewildered by our sudden
intense action that they no longer dare to defend
themselves.'[104] Actually the fact that nothing happened to
justify the excitement on the night of the fire does not
indicate great astuteness on the part of the National
Socialist leadership. The headquarters of the Communist
conspiracy had not been discovered. Everyone could read
in the papers that the police were working on pure
conjecture. At the cabinet meeting of 28 February Göring
raised the question of why the Communists had set fire
to the Reichstag and answered it by saying – a typical
blunder – that they had been unable to accept the
confiscation of the secret material in the Karl-Liebknecht
House, which allegedly incriminated them gravely.[105] In
his much heralded radio speech of 1 March he admitted
that the KPD had not yet completed its preparations for
civil war. He documented his allegation that the
Communists had planned a large-scale campaign of

terrorism with obsolete material borrowed from the white elephants of anti-Communist propaganda. Commenting on the alleged flight of Torgler and Koenen from the burning Reichstag, reported over the radio on 27 February, as proof of Communist guilt, he declared that 'in one form or another there has been a plot which the Public Prosecutor's office and the police are doing their utmost to elucidate'.[106] It was not until 2 March that he came into possession of concrete incriminating evidence, which was authentic as far as it went but not very significant.[107]

Most of the charges against the Communists were based on material which had been provided by the Political Police, but the significance of which was of course exaggerated. Only a few assertions, for example, that van der Lubbe had admitted his connection with the KPD or that large-scale looting expeditions had been scheduled for the afternoon of 28 February in Berlin, were pure invention. The absence of really damaging material does not diminish our impression that Hitler and Göring were convinced of the Communist determination to stage an uprising; conversely, if the National Socialists had invented such an accusation in order to make tactical use of it, it seems unthinkable that they would not have taken the trouble to obtain proofs, or forge them if necessary. Actually they had no serious material with which to counter the anti-National Socialist stories in the foreign press.[108] Finally, when the foreign press persisted in suspecting Göring,[109] the National Socialist leadership instructed the examining magistrate to compile material incriminating the Communists.

In order to understand why the National Socialists let themselves in for the Reichstag fire trial against van der Lubbe, Torgler, Dimitrov, and his two fellow Bulgarians, one must be familiar with the grotesque image of Communist activity which in the first days of March occupied the minds of responsible figures including Göring. This image was pieced together from uncritically interpreted Communist propaganda pamphlets, from the questionable statements of Communist renegades, some of them common-law criminals, and from the exaggerated, misleading reports of regional police authorities; it included notions about the technique of Communist conspiracy that strike us as utterly childish even if we take into account the contradictory tactics of the KPD at that time.[110] Up to the last moment the National Socialist leaders looked for further incriminating material.[111] The trial was brought about by fear and resentment of the Communists and was conducted accordingly from start to finish. The political naïvety of the Public Prosecutor, the judges, the experts, the witnesses, and a large part of the press correspondents is almost unbelievable; it shows, however, why National Socialist propaganda was able to meet with belief especially among the bourgeoisie, and why the voters did not give a negative answer to the emergency decree of 28 February.

But from the standpoint of foreign propaganda the Reichstag fire affair was a disaster from the start and resulted in a serious loss of prestige which infuriated Hitler. Münzenberg's [Willi Münzenberg, 1933–40 in charge of KPD propaganda in Paris *Ed.*] propaganda was enormously successful, thanks in part to the constant blunders of the government and of the Reich Court. As we have seen, the case for the prosecution collapsed at the outset; Hitler had wanted a quick trial; instead, the preliminary investigation dragged on until the end of June and the trial itself from September to 23 December 1933. Only when it was too late did Goebbels attempt, through his control over the National Socialist press, to cover up the bad impression.[112] In the end the *Völkischer Beobachter* protested vainly against the acquittal of the Communist defendants, which amounted to a conviction of the National Socialists. It is the fate of dictators to be taken in by their own propaganda, which blinds them to reality. That is exactly what happened to Hitler in connection with the Reichstag fire; it is characteristic that in later years he tolerated no mention of the topic.[113]

The acquittal of the Communist defendants was no particular act of heroism on the part of the court. In the face of foreign opinion, which followed the proceedings in every detail, the court could not have convicted them if it wished to preserve a vestige of credibility. The Public Prosecutor's final plea was lamentable; if he still included Torgler in the indictment, it was because he could not openly confess his mistake.[114] At times the trial proceedings were merely an attempt on the part of the National Socialist members of the government to vindicate themselves against the well-known Brown Books – with so little success that to this day historians find it necessary to prove that the National Socialists had nothing to do with the fire. In this point the government was so much on the defensive that they had no other recourse than to release Dimitrov, Popov and Tanev.[115] The execution of van der Lubbe, which quite apart from the inadmissible retroactive introduction of the death penalty[116] seems at least questionable from the juridical point of view,[117] was carried out quietly. The plan for a public execution of the incendiaries, still demanded by Hitler in a government declaration of 23 March, was dropped.[118] Marinus van der Lubbe, who had protested in vain against the systematic injustice of the new Germany, went to his death with composure.

SUMMARY

Our investigation, which would have been impossible without the basic research of Fritz Tobias and largely confirms his findings, shows that even the political aspect of the affair precludes the possibility of National Socialist complicity in van der Lubbe's act of incendiarism. Not only the National Socialist leadership but their German National coalition partners as well were convinced of the Communist authorship of the fire. Precisely because they could not fully understand the political purpose which they felt obliged to impute to the KPD in connection with the fire,[119] they fell a victim to their own hallucinations, induced in part by their propaganda. They truly believed that an armed Communist uprising was imminent; it was more than propaganda when they undertook to save Germany from 'Marxism', it was an integral part of their political creed. The Fascist cult of the leader obliged them to regard Hitler's political activity after the Reichstag fire as the self-assured conduct of a man who fully mastered the situation and was clearly conscious of his aims. Goebbel's entries in his diary during these weeks show to what extent the habit of representing their actions as 'heroic' and 'historically significant' had affected the very thinking of the National Socialist leaders. When Goebbels spoke of the Reichstag fire as 'the last mishap',[120] when Göring represented himself as the saviour of state authority from the Communist threat, or Hitler felt himself to be the champion of Europe against the 'Asiatic plague' of Bolshevism[121] – in every case they were the playthings of their wishful thinking.[122]

Incapacity for calculated tactical exploitation of the situation and blindness to reality induced by their own aims and resentments were the determining factors in the action of the National Socialists after the Reichstag fire. Their reactions were not guided solely by propagandist considerations but also by a false estimate of the political situation. Not only did they exploit the powerful emotional currents with which the political life of Germany was then charged, especially certain social groups' exaggerated fear of Communist and Marxist strivings for power; they were themselves driven by these currents. Under normal political circumstances, this lack of perspective would have been fatal to them – but not in the overheated, irrational atmosphere of Germany in the spring of 1933. The National Socialists were relatively successful in the elections of 5 March 1933, though less so than they had expected. But this success was largely a product of their spontaneous, unconsidered reactions and not of any shrewd, well-thought-out plan.

After having steered a seemingly moderate, pseudo-legal course, accompanied to be sure by increasing terrorist activity on the part of the SA and the SS, Hitler, on the night of the fire, suddenly entered into a phase of totalitarian experimentation. The emergency decree was a kind of *coup d'état*, anticipating the parliamentary Enabling Act at which the National Socialists had been aiming. It was not planned in advance, but resulted from the nervous impatience with which the National Socialist leadership reacted to the imaginary Communist counter-blow. Hitler had no way of knowing that he would gain unlimited power without a struggle, at the very first try. In response to the supposed signal for total Communist resistance, he put down all his chips like a poor roulette player, and won. Obviously a civilian chancellor did not, as Fritz Tobias quite mistakenly puts it,[123] become a power-intoxicated dictator overnight, but it cannot be denied that the state of hysteria into which the fire drove him was an important factor in making Hitler overcome his last inhibitions and throw himself completely into the battle for power.

In our account of the genesis of the Emergency Decree for the Defence of Nation and State and of the policy pursued by the National Socialist leadership in the interval between 27 February and 5 March, we have striven, without losing sight of individual motivations, to analyse an abundance of data, some of which are in part mutually contradictory and some of which have never before been taken into account, including the statements of the National Socialist leaders, which cannot be fully understood if they are interpreted as pure propaganda. In view of the inadequacy of the source material, in particular the lack of official documents not intended for the public, we are reduced to hypotheses in certain matters, such as the question whether the National Socialist leadership actually thought for a time of calling in the Reichswehr or whether the idea was brought up solely in order to move the Reichswehr to tolerate National Socialist terrorism. We do not know how much Hitler himself had to do with the emergency decree. In any case it responded to the needs of various government agencies, and quite possibly was not a deliberate step toward unrestricted dictatorship but only the simplest possible means of crushing an adversary whose strength had been overestimated – which does not mean that

Hitler did not immediately perceive its value as a totalitarian instrument. The decree shows that the first 'crisis' – and it seems likely that the Reichstag fire was at first regarded as a crisis – convinced the National Socialist leadership that the normal resources of an authoritarian state apparatus were no longer adequate. The centrifugal tendencies that became so pronounced later on – conflicts between government departments, lack of coordination between party and state, the far-reaching influence of personal rivalries among leaders – were already apparent at this stage. An example is the tendency of the SA and SS, beginning with the above-discussed campaign of arrests, to set up private concentration camps. But perhaps themeasures made possible by the Reichstag fire – the seizure of absolute control over the state and the police through the emergency decree – also helped to enable Hitler to resist the radical National Socialists' demand for a revolutionary *coup d'état*; in any case the conferences between the National Socialist leadership and the heads of the Reichswehr make this a plausible hypothesis.

The Reichstag fire hastened the unrestricted dictatorship of National Socialism. Dictatorship, however, is never solely the work of those who strive for it, but is also a product of the circumstances. Germany fell a prey not to coldly planning practical politicians, but to brutal, unscrupulous, uncontrolled, and grossly cynical *condottieri*, who displayed their motives more openly than a good many people wished later to admit. The factors that enabled Hitler to take power were the opportunistic support of the conservative right and a lack of political clearheadedness or sense of justice in those German voters who were accessible to mass psychoses. The historical significance of the Reichstag fire is to be sought not least in the fact that it shows the enormous importance of political myths for the breakthrough of totalitarian forces.

4. Social and Psychological Aspects of the *Führer's* Rule

LOTHAR KETTENACKER

The well-known phenomenon of psychological suppression has been named *Vergangenheitsbewältigung*, or 'overcoming of one's past', when describing the reluctance of the German people to acknowledge and come to terms with the crimes committed in their name by the Nazi regime. Questionable as it may be to speak of collective guilt, nevertheless the responsibility of a society for its most recent past is undeniable. It is not without reason that Alexander Mitscherlich laments the 'inability' of the Germans to 'mourn', which he explains as their disillusioned love for the *Führer*, who *post bellum et mortem* is now attributed with the sole guilt for everything.[1] Despite a considerable amount of research, historiography has been unable to convince the public, beyond an enlightened few, that it should change its mind. For the most part this is the result of difficulties in communication between the 'researchers' and the 'consumers' of historical knowledge, and not least of an increasing obsession with the theory[2] of a subject whose most important aspects have already been widely researched. More important is the impression that is probably given, that the process

From C. Hirschfeld and L. Kettenacker (eds), *Der 'Führerstaat': Mythos oder Realität?* (Stuttgart, 1981). Translated by Brian Follett.

of psychological suppression did not stop with mere historiography. Even when all claims to historicism were refuted, what has concerned contemporary research most is the question of how Hitler came to power and how he used it. What went on behind the scenes, concealed from contemporaries and which at last can be revealed, has exerted the greatest fascination. At the same time, what was suppressed was the inadequately explained problem of why countless Germans, indeed after 1933 apparently the great majority of Germans, identified themselves with the Austrian demagogue. This question is rarely asked, and even where there is the slightest hint of agreement with the assertion implied in it, that is, the concept of 'acclamation by plebiscite',[3] it is basically the system of rule which is of interest rather than the motivation of the ruled. There are certainly good reasons for approaching the apparent popularity of Hitler, which neither his opponents nor foreigners could deny, with critical open-mindedness. But this fact cannot simply be ignored or regarded as historically unimportant and dismissed as 'affective integration'.[4] Behind this lies the excessively elitist self-consciousness of historians who see themselves and their progressive attempts at interpretation as more significant than the historical phenomenon of the Hitler Movement itself. It is not therefore surprising that journalists and political commentators are the best writers of history in this respect[5] because for them the relationship between leader and led need not be explained with some theory or other about Fascism. The latest research has concentrated almost exclusively on the system of rule, on its success at home and its initial successes in foreign policy and on the rivalry of these new masters, but has scarcely shown any interest in the mentality of the small, insignificant man in the stress who meant *'Heil Hitler'* quite seriously. As if, with the seizure of power in the beginning, the functioning of the ruling system and the opposition at the end, all had been said and done!

Although there has been no lack of attempt at social-psychological evaluation, which thankfully has made some important revelations, it is nevertheless remarkable that this is unable to escape from psychoanalysis imbued with a strong individual-psychological approach. Consequently the historical dimension is missing. This is true of the so-called 'sexual-economic' theory of Wilhelm Reich and of the ideas of Theodore W. Adorno and Erich Fromm, who both sought to analyse and identify the main elements of the authoritarian personality.[6] Sigmund Freud was always looking over their shoulder, the father-figure overshadowing a new breed. However, the assertion was made, from election analyses taken at the end of the Weimar Republic, that the *Mittelstand* [A term difficult to translate; although part of the middle class, it refers in the main to its economic sector, i.e. small and medium businessmen as well as to higher income brackets of employees. *Ed.*] were the 'central supporting troops of the Swastika'[7] and that the industrial workers, following an improvement in their standard of living, were not immune to the assaults of Fascism, with its promise of overcoming the spreading phenomenon of alienation caused by the process of forced and rapid industrialisation.

However, previous research should in no way be questioned or devalued. In the research into the conditions which created Hitler, historiography to a certain extent got in its own way, on the one hand because of the embarrassment of most German historians after 1945 and, on the other, because of the significant methodological difficulties. After the war there was an understandable consensus among conservative and liberal historians in view of the fundamental rejection of the political culture of Germany, instigated by the Anglo-Saxon Re-education Concept,[8] to emphasise the main feature of National Socialism as being the seizing of power by Hitler and to portray the opposition to it as 'a revolt of conscience'[9] by the nation. For Marxists the problem of the joint responsibility of German society did not at first arise, because National Socialism before 1933 had been stamped as a by-product of the crisis of capitalism;[10] the mentality of large groups of the population vulnerable to Fascism is completely unimportant to a dogmatic consideration of history. The phase of moral evaluation was followed by a sober interest in the processes leading up to the seizure of power and in the functioning of the new system of

government, accompanied by concern about the placing of
the German development in its position within the wider
framework of international Fascism. But even then the
original suppressive impulse was still present, as if an
analysis of the system and its origins and the way it
operated, the phenomenon of the popularity of Hitler, could
be made to disappear. By reference to the last, only partially
free, election, in which the Hitler Movement was unable to
obtain an absolute majority of votes,[11] the Germans could
claim exoneration in a more or less democratic way. Not
only for Hitler, with his cynical contempt for the masses,
but also for historians, the population became, after its
incapacitation through the Enabling Act and the process of
Gleichschaltung which covered all areas of public life, little
more than the victim of cunning manipulatory techniques
and terrorist intimidation. In the mean time, every sane
German knew that events were only being represented as
half-truths and that, despite all the results of research, the
impression given of the relationship between Hitler and
the Germans was simply not right. The divergence between
the professional and the popular conception of German
contemporary history is at its greatest here.

If the importance of Hitler as one of the most relevant
and basic proofs of the legitimacy of the National Socialist
regime was never seriously questioned, then the attempts to
delineate the charismatic nature of the effect he had came
very close to previously practised historical methods,
comparable to some extent with the problem with which
the constitutional lawyers were confronted over the definition
of the term *Führer*.[12] The identification of the *Geführten* (the
led) with the *Führer* (the leader) by far outreaches any
source-based or quantitative analysis. Even the secret
SD Reports [*Sicherheitsdienst*, security service, Himmler's
intelligence agency headed until 1942 by Reinhard Heydrich
and from May 1942 by Dr Ernst Kaltenbrunner. The *SD*
public opinion reports were compiled by Otto Ohlendorf
with the object of supplying the NS leadership with an
unvarnished picture of public opinion on all crucial issues.
Ohlendorf succeeded so well that Bormann put an end to
them by late 1944. *Ed.*] on the mood of the people are of

little assistance because they depict only reactions to individual measures taken by State and Party, to foreign political events, to difficulties in supply, and the like[13] and do not criticise the person of the *Führer*. Even in the conscious mind of the people Hitler seems to have been sacrosanct.[14] As the *Reichskanzler*, the Commander-in-Chief, the Head of State, his decisions and their effects can be analysed precisely, but not his influence over the masses, which was the result of his personal magnetism, and which was the basis of his power as well as of his historical significance. An insight into this phenomenon is made difficult by the closeness of the subject to the mentality of the common man.[15] The aspects of foreign policy of the inter-war years, and also the methods of government of the NS regime which dissolved the traditional concept of state, have become rigid historical structures, like the rival Upper Italian city-states at the time of Machiavelli. The Hitler myth too has become objectivised as a topic of historical research, but the mentality of the broad layers of German society which made the myth possible has not assumed the character of a unique and inimitable process with the same calm certainty. Apart from exceptions such as Broszat's examination of social motivation and loyalty to the *Führer*[16] research has failed to consider how the conjunction between Hitler's own predisposed attitudes and the ideological disposition of the masses formed the basis of his policies. There is no lack of allusion to the manipulation techniques of Nazi propaganda. That there was a certain receptivity on the part of Hitler's supporters is generally played down. Similarly suppressed is the historical recognition, now out-moded, that ideological and spiritual needs existed among many social groups who had become insecure socially and psychologically, which cannot be explained purely in economic terms. To Hitler and to the economy as the war approached, craftsmen and small businessmen may have seemed to be 'the expendable class'[17] but nevertheless the *Führer* remained the indispensable instrument of integration for the petit bourgeoisie. The political awareness of the first Republic is measured with such naïvety against the criteria of the democracy which was only successful at its second attempt. Thus it is that electoral decisions based on economic factors, which would be seen as rational electoral behaviour in a democracy, are treated as the major reason for the rise of National Socialism. As if an objectionably primitive ideology, just because it appears today to be ridiculous, could be claimed to have no sense historically. Even though it was not until the world economic crisis brought the Nazis to power, it should still not be assumed that the loyalty of the masses to the *Führer* was of primarily economic origin. This would be to confuse cause and effect. To explain the basis of Hitler's success as his promise to save every professional group and section of the populace from economic distress is far too narrow an interpretation. The party programme of the NSDAP made the same promise and was taken seriously only by a few, least of all by Hitler himself.[18] After his seizure of power, Hitler did quite well enough without having to resort to such tactical considerations.

In view of the methodological problems, it seems justifiable to approach the phenomenon of *Führer*-rule in a speculative way. Four theses will therefore be discussed:

1. The assumption of power by the National Socialists was the revolution of the petit bourgeoisie, numerically the most rapidly expanding but socially and ideologically the most insecure of the lower middle class.

2. The idea of 'National Community' was no mere slogan of propaganda to conceal class differences, which persisted as before. It corresponded, notwithstanding the social reality, with an historical force which was not to be underestimated.

3. Hitler exemplified the German petit bourgeois of his age, and in this respect was not only *Führer* but also the exponent or 'representative individual'[19] of an extreme form of that German nationalism which, although a continuation of it, was nevertheless distinct from the more middle class nationalism of Wilhelmine Germany.

4. Hitler's charisma was based primarily on his being 'overlord' of an unbureaucratic system of government

which could most accurately be described as neo-
feudalism, and which appealed to some atavistic
instincts of a still strongly dynastic-orientated society.

I

The proposition that the unopposed acceptance of the
assumption of power by Hitler cannot simply be explained
by the process of *Gleichschaltung*, but has to be seen as a
revolution corresponding to the due requirements of the
period, has been emphasised in particular by Ralf Dahrendorf
and David Schoenbaum.[20] In fact, the National Socialist
assumption of power shows many basic traits of the modern
theory of revolution as propounded by, for example, Karl
Griewank, especially in the concept of the overthrow of
existing political and social conditions, on the basis of a
new ideology brought about by a mass movement.[21] The
description of the events of 1918/19 as a revolution has
found general acknowledgement, but not for those of 1933.
This has less to do with the events themselves than with the
long-held view of the idea of revolution through the
Enlightenment and Marxist theories of revolution. In
addition there is the attraction of the idea of the myth of
revolution steeped in anarchy. Theodor Schieder is of the
opinion that the question of whether the overthrow of a
bourgeois-liberal state should be considered as revolution
'in the true sense of the word, could not be unequivocally
answered because, while it was true that revolutionary
elements came into play, nevertheless events themselves
were inconclusive in a specifically emancipatory sense'.[22] In
view of this ideological historical designation, it seemed
obvious to the National Socialists that they should accentuate
the conservative, anti-Enlightenment and legal character of
their revolution, in contrast to the 'November Revolution',
carried out by them with oath and excommunication,
something more in tune with our modern understanding of
revolution. Nobody would contest the revolutionary changes
inherent in the transition from the Roman Republic to the
Empire, merely because Augustus was capable of retaining

the external forms of republican legality. Whereas the
Revolution of 1919 had been brought about by an externally
initiated collapse of imperial Germany and not by the
conscious seizure of power by leftists intent upon planned
revolutionary changes,[23] the National Socialists had worked
directly towards the overthrow of existing political conditions.
Even if the lower middle-class purveyors of this revolution
were anti-modernistic in their motives, nevertheless the
National Socialists can lay claim for themselves, in its
consequences, to having evolved the criterion of social
reclassification. Although they put to one side the political
changes of the Weimar Democracy, which had been imposed
from without and unwillingly accepted in expectation of a
moderate peace settlement, they nevertheless, as a result of
a process not intended to have that result, brought about
the social modernisation which had been initiated in the
Weimar period but not put into operation. 'The brutal
break with tradition and push into modern times', as this
process is called by Dahrendorf, 'is the essential characteristic
of the social revolution of National Socialism'.[24] Schoenbaum
propounded this argument in his thesis which appeared in
the same year, in which, however, he limited himself to an
examination of the social reality of the ideology of 'National
Community'. Any interpretation of the NS revolution must
consist, however, not only of an examination of the
beginning, the logical fact of it, but also of the catharsis of
the catastrophe – the social consequences of total war and
the no less total defeat. A revolution can never be just that
which it appears to represent. Even if Hitler, looking to the
primary aims of his programme which lay in foreign policy,
prevented any direct transition from the political to the
social revolution with his liquidation of the *SA* leaders, he
never professed himself to be satisfied with the conquest of
state power and always considered National Socialism as a
'movement'. Before 1933, the term 'Hitler Movement',
which expresses far more about the whole phenomenon
than the party name coined for propaganda purposes, is to
be found alongside it in the official common parlance.[25] In
fact the regime, for the whole period of its existence, was in
a permanent state of change. Hitler could never completely

disentangle himself, to the end of his life, from the gulf between tactical considerations and racist utopianism.

Thus the pact with the conservative elite served the purposes of Hitler's seizure of internal power and the extension of his power externally, but was not primarily aimed at the preservation of the traditional propertied section of the upper classes, as some left-wing theoreticians of Fascism, on the basis of superficial thoughtless utterances about the nature of capitalism, would have people think. It is beyond my comprehension to see why the readiness of a politically and economically unstable leading class to assure itself of the favour of a people's tribune which held sway over a mass of supporters should immediately be seen as one of the constituent elements of Fascism or even of capitalism. The responsibility of the traditional elites, who hoped to save or further their own interests by collaborating with the new regime, whose only concern was to bring about the overthrow of the political order, is not to be questioned in this way.[26] The very nature of National Socialism, which should be the main consideration in any assessment of Fascism, is still not adequately described, nor is the mass support which made it capable of collaboration in the first place. In Italian Fascism, the phenomenon of the mass movement preceded the alliance of Mussolini with the conservative elite, which became important only during the period of the regime.[27] Even in a stable democracy the responsibility for government would have devolved, sooner or later, on a party leader having Hitler's type of support, combined with the loyalty of the leading social class. But even then, a politician who offered protection in public even to the murderers of Potempa would never have induced such a mass of followers.[28] [In 1932 several *SA* members murdered a political opponent in Upper Silesia. They were sentenced to death, but the death sentences were commuted to life sentences on the grounds that the presidential decree imposing the death sentence on political murder could not be known to the perpetrators at the time of committing the crime. Hitler fully backed his men and after 1933 they were pardoned. The roots of this particular crime go back as far

as 1919–21 when Upper Silesia was in the throes of brutal
struggle between Germans and Poles and was the stage of
three irredentist Polish risings. *Ed.*] And just as it was
impossible for the Catholic church to maintain its basic
organisation by the invocation of a concordat, it was equally
impossible for bureaucracy, industry and the army to escape
a gradual dispossession, which could not be avoided either
by victory or defeat but at best only by a successful *coup
d'état* at a propitious moment. National Socialism was
capable of anything, and certainly of a policy which in
practice could turn out to be more anti-bourgeois and anti-
capitalist than might seem theoretically admissible even to
later generations who are permeated with just these attitudes.
It is quite possible that if Germany had won the Second
World War even the Prussian-German upper classes would
have been dealt a death blow, in the same way as it was
intended to treat the Catholic Church. The relentless and
ugly murders of the Prussian nobility who took part in the
20 July plot scarcely indicate any special inhibitions in
dealings with the upper classes. 'In Hitler's outrageous
reaction', writes Fest, 'there reappeared that never relin-
quished resentment of the old world, that hate which also
so ambiguously permeated his relations with the middle
classes'.[29] He would, at that moment, have preferred to
have weeded out the officer corps just as Stalin had.[30] If one
can include Napoleon within the whole process of the
French Revolution, so too can one characterise Hitler and
his twelve-year rule as the 'German Revolution', ascribing
to it neither attribute nor condemnation. In its degree of
political mobilisation and the international political changes
brought about by it, the whole epoch was a single *levée en
masse*, the like of which German history before and since has
never known. One would never wish to mobilise the masses
in Germany again without considering the effects of this
development.

Beginning and end, seizure of power and unconditional
surrender are equally to be considered as a unity in so far
as they demonstrate the ability of the revolution for
integration. It must surely give rise to thought that the
Weimar Republic did not collapse after a civil war as many

contemporaries believed it would, but in a rush of national fervour which in many places called to mind the eruption of national feelings of August 1914.[31] 'It would not be possible simply to eliminate the opposition', conjectured the writer Fritz von Unruh in the spring of 1931, 'otherwise there would be a general strike. The trade unions would give backing with bitter resistance; in addition there would be the Reichsbanner and the support of all those concerned for the future. And even if Hitler were to win over the Reichswehr, and bring up the big guns, he would discover millions of decided opponents.'[32] Nothing like this happened;[33] instead there was the old pals' act, personal realignment, voluntary stepping into line, at worst resignation and emigration. In days to come the German dictator was not destined to fall prey to any assassination, although he presented himself to the masses more often than any other European statesman and was often driven about the country in an open vehicle. Only after a long and exhausting war, in the course of which almost the whole of the civilised world united against Germany, could the breath be blasted from the Hitler Movement. The end was not hastened by a fighting resistance movement as in the countries occupied by German troops. Even shortly before the end of the war, opinion polls among German POWs still showed an actual opposition to National Socialism of only 9 per cent plus 15 per cent 'passive anti-Nazis'.[34] Even in the autumn of 1945, after the German people had been confronted with the horrific reality of the concentration camps, the British Occupation authorities announced that there were still 10 per cent out-and-out Nazis and about 60 per cent 'drifters', but all bearing that same mark of authoritarian mentality.[35]

That National Socialism had to be thankful for its popularity above all to the middle classes who had been particularly unsettled by the economic crisis, was a premise which occurred to the German sociologist Theodor Geiger as early as the September 1930 elections. Election results in subsequent years altered nothing in this trend towards the decline of the bourgeois liberal parties in favour of the NSDAP. The first large party statistics of 1935 show,[36] in addition, that among members of the party before 14

September 1930 there was a predominance of members of the old and new middle classes, that is to say, craftsmen, small businessmen and white-collar workers: there were 33,944 artisans and 3,586 self-employed persons as opposed to no less than 52,044 members of the lower middle class; if farmers and civil servants are counted, then the figures rise to 79,240, with a party membership of 69 per cent, as opposed to 26·3 per cent artisans and 2·8 per cent self-employed. On the other hand, the proportion of civil servants and white-collar workers was only 16·5 per cent, with 31·7 per cent the largest group of the total number of employed persons in 1925. If one considers the number of political activists in the party before 1930, then the middle class reaches a percentage of 73 per cent, as against 18·5 per cent artisans and 2·3 per cent self-employed.[37] Civil servants and teachers had not yet penetrated the party. Their number only rose considerably after the assumption of power, and they are the only 'March Victims'. Nevertheless a high percentage of these party members, almost one in two, were already working as political activists. Even before the onset of the economic crisis, the different cadres of the party and its adherents were composed mainly of the lower middle class. Despite all the promotions into the upper ranks, even after 1933, nothing was to alter this 'intellectual predominance of the petty bourgeois'.[38]

This quickly recognised affinity between the middle classes and National Socialism has, up to now, mainly, if not completely, been examined only from the socio-economic point of view.[39] In only isolated cases can points of comparison be found with wider socio-psychological aspects.[40] Most revealing in this respect are the studies dating from the final years of the Weimar Republic carried out by sociologists and not by historians using sociological arguments. In particular, the research carried out by Theodor Geiger[41] and Hans Speier[42] whose conclusions were then taken up after the war by Rainer Lepsius.[43] Leading the way is the differentiation of ideology and mentality undertaken by Geiger. The latter of these two entities is defined as an 'intellectual-spiritual disposition', the 'direct influence on a person through his social environment and

the experience of life radiating from this and caused by it'.[44]
It may be questionable to speak of a 'false consciousness' or
of a 'false ideology' in terms similar to the thinking of
Marxist categories,[45] but it is none the less welcome that
Geiger dismisses the question 'correct or false', when applied
to the concept of mentality, as logically inadmissible, and
only recognises such attributes as being typical or atypical.
'To be within the field of influence "of false ideologies" ', as
he says, 'can just as easily correspond to the typical
mentality of a whole class, when the social circumstances or
the historical connections are of such a kind that the class
would not be able to make itself understood'. [46] Unfortunately,
in an otherwise excellent discourse on the middle classes
under National Socialism, there is a lack of supporting
concrete evidence for this suggestion. It has always been
pointed out that Hitler's unique talent consisted mainly of
being able to put into words, within his speeches, the anger
felt by his listeners. In this is revealed the relationship
between Hitler's Social-Darwinistic ideology and the specific
contemporaneous mentality of the middle classes, located in
the no-man's-land between capital and labour and beset
with their own anti-bourgeois affectations and imagined
fears of proletarisation.

Hans Speier goes even further afield than Geiger in his
research, published after the war, into the employed section
of society as affected by National Socialism, in which he
also includes questions concerning the function of education
and national feelings as criteria of status. He suggests that
'the poorer among the middle classes believed that they
were immune from being confused with the proletariat by
insistence upon their national feeling'. Socio-discriminatory
prejudices are always more sharply defined among border
classes which stand in close proximity to the victims of
prejudices, that is those discriminated against in geographical, economic, religious or other terms. He is able to show
that the middle classes, threatened by proletarisation,
considered themselves to be the *Volk*, purely and simply,
which he saw threatened, not only by the 'atomising effect
of the liberal-democratic idea', but also by the destructive
impetus of the Marxist class war.[47] The way to the National

Socialist *Volksgemeinschaft*, the national community of a 'classless society', which is modelled on the organisation of the army, was thus depicted here.

Lepsius, in his inaugural lecture on extreme class-specific nationalism, examined the claim of the middle classes to be the bearers of the 'moral norms of society'.[48] The battle against class struggle, for the attainment of a socially healthy world of a pre-industrial kind, set loose an incredible potential of aggressive energies with its 'dictatorship of virtue'. Viewed in this light, there came to power in 1933, not the bearers of a well-defined ideology, but a man who pretended that he would bring about a *Volksgemeinschaft* based upon certain bourgeois norms of integrity. The contemporary term for that middle-class mentality raised aloft to being the state morality was *gesundes Volksempfinden* (the inherently healthy feeling of the people), a 'purity of national sentiment'.

II

The National Socialist *Volksgemeinschaft*, the ideology of the classless society, which was directed against the democratic multi-party state, drew its inspiration from memories of the *Burgfrieden* [the suspension of political, social and economic conflict for the duration of war. *Ed.*] of 1914, which was to become a permanent institution and not only in times of war. Even after all the radical changes there still remained that one objective – the breaking down of class differences, the reconciliation of the working class with the nation – which was not yet attained even by the outward means of enforced integration and co-ordination, *Gleichschaltung*. Although the NSDAP was able to obtain considerable gains in industrial areas, above all in Silesia and Saxony,[49] and also among young voters and unemployed persons, the electoral statistics nevertheless clearly showed that the working classes had more confidence generally in the conventional parties of the Left than in any National Socialist propaganda. Even after the assumption of power, the membership at first remained far below their representation in the population, while white-collar workers, self-employed people and especially civil servants were over-represented, with the result that in 1935 the Reich's organisation leader, Ley, insisted upon a 'more energetic' recruitment drive to engage workers and farmers as new party members and political leaders (*Politische Leiter*). 'We must depart somewhat from the basic principle', he declared, 'of accepting into the party only those who wish to come into the party. We should now, as in a period of struggle, again set about recruiting for us men whom the party wishes to have as members.'[50] In addition came a denunciation of bourgeois class prejudices by means of National Socialist propaganda. Many of the working class may still have been sceptical when Hitler made out that he wanted to nationalise, not the means of production, but people.[51] For the rest of society, and above all for the lower middle class, the class with the greatest rate of growth as a result of industrial upheavals, this particular idea, as Sebastian Haffner quite rightly suggests,[52] had much more power of conviction than it is at present thought to have had. Socialism as a nationalisation of industry means even more bureaucracy, which was seen to be spreading like a malignant cancer and was felt increasingly to be causing alienation between state and citizens. It was particularly the millions of white-collar workers, craftsmen and business people who regarded the Weimar state as a sinecure of politicians and bureaucrats on the expense account of the national community.

The upsurge in the economy, especially the reduction of unemployment and the success of Hitler's foreign policy, had won over to the regime both the liberal middle class and large sections of the uncommitted working class. For the main supporters of National Socialism, the lower middle class, this was merely a confirmation of the expectations raised by the new system. The national community was the expression of a certain mentality and needed no precisely defined ideology, any more than Catholic bodies are dependent upon theology whenever it can be supported by a broad, interwoven system of social limitations and norms of behaviour. Thus, as Renan defined the nation as the '*plébiscite de tous les jours*', the national community was the

daily, practised, satisfying, communal experience of a society
that had been suffering from increasing alienation. It was
the infinite stereotype, based upon the outward manifestation
of the military, of the closely-knit lower middle class club
life. The *Stammtisch* [table in German pubs reserved for
the 'regulars' *Ed.*] mentality of brothers round their own
pub table, as was manifest in countless suburban and
provincial pubs, was the true terrain of that 'purity of
national sentiment', the *gesundes Volksempfinden*, and of the
'middle class moral norm' (Lepsius): the 'household' year
for middle-class daughters, national labour service for flabby
middle-class sons, national service as the 'school of the
nation', the proverbial 'short trial' of National Socialist
legal terminology for criminals of all kinds,[53] the rooting out
of 'degenerate art' [not a NS term but first used by the
Zionist Max Nordau *Ed.*] from all museums and, as a
reward, the gold medal accolade of the Olympics; watching
over all the omnipotent yet mundane *Führer*, not creeping
away behind piles of documents, but showing himself to the
people at every opportunity,[54] speaking to them, praising
them, urging them, admonishing them and finally challenging
all foreign-comers. His swaggering speeches, either in the
pose of *pater familias* or of *Praeceptor Germaniae* in which he
railed at the decadence of the Weimar 'system', and invoked
the good, the strong and the healthy in the German people,
were perfectly tailor-made for the unpolitical, naïve
personality of the German provincials, with their antipathy
to the metropolis and the unclean spirit of the times
prevailing there. He acted as if he were the German
Messiah – he always considered the Lord God, or the
Almighty, or at least Providence to be on his side[55] – who
chased the Jewish traders, the internationalists and Marxists
out of the temple of the nation in order to make room for
the faithful in the community, who were then only required
to act on impulse instead of always having to try to
understand the world, its changes and its crises. Even if
Hitler continually advocated the importance of a healthy
peasant-farmer class, drove out women from the employment
market by extolling their role as mothers,[56] warned youth
against immoderate beer consumption[57] and urged them to

take up physical training, stormed against the carping of intellectuals with their consuming desire for criticism[58] and generally provided fatherly advice on all possible topics, then one cannot put too high a value on the effect of his words across wide reaches of the population, who were generally unaccustomed to such addresses by politicians. And if not all voices of opposition had been silenced, then the National Socialists made the best possible use of the manipulative techniques available to them in the form of the new mass media. Among the young generation radios and gramophones exercised a great fascination. Before the election of 31 July 1932, in which the NSDAP was able to double its proportion of votes in the Reichstag, Hitler made a record so that, even in places in which he could not make a personal appearance, at least his voice could be heard. [The initial reason for producing this record was the fact that the NSDAP was not allowed to broadcast on the radio. This was also the reason for Hitler's flying from city to city to deliver his speeches, though of course it was quickly realised that this was of greater effect than the voice coming out of the radio set. *Ed.*] His standard speech in this election battle was a call to the mentality of national community of the man in the street, who was annoyed by the plethora of Weimar parties and their promises. So Hitler let it be known that 'these attempts to divide the nation into classes, groups, professions and faiths, and to inch forward clumsily towards the economic fortune of the future, have today finally collapsed'.[59] No politician of his time had ever addressed such masses of people in election campaigns as Hitler. Just to quote one example: on 28 July 1932 he was speaking in Aachen and Cologne, in the Festival Hall at Frankfurt and on the sports ground at Wiesbaden, perpetually on the move by plane from one assembly to another, and quite often landing in the midst of the throng. Later Hitler's voice would be relayed by national radio into all outlying areas. For general radio reception organised by the party since 1935 in factories and larger assembly rooms, the efficient *Volksempfänger* (people's receiver) was available.[60] Through a reduction in purchase price from 76 Reichsmark to 35 Reichsmark, the poorest party member could soon afford the cheapest wireless in the world at that time, the German *Kleinstempfänger*. Small wonder that the annual increase in listeners was about a million, and in the crisis year 1938/39 even 1·8 million.

The effect of films was to be even more intensive. This was the first generation to be subjected, however psychologically unprepared, to the illusory products of the film industry. Even in the smallest hamlets cinemas grew out of the ground. The public would take more part than today in the emotive happenings on the screen: there would be unashamed sobbing, laughter, and expressions of fear. At the appearance of the *Führer* – probably the majority of Germans only came face to face with him as a 'film star' – it was noticeable that a quasi-religious thrill would be induced in many onlookers. Thus the national community was also to be experienced at the cinema. What served NS propaganda best though, was the weekly newsreel, the *Wochenschau*, an invention of the early 1930s.[61] With a society so addicted to films, this free accompaniment to the main film had a fantastic publicity effect. [During the war German newsreels became rather repetitive and boring, so much so that German cinemagoers purchased their admission tickets but did not enter the cinema until the newsreel had ended. This caused Goebbels to issue a decree which prohibited admission to those who had missed the newsreel. *Ed.*] The political importance of the *Wochenschau* had already been recognised by the Weimar republic. It was in this way that the SPD, with its *Emalka-Woche*, tried to have an influence on the nation, while the Communists extended their influence with their *Hektor-Woche*, but these were all vain attempts to compete with the popular *Ufawochenschau* of Hitler's 'friend' Hugenberg [from which, however, the NSDAP profited little before 1933. *Ed.*].

Furthermore, the Weimar republic had not been able to give the state that representative dignity which meant so much to the firmly-held dynastic feelings of the Germans. Following defeat and revolution, there was no replacement for the pomp and splendour of the empire, for the glittering army or fleet parade. The ruling parties had not considered it necessary to devote any particular attention to the image of the state. From one day to the next, regardless of its political culture, all that was required of German society was a completely rational political awareness. They were far too keen to leave the political show business, flags and uniforms, parades with drums and trumpets, to the opposition parties of the right and left. [This requires some qualification. As the abundantly available film material shows, by the early 1930s military structures, ranks and appearance were as dominant among the parties of the left as of the right. Today's viewer will find it difficult to distinguish between Stormtroopers and *Stahlhelm* formations and those of the *Reichsbanner* or the Red Front. This applies particularly to their youth organisations. *Ed.*] The corresponding events of the ruling parties had the character of boring collections of old gentlemen receiving doctorates compared with the Party Days of the NSDAP before 1931, in which thousands of supporters would arrive by special trains, on open lorries and even by long marches on foot, demonstrating their true party colours for all to see.[62] This remarkable lack of image-building by the Weimar republic, which could not be offset even by the person of the ageing Hindenburg (the 'wooden titan' as Wheeler-Bennett called him),[63] was particularly fatal for Germany, because there were quite different socio-psychological conditions present here from those in the western democracies.

After the unfathomable defeat and sudden disappearance of the monarchy within the Reich, as in the individual states, the dynastic connections and socio-psychological dispositions which had grown over the centuries had at one fell swoop lost their central point of contact. Even at the beginning of this century, the petty courts of the provinces had still maintained considerable pomp.[64] The value judgments and integral structures of consciousness were not able to adapt to the sudden change of conditions. The failure to create a People's Empire, as put forward by Naumann, caused mainly by the rapid loss of authority of Wilhelm II in the course of the First World War,[65] made the way free for that demagogue rising from the anonymity of the trenches who exploited the general psychosis of the post-war period to take his place, after 1933, on the now vacant plinth of the dethroned monarchy. That Hitler succeeded in raising himself in such a short period from a demagogic party leader to a charismatic leader of the people, to say nothing of being a people's emperor, can certainly not be explained simply by the cunning manipulative techniques of the regime. The mobilisation of the population in peacetime towards more and more massed demonstrations, unique in the whole history of Germany, from the local party gatherings to the huge party rally of the Reich for the NSDAP in Nuremberg was no enforced occurrence. People today will simply not understand that in the NS 'national community' a truly incomprehensible, irrational participation was manifested which did not form political opinion, but was nevertheless a serious expression of will, not merely an act of plebiscitary acclamation. One may well pose the question whether this kind of 'national sentiment' with its dubious attribute of being 'healthy' can in any way be compared with concepts such as pragmatic 'common sense' or revolutionary *volonté général* (general will) and held to be the 'moral norm' which, as Lepsius acknowledged, is specific to certain classes of society without being class ethics.[66] Perhaps one should introduce here the concept of '*Volk* ethics' as a synthesis of the dialectic opposites of 'private ethics' and 'state ethics'. This 'purity of national sentiment' was in many respects a usurping categorical imperative by the National Socialist state which was supported by the inherent intolerance of lower-middle-class integrity as the basis for its legislation and administration of justice. The sense of justice of the individual, on which Kant originally based his ideas, was thereby yet again corrupted. Indeed, one must take great care not to assume here any direct causal connection with the phenomenal crimes of the regime, the destruction of the Jews and the similar genocidal character of *Lebensraumimperialismus* (living-space imperialism). As we know, neither the *Kristallnacht*, the night of the broken glass, nor the war against Poland were particularly popular events,[67] to the dismay of the German dictator. Quite rightly, Broszat points to the fact that, in the phase of assumption of power, it was not anti-Semitism and the ideology of 'living space' which stood in the forefront of National Socialist propaganda, but the battle against Marxism and the democratic multi-party state as well as the expression of national rebirth,[68] themes which corresponded with the concept of the 'healthy national sentiment'.

The ideology of the national community is usually measured by how far it succeeded in integrating the working class. To prove this is nevertheless an extremely difficult undertaking for the time after 1933. The question is by no means answered by the fact that in the Third Reich no fundamental change took place in industrial relations. Even the central examination by T. W. Mason of the struggle for power between industry and DAF [the *Deutscher Arbeitsfront*, which replaced the trade unions and in which employers and employees were organised. *Ed.*] in Hitler's state can only be regarded as a preliminary stage,[69] unless one takes the view that only marginal importance can be attributed to the subjective attitude of the workers to the regime. Nevertheless, new results of research into electoral relationships before 1933 have shown that the NSDAP with its extreme National Socialism and its ideology of the national community was successful in 'mobilising for itself' Germans of all ages, classes, groups and faiths 'in such high proportions that, in all over-representations of the Protestant middle-class stratum, it bore the nature of "People's Party" more definitely than any other political group at that time'.[70] It may be assumed that this process obtained considerable impetus from the authority implicit in the attainment of state leadership. For Hitler, capital and labour were of equally subsidiary importance in themselves.[71] He favoured free enterprise merely because it represented a more compliant instrument for his purposes, due to its continual vulnerability, and a more efficient one for his strategy of 'living space' than would any totally bureaucratised economy directed, as it were, by retired Austrian white-collar workers. Important as the development of prices and incomes may be, one must nevertheless also consider closely the activity of the industrial and disciplinary courts and ask oneself whether the regime was successful because of its ability to communicate to the workers the feeling that even the industrialists had to stand to attention in front of the *Führer* and that every factory owner was well advised not to cause trouble with the NS Political Leaders among the staff.[72] It was of far-reaching importance for the 'education in awareness' of the workers that NS propaganda did not become lax, as happens today in many eastern bloc states, in emphasising the equal status of manual and mental work, combined with the depreciation of the intellectual as a type. When asked by the NS poet Hanns Johst why he had given his movement the name of Workers' Party, Hitler explained that he had wanted to 'reacclimatise' this concept 'to the power of the German language and to the sovereign rights and duties of the German people'.[73] Every fellow German was to consider himself to be a citizen and a worker, being neither middle class nor proletarian. National Socialism was the attempt, as Schoenbaum so appositely remarked, to reform the idea of interdependence of existence and awareness as defined by Marx.[74] A dissertation written in Munich about the NS organisation 'Strength through Joy' (*Kraft durch Freude*) comes to the rather unwilling conclusion that the regime had in fact succeeded in the integration of the labour force by means 'which did little to change the actual inequality of the workers and the existing class structure, and that, in fact, this integration had taken place outside the full awareness of the people'.[75]

Conclusive proof is not available for this assumption unless, as for Dahrendorf, the evidence is to be seen in the tendency towards bourgeoisification of the working classes after the Second World War.[76] In fact, the workers in 1935, with 32 per cent membership of the NSDAP, were still considerably fewer in proportional numbers than their 46 per cent proportion of the working population.[77] The same picture is also shown by party members of peasant stock, who were not known for any lack of loyalty to the regime, for the simple reason that most of the Political Leaders were recruited from their ranks.[78] Nevertheless, by now one in twenty workers belonged to the party. Furthermore, they provided more Political Leaders (a total of 112,328) than any other professional group.[79] If the working class before 1933 generally kept its distance from the NSDAP, then it was not only because it mistrusted National Socialist propaganda, as a consequence of its stubborn Marxist beliefs, but also because the SPD, in competition with middle-class conviviality, had established its own pseudo-lower-middle-class environment, together with skittle clubs, gym clubs and music clubs. The lower-middle-class mentality, from which the ideology of National Socialism grew, was, in any case, by no means unknown to the workers.[80]

III

'Charismatic rule', according to Max Weber, 'as the expression of the extraordinary, is in sharp contrast, not only to the rational and more especially the bureaucratic, but also to the traditional and more particularly the patriarchal and patrimonial or immutable.'[81] Fundamentally little is expressed by this negative definition, because it could as well refer to Jesus Christ as to Adolf Hitler. With the attribute of 'charisma' is too often associated the assumption that one is dealing not only with an irrational phenomenon, but also one which is incapable of being expressed in rational terms. In what follows I will attempt to delineate this vague concept with more precision in the case of Hitler, and to see Hitler himself as a 'representative individual'[82] who was, as Broszat points out, 'on the one hand, only the exponent of a broad, nationalistic psychosis and on the other hand the integral figure of this "movement" '.[83] The German dictator's successes are generally attributed to the special circumstances prevailing at the time and to his capacity for making these suit his own purposes. It is disputable, however, whether or not this analysis should go a stage further. The socio-psychological connection between *Führer* and followers – without taking political legitimacy into consideration – lay, in Hitler's case, not in his so-called 'aims' but in the incarnation of a lower-middle-class mentality. In this respect incarnation means the outlining, or, as it were, the casting of this initially quite natural and ordinary mentality into an ideology. That

Hitler's philosophy of life was indeed an irrational collection
of thoughts but at the same time coherent and of a type to
be taken seriously, has been shown conclusively by Jäckel.[84]
The declaration of Robert Wagner, *Gauleiter* in Baden in
1941, is characteristic of the experience of awakening among
many of the earlier young adherents of the Hitler movement,
which can be expressed in another way as the crystallisation
of lower-middle-class mentality towards National Socialist
ideology: 'When I heard this man speak for the first time,
the scales fell from my eyes. He expressed in words what I
would have liked to have said, but at that time was unable
to say'.[85]

It was not only Hitler's talent as a demagogue, but also
his self-perception as an artist, which he often enough
invoked, and whose function for the regime has generally
been ignored by researchers up to the present. In his
spiritual derivation and his way of life Hitler was an artist,
a Bohemian. The lack of social recognition alters nothing of
this. It was just his mediocrity as an artist, his affinity for
mass cultural taste, together with his desire for recognition
of his misunderstood genius, which enabled him to form a
powerful mass movement from the chaos of a malaise which
was universal yet mainly to be found among the lower
middle classes. In his study of the cultural-historical roots
of National Socialism, Fritz Stern has referred quite rightly
to the considerable impact of that confusing book by Julius
Langbehn about 'Rembrandt as an Artist', that defiant
revolt against scholasticism and modernity in the name of
art.[86] [There is no evidence showing that Hitler was familiar
with Langbehn's work. *Ed.*] Hitler's repeated criticism of
the intellectuals and 'men of learning', of their inability for
constructive and devoted cooperation, had its roots at a
deeper level, though probably it had additional effect
through its denunciatory nature. It was through him that a
certain so-called appreciation of art, that bordered on kitsch
and was taken straight from grandfather's wood-whittling
attic, reached the realms of the sublime, of the everlasting
and infinite, against which the unstable spirit of the times
could never compete. In art time stood still, and where
there was an incontrovertible measuring stick for all things

was to be found the birthplace of the utopia of the thousand-year Reich. Hitler's countless addresses on cultural occasions[87] are a verbal testimony of the ideal of beauty of the 'little man', who repeatedly looked up to his *Führer* as if to the keeper of the Holy Grail of 'the good, the true and the beautiful'. Resentments and inferiority complexes were built up into a monument of defiance, in a pathetic gesture of negation, so that the 'little man' then stood deeply touched before his own misery as if before something which could objectively be considered magnificent. Hitler knew how to give real meaning and shape to such things as the collective denunciation of reality, the rejection of both the defeat and the peace treaty, and the new constitution which, from that time onwards, could no longer be recognised as primarily German. The peace, according to his message, was not definitive: it was basically only the continuation of the war by other means; by means of political struggles on the basis of military forms of organisation, like the *Führer* principle and the uniformed unit and all other requisites of the war game, to the fascination of the opponent. One needs only to think of many *SA* units set out in full marching order, the presentation of the colours, party inspections, propaganda parades, or even life in the camps surrounding the party rallies: all this was thought-provoking. That the seizure of power at home should be followed by the war of conquest abroad was only known by a few,[88] and was generally just as unanticipated as the revolutionary consequences of the change of system. Identification with the successes of the regime in the economy and in foreign policy, and with the political milieu created by it, thrust aside any thoughts of the dogma underlying them. The transition from war game via the systematic preparations for war to the cold-blooded outbreak of the bloodbath itself took place in as theatrical and unreal a way as the descent of Hitler from the rostrum of the demagogue who interpreted the world only fleetingly, to the revolutionary who set himself the task of actually changing it. Bracher quite rightly emphasises the fact that National Socialism has always been underestimated.[89] (Fabrys' fascinating book on Hitler in the judgement of others[90] is one single confirmation

of this point.) It was because of the confusion which resulted
that appearance and reality, claim and actuality, anti-
semitism as an ideology and as a final solution, were all
closely interwoven. The reality of the Third Reich, being
expressed in an exaggerated way, had a certain synthetic
quality. For Hitler, who, at the table, would quote whole
passages of Schopenhauer,[91] the world was, in all seriousness,
the expression of whatever notion a decisive willpower
wishes to make it. The real power of his words and of his
lower-middle-class prejudices, always expressed with a surge
of conviction, further extended his tendency to day-dreams.
It has been shown that he was capable of pulling the wool
even over his own eyes and that he was often carried away
by his own hysterical torrent of words and theatrical
manner.[92] He was the actor who identified with his part so
closely that he actually committed the very murder which
he was meant only to act, without the applauding audience
really becoming aware of it. His cynical observations about
the gullibility of the masses[93] are not counter-evidence, for
even they mirror his lower-middle-class notion of the great
statesman. Just in the same way as he once spoke, in
connection with the reform of the Reich, of the *Tonmasse*,
the 'lump of clay' from which he intended to model the
permanent shape of the new Germany,[94] so too, for him,
everything was freely at his disposal and could be
manipulated in any way he liked. So too, the masses were
just the raw material to enable his political visions to take
their shape. His success can only be explained by the fact
that he himself had been cut from the same tree. In this
respect, it is not his philosophy of life, the second stage of
the process of transformation from thought to reality, which
is of interest, but the other things which bound him to his
massed followers: above all the implications of his social
background and his experiences in the First World War.

Enough is known about the fact that Hitler came from a
lower-middle-class environment, from which he did not
emerge until his thirties and, in fact, was threatened by
social demotion. In *Mein Kampf* he even describes himself as
an 'upstart', and stamps the milieu of his youth with the
words, 'the fear of the social group, which has only recently

raised itself above the level of the manual workers, of sinking back into the old, less respected class, or at least of still being reckoned among them'.[95] As a member of his earlier class background, Hitler was numbered among the fastest expanding class group (between 1882 and 1925) of the small officials and white-collar workers who, after defeat in the war and the current inflation, were worried about their status and were afraid of being crushed between the millstones of 'organised' capitalism and the 'organised' working class. Hans Speier pointed out the ideology of the national community which resulted from this, and also the function of education and half-education as a mark of class that nevertheless stood in direct contradiction to it. Just as, for the broad and still amorphous social group of the so-called 'new' middle class, the petty officials, white-collar workers and deproletarised employees, so too in Hitler's eyes, art and education, seen in their unchallengeable, classical form, were not only worth striving for in themselves, but were features of demarcation from the working class. The workers as he knew them from pre-war times in Vienna simply did not frequent the Opera House or the National Library, and they lacked that certain sense of 'higher values'. This will for self-advancement, so strong in Hitler's case, stood in sharp and painful contrast to the actual chances in life which were offered to him. He preferred the wandering life of the unattached artist to the Customs Office in Linz which was the final point of his father's career, and was the symbol of that same bureaucracy which he despised his whole life long. It was an attitude which also characterised his later life and the spiritual disposition of many contemporaries after 1918, that of not coming to terms with the existing realities, of not 'adapting' as it was called in Austria, but of always being ready, for the sake of some grandiose success, to run the risk of defeat and failure – but still a heroic failure and, in view of the circumstances, a by no means shameful one. Hitler felt himself threatened not only by social degrading, which he sought to avoid by reason of his self-awareness as a painter and by his eagerness for culture as a self-educated man, but also, as a member of the multinational Austrian state, by the infiltration of foreign Slavs, who were adjudged to be racially, as well as culturally, inferior. This was an experience which he shared with the Germans on the border in the East, among whom the NSDAP, at the time of the later elections, could count on 50 per cent of the votes for themselves.[97] Less well-known is the fact that Hitler, in his private life, remained a lifelong member of his lower-middle-class background. The evidence for such an attitude can only be mentioned briefly here: the primitive meditative landscape pictures of those early days, which were by no means of the Wilhelmine style of art; the enduringly modest life style, which was later ideologised by propaganda as 'spartan'; the furnishings of the Berghof before its extension[98] which were described by Rauschning as lower-middle-class; the preference for the simple, straightforward world of the lower-middle-class Karl May;[99] the efforts made for the support of his always anonymous relatives.[100] It was a side of him which made the *Führer* appear human, especially when it served the purposes of propaganda. In addition there was Hitler's brand of 'taste for the theatre', which is central to most assessments of his life, that taste which once again derived from his lower-middle-class mentality, of letting no individualistic traits be seen. It was nevertheless the form of expression of the demonstrative will for power, the style of Germany and of its *Führer* who represented its universal reputation. Instead of speaking simply of 'Hitler's taste',[101] like George L. Mosse, the central theme here should be as in Thies' portrayal of Hitler as the 'architect of world power',[102] the importance of power symbolism.

Both directions in taste are closely related to one another, like thought and ideology, or, to quote a pairing of Theodor Geiger's, like 'skin' and 'garment'. Hitler had, in more casual terms, a lower-middle-class 'skin', but to his humbled, and spiritually and culturally totally confused followers, stood clothed in the tunic of the *Imperator Positur*, with proudly raised head, noble expression, searching look and outstretched arms, exactly as envisaged by the stage director's brief for any provincial pre-war theatre, or like the script instructions for any film dealing with antiquity. The only difference was that this was not a drama for the normal stage, but on the grand platform of the Nuremberg Reichsparty rally arena, in full view of the faithful followers paraded into a symmetrically arranged throng. This *Führer* corresponded exactly to the picture which the 'little man' of the 1930s had made for himself out of the celebrated and heroic greatness of his *alter ego*, for which history had already set up a monumental plinth. What has been described as Hitler's mass instinct, a concept which betrays something more than charisma, is just this feel for the *mise en scène* of lower-middle-class cliché, the inherent ingredient of the 'flicks' of the period. The relationship between *Führer* and followers was quite different from that between Kaiser Wilhelm and his middle-class subjects: not class-distinctive hierarchy, but a voluntary, unbridled submission of the people. Wilhelm II could never have claimed to be a man of the people, without family or title and without means. Hitler was able to do this and knew how to present himself by various demagogic twists as the selfless, classless son of the people, whose heart yearned only for one thing – the strong and unified *Volksgemeinschaft*, the national community. Thus in 1936 he appealed on behalf of rearmament to the Krupp workforce with the assertion, 'I am perhaps the only statesman in the world who does not possess a bank account. I have no investments, I have no shares in any sort of business concern. I possess no dividends.'[103] Such honest apologies probably made more impression on the workers than many a learned treatise about the nature of capitalism, even if there did seem to be a marked possibility that there was something called capitalism without capitalists.

Now to consider the war experience. One could, of course, trace back the ideological pre-history of National Socialism in any way one likes, back into the German past, without ever finding a point of departure. In any search for the socio-psychological congruencies between Hitler and society it is useful to limit oneself to an analysis of the First World War and its effects on the collective subconscious. To this end belong the so-called 'Ideas of 1914',[104] that is, the emotional destruction of class differences in the ecstasy of the outbreak of war and the glorification of militarism. Also of importance is the erosion of the monarchy and of the middle-class pre-war world in the trenches, the propaganda of the top army leadership and their nationalistic charge-hands,[105] the shock of the unexpected defeat. The war gave Hitler's life both sense and direction, shaping from the Bohemian and ideological wanderer an organiser, schooled in militarism, a demagogue exuding political virility. As he had no family, personal ties or involvement, he identified utterly with the well-being of his chosen nation – although without consideration for its traditions – and with the fate of the German people to which belonged, though less with the Bismarckian nation that had made Austria an outcast. He took quite literally the pseudo-intellectual war propaganda which appealed so much to his half-educated mind. The anti-middle-class resentments of the artistic youth who had been rejected by pre-war society now concentrated themselves into the social protest of the front-line soldier against the administrative and supply organisations in the rear, against the bourgeois war profiteers and socio-democratic opponents of the war. Subsequently, the highly decorated but yet simple front-line soldier was able to gain a reputation as the mouthpiece for the generation that had been cheated of its victory. The matrix of a National Socialist mentality was formed at the battlefront. This artist from lower-middle-class surroundings, an Austrian and a Catholic and as such in the German army subject to prejudices, got to know all levels and classes of society as well as Germans from other regions and faiths. The concept of the national community is an idea from the trenches, from which nobody again was ever to be released into the middle-class world, in which old regional and class differences would have to make their own way. The middle-class hierarchy belonged to the past.[106] The hierarchy of the future was not to be based on education, on that derided school knowledge with which one could become a lieutenant without any previous experience of the front line, or on a specialist knowledge which enabled jurists, for instance, either based behind the lines or even staying at home, to have a 'cushy' time. Even more resentment was aroused by the propertied middle class. 'Madness', Hitler later calls it in conversations with

Rauschning, whose 'democratic ideas of rank are based on the purse', or on the 'chance speculations of smart business people'.[107] The vocabulary of the front-line soldier who, in his lowly class, criticises the civilians, is quite unmistakeable here. Against the whole of the bourgeois world is ranged the rank and file of battle. Hitler's model of society is the fanciful utopia of the front-line soldier, later to be invoked at all times.[108] In place of the degenerate nobility and the better-schooled middle class a new class of gentleman was to appear, a new military nobility as at the beginning of feudal society, with no other pre-conditions than resoluteness in battle and loyalty to the *Führer*. The symbolic figure of the decadent bourgeois world was the Jew, who was nicely tucked up at home while others kept their heads down, or who, as a journalist and therefore a socialist, weakened the home front with demoralising speeches about international understanding. In order to be able to carry on his business, he objected to annexation, that necessary living-space which alone could protect the people as much from blockade by the English fleet as from international industrial plutocracy. The great conspiracy of world Jewry is quickly at hand, almost exactly like the panic of soldiers fearing syphilis brought on by prostitution, the 'Jewish influence on the spirit' and 'money maker from our copulative instinct'.[109] The personalising of misunderstood powers, the reduction of decisions and arguments to a clearly outlined, chalk-and-cheese view of the 'enemy', was typical of the needs of the front-line soldier with his extremely limited horizons of experience in an unusually condensed psychological situation. At the same time, trench warfare by a few square metres a day gave rise to the atavism of 'living-space'. At Verdun hundreds of thousands gave up their lifeblood, while just over to the East the great land race was starting.[110] Hitler was particularly impressed by the great organisational efforts of the German army in the war. With the invalidation of middle-class and civilian values, substituted by orders and obedience, suddenly nothing seemed impossible. The mass of humanity became the compliant instrument of a higher purpose. As long as there was no lack of brute determination in this, no objective was unattainable and the utopia of today could become the reality of tomorrow. 'If one day I shall command the war effort', Hitler said to Rauschning as he took on the guise of the Lord over life and death, 'I shall have no second thoughts about the 10 million young men whom I shall send to their death'.[111] This was typical of his brutal way of thinking which could at any time become deadly earnest. Other attitudes can be mentioned only briefly here: right is always on the side of the strong and the brave; court martial is the best, because it is the quickest, form of justice;[112] art is archaic reality, the representation of everlasting values, like the heroism of battle, it serves to raise self-awareness and give morale in battle; the economy is the servant girl of politics, inflation merely a question of discipline;[113] existence is terrible and simple – victory or defeat, hammer or anvil. It is the simplifying perspective of the front-line soldier and eventual *Stammtisch* veteran in the pub who knows everything better because in his own life he has had certain experiences which had been incomprehensible to him and which he had been unable to cope with in any psychic way: 'If I were the Kaiser ...'[114]

By making absolute any unusual experiences which he shared with others of his generation, together with upgrading them into an ideology in themselves, Hitler formed the socio-psychological conditional framework for his later success. If anyone wanted to erect a statue to him, then it would have to be represented as the blustering cavalryman planted firmly on the *Stammtisch* in the pub, its visionary eyes directed at an imaginary audience, and at the same time surrounded by beery war veterans and lower-middle-class men glancing up from their game of taroc cards.

IV

In the meantime, research has adequately shown that the impressive façade of structuralised unity which Hitler's state outwardly represented was in reality a sham, behind which, unseen by the national community and people abroad, a continuous battle was being fought. New findings will no longer be able to contradict this assertion so it is high time that this phenomenon is given a definite interpretation which can explain in a rationally convincing way the contradiction between appearance and reality. It was not by chance that the American historian Robert Koehl was one of the first to point out the feudal aspects of National Socialism.[115] While European research is always sceptical about the question of the universal feasibility of the concept of feudalism, in America a higher degree of recognition is given to this very point, especially since the appearance of a collection of works about *Feudalism in History*.[116] Robert Koehl, in his research into Himmler as the Reich Commissioner for the Consolidation of the German Race[117] had stumbled on certain neo-feudal indications in National Socialist ideology. From the fanatical notions of a 'new blood and soil aristocracy', as propagated by Darré from 1935 onwards,[118] to the conception of the *Volk* state which was acceptable also to the National Socialist left wing, or the casting (so zealously pursued by Himmler) of the *SS* as a new order of knighthood,[119] all these indications pointed in the same direction. Most significant of all was, of course, Hitler's own obsession with *Lebensraum* which, in his imagination, involved the birth of a new master race of Aryan blood.

What is of interest in Koehl's proposition today is perhaps not so much the ideological aspects of the National Socialist structure of government as its trends in reorganisation of the state, which show a surprising similarity to developments at the beginning of the feudal age. Although it must seem questionable whether, for the sake of the definition of one theory, the development of yet another should be introduced, one cannot help pointing out the differing roles of the Fascist and National Socialist states as the criterion for a differentiation of these two concepts. Mussolini's utopia was based on the centrally and legally administered *Imperium Romanum*, whereas the National Socialists, and especially Hitler, dreamed of the rebirth of the medieval feudal empire of the Ottonians and Hohenstaufen. Hitler, of course, was an Austrian and as such retained traces of the traditions of the old empire: out of the Holy Roman Empire of the

German Nation should arise a modern Germanic Imperial State under German leadership. Care should be taken lest the state which, like the economy, had only an instrumental function, should stand like a bureaucratic hurdle in the way of the attainment of this vast objective. Indeed, as Koehl emphasises, 'to National Socialist theorists the Roman tradition as well as all modern state bureaucracy was anathema'.[120] That Hitler, at the same time, was as fascinated as a young schoolboy with the ancient Roman empire[121] changes nothing of his extreme anti-bureaucratic attitude and way of governing.[122]

This last point takes on special significance in respect of the socio-psychological basis of the *Führer* rule. Hitler was the embodiment of the subjection of bureaucratic power against which increasing numbers of Germans were now turning. Bureaucratisation meant on the one hand the rationalising of political rule but, on the other, depersonalisation and deglorification. Kaiser and princes had disappeared from the stage, great and small war heroes had no place, and what followed was the growth of those anonymous bureaucracies of the parties and the central and local public services. Then came the somewhat archaic embodiment of power through Hitler, firstly as partly Duke, who possessed the boldness to set his *Führer* principle against all democratic legality, subsequently as 'People's Kaiser' who – like the Roman emperors before him – swept across the land, not high on his charger, but in an open car next to his chauffeur, showing how close he was to the people. Just as the picturesque and anachronistic princely ways of the Bavarian King Ludwig II had met with approval among the simple people, so too did Hitler's popularity with the masses lie in the fact that the power of the state was clearly to be seen in his person, as 'Overlord'. He was no puppet in the hands of a huge state bureaucracy or of industry, but, like the legendary ruler of yore, the provider and distributor of fundamental power. With his signature to a *Führer* order he was able to hand out areas of power like feudal tenures, whole provinces, funds for the economy or for resettlement measures in the East and the like, taking no consideration of bureaucratic structures and answerable only to the principle of 'healthy national sentiment'.[123] Simultaneously he was the source of power for thousands of posts and jobs within the party and its member sections, for the minor authorities and administrators, for many who, before his arrival, had only dreamed of even the smallest measure of power or exclusive, independent responsibility, or who had possessed this power only for the limited duration of the war. What was decisive now was the personal sense of loyalty to the *Führer* of these new vassals. But his prestige was never put in question by the rivalries of these minor *Führers*. On the contrary, they only enhanced his authority as the final arbiter and law-giver. Hitler guaranteed by his person that no bureaucratic fossilisation would arise and that the wheel of history would remain in motion. What was so fascinating about him, above all else, was that he, and he alone, decided on the *ultima ratio*, on war and peace, the prerogative of all true rulers, out of sight of his people.

It was not just Hitler's methods of governing that were feudalistic, but more especially his policy of *Lebensraum* and more global vision, the active resumption of the medieval colonisation of the East. The East was, so to speak, declared the 'Wild West', where law and order at first counted for nothing. The territorial annexations had, at the same time, served as a training ground for a new 'nobility of the sword' who were not likely to proceed with kid gloves. His vassals were obliged, after ten years, to assure him of the completion of the Germanification of their tenures, without having to account for their methods. By the introduction of border districts a central administration spanning the whole empire was to be avoided. The danger that *Gauleiter* could become petty 'Reich-princes' was considered by Hitler to be minimal because they were subject to dismissal at any time, and were not allowed to bequeath their power.[125] The huge Reich was to be opened up by the most modern means of communications technology, with a network of railways with 4-metre lines and with an 11-metre wide system of *Reichautobahn* radiating from Berlin.[126] While on the one hand Hitler could see himself being 'handicapped and hooked' by bureaucracy, he nevertheless allowed himself to drink the intoxicating liquor of the possibilities of the modern communications technology. His schizophrenia, too, Hitler shared with many of his contemporaries. It was only his initial inspiration that was anti-modernistic: the political fulfilment of his plans was not possible without the huge operational involvement of modern technology. Furthermore, it was a question of a completely new civilisation, the attainment of a utopia. To this extent the National Socialist 'living-space' vision was an imperialism *sui generis* but, despite all 'continuity of the power structures' through the alliance of the old and the new elites, it was nevertheless different in a qualitative sense from the middle-class mercantile imperialism, based on foreign competition, of the pre-war era.

Most theorists of Fascism agree that the middle class, and especially the lower middle class, represented the actual basis of the National Socialist movement.[127] But generally no further conclusions are drawn from this verdict for the interpretation of the phenomenon of National Socialism, because the stringent logic of the theory, which makes certain aspects so absolute, might thus be damaged. The most prominent feature of German Fascism is, without doubt, its strong association with the person of Hitler, so that one could define National Socialism most precisely with the contemporary term 'Hitler Movement'. Hitler as the medium (which it was the purpose of this essay to analyse) is not explained adequately by the mere location of the man as the *Führer* within the National Socialist ruling system, nor even by the strongly manipulated function of the *Führer* cult as it was systematically presented by Goebbels. The unique appeal of this man, as is often maintained, consisted mainly in his being the exponent of an initially non-ideological – to say nothing of politically articulate – mentality, in fact, of that 'healthy national sentiment' which in political practice became extremely impure and intolerant. In the Hitler Movement Germany experienced its own genuine revolution, even if this did not correspond exactly to the theoretical model of revolution. National Socialism embodies a fundamentally new variant

of the concept of revolution, namely the delayed revolt of
the lower-middle-class masses against modernity and against
the consequences of an unnatural and politically and socially
unbearable industrialisation. From this 'delayed nation'
there had suddenly developed, with a certain logical
consistency, the delayed and socially and psychologically
disturbed industrial monarchy (in the symptomatic language
of propaganda, the 'young people') that, at any cost, did
not wish to become the industrial society but remain the
Volksgemeinschaft.

5. The Structure and Nature of the National Conservative Opposition in Germany up to 1940

KLAUS-JÜRGEN MÜLLER

I

The development of research into what is called 'the German resistance' or 'the German opposition' has gone through various phases.[1] In the first of these phases research was centred on the proof of its factual existence, its activities, motives and political attitudes. This corresponded on the one hand to a politico-psychological need in respect of the view popularly held abroad of German collective guilt, and on the other to a need to legitimise the new state of the Federal Republic.

At the second stage, historical science abandoned its narrow focus on the complex events of 20 July and

Original contribution to this volume. Translated by B. J. Follett.

the national conservative opposition and included other politically differing opposition and resistance groups from the widest social backgrounds. At the same time, following a dominant tendency of modern German historical science, the problem of continuity was taken up in connection with the phenomenon of resistance or, as the case might be, opposition.

For some time a third developmental stage has been apparent,[2] characterised mainly by an intense concern to define qualitatively the phenomenon of resistance, whose multi-layered nature has already been identified by research, and thus to find a complete historical definition. This concern grew from two roots simultaneously. In the first place, more recent research into the structure and nature of the National Socialist system of rule, expressed in the dichotomic terms 'monolithic system' and 'polycracy', made it clear that there was a need for a specific theoretical basis for the NS system, which naturally affected the concept of resistance. In the second place, as a result of research into the characteristics of wide areas of social classes in the Third Reich – for example, non-conformist attitudes to the system by some Catholic rural populations or by parts of the industrial working class – the analytical inadequacy of the traditional, very politically and morally defined concept of resistance had become extremely obvious. Modern research into the resistance is therefore concerned to a great extent with developing more extensive (compared with past interpretations) alternative analytical and conceptual models. In this respect it must be said that this is by no means a question of wanting to disclaim, with the arrogance of a later generation, the political and moral content of the revolt of 20 July and of other resistance groups not belonging to the national conservative opposition, or the fact of the existence of a serious anti-Hitler opposition, or of wishing to despise it. It has more to do with an historically consistent analysis – and that means above all an appropriate conceptual and categorical survey – of a phenomenon that has since proved to be more stratified, more differentiated and more problematic than previous examinations and interpretations show. Furthermore, it is a question of making sure that research into the resistance keeps pace with the developments of the historical debate about the National Socialist system.

Within the context of our present discussion, two problems will be examined: first, the national conservative opposition has to be placed in its historical framework. To do this it must be freed from the usually predominant moral-political aspects of the question and placed in a purely historical perspective. It will need to be considered as an historical phenomenon in its own right, and not merely as an integral part of one all-embracing homogeneous and monolithic concept of 'resistance' which, together with other integral parts such as 'Church resistance', 'working class resistance' and others, went to make up the collective concept of 'German resistance'.

What may be regarded as the 'resistance of the working class' was an attempt on the one hand to bring down the regime by the creation of a mass-based opposition (KPD) and on the other hand to maintain a certain organisational and political solidarity (SPD and trade unions).[3] The 'Church resistance' may be understood as ecclesiastical concern for defence against 'totalitarian claims to sovereignty, and as such is a phenomenon which is not limited to the Third Reich alone'.[4] The 'youth resistance' became extremely multi-layered and could cautiously be considered as a conglomeration of defensive reactions to the excesses and opportunism of the totalitarian system.[5] However, what is known as 'national conservative resistance' is fundamentally an independent phenomenon in so far as it represents a specific manifestation of the attitude of traditional elites towards National Socialism and the Nazi regime. In this respect a further examination is introduced of the wider framework of the attitudes of traditional power elites in a political and social environment which is experiencing profound secular change. From such a proposition the conservative opposition is conceived as being a specific symptom of politico-social change. It is therefore a question of the activity and attitudes of opposition groups from the areas of the traditional, national conservative ruling elites, mainly those of the military, diplomatic and upper administrative groups from within and (with few exceptions) also outside the apparatus of state.

Secondly, there must also be an attempt to define this national conservative resistance in exact conceptual terms. In the case of the traditional ruling elites, the commonplace term 'opposition' already presents a few difficulties. What does 'opposition' mean in these contexts? What does 'resistance' mean? What is the fundamental difference between 'opposition' and 'resistance'?

Is every contradiction of any high-ranking state functionary on any important political question immediately to be termed 'opposition' within the NS *Führer* state, especially when fundamental aspects of the ruling system, as invested in the functionary concerned, have been accepted and the conventional procedures (lectures, memoranda) adhered to? Is it 'opposition' when actual or implicit agreement on aims exists, although divergencies of method are both apparent and expressed? Does the concept of 'opposition' presuppose not only contradiction and dissent, but also a certain basic consent, whereas 'resistance' is distinguished from 'opposition' precisely by the lack of basic consent? A glance at existing literature very quickly shows that relatively little consideration has been given to these problems of terminology. The terms 'opposition' and 'resistance' are often used synonymously. Only in more recent times have there been a few significant efforts to clarify the terminological problem by a more comprehensive and theoretical framework. A valuable and comprehensive proposition has been put forward by Hüttenberger[6] as a theoretical basis for discussion. He understands the term 'resistance' in general as the specific form of argumentation within any unbalanced form of government; it can cover anything from non-conformist attitudes to dissentient attitudes, from civil disobedience to conflicts inherent in the system, and even go as far as conflicts designed to overthrow the system. This is undoubtedly a flexible and conceptual framework appropriate to the complexity of the historical phenomenon under discussion here. Within this framework the 'national conservative opposition' may be defined in purely formal terms as dissentient attitudinal behaviour by parts of a governing body against predominating parts of this same body. Nevertheless, the problem still remains of the application of this formal proposition in concrete terms. In order to arrive at a specific description and a complete explanation there is a need not only for formal criteria but also for substantial definitions which are deduced from known facts.

We need to proceed in two stages:

1. an interpretative data network is to be drawn up which will allow for a consistent *historical location* of what will be called 'the national conservative opposition' in specific terms;

2. centred upon the events and developments of the years 1938/39, this phenomenon is to be examined structurally as regards personnel, politics and activities, in order to make possible a specific and conceptual survey consistent with the known facts.

The historical data network[7]

The attitude of the traditional power elites in state and society must be viewed against the background of the history of the German state and its politico-structural problems. There were two main elements of this state: the feudal *Junker* tradition of the Prussian military state from which grew the German Reich, and the modern capitalist industrial society, since the foundation of the German national state coincided with the industrialisation of Germany.[8]

These two elements were the main contributors to the conditions prevailing at the end of the 1920s and beginning of the 1930s, in which traditional power elites saw themselves confronted by National Socialism. Both elements had been the governing factors of historical development. Basically, the German national state of the late nineteenth and early twentieth centuries can be defined as a dynamic industrial state, founded and led by a predominantly agrarian, pre-industrial, *Junker* elite, which had adapted well to the economic and cultural bourgeoisie both in its political and social direction and in its socio-economic interests,[9] which had considerable influence upon it. Other social strata were, however, either excluded from the fundamental decisions about the political and social shaping of general life in this 'uncompleted national state'[10] or else were not fully consulted. This was true not only of national minorities such as Danes, Poles or citizens of Alsace-Lorraine, but also of certain social groups, who for political and other reasons had gathered in the republic, and of (at least temporarily) large parts of the Catholic population.

Herein lies one of the central problems of this new German Reich. The fact that the 'industrial revolution' took place at the same time as the foundation of the national state under the leadership of the *Junker* Prussians presented a fundamental problem of integration. The young Reich not only had the task of uniting the German provinces, the *Länder*, which had very different historical developments, into one national state, but it also simultaneously had to integrate the traditional pre-industrially-orientated ruling elite with social strata which had just grown up as a result of the industrialisation process. This difficult situation was further heightened by the progressive development of the industrial state: from this point onwards the discrepancy between 'feudal' and 'feudalised' ruling elites on the one hand and on the other those classes of the people who had not been widely included in the shaping and governing of the Reich, had to be overcome. Simultaneously, the clash of interests among ruling elites, and between these and other groupings within the political, social and economic system, had to be settled. They were increasing in sharpness and complexity with the widespread process of industrialisation. This integration problem gradually became a decisive aspect in the shaping of the German national state. Even the numerous manipulative attempts at secondary integration and political stabilisation such as, for instance, civic mass mobilisation on ideological and organisational levels, were never able to settle this problem completely, but became, in fact, even more indicative of the permanent structural dilemma of the Reich.[11]

The problem of integration also became one of legitimation for the ruling elites, a problem that became even more acute as social change in the wake of the developing industrial state made itself more noticeable. The high-ranking civil servant group, accustomed to functioning within the traditions of the upper-class state regime, the industrial and cultural bourgeoisie whose only articulation was through their own particular interests, and parts of the military elite which remained alienated from the industrial society, all these were overwhelmed by this dual problem. High administrative bodies were similarly overwhelmed by the task of making wider political participation possible in a more and more strongly differentiated society, as were the cultural and propertied bourgeoisie, faced with the task of exercising such rights, to say nothing of how to gain them for themselves. The military elite, on the other hand, considered itself to be not merely a professional elite but primarily a politico-social elite. This historically based state of affairs was to be the main instrument in bringing about the confrontation of the different elite groups with National Socialism.

The position of the military elite in the state was never to be fully accounted for just by its prime functional, military role. The officer corps was a fundamental part of the traditional socio-political ruling class of the German state. It was the embodiment, in a way, of its traditional values.[12] That meant more than social privilege: the military elite, because of the tradition of the Prussian military state, also possessed a fundamentally political quality which found expression in the pseudo-autonomous special position of the military leadership with respect to the politico-administrative executive, the government. But above all it found expression in the claim to political rights of discussion and decision-making, a claim which was expressly insisted upon again and again by the chief representatives of the military elite: joint power through joint decision-making. This was a fundamental element in the self-appraisal of the traditional military elite. This dualism of a military and political-administrative rule, which formerly had cohered only in the crown, in the person of the monarch, had been inherited from the Prussian military monarchy and its importance for history cannot be underestimated.[13] Not only with respect to the claim of a few high-ranking military members of the resistance – such as, for example, Colonel General Beck [though, like a large number of the national conservative opposition, he was not a Prussian by birth, *Ed.*] – to bear a high proportion of the responsibility for the state, but also to the inbuilt civilian opposition to the traditional ruling role of the military, and not merely from the fact that they possessed all the necessary physical means of power for a state coup.

The problem of integration and legitimation with which the traditional ruling elites saw themselves confronted hit the military elite especially hard. The disintegration of the old social structure in the course of the industrialisation process, but above all the First World War, civil political reorganisation, inflation and the world economic crisis, had greatly intensified this problem. The First World War had clearly offered a further challenge to the military elite: they now not only had to deal with socio-political change, but they were also faced with a fundamental change in the manner of warfare. The technological war between highly industrialised states presented an enormous challenge to the traditional military caste and to the traditional conception of officership, just as socio-political change had previously put their position strongly in doubt. There now appeared a new set of stress elements which became apparent in such pairs of opposition as traditional military caste against technology military specialists, exclusive military elite against modern mass armed forces, or 'military specialists against total social mass mobilisation'.[14] It was in such a dichotomy that the second secular challenge to the traditional military elite was expressed.

Socio-political change and change in warfare fused into a threatening syndrome because the officer corps reacted to this complicated situation in many different ways. However, all the different types of reaction may be reduced to one pattern: namely, the idea that this dual problem could only be solved in the long term, first, if the structure of the state was reorganised along authoritarian lines and, second, if a new legitimising mass basis could be gained for the traditional elite classes. This is the common denominator to which the various and very controversial conceptions within the military elite can be reduced. It included not only those who were aiming mainly at ensuring their own political and social influence, but also those who regarded the military and military technical superiority as a justification for the continuation of the traditional power structure. These agreed on both points. This was also the point of agreement between the military elite and the other fractions of the traditional elite groups. In view of the impossibility, within the excessively pluralistic political structure of the Weimar Republic, of solving the increasing economic and social problems according to traditional values, or of improving the international status of the Reich, which had been created as a result of the First World War, these groups tended more and more towards an authoritarian solution, whatever else they may have understood by this solution.

In these political objectives the other groups of the traditional elites identified themselves with the aims of the military elite: first, the regaining of Germany's 'great power' status in Europe, which had been lost in the First World War – a position which was defined mainly in a military and power-political sense[15] and, in fact, not only by the military elite; second, the regaining of an authoritarian structure of government and administration; this was seen by the civil elite as a precondition for effective government in a modern society, and the military elite strove for an authoritarian form of state in order to be able to obtain the organisation of the whole nation, as conceived and led by themselves, together with its resources for modern warfare, now defined as 'total'.[16]

Up to 1933, however, the different routes towards the realisation of this concept had either failed or had shown themselves to be impracticable: this was true, on the one hand, for the *putsch* strategy of the civil-military forces of reaction centred around the *Generallandschaftsdirektor* Kapp and General von Lüttwitz in 1920; it was true, on the other hand, of the conception of General von Seeckt, whose characteristic policy, *étatism*, meaning the separation of the army from the republic ('State within a State') [Seeckt's policy, while accepting the Weimar Republic as the lesser of a number of evils, was orientated along an abstract conception of the German Reich, but not along the *concrete reality* of the republic. *Ed.*], could not be maintained for any length of time;[17] and finally, it was also true of the alternative concepts which were developed by Generals Groener and Schleicher.[18]

Under these historic conditions, in January 1933 came the foundation of the government under *Reichskanzler* Hitler, a government in which the National Socialists were in a minority against the representatives of national conservative organisations. Hitler's government was formed at that time on the basis of an 'entente' between substantial organisations of the traditional power elites and the leaders of the National Socialist mass movement. All of the groups which formed this 'entente' saw in it particular advantages for themselves. The old elites no longer felt capable of maintaining their traditional positions by themselves, or of realising their political objectives either inwardly or outwardly. They lacked, in addition, any basis within society. Hitler, however – or so it seemed to the defenders of the idea of an 'entente' with the NS movement – was able to give them the necessary basis with the masses and thereby solve for them the problem of integration. Hitler, for his part, had to accept that he was unable to get to power on the strength of his own organisation. The events of 9 November 1923 had shown the impossibility of any *coup d'état*; the November elections of 1932 had shown the hopelessness of obtaining power through a parliamentary majority. The mass movement had brought Hitler to the threshold of power, but only the old power elites, who still held the decisive posts within the state apparatus, could help him across it. They alone could procure for him any share of power.

For the military elite, who were not in a position during this phase of rapid politico-social change to achieve any substantial basis of legitimation and action on their own, conditions from now on seemed to be assured for the realisation of most of their fundamental objectives: in home politics there was the recreation and securing of that traditional division of power within both state and society which had been considered since 1918 to be particularly threatened; in foreign politics there was the regaining of the 'great power status' of the Reich, defined as military power politics; and finally, in military politics, there was the permanent and total mobilisation of society, called by the euphemistic name 'defence capacity of the nation', which was considered to be the incontrovertible prerequisite of any status as a great power, given the conditions of an industrial-technological era.

There were also advantages, *mutatis mutandis*, for the non-military elites, who saw their basis in society rapidly dwindling as parliamentary and social change increased and as the power structures, monopolised by the conservative bourgeoisie, were eroded. In this entente the army were allotted, according to their own self-appraisal, a privileged status; Hitler paraphrased this with the formula of the 'two pillars' on which the regime rested − army and party − thereby, through clever tactics, cunningly limiting the expectations of the military.[19] But in foreign ministry circles also, despite the indolence of the Reich foreign secretary von Neurath, 'who considered it more important merely to be in attendance rather than to put through any sensible foreign policy',[20] a tradition of joint responsibility and sharing of power endured. This was embodied by Ernst von Weizsäcker who, on his appointment as secretary of state (February 1938) described this concept with the metaphor that it was a matter of 're-engaging the neutral gear of the Foreign Office to the state engine so that it would help to pull'.[21]

For the representatives of the traditional power elites, this entente promised to create those prerequisites which seemed necessary for the successful attainment of their main objectives. Because of the nature of the entente with the National Socialists in the coalition, the twofold objective described above, with its foreign and home policy components, took on a decisive function in the relationship between the traditional ruling groups and the National Socialist regime. The future development of this relationship was thenceforward fundamentally governed by the degree of fulfilment, or as the case may be, disappointment, of those expectations which had united the elites within the collaboration implicit in the 1933 entente. In concrete terms this meant that this relationship developed, in domestic policy, according to the measure of attainment (or failure) of any joint decision-making power within the state, which assumed a greater importance for the military than for the upper ranks of diplomats; in foreign policy, according to the guarantee (or endangering) of success in the aspiration to be a great power.

A suitable interpretative framework has thus been constructed which enables a sufficiently precise historical definition of the phenomenon 'national conservative opposition' to be made. What is formulated in Hüttenberger's conceptual system as 'resistance by integral units of a ruling body against other more predominant parts of that'[22] is represented in the historic fact of the national conservative opposition as a definite complementary feature of the entente of the traditional elites with Hitler and his movement. National conservative opposition was thus a specific phenomenon of conflict within the framework of this entente.

At the same time, differentiation between national conservative opposition and the resistance of '*a prioristic* opponents' becomes possible. Those opposition groups' very being (like that of the National Socialists themselves) in principle allowed them no choice between opposition, neutrality or coalition (or perhaps collaboration) with the National Socialists: groups like the Jews, to whom the NS racist ideology allowed of no possible option; or groups for whom there was no option on philosophical or religious grounds, such as, for instance, Christian fundamentalists. This applies also to supporters of political movements who, like Communists or anarchists, were fighting in principle against the existing social order, irrespective of whether it was a National Socialist or a middle-class parliamentarian order. Therefore the whole spectrum of this particular phenomenon of conflict, which was a complementary feature of the entente of the traditional ruling classes with NS leaders, needs to be fully described because of its varying stances, ranging from those inherent in to those opposed to the system. Also the form, as well as the degree of intensity, of different reactions by individual representatives of those traditional elites to the various demands made by the regime must be fully evaluated. In this respect the following additional analytical categories must be introduced. First, the phenomenon of conflict is to be analysed from the point of view of which of the two essential objectives appeared to be most endangered in the eyes of a cross-section of representatives of the elites; the 'entente' character of the system or the great-power conception in world politics, or both? Given that this consideration of objectives was of all-consuming fundamental importance, it can, for example, be shown as quite plausible that while certain immoral practices and features of the regime in the first years of the Third Reich certainly caused disquiet and criticism in military and diplomatic circles and in the ranks of the upper civil service (as, for example, the suppression of political and ideological opponents, and various anti-semitic and anti-religious measures which directly violated all ideas of tolerance and human rights), it was not until the *vabanque* game of 1938 or the intrigue against Fritsch, and immediately prior to that the ambitions of the *SA* Chief of Staff Röhm in national defence policies, that any politically significant moves were made by the opposition.

Second, the question has to be asked, by whom and in what way was this endangering of objectives behind the backs of the traditional elite effected? In other words, opponents and dangers must be assessed. With this answered, the possibility then exists of describing and explaining with more precision the breadth of the respective reactions in cases of conflict, and therefore the gradual development from, for instance, defensive assurance of an individual position to offensive stabilisation of the position (such as 'the purging of "radical" elements from the regime' or their elimination from the decision-making process in foreign policy) and thence to plans and attempts to destabilise and overthrow the system. In this respect it was of considerable significance whether certain threats to the essential objectives, as envisaged by representatives of the elites, emanated from individuals and certain groups within the NS movement or from Hitler himself. The quality of their reaction was significantly governed by this: the following three examples show variant combinations.

1. The Röhm affair[23] of June 1934: why did the murder of some conservative adherents in the course of the elimination of the *SA* leadership not produce any significant political reaction on the part of the elected representatives of the officer corps? The answer is clear when the interpretive framework is referred to: Röhm's policy was, for the *Reichswehr* leadership, the first threatening attack on the inner-political position of the army both in its capacity as the monopolist of national strength and as one of the two constituent 'pillars' of the regime. Röhm and his *SA*, with their internal and military political aspirations, were endangering the 'arrangement' of 1933. Hitler, on the other hand, had by his action shown himself to be a loyal partner to the alliance who was merely stabilising the system of the 'two pillars'. Seen in this light, the passivity over the murders, the decision to accept Hitler as Hindenburg's successor and the oath to Hitler are all quite logical.[24] [The decision to fuse the offices of Chancellor and President was made by unanimous cabinet decision on 1 August 1934 and sanctioned by a plebiscite. The result of the latter caused some disquiet in the NS leadership because the votes in favour of it were 3 million down compared with the plebiscite of November 1933 which endorsed Germany's withdrawal from the League of Nations. *Ed.*]

2. In certain phases of the German-Polish crisis, which in turn led to the outbreak of the Second World War, the conduct of the secretary of state, von Weizsäcker, was influenced for quite a long time by the conviction that the Reich foreign minister, von Ribbentrop, was the only warmonger, while Hitler had merely fallen prey to an erroneous, if fatal, assessment of the international situation; it was just a matter of correcting this by means of informative manipulation. The secretary of

state therefore did all he could to gain influence over Hitler's decisions, to the exclusion of the foreign minister. One thing he tried was to persuade the British to issue a warning to Hitler, so that he would have no illusions at all about the reaction of the British government to any German aggression against Poland. This warning was, on the one hand, to be discreet, that is, it should not be made public in order to save the *Führer*'s prestige (every kind of destabilisation of the system was to be avoided) and, on the other hand, it was to be effected, if possible, without the involvement of the foreign minister. Weizsäcker even went so far as to suggest to the British ambassador that he should discredit Ribbentrop.[25] It was a classic case of contra-diplomacy within the framework of a system-adherent power struggle for influence with Hitler.

3. Another example is the Blomberg–Fritsch crisis.[26] If, in the opinion of some national conservative representatives during the Röhm affair and in certain phases of the Polish crisis, it seemed that Hitler could either be relied upon to defend the entente character of the regime or could not himself be numbered among the radical warmongers, he nevertheless played a less distinct role in the Blomberg–Fritsch crisis, at least in the eyes of many of the military. It was mainly the Gestapo and *SS/SD* who had perpetrated a treacherous coup against the army in the intrigue against Fritsch. Hitler's conduct, however, was now at best unfathomable; the solutions, in staff and organisation, which he eventually imposed no longer enabled him to appear to be an arbiter favourable to the army. The Fritsch crisis was therefore a decisive turning point for certain key figures in the later resistance, as is shown in the cases of Admiral Canaris and General Oster.[27] [However, the suggestion for Hitler to assume direct supreme command came from none other than the retiring Field Marshal von Blomberg. *Ed.*]

A few officers at that time proposed different measures for the internal purging of the regime, in other words, offensive steps by the army to stabilise its position within the regime, because Hitler was no longer obviously functioning as a regulating factor.

A similar example is that of Carl Goerdeler, one of the main figures in the civil conservative resistance.[28] He was a prime example of those in the entente of the conservative organisations with Hitler, whom he served as Reich commissioner for prices in 1934, fully convinced that only an authoritarian state was the right type of government for Germany. At the end of 1935 he was influential in working out for Hitler a new law for city administration. He often sent Hitler reports, fully convinced that the *Führer* was an 'enlightened dictator' with idealistic intentions, who could be won over by factual arguments. When Hitler did not follow his advice but set out on that financial and credit-based policy which was so hazardous in his eyes, and when party organs allowed massive debts to be built up in his area of responsibility as mayor of Leipzig, he gave up his civil and civic posts and made his way into the opposition. Nevertheless, he still hoped for a long time to be able to influence Hitler by means of reports and memoranda, though he became more and more adamant about not joining the party. It was only when he realised that Hitler was throwing the Reich into a war that he went over to fundamental resistance. Similarly, there were other high-ranking officials, such as the Prussian finance minister Popitz who, in some illusionary, mistaken interpretation of the system, believed for a long time that the basic idea of their entente could be saved by cooperation with Hitler against the party and then later with Göring against Hitler. By so doing they lost their lives. [And even with Himmler! *Ed.*]

The development of Henning von Tresckow,[29] who was one of the greatest key figures of the military resistance in the war, shows very clearly how our categorised interpretational pattern can prove to be accurate, apart from isolated individual moments. In 1934, despite domestic political concern on account of National Socialist machinations (for instance, in the field of religious policy), Tresckow had affirmed his oath to Hitler. The entente with Hitler had a higher priority for him at that time than thoughts of any particular negative feature of the regime. Two years later he was demanding that the army take measures against the *SS* and Gestapo, while he was working intensively on the plans for the invasion of Czechoslovakia. He found himself in accord with the regime over German efforts towards great power status, but saw the position of the army as threatened by the *SS* and Gestapo (though not at this time by the claims of the regime to totalitarianism). He therefore advised an offensive attitude of positional retention, as he also did during the Fritsch crisis. Then, in 1938/39, concern about the impairment of the 'great power' objectives prevailed over his positive attitude to the system of the entente: the war had to be prevented, since it could not be won. Hitler, the 'dancing dervish', would have to be assassinated. These were strong words from a young officer of the general staff, but above all, a clear statement of priorities: the maintenance of German 'great power' objectives was more important to him than the preservation of the system. In due course, after the victory over France in 1940, he reverted to his previous enthusiasm for a period of time, in the hope that the war could then be concluded and the position of the Reich as a great power could be retained. The system had clearly not threatened the future of Germany after all. Then with the Russian campaign he foresaw the imminent catastrophe of the system whose criminal character had in the mean time become clear to him ('Barbarossa' and 'Commissar Order'). [Hitler's order drawn up in consultation with the army leadership to liquidate all Russian commissars upon capture. *Ed.*] The path towards the planning of a *coup d'état* was once more open.

In the cases mentioned, the intensity and quality of the reactions, like their objectives, were exclusively governed by how far and by whom their position within the ruling system was threatened (or assured) or who was the cause of the threat to their objectives in foreign policy.

A third element in the analysis can be formulated as the question of priority of objective. Within the military elite there were divergent ideas on the order of priorities within the accepted fundamental objectives. These divergencies were in turn the cause of the different strategies used to pursue these objectives. Not only were attitudes to the regime decisively governed by this, but also the type of reaction within any situation of conflict. In the Sudeten crisis, for example, the cooperation and will to act of the opposition organisations was deeply undermined by their divergent views on priorities.[30] The groupings around Oster and Gisevius [Major General Hans Oster, departmental chief of the *Abwehr*; Hans-Berndt Gisevius, erstwhile Gestapo member, later in the consular service of the German foreign office, *Ed.*] were primarily concerned with having a campaign to purge Germany's domestic scene which went as far as the overthrow of the regime, and they wanted to take Hitler's militant *vabanque* policy as grounds for a *coup d'état*. On the other hand, for Halder [successor in 1938 to Col. General Ludwig Beck as chief of the army's general staff, a position he held until the late summer of 1942, *Ed.*], Canaris and Weizsäcker what was obvious was not primarily considerations of internal policy, but the endangering of the Reich's previously obtained improvement in external political status, and the imperilling of any future expansion of power by a war policy about the motivational power of which they again had differing views, as well as over the exact moment to act. Their reactions to certain actual events, such as the Munich conference, were equally divergent.

With Tresckow, on the other hand, there had been a gradual interaction of elements in a complex individual development: the threat to the essence of the entente, the ever-increasing danger for the great power objectives, and finally the discovery of the criminal nature of the regime, all contributing to his view that Hitler and his rule were the absolute source of all evil and needed to be confronted with all the means at his disposal.

Assessment of opposition and alternative strategies, as well as differing orders of priority and divergencies in methods were therefore of vital importance for the actual stance taken towards the regime, especially with regard to the intensity and radicalism of opposition activities. [One might add here that Tresckow as late as 1943 was approached by a subaltern officer whose opinion it was that

Hitler's assassination would not do, instead an army unit would have to take over Hitler's entire HQ. Tresckow's reply highlights the dilemma of the German 'opposition': 'Well, I might find a divisional commander, but will I find the division?' *Ed.*]

II

The analytical data network that has just been drawn up makes it clear that, in the first place, a qualitative assessment of national conservative opposition in the years 1933–9 cannot (as is still quite commonly found) take place within the framework of an investigation which conceives of the opposition as a coherent and united whole. In the second place, it becomes evident that the phenomenon of national conservative opposition can, in essence and in many ways, be conceived of as the reflex of a struggle for power between constituent organisations of a regime, which in turn had an inherent tendency to overstep the boundaries of system-adherence at different points.

On the basis of this proposition, it will now be necessary to analyse the complex conflict of national conservative opposition in the years 1938–9 in respect of its personnel, politics and activities.

Before the Blomberg–Fritsch crisis, certain activities took place on two levels which were frequently claimed by writings exclusively aligned to aspects of the resistance to be evidence of determined resistance, but which a closer perusal shows were anything but that. First there were the activities of the internal political information and news service, built up by the then Lt. Colonel Oster under the auspices of the *Abwehr* and accepted and supported by Canaris, which mainly focused its attention on those party organisations (particularly the *SS* and *SD*) which were opposed to the army, and on their criminal machinations.[31] Oster had extended the information facilities which were at his disposal in his official *Abwehr* post by building up a loosely connected network of information sources. He kept in touch with countless individuals who were fundamentally critical of the party or of the regime, and who were mainly from the rightist conservative circles, such as Gisevius, Schlabrendorff, Halem, Kleist-Schmenzin and Beppo Römer, who were known to him from time spent together in the *Freikorps* or because of social or in-service contacts. [Römer in fact was to end up as a Communist. *Ed.*] They were relevant to his purpose and possessed countless interesting and valuable contacts. But this was by no means that 'significant inter-cooperative and vast organisation of a conspiracy begun in the second half of the thirties'.[32] There can be no question of this being a 'conspiracy', in the sense of a conspiratorial organisation pledged to overthrow the status quo or determined upon a *coup d'état*. On the contrary, the truly discerning eye can see a sort of very loose 'old boy network', made up of former *Freikorps* members and right-wing conservatives, extended by accidental or socially established contact with critically aligned individuals, which together formed the basis of Oster's internal political system of information and contact. But it was nothing more than that.

Second, Fritsch and Beck had also been busy building up direct and all-embracing internal and foreign information sources. Military attachés [during the Sudeten crisis these did not help Beck very much, since in contrast to Beck's own convictions they assured Hitler that France and Great Britain would not come out in support of Czechoslovakia. *Ed.*] with allegiance to them personally, such as Geyr von Schweppenburg in London or Kühlenthal in Paris, sent numerous bulletins of information outside the normal service channels. In addition, private individuals from their private and official circles served as sources of information.[33] Goerdeler also belonged to them, and he had developed an active series of tours abroad since the summer of 1937, as a result of which he had contacts in the British Foreign Office. He ensured that his reports reached the two important men in army headquarters in exactly the same way as he tried to send them to Hitler via the latter's adjutant Wiedemann.[34] However, to his foreign contacts, Goerdeler, whatever he might actually have said, could only give his own private and personal opinion; there was no kind of organised opposition group behind him and at best he only echoed the feelings of certain circles within the national conservative milieu.[35]

Goerdeler's activities are in fact a good example of the multi-layered nature of the 'opposition phenomenon'. On the one hand his supply of reports was, for the army leaders, a means towards better personal information within an otherwise fairly closed system of information; on the other hand, from Goerdeler's own point of view, it was a classic case of an attempt to infiltrate the sphere of the decision-makers from an area outside the whole apparatus of state. Furthermore, this example shows the dialectics of information, both about and from foreign countries. Above all, however, it must be remembered that he was in no way the bearer of a mandate, either on the part of the army leaders, for whom he was nevertheless a competent and first-class informant, or on behalf of any sort of existing opposition group. [Though as the detailed reports now held in the PRO show, he presented himself as the spokesman of both the civilian and military opposition. *Ed.*]

These two activities, both partially overstepping the narrow confines of officialdom – Oster's setting up of an information network and Fritsch and Beck's less well-organised efforts towards information improvement – were anything but preparations for an opposition conspiracy, and were purely and simply initiatives towards improving the lack of information input to high-ranking officials which was so symptomatic of a totalitarian society. The fact that these kinds of initiative also brought results which were valuable within the context of the system-adherent struggle over the position of the army within the state is symptomatic of the system itself, as shown, for instance, in the partial autonomy implicit in the information activities of Goerdeler abroad and in his attempts to inform Hitler.

The Blomberg–Fritsch crisis[36] in more ways than one forms a decisive landmark in the history leading up to the later military opposition. In the first place, for many national conservatives, already critical of isolated events as well as of certain tendencies developing in the regime, it was a turning point and the beginning of an increasing disillusionment with the nature of the regime itself. At this point some decisive moves were made in the direction of later resistance activities. In the second place, the crisis also had the effect of a catalyst: many different individuals who had previously only been in loose contact with one another now, for the first time, united in closer and more direct association. A more exact analysis shows that it was still in no way a case of the formation of a kind of unified, coherent opposition grouping, but a move towards activities and cooperation on very different levels, with extremely diverse motives, objectives and methods, carried on by a whole variety of persons and groups.[37]

To begin with, the lawyer Count von der Goltz, who was acting as legal adviser to Col. General von Fritsch, together with a few representatives of military judiciary who strongly supported him, was concerned not only with exonerating his client, but also with illuminating the background to the affair at the same time. Oster gave valuable help to these, at first, basically unpolitical efforts.

Next there were a few generally uncoordinated activities by individuals from outside the armed services, which aimed at informing some high-ranking officers about the reasons behind the crisis, which in the beginning were more assumed than proven, in the hope that somehow they could get them to become involved. At any rate, none of them knew exactly how, by what means or to what end this should actually happen. Goerdeler, Gisevius, Schacht and also the *SA* chief of staff, Viktor Lutze, worked with this in mind to influence some commanding generals and even Fritsch's successor. However, these were completely illusionary interventions in as far as they were meant to have more effect than just forcing the reinstatement of Fritsch. The intention behind these initiatives was in inverse proportion to their actual effect.

Meanwhile Oster, with a few like-minded friends from the *Abwehr* (Liedig, Heinz) and from former *Freikorps* days (Nebe) [Naval Captain Franz Liedig, Lt. Colonel Friedrich-Wilhelm Heinz and SS *Gruppenführer* Arthur Nebe, chief of the criminal police. These 'resistance' activities did not stop Nebe, after the invasion of Russia, from heading an *SD* extermination squad which is alleged to have murdered some 40,000 Jews. *Ed.*] together with the dynamic Dr von Dohnanyi, the personal consultant of the Reich minister of justice, developed considerable activity with the dual aim of revealing the *SS*, *SD* and Gestapo as the originators of the malicious intrigue against the top-ranking military leadership, and of bringing about a kind of unusual, powerful self-help campaign by the army against these organisations. In this way they hoped to eliminate the main source of danger to the position of the army within the state and to put through a reform of internal political organisation which would restore the entente nature of the regime.

Finally, in connection with the settlement of the Fritsch case and on the highest military levels, Beck, the chief of the general staff, Canaris, the chief of the *Abwehr*, and Hossbach, the recently deposed chief adjutant of the *Wehrmacht* to Hitler, became active in putting through some fundamental changes intended to stabilise the position of the armed services in the state and restore the regime to its original form as envisaged by them.[38]

Beck was occupied at the time with a reorganisation of the highest military leadership structure, through which the army chief of staff was to take over a key military and military-political position within the *Wehrmacht*. Further, Canaris and Hossbach devised a plan which proposed the intervention of the army leaders with an ultimatum to Hitler aimed at stripping the *SS* and Gestapo leaders of power and forcing the 'release of the Wehrmacht from the nightmare of a Tscheka'.[39] In contrast to the conspiratorial plans of the Oster–Gisevius group, which incorporated violent measures, the initiatives and plans of the three top-ranking officers did not overstep the limits of official procedures, even if they were somewhat unusual.

Thus, at that time, many separate groups aspired to very different objectives, using very different means and methods. Moves to exonerate *Generaloberst* von Fritsch combined with attempts to reveal the *SS*, *SD* and Gestapo for what they were. These, again, partly combined with the attempt to dispossess the NS organisations of their power, which would at the same time stabilise the internal-political position of the armed services within the state, and perhaps would have modified the whole nature of the regime without fully eliminating it. What these activities all had in common was the initial cause – the rehabilitation of Fritsch – and their alignment against the *SS* and its operations, as well as the Gestapo and the *SD*. They differed over the breadth of their intentions, the intensity of their desires and the extent of their objectives. At variance between them were the possibilities for action and the methods envisaged. The circles round Oster and Gisevius wanted to modify internal political arrangements by a violent purge campaign, and to eliminate the power of the *SS* as being the main threat to the entente of 1933. Among the army leaders, on the other hand, there was more thought of an officially legitimised redistribution of responsibility, and the pruning of problematical offshoots within the NS organisational jungle, all to be set in motion with more or less gentle pressure. Their objective was not the modification of the regime but the strengthening of the army leadership's position within the system, together with the reinstatement of von Fritsch. In an attempt to standardise all this, one could say it was a system-integrated power struggle whose essence contained trends towards both evolutionary reform of the regime and violent purge of it.

Thus the Fritsch crisis mainly brought about a climax in the internal political struggle for power which was inherent in the system, but was in no way a conspiracy aimed at the overthrow of the system, even in its initial stages.

It was not until the Sudeten crisis,[40] between April and September 1938, that further crucial moves were made. In this international crisis there arose for the first time a few loosely-knit organisational groups which could be termed an 'anti-war party'. They lent a new dynamism both to the trends of evolutionary regime reform and to those of violent regime purging. These three components – anti-war party, evolutionary regime reform groups and violent regime purge groups – provided the phenomenon which was often called (in much too unspecific and abbreviated a way) 'the German opposition' or 'the German resistance'. It was a very complex structure which was prohibitive of any all-inclusive label giving the idea of a united movement.[41] Concepts such as 'plot', 'conspiracy' or 'anti-Hitler fringe' can be considered as only very indistinct approximations; they fall well short of the truth and do not possess the analytical strength and selectivity required in this matter.

The outstanding representatives of this 'anti-war party' in the international crisis of 1938 were, on the military side, the chief of the general staff, Beck,[42] then his successor General Halder[43] and the *Abwehr* chief Admiral Canaris;[44] on the German diplomatic side it was secretary of state von Weizsäcker.[45] The partial and short-term combination of efforts towards the prevention of war, together with indications of the internal political power struggle (in its evolutionary-reformative form), and above all the political motive structure of the 'anti-war party', and the consequent effects of these three components, were all crucial factors in determining the nature of the activities and the limits of capacity for action of these elements.

For all four representatives of the 'anti-war party' the central issue of their external political objectives was the idea of a German great power status in central and eastern-central Europe. This objective was self-evident and beyond question. It went beyond any mere revision of the Treaty of Versailles. What was intended was a fundamental reshaping of the central European scene envisaging German hegemony.

As far as the methods with which such a concept was to be carried out were concerned, there was also agreement in principle between these individuals. None of them denied the possibility of the involvement of military power or even of war. Moreover, military power and its possible deployment was an integral part of their calculations, even if in varying degrees of importance. Again, they were in agreement over the stipulation that such a policy should never lead to an all-out European war. Limited and politically controlled martial conflicts were not excluded from this concept, even if they were not a foregone conclusion in any plans. A combination of diplomacy (assurance through alliances and agreements between the great powers) with military deployment was the basis of the concept on which these men, with all their individual differences, were agreed.

These common external political objectives and the methods envisaged for their achievement forced their adherents, in view of the international situation in the second half of the 1930s and the conscious decisions of the German dictator, into an unusual and completely insoluble situation. This was particularly true in the case of Beck, but also of von Weizsäcker.

For Beck, the availability of strong German military forces was a necessary prerequisite for the attainment of his external political objectives, which, moreover, incorporated plans for the elimination of the state of Czechoslovakia as a political power in Europe. This corresponded to his definitive policy of rearmament which he conceived and carried out at the end of 1933 as a unilateral autonomous military preparation not to be restricted by any international negotiations. From the end of 1933 he made several military-political and rearmament demands which, to a certain extent, went far beyond any plans envisaged by Hitler. From the beginning of 1936, mainly because of rearmament in other great powers, he conceived the construction 'of an army capable of carrying out a rapid conclusive offensive' with a central feature of strong motorised and tank units. This he persisted with, despite all economic and financial considerations. For a time he even consciously allowed for a short-term lessening of quality among the officer corps. The rationale of this unilateral and excessive rearmament lay in the desire to get through the accompanying phase of external political risk as rapidly as possible and, also, in the calculation of Germany becoming militarily so strong that while it was attaining its external political objectives, either other great powers would continue to remain uninvolved, or German military campaigns would be over so rapidly and conclusively that any intervention by a third power could no longer be timed effectively.[46] [One must emphasise that Beck's plans remained dormant after his departure. Halder, in terms of military plans, offered Hitler the conventional wisdom of First World War vintage. This applies up to and including the campaign in the West. Only in the case of the latter a relatively junior general, von Manstein, proposed a solution utterly alien to Halder which, however, Hitler adopted. Nevertheless, not only Halder but also Hitler were surprised at the speed and magnitude of the German success. *Ed.*] In certain circumstances the desired political ends could be obtained merely through a demonstration of military strength without direct intervention.

Beck wished to ensure the necessary external political requirements for his policy of expansion (or, in other words, German superiority in power politics) by supplementing the military and arms capacity of the Reich by treaties and military alliances. On this matter, he pointed out in a memorandum of 12 November 1937 that 'various facts' indicated the need 'for an imminent solution by force' of the Czechoslovak problem and that someone should prepare 'the political ground among those powers who stood on our side or who were not against us', and even enter into 'military discussion in either the one case or the other' and that this should have happened long ago.[47] Since 1935 he had been considering with secretary of state von Bülow and the Hungarian chief of the general staff a German-Hungarian contract 'for the division of Czechoslovakia'. Hitler based his whole martial policy of expansion mainly on the time schedule that had been produced by the arms race. He realised that in a few years potential opponents would have become stronger than the Reich. That Hitler could take this line was mainly the result of Beck's own military and arms policy. He was therefore not critical of Hitler's immediate expansionist objectives and in principle agreed with them. The existence of the CSR 'in its present form' was inconceivable for Germany, he wrote.[48] So there was no conflict in principle about 'whether' but a distinct disagreement about 'how' and 'when'. This disagreement was to gain more depth because Beck foresaw only catastrophe if Germany entered a war at an inappropriate time or in unfavourable circumstances. [However, the question which Beck never answered was when, in the light of Germany's foreign and domestic policy, the appropriate time would be. *Ed.*] In his view, such a war could only be a threat to the aim of Germany's attaining great power status.

Weizsäcker too had always demanded not only the revision of Versailles but also, increasingly, a restoration of

German hegemony in central Europe as the aim of German policy. Germany's economic and military strength was for him an absolute prerequisite for this. From the end of 1937 to the beginning of 1938 he had been saying that 'we require from England colonies and a free hand in the east'. He was clear about the fact that 'the realisation of our expansionist ideas requires English toleration' but felt that a compromise settlement with Britain should not be impossible.[49] On no account, however, should it come to a European war caused by German ambitions. He also supported the political elimination of Czechoslovakia as the external political aim, but it appeared clear to him from as late as spring 1938 that the localisation of a German-Czechoslovak war would not be possible. The western powers would, under the present circumstances, certainly get involved.

For Beck, the famous 'weekend crisis' of May 1938 was a turning point. [Benes announced the massing of German forces on Czechoslovakia's frontier — an entirely fictitious assertion. *Ed.*] While he had still been pushing on with military and military-political plans against the CSR between November 1937 and spring 1938, always supposing that a military intervention against the CSR could only be reckoned with at the earliest in 1940 but by no means in 1938, Hitler's reaction to the 'weekend crisis' shocked him to the core. The dictator spoke not only of a martial conflict with the CSR in 1938 but also possibly with the western powers. Thus almost the whole basis of Beck's military plans and even his whole military policy lay in ruins. Since the end of May, he confided to a close friend in November 1938, he had had only one thought in mind: 'How can I prevent a war?'[50] For Canaris and Halder the May crisis was also the crucial moment of their disillusionment about Hitler's external political *vabanque* game.

Weizsäcker reacted somewhat differently to the events of the end of May. In view of the deepening international crisis he developed his own concept, which sought to combine the destruction of the CSR as a sovereign state with the avoidance of a European war. He described this concept with the metaphorical idea of the 'chemical dissolution process' of the Czechoslovak state, in other words the disintegration of the CSR by external pressure beneath the cloak of war and by internal subversion. He preferred – so he maintained – 'a purely political dissection of the Czechs' rather than a war. This remained, for the whole summer of international crisis, the main line of his policy.[51] Whereas Beck had already realised Hitler's war intentions at the end of May, Weizsäcker spent the whole of June and July in 'continual guessing games about Hitler's real intentions'.[52] On the one hand, he believed that Hitler had set in motion a vast strategy of bluff, a huge intimidatory manoeuvre to soften up the Czechs, but no war; on the other hand, after vain efforts to win over the foreign minister to his concept of 'chemical dissolution' and after a few confrontations with Ribbentrop, he became more and more convinced that the latter was forcing Hitler into war. From the beginning to the middle of August he then tried, partly by-passing Ribbentrop, to influence Hitler, directly or indirectly, in order to prevent him from making any possibly risky political decisions.[53]

The concern that too aggressive a German policy would bring about the risk of a war with Czechoslovakia which could not be contained, since German rearmament was incomplete and there had been no external political assurances, caused many high-ranking officials to become converted opponents of a thoughtless power policy, the foundations of which they had nevertheless to a considerable degree helped to create. What often used to be called, in this connection, 'German opposition' was, as previous analysis shows, neither an alternative to the system nor, in essence, any fundamental alternative to the external policy. It was more a case of an 'anti-war party' of high-ranking state functionaries being formed out of different views on opportunities, methods and risk factors concerning German power politics in Europe.

The conflict which broke out at that time between Beck and Hitler, and in which Canaris and Halder supported Beck and even Weizsäcker had sympathy for him, has frequently been described. But to call it the first attempt at a *coup d'état* misses the mark;[54] to call it simply 'struggle against the war' and to see it as essentially an internal political power struggle is to miss its wide military-political dimension, and would be an inappropriate abbreviation.[55] Beck's efforts in summer 1938 developed methodically in two stages: first the chief of the general staff tried to obtain his goal through the normal official channels of persuasion, in other words by memoranda and reports. He wished to influence Hitler to give up his war plans. His essential arguments were of a political and military nature. In a second stage, in which Canaris obviously exercised an important influence on him,[56] Beck attempted to prevent the threat of a war by more unusual means; by the collective resignation of the generals. Finally he resorted to the plan worked out by Canaris in conjunction with Hossbach in the Fritsch crisis, modified it somewhat and began to consider putting heavier pressure on Hitler himself, which was to be pursued to the very limits of rebellion; namely, a campaign by the military, coupled with the threat of resignations, against those radical elements of the NS movement which he and other generals saw at work behind Hitler's intentions of war. The political upset which would probably result from the collective resignations was to be used as an internal political ground-floor purge, in fact to strip of all power those 'radical organisations' who were apparently collectively responsible for the external political *vabanque* game and who had revealed themselves previously to be internal political opponents of the army. Beck's suggestions combined simultaneously the struggle to prevent the war and the long-term internal power struggle for the maintenance, or rather the restoration, of the 'two-pillared' concept of the system.[57]

In all the differences between Beck's and Weizsäcker's activities there is at least a parallel to be seen here. Just as Beck, to give depth to his struggle against the war, had tried a campaign against warmongering 'radicals' in the NS movement who had already previously tried to undermine the position of the army within the system and now in his eyes were driving Hitler to war, so too did Weizsäcker endeavour to break down what he considered the unhealthy influence of Ribbentrop upon Hitler, and at the same time to reinstate into the decision-making process the whole weight of the traditional diplomatic ruling elite of the Foreign Office, whose professional leader he was.

It can therefore be maintained that, at the very moment of the acute international worsening of the Sudeten crisis, an anti-war party arose among high-ranking officials[58] which wanted to avoid a conflict that in their opinion could not be contained and isolated at the time, but which completely backed the objectives of German great power policy; in short, the setting-up of the hegemonial position of the Reich in central Europe, implicit in which was the destruction of the CSR; and which, at the same time, by no means fundamentally opposed the use of military force (Beck, Halder),[59] political-military pressure (Weizsäcker) or definitive means of subversion (Canaris). It was opposed to a purely military solution of the conflict at that particular time on the grounds of inopportunity and calculation of risk. On a deeper level, the anti-war policy of these high-ranking state functionaries was simultaneously an attempt to hold personal sway over the consequences of a German great power policy which they themselves had helped to conceive and the means for which they had to a great extent helped to create.

On a third dimension, the anti-war policy was linked with an internal political power struggle in which, by the use of various means, it was aimed to re-establish the position of the army leadership and diplomatic ruling elite within the regime, especially within the political decision-making centre, thereby also delaying the war policy.

In order to be able to answer the question of the chances of this anti-war party and also of its political weight, the following must be taken into consideration: Beck and Canaris – certainly not Weizsäcker – since they were not thinking of a military *putsch*,[60] and since they were in high-ranking positions but not at liberty to give orders to the whole army or even to the *Wehrmacht*, could influence nothing without the help of the person holding the highest power of command. The leadership of the army, in other words the supreme commander [General von Brauchitsch, *Ed.*] would have to identify himself with and support their efforts at putting off the war, in full agreement with the other commanding officers. It was just these decisive functionaries that they were unsuccessful in winning over to their anti-war policy. That, of course, had a lot to do with the various personalities of the relevant high-ranking officers. There was, however, something even more important: in the first place, it was obviously quite impossible to persuade the commanders of the navy and air force to cooperate. Göring, regarded by the army leaders with deep suspicion since the Fritsch crisis, was not yet seen to have turned to an anti-war policy; and the naval command, disinterested in the CSR conflict, was completely absorbed in long-term plans for reconstruction and in strategic considerations, within the framework of a 'world power policy' of a definitely anti-British nature.[61] In the second place, however, and this was even more crucial, Canaris and Beck were unsuccessful in convincing the supreme commander of the army and the leading generals that Hitler's intended military conflict could not be contained and that the western powers would certainly attack. From a purely military standpoint, Beck was unable to put forward any convincing proof for the correctness of his prognosis or, as a result, for the correctness of the promises for his proposed action. Neither the reports of the military attachés nor the comprehensive studies of the combat operations department of the general staff, nor the results of the war manoeuvres carried out by the general staff, nothing supported his hypothesis[62] – in fact the opposite was the case. It therefore came as no great surprise that the high-ranking generals were wary, in these circumstances, of supporting Beck's and Canaris' unusual proposals. From a purely military point of view a war against the CSR held out many opportunities. Beck's rearmament and military policy had borne extremely ambivalent fruits: his own achievements were turned against him. Again on the political front, he was not able to convince them, for the simple reason that it was in no way certain that the western powers really would attack. This was of crucial importance for the efforts of the anti-war party.

Weizsäcker had the same handicap. As the highest ranking official in the foreign office, he did not have direct or continual access to Hitler, Ribbentrop being his superior and reference partner. Since the latter, however, was in his view one of the most influential warmongers, he found himself faced with the problem of preventing him from continuing in his fatal train of thought and at the same time from adding strength to the *Führer*'s policy of risking a war,[63] and to a greater extent he had the problem of influencing the *Führer* himself in the matter of his own political thinking. Here, however, lay yet another huge dilemma for the secretary of state. Quite apart from the obstacles implicit in his official position, certain other limits were imposed on him here, in as far as he was likewise striving for the destruction of the CSR, with the debate revolving around the appraisal of the situation, which in itself presented difficulties of definition and proof, and the question of any ensuing operations, which were themselves dependent on the perception of the situation, which again was so controversial. Weizsäcker's long-held view that Hitler was pursuing a huge policy of bluff is a typical expression of this dilemma.[64]

At this point in the analysis the functional importance becomes clear of those often quoted discreet missions by different emissaries and some direct interventions, which were not always coordinated in any way, but which were all activated with the same end in mind.[65] They were initiated by Canaris and by the circles around Oster and Weizsäcker, with the prime aim of justifying the correctness of their premises that the western powers, in the event of a German attack on the CSR, would attack – as Beck always maintained they would, but without any definite proof. This was the function that was to be served by Kleist-Schmenzin (from 18 May) and the brothers Kordt (Erich through his influence upon Brauchitsch, Theo in London, between 23 August and 7 September) and also C. J. Burckhardt (end of August and beginning of September); these were supporting activities for Weizsäcker, Beck and Canaris' anti-war policy. In addition, Canaris sent a colleague who was critical of the *SS* and of the party (Groscurth) to Budapest (22 August) and himself spoke to Pariani [General Alberto Pariani, under-secretary of state, *Ed.*] in Rome (2 September) in order to provoke negative attitudes to Hitler's war policy among the most important of Germany's allies. Weizsäcker was not only the prime instigator of the Kordt mission, but also collected a consensus of opinion from the heads of missions in the most important German embassies in Europe about the impossibility of isolating a German-Czech conflict *rebus sic stantibus*.[66] It is well known that these efforts were fruitless. The expected signs did not come from London, at least not in the form required, and it was not possible to prevent Ribbentrop from continuing his warmongering, or to convince Brauchitsch and the commanding generals of the correctness of the appraisal of the situation set before them, or finally to influence Hitler himself towards a degree of moderation. Beck therefore, despite the attempts of Weizsäcker to change his mind, resigned his post – more a sign of giving up than of rebellion.[67]

The nature of the anti-war party and its opportunities can be further clarified by an analysis of its structure. Its actual nucleus – and this word is not used in the sense of its organisation but as an identification of the principal representatives of that central and all-exclusive objective, prevention of war – consisted of the high-ranking officers already mentioned and, in the diplomatic field, Weizsäcker. From him emanated activities which ran parallel to those of Canaris and Beck, and which – so it seems – took place partly and temporarily in coordination with them. Beneath this small central group there was the circle round Oster and Gisevius. For them, in contrast to the Beck–Canaris–Weizsäcker group, the efforts to prevent a war rapidly became a vehicle for considering a *coup d'état*. For them the overthrow of the regime was the prime objective, in the face of which the prevention of war took on a secondary and instrumental function. In their oppositional aspirations they were more radical, but in their means and possibilities, because of their subsidiary posts within the apparatus of power, they lacked any significant opportunities for influence. For this reason they were constantly on the lookout for a general who would be prepared to support their subversive manifesto, and to cooperate with Beck and Canaris. They were also concerned with broadening the basis of their campaign, if possible by the involvement of more high-powered statesmen. With this in mind they made contact with Schacht, put out feelers to Brauchitsch and made overtures to some younger members of the foreign office who were critical of the regime.[68]

On a third level there was a string of individuals who were activated by both these groupings in complete independence of each other. They took over (as previously mentioned) various supportive functions for the anti-war party, either as emissaries on secret diplomatic missions or for the purpose of exercising influence internally on various high-ranking officials. They were made up both of individuals from the critical and dissatisfied national conservative milieu who found themselves outside the apparatus of state, such as Kleist-Schmenzin, and of men who fulfilled functions at a wide range of levels within the state service, such as Groscurth, Count Schwerin, the brothers Kordt or, on a higher political plain, Schacht. These were people with a wide variety of oppositional attitudes. Many had their own, highly individual, political ideas which (as Kleist-Schmenzin did, for example) they expounded on their own account to their foreign counterparts in completely independent extensions of their allotted foreign missions. This contributed in no small way to the fact that the view of the German opposition was made no clearer, and even became more distorted.[69] Within the framework of our enquiry, they nevertheless play a subsidiary but instrumental role as 'auxiliary organs' with the anti-war party or the subversion groups. They did not, however, possess any oppositional importance in their own right.

These functional activities, which took place within the framework of the war-prevention policy of the high-ranking officials, should be clearly distinguished from the activities which were undertaken on their own account by some national conservative opposition elements in contact with foreign counterparts, as for example, von Koerber in his talks with the British military attaché or Goerdeler on his journeys abroad. These individuals always spoke of their connections with high-ranking military circles but, in fact, had no mandate from them. [The PRO documents appear to contradict this assertion. Simply because no written documents were made, or at any rate not survived, does not automatically exclude the possibility of an oral mandate. *Ed.*] They styled themselves supporters of 'the German opposition' but this existed only in their pipe-dreams. At best they described a vague trend of feeling in national-conservative circles. It was certainly not incorporated in either the anti-war policy of the Beck–Canaris–Weizsäcker group or in the *coup d'état* dreams of the Oster–Gisevius group. Therefore those foreign contacts, often exclusively attributed to *the* opposition, are clearly to be distinguished from the activities of the anti-war party, which in different ways were at that time a part of the official or semi-official German-British talks,[70] as for instance, the contacts made by Wiedemann, Hewel and also, to a certain extent, by Weizsäcker, in whose activities the dividing line between official business and personal political accentuation is very difficult to draw.[71]

Such a differentiation, at first sight somewhat schematic, is appropriate for analytical reasons to counter any misconceptions which may attribute a coherence and unity to the concept of 'opposition' which does not in any way correspond to reality.

The structural analysis of the anti-war party also shows that its nucleus was composed of high-ranking officials in the military, diplomatic and secret services who had come together to form a policy of war prevention. This policy, however, always retained its dimension of being an internal political power struggle. From within this party a small group of radicals tried to extend the war-prevention efforts in the direction of a *coup d'état* or at least to an action by force to change the regime. However, it must be emphasised that, in this phase, the inherent trend in the internal political power struggle towards an enforced purge of the regime had intensified, in view of the threat of war, towards a campaign of force aimed at the destabilisation of the regime. The group that represented this trend did not gain any impetus, however, because of their political and functional lack of weight.

This constellation changed significantly in the next phase of development which began with Halder's assumption of office on 1 September 1938.[72] The Oster–Gisevius group used the changeover of office to initiate (via Canaris) direct contact to Halder and to obtain from him a mandate for the preparation of a *coup d'état*, and also to place their own personal opposition potential at the disposal of the anti-war group. With these contacts the policy of war prevention took on a new dimension: from now on it could be made operational on two different planes. It therefore became characteristic of this phase that activities in the planning of the conspiratorial *coup d'état* on the one hand, and on the other the political secret diplomatic efforts towards war prevention on the home and foreign fronts, were acting side by side, even if they often lacked coordination. Thus the secret contact already begun in Beck's time, and especially the initiatives taken by Weizsäcker and Canaris, and also by Halder (the Böhm–Tettelbach mission) continued apace at the same time as efforts to win over high-ranking officials such as Keitel and Brauchitsch, by the well-directed and selective infiltration of information, to a policy of war prevention and a corresponding campaign to influence Hitler. Simultaneously, however, the Oster–Gisevius group, with permission from Halder, began the technical preparations for the *coup d'état*.

In contrast to Beck's time in office, there was now a certain coordination between the representatives of the war-prevention policy in high offices and the conspiratorial activist elements in more subsidiary posts. Through this had grown up an extension of its personnel base that was important in both its political and technical aspects.[73] Now, for the first time, a campaign directed against the leadership of the regime can be referred to, in both military and political circles, and this could be generally termed the 'opposition', although the complexity and multi-layered nature of that opposition should not be forgotten.

This opposition was, however, characterised by intrinsic divergencies in motives and objectives. What for Halder and Canaris represented a last desperate means to prevent a war and was being prepared to cover all emergencies – in other words, the *coup d'état* – was for the Oster–Gisevius group the real objective and in their opinion would be the best course in view of the imminent threat of the outbreak of war. This group, which for some time had been seeking a platform for a coup, now began preparations for the overthrow with more far-reaching intentions than Halder ever anticipated. In short, one can speak of a conspiracy within a conspiracy: acting on the basis of the Halder–Canaris mandate, Oster and his friends were nonetheless also working on their own account. Furthermore, even their preparations were to a certain extent being undertaken in different, independent ways. Whereas Oster and Gisevius, in conjunction with General von Witzleben [Looking at Witzleben's career as a whole, particularly the lamentable role he played in the July 1944 plot, it seems doubtful that he acted without Halder's backing. *Ed.*] were planning to arrest Hitler within the course of a *coup d'état*[74] the leaders of the detail which was to carry out the deed against the *Reichskanzler* (F. W. Heinz and Liedig), themselves originating from the romantic national revolutionary milieu of the former *Freikorps*, had decided, apparently independently, to kill him on the spot. Within the framework of the war-prevention policy anticipated by the anti-war party (Halder, Canaris) a fatal multiplicity had therefore developed. Whereas Halder and Canaris were primarily aiming at the prevention of war, Oster and his friends were striving exclusively for the overthrow of the regime. This subversion group was itself in the process of being outmanoeuvred by an assassination group. If therefore there can be any reference to an 'opposition' in connection with the events since Halder's assumption of office, then one may only use this vague concept in the sense of a rough, all-inclusive term to cover three groups with fundamental differences in objectives and methods.

This disparity was also the reason why, after Halder had allowed immediate preparations for the *coup* to gather momentum during the crisis of the Godesberg talks,[75] the various elements in this differently motivated group rapidly disintegrated because of the news of the approaching Munich Conference, and thereafter, for some months, were practically paralysed. For the actual anti-war party, every reason for any measures to destabilise the system disappeared with the Munich Conference since, with the apparent elimination of the threat of war, the main objective of their war-prevention policy had been attained. From now on (until the next perilous crisis) there was for them a return to normality, to the normal pursuance of their business of office. After Munich Weizsäcker tried again to put his conception of German foreign policy to the Reich leaders. Halder devoted himself to the completion of the reconstruction of the army and the working-out of operational plans, while Canaris returned to the everyday problems of business in the secret service.

The subversion group, on the other hand, considered itself robbed of the crucial requirement of its means for action by the Munich Conference – spectacular diplomatic defeat of Hitler or immediate imminence of the outbreak of war – and resented the hand the western powers had in it all ('Chamberlain has saved Hitler!').[76] But the subversion group within the opposition which had been formed during the Sudeten crisis was only one of several elements of this organisation and, in addition, one of the weakest, measured by its small political importance and by the posts attained by its supporters within the civil-military apparatus. The assassination group, furthermore, was of minimal importance in all respects, especially as the actual preparations for the coup had at no point developed beyond the stage of improvisation.[77]

A structural analysis of the workings of opposition, also termed the 'September Plot' in the relevant literature, results in the following assessment: in essence it was a matter of the continuance of an anti-war policy; this subsequently, however, took on a dual nature – political and secret diplomatic activities were supplemented by a contingency plan for a *coup d'état*. The primary aim, nevertheless, remained the prevention of war and not the overthrow of the regime. Within this system-destabilising, anti-war contingency planning there ran an independent and self-propagating subversion plan, which aspired to more all-embracing objectives than mere prevention of war, namely, the overthrow of the regime and even assassination, with the intention not only of eliminating the source of the threat of war within the regime, but also of pressing on towards a new political and social order. As far as all the participatory elements were concerned, it can be maintained that the radical nature of their objectives stood in inverse proportion to their official and political status. The anti-war party consisted of high-ranking officials within the power set-up; the subversion group, on the other hand, and to a greater extent the assassination group, represented in itself no really serious political strength. To sum up, it was a case of completely heterogeneous and disparate groups being active on widely differing levels, lacking a unified political basis in any positive sense and also showing in their negative objectives a wide variety of different angles – prevention of war, or overthrow of the regime or even assassination.

The time span between the Munich Conference and the outbreak of war was characterised by the disintegration of the contacts and coordinated action between the different opposition individuals and groups which had become more closely identified with one another in the phase between the Fritsch crisis and Munich, and also by the complete divergence between those groups which were concerned with the prevention of war and those which were working mainly towards subversion and fundamental change in the regime.[78]

Within circles critical of the system considerable tensions now prevailed. Old contacts among conservative opponents of the regime broke down; different individuals launched into noncommittal discussions with other individuals who found themselves out of office (Beck, Hassell, Goerdeler, Planck and so on), accompanied all developments with great criticism[79] and got no further than either vague deliberations based on long-term developments (Witzleben, Sodenstern)[80] or illusory *ad hoc* plans (Gisevius, Schacht). After Munich the basis of action which deteriorated most was that of the operational group intent on a policy of subversion; they had completely lost contact with developments.[81] Oster and Gisevius destroyed part of their documented plans for an overthrow of the regime; Witzleben was dismissed from Berlin and took over a *Gruppen-Oberkommando* in Kassel. Halder insisted on keeping his distance from the radical conspirators.[82] It was not until the late autumn, after the Polish campaign, that the subversion group again emerged within the field of opposition operations.[83]

The exponents of the anti-war policy, on the other hand, from the taking of Prague up to the outbreak of war undertook an intensive and largely uncoordinated campaign on a variety of different levels, which in the end also bore no fruit. Its membership during this period had remained relatively consistent: on the one hand, there were representatives of the traditional power elites in top positions within the power structure; on the other hand, there were also persons more or less critical of the government who came from outside the power structure but had access to ways of approaching high-ranking officials as well as good foreign contacts. So nothing had changed, in principle, within the membership apart from the fact that, in the decisive phase before the outbreak of war, Göring's endeavours partly converged on the war-prevention policy of these circles.

The structure of activity linked with this war-prevention policy was varied and multi-layered. The main aim of even the most diverse activities, depending on different assessments of Hitler's role in the German-Polish crisis, was either to keep the *Führer* away from the warmongering influence of the so-called 'radicals' in the NS leadership, or to hold Hitler back, or even to frighten him off from any war policy. Accordingly, these activities were deployed on very different levels and with a variety of different objectives. Attempts were made to influence the decision-making process at the highest levels by all kinds of dissemination of information in order to change the course of German foreign policy which was felt to be so fatal. They tried to prove that, in the event of armed conflict between the Reich and Poland, the western powers would certainly become involved, the Italian Axis partner would not stand on the side of the Reich in the event of war, that the army and economy were not yet ready for war and, finally, that the envisaged objective could not yet be obtained without use of arms. Thus attempts were made from very different quarters – from Halder and Canaris, from Goerdeler, Beck, Hassell and Schacht – to influence von Brauchitsch and the chief of OKW, Keitel, so that these generals in responsible top posts should bring influence to bear on Hitler to avoid war.[84] Weizsäcker once again made great efforts, as he had a year before in the Sudeten crisis, to convince both Ribbentrop and Hitler of the dangers of a policy aimed at an anti-British conflict.[85] At the same time, this meant an attempt to influence German foreign policy through official channels which brought him into fierce conflict with Ribbentrop.[86]

Also, the different organisational groups within the anti-war party were endeavouring to obtain their aim of avoiding war through talks with foreign diplomats and through diplomatic steps in London and Rome. Halder told the French ambassador that someone would have to point out in no uncertain terms to Hitler the full seriousness of the situation; and he impressed on the British ambassador that he should make Hitler understand that Great Britain would not yield any further but would be obliged to reply to a German attack on Poland with a declaration of war. A whole list of emissaries and go-betweens gave speeches in London.[87] These were people acting on their own initiative, such as Schacht or Goerdeler and sometimes the Kordt brothers, Moltke, Trott zu Solz, or confidential agents of Canaris' *Abwehr* or of Weizsäcker (as, for example, Schlabrendorff, Selzam, Schwerin-Schwanefeld, C. J. Burckhardt). Canaris himself tried, as in the previous year, to persuade the Italians to make a clear denunciation of a war policy.[88] In addition, certain collaborators of Canaris, namely the circle around Oster, acting on their own account, infiltrated information to the British with the dual purpose of warning the western powers of the danger that Hitler was turning from peaceful intentions, and at the same time of provoking some energetic reactions and counter-measures by the British that might then make Hitler shrink from any risk.[89] Weizsäcker, for his part, was active on at least three different levels: first, as already mentioned, he was trying to bring his influence to bear through official channels on the central decision-making arena of German foreign policy; second, as a peripheral plan, he was endeavouring to set a peace initiative in motion by having talks with foreign diplomats, especially with Nevile Henderson, but also with Attolico. This (as has justifiably been pointed out[90]) was almost a repetition of the crisis procedure he so successfully employed during the Sudeten crisis, which was directed towards a political solution to the Polish conflict. Third, it should also be mentioned here that Weizsäcker tried to introduce a diplomatic scheme which could work as a detente in the situation of European conflict in the summer of 1939.[91]

In the relevant literature, the many and varied efforts which have been described have always been examined in connection with the complexities of 'resistance' or 'opposition'. At a closer look however, the question arises whether these two concepts adequately describe the instances just depicted. They were certainly anything but 'resistance' in the sense of activities consciously aimed at destabilising the system.

These sort of activities (especially in view of the conditions prevalent in a totalitarian regime) should rather be considered as built-in opposition, as opposition in traditional political parlance, namely as attempts to introduce and carry out an alternative policy. That is not to say that the ethically significant intention of preserving peace for Europe and the Reich should be considered any less important; it is merely that, for these activities, the term 'opposition' is simply not appropriate in the sense of a resistance opposed to the system; it was rather opposition as an attempt to put through an alternative policy within the system. This in turn clarifies the nature of the activities of the anti-war party in this phase. These consisted of bringing influence to bear on the process of decision-making both by means of normal procedures along official channels with peripheral measures based on the usual diplomatic political tactics, and also of activities which would be considered as a kind of counter-diplomacy: an interplay with allies and representatives of states with which the Reich leadership was in controversy at the time but which were likewise interested in the prevention of war. Whatever form the attempts at gaining effective influence on the central foreign policy decision-making process may have taken – information, counter-information, occasional false information, back-room talks and talks to gain opposite effect - it nevertheless all remained the type of opposition inherent in the system.[92] In this phase of development before the outbreak of war there was no earnest consideration or even preparation for war prevention using measures likely to destabilise the system. In May 1939, when Goerdeler reported to his British counterparts that the German army was still prepared for the overthrow of the regime but that it was a question of choosing the right time, that although he himself was ready for action, 'the leaders of the whole movement . . . still considered it too early', then this was either an assessment of the situation stemming from his own pipe-dreams or a conscious delivery of false information [such as a completely falsified version of Hitler's speech to his generals of 22 August 1939 designed to harden British attitudes against any compromise solution. *Ed.*] by which he intended to make the British take some action.[93] Gisevius states here, quite relevantly, with bitter self-criticism: 'In these dramatic days before the outbreak of war there is absolutely nothing heroic to be reported about the attitude of the German opposition . . . we must be content with the simple fact that nothing notable has been done.'[94] This was the situation as expressed by that small group of radicals opposed to the system, but it was equally, if not more, relevant to the anti-war party which wished to retain the system. Their efforts had been in vain on at least three accounts. First because of the lack of coordination in their activities, they provided their foreign counterparts across a broad front with a confused and even contradictory view of things.[95] Second, many of their interventions and much of their advice were contradictory and even countermanding.[96] Third, the greatest reason for the failure of their efforts lay in the fact that they failed to recognise Hitler's absolute war intentions. Weizsäcker still believed for a long time in summer 1939 in a 'huge bluff on Hitler's part with the intention in the end still of giving in',[97] and that their Prusso-German revisionist and 'great power' views coincided almost completely, in the case of Poland, with Hitler's immediate objectives as he continued his course of confrontation with the Reich's eastern neighbour. Canaris furthered the anti-Polish nationality and Ukrainian policy while Weizsäcker, at the end of 1938, tried to distract Ribbentrop and Hitler from the Czechoslovak problem and on to the question of Poland (Danzig and the Corridor) [Did Hitler need to be distracted in view of the Polish initiative? See p. 287 below. *Ed.*] and some time later he advised 'being clearer to the Russians in Moscow on the question of the division of Poland'.[98] There can be no question but that all this contributed not only to the fatal momentum of the developing crisis between Munich and the outbreak of war, but also to the final futility of all efforts of the anti-war party.

If, in conclusion, one is required to attempt to answer the question posed at the beginning, as to a specific conceptual assessment of the phenomenon of national conservative opposition, this answer will not be found by replacing the word 'opposition' simply by another single term. On close examination, the historical reality has shown itself to be too complex for this. Such a reality can only be adequately contained within a system of interrelated concepts which offers the necessary analytical selectivity. The complex phenomenon of conflict, 'national-conservative opposition', within the time scale we have considered presents itself primarily as a system-inherent power struggle for the purpose of stabilising national conservative positions of power and influence which had as its main objective an evolutionary reform of the regime, but within which certain weaker trends towards an enforced purge of the regime were present. This built-in power struggle then converged with the war-prevention policy of an anti-war party. This, borne by high-ranking functionaries of the regime within the army and the foreign office, had likewise set itself the objective of putting through an alternative foreign and military policy. At a critical stage in international affairs some system-destabilising tendencies could nevertheless be detected in its activities. At the climax of the Sudeten crisis the anti-war party, parallel with its system-inherent efforts towards an alternative policy, developed a new scale of activity with contingency plans for a *coup d'état*. For a short time this was linked with a number of marginal operational groups following a policy of subversion and assassination. After Munich, however, this ephemeral radicalisation of the anti-war policy collapsed. In the last year before the outbreak of war, therefore, there can be reference to only one absolutely system-inherent anti-war party with its alternative policy of war prevention. In this phase, the anti-war operational groups sought to obtain the goal of their policy by means of departmental influence on the external political decision-making process and by discreet counter-diplomacy.

PART II

Introduction

National Socialist foreign policy remains in the forefront of
scholarly debate but a general consensus has never been
achieved. One of the first major works to break new ground
was Hans Adolf Jacobsen's *Nationalsozialistische Aussenpolitik
1933–1938* a work which not only looks at German foreign
policy during this period but also analyses in great detail all
the other NS agencies which operated in or tried to influence
German foreign policy. Jacobsen examines their structure
and composition and the sources from which their personnel
was drawn, and assesses the actual influence exercised, but
he stops before the outbreak of war in 1939.

Here A. J. P. Taylor's *Origins of the Second World War*, first
published in 1960, still represents a milestone, and now, as
then, causes heated discussion. It is doubtful whether
without Taylor's work the issue of 'war guilt' would ever
have been raised among serious historians. Up to 1960 the
conclusions reached at the trial of the German Major War
Criminals in Nuremberg were also accepted by historians.
But even Alan Bullock, a major opponent of Taylor's
interpretation, has found it necessary to revise some passages
in his biography of Hitler. The reaction of Taylor's argument
was at first very hostile, but in Britain at least the debate
has now subsided a little. It still rages in West Germany
where, for instance, the publication of a volume of essays on
the outbreak of the Second World War, *Kriegsbeginn 1939*,
edited by Gottfried Niedhart, caused a polemical and
vitriolic attack from the Swiss historian Walter Hofer, who
had himself published a small documentary volume many
years previously under the title *War Premeditated*. Hofer
attacked Niedhart simply for including A. J. P. Taylor's
essay 'Second Thoughts', which he had added to the second
edition of his *Origins of the Second World War*. Much of the
revisionist work done inside as well as outside Germany still

encounters silence, or at best some marginal comment from German historians. For example the editor's own minor contribution, a critical source analysis entitled 'Hitler and the Origins of the Second World War: Second Thoughts on the Status of some of the Documents' published in the *Historical Journal* in 1968, when included in the collection of essays edited by E. Robertson, *The Origins of the Second World War* (London, 1971) drew from Andreas Hillgruber in his review of the volume for the *Historische Zeitschrift* the comment that the argument was vulnerable to attack. But he did not specify in what way, nor did he attack it. Simon Newman's recent study, *March 1939: The British Guarantee to Poland* attracted three German publishers interested in a German translation. Massive pressure was brought to bear on at least one of them not to handle it, coupled with the threat that a German translation would be submitted to the Federal Office of Examination of Writing Likely to Endanger Youth (*Bundesprüfstelle für jugendgefährdende Schriften*). Needless to say, no translation materialised. Oswald Hauser's recent two-volume study (a third is to follow) *England und das Dritte Reich* has elicited very favourable responses among reviewers in Britain, whereas in Germany the implication is that although it cannot be ignored completely, it is better not to pay it too much attention.

On the whole, the debate on most aspects of the Third Reich has now produced two schools of interpretation: The intentionalists and the functionalists. The former, including Hofer, Hillgruber, Bracher, Hildebrand, to name but a few, took up the argument first formulated by Hugh Trevor-Roper in his essay on Hitler's war aims. Crudely summarised, it portrays Hitler in his domestic as well as in his foreign policy as a man who with remorseless consistency followed the programme formulated as early as in his book *Mein Kampf*, in his *Second Book*, in his conversations with Rauschning (on the dubious nature of this source see p. 13) and in his *Table Talk*. This school of interpretation spends little time on the historian's first and most arduous task: the critical evaluation of sources. Thus little or no time is spent in examining the 'genesis' of *Mein Kampf*. Apart from being in the most literal sense popular oratory made literature, it was written when Hitler's thoughts on foreign policy were still heavily influenced by Baltic Germans such as Rosenberg or v. Scheubner-Richter. They considered Soviet Russia as the product of an essentially Jewish revolutionary intelligentsia which, deprived of the Baltic German stock which had provided so many leading figures in Tsarist Russia, was bound to fall and to disintegrate under its own weight. When this happened, all that Germany needed to do was to pick up such pieces as were essential for the supply of raw materials and for the provision of living space.

By the time Hitler was appointed chancellor this view hardly corresponded with reality. The Soviet Union as a consolidated power was a fact. This may be one reason why Hitler never fulfilled Rosenberg's lifelong ambition of becoming Germany's foreign minister. By that time all Rosenberg's prophecies had been contradicted by actual events. But Hitler, always with a strongly developed sense of loyalty to those who had followed him, did not reject Rosenberg but shunted him into a siding where he could develop his various schemes but rarely realise them.

Intentionalists ask, for example, why Hitler involved the Third Reich in the murderous struggle of the Second World War, and provide the equally simple answer that this was precisely his intention. Evidence is produced in abundance, but when it is scrutinised closely it emerges that it has been used very selectively to fit a preconceived notion. Hence also the feature highlighted above, the virtual absence of source criticism. Apart from one other work, to be discussed below, this is most notably demonstrated by Norman Rich's two-volume work, *Hitler's War Aims*.

The intentionalist interpretation still dominates, for the functionalist interpretation, as represented in the work of Hans Mommsen and latterly also by Martin Broszat, has so far concentrated more on Hitler's domestic than on his foreign policy. The work of Peter Hüttenberger, in particular, with some support from the more detailed work of Martin Broszat's *The Hitler State*, has demolished the notion of the Third Reich as a monolithic power bloc, a dictatorship organised in the smallest detail, affecting every sector of

German life. An early American pioneer of this revision was Edward N. Peterson in his *The Limits of Hitler's Power*. Sociologists such as Ralf Dahrendorf in his *Society and Democracy in Germany* have already at an early stage pointed to the obvious conclusion that National Socialist Germany was for most of its existence nowhere near as totalitarian as it and historians subsequently claimed, a point driven home with a vengeance in the cultural sphere by H. D. Schäfer's *Das Gespaltene Bewusstsein: Deutsche Kultur und Lebenswirklichkeit 1933–45*. In place of the monolith of the intentionalists, there was what Hüttenberger has called the National Socialist Polycracy which by definition excludes the idea of a type of rule by which Hitler and his close associates could exercise rigid control over all spheres of German life. It also negates the Marxist approach which sees in National Socialism the most aggressive form of capitalism. Instead Hitler's rule was based on an entente between the NSDAP, the army and the traditional elites, which only dissolved during the latter part of the Second World War, when the ultimate fate of the Third Reich was sealed anyway. In other words, in order for Hitler to remain chancellor he had to make compromises – with the traditional elites, with industry and, significantly, also with the churches, notably the Roman Catholic church. Hence his polycratic regime consisted of several different oligarchies, representing different and often mutually exclusive interests and ideologies, different personnel structures which cooperated with or obstructed the NSDAP which was based on the leadership principle. Within this polycracy, National Socialism represented the most dynamic element, because during the initial phase of Hitler's rule his position and that of his party were still very precarious. The precondition for the expansion of power by Hitler lay in the fear of the other partners that they would not be able to maintain their own respective positions in the face of the revolutionary forces generated by the world economic crisis.

The administrative confusion which marks the Third Reich, a picture of which in the sector of the war economy Albert Speer has drawn in his *Inside the Third Reich*, cannot be explained away as a deliberate *divide et impera* policy of

Hitler's or as the practical application of the Social Darwinian process to the institutional structure of the Reich; it can only be credibly explained in terms of the permanent attempts at penetration by and of compromises with the various oligarchic bodies or individuals. Nor can it be explained in terms of improvisation on the one hand and planned action on the other because Hitler and his regime utilised every opportunity to consolidate their political position, but in so doing often met with outright resistance and thus reached the limits of their power. On the other hand, however, Hitler resisted any attempt to introduce a specifically National Socialist Constitution, something which his minister of the interior Dr Wilhelm Frick and the NSDAP's foremost legal brain Dr Hans Frank aimed at over many years. He did so because whatever powers a new constitution might have conferred on him, there would inevitably also have been constraints, and in freeing him from constraints the Weimar Constitution, suspended in vital parts, was of greater service to him than any new constitution. Another and final characteristic of this polycratic structure was that its constituent members were for many years dependent upon one another and hence had to cooperate and compromise with one another in ways which to the outside observer conjured up the image of a monolithic power structure.

The functionalist interpretation therefore proceeds from the premise that the political development of the Third Reich was determined to a much greater degree than has hitherto been assumed by the respective decision-making processes rather than by fundamental motives or planned intentions. Hitler projected the image of the decision-maker, but in reality had great difficulty in reaching decisions on crucial issues. Under this dynamic guise a wave of activism was unleashed, but being devoid of any supreme coordination it degenerated progressively into radicalisation and thus into situations which forced decisions that drove Germany into the abyss. In short, it was not simply and exclusively the arbitrary will of the dictator that was decisive, but also a chain reaction caused by and based on a somewhat naïve and crude understanding of politics directed by its impulses.

The functionalist approach has so far had the advantage that when applied to concrete situations it fits – admittedly almost too perfectly for the historian's comfort. However, it does not have to rely on often highly controversial evidence, let alone conspiracy theories; it does not take refuge in writings which by 1933 had become largely irrelevant or take quotations out of their original context as the intentionalists do to prove their case.

Unfortunately in their analysis of National Socialist foreign policy the functionalists, Hauser apart, have yet to provide a major work; indeed for both functionalists and intentionalists such a major work is still lacking. Great hopes had been placed in Gerhard L. Weinberg's *The Foreign Policy of Hitler's Germany*, of which so far two volumes have appeared. These hopes were based on his reputation as an expert in and master of the vast amount of German primary sources. Doubts about his expertise occurred only when he was one of the two 'experts' who in 1983 authenticated Hitler's so-called diaries, which quickly emerged as the handiwork of a crude forger.

This lapse apart, when the first volume of Weinberg's foreign policy study became available, it provided nothing more than the traditional diplomatic history approach which was superseded long ago. No new sources were offered except the private papers of some rather obscure American individuals to whom Hitler had allegedly offered his innermost thoughts. Nevertheless, this criticism could probably have been discounted or minimised if the work submitted had actually shown competence in the mastery of its sources. In the early 1960s an American compatriot of Weinberg, David L. Hoggan, wrote a massive tome, accompanied by an equally massive and impressive scholarly apparatus, trying to exonerate Hitler from starting the war in 1939, laying the blame mainly on Halifax and Roosevelt. But once the sources cited are examined it quickly appears that what Hoggan said was one thing and what his sources said was quite different. He had in fact written his book against his sources. It seems that the service which Hoggan rendered to the cause of historical 'revisionism', Weinberg renders to that of current historical orthodoxy. He uses all the well-known sources, discredited or otherwise; source criticism is not only absent but explicitly negated. For instance, any source criticism of the so-called 'Hossbach Memorandum', i.e. the document in the form in which it was submitted in evidence at the Nuremberg trial, he blandly dismisses as 'silly speculation'. This is perhaps pardonable, but the entire work begins methodologically in the worst possible manner. Thus in vol. i, p. 22, he produces a direct quote from Hitler: ' "I believe that I have enough energy to lead our people whither it must shed its blood (*zum blutigen Einsatz*) not for the adjustment of its boundaries, but to save it into the most distant future by securing so much land and space that the future receives back many times the blood shed" Hitler said on 23 May 1929'. Looking back at the source quoted by Weinberg, the *Völkischer Beobachter* of that date, what one reads is the following: 'We National Socialists do not follow a policy which could not secure the existence of the Volk for all eternity, because in contrast to these Marxist panjandrums I have been a soldier and for years stepped over enough corpses to know what war means. I believe that I *would* possess enough energy to lead our people *even* whither it must shed its blood, *but* not for an adjustment of its boundaries but to save it into the most distant future.' The words italicised are those which Weinberg has omitted or changed in order to alter the entire context. Weinberg goes even further, stipulating an alleged identity of interest in the quest for war between Hitler and the German people and ends: 'His people were not to be disappointed. They would get all the wars he had promised. . .' Reports by foreign journalists in Germany at the outbreak of war, or for that matter the reception by the German public of Chamberlain the year before, speak a different language.

In vol. i, p. 176, Weinberg writes: 'In June 1934, Hitler and Admiral Raeder, the commander-in-chief of the German navy, discussed new warships, including a series of submarines, that Germany was building in violation of the peace treaty and agreed that the fleet – originally planned mainly with France and Poland in mind – would eventually have to be developed for use against England'. Weinberg's evidence is provided by documents of the Nuremberg trial, vol. 34, p. 775 (Document C–189). However, the document cited states 'Commander in Chief of the Navy expresses the opinion that the navy might nevertheless later have to be developed against England'. Weinberg does not identify to whom Raeder's alleged remark was made. It was reported in 1961 by Admiral Zieb of the navy engineering branch. Whether Raeder made this remark or not is a minor issue: What is important is that Weinberg postulates a naval policy jointly agreed by Hitler and Raeder for which there is not a scrap of evidence, and at a time when a close rapprochement between Great Britain and Germany still occupied the first place in Hitler's foreign policy desiderata!

Given this cavalier treatment of sources it comes as no surprise that Weinberg accepts without qualification Hitler's 1935 claim to have achieved parity with Great Britain in air armaments, thus discounting not only the more accurate figures available to the British Air Ministry at the time, but also the substantial body of research on this topic published since the end of the Second World War. On Hitler's speech of 21 May 1935, in which he renounced publicly the military clauses of the Versailles treaty, Weinberg comments as follows: 'He offered bilateral non-aggression pacts to all neighbours . . .; he assured the world that he wanted only peace; he promised to observe the Locarno Treaty including the demilitarisation of the Rhineland. . .' According to the same source as that cited by Weinberg, what Hitler said was rather different and more qualified than Weinberg would have us believe: 'The German Reich government will find itself bound by the obligations, especially those arising out of the Locarno Treaty, as long as the other signatories are prepared to stand by the pact. As regards the demilitarised zone the German Reich Government considers it an immensely heavy burden to bear for the pacification of Europe. It believes it must draw attention to the fact that the continuing increases of forces on the other side cannot be considered as a supplementation of these endeavours.' A little later on in the speech Hitler became more specific: 'The German Reich Government will be particularly grateful to receive an authentic interpretation of the repercussions and consequences of the Russo–French military alliance upon the treaty obligations of the individual signatory of the Locarno Pact. It does not want to leave any doubt about its own attitude, which is that it considers these military alliances as irreconcilable with the spirit and the letter of the Covenant of the League of Nations.' In other words, Hitler made no blanket promises but quite clearly pointed to the consequences once the Russo–French alliance was ratified.

Weinberg even manages to find an American citizen sentenced to death in 1937 and executed 'for supposedly having some anti-Nazi leaflets in his possession'. This 'American' citizen he identifies as Helmut Hirsch, who was never an American citizen, but a German émigré and member of Otto Strasser's 'Black Front' who was sent into Germany equipped with explosives to assassinate National Socialist leaders, possibly Hitler himself. When caught, he was tried, sentenced to death and executed. The only American citizen detained in Germany was a merchant navy seaman by the name of Simpson, who also acted as a courier for the Communist Party in exile. He admitted his activities in court and also to members of the US embassy in Berlin and was sentenced to three years' imprisonment, released after two months and deported to the USA as an undesirable alien: but all that had happened in 1935 and not in 1937.

These are only a few examples which could be developed in a more extensive review article for which this volume is obviously not the place. However, the examples cited demonstrate just how carefully not only the student but also the scholar has to tread in recent contemporary history, that without checking nothing can be taken for granted. In addition, they raise serious doubts about reviewing standards and expertise when one established historian comes to the conclusion: 'Turning to the events of the 1930s, the most reliable account is G. Weinberg, *The Foreign Policy of Hitler's Germany* . . .' and praises it as 'a model of meticulous scholarship. . . .' Even within this volume it is evident how risky it is to adopt unchecked primary sources quoted in secondary works.

In the selection of essays which follow, Esmonde Robertson sets the scene with his contribution on Hitler's planning for war and the response of the Great Powers. In so far as the anti-semitic component of Hitler's thought is concerned, comment will be reserved for Part IV. Robertson dates the notion of an 'international Fascist conspiracy' as far back as the early 1930s, although it appears not to have come into general use until the conclusion of the tripartite pact between Germany, Italy and Japan in September 1940. It is obviously very difficult to evaluate Hitler's early utterances about his aims to the German generals in 1932/33. The intentionalists of course see in them evidence for a general 'master plan'. On the other hand there is also the problem of how Hitler assessed the aims of Germany's military leadership. There is ample evidence that in January 1933 he expected them to be a 'bunch of hounds' held tightly on the leash by previous governments. His disappointment proved all the greater when on coming to power he found the opposite to be the case. On 3 February 1933 he informally addressed his generals and admirals at a private gathering, of which General Liebmanns' notes have survived, and of which Weinberg produces a highly distorted summary. Nevertheless, the tenor was deliberately aggressive; Hitler believed he was articulating what the military leaders themselves felt. However, the reception he received was, to put it mildly, cool. Not, as already mentioned, that they differed with him over aims, but rather they considered the methods suggested extremely dangerous in the light of Germany's geostrategic position and state of armaments. Yet, up to 1939, or for that matter up to 1941/42, it was his assessment which proved correct in the short term and not that of his military experts. On all the issues, the renunciation of the military clauses of the Versailles treaty, the remilitarisation of the Rhineland, the *Anschluss* with Austria, the Sudeten crisis and ultimately the annexation of the Czech rump-state, Hitler had been proved right. He seemed to have been right in his forecast that neither France nor Great Britain would do anything actively to assist their Polish ally, though they declared war over Poland. In the conduct of military operations he held back until the planning stage of the campaign in the West, when all his chief of the general staff, Col. General Franz Halder, could offer was little more than a revamped version of the Schlieffen Plan. It was at this point that Hitler's *Wehrmacht* adjutant, Colonel Schmundt, drew attention to Manstein's alternative *Sichelschnitt* plan, cutting straight through the Ardennes. This was precisely what Hitler wanted; he imposed it upon his general staff and as so often before was proved right. The only occasion where Hitler and the bulk of his generals were unanimous was in their assessment of the attack upon Russia. They all expected Soviet Russia to collapse like a house of cards.

A considerable blind spot in our knowledge is the role F. D. Roosevelt played in the origins of the Second World War. Here differentiation is necessary between the official policy pursued by the State Department and F. D. R.'s 'private diplomacy' to which he remained addicted to the day of his death. Against the assertion that US–German relations did not deteriorate until just before Munich one must set Roosevelt's 'Quarantine Speech' of 1937, the despatch of his personal emissaries to the governments of the European powers 'to stop Hitler' and his never-ceasing attempts to get back from Congress greater discretionary powers in the conduct of US foreign policy. Up to 1939 Congress would not play, for the isolationist and non-interventionist impulse was too strong. (Roosevelt was a man with a set of very strong dentures, only the dentures were in the hands of Congress.)

In the meantime, however, Hitler held the floor in Europe. From the conclusion of the German–Polish non-aggression pact in 1934 up to Munich he held the diplomatic initiative and piece by piece dismantled the French system of security. Robertson rightly emphasises an important fact which is often forgotten, namely that the German–Polish pact sacrificed the interests of the substantial German minority within Poland's frontiers. Since Germany had joined the League of Nations in 1926 their grievances had been raised time and again on the floor of the League, without ever getting further than the committee stage and with no action following. In the interests of his policy Hitler sacrificed them in 1934 as he sacrificed the interests of the German South Tyrolians for the sake of closer relations with Italy. Yet the grievances of that German minority were real enough, as were those of their counterparts in Czechoslovakia. Diaries of members of the military resistance such as Lt. Colonel Groscurth noted the genuine feelings of liberation when the Germans occupied the Sudetenland, while the outbreak of war with Poland was accompanied in the early days by large-scale massacres among Poland's German minority.

It is one of the tragic ironies that it had to be the Munich agreement which was the last agreement of Europe's great powers which was signed without being under the shadow of the superpowers, East and West. The signatory powers pledged themselves to guarantee the new borders provided, however, that the government in Prague succeeded in settling its minority problems for itself. That this was not the case gave Hitler the pretext to march into Prague, while neither Great Britain nor France initially saw in that occupation a violation of the Munich treaty. Nevertheless Hitler had crossed his diplomatic Rubicon. Though objectively the German claim on Poland had been considered justified before the ink on the Versailles treaty was even dry, Hitler had lost the last diplomatic credit he had with this first 'step across frontiers'. However justified the issues he raised may have been in themselves, having abandoned the role of the last executor of 'Wilsonian principles', no one believed him; behind every demand stood the question 'what next?'. Even in spite of this it seems doubtful whether Great Britain or France would have guaranteed Poland, had they known that it was the Polish foreign secretary, Colonel Joseph Beck, who had at the height of the Munich crisis initiated bilateral talks with Germany to settle the problem of Danzig and the Corridor and in which, after Germany had let him have the Teschen area of Czechoslovakia, he then refused to make concessions. Beck played his cards skilfully; only after having been offered and having accepted the British and French guarantees did he reveal that the Germans were making actual demands. In itself a diplomatic masterpiece, this had consequences for Poland which were hardly worth the gamble.

With the outbreak of the Second World War the question of Hitler's war aims finds its brilliant classical intentionalist formulation by Hugh Trevor-Roper, as relevant in any discussion now as when it was first published in German in 1960. That it is in need of revision will become apparent in the contributions that follow. But that does not deprive it of its intrinsic importance which lies in the fact that it provided a new impulse to further research in new directions and dimensions. Some doubts arise over whether Trevor-Roper pays too high a tribute to Sir Robert Ensor. He is said to have seen it all coming in detail, because of having read *Mein Kampf*, though it does not contain a single reference to Czechoslovakia. Also, it seems that Rauschning's foresight as regards a Russo–German alignment does not deserve the praise Trevor-Roper gives it. Rauschning's book was a product of the late autumn of 1939 and was first published in December of that year, enough time for the author to introduce into it events that were taking place while he was putting the book together.

Dietrich Aigner, one of the foremost specialists in Anglo–German relations during the inter-war years, attempts in his essay to bring about a conceptual clarification of such nebulous terms as world power, world dominion and world domination which are frequently bandied about, often as synonyms of each other. Esmonde Robertson has raised the question of whether Hitler aimed at 'world conquest'; Weinberg, moderate for once, argues that Hitler aimed for 'world dominion'. Or does he mean conquest? It never becomes clear. Aigner isolates concepts which have degenerated into slogans from their propagandistic context and suggests implicitly that the belief in National Socialist 'world rule' or 'domination', 'dominion' or 'world conquest' began to develop their own semantic dynamism and ultimately played much the same role within the context of Hitler's foreign policy as did the 'protocols of the Elders of Zion' within the context of modern anti-semitism. Hitler's own ambivalence and careless use of language have contributed considerably to this terminological confusion. Ultimately, however, Aigner poses the question whether his was in fact a rationally planning ice-cold intellect. This is a question the historian of the traditional mould cannot really answer. It requires the answer of a psychologist, though the answers 'psycho-history' has come up with so far in the 'Hitler case' are, as will be shown below, far from encouraging.

One of the gaps still existing in the historiography of National Socialist foreign policy is a biography of Joachim von Ribbentrop, Hitler's foreign policy adviser, special envoy, ambassador in London and then from 1938 until 1945 German foreign minister. Coming from outside the 'establishment' of the German foreign office his activities were considered as those of an unwelcome intruder, so much so that as foreign minister he could never be sure of the loyalty of his own staff. Just as in the post-war literature Hitler has become the scapegoat of the German generals, on whom all military failures and ultimate defeat are blamed (aptly summarised by the title of von Manstein's memoirs *Lost Victories*), so Ribbentrop is blamed for all the excesses and shortcomings of German foreign policy. Yet if one delves deeper into the sources rather contradictory outlines emerge. From the files of the British Foreign Office emerges a narrow-minded, arrogant individual, with a very limited horizon, convinced of Great Britain's decadence, in fact the same picture which Ribbentrop's subordinates in London and Berlin continuously conveyed to the British Foreign Office. From the French files almost the opposite emerges, a well-versed man of the world, a good negotiator quick to come to the core of any issue. André François-Poncet's despatches convey rather a different picture of Ribbentrop from the one he renders in his memoirs. The French foreign minister Louis Barthou considered him a man of extreme politeness, well educated, with whom he found it much easier to discuss for instance Richard Wagner than with the German ambassador in Paris. Jacobsen attests to Ribbentrop's having both francophile and anglophile attitudes. Up to 1938 he was certainly reputed to hold much more liberal views on the issue of 'non-Aryans' than other members of Hitler's close entourage, views which were noted with misgivings and were also potentially dangerous since, like Speer, Ribbentrop lacked his own personal power base within the National Socialist polycracy. However, the widely prevalent notion that he was an engrained anglophobe and that he discounted British power can be dismissed. Disenchantment set in during his spell as ambassador in London, when Ribbentrop realised that Britain could not be won over to a large-scale revision of the territorial provisions of Versailles in Eastern Central Europe. His final report on his period as ambassador in London makes it quite clear that Hitler could not count on British *désintéressement*, let alone their support with regard to any German expansionist move in Europe. If Germany was determined to become a world power by militant means it would encounter British opposition.

Wolfgang Michalka in his essay paves the way for what might lead to a fundamental reassessment of Ribbentrop's role. Far from being Hitler's lackey and 'yes-man' he was quite capable of developing an alternative foreign policy to that of Hitler, the forging of a Eurasian continental bloc which was to include the Soviet Union and would either neutralise Great Britain's role in Europe, or in the case of war, keep her and ultimately also the United States in check.

What role this concept played once war had broken out is further elaborated upon on a functionalist basis by the editor's own essay on Hitler's alleged 'programme' and the genesis of 'Operation Barbarossa', a case-study which, so the writer believes, bears out the usefulness of the functionalist approach in the realm of foreign policy. While 'Barbarossa' also implied the bankruptcy of Ribbentrop's own alternative concept, it will emerge in the course of the chapter that this cannot simply be blamed on Ribbentrop, or even for that matter exclusively on Hitler.

6. Hitler's Planning for War and the Response of the Great Powers (1938–early 1939)

E. M. ROBERTSON

It is the purpose of this study to establish whether in the months after Munich Hitler overtly intended launching a great ideological war for the acquisition of *Lebensraum* in eastern Europe and, if this were his aim, whether its concomitant was a radical implementation of his drive against the Jews which was to culminate in the death camps of 1942. Enquiry will include not only a discussion of Hitler's priorities in armaments but also his attempts to deflect unfulfilled expectations inside Germany to warlike ends. The reactions of the governments in London, Paris and Washington to events inside Germany and into whether the new alignments, already perceptible early in 1939, emerged as a result of fears that Germany had taken the lead in an international Fascist conspiracy for world domination will be considered.

It is essential in a discussion of this kind to summarise the changing historiographical interpretations of Hitler's policy especially for the period under review, and to reassess

Original contribution to this volume.

certain ideas which I myself advanced over twenty years ago. At that time I stressed how Hitler's hostility to Britain became predominant late in 1937.[1] A reassessment, now that so many documents and books are accessible, is a formidable task. Indeed, it has been contended that with the possible exception of Jesus Christ more has been written about Adolf Hitler than any other personage in human history.[2] In the 1960s the controversy, with which many people are now thoroughly familiar, had turned mainly on the ideas advanced by A. J. P. Taylor and Hugh Trevor-Roper, now Lord Dacre. This controversy is no spent force and needs to be summarised. According to Taylor, Hitler was the supreme opportunist who took advantage of circumstances, created by others, to reverse the Treaty of Versailles and to convert Germany once again into a great power. Hitler was another German who continued the policy of his predecessors. Trevor-Roper had already advanced the more radical thesis that Hitler adhered to a programme systematically worked out in advance, and that his principal ideas were elaborated in *Mein Kampf* and confirmed by utterances made publicly or in private later in his career. While certain of Trevor-Roper's theses, at least until the late 1960s, have gained acceptance in Britain and Germany, Taylor has won new adherents mainly in Britain.[3]

After publication of Hitler's *Secret Book* in 1958[4] several German historians, notably K. Hildebrand and A. Hillgruber, systematically reassessed Hitler's ideas and examined them closely within the framework of the changing social context of the Third Reich. According to these and other scholars Hitler was thinking in terms of German expansion in two or three stages. This is described as the *Stufenplan*. Germany should first arm within her existing frontiers and achieve partial autarchy (economic self-sufficiency) by about 1939. Next, either before or after a short war in the West primarily against France, she should seize living space in the East for German colonisation. Having achieved full autarchy on the continent Germany could pass to the third stage and carve out an empire for herself overseas and, with Britain as an ally, a neutral or an enemy, turn against the USA.[5] J. Dülffer in his magisterial history of the German navy accepts the *Stufenplan* as a working hypothesis. It will be seen how he draws the conclusion that, late in 1938, Hitler was making parallel preparations for a *Blitzkrieg* in 1940/41; for a long war, to be fought mainly at sea and in the air, after 1944.[6]

In criticism of the *Stufenplan* theory it should be remembered that Hitler himself never explicitly enunciated the two or three stages through which German policy was intended to pass. He admitted that he had never finalised his political ideas, and that he was a man who kept his own counsels.[7] He was at first clear on one issue alone: psychological rearmament must precede both technical rearmament and war.[8] It will be seen how after Munich this formidable problem had still to be tackled.

Expressions such as 'world power or collapse' used for instance in *Mein Kampf*, are moreover open to several interpretations, and there is a good deal of confusion between his ideas on what Germany might, or what she should do, after the subjugation of Europe, which was his central aim. In his *Secret Book* he talked more explicitly about a future conflict between Britain, who was cast in the role of Germany's ally, and the USA than a war between Germany and the USA. Indeed, Hitler's analysis of the future tasks he set for British statesman might have mirrored something of what he himself or some future German statesmen should do.[9] There is also confusion about what Hitler meant by 'world power'. The expression can be taken to mean that Germany should be converted into the greatest of all other world powers, each of which would be self-sufficient and organised on a military basis. Alternatively, world power can mean 'competition for blood purification' in which the Ayrian race, with its natural home in Germany, should dominate all other races, not only in Europe, but in Africa and in the western hemisphere.[10] He most certainly favoured the idea that anti-semitic Anglo-Saxon nationalists in Britain, and perhaps in the USA, should win power at home and share in Germany's destiny abroad. In a talk to senior officers of the armed forces on 22 January 1938 he was quite specific: 'There is only one great consolidated group of people on this earth which, because of union of race and language, lives crammed in the heart of Europe. This is the German people with its 110 million [sic] inhabitants. . . .' A comparison with the population figures of other states 'fills me with the joyful hope; that to this solid block in Central Europe the world one day will, and must, belong'.[11] Here the implication is that Germany must be a world power in order to defend the Europe which she dominated, not that domination of the continent was to be a stepping-stone to world power. Stress was also laid on the racial homogeneity and the numerical superiority of the Germanic race rather than on the extent of the Reich's future frontiers.

Such ideas were to be repeated time and again at meetings with leading party men and soldiers later in 1938 and early in 1939. Only a few examples need be cited here. In a talk to junior officers of the armed forces on 18 January 1939 he described the German people 'above all because of its racial values' as 'the strongest in the world'. They must in future be fed by the whole of Europe.[12] Speaking to senior officers a few days later, he alluded to the contribution of the Roman Empire to the white races, a theme which was to be developed in his Reichstag speech of 30 January 1939, as a prelude to a song of praise on Fascist Italy.[13] He also told his audience that one day the Aryans would conquer the world. In a further address to senior commanders of all three services of 10 February he spelt out how, in the process of 'realizing a preconceived plan', he would have behind him not only the 'strongest people in Europe' but, and 'perhaps this will surprise you, virtually the strongest in the world'. Germans should not be content with what had been achieved in the last six years. They stood at the starting point, not at the end of the road to expansion. 'The solution of the problem of *Lebensraum* must be solved, so far as it can be solved', in this generation. 'For in the next hundred years no German statesman would possess the same authority as he possessed.' There can be no doubt that because of the rearmament of other powers and, because Hitler himself was still in the prime of life, he would in the near future pass from words to deeds and go to war; according to some of his listeners his aim was, first domination of Europe and then, for hundreds of years Germanic domination of the world.[14]

Despite adjustments made on account of changing conditions, his policy had until that date, he claimed, unfolded in a logical and orderly sequence. While Germany had first to win military sovereignty within her existing frontiers, the actual date chosen for leaving the League of Nations and for the reintroduction of conscription depended on circumstances. The next logical step, the reoccupation of the Rhineland, was at first intended for the year 1937. But he took advantage of the disarray of his opponents and acted in March 1936 a year earlier than he had intended.[15] For a time he thought that the conquest of Czechoslovakia should take place simultaneously with, or precede, an *Anschluss* with Austria. Circumstances required him to readjust his priorities and to annex Austria before taking on Czechoslovakia. This document might be interpreted to mean that Hitler was strictly following a *Stufenplan*. But sufficient stress needs to be laid on the second section of the address. Instead of fulfilling a promise, made to his listeners, by declaring what his specific aims were, as for example the oocupation of Prague or an attack on Poland, Hitler merely said that he would take advantage of the weaknesses and divisions of Germany's potential enemies for further expansion in whichever direction he chose. He would harass them and keep them guessing. One tentative conclusion can be drawn from the available evidence. Looked at retrospectively, Hitler's policy, especially in the early years, has every appearance of corresponding to an existing plan; seen prospectively, Hitler still regarded himself as the master opportunist who would allow the mistakes of others to decide how to formulate foreign policy.[16] This has given rise to considerable controversy.

There is a debate surrounding Hitler's intentions on another issue. Hitler, according to many scholars, no longer monopolises the centre of the stage. While we certainly cannot understand the Third Reich in terms of Hitler alone, we must remember that he always worked with or through others. Hence the 'totalitarian' interpretation of his policy is much less in evidence today than it was twenty years ago.[17]

Indeed David Irving carries this view to an extreme. He maintains that during the war Hitler was not fully in control of his Reich and that the policy he pursued was either forced on him by others or that he was just bypassed.[18] This theory is supported in certain respects in an important work, based mainly on British documents, by Simon Newman, who argues, with loud applause from A. J. P. Taylor, that Chamberlain's guarantee to Poland of 31 March 1939, given under pressure from Halifax, the foreign secretary, provoked Hitler into doing something which he did not previously intend, namely into ordering a plan for the invasion of Poland which duly took effect in September 1939. Newman rejects the idea that the guarantee was a deterrent.[19] He and other scholars, while admirable in discussing appeasement, frequently misunderstand Hitler's character. They either misinterpret, or use a faulty translation of Hitler's Reichstag speech of 30 January 1939, which they describe as moderate.[20] They had not, moreover, at their disposal other vital German evidence, which strongly suggests that irrespective of Poland, Hitler early in 1939 was intending a general war of conquest, and of annihilating European Jewry.

Whether in the year ending in 1938 Hitler still adhered to the *Stufenplan* or not he was, according to certain authorities, also driven by a pathological impetus, a naked fanaticism, which was so strong that it blinded him from recognising the scope and consequence of rational planning. Therefore the ideas of those who maintain that an understanding of Hitler depends on the correct application of depth psychology, combined with accepted critical methodology in the interpretation of historical evidence, must be taken seriously.[21] That Hitler was spurred into action by vengeance, as this school of thought cogently maintains, and not merely by calculation of advantage, stands out on several occasions. Dollfuss had defied him in 1934. Therefore, regardless of the international consequences, Hitler was glad to see him go. He might conceivably have ordered his assassination.[22] Beneš had defied him in May 1938, therefore the rump Czechoslovakia, whose rulers after Munich were in fact behaving as obedient vassals, had to be destroyed.[23] Britain had to be defeated, not because Germany wanted to become the succession state of the British empire but because, contrary to her real interests, Britain's rulers had made their country the most formidable centre of resistance to full-scale German military expansion in Europe. Since Britain was breaking the laws of history by going to war with Germany, a radical change of course, not a mere readjustment of priorities, was called for. By the summer of 1939 Hitler needed the friendship of Soviet Russia, and this meant the renunciation, at least temporarily, of hopes of acquiring that vital living space in the Baltic States and the Ukraine where, according to Hitler, Germany's destiny lay. In 1939 Hitler had, as I have claimed, involved Germany in the wrong war, a war in which even victory was not enough.[24] Hence he was forced by outside pressure to achieve his long-cherished ambitions simultaneously. The war was thus to spread and involve powers which were much stronger than Germany and end in total defeat.

There is hard evidence to suggest that in the summer of 1938 Hitler was not only determined to seek *Lebensraum* at the expense of Czechoslovakia but to punish the Czechs for precipitating the May crisis.[25] In September he was again furious with Beneš for expelling the leaders of the Sudeten Germans. Reflecting on events shortly after Munich, Ernst von Weizsäcker, the state secretary at the Foreign Ministry, observed: 'For us the will for a solution through a war of revenge and for the annihilation of Czechoslovakia prevails'. The belief, expressed in Britain, that Hitler had backed down because of the firm stand taken by other powers against him merely added fuel to his anger.[26]

Moreover, the fact should not be overlooked that in certain respects Hitler had come to dread British appeasement as much as, or even more, than a possible show of British strength.[27] Appeasement was plausible. In this connection Weinberg rightly points out that the British, in their efforts to achieve a compromise between Beneš and the Sudeten Germans, inveigled Germany into tiresome negotiations from which there was no escape. Haggling at a conference table was precisely what Hitler did not want since it deprived him of the chance of launching a short war to thrash the Czechs in order to test the new *Wehrmacht* and make a triumphant entry into Prague.[28]

Thwarted at Munich, the revenge theme comes to the surface even more conspicuously and, whereas Hitler still recognised that certain of Germany's vital interests should not figure too prominently in propaganda, he no longer chose to conceal his anger against the growing number of his opponents both at home and abroad. In an address to approximately 400 journalists on 10 November 1938, he declared: 'Circumstances have forced me to talk almost solely of peace for a decade'. Only by repeatedly emphasising the German wish for peace could he provide the country with conditions to go ahead with rearmament which was the one 'indispensable prerequisite for the next step'. Some people, he went on to say, were now gaining the mistaken impression, which was exploited by intellectual defeatists, that he really wanted peace. The German people must be made to learn that 'there are certain things which, if not achieved in a "friendly manner", must be realized by means of force'. Hitler also reminded the party leaders not to air their differences in public. They were to stand firmly behind him especially on occasions such as the annual parade of 9 November. This warning was obviously intended for two mortal enemies, Rosenberg and Goebbels, who, together with Hess, were in the stadium. There had, Hitler insisted, to be a united front which alone would make full social control possible.[29]

Even before this address Hitler could not, or would not, conceal this change of attitude from foreigners. In a speech at Saarbrücken, delivered on 9 October, he lashed out against the British opponents of appeasement, namely Churchill, Eden and Duff Cooper. The speech had immediate repercussions abroad. British rearmament was greatly accelerated, that of the United States was ordered to start. By ventilating his anger Hitler had alerted Germany's potential enemies. By doing so he was to lose the initiative. In November he made even fiercer attacks on British statesmen. But, because of horrific events inside Germany itself, these attacks were overlooked by London and

Washington. Also on 22 October a propaganda campaign in favour of increased German armaments was launched.[30]

Hitler did not only vent his rage on the British. No people had annoyed him more than those military and economic experts in his own country who were accused of preaching defeatism and despondency. Men such as Col. General Ludwig Beck, ex-diplomats such as Ulrich von Hassell, Carl Goerdeler, former mayor of Leipzig, Hjalmar Schacht, minister of economics, and other economic experts, including the unfortunate Rudolf Brinkmann, belonged to what he described as 'the overbred intellectual circles' who were trying to prevent him from fulfilling his providential mission. He railed against them. Unfortunately, he admitted, he needed their expertise, 'otherwise, perhaps, we could someday exterminate them or do something of this kind to them'. On 30 January 1939 Hitler again attacked the 'intellectuals' and spoke of creating a new ruling elite which was to be racially pure. No wonder that, because of Hitler's open threats, the resolve of the conservative opposition to the regime was strengthened. This theme will be dealt with later.[31]

If for reasons of political expediency Hitler held back from unleashing a bloodbath against his conservative opponents, there was one group in Germany against whom he had no such scruples and who were defenceless, the Jews.[32] The reciprocity of Hitler's need for living space and his determination to destroy European Jewry has not been sufficiently explored and will be dealt with later.

The revenge theme in Hitler's policy after Munich should, however, not be overstressed. Hitler still possessed a remarkable grasp of two central problems in modern war. However ineffective his propaganda might have been before Munich in whipping up war fever among German citizens, who according to Weizsäcker, would have responded to war with 'silent obstruction',[33] Hitler boasted about how attacks in the press and on the radio, combined with ostentatious troop movements and target practice near the Czech frontier, had broken the nerve of the 'Gentlemen of Prague'.[34] German propaganda was not of course the only factor behind his success, and Hitler made no mention of those

German Army Intelligence reports, according to which it was Czech acceptance of the Anglo–French Plan of 20 September which had destroyed the morale of the Czech army, rather than German propaganda. Nevertheless, the telephone wires linking Prague with London and Paris were tapped. By this means Hitler had learned that the Czech minister in London, Jan Masaryk, was thoroughly defeatist.[35] Despite the continued success achieved, through psychological terrorism and the exploitation of telecommunications, Hitler did not believe that if there were to be a repeat performance of the Czech crisis Germany would again enjoy the element of surprise. This might in part explain the reckless manner in which he and Ribbentrop attacked British and promoted German rearmament. Both were wrong in assuming that since Britain was rearming in any case attacks in the press against her would make no difference.[36]

Even before Munich Hitler was giving serious consideration to the possibility of first incorporating the Sudeten areas of Czechoslovakia into Germany that autumn and invading the rest of the country in the spring of 1939. He was at that time determined to go ahead with his plan for the conquest of Czechoslovakia in two stages even if it led to war with the western powers.[37] After Munich Czechoslovakia was progressively reduced as a power factor. In October she was still capable of pinning down 25 German divisions: the figure before Munich was 35. In October an attack from German Silesia and Austria was planned, the aim of which was to cut Czechoslovakia at her waist. At this stage Czechoslovakia had ceased to count as a power factor. On 17 December this plan was to be implemented regardless of Czech provocation but no date was given when it was to take effect. It was more than just one among several contingency plans as contended by Newman.[38]

The strategic situation resulting from the emasculation of Czechoslovakia resulted not only in a revision of German plans for future war with the West, which will be considered later, but of the military and political role the Soviet Union was expected to play in Europe. After the military purges, which had started in the summer of 1937, Hitler had virtually written off the Red Army as a force capable of influencing European affairs.[39] There were further purges in 1938, and in September no military activity was observed in the western military districts of Russia. Admittedly Moscow had warned the Poles that if they joined in the scramble for Czech territory the Russo–Polish Non-Aggression Pact of 1932 would be repudiated. But after the Poles seized the Teschen area, shortly after Munich, Russia, apart from sending aircraft to Czechoslovakia, remained remarkably inactive. Russia's attention seems to have been fixed on the Far East. According to Erickson the purges in this area lacked the ferocity and intensity exhibited elsewhere.[40] For their part the governments of Poland, Romania, Hungary, Yugoslavia and even Czechoslovakia were only too glad to see Russia elbowed out of eastern Europe. One reason for this was the increased activity of the Comintern resulting from the Spanish Civil War and fear that civil war might spread to their own countries.[41] The Comintern was also active in France, which was suffering yet again from an economic crisis resulting from the third devaluation of the franc in May of that year. This caused the French right, with strong British encouragement, to look with suspicion on the alliance with Russia.[42] With Russia weak Hitler did not consider it necessary to concentrate on expanding the German economy for a major war involving mainly the army. According to Deist the army was only ready for a *Blitzkrieg* after the capture of Czech weapons and war material resulting from the occupation of the rump of Czechoslovakia on 15 March 1939.[43] It seems that even during the Czech crisis Hitler himself did not believe wholeheartedly in the efficacy of a *Blitzkrieg*. Early in September he told his generals that just as cavalry attacks had proved abortive in the past, so too tank attacks might prove ineffective if made against fortified positions in the future.[44] In 1938–39 Hitler still assumed that the main fighting would be in the West; territorial expansion in the East. It must therefore be asked how the two prospective theatres of operations stood in relationship to each other.

Late in 1938 Hitler was so uncertain about his own immediate military objectives that, apart from a possible

seizure of Danzig and Memel and an invasion of the rump
of Czechoslovakia, no general directive could be issued to
all three branches of the armed forces. In these circumstances
Weizsäcker told a fellow diplomat, Ulrich von Hassell, who
was completely disillusioned with the regime, that 'the
foreign policy of Ribbentrop and Hitler was aimed at war.
There was merely vacillation on whether it should
immediately be directed against England, for which purpose
Polish neutrality would have to be preserved, or at first in
the East in order to solve the German–Polish and Ukrainian
problems.'[45] But if Hitler was uncertain about his immediate
military objectives, it must be asked whether he acted with
a clearer grasp on the priorities of Germany's armaments.
Since changes in naval policy indicate which enemy, or
enemies, Hitler had in mind, they will need to be stressed.[46]

Seldom, according to Dülffer, did Hitler in his discussions
with his naval staff explicitly state which enemy he had in
mind. For instance, in 1937 it was considered dangerous
even to discuss the prospect of war with Britain. Hence,
bearing in mind Deist's stricture that Hitler was interested
in ships not plans, his policy has to be reconstructed from
those projects which he seriously intended to implement.[47]
By 1937 he no longer believed that Great Britain would
automatically allow Germany to seek her *Lebensraum* in
Europe in return for German support in maintaining her
empire. But, given the choice of an alliance with Germany
or the United States, Hitler persistently hoped that Britain
might be persuaded to opt for Germany. Two factors
confirmed him in this optimism. Britain, whose economic
power was on the decline, was not only aware of Germany's
growing strength, but she realised that, whereas the Third
Reich might allow her to retain her status as a great power
with a large empire, the USA had no such interest and
might even compel Britain to seek an ally, such as Germany,
so as to defend Canada.[48] Towards the end of 1937 Hitler
also realised that new plant was being installed in British
armaments factories and that the emergence of a coalition
between Britain and France, with the strong economic
backing of the USA, could not be ruled out. In an all-out
arms race this coalition would outstrip Germany by 1943–5.

Hence at the Hossbach conference of 5 November 1937 the allocation of steel for the navy (which was now to have battleships exceeding the limits of the 1935 Naval Agreement with Britain) was given priority over the demands of the two other branches of the armed forces. Germany, he declared, had to be prepared for war with the West while she still enjoyed a lead in armaments, namely before 1943. Had Hitler decided on preparations for war with Britain before this date he would not have ordered the construction of battleships, which took several additional years to complete, rather than the cruisers and submarines which his naval staff valued.[49]

Early in 1938 he still believed that Britain was unlikely to intervene if Germany annexed Austria or the Sudetenland. She was more likely, however, to do so at a later date in order to prevent Germany from dominating the entire continent. But his service chiefs, who were by April 1937 more aware than Hitler himself of growing British antagonism, had to decide on plans in the event of war breaking out prematurely. At an inter-service meeting of 20 May General Jodl of the Armed Forces High Command discussed the possibility of an occupation of Holland and Belgium. Whereas the German air force recognised the value of acquiring air bases in the Low Countries, if only to prevent them from falling into British hands, the idea was rejected by representatives of the other two branches of the armed forces, mainly because of the effect such action would have on neutrals, especially the United States.[50]

After the May crisis Hitler himself took the initiative in planning for war against Britain. Two programmes were sanctioned: the first being for the construction of an emergency fleet which was to consist mainly of submarines and cruisers. As part of this programme two new battleships of 42,000 tons were to be built and two existing ships of 25,000 tons were to be refitted with guns of a heavier calibre. This programme was to be completed by 1940–1, which was the deadline, according to Dülffer, for war on land against either France or Russia. With this relatively small fleet Hitler hoped either to deter Britain from intervention or, as suggested by Henke, to launch an interim war against Britain in order to drive her off the continent but not to destroy her as a power factor. Hitler also decided on a more grandiose programme. Six additional battleships of up to 56,000 tons were to form the nucleus of a great battlefleet which was to be ready for war probably in 1944–5. By these dates Germany was expected to have achieved full autarchy in Europe and to be ready to make a bid for world power, which meant the acquisition of colonies and bases overseas. If necessary, Dülffer maintained, she might even have to wage war against the USA, especially if Britain became too dependent on that country. Bases in Norway and the Atlantic Coast of France, and not just in the Low Countries, were now needed. Because of bureaucratic muddle and for technical reasons, such as inadequate building yards, work could not even start on the second programme for several months.[51]

After Hitler had announced his decision to attack Czechoslovakia, at a meeting with his generals and senior officials on 28 May, he also spoke of a war with the West, the aim of which was to extend the German coastline to include Holland and Belgium. He had nothing to say on what Germany would do, despite earlier discussions on air attacks on the British fleet and ships approaching British ports, if Britain continued hostilities after defeat in France. There was not the slightest hint of an invasion.[52] With Czechoslovakia unconquered his major preoccupation was still a defensive war on land. Hence in the later stages of the Czech crisis his naval programme was no longer to be a top priority. Cement and steel, as well as the commitment of 400,000 workers, were needed for strengthening the West Wall which accounted for 21 per cent of the total military expenditure for the second half of 1938. Whereas naval expansion continued at its existing rate in absolute terms, its share of expenditure in the second half of 1938 fell from 19 to 12 per cent of the total, while that of the air force rose from 21 to 22 per cent. One of the aims of the crash programme, called *Operation Limes*, for the construction of the West Wall, undertaken mainly by organization Todt, was to deter Belgium from joining the French in an attack on the Reich.[53]

After Munich there was a distinct switch of emphasis in German military planning from the defensive to the offensive. As a result of experiments conducted with artillery against Czech fortifications the German High Command came round to the view that the Maginot Line could be pierced.[54] Because the army was now considered to be adequate for an offensive in the West Hitler decided once again to switch the emphasis of armaments to the *Luftwaffe* and navy. In October 1938 expenditure on the former was increased fivefold. Work was to be well advanced by 1942 when 20,000 aircraft were expected to be produced annually in peacetime and raised to 30 or 40,000 in wartime. Needless to say such totally unrealistic estimates could never be realised. For one thing Germany could not procure the vast quantities of fuel oil or produce the munitions which were needed. Also work on the fortifications, which were to include Germany's new frontiers in eastern Europe, was to be complete by 1950.[55] The most spectacular expansion, however, was intended for the navy.

Within the Naval High Command there was by no means unanimity on what sort of ships should be built. In the autumn of 1938 Admiral Heye and other members of Admiral Raeder's staff favoured the construction of submarines, combined with pocket battleships and cruisers, for war against British commerce. Raeder accepted most of Heye's ideas and in November 1938 proposed postponing the construction of the ten heavy battleships until 1946-7. Towards the end of November Hitler roundly rejected Raeder's views. In the resulting bitter controversy Raeder for a time considered resignation. But Hitler got his way and Raeder acquiesced. The programme for heavy ships rather than for light cruisers and submarines, which had had to be postponed on Hitler's explicit orders, was to be completed by the end of 1944. Raeder, with Hitler's backing, now had the whiphand in rivalry with the other branches of the armed forces. By the end of 1938 Göring, commander-in-chief of the air force, gave him full support.[56]

In his correspondence with Hitler in January 1939 Raeder no longer assumed that Britain alone would be Germany's future antagonist. From now on Germany had to brace herself to fight 'the strong naval powers' which could only have included the USA. On 27 January 1939 Hitler reaffirmed his decision that, 'the construction of the Navy, as ordered by me, must have priority over all other tasks in armaments including those of the other two branches of the Armed Forces as well as over production for export'.[57] According to the Z-programme 10 battleships of 56,000 tons or more, 3 battle cruisers, 4 aircraft carriers, 8 heavy cruisers, 44 light cruisers (for colonial service), 68 destroyers, 90 torpedo boats and 250 submarines were all to be completed between 1944 and 1946. A start was in fact made on the Z-programme early in 1939. In the first half of that year the allocation of iron and steel to the navy rose from 14 to 16 per cent. Work on the Z-programme was continued until the outbreak of war. But it was to prove an extravagant pipe-dream. German provocation and not Hitler's preferences was to determine armaments policy.[58]

It is significant that the initial impetus for a large navy can be detected in the period before Munich. Although the United States at that time was expanding her fleet in the Pacific there had been no serious deterioration in German–American relations. That the Z-programme was imposed on the reluctant service chiefs late in 1938 and in January 1939, precisely at a time when not only Britain but the USA had become a target of bitter German propaganda, is significant. It indicates that the great racial war which lay ahead might have to be fought not only against Bolshevik-and Jewish-infested Russia but also the USA, whose president had made himself the 'mouthpiece of Judah and the instrument of the Comintern'.[59]

The Z-programme, considered side by side with the expansion of the *Luftwaffe* and of work on fortifications, which would take several years to complete, raises an important question. Previously experts on the German war economy have emphasised that while Hitler was planning a *Blitzkrieg*, expenditure on armaments should not hit the consumer,[60] but Richard Overy, using a wealth of evidence of a technical kind, has recently concluded: 'Hitler's plans were large in scale, not limited, and were intended for a major war of conquest to be fought considerably later than

1939. . . . Hitler's object, in the long run, was European conquest and world hegemony.' Overy's last sentence can be substantiated by the words Hitler, Göring and Himmler frequently used to party and military leaders late in 1938 and early in 1939. Overy's conclusions lend support to the view that Hitler was serious in his plans for a large air force and navy for a war to be fought after 1944 against Britain or perhaps the United States.[61]

There is one argument, however, which Overy might not have stressed sufficiently. Hitler believed that he alone could lead Germany to victory. His premature death would have the disastrous effect of denying Germany a leader with that charismatic genius needed for fulfilling her providential mission. Hence, he told his commanders on 28 May 1938 and again on 10 February 1939 Germany would have to be ready for war in the near future. But plans for a long war did not rule out the idea of a *Blitzkrieg*. Dülffer reaches the interesting conclusion that after Munich Hitler intended the army to fight a *Blitzkrieg* against France or Russia in 1941–2; the navy was to be ready for a long war after 1944; the *Luftwaffe* to be prepared for either contingency. Hence it makes better sense to speak of parallel preparations for war based on two time-scales rather than in three discrete stages. The fact should not be overlooked, however, that Hitler simply might not have made up his mind. He himself admitted that this was sometimes the case.[62]

In the period before the new navy and *Luftwaffe* were complete, Germany had to pass through a danger zone with a relatively small fleet. In order to achieve a degree of immunity from a pre-emptive strike she needed either an alliance with those naval powers, Italy and Japan, who were also opposed to the West, a course advocated by Ribbentrop, or to take advantage of the warlike acts or demonstrations of hostility by these two predatory powers against the western democracies, a course favoured by Hitler.

After the May crisis Hitler was more anxious than ever to secure Japanese support, and in his address to his generals of 28 May he spoke of the desirability of an alliance with Italy and of rendering support for Japan. In the summer of

1938, after much haggling, the Germans renounced certain vital interests in the Ear East in favour of Japan. For instance, the export of war material to China in exchange for valuable raw materials was stopped and, in face of strong Chinese protests and a threat to break off diplomatic relations, a German military mission was withdrawn from China and a Russian mission took its place. The 'policy of balance,' as Fox points out, had broken down. Germany was now virtually on Japan's side in the war in China.[63]

But one question had yet to be resolved. If political cooperation was to be followed up by a military alliance between the three Axis powers, against whom should it primarily be directed? There had been a severe frontier clash between Japanese and Soviet troops at Chankufeng about 70 miles southwest of Vladivostok, lasting from late July until 10 August 1938. As a result approximately 20 Japanese divisions, which were badly needed in the war against China, had to be held in readiness on the borders between Japanese- and Russian-controlled territory.[64] To the relief of British naval authorities, sections of the Japanese Army High Command continued to regard war with Russia as inevitable.[65]

Hitler was fully aware of Japanese anxiety as regards Russia, and late in May he instructed General Ott, his new ambassador in Tokyo, to try and divert Japanese attention away from Russia to Britain.[66] After Munich Hitler unsuccessfully continued to pursue this policy for which reason no tripartite alliance was signed until September 1940. There is, however, one fact which might have influenced Hitler more than Ribbentrop against close friendship with Japan, namely NS racial doctrines. Already, in a speech to students at Munich on 22 January 1936, Hitler had declared: 'the white race is called to rule, lead and dominate the rest of the world'. The Japanese reacted fervently.[67] Even in the speech of 20 February 1938 in which he announced his intention to recognise Manchukuo he added a rider: Japan's greatest victory would not affect the 'civilization of the white races in the very least'. Despite the conclusion of a cultural agreement between Germany and Japan on 25 November 1938, there could be no real community of fate between Germany and Japan in the same sense as between Italy and Germany.[68]

Hitler was, however, determined to exploit Japanese warlike actions to Germany's advantage. He was not to be disappointed. After Munich the Japanese launched an offensive down the coast of China, capturing Canton and Hankow before the end of the year. A possible clash with Britain, who feared that Chiang Kai-shek might do a deal with Russia or worse still with Japan, was at this stage a distinct possibility. The British Foreign Office, after deliberations with the Admiralty, considered the circumstances in which units of the fleet might have to be sent to Singapore, a course of action favoured by the Australian government. The prospect of hostilities in the Far East was clearly to the advantage of Germany.[69] Nevertheless in negotiations for a tripartite alliance the Japanese feared that, if it were directed against Britain and France, they might be involved in war with the United States. They still wanted an alliance directed mainly against the Soviet Union.[70]

Mussolini also had misgivings about an alliance. These were aggravated by the desire of the Germans in the South Tyrol for union with Germany which was vocally expressed after the *Anschluss*. No wonder that when Ribbentrop raised the question of an alliance late in October, Mussolini replied that the Italian people were not spiritually ripe to accept the idea.[71] Nevertheless, during the summer and autumn of 1938 the Fascist regime was assuming a new character, and this was to influence German–Italian relations. Already in 1937 laws against miscegenation had been introduced into Ethiopia and, for reasons of imperial prestige, also because the Jews favoured the League of Nations, and not merely to gratify Nazi Germany, anti-semitic legislation was introduced into Italy itself. The racial laws took effect on 10 November, the same day as *Kristallnacht*.[72]

This caused Hitler and his henchmen profound gratification. It now seemed that a real community of fate between the two dynamic regimes would solidify. A formal military alliance would mean that in North Africa alone

Italy would pin down 21 French divisions.[73] But Mussolini was suspicious of the western powers as well as of his German partner. When, for instance, Chamberlain and Halifax visited Paris on 23–24 November he mistakenly feared that Britain and France had already concluded an alliance against the Axis powers. This acted as an additional inducement for Italy to draw closer to Germany. But there were more sinister reasons which spoke in favour of an alliance. Mussolini always feared that if Germany defeated France or Britain, Italy at the peace conference might be cheated of the spoils of victory. A far worse contingency would arise if Hitler did a deal with the West before war broke out. Hence, Ribbentrop's visit to Paris on 6 December to sign a Treaty of Friendship was viewed with such suspicion in Rome that on 30 November a crisis with France, which is described elsewhere, was deliberately staged in Rome. A propaganda war, accompanied by military preparations, ensued between Italy and France and was to continue from December until April 1939.[74]

Mussolini was determined at all costs not to subordinate the interests of his country to those of Germany. Suspicion was mutual and found expression in a memorandum, drawn up late in November by the German High Command, for military cooperation between the two countries. In it no mention was made of Mussolini's long-cherished ambition to invade Albania or of Hitler's intention to occupy the rump of Czechoslovakia.[75] But the German leadership no longer had such a compelling reason to fear that an alliance might embroil Germany in war on account of a rash unilateral Italian move in the Mediterranean. The Anglo–Italian April Agreements, providing for the reduction of Italian troops from Spain, came into force in November. This meant that if Italy were involved in war it would primarily be against France, in which case Britain could not, as was feared earlier in 1938, scuttle the Mediterranean and concentrate her fleet in the North Sea and Atlantic.[76] Close partnership with Italy though, could still prove dangerous. In the middle of December Weizsäcker told Admiral Canaris, head of the *Abwehr*, that because of the planned German measures in the East, by which he meant action in the Ukraine, a conflict with Poland was inevitable. 'We have a preponderance over the Polish Army.' In such a conflict France and Britain would remain neutral. But if Italy exploited it by taking action against France, then a 'world war would not be improbable'. Later Weizsäcker had reason to assume that because of her military weakness Italy would not involve Germany in a war on her behalf.[77]

While Hitler's armaments and foreign policy were both being geared for war it is necessary to examine whether by adroit propaganda he could wean his people from a hankering after a peaceful existence and enlist their support for a forward policy based on *Boden* (soil) which meant that Germany needed food-producing and industrial areas, and *Blut* (blood), the liberation of racial Germans from foreign oppression and the elimination of 'contagious political and physical diseases' borne by 'undesirable' ethnic groups.

There is evidence to suggest that by 1938 Hitler himself was coming round to the view that his own aims were ceasing to correspond with social reality and that he was trying to put the clock back. This might have been an additional reason for his bringing forward the date for armed action. Admittedly after 1933 there was a marked increase in the number of marriages. But, despite the rise in the birthrate, Hitler on 5 November 1937 complained that sterility was settting in not only in Austria and the Sudetenland but in the Reich.[78] For additional reasons all talk of *Lebensraum* in the East was making less sense. The number of Germans living on the frontier with Poland was on the decrease while the number of the Poles to the east of the frontier was rising. Moreover, while those Germans still living in Poland were being Polonised, German farmers in Pomerania were marrying Poles.[79] But oblivious to these facts, Hitler and his intimates left no doubt that territory had to be acquired, first to provide Germany with food, which had become a matter of some urgency after the 1937 recession, second, in order to establish the infrastructure for a vast armaments programme. The acquisition of Austria, Czechoslovakia and parts of Poland would provide Germany with the finance, labour and raw materials to make a start on the programme. But if Germany were to make a bid for world power, then the raw materials of the Donetz Basin and the oil of the Caucasus were needed.[80]

Expansion beyond the areas occupied predominantly by ethnic Germans posed a problem in that it would lead to a contradiction in Hitler's equation between territory and population on which he laid such stress. The equation can be stated simply. Late in 1938 he boasted that the population of Germany was racially purer and more cohesive than that of the USA, Britain, France and Russia, and he produced figures to prove his point. In this mathematical exercise he wisely omitted Japan.[81] If, even before the outbreak of war, the influx of foreign workers was, according to Hitler's critics, beginning to jeopardise his racial policy, what would happen if Germany expanded? The number of helots would increase and the population become less homogeneous.[82]

A further problem arose as a result of the incorporation of Austria and the Sudetenland. However much the inhabitants of these areas welcomed their liberation, Hitler was fully aware that they had lost their traditional symbols and local identity. He told the newcomers on 30 January 1939 that just as primitive German tribesmen of the past had to transfer their loyalty to the German nation, local particularism in modern times would have to be transcended by something of greater value, size and durability.[83]

In spite of systematic indoctrination and coercion it cannot be claimed that in 1938–9 a binding consensus existed between the regime and population. Before 1939 there were no Navy Leagues, no voluntary associations of farmers and artisans clamouring for *Lebensraum*. There was no war fever, no mass anti-semitism, little 'hurrah' patriotism. But the National Socialist leadership exerted a remarkable degree of social control and it optimistically thought that it could divert such popular discontent as existed from protest to war and expansion. Nowhere is this more pronounced than in the view it adopted to economic hardship in rural areas.[84]

Many party ideologues were convinced that the fundamental character (*Lebenssubstanz*) of the regime was in some way represented by those classes living in the country, and it was precisely these who were most severely hit by the 1938 economic crisis. One group, led by Walter Darré, known as the agrarian radicals, were especially concerned with conditions on the land and, as far back as the 1920s, they had favoured the acquisition of *Lebensraum* in the East for German warrier farmers.[85] By 1938 these and like-minded party men had won a formidable ally in the person of Heinrich Himmler, head of the SS.

Himmler was more than a cold-blooded executioner. He was fully aware of the need to overcome social distress. By the end of 1938 both the coercive and political powers of the SS were tightened and extended. On 2 July 1938 the *Volksdeutsche Mittelstelle*, concerned with ethnic Germans living outside the Reich, was given greater powers. While it came under Himmler's personal command, it took its orders either from Hitler personally or from the Foreign Ministry.[86] It acted as one pressure group among others in the formulation and implementation of policy.

Himmler, now in command of the entire police with an elaborate network of agents at his disposal, made himself the spokesman of the rural population. In an address of 8 November 1938 to senior SS officers, which was evidently attended by Ribbentrop, he declared: 'We suffer today to a dangerous degree because of the flight from the land. Our industrial expansion soaks up the good blood from the land.'[87] As a result those who remained on the land, especially women, were so overworked that they were incapable of or had little inclination for procreation. He mentioned two stop-gap solutions: the commitment of troops, the Labour Service and the Hitler Youth to harvest the crops as well as new time-saving devices in industry. This would enable people to leave the towns for the country. After this exodus had gained momentum there would not be enough land to go round. Therefore the forcible annexation of territory, preferably in those areas immediately adjoining the Reich, where there were already nuclei of racial Germans, was imperative.[88] Significantly, Himmler expressed no interest in the Donetz Basin and the Caucasus which were of value for raw materials but contained no racial Germans.[89] Possibly because Ribbentrop was present, he did not discuss specific goals of future foreign policy. He explicitly declared, however, that the occupation of Austria and the Sudetenland constituted nothing more or less than the base for the great German empire of the future. It would be the 'greatest empire established by mankind and which the earth has ever seen'. The war that would inevitably bring it into being would not be that contest between states, which had only been postponed at Munich, but a life and death struggle against the Jews, Freemasons and the churches. This war would break out within the next ten years and prove of long duration. Using the first person singular he declared that the Jews were the negation of everything he stood for. Unless they were annihilated by Germany and Italy, these countries themselves would, in the event of a defeat, be annihilated. If victorious the Jews would kill off not only every National Socialist in Germany but every single person with a German mother.[90] While Himmler spoke of the liquidation of the Jews as a central war aim, Germany's mission for the present was to act as the centre for the dissemination of anti-semitism in the world at large and as the home of the Aryan race.

The Jews, however, were not the only danger to the survival and purity of the German race. In his mind nothing was more dangerous than if ethnic Germans, living abroad, allowed themselves to be assimilated by the host country, above all if they were Slavs. To obviate this danger Germans and other members of the Nordic race were, where possible, to be enticed into leaving their host countries and living in Germany. 'The German Reich is the home of Nordic blood.' The Reich 'is the strongest magnet through which German blood could be attracted'.[91] Paradoxically, while Himmler was advocating the homecoming of ethnic Germans before additional *Lebensraum* had been conquered, the *Volksdeutsche Mittelstelle* was ordered to implement a policy which seemed to be at variance to Himmler's principles. Its head, Dr W. Behrends, was, on Hitler's orders, reminded that those Germans still living inside the frontiers of Czechoslovakia were not to leave the country. They and other pockets of Germans in eastern Europe were to remain in their respective countries where they would later assist the authorities in restructuring society on German lines.[92]

The racial Germans in Poland constituted an exceptionally delicate problem. They numbered approximately 1,951,000 and, according to Jacobsen, they felt left in the lurch on account of the German–Polish Treaty of Friendship of January 1934. Henceforward, for reasons of political expediency, they were given little help from the authorities of the Reich to resist the process of Polonisation.[93] After Munich a new problem arose. Approximately 15,000 impoverished Polish Jews, then living in the Reich, were forcibly expatriated. While the Polish authorities treated them as humanely as circumstances permitted, they retaliated by threatening to expel German citizens living in Poland.[94] They also intensified the process of the Polonisation of the German minority. Early in November the *Volksdeutsche Mittelstelle*, which acted as spokesman for this minority, presented Ribbentrop with a report describing their 'intolerable situation' and requested intervention on their behalf. The report was brought to the attention of Hitler, who commented that he 'did not intend to put up any longer with the conduct of our eastern neighbours towards his fellow Germans'. But Hitler took no action. No wonder that early in 1939 the German minority in Poland remained bitterly opposed to the idea of a German–Polish agreement on concerted action against the Soviet Ukraine in return for a guarantee of Poland's western frontier. This agreement would put an end to their national identity, their *Deutschtum*.[95]

Political expediency, as for instance in the South Tyrol, and later military necessity, were later to determine Hitler's policy towards racial Germans and to vindicate Himmler's principles as outlined on 8 November. After the Non-Aggression Pact with Russia was concluded in August 1939 those Germans living in the Baltic States and Bessarabia were left with no choice but to return to the Reich. Germany's new frontiers in Poland, on the other hand, after the outbreak of war, were to include most of the German minority in Poland. For every German coloniser two Slavs or Jews had to be expelled or liquidated. After the attack on Russia in June 1941 German control was extended to those areas where the Jews of eastern Europe were highly concentrated.[96] For geographical reasons therefore Himmler's ideas on extending the areas for Germanisation and for exterminating Jews and Slavs were closely related. The acquisition of soil and the purification of blood were part of the same process.

It is significant that Himmler dropped no hint of the imminence of the great pogrom, *Kristallnacht*. He was evidently only informed of the fact on the evening of the 9th.[97] It should not be supposed that Himmler's ideas of *Lebensraum* corresponded in every respect with those of other paladins of the regime, among whom there was much infighting. Although Alfred Rosenberg stood on the fringe of the small circle of top men, he could occasionally perform useful tasks. Instead of colonising the East on a large scale, Rosenberg laid stress on encouraging national liberation movements within the territories of the Baltic States, Soviet Russia and Poland. In this way he hoped that the process of the 'decomposition' of Soviet Society could be hastened. He cooperated with the *Abwehr* and resented the fact that in November Himmler was made responsible for propaganda directed from the Reich in favour of the Carpatho-Ukraine.[98]

Göring and members of his staff, working on the Four-Year Plan, had their own ideas on *Lebensraum*. As far back as 1937 they were planning how to integrate Polish Silesia into the economy of the Reich. Their plans were to be intensified in April 1939.[99] Conservatives outside the party, such as Weizsäcker and members of the Army High Command, as well as Goerdeler, later leader of the opposition, had no time for Poland. They believed that Germany should have approximately her pre–1914 frontiers in the East. They were, however, resolutely opposed to the expulsion or annihilation of the Slav inhabitants. While Schacht and the financiers stood for informal imperialism and sought economic control over Europe, they welcomed Hitler's demand for the return of colonies in full sovereignity, which was first made in December 1935, and repeated at the end of 1938.[100] The eastward thrust of Hitler's policy, which appealed mainly to party members and the *SS*, stands out in directives issued by Hitler himself or by the Foreign Ministry, to the local press and party organisations through a special office controlled by a certain Georg Dertinger. On

10 November Hitler told Dertinger: 'Germany's claims for domination over territory which are bestowed on her by fate, lie naturally in the East'. Austria and the Sudetenland were 'the first two courses of the meal'. Others were to follow. Hitler made it plain to Dertinger that he had gone over to a policy of imperialism (a word to be reserved for private conversation).[101]

Although Hitler was determined on establishing a new German empire he could still use the principle of self-determination to Germany's advantage. But the principle had now acquired a new meaning. Until the middle of September 1938 Hitler had addressed his appeals almost exclusively to the Sudeten Germans and he thereby won considerable sympathy in London. But even before the Bad Godesberg meeting of 23 September he realised that he could not dismember the Czech state if Germany were merely to obtain the fringe areas. He therefore turned to Czechoslovakia's external and internal enemies. Because the Poles were active in asserting their claims, they were rewarded handsomely with the town of Teschen and its environs as well as areas to which Germany had a better claim. The Hungarians, on the other hand, who were anxious to improve their relations with Yugoslavia in the summer of 1938, proved sluggish and thus became dependent on German generosity.[102] Paradoxically, while those Germans still living in Czechoslovakia were explicitly ordered to stop all agitation in favour of incorporation into the Reich, the Slovaks and the inhabitants of the Carpatho–Ukraine on the eastern areas of Czechoslovakia were granted autonomy.[103] Partly to remain on good terms with the Romanians, whose communications with Prague ran through the Carpatho–Ukraine and who feared Hungary, partly to keep the Poles guessing on Germany's future moves, Czechoslovakia was grudgingly allowed to exist as an independent hyphenated state, provided that she disowned Beneš's policy and cut her links with France and Russia.[104]

Despite disagreements between his lieutenants[105] there was, from Hitler's point of view, much to be said in favour of keeping open his options for eastern Europe. While the Soviet Union remained weak and isolated, the western powers had suffered such a devastating blow to their prestige after Munich that the whole area between Germany's eastern and Russia's western frontiers from the Baltic to the Black Sea seemed to be open to German penetration or subjugation. Eventually this area could be converted into a great springboard for a military advance into Russia.[106]

There was one relatively powerful state which had still to be persuaded to accept Hitler's plans. During the Czech crisis, at a time when the Polish government was still proving 'cooperative', Hitler brushed aside a Polish proposal to discuss the future of Danzig and the Corridor in return for a guarantee of the German–Polish frontier. On 23 October, when Hitler's attention was no longer fully absorbed with Czechoslovakia, discussions were opened between Ribbentrop and Colonel Joseph Beck, the Polish foreign minister, in Warsaw and resumed on 19 November. It was believed in Berlin that the Poles might be prepared to compromise over Danzig as well as over German communications across the Corridor.[107] Significantly Ribbentrop did not raise the question of the future of Polish Upper Silesia, which previously had belonged to Germany and which was rich in coke. One factor was to cause real optimism in Berlin. After Ribbentrop met Bonnet, the French foreign minister, in Paris on 6 December 1938, he formed the impression that the French had written off their allies in eastern Europe, which included Poland.[108] There were also encouraging indications on Britain's attitude. Reports from von Dirksen, German ambassador in London, received early in January, indicated that while Britain suspected future German policy in the West she would stand aloof if Germany sought expansion in whichever direction she chose in eastern Europe.[109]

When Beck arrived in Berlin for further negotiations in January 1939 Hitler told him that he was not interested in the Ukraine. He added that his policy was not only directed against the Comintern but against Russia itself. But neither Hitler nor Ribbentrop, when negotiations were resumed later in January, succeeded in persuading Beck that Poland should join the Anti-Comintern Pact. To do so would have been tantamount to an abdication by Poland of her status as a sovereign state with control over her own foreign policy.[110] At this stage Beck believed that if he took a firm line Poland would eventually break free from her isolation. He hoped to achieve this by a visit to London in mid-March. He had one reason to be hopeful about the outcome of this visit. His country was already winning sympathy from an unexpected quarter.

There was considerable sympathy in the USA for Poland. The idea that Poland should have a corridor to the sea was not only provided for in the Treaty of Versailles but formed part of Wilson's Fourteen Points. Colonel Beck was also on especially friendly terms with the American ambassador, Anthony Biddle, who gave Poland a good press in Washington. Biddle had a formidable ally in William Bullitt, American ambassador in Paris who in turn was on really close terms with Roosevelt. Bullitt was also kept informed by the Polish ambassador, Lukasiewicz, on the state of German–Polish relations. By December 1938 Biddle recognised that Poland was threatened by Germany and that she would fight, if necessarily, alone.[111] Hitler seems to have been aware of American sympathy towards Poland, for in his talks with Beck and Lipski, Poland's ambassador in Berlin, early in January he missed no opportunity of castigating Roosevelt.[112] Later the German Foreign Ministry became thoroughly suspicious of Biddle.[113]

By 26 January German–Polish negotiations had reached deadlock. But even at this stage Hitler was not thinking of war with Poland: the German occupation of Danzig which was planned since October would, Hitler thought, face Beck with a *fait accompli* which would render it easier for him to persuade his countrymen that there was no alternative other than making territorial concessions.[114]

Also towards the end of January there was a switch of emphasis in German propaganda which eventually contributed towards a new *Ostpolitik*. Despite a few disparaging references to Soviet Communism in connection with the Spanish Civil War, as well as in Germany's relations with Japan and Hungary, Hitler in his speech of 30 January was remarkably quiet about Russia. This might have resulted from a press truce informally agreed on in October 1938.

Economic interests, as represented by Göring, also spoke in favour of better relations with Russia.[115] Moreover, high-ranking army officers were far less averse to war with Poland in 1939 than with Czechoslovakia in 1938. Some of them were born within the frontiers of post-war Poland and they looked gleefully forward to seeing the reversal of the territorial status quo. How else could this be achieved except in cooperation with Russia? Hitler might not have been fully aware of how strong this anti–Polish feeling was, and he perhaps feared that the influence of men such as General Ludwig Beck, who had opposed war in 1938, would prevail if a new military operation should be decided on. At all events, late in January, shortly before new operational plans were drawn up, Hitler started to curry the favour of the officer corps. Not only did he subject them to homilies on German racial superiority, which have already been discussed, but he praised their traditions and spent a few days at Bismarck's estate in Friedrichsruh. He even went so far as to tell them that, if the party betrayed him, army officers would stand by him with swords drawn. Flattered by Hitler's attention, General von Brauchitsch, the com-mander-in-chief of the army, succeeded, to the intense annoyance of Himmler, in conferring military privileges on the *SA*. The officer corps was now being tamed and was all the more ready to accept a tougher line against Poland.[116]

In the second half of January Hitler had to revise his policy towards Prague in the light of worsening relations with Poland. In the previous November German authorities went so far as to cooperate with the Czechs in taking counter-measures against Polish subversion in the Carpatho-Ukraine, and in the middle of February Hitler for the second time had to stop the Hungarians from entering the territory, a course of action which would have found favour in Rome, Warsaw and Moscow.[117] He was, however, determined on a German military occupation of Slovakia, for this would enable German forces to threaten Poland on her long, exposed southern frontier. So far Hitler had no reason to suspect that this operation would seriously jeopardise relations with the western powers. In fact the Cabinet in London considered that Czechoslovakia had alienated her independence.[118] A. J. P. Taylor rightly contends that it was an event inside Germany itself, not a new course in foreign policy, which finally persuaded influential Britons that appeasement should be abandoned.[119]

On 4 November vom Rath, a member of the German embassy in Paris, was shot dead by Hershel Grynzpan, a Polish Jew, whose father had been sent back to Poland from Germany. On the 7th the German press told its readers to draw their own conclusions from this act. On 9–10 November Jewish shops and synagogues all over Germany were destroyed or pillaged. Approximately 100 Jews were killed and the police stood idly by.[120] The question arises who gave the order or the nod for the pogrom to go ahead? Late in the Czech crisis Joseph Goebbels, the propaganda minister, was out of favour for telling Hitler, in the presence of other leading men, that the German poeple were not ready for war. He was also involved in a sexual scandal which was the cause of a certain disgust, tempered by amusement.[121] Goebbels needed to get back into favour, and on the eve of the intended pogrom spoke to certain party and SA leaders. He was ordered not openly to urge resort to violence, for the fiction of legality had to be preserved. But Goebbels did not act entirely on his own volition. Hitler himself regarded 9 November, the anniversary of the abdication of the Kaiser in 1918, as the day of infamy and he certainly favoured the action. The pogrom marks a turning point in his foreign policy. He now quite openly told foreign diplomats that while National Socialism was not for export anti-semitism was. In this connection he mentioned a number of states such as Italy, Hungary, Romania and Poland which were becoming anti-semitic. [Up to November 1938 Poland actually had more stringently discriminatory anti-Jewish legislation than NS Germany. *Ed.*] And on account of the recession he was not altogether wrong in taking this view. Provided that those Jews who were deported were first thoroughly pauperised before reaching their destination, the spread of anti-semitism was, so he thought, assured.[122] Hitler, however, did not disguise his belief that the Jews only wanted to transfer their financial assets from Germany to other countries. They themselves wanted to stay in Europe and not to emigrate. The reason for this, he said, was simple. The Jews regarded themselves as the vanguard of revolutionary communism. 'World Jewry in no way wishes that the Jews should vanish from Europe', Hitler told Pirow, the South African minister of defence, on 24 November 1938.[123] In a talk with the Czech foreign minister, Chvalkovsky, on 21 January he went a stage further. 'The Jews must be destroyed by us. The Jews did not create the 9th of November for nothing. This day will be avenged.' Hitler had used equally vitriolic language in his recent conversation with Beck.[124] On 30 January 1939 Hitler threw down the gauntlet. He told the Reichstag that he had at one time prophesied that he would come to power in Germany. The Jews had merely laughed. 'Today I will again be a prophet. If international Jewish finance, both inside and outside Europe, succeeds in driving the nations once again into a world war, the result will not be the Bolshevization of the earth and thus victory of Jewry but the annihilation of the Jews as a race in Europe.' In uttering these words Hitler had proved that if ever there was such a person 'as the liar who spoke the truth' it was indeed himself.[125]

Roosevelt's reaction to Hitler's speech, which was also bitterly anti-American, was much more spirited than Chamberlain's. This is partly to be explained by the fact that both Chamberlain and Halifax had decided after 10 November that Hitler's policy of anti-semitism was a domestic German issue which precluded intervention by his Majesty's Government. Hence, Hitler's hostile reference to the Jews made little impact in London. Chamberlain, however, was pleased to learn that Hitler lodged no ultimatum for the return of colonies and he took pleasure in the fact that Hitler wanted to increase trade. He therefore took a sanguine view of the future of Anglo-German relations. Throughout February and early March he continued to regard Hitler's Germany as a normal state with which agreements could be concluded. Sir Nevile Henderson, the British ambassador in Berlin, shared Chamberlain's views and this caused intense annoyance in

Washington. Halifax, it must be admitted, favoured a stronger line in opposing Hitler.[126]

After *Kristallnacht* indignation among most sections of the American public was so strong that Roosevelt had to recall the American ambassador from Berlin. The American government once more intensified rearmament, especially that of the air force. While Roosevelt was still strongly aware of isolationist feeling in Congress, he was determined to galvanise the British and French into resisting the dictators. On 17 November 1938 an economic treaty was concluded between the USA and Britain. Next month Chamberlain was informed by Roosevelt, through a mutual friend, a certain Colonel Arthur Murray, that if Britain and France became involved in war to resist aggression they could depend on receiving support from the vast resources of the United States. This assurance was heartily welcomed by Chamberlain. The French, too, were especially in need of American aircraft and hoped for the continuation of deliveries in time of war, after the expected revision of the Neutrality Acts had been passed by Congress.[127] On 4 January Roosevelt in his State of the Union address strongly condemned the dictatorships and spoke of measures short of war to resist them. While this statement was welcomed noisily by the Polish press, it infuriated but did not deter Hitler.[128]

American aid to the western democracies could take several forms: the exchange of technical information in staff talks; an embargo on German imports on the grounds that they were subsidised. Hitler dismissed the second danger by declaring on 30 January that if there was to be an economic war Germany and not the flabby democracies would prove victorious. This is the context in which he used the words 'export or die' in his Reichstag speech. Above all the American Fleet, which between May 1938 and April 1939 was concentrated in the Atlantic, partly as a warning against a pro-Fascist coup in Brazil, partly against the Axis powers in Europe, could be sent to the Pacific where the Japanese were menacingly poised to pounce on areas, rich in raw materials, in south-east Asia. By January Halifax fully recognised Britain's strategic dependence on the United States.[129]

But however sympathetic Roosevelt personally might have been to Britain and France, the isolationist senators, who were a strong pressure group, would not allow America to be involved in war merely for the protection of the British or French empires. Nearer to American hearts were the states of Latin America which were exposed to the repercussions of the Spanish Civil War. It was, for instance, feared in Washington that a Franco-style coup might succeed in Brazil and that the Germans or Italians might subsequently use north-east Brazil for an attack on the Panama Canal.[130] There was also an economic threat in that 80 per cent of Argentine's exports were with Europe, mainly Germany. If Germany gained mastery over Europe she could use the threat of cutting imports as a means of making Argentine subservient to Germany. Late in January Roosevelt feared that by economic means alone Germany could pose a threat to the United States 'without having landed a single soldier on American soil'.[131]

Roosevelt, no less than Chamberlain and Halifax, might have been well off the mark in his assessment of Hitler's immediate intentions. But the danger was real. The fact, unknown to their military staffs, that Hitler was accelerating plans for the construction of a great battle fleet and a strategic air force, which were intended to be completed by 1944, constituted an unknown but genuine future threat not only to the British and French empires but also to the western hemisphere. Hitler the man was even more dangerous than Hitler the ghost.

After the occupation of Hainan off French Indo-China by the Japanese on 10 February and further provocation from Italy the French, who needed American aircraft, sent alarmist reports to Washington about the existence of a world-wide Axis conspiracy. Although there is no evidence to suggest that Germany, Italy and Japan were in fact concerting their actions, a number of coincidences created the impression that this was the case. It can therefore be claimed that the Rome, Berlin, Tokyo Axis acted as if it existed.[132]

Early in 1939 a new factor was to influence Roosevelt's policy. Hitherto he had listened to the advice of Brüning, a former Reich chancellor, Schacht and the Nazi 'moderates' on likely changes in German policy. But in 1938 more determined opponents of the regime took to the field. There can be no gainsaying that Goerdeler and other members of the opposition were appalled by the downright criminality of Hitler's regime. Before 10 November they were aware of the adverse effects at home and abroad of the continued detention of Pastor Martin Niemoeller. Hitler therefore devoted a large part of his Reichstag speech of 30 January to defence of his church policy.[133] Far more serious was the systematic brutality of *Kristallnacht* and its sequel. Hitler, as we have seen, was fully aware of the moral attitude of those 'overbred intellectuals' who condemned his policy. The opposition courageously warned the British and Americans of the dangers which lay ahead. By 26 November the Foreign Office evidently obtained the full text of Hitler's address to the press of 10 November from a certain Count von Toggenburg. On 26 January, at a time when Hitler was giving a series of pep talks to army officers on German racial superiority, a report by Lieutenant Colonel Gerhard von Schwerin, the new head of the British empire section of the army intelligence *Fremde Heere West* was sent to Halifax. It was discussed by the Cabinet on 1 February. Schwerin claimed that Hitler's aim was world conquest.[134]

As a result of information from Germany the Cabinet and Foreign Office came to some interesting, but at times inaccurate, conclusions, not only in Hitler's plans but on his personality. Writing on 19 December 1938 Gladwyn Jebb, private secretary to Cadogan, the permanent under-secretary of state for foreign affairs, correctly maintained that Hitler regarded Germany's domination over Europe as a step to world domination. Jebb went on to say that Hitler was 'barely sane', and 'consumed by an insensate hatred of this country'.[135] In this he was mistaken. Even Chamberlain, who was willing to give Hitler the benefit of the doubt, to a greater extent than Halifax, confided in mid-December 1938 to Colonel Murray that having met Hitler at Munich, 'I see that he is a man who gets an idea in his head and the idea swells and swells until it gets near to bursting'. Chamberlain believed that the army, but not Hitler, might respond to a deterrent such as a trade embargo.[136] But Chamberlain also failed to appreciate that Hitler could use his oratorical gifts to tame his generals and that he was still quite capable of weighing the balance of advantage before taking action.

Meanwhile Goerdeler was distributing to his British contacts hair-raising reports on likely German action. Hitler allegedly was pushing Italy into war with France. He either intended launching an air attack on London, or an invasion of the Low Countries and Switzerland, as a prelude to an offensive in the West. The date given for such action was the second half of February.[137] So exaggerated were these reports that, perhaps unknown to Goerdeler, they were fabricated. Their authors, however, were so well acquainted with the kind of information which was calculated to make the blood of British decision-makers curdle that, as suggested by D. C. Watt, they must have emanated from those who were in responsible positions. At all events the reports provided an additional stimulus for the Cabinet in London to take immediate precautions for air defence and for raising the size of the army.[138]

On 10 January Halifax sent a copy of an alarming report to Roosevelt who later received one directly from Goerdeler. Having received it Roosevelt could not give the British additional assurances due to an air crash involving a French official which was to cause an outcry from the isolationists.[139] Nevertheless, the expectation of American support at a future date made it easier for the British and the French to start, very cautiously, to assume new commitments. Early in February it was decided by the British Cabinet (which for some years expected war in 1939) that if the Netherlands or Switzerland were attacked by Germany, and if these powers resisted, they could count on receiving British military aid. No such intervention would take place if Hitler's troops entered Czechoslovakia, which allegedly had alienated its independence, or if they entered Memel. Later, as Weinberg correctly maintains, any power, regardless of its geographical location, would receive military aid if attacked, provided it put up a fight.[140] In February, after the crisis had died down, Chamberlain hoped that Britain, who had implemented her Agreements with Italy of April 1938 in November, could assuage the French and detach Italy from Germany.[141] He was to be disappointed. On 30 January Hitler declared in his Reichstag speech that if a third party were to pick a quarrel with Italy, regardless of the motive, and use it as a pretext for going to war, Germany would stand by Italy.[142] Now that he was sure of German support, Mussolini became all the more bellicose, and on 4 February he discussed with his generals and officials plans for a war with France which he expected would break out in 1942.[143] In answer to Hitler's declaration Chamberlain informed the House of Commons on 6 February that if France were subject to an Italian attack she could count on British cooperation. The British were not ready for staff talks with the French and soon decided to send a more substantial expeditionary force to France.[144]

The chain of the events leading up to the German occupation of Prague on 15 March and its repercussions has been discussed elsewhere.[145] Here one neglected subject needs attention. Late in 1938 it was still feared in Moscow that Germany might either come to an agreement with Poland and launch an attack on Russia and partition the Ukraine or that German troops might invade Poland as a first step towards their gaining control over the whole of the Ukraine. Mutual fear of Ukrainian nationalism, which was being stirred up by several German agencies from the Carpatho-Ukraine itself and by the Vienna and other radio stations in the Reich, had brought about that short-lived Russo–Polish rapprochement which found expression in the renewal of the 1932 Non-Aggression Pact late in November 1938.[146]

The Soviet leadership at that time not only distrusted German intentions towards the Ukraine but, with some justification, believed that the British and French were at best indifferent to the problem.[147] This suspicion was ventilated openly in the famous speech delivered by Stalin to the XVIII Party Congress of 10 March 1939. Although he attacked the Axis powers for warmongering, he also chastised the western powers for their policy of 'non-intervention' which he described as 'something very like encouragement of the aggressor'. In saying this Stalin clearly had the Ukraine in mind. According to E. H. Carr, the speech 'was an extraordinary astute exercise in political tight-rope walking'.[148] Hitler realised that a rift was now opening between Russia and the West. After some hesitation, and to the dismay of both Rosenberg and the *Abwehr*, who promoted Ukrainian nationalism, Hitler refused to accord independence to the Carpatho-Ukraine which it enjoyed for one day only. On 12 March he decided to hand it over to the tender mercies of Hungary, whose government would take no nonsense from Ukrainian nationalists.[149] Late in March Hitler told General Brauchitsch that if war broke out with Poland Germany did not intend an invasion of the Ukraine.[150]

This change of German policy, news of which almost certainly reached Stalin, had immediate international repercussions. The Romanians, who were anxious to annex at least a part of the Carpatho-Ukraine for themselves, now feared that Hungarian irredentism, having succeeded in former Czechoslovak territory, would next be directed against their own country. But the people most immediately affected were the Western Ukrainians. They formed the largest minority in Poland and were concentrated mainly in Eastern Galicia. After 15 March they felt betrayed, and they vented their rage on the Organization of Ukrainian Nationalists (OUN), a body supported by the *Abwehr*, and their German protectors. The Ukrainian problem was now taken out of German–Soviet relations.[151]

As a result of the German decision on the Carpatho-Ukraine, the community of interest between Russia and Poland came to an end. Whether either Hitler or Stalin would go a stage further and seek a real rapprochement depended on whether the Poles would reject the German demands; the reactions of the western powers to the events of 15 March; developments on the Soviet–Japanese frontier. German–Polish negotiations finally broke down on 26 March. At the end of the month Dertinger's press office reported: 'The compass points at Poland, Poland carries within herself the seeds of death'.[152]

Soon after 15 March the British Cabinet, but not the service chiefs, regarded Romania and Poland as more reliable as allies than the Soviet Union. Halifax was also aware that if no guarantee were given to either country, the USA, which was now thoroughly disillusioned by Chamberlain's optimism as regards appeasement, might not support Britain or France in the event of a fresh crisis. Subsequently Beck, through two sources, Biddle in Warsaw and Ian Colvin, a British journalist, requested a guarantee from the British. Chamberlain complied on 31 March.[153] Although it cannot be determined with precision which came first, the British guarantee of Poland or Hitler's decision to invade that country, which, according to Henke, seems to have been taken reluctantly, the British Cabinet was sufficiently aware that Hitler could only be prevented from striking in whatever direction he chose if he knew that armed resistance must automatically be expected from Britain and France. Indeed, the Cabinet in London was right in supposing that if Hitler feared anything it was a war on two fronts. Chamberlain might have been ill-advised not to have consulted his service chiefs before giving the guarantee, but given the way Hitler was behaving, the guarantee was certainly not a 'deliberate challenge' to Germany.[154] While it was intended as a deterrent it did not close the door to negotiations and appeasement.

As a result of the Italian occupation of Albania and complex diplomatic manoeuvring, which has been described elsewhere, the British and the French guaranteed Greece and Romania on 13 April. The United States Fleet was ordered to sail for the Pacific on the 16th. That day Mussolini was informed by Göring that a Russo–German agreement was in the offing.[155] The realignments, already perceptible in April 1939, were to harden in subsequent months and pave the way to the coming of the Second World War.

7. Hitler's War aims

H. R. TREVOR-ROPER

Hitler's war aims are written large and clear in the documents of his reign. They are quite different from the war aims of the men who, in 1933, admitted him to power and who, after 1933, served him in power. They are also, in my opinion, different from the aims which have sometimes been ascribed to him by historians who regard him as a mere power-loving opportunist. In this essay I wish to show these differences. I shall do so with the aid of four personal sources. Other more casual documents could easily be used to confirm these sources, but for the present I will be content with these four.

These four sources to which I refer are, first, *Mein Kampf*, Hitler's personal credo, written in prison in 1924 after the total collapse of his first bid for power; secondly, Hermann Rauschning's *Gespräche mit Hitler*, which were first published in 1939 and are the record of Hitler's private political conversations at the time of his second and successful bid, that is, in 1932–4; thirdly, the official record of Hitler's *Tischgespräche*, at the time of his apparently universal military triumph in 1941–2; and, finally, the similar record, discovered last year and still unpublished in Germany, of his *Tischgespräche* at the time when he first acknowledged final defeat, in February 1945. These four documents are like four windows, opened, by different hands, into the inmost recesses of Hitler's mind at four crucial moments of his career: the moments of political defeat, political triumph, military triumph, military defeat. The first window was flung wide open by himself: it was his challenge to the

First published in German in *Vierteljahrshefte für Zeitgeschichte* (Munich, 1960).

world to show that he did not accept the defeat of 1918.
The second he would no doubt have preferred to keep shut:
in 1932–4 he had no wish to publish his radical programme
before he had built up the political and military base that
was to sustain it; it was an enemy's, or rather a traitor's
hand which opened it. The last two windows were opened
by Hitler himself, but privately. The world was intended to
look in, but not yet. Posterity, not the present generation,
was to see the secret of his triumph, the cause of his defeat.

Now the interesting thing about all these documents is
that though spread over a period of 22 years, and issued in
these very different circumstances, they all show an absolute
consistency of philosophy and purpose. This consistency,
this purpose has often been denied. It was denied at the
time by those, in Germany and abroad, who wished to
disbelieve it: whether, like some western statesmen, they
feared to contemplate this hideous new power or, like some
German statesmen, they hoped to harness it to their own
more limited aims; and it has been denied since, by
historians who are so revolted by Hitler's personal character,
by the vulgarity and cruelty of his mind, that they refuse to
allow him such virtues as mental power and consistency.
But in fact I believe that all these denials are wrong. The
statesmen were proved wrong by events. The historians, in
my opinion (though they include some distinguished names
among my own compatriots – Sir Lewis Namier, Alan
Bullock, A. J. P. Taylor) err by confusing moral with
intellectual judgments. That Hitler's mind was vulgar and
cruel I readily agree; but vulgarity and cruelty are not
inconsistent with power and consistency.

Let us take first the evidence of *Mein Kampf*, once the
most widely distributed though by no means the most
widely read book after the Bible. The dreadful jargon in
which *Mein Kampf* is written, its hysterical tone and
shameless propaganda, should not blind us to the crude but
real mental power which underlies it. The book is the
expression of a political philosophy fully formed. In it Hitler
declares himself to be a student of history convinced by his
studies that a new age of history is now about to begin. He
also declares clearly what kind of an age this will be. The

age of small, maritime powers ruling the world through sea-communications, seapower and the wealth built up by overseas colonisation, he says, is now closing. With them, the whole world that they have created must gradually dissolve. Instead of distant overseas colonies, which have become useless, power will now depend on great land-masses such as modern techniques can now at last mobilise. Moreover, thanks to those same techniques, whatever power succeeds in mobilising such land-masses can base upon them a lasting empire. The only question is, what power can mobilise them first? When he asks himself this question, Hitler obviously has in mind only two powers, Germany and Russia. In 1923 both Germany and Russia were defeated powers. Was it conceivable that either of them could rise from such defeat to seize this unique historical opportunity?

To an outsider, without faith, it might well seem that neither Germany nor Russia was equipped for such a task. But Hitler had faith. He believed that Germany could do it. Not Weimar Germany of course, defeated, demoralised, disarmed. Nor even monarchist Germany: the monarchy was too weak. It has had its chance and failed. History has condemned it. Moreover, it is also too conservative. The monarchists aim only at restoration, the restoration of the frontiers of 1914, the colonies of 1914. But the frontiers of 1914, says Hitler, are anachronistic in the new age, and so are the colonies: such an ambition is, to him, meaningless and contemptible. 'Monarchies', he would say later, 'serve to keep empires; only revolutions can conquer them.' And so, in 1923, Hitler advocated a revolution: not a mere palace revolution, but a historic revolution, comparable with the Russian revolution: a revolution which would release a new historic force. Moreover, Hitler made it perfectly clear that he was himself the demiurge of such a revolution. He was, he said, one of those world-phenomena which occur only at rare intervals in time, at once philosophers able to understand and practical politicians able to exploit the turning-points of world history. If only he could obtain power, Hitler wrote in 1924, he would create, out of German nationalism, now red and raw with defeat, a revolutionary force which would resume the historic mission of Germany and conquer, not distant colonies, the chimera of Wilhelmine Germany, but, from infamous Bolshevik Russia, the vast land-spaces of the East. To show his credentials, Hitler reminded his readers that his own first speech, in 1920, had been on this topic: he had spoken in praise of the 'infinite humanity' of the Treaty of Brest-Litovsk, whereby Germany had devoured the industrial heart of Russia, as against the shocking brutality of the Treaty of Versailles, whereby she had lost her own industrial toenails.

The importance of *Mein Kampf* as a real declaration of Hitler's considered and practical war aims, even in 1924, is often overlooked. But it is shown by one small fact among many. Although every German was enabled and expected to read it, Hitler consistently used his copyright to prevent any full translation, at least into English. The authorised English edition was a miserable abridgement, one-fifth of the full length, and it was not until 1939 that an English publisher broke the ban and published a pirated translation. And so English (and other) politicians and political writers consistently ignored the plain statements in *Mein Kampf*, or wishfully maintained either that Hitler did not mean what he said, or that he could not do what he meant. One notable exception was the distinguished English historian and publicist, the late Sir Robert Ensor. After 1933 Ensor consistently maintained that Hitler would make war, and in 1936 he declared roundly that he would annex Austria in the spring of 1938 and either cause a European war or a European surrender to avoid war over Czechoslovakia in the autumn of 1938. When his predictions were verified and he was asked to give his reasons, Ensor gave them: their starting-point was, 'I had the advantage – still too rare in England and then only just not unique – of having read *Mein Kampf* in the German'. I particularly remember this incident, because it was thanks to it that I also mustered the energy to read through the turgid pages of that barbarous, but important work.

If men would not take *Mein Kampf*, which Hitler himself had written, seriously, they would hardly pay much regard to Rauschning's revelations, whose authenticity could not be proved. [See pp. 13–14 above. *Ed.*] Indeed, I am told that, when they were published in 1939, Neville Chamberlain, obstinate in his illusions, declared that he simply didn't believe a word of it, but to anyone who has read *Mein Kampf*, Rauschning's revelation of Hitler's vast ambitions of world conquest has few surprises. Perhaps the most interesting thing about Rauschning's book is its date: the date both of its contents and of its publication. Its contents, being of 1932–4, show that the passage of ten years and the acquisition of power and its responsibilities had not reduced Hitler's vast and revolutionary aims in the least. The date of publication, 1939, shows that Rauschning was equally faithful in recording the expression of those aims. For in 1939 Hitler had made a pact with Russia in order to make war on Poland and the West. Many people in the West and in Germany accepted this pact as evidence that Hitler was now committed to the old, Bismarckian, *Kleindeutsch* programme. If Rauschning had really (as was said) merely written a topical work, he would hardly have included one passage, which then seemed false but which history has since shown to be true – but in fact he did include it. It is the passage in which Hitler, having repudiated the acquisition of colonies and disdained the pre-war frontiers of Germany, went on to speak of Russia. 'Perhaps I shall not be able to avoid an alliance with Russia' he said. 'I shall keep that as a trump-card. Perhaps it will be the decisive gamble of my life. . . . But it will never stop me from as firmly retracing my steps and attacking Russia when my aims in the west have been achieved. . . . We alone can conquer the great continental space, and it will be done by us singly and alone, not through a pact with Moscow. We shall take this struggle upon us. It will open to us the door to permanent mastery of the world.'

Thus from 1920 to 1939 Hitler's aims were clear: repudiation of colonies, repudiation of the old imperial frontiers (those, he said, were an ambition 'unworthy of our revolution'), and instead the creation of a revolutionary, nationalist force able to conquer permanently 'the great continental space' of Russia. In the face of this reiterated clarity, it seems odd to me that distinguished historians should insist that Hitler had no such consistent war aims: that F. H. Hinsley, for instance, in his work on *Hitler's Strategy*, should argue that Hitler only made war on Russia in 1941 in order to acquire the means of breaking the obstinacy of Britain, and that A. J. P. Taylor, reluctant to allow Hitler any consistency, should maintain that he had a series of interchangeable philosophies – i.e. convenient theories – which he would produce at will, as occasion required. Had he not, in *Mein Kampf*, spoken of the decisive struggle against France – *Frankreich muss vernichtet sein*? [A phrase not in *Mein Kampf*. *Ed.*] Would he not later speak of the decisive struggle against America? But since these historians use these arguments, let me answer them.

Of course it is true that, at different times, Hitler was prepared to say almost anything, and we can never believe anything to be true *merely* because he said it. However, since some of his statements of aims must have been true, even if at other times contradicted by him, we cannot reject everything out of hand: we must find a criterion of veracity. Now I believe that such a criterion is easily found. Hitler's statements of his aims can be accepted as true provided they are explicable not merely by immediate tactical necessity but, first, as part of a general philosophy regularly expressed even in adverse tactical circumstances, and secondly by long-term practical preparations. Once we apply these tests, Hitler's alternative 'philosophies' soon dissolve: only the philosophy of an eastern empire remains. If Hitler raged at France in 1923, that was merely because France was then the centre of a system of eastern alliances. As Göring explained to the American ambassador in 1937, 'the sole cause of friction with France was France's policy of building up alliances in eastern Europe to prevent Germany from achieving her legitimate aims'. If Hitler told Ramón Serrano Suñer, the envoy of General Franco, in 1940, that the real war was against England, that was obvious advocacy: what had Franco to gain from the spoils of Russia? Similarly, in 1941, when he had to explain away to an outraged Mussolini or a dismayed German naval command his sudden war on Russia, he naturally explained to them that this was really the best way of winning their war against England. However, Mussolini on 3 January 1940, in a letter to Hitler, had asked him not to 'betray his revolution' but destroy Bolshevism and secure living space in Russia. Hitler took two months until he wrote a negative reply. But in fact his practical preparations, his systematic policy, show that he was not interested in either England or France: his real war was, as he so consistently stated, not a conservative war against the West but a revolutionary war against Russia.

In this matter of his real aims it was not only foreigners and historians whom Hitler deceived. He also deceived what for convenience I shall call the German Establishment. By this term I mean the German conservative civil servants and generals and politicians who, in 1933, brought him to power and who, from 1933 onwards, at least for a time, served him faithfully, only to be bitterly disillusioned and sometimes, from dupes, to become martyrs: men like Neurath and Weizsäcker and Hassell and Schacht and many others. These men, I have already suggested, had war aims: or rather, political aims which might have to be realised by war, though they hoped to achieve them peacefully. They wanted, naturally, to restore German pride, shattered by defeat. They wanted to restore the army as an essential institution of state. They wanted to recover lost territory. But their territorial aims were limited: they did not want to swallow again the indigestible morsel of Alsace-Lorraine. What they wanted was land in the East only – but old lands, not new. They wanted the old imperial frontiers in Poland. If they were prepared to go a little further than the Kaiser and absorb Austria and the Sudetenland also, that was rather a necessity imposed by the Habsburg collapse than a sign of political ambitions in south-east Europe. For the demands of these men were essentially limited, essentially conservative. They might hate Russia for its Bolshevism, but they had no desire to conquer it. A war of conquest against Russia, quite apart from the cost and the risks, would entail (as Hitler himself said, it would necessitate) a German revolution. A German revolution was not wanted by the German Establishment.

How then, we may ask, could the German Establishment be so mistaken as to give themselves, as indispensable agents of his policy, to a man who was not only so criminal in his methods but also so completely opposed to them in his aims?

The reasons, of course, are many. There was weakness, there was self-deception, there was subtle bribery. In many ways the German Establishment was not an establishment: it was not an aristocracy, rooted in tradition or bound together by common principles: it was a caste, an interest-group, rotted within; and Hitler exploited the rot. But also there was a hard fact of geography. One has only to look at the map of Europe to see that in order to carry out his large policy, Hitler had to begin by carrying out their small policy. Their policy was to increase German respect and self-respect by the possession of an army, in which also they were professionally interested; to knock France out of eastern Europe; and then to recover the old eastern frontiers at the expense of Poland and seal off the Habsburg gap by incorporating the Austro–Germans and the Sudeten Germans in the Reich. Then they wanted to stop. For such limited aims Hitler of course had, and expressed, nothing but contempt. He wanted to conquer Russia and occupy it permanently, up to the Urals, perhaps beyond. But how could he reach Russia except through Poland, or Poland except by detaching France? For sheer geographical reasons Hitler had to begin his revolutionary policy by carrying out the conservative policy of the Establishment. This was very convenient to him. It enabled him, by playing down his ulterior aims for the time being, to buy their support. Then, when he had carried out their policy for them, he could afford to come out into the open. He was armed, victorious, unstoppable. He went on to realise his own. The full achievement of their aims was merely the essential preliminary for the achievement of his.

Thus the years 1940–41, the years of Europe's greatest crisis, were the years also of the parting of policy in Germany. It is instructive to look at the diary of Ulrich von Hassell, a perfect representative of the German Establishment, indeed its martyr. In the years before 1939

Hassell had helped to carry out Hitler's policy as ambassador in Rome, and his support of that policy, when it was revealed by the publication of the documents, shocked many westerners who, from the earlier publication of his later diaries, had come to regard him as one of themselves. But in the spring of 1940 Hassell and his friends saw all their aims realised, and they longed to make peace before the monster whose criminal genius they had used, and whom they had armed, ran amok. So they formulated their peace aims. These were 'das Prinzip der Nationalität, mit gewissen, sich aus der Geschichte ergebenden Modalitäten' – that is, of course, such 'Modalitäten' as history had made in Germany's favour. In concrete terms Hassell required 'dass die Vereinigung Österreichs und des Sudetenlandes mit dem Reich ausserhalb der Erörterung stehe'. 'Ebenso', he added, 'kommt ein Wiederaufrollen von Granzfragen im Westen Deutschlands nicht in Frage, während die deutsch-polnische Grenze im wesentlichen mit der deutschen Reichsgrenze im Jahre 1914 übereinstimmen muss'. With these 'modifications', achieved for them by Hitler, Hassell and his friends would have agreed to the 'Wiederherstellung eines unabhängigen Polens und einer tschechischen Republik'. To crown the work of conservative restoration, 'eine Monarchie is sehr erwünscht'.

The views of Hassell and his friends can be traced, backward and forward, in peace and war, in office and resistance, with but little variation. They are as consistent as Hitler's. They form the aspiration, the apologia, the alibi of a whole class, the burden of the documents of the *Auswärtiges Amt* in the 1930s, of the conservative resistance of the 1940s, of the self-justifying memoirs of the years after 1945. But of course they are academic, at least after 1940. Till then, these men had served Hitler; after that, they did not seriously hinder him. Power once given, once used to create its own basis, could not be taken away. And yet these men, it must be admitted, had not the excuse of foreigners. They had read, or could have read, and ought to have read, *Mein Kampf*.

So Hitler set out in 1941 to realise his permanent war aims. Leaving the irrelevant West to its impotent, meaningless resistance, he turned east to conquer, in one brief campaign, the prize of history. After the war there were many who said that Hitler's Russian campaign was his greatest 'mistake'. If only he had kept peace with Russia, they said, he could have absorbed, organised and fortified Europe, and Britain would never have been able to dislodge him. But this view, in my opinion, rests on a fallacy: it assumes that Hitler was not Hitler. To Hitler the Russian campaign was not a luxury, an extra campaign, a diversion in search of supplies or the expedient of temporary frustration: it was the be-all and end-all of Nazism. Not only could it not be omitted: it could not even be delayed. It was now or never that this great epochal battle must be fought, the battle which he likened to the battle of the Catalaunian Plains between Rome and the Huns. So urgent was it that Hitler could not even wait for victory in the West. That, he said, could be won afterwards: when Russia was conquered, even English obstinacy would give in: meanwhile he must strike, and strike quickly in the East.

Why was Hitler in such a hurry? Because, he believed, time was against him. If he waited, there was the added cost of the huge armed forces which he had created, the danger that their weapons would become obsolete while he waited, the fact that the Nazi leaders were ageing, the German birthrate declining, the fear that 'some idiot with a bomb' might assassinate the only man strong enough to carry through that 'Cyclopean task', the building of an empire. On the other hand the Russian population was increasing, Russian industry was expanding, and in ten or fifteen years Russia would be 'the mightiest state in the world'. Therefore, Hitler had said in 1937 'it is certain that we can wait no longer. . . . If the Führer is still living, then it will be his irrevocable decision to solve the German space problem no later than 1943–5. . . . After that date we can only expect a change for the worse.' If Hitler had merely contemplated war against the 'decaying' West, there was no hurry. It was the eastern war in which time, even history, was against him: history which by haste and willpower he hoped to reverse. He would reverse it by rolling back, at the last possible minute, the Asiatic barbarians from 'the Heartland'.

Whoever controls the Heartland, controls the world.' Such was the view of the Englishman Sir Halford Mackinder, the founder of Geopolitics, from whom – indirectly through Haushofer and Hess – Hitler derived his views or at least some of them. 'The Heartland' was East Europe and European Russia. Hitler saw himself and Stalin as two giants competing, with revolutionary force, for control of this Heartland; and he knew that whichever of them won was ruthless enough to make his conquest permanent. The politicians of the Establishment could have no such ambitions because, apart from anything else, they were too mild. In a memorandum to Hitler Schacht had pointed out, in 1934, that a policy of eastern colonisation was impossible because eastern Europe was already fully populated. What – in Hitler's phrase – ridiculous *Humanitätsduselei*! It only showed that the Establishment had no conception of his aims. They thought in terms of conventional wars, wars for power. Hitler might fight such a conventional war in the West, and therefore in the West he would respect the old conventions of war; but this eastern war was quite different: it was a war for the wholesale possession of land and the right to clear off, or reduce to abject slavery, the former inhabitants of the land. Conventions would be ignored; quarter would be neither given nor asked; Moscow itself would be razed to the ground, and its name and memory blotted out from history and geography alike.

In 1941, when Hitler had launched his final war, and felt the crunch of victory on all fronts, he thought that his great hour had come. Now at last the consistent aim of twenty years was about to be fulfilled. Therefore, he judged, it was time, once again, to declare his testament, to open another window into his mind. And so his faithful high-priest and secretary, Martin Bormann, made all the arrangements. At his headquarters, in East Prussia or in the Ukraine, Hitler sat and talked, and obedient stenographers, placed behind screens, took down the holy writ: Hitler's *Tischgespräche*, or rather his monologues, on the power he had achieved and the empire he was now at last about to create.

Hitler's *Tischgespräche* is a dreadful document, repellent and yet fascinating, the multiple mirror of a mind completely empty of humanity and yet charged with fierce, systematising, sometimes clarifying power. 'I have the gift', Hitler once said 'of reducing all problems to their simplest form': and here he reduced them. Sometimes the simplicity is terrifying: Hitler was indeed one of Burckhardt's *terribles simplificateurs*; but at least it is always clear; and nothing is more clear than his picture of the New Order now about to be established in the East; a nightmare, barbarian empire, without humanity, without culture, without purpose, 'a new Dark Age', as Sir Winston Churchill once described the consequences of a Nazi victory, 'made more sinister, and perhaps more protracted, by the lights of perverted science'. For the sole purpose of empire, Hitler declared, was to sustain itself, to minister to national pride. 'Who has, has': that is the sum of political morality; and the greatest folly that a master-race can commit is to give anything up or so to arm its subjects that they may enforce a claim to freedom. Therefore, in the new German empire, subject peoples must possess no arms; they must acquire no education (except the knowledge of enough German to obey orders); and they must be taught contraception and denied hospitals in order that both dwindling births and unhampered death may keep their numbers down. Thus reduced, the enslaved Russians can live on as a depressed Helot class, hewing wood and drawing water for a privileged aristocracy of German colonists who will sit securely in fortified cities, connected by strategic autobahns, glorying in their nationality and listening to *The Merry Widow* for ever and ever. For 'after National Socialism has lasted for some time, it will be impossible even to imagine a form of life different from ours'.

Such was Hitler's ultimate millenium. In 1941 he thought he had realised it. In February 1945 the hope of it had gone, apparently for ever, and even Hitler was forced to admit it. It was a desperate admission, and he had long refused to make it, but now there was no evading it, and the only question was, how had such a disastrous reversal of fortune come about? How indeed? As Hitler reflected on it, he decided that once again it was his duty to enlighten posterity by opening a window into his mind. So in Berlin, as formerly in Rastenburg and Wynnitza, the machinery was mounted, the screen set, the stenographer placed, and Hitler opened the fourth window into the working of his mind, the last chapter of his holy writ: his explanation of defeat.

And how did he explain it? Did he ever suggest, as so many others have suggested, that he was wrong to have made war on Russia, that he should have stopped, as the German Establishment would have liked to stop, in 1940? Certainly not. Admittedly, he allows, a useful peace could have been made with England in 1940 or 1941, with advantage to both sides: for both had gained victories over their degenerate Latin enemies – Germany over France, England over Italy. But Hitler was quick to add that this peace would have been merely tactical not final: its purpose would have been not a final settlement but the redirection of Germany's war effort. 'Germany, secure in her rear, could then have thrown herself, heart and soul, into her real task, the mission of my life, the *raison d'être* of National Socialism: the destruction of Bolshevism'. 'It is eastwards, only and always eastwards, that the veins of our life must expand.'

How then did Hitler explain his disastrous failure? In these last conversations he goes through many possibilities. Was it in going to war at all? That suggestion is made only to be dismissed: from the very beginning the whole purpose of Nazism was war. Was it then in launching his war too soon? No, he would not admit that. Russia had to be attacked: a dozen reasons demanded haste. In fact, he now maintained, it would have been far better if he had begun earlier, if he had launched his essential preliminary war against the West in 1938 instead of 1939. But alas, at that time Germany, though materially armed, was morally unprepared, encumbered with reactionary generals and diplomats. And then there was the infamous behaviour of Chamberlain who, at Munich, surrendered to all Hitler's demands and thus deprived him of his excuse for war. 'They gave way on all points, the cowards! They yielded to

all our demands! In such circumstances it was very difficult
to take the initiative and launch a war.'

What then could the hitch be? In the end, after long
fumbling, Hitler found it. It was his trust in Mussolini, he
decided, which had ruined him. Of course he greatly
admired Mussolini, he owed much to his example, much to
his friendship, especially in 1938 at the time of the *Anschluss*
with Austria; but in 1941 Mussolini had been a disastrous
ally. By his misadventures in the Mediterranean, and
particularly by his ill-timed and unannounced adventure in
Greece, Mussolini had dragged Hitler into the Balkans to
rescue him, and had forced him, by that diversion, to delay
by five weeks his attack on Russia. For the attack on Russia
had been planned for 15 May: in fact, owing to the demands
of the Balkan campaign, it was not launched until 22 June.

And what was the result? To Hitler, at least in retrospect,
it was clear, his Russian campaign had been designed as a
Blitzkrieg: it was to be over in one summer; and if he had
only had one full summer, it would have been. But he had
started late, five weeks late, and then the winter, that
terrible Russian winter, had come unexpectedly early: and
so the armies had been snowed up, the programme halted,
the Russians had had time to recover, the English to plot
new alliances, new campaigns in the rear. . . . When Hitler
looked back and thought how nearly he had won everything
that he had ever sought in 1941, and how his triumph had
dissolved even as he was celebrating it, he could almost
weep with chagrin. 'That idiotic campaign in Greece!' he
would exclaim, 'If the war had remained a war conducted
by Germany and not by the Axis, we should have been in a
position to attack Russia by 15 May, 1941. Doubly fortified
by the fact that our forces had known nothing but decisive
and irrefutable victory, we should have been able to
conclude the campaign before winter came. How differently
everything has turned out!'

Thus to the end Hitler maintained the purity of his war
aims. To him, from 1920 to 1945, the purpose of Nazism
was always the same: it was to create an empire, to wrest
the 'great continental space' of Russia from the Russians.
Even after defeat he did not seek to cloak it. A month after

issuing this last testament, he told Albert Speer that
Germany had failed him and deserved to perish: 'the future
belongs solely to the stronger Eastern nation'. And the day
before his death, the last words of his last message sent out
of the Bunker in Berlin to the Wehrmacht was an adjuration
that 'the aim must still be to win territory in the East for
the German people'.

Thus Hitler's ultimate strategic aims can be detached with
absolute clarity, absolute consistency, from the tactical
necessities or concessions which surround them. At different
times he was under different necessities and made different
concessions. In 1923 France, in 1940 England stood between
him and his goal. But these were not his real enemies.
France, once conquered and rendered harmless, was let
alone, even pampered: the British on landing in Normandy
were astonished at the plenty they found there. Britain,
Hitler was always willing to 'guarantee': he had even, in
1928, written a book on the necessity of an Anglo–German
understanding. The book does not survive, but it was
because of his familiarity with its contents that Rudolf
Hess – the channel through whom Hitler sucked his
'geopolitical' ideas of eastern conquest – made his dramatic,
solo flight to England in 1941. This was written before the
discovery of Hitler's *Second Book*, which was published in
1961. This book in fact confirms my thesis: its argument is
that tactical surrenders – even surrenders which may seem
a betrayal of Nazi ideals – must occasionally be made in
the interests of a long-term policy for the realisation of
those ideals. In 1928 the tactical surrender would be the
cession of the South Tyrol to Italy, just as in 1939 it would
be the Russo-German Pact. But in 1928, when he was on
the way to legal power, Hitler did not think it prudent to
republish his aggressive long-term plans. Similarly, inside
Germany, the Establishment, the old conservative classes,
with their limited aims, stood between him and his policy.
Hitler's tactics took account of these obstacles. Throughout
the 1930s, although *Mein Kampf* sat in every bookcase, its
doctrines were muted, at least in public and abroad, and
Hitler was quite content that they should be written off as

juvenile indiscretions. In 1939, he would make 'the greatest gamble in his life': the Russo-German Pact. But all these were tactical necessities. In private Hitler never ceased to utter the doctrines of *Mein Kampf*. And in 1941, when France, England and the German Establishment were all defeated, he threw off the mask. The original authentic voice rang out again. He set out, over the corpses of enemies and accomplices alike, to achieve 'the ambition of my life, the *raison d'être* of National Socialism' – the conquest of the East. When final judgment is made both on the German Establishment of the 1930s and on Russian policy in respect of Germany since the war, these facts may help to make it.

8. Hitler's Ultimate Aims – A Programme of World Dominion?

DIETRICH AIGNER

Any discussion of Hitler's alleged 'programme' for achieving world dominion should be preceded by an attempt at terminological clarification. 'World Dominion' or 'World Domination' obviously convey something different from 'World Power'; all the same and all grammatical incongruities notwithstanding, both terms are often used as synonyms.[1] To illustrate the point: there is no need to elaborate further on the statement that Hitler wanted the Third Reich to achieve or regain world power status. This has never been in controversy, but in the early and mid-1930s Hitler's foreign policy already gave rise to a widespread tendency abroad to interpret his 'real' aims as the 'achievement of world domination'. Hitler's often quoted dictum 'Deutschland wird entweder Weltmacht oder überhaupt nicht sein' should – so it was conjectured – be plainly read to mean: Germany must achieve world domination or it will perish.[2]

There is an obvious need for terminological clarification, all the more so as the concept of 'world domination' pertains to something so exorbitant as to transcend all human experience. Not even the largest empires in history – the

From W. Michalka (ed.), *Nationalsozialistische Aussenpolitik* (Darmstadt, 1978), pp. 49–69

Roman and the British – ever really lived up to this claim. In an age when the 'known world' has become identical with the globe itself, such exorbitance could not fail to make 'world dominion' or 'world domination' a propaganda slogan closely allied to the related and hardly less dubious idea of a 'world conspiracy'. Both catchwords have had a not inconsiderable impact on the course of history and must, for this reason alone, be accorded eminent historical relevance irrespective of their validity. We have, to cite an instance, to accept as a fact Hitler's sincerity in believing the 'Protocols of the Elders of Zion' to be an authentic piece of evidence for 'a Jewish world conspiracy aiming at Jewish world domination',[3] just as we have to accept at face value Neville Chamberlain's sincerity when airing, in his Birmingham speech of 17 March 1939, a prevalent suspicion: 'Is this [breach of faith on Hitler's part] in fact a step in the direction of an attempt to dominate the world by force?'[4]

Speaking of Hitler, it is self-evident that he and National Socialism were credited, right from the start, with hatching global ambitions. His accession to power meant nothing less than a universal challenge directed at the whole range of forces which, in the political, religious and cultural fields, were shaping our age; there was – all over the globe – no country wholly unaffected by what was happening in Germany, and there were sizable groups of opinion-makers nearly everywhere that felt, for political, racial, or religious reasons, the National Socialist impact most acutely. This atmosphere of a world-wide affliction found expression in the all but universally antagonistic attitude of the media.[5] Even though this failed to produce a common, politically feasible response going beyond the largely abortive efforts at establishing anti-Fascist 'People's Fronts', it nonetheless served as a sounding-board for forces that – for reasons of their own – tended to project all of Hitler's moves in the foreign policy field on a world-wide scale. We may, without risking oversimplifying a highly complex historical situation, differentiate three distinctly motivated groups:

1. No one was more immediately threatened by Hitler's expansionist designs as expounded in *Mein Kampf*

than the Soviet Union. Moscow and international Communism had, for this reason, a very vital interest in counteracting the potentiality of any anti-Soviet alignment by insisting on the 'general' character of the 'German menace' and by working for an implementation of Litvinov's formula of 'peace is indivisible' in the guise of 'Peace Front' based on the principle of 'Collective Security'. Central to the far-reaching propaganda efforts directed not only at Popular Front adherents but at pacifists, 'patriots' and League of Nations enthusiasts at large was the 'revelation' of Hitler's 'plan for world conquest by stages'; neither the British empire nor the United States would eventually escape, his wooing of the British only being meant to lull them into false security, inviting them, as it were, to dig their own graves.[6] The Comintern propagandists' task was greatly facilitated by their being able to draw on ideas that had gained currency in the Allied countries during the First World War.[7]

2. 'Pangermanism's Drive for World Conquest' was a staple argument no Allied propagandist in the 1914–8 war could have done without. If any proof was needed, the slogan 'Deutschland über alles' was considered sufficient.[8] In the case of Britain there was moreover an early recognition that for a global power any challenge of a more serious kind – in foreign commerce no less than in naval strength – had to be perceived as a global one. It is a measure of the persistence of 'plausible' stereotypes that the challenge of Hitler's Germany was conceived, after 1933, in traditional patterns and that 'Pangermanism's revival' was documented preferably by the authority of people who, like the geographer Ewald Banse or the geopolitician Karl Haushofer, were at most peripheral figures in the National Socialist power set-up. When Hitler's aggressive moves in 1938 and 1939 had finally eliminated all further doubt about his 'real aims' – doubts largely generated by his persistent wooing of British friendship in the earlier years – 'Germany's

drive for world domination' became once more the
staple diet of Allied war propaganda.[9]

3. German global aspirations had been a central theme
of interventionist propaganda in the United States
even before US entry into the First World War.[10]
When organised anti-semitism took over in Germany
and American sympathisers – mostly of the anti-
semitic brand – felt prompted to activities of their
own, the old bogey of the 'German menace to the
Western hemisphere' surfaced again right after 1933,
soon gaining in credibility from German incursions
into Latin American markets. It was instrumental in
the Roosevelt administration's efforts at gradually
revising neutrality legislation after 1936, in getting
assistance to Britain under way in 1939–41, and in
finally edging the country towards full-scale war entry.
No one was more vocal in denouncing Hitler's 'Program
of world conquest' than President Roosevelt himself,[11]
one of his chief authorities being Hermann Rauschning
who, in 1939, had been entrusted by Sir Robert
Vansittart with cultivating US public opinion in favour
of the Allied cause.[12]

Rauschning with his alleged Nazi past as a Hitler confidant
was a godsend for Allied propagandists, for as far as 'global
designs' were concerned there was nothing else in their
hands that could stand close scrutiny.[13] How utterly devoid
they were of hard and incontrovertible evidence came to
light during the Nuremberg trial against the Major German
War Criminals. Not one of those 'secret documents' the
President himself had made so much of was presented to
the tribunal, and 'Hitler's confidant' Rauschning himself
took care to avoid the confrontation. Even the so-called
'Hossbach Protocol', surfaced in the very last minute and
used as a key document by the prosecution in its case
against 'conspiracy and aggression', was plainly unsuited as
evidence for a 'plan for world conquest'. The Nuremberg
formula of 'conspiracy and aggression' had, for this reason,
to evade the whole question of Hitler's foreign policy 'aims'
let alone 'ultimate aims'; the verdict went so far as to

qualify the relevance of *Mein Kampf* for the actual course of
Hitler's foreign policy, establishing instead 'aggressive intent'
and 'conspiratorial preparation of aggressive wars' as the
decisive elements for reaching judgment.[14] In view of the
dearth of hard factual evidence the propagandist slogan of
'Hitler's plan for world conquest' had obviously to be
discarded; whenever it surfaced thereafter it based its claim
on an interpretation of Hitler's personality as someone
'power-drunk' and basically 'insatiable'. As a consequence
discussion of Hitler's 'aims' lost its rational and verifiable
basis in favour of psychologising analysis. Viewing Hitler as
an 'unprincipled nihilist' and 'opportunist' in foreign policy,
devoid of anything like a capacity for long-term planning
and consistent action, may also be seen as a response to
those glib propaganda slogans that had served their purpose
and were now felt to be a liability rather than an asset in
scholarly debate. This may, partly at least, also explain
why British and American historians tend to view with
diffidence the resurrected tableau of 'Hitler's plans for world
domination' as elaborated by some younger German
historians.[15] It should be stressed, therefore, that this novel
interpretation of Hitler's foreign policy aims is a departure
from propagandist formulas and should be taken seriously.

   This is not the place for summarising the present state of
historiographical research in so far as Hitler's foreign policy
is concerned. As a consequence of the work done in this
field by H. R. Trevor-Roper, Andreas Hillgruber, Eberhard
Jäckel, Norman Rich *et al.* the existence of long-term
political aims is no longer a matter of controversy and there
is a certain consensus among historians of the period that
Hitler – all his tactical manoeuvrings notwithstanding –
never lost sight of those basic aims. There are, to be sure,
dissenting voices. For Marxists Hitler never amounted to
more than a pawn ('Agent') in the service of powerful
interests quite beyond his reach.[16] More or less close to this
view are those who see Hitler's *actions* largely determined
through domestic, that is socio-economic constraints,[17]
whereas a third group of historians regards Hitler as *one*
actor on the international stage among several others,
subject to the constraints and pressures inherent in the

256 ASPECTS OF THE THIRD REICH

process of international power politics, setting a course the pursuit of which went far beyond his capacity – thus depriving the historian of any valid inferences for possible long-term aims.[18]

However much these different approaches may vary from each other, they do not in themselves deny that Hitler did in fact hold foreign policy aims. Real controversy centres around the question of *how* Hitler's 'aims' are to be *interpreted* and what validity is to be accorded to them within their geographical and chronological context. The dispute is essentially between two 'schools of thought', between those who – on the strength of a number of well-known passages in *Mein Kampf* and in Hitler's *Second Book* – arrive at *continental* aims, and those who – by stressing the ideological content of Hitler's testimonies – conclude on *global* aims. The first group of German historians, with Eberhard Jäckel as their chief proponent, hold the view that Hitler's undeniable aim of *Weltmacht* status would have found fulfilment with the establishment of a continental empire based on German *Lebensraum* in eastern Europe. For their opponents – centred around Andreas Hillgruber and Klause Hildebrand – this continental empire has to be considered only as a 'first step' in a long-term 'plan of world conquest by stages' (*Stufenplan*) with the ultimate aim of world domination through elimination of the United States. Whereas the 'continentalists' are satisfied that Hitler's idea of *Weltmacht* was pertinently circumscribed in *Mein Kampf* in terms of 'a sound relationship between the numerical strength of a people and its *Lebensraum*',[19] that his principal aim in foreign policy was the 'conquest of *Lebensraum*' in eastern Europe and – as an ancillary to this end – the establishment of an Anglo-German alliance with Britain directing its energies overseas, the 'globalists' regard attainment of continental invulnerability as a mere preliminary for world-wide expansion, the further stages of which would have been the securing of colonial territories (*Ergänzungsraum*) [supplementary living space *Ed.*] in Africa and military bases in the Atlantic Ocean in preparation for a 'final fling' at the United States as the 'last stage' in Hitler's pursuit of world hegemony. There is some latitude, among globalists, in defining this process of global conquest; no longer do they talk about a precise 'time-table' and most of them are now inclined to view Hitler's 'programme' as something to be realised by future generations. At the same time they hold to the belief that the 'globalist' view provides an explanatory model for gauging Hitler's decisions and actions during the years 1938 to 1941, when, in their view, the different 'stages' of his programme became mixed up under the impact of unforeseen international developments forcing him to compress his long-term plan into a short-term 'global *Blitzkrieg*' (*Weltblitzkrieg*).[20]

The basic difficulty in assessing Hitler's 'ultimate aims' derives in large part from the multi-faceted character of his personality and his contingent inability to differentiate clearly between a 'philosopher's' speculations, a visionary's effusions, and a politician's down-to-earth practical aims. The task is further complicated by the bewildering fact that, even when Hitler's intentions seem to have been clearly stated, there is an obvious divergence between what he said and what he subsequently did. One flagrant instance is the problem of an Anglo-German alliance. In *Mein Kampf* and in his *Second Book* he had, for its sake, abjured all ambitions at colonial expansion overseas and a concomitant naval programme. This, however, did not prevent him after 1936 from declaring the return of Germany's former colonies to be 'the only important direct issue between the German Reich and Great Britain' and – by authorising the 'Z-Plan' in January 1939 – from launching a naval programme of gigantic dimensions. Another instance is the problem of *Lebensraum*. Taking his 'programmatical' book as a guide there could never have been the slightest doubt that German living space had to be gained in the East at Russia's expense. Contrary to expectations there is nothing to suggest that Hitler had seriously envisaged war against the Soviet Union prior to July 1940. (For a more detailed elaboration of these inconsistencies and even contradictions see 'Hitler and the Origins of the Second World War: Second Thoughts on the Status of Some of the Documents', *Historical Journal* (Cambridge, 1968); reprinted in E. M. Robertson (ed.), *The Origins of the Second World War* (London, 1971), pp. 158–224).

The flagrant inconsistencies just mentioned should help to draw attention to the simple but generally under-estimated fact that Hitler went to war in 1939 with front lines diametrically opposite to all his known intentions – with the Soviet Union as an ally and Britain, France and Poland as adversaries.[21] When trying to assess the evidence which indicates Hitler's 'ultimate aims', one is bound to disregard, for this reason, all decisions derived from a course of events that departed even further from what Hitler had anticipated. This should apply in the first place to all those ideas in the strategic and foreign policy fields conceived as a means of achieving victory in a kind of war Hitler himself felt had been 'forced upon him'.[22] On the strength of this argument it would be inadvisable to conclude – from the global character this war rapidly assumed – there were global designs of long standing on Hitler's part, the 'reversed' constellation of 1939 having already been a global one when considering US involvement right from the start.[23] Even 'globalists' admit that Hitler was forced to resort to short-term global planning in view of what he judged to be the inevitability of the US entering the war.[24] This does not, of course, exclude the possible existence of long-term global designs; it should only warn against the validity of evidence originating from Hitler's position in 1940/41 being used for far-reaching conclusions. No consideration will be given to it here for this reason.

It is no longer possible to hinge the constellation of September 1939 – regarded by Hitler as 'perverse' and 'forced upon him' – on Britain's sudden about-turn after the Prague *coup* of 15 March 1939. Recent research has rather established the basic continuity of British foreign policy for the whole of the period. Generally speaking there is little doubt now that Hitler's Germany brought about, right from start, fundamental antagonisms on a world-wide scale, that – by its very existence – it generated fears and apprehensions that grew in intensity with the degree of German rearmament, culminating in an all but universally accepted notion of 'Germany being World Menace Number One'. It is a sorry reflection on international historiographical research that this basic simple fact has – for more than two decades – been obscured by a largely emotional and politically motivated debate about *appeasement*.[25] Recent research makes it plain that Hitler, far from being *encouraged* by British *appeasement*, realised his failure to come to terms with the British as early as autumn 1936 and acted accordingly by initiating, in 1937, a foreign policy reversal of his own. This reversal was of a decidedly, though not yet definitely, anti-British character.[26] There is authentic evidence for these years that Hitler credited his 'hate-inspired enemies' with planning to wage war upon him.[27] One crucial consequence was a progressive rapprochement towards Italy as an ally to be counted upon in the impending conflict with the western powers. While the *Anschluss* with Austria gave practical expression to the Rome–Berlin axis, it heralded at the same time a new stage of open confrontation with Britain and France culminating in the so-called 'Week-end Crisis' of May 1938, an episode that may now be seen as the decisive turning-point in the pre-history of the Second World War. It certainly served to confirm Hitler's lingering fears and suspicions as far as Britain was concerned. With the contingency of an Anglo-German conflict now hard upon him, he concluded on the near inevitability of a contest with the western powers. Whatever he thought and did thereafter was dictated by the prospect of impending war – a prospect that gained in acuity through a belief, shared on both sides of the Channel, that time was on the respective opponent's side. The 'Z-Plan' for large-scale German naval rearmament originated during the days of the 'Week-end Crisis' and should be properly assessed in this context. Hitler's actions during the 'Cold War' era from May 1938 till August 1939 *per se* can obviously not be taken as conclusive evidence of his long-term aims and should best be considered as belonging in the same category as his wartime decisions. No really strong inferences can be drawn from them for the alleged *Stufenplan*.

A close analysis of those documents presented by the 'globalists' as evidence for Hitler's genuine and original foreign policy 'programme' may thus be summarised:

1. For Hitler Britain and her empire constituted – to a quite extraordinary degree – a model of highly successful

statesmanship on a world-wide scale. Additional to power-political calculations aiming at an Anglo-German alliance there is ample evidence for an all but 'erotic' fixation as regards his infatuation with what he took to be the manifestation of racial superiority by a representative of the Germanic 'master race'. Historians have usually described this attitude as 'hate-love'. This seems inadequate as it may be too shallow an explanation for something far more elusive.[28] When assessing all the relevant evidence it appears unlikely that Hitler thought of Britain only as a 'junior partner' in his 'grand scheme' of Anglo-German global partnership. Some help may be derived from drawing an analogy with the young politician's self-conceived role as a *drummer* (*Trommler*) rather than a *Führer*,[29] suggesting that 'drummer' Hitler might conceivably have been prepared to acquiesce in the world political leadership of some 'strong man' like David Lloyd George or Winston Churchill, always provided both countries had previously arrived at a 'demarcation of spheres of interest', that is, agreed on giving Hitler 'a free hand in the East'.[30] To put it bluntly: there is not a shred of authentic evidence to suggest that Hitler was intent on a diminution of British power, let alone destruction of the British empire; there is, on the contrary, overwhelming and unanimous evidence bearing witness to Hitler's high regard for British imperialism as an element of overriding importance for the perpetuation of white man's rule over the globe. The one lone voice among contemporaries dissenting, Hermann Rauschning's, may safely be dismissed.[31]

2. Hitler's early writings contain nothing to suggest that he believed the British to be a decadent people. What he visualised was rather the vulnerability of the British empire menaced in his view by (a) international Communism, (b) world Jewry, and (c) US expansionism. The 'American Menace' is dealt with in some detail in his *Second Book*; reference to it obviously serves the purpose of enhancing the value of German 'friendship' when defending Europe and the British

empire against US ambitions. It should be borne in mind, however, that Hitler is merely echoing a current trend in contemporary political thinking and that the wording of Hitler's thoughts follows rather closely the prevalent 'defensive' stance.[32] No inferences should be drawn of a 'last stage' in Hitler's long-term planning for world conquest. In 1930, for instance, two years after having written his *Second Book*, Hitler regaled Otto Strasser, his opponent in foreign policy matters, with a glittering vision of 'Anglo-German-American harmony in organizing world economy';[33] the following years are utterly devoid of any testimony that could be properly fitted into Hitler's earlier and largely 'borrowed' image of the United States as a 'menace'.

3. The concept of *Lebensraum* looms large in Hitler's ideas on foreign policy. This term was borrowed from geopolitics and twisted in such a way as to give expression to NS 'Blood and Soil' romanticism as a reaction against industrialisation and urbanisation. It may additionally have gained in importance through memories of widespread famine in the years 1917–19, when Germany's 'collapse of morale' was largely attributed to the British blockade. There is no doubt that *Lebensraum* adequate for nourishing the German people could be gained only by means of an aggressive and expansionist foreign policy; *achievement of world hegemony*, however, is quite a different matter.[34] Even when National Socialist clamouring for the return of Germany's former colonies was at its loudest, nobody seriously thought of German mass settlements overseas. Colonies were primarily regarded as providing raw materials and thereby strengthening German autarky, but even this idea was voiced only when any feasible prospect of an Anglo-German alliance had all but evaporated. In conclusion it may safely be said that for Hitler Germany's colonial claim was more or less a bargaining counter, certainly not an issue worth anything approaching Anglo-German conflict. His central idea – the real core of his foreign policy reasoning – seems to have been the vision of a large

German empire based on eastern conquests, in alliance with the British empire the 'natural' incumbent to continental hegemony.

4. Since the days of Mahan and Ratzel [Alfred Thayer Mahan the American navalist, whose book *The Influence of Seapower upon History* (New York, 1890), made a profound impact upon the navalists of all the great powers. Friedrich Ratzel is considered to be one of the founders of 'Geopolitics', especially his work *Politische Geographie* (1897). *Ed.*] *naval supremacy* has been seen as a prerequisite for world domination. In *Mein Kampf* and in his *Second Book* Hitler had expressly renounced all German naval pretensions in favour of securing Anglo-German partnership. Recent research, notably by Jost Dülffer, has made it plain that Hitler took a more active interest in naval technicalities than had hitherto been assumed. There is nothing, however, to suggest that the Anglo-German Naval Agreement of 1935 with 'self-imposed' German limitations was meant to serve any other purpose save as a first step in bringing about Anglo-German partnership.

5. Besides living space *race* was another key concept in Hitler's ideology. Judging from the early use of the term it is virtually inadmissible to reduce its meaning to 'Germandom'. Anglo-Saxons always took pride of place in Hitler's hierarchy of 'racial excellence', Germany's predestined partners in 'the common mission of the Nordic master race' when safeguarding civilisation against Bolshevism, Jewry, and 'the Coloured World'. The idea of 'world leadership' as proclaimed in Hitler's early writings does *not* imply exclusive German world supremacy.[35]

6. Hitler conceived of himself primarily as an artist, a visionary, and a philosopher of history. 'Practical politics' was, for him, not the 'art of the possible', but the emanation of 'deep insights' gained through an apperception of those motive forces that dominated world history. This vision of history was largely based on a bowdlerised version of Social Darwinism as it had been handed down to him – presumably from English

sources – through the intermediary of Houston Stewart Chamberlain.[36] For Hitler the 'Struggle for Existence' and 'Survival of the Fittest' (i.e. those of the highest racial quality) were unalterable 'Laws of Life'; doom was reserved for he who ignored them, even a 'deficiency in success' (*unvollkommener Erfolg*) was preferable to passivity. Fighting for power and domination was perceived as the basic motive force in history, the validity of this 'law' being irrevocably bound up with the existence of mankind. There is no room in this vision for anything like chiliasm or finality, the idea of peace – peace also as a correlative to domination – is entirely alien to Hitler's way of thinking; he even postulates the necessity of always leaving a chance for future war when concluding peace treaties.[37] The essence and purpose of this eternal struggle is for him *not* the achievement of territorial gain and political domination, but the contest itself as a means of self-assertion. No target, however highly placed, would ever be adequate to this end, no victory could ever bestow final contentment but serve only as a further incentive for he who is destined to fight the eternal struggle. It is in his theoretical writings, notably in his *Second Book*, that Hitler has so frankly exposed these 'philosophical' foundations of his *Weltanschauung*; when he pronounced them in public – as was the case at Erlangen in 1930 – he characteristically did so for the benefit of an exclusively academic audience.[38] Caution should prevail when interpreting such reflections in terms of a foreign policy programme aiming at world domination.

Finding sufficiently powerful evidence for Hitler's 'ultimate aims' in support of the *Stufenplan* hypothesis is obviously no easy undertaking. There are, however, a number of aspects to the matter that plainly contradict such rationalisations. In the first place it would be wise to consider the so-called 'Hossbach Protocol'. As a result of recent research its importance as a 'key document' has been deservedly downgraded and fitted into the broader context of Hitler's whole set of ideas on foreign policy. But this should not obscure the fact that this is the *first* ascertainable instance of Hitler expounding long-term foreign policy aims to the highest-ranking representatives of the Reich government, and of the *Wehrmacht*, and that he took care to characterise these disclosures as a sort of 'political testament', a reflection, possibly, of his current presentiments of early death.[39] It is worthy of note that even among the top echelons of the NS leadership there had been, to the best of our knowledge, no talk of long-term foreign policy aims prior to November 1937, and that relevant measures undertaken in the preceding years – the speeding-up of rearmament, the launching of the 'Four-Year Plan', etc. – had heretofore never been expressly placed within the framework of a foreign policy 'programme'. This may serve as additional evidence for what has been stated above, that Hitler did not embark on concrete expansionist planning until he was satisfied that his prime object of an Anglo-German alliance, premise of all his foreign policy conjecturing, had been wrecked by his 'hate-inspired enemies' across the Channel. We may therefore assume that no global intentions going beyond the idea of an 'Anglo-German world partnership' had found expression before that date and that nothing has come to light in the way of a 'political testament' exceeding the *continental* bounds of the Hossbach exposé.

Additional confirmation for such an assumption may be perceived in the absence of a 'dauphin', an 'heir' initiated into Hitler's far-reaching intentions and to be entrusted with executing further stages of a long-term programme. Hitler, instead, thought of himself increasingly in terms of his personal singularity, and it is here that the relevance of his growing fascination with projects of architectural gigantism comes in. For the 'would-be artist' and 'would-be architect', art and architecture provided a chance of materialising his heroic and fatalist beliefs, instituting as it were testamentary monuments and mementos capable of generating integrative strength for future generations. Once again one would be well advised not to project this into the framework of a 'foreign-policy programme'.[40]

It is interesting to note within this context that, even at the apex of Germany's military victories, political indoctrination of the *Hitlerjugend* carefully eschewed anything approaching concrete war aims, stressing instead the necessity of unrelenting readiness for the 'eternal struggle'.[41] There is nothing in NS ideology to suggest a possible and intelligible synthesis between the 'nationalist' and the 'imperial' ideas; they never ceased to be in contradiction to each other as evidenced by the emergence, late in the war, of the 'European idea'. [This is also borne out when perusing the syllabus of the officers' schools of the *Waffen-SS*, the SS-*Junkerschulen*. See R. Schulze-Kossens, *Militärischer Führernachwuchs' der Waffen-SS* (Osnabrück, 1982) and Bernd Wegner's work cited in the bibliography below. *Ed.*] If further proof is needed for National Socialism's inherent inability to overcome nationalist parochialism in favour of a truly globalist set of ideas, we may just throw a look at NS *Volkstumspolitik* (cultivating Germans abroad), above all in the United States. The much-vaunted 'Fascist International' or 'Nazi Fifth Column' pertains to the realms of imagination and propaganda.[42]

From whatever angle we may consider the matter of Hitler's 'ultimate foreign policy aims', it all boils down to the question whether or not he was, as he claimed for himself and the 'globalists' claim again, the coolly planning master-mind on the political stage.[43] This, it would seem, is a matter for psychologists to decide. Historical evidence hardly supports this view. Neither was the 'polycratic system of inter-departmental anarchy', now generally recognised as the true basis of his personal regime, of his deliberate making, nor can it be said that he 'foresaw all the contingencies of his actions'. No doubt, Hitler more than once gave proof of an uncanny instinct for future developments, but the actual course of European politics following his accession to power went far astray from what he had anticipated. If an analogy may be drawn: just as in matters of governmental and administrative policy he put his trust in the selective process of the jungle, so it seems that for him the stage of international politics was set by a dark and elusive power called 'Providence' whose ultimate intentions had been revealed to him in his vision of history. This 'Big Idea' opened up the vista on the course of human history, making human developments 'comprehensible' in spans of centuries and promising him light in a world populated by evil and demonic forces. But this 'Big Idea' did not signify: go and seize the world, overcome those demons and bring eternal peace to mankind by subjecting it to your will. What it did signify in effect was: be prepared for the eternal struggle, progenitor of all things, creative genius till the end of days; fight against powers whose defeat will beget new struggles against new powers. If we take this to be the very core of Hitler's politico-philosophical beliefs, we may visualise, on a level far removed from practical political planning, National Socialism in so far as it is to be understood as 'Hitlerism' to have been a combative and destructive force *par excellence* whose 'aims' were, by its very nature, boundless and which, in an entelechy of its own, had to run its course towards destruction – of mankind or of itself.

9. From the Anti-Comintern Pact to the Euro-Asiatic Bloc: Ribbentrop's Alternative Concept of Hitler's Foreign Policy Programme

WOLFGANG MICHALKA

Even before the entry of Italy to the Anti-Comintern agreement on 24 October 1937, Joachim von Ribbentrop had explained to the Italian foreign minister, Count Ciano, that the ideological union with Japan would be extended into a powerful political bloc. He said that, in the case of the Anti-Comintern pact, the need was for a wooden bridge to be built which would later make it possible for a great durable iron bridge to be erected.[1] Referring to the inevitable conflict with the western powers, and especially with Great

From Wolfgang Michalka (ed.), *Nationalsozialistische Aussenpolitik* (Darmstadt,

Britain, he emphasised 'the necessity of a military alliance between Rome, Berlin and Tokyo'.[2]

The American ambassador in Tokyo, Joseph C. Grew, assessed the ideological alliance between the three Fascist powers with great insight when he wrote, 'Anti-communism is merely the banner beneath which the "have-nots" unite. The threat to England is very real and immediately apparent, when one considers that, through Japan's joining the Berlin-Rome axis, the "life-line" of the British Empire from the North Sea through the Mediterranean as far as Singapore is threatened.'[3] Grew's analysis of the Anti-Comintern pact in 1937 corresponds exactly with what Ribbentrop, as German ambassador to the Court of St James, had recommended to the *Führer*, Adolf Hitler, in his Main Report of 28 December 1937 and in his Final Conclusions of 2 January 1938:[4] the formation of a strong anti-British alliance of powers which could threaten the British empire in different vital areas in order to compel it to neutrality or, in the event of a conflict, could defeat it. Ciano was also very conscious of this anti-British direction in the Anti-Comintern pact: 'London will have to examine its position anew';[5] 'if we are to sign the pact of three, which seems anti-communistic yet in reality is anti-British',[6] he remarked in his diary, then the ring of alliances would close around England.[7] On 6 November 1937, after the signing ceremony of the anti-Comintern Pact, he noted: 'Three peoples are pledging themselves to go the same way, the way which will possibly lead to war, to a necessary war, if one is to crack this shell which is stifling the energy and the aims of these emergent nations'.[8]

This alliance of the three powers formed a significant turning point in international politics, and above all, in German foreign policy which had been fundamentally determined since February 1938 by Ribbentrop, as foreign minister, and had served to realise his concept of foreign policy as it developed up to 1937, in complete contrast to Hitler's foreign policy programme.[9] That this change in German foreign policy was apparent to other nations is shown, for example, in a paper by the German ambassador in Rome, Ulrich von Hassell,[10] who soon had to leave the foreign service: 'Here it is a question of a new orientation of German foreign policy, which, at the instigation of no less a person than the ambassador in London [Ribbentrop himself], sets itself in open opposition to England and directly contemplates a world conflict'.[11]

As can be seen from Ribbentrop's memoranda and embassy reports,[12] he too saw an international crisis coming. In view of the incompatibility of German foreign policy objectives as outlined by Hitler with the underlying principles governing British objectives, he came to the conclusion that a German-British conflict was unavoidable. In contrast to Hassell, however, and to the foreign office generally,[13] he did not wish to delay this at any price, but rather to make direct diplomatic and military preparations in order to ensure victory for Germany. The fact that there were differing concepts of objectives and methods between him and Hitler[14] should be taken into consideration when analysing German foreign policy.

From the end of 1937 NS foreign policy was thus aimed at obtaining territorial gains in the face of British opposition and preparing for the resultant and almost inevitable German-British confrontation. If Ribbentrop recommended to the *Führer* 'the creation of an alliance against England, in utter secrecy but with absolute determination',[15] he there anticipated his policy from 1938 onwards. His final ambassadorial report of 28 December 1937, which can be evaluated as a supplement or even a continuation of the thoughts of Hitler as set out in the 'Hossbach Memorandum',[16] therefore offers an important clue to understanding the changes in German foreign policy in 1938. In connection with this, the three-power alliance between Germany, Italy and Japan, which Ribbentrop intended to extend into a military alliance in the immediate future, can also be seen as the guiding theme of his policies over the next few years. 'Whatever significance for the total policy of the Reich in the two years before the outbreak of war is to be attributed to the three-power pact negotiations, needs no further elucidation when considered in the light of some quotations from Ribbentrop's memorandum. It contained the grand design of the NS leaders to neutralise their most dangerous opponent, Great Britain, and with their freedom of movement thus protected by political manoeuvre, to rearrange the map of eastern central Europe according to their own wishes'.[17] Countless documents and references can be found showing Ribbentrop's direct aim for this goal and his tenacity in maintaining the policy outlined by him at the end of 1937. His intentions were, moreover, quite clear in his wooing of Japan towards a close military alliance, on the one hand that he should not press his Asiatic partner too far, and on the other that he still needed to include Italy as well. Already in his 'Note for the *Führer*' of 2 January 1938 he had requested Italy's entry into the 'great alliance' directed against England. Immediately after the successfully organised *Anschluss* of Austria with the German Reich, he believed he could begin an initiative towards Rome. A German-Italian treaty would insure them in their next step – the solution of the Sudeten problem – against the possible involvement of the western powers. For 'against France and England, the only solution to the Czech problem was close cooperation with the Italians', as Hitler's *Wehrmacht* adjutant, Schmundt, was quoted as saying in April 1938.[18]

The envisaged pact was due to be concluded in May 1938 on the occasion of a seven-day state visit to Rome.[19] But Ciano knew very well how to torpedo and drown his German colleague's plan. He gave the German delegation to understand that the forthcoming Italian-English discussions made any close German-Italian alliance seem inadvisable. The 'weekend crisis' of 20–21 May 1938[20] forced Ribbentrop and Hitler to press for renewed alliance talks. For Hitler, who felt personally affronted by foreign reactions to alleged German troop movements, only a 'military solution' now remained, which was nevertheless to be secured by diplomatic measures.

Thus, Japan as well as Italy again assumed great significance. At the end of May 1938, the German leader explained in no uncertain terms to Ott, the German ambassador in Tokyo, that he was firmly expecting a German-English confrontation, because London would always oppose any German territorial conquests in eastern Europe. And as he was unable to abandon his plans for territorial gains, he considered it essential that German diplomacy should realign Japan from her hitherto anti-Russian policy to an anti-British one.[21] Hitler's words are of interest, because on the one hand they pinpoint the direction of future NS foreign policy, and on the other they reflect, not only in their tone but even in their formulation, Ribbentrop's evaluation of Anglo-German relations, and as a result subsequent German political moves. Hitler thereby identified himself with the policy proclaimed by Ribbentrop, which had already made some initial gains.

On 19 April 1938 the new chief of the Foreign Office, *Reichsaussenminister* von Ribbentrop, showed to the likewise newly appointed state secretary in the Wilhelmstrasse, Ernst von Weizsäcker, a memorandum intended for Hitler, with which he was attempting to commit the *Führer* to an anti-British policy. As so often in 1937, Ribbentrop repeated that German plans for expansion could not be carried out without English resistance. Therefore reason demanded that they should designate Russia as the ostensible opponent, but in reality they should orientate everything against British world power. It was not necessary to fear the Soviet Union at that time because it was 'eliminating itself'.[22] This current appraisal of Soviet politics can only be attributed to the effects of the purging of the Red Army, which was expected to lead to a considerable weakening of the military potential of Soviet power. For this reason, as Ribbentrop assured Weizsäcker, there was no need, in contrast to the period before the First World War, to fear a war on two fronts, that is a confrontation with England, France and the Soviet Union simultaneously. The German-Italian-Japanese power combination was therefore a guarantee of the success of German expansionist policy.[23]

The persistence with which Ribbentrop tried to accomplish the aims of his concept of foreign policy is also demonstrated in his efforts to achieve coordination of the news media with Tokyo and Rome. Already in his 'note for the *Führer*' of 2 January 1938 he had written: 'It is my opinion that Germany, Italy and Japan must on the other hand stand firm together. . . . Also with regard to news services and propaganda, one can, in my opinion, never have enough such friends when the pressure is on'.[24] As a result of the anti-German press campaign sparked off by the May crisis, he approached Oshima, the Japanese ambassador in Berlin, on this very topic on 17 June 1938.[25] He tried systematically using various methods to win Japan over to a close alliance with the German Reich. Two days later he revealed his actual objectives to Attolico, the Italian ambassador in Berlin. He set out in great detail his view that the gulf between the democracies and the totalitarian states would become even greater. The western powers wishing, as initiators of the Versailles system, to maintain the status quo in world politics, were eager to obstruct every justifiable and legitimate objective of the 'young' nations. They would even go so far as to drive Italy out of Abyssinia, and with this threat Ribbentrop was attempting to put pressure on the Italians.

In view of the polarisation of world politics, there was only one way open for the totalitarian states: to form a strong bloc in order to be able to attain their objectives together. Attolico therefore informed the German foreign minister of his own instructions, which were, of course, too restrictive for the German. In reply to this, Ribbentrop emphasised that only a strong military alliance would offer the expanding powers any possibility of retaining what had been gained, and above all of attaining their further objectives. Finally both diplomats agreed that they should win Japan over to the idea of a pact.

The countless attempts by Ribbentrop to achieve a closely united three-power pact with Italy and Japan, an 'international political triangle', against Great Britain, were, however, largely unsuccessful during 1938. The phase of mutual probings and soundings finally came to an end at the turn of the year 1938–39. The following months were marked by official tripartite discussions at the highest level. This time it was Mussolini who set things in motion. Reacting to the deepening tension between Paris and Rome, and in view of Fascist Italy's plans for an offensive against Albania, the *Duce*, after long hesitation, felt himself compelled to give up his 'diplomacy of two-shouldered water-carrying',[26] a policy which strove to keep the doors to either Berlin or

London from closing finally, and come out fully in favour of Hitler's Germany. To his son-in-law, foreign minister Ciano, he expressed his wish to seal the pact between Germany, Italy and Japan so often suggested by Ribbentrop, by the end of January 1939. 'More and more he considers a collision with the western democracies to be unavoidable and he would like to complete the disposition of the forces well beforehand. In the course of this month, he wishes to prepare public opinion, which he holds in low esteem in any case.' Thus did Ciano describe his father-in-law's changed outlook.[27]

It is worth noting here that Mussolini had now swung over completely to Ribbentrop's anti-British policy. The *Duce* too was now advocating the involvement of Jugoslavia, Hungary and Romania in the German-Italian-Japanese alliance which, now independent in sources of vital raw materials, 'can defy every coalition'.[28] It was exactly this idea that Ribbentrop had in mind when he was working towards the possible inclusion of other countries in his own plans for a continental union against Great Britain. And just as Ribbentrop intended to use this anti-British combination of powers for the realisation of plans for eastern Europe, so Mussolini hoped to obtain 'supporting cover' for his own planned Albanian adventure.[29]

The NS foreign minister therefore greeted Mussolini's readiness to form the alliance with the bombastic words that this political step was 'one of the greatest deeds in history'.[30] Hitler declared in his Reichstag speech of 30 January 1939 that National Socialist Germany understood completely 'that other peoples also wanted to secure their share of the good things of the world, in direct proportion as to their numbers, their fortitude and their worth'.[31]

'The idea of a mutually acquisitive society could scarcely be put in a more blatant way. Hitler knew exactly how he could bind Mussolini in this way most tightly and firmly to Germany, and knew that he was goading him forwards on the path of Roman expansionism and thereby widening the gulf between Italy and the western democracies even more.'[32] This recognised and practised tactic of Hitler's had already proved successful during the Abyssinian war.[33]

The Italian draft for the treaty, in which the anti-Communist direction was completely lacking, met with Ribbentrop's unqualified approval. However, the Japanese were of a different mind. The clearly anti-British function of this alliance appeared to them to be too risky. The differences in the terms of the alliance, between Germany and Italy on the one side and Japan on the other, were increased by the crisis in world politics[34] which had been created by Germany's annexation of Czechia and the creation of the 'Protectorate of Bohemia and Moravia'.[35] Japan feared a European conflict and now tried to distinguish clearly between an anti-Soviet and an anti-British alliance. The changes in the pact which Ribbentrop had demanded again and again were therefore rejected by Tokyo and reduced to a clear emphasis on the anti-Communist nature of the tripartite alliance, a requirement which completely contradicted Ribbentrop's intentions. Nevertheless, whether through arrogant optimism or lack of insight, he simply could not accept this Japanese reluctance. 'The Japanese alliance still lay closest to his heart. In it he saw the "grand design" that would surely change the increasing deterioration of the German position.'[36] The balance had shifted since the March crisis to the disadvantage of Germany, and Ribbentrop was hoping to redress this by binding Japan more tightly to the Berlin-Rome axis, thereby creating an all-embracing, global balance of power.

With the help of threats and pressure he was still trying to persuade the hesitant Japanese to join his ideal alliance. He held out to them both the possibility of an exclusive German-Italian alliance and the spectre of a German-Soviet rapprochement. In spite of all this, Japan remained cautious, even to the extent of rejecting the three-power pact. Ribbentrop had to be content with a two-power alliance between Rome and Berlin.

On 22 May 1939, with a great accompaniment of propaganda, the 'Pact of Steel' was signed and was openly declared to be the main persuasive weapon for any future *Lebensraum* policy. This mighty alliance could scarcely be described more appropriately than in the words of Count

Ciano, writing in his diary: 'I have never before read such a treaty as this. It is real dynamite'.[37]

We can therefore agree with Theo Sommer's metaphorical analysis of the importance of the Steel Pact:

> Hitler was the Roman sparrow in the clenched fist rather than the triple pact dove upon the roof. If there is to be no three-cornered system, he must have said to himself, then rather an axis of steel which may also serve as a crowbar. The Steel Pact smoothed the way for him, in diplomatic terms, in the dispute with Poland. This, however, represented a close-range objective, the attainment of which did not appear to require Japan's support, especially as a prospect was now gradually appearing with the Kremlin at its centre, standing as a possible collaborator in the solution to the Polish problem.[38]

Ribbentrop, who had still not completely given up the idea of a tripartite pact, gave the Japanese ambassador in Berlin his interpretation of the German-Italian alliance, while simultaneously holding a door to this alliance open to the Japanese. At the same time, however, he did not hide his annoyance at the Japanese delaying tactics which had finally forced Germany and Italy to closer alignment with one another without Japan. Nevertheless, he asked the Foreign Office in Tokyo to make up their minds quickly and join the Steel Pact. Ribbentrop's eagerness, in spite of everything, to accomplish his global concept of an international political triangle against Great Britain, first envisaged by him in 1937, is clearly seen here.

The continued lack of response by the Japanese government caused such scepticism in Berlin that the possibility of reaching an understanding with the Soviet Union was no longer ruled out, and in fact was even considered a probability.[39] For Ribbentrop, who preferred to think in terms of opportunism in power politics rather than ideological dogma, the change from the Anti-Comintern pact to an alliance with the Soviet Union was a procedure virtually free of problems; for the Anti-Comintern alliance was, in his view, primarily an anti-British and only secondarily an anti-Soviet alliance, which could now easily be seen in its true light.

Already, in May 1939, he had given the German ambassador in Moscow, Count von der Schulenburg, appropriate instructions for a German-Soviet rapprochement. [The feelers for a Russo-German rapprochment had already been put out by both sides at lower levels during the latter half of March 1939. *Ed.*] The main factor in German foreign policy, he pointed out, was the alliance with Italy which, however, was not directed against the Soviet Union, but exclusively against the Anglo-French alliance. On the subject of German-Japanese relations, he then explained that these had developed historically out of the Anti-Comintern policy.

> This device does not represent, however, the actual central political issue of what we intend at this present time, of cultivating German-Japanese relations. We are thinking more in terms now of concerted opposition to England. In view of our good relations with Japan we consider ourselves now to be in a position of being able to counteract any Japanese-Russian friction ... and ... to contrive that Japanese foreign policy should gradually assume a direction which would not bring her into conflict with Russia.[40]

These words were undoubtedly received with astonishment in Moscow.

The same instruction shows Ribbentrop's concept of a European-Asiatic continental bloc, which was to stretch from Gibraltar as far as Yokohama and was to have an unambiguously anti-British alignment. This concept of a bloc of four was often to be repeated by Ribbentrop in the future; in his opinion, it was the only effective provision which could promise any success against an Anglo-American coalition. For him this policy could be considered as an alternative to Hitler's 'push to the East'. At the end of May 1939 Hitler's foreign minister had already toyed with the idea of using a Japanese-Russian settlement, arranged by him, as a form of cost price payment for a German-Soviet detente – an idea which two months later was to thrust itself more and more to the fore in his political thinking.[41]

On 5 July 1939 Ribbentrop expressed to the Bulgarian prime minister Kiosseiwanoff his hope for an agreement between the powers of the Anti-Comintern pact and the Soviet Union. He gave his assurance that there was no conflict of interests between the German Reich and Soviet Russia. In support of this declaration, which sounded so incredible in view of Hitler's *Lebensraum* policy, the German foreign minister emphasised that 'the *Führer* was not a Napoleon in search of a Moscow adventure'.[42] It is not really clear whether, in making this remark, Ribbentrop was merely counting on making Bulgaria completely dependent upon Germany, or whether he was declaring his own foreign policy, which could not condone an expansionist and ideological war of destruction against the Soviet Union. However, if one compares the conversation Hitler had had immediately beforehand with his Bulgarian guest, at which Ribbentrop was also present, then the difference in emphasis between Hitler and his foreign minister is remarkable. The *Führer* was arguing in general terms without entering into precise details,[43] whereas the head of the Foreign Office was offering the Bulgarian head of state a declaration of the principles governing a definite foreign policy. As there was no compelling reason for this within the German-Bulgarian discussions, Ribbentrop's remark can only be considered as a restatement of his own policy. It was probably a supplementary justification for a previously developed concept which had frequently been presented to Hitler, and which, in view of tentative Soviet steps towards alliance, now seemed close to becoming reality. In contrast to Hitler, who was striving for an alliance which would make possible his *Lebensraum* war in the East, Ribbentrop's aim, at least since 1937, was the creation of a political situation in which either Britain, as the main opponent (in his view) of German revisionary and colonial power, would be compelled to wait in the wings if war came, or – if British neutrality could not be achieved – Germany in its struggle against Britain would be backed by an alliance of such overpowering magnitude that victory would be assured in any military conflict. The 'international political triangle' between Berlin, Rome and Tokyo had been conceived originally with this in mind. Now, however, a replacement structure seemed to be developing, with a possible extension towards a European-Asiatic bloc of four. A German-Soviet liaison at that moment offered Germany everything that it could require in the present circumstances:

> the chance, slim as it may have been, that the European democracies, merely through the very completion of the pact, would be shocked into a state of inactive torpor; but above all, the certainty that it would not come to a war on two fronts, with Germany being protected even more effectively in the East than by any Japanese demonstration in Manchuria or outside Vladivostock. Furthermore the pact, as signed by Ribbentrop and Molotov, laid no kind of premium on the good conduct of the Reich. The security of its eastern borders remained fully guaranteed, even if Germany itself were to be the aggressor [as Hitler of course had in mind].[44]

After the completion of the German-Soviet Non-Aggression Pact on 24 August 1939, German-Japanese relations reached their lowest ebb. The Japanese felt themselves to be deceived and betrayed by this diplomatic coup. Yet despite his feeling of triumph at having trumped the French and especially the English, in September 1939 Ribbentrop was still giving voice to his original plan of alliance, the anti-British continental bloc of Berlin-Rome-Moscow and Tokyo. He therefore renewed his efforts to win over Japan. Immediately after the beginning of the war, on 9 September 1939, he revealed to Oshima, the Japanese ambassador in Berlin, his 'global' concept. He proceeded cleverly with this, pointing out to the annoyed and distrustful Japanese the advantages and the necessity of a 'political world-wide square'.[45] If Germany were to lose the war, he argued, then the western democracies would form a world-wide coalition and drive Japan into a corner, so that any Japanese policy of expansion would be impossible and even their Chinese possessions would be snatched away. A German victory, on the other hand, which in view of the newly created situation seemed to Ribbentrop a foregone conclusion, would finally confirm Japan's hegemony in the Far East, provided that previous good relations were maintained and strengthened. In this respect the German-Russian agreement would also be of great advantage for Japan. If an agreement could be reached between Moscow and Tokyo – which was his especial aim – then Japan could immediately turn south and expand in the very area where her vital interests lay. The idea of close political cooperation between Berlin, Rome and Tokyo was therefore far from dead. 'Ribbentrop left them in no doubt as to whom they should direct this cooperation against: entirely against England. According to his interpretation, this would put the policy of the three powers and also that of Russia on a unified course, corresponding exactly to the practical interests of all parties.'[46]

The German successes in the Polish campaign caused Oshima and his colleague in Rome, Shiratori, both of whom had originally requested their recall to Japan, to swing over to Ribbentrop's plans. Both set themselves from then on to work for a Japanese-Soviet rapprochement directed towards an international political bloc of four. Yet although the Japanese government felt itself compelled to disregard any border incidents with the Soviet Union, it could not feel enthusiastic about an alliance with Moscow, and the Japanese-Soviet truce therefore did not correspond to either Oshima's or Ribbentrop's ideas. Apparently the German government was not even informed of the negotiations between Tokyo and Moscow, so Ribbentrop's offer to be the negotiator was rejected out of hand.[47]

'On his debut as a peace negotiator, Hitler's foreign minister had therefore sadly suffered disaster. Both the Russians and the Japanese had cold-shouldered him. Thus both his plan for a four-power pact and the attempt to manoeuvre Japan into an anti-British channel were condemned to failure.'[48] This is the verdict passed by Theo Sommer on Ribbentrop's policy in September 1939. His pro-Japanese concept, which he had pursued more or less successfully since 1934–35, had received a severe setback.

Ribbentrop expressed his changed views of the formerly oft-courted Japanese to his Italian colleague on 1 October 1939. 'With the upsurge of the new love for the Soviets in Ribbentrop's thinking', writes the Italian foreign minister, 'the old passion for Japan has disappeared, that Japan which – as he was wont to say – was no longer one of the fundamental powers of the modern world, an unconquerable country, an heroic people etc., etc., but instead of this, just another Asiatic state, which has the misfortune to be governed by a clique of out-dated militarists of little intelligence.'[49]

Despite this change of opinion, Ribbentrop's interest in Japan was not to cool completely. Already, in the spring of 1940, the situation had improved, in both his and Hitler's view. The immediacy of the expansionist policy in Scandinavia and in France caused Japan to become an important counterbalance to Great Britain, but more particularly to the USA, which in 1940 had more and more to be taken into consideration by German politicians. For the first time, therefore, Japan took on an anti-American role which was to lead to a declaration of intent at the sealing of the tripartite alliance six months later.

In this connection, it must not be forgotten that when in March 1940 Ribbentrop again took his four-power plan out of the drawer and set about its accomplishment, it was against a changed international background. Once again he tried to intercede between Japan and the Soviet Union, but again with no significant result. Success, however, (though coming in different circumstances) was to lie in the fact that this led to the summer of 1940 which was rich in military and political gains for Germany. After Holland had been overrun by German troops and the defeat of France was virtually assured, with the result that Germany's chances of victory over England were increased, the government in Tokyo felt itself compelled to revise its existing policy towards Germany and Italy.[50] The unexpected and rapid German victories over the colonial powers of Holland and France opened new perspectives for Japanese policy which had scarcely been considered possible before. An expansion to the south-west, to the Dutch East Indies and French

Indo-China, would be a mere formality. All that remained to be clarified was how the German victors would react to the Japanese territorial claims. Now it was not only Great Britain and the USA who were the main challengers to Japanese imperialism but also the German Reich. Concern spread in the Japanese ministries that Germany would degrade Holland and France to being vassal states and then send a protective army to the East Indies and Indo-China in order to make these colonies into dependencies. However, against all expectations, Ribbentrop calmed these Japanese fears. He had a declaration made in Tokyo that the German Reich had no possessions in the Far East. What motives could there be behind this 'renunciation'?

Theo Sommer points out that Ribbentrop – as a year earlier in the case of Italy – wanted to press Japan towards expansion in the East Indies in order to involve her in opposing Britain and the USA, with the aim of causing Tokyo – under pressure – to have to decide ultimately for Berlin.[51] In addition, of course, there were also military and strategic factors to be considered.

The German-Japanese-Italian talks which finally led to the three-power agreement in September 1940 illuminate Ribbentrop's endeavours to attain his original plan of the 'international political triangle' and to fit it into the new political situation, which had undergone changes due to the German-Soviet alliance, and finally extend it to an 'international political square'. When he met the former Japanese foreign minister, Sato, who came to Berlin via Rome in order to sound out the German position with regard to the 'ownerless' colonies in the Far East, Ribbentrop gave a clear idea of the alterations in the pact. He described the prospects for the future in glowing colours to the Japanese guest: 'Under the new world order, Japan would hold sway in Eastern Asia, Russia in Asia itself, Germany and Italy in Europe; and also in Africa it would be exclusively Germany and Italy, perhaps with a few other interested nations, who would gain ascendancy and rule.'[52] But Ribbentrop took his vision of external politics one step further by giving the Japanese diplomat the impression that South American states were already turning to the German

Reich in order to maintain or instigate economic agreements with this new world power, especially in view of the distinct possibility of a rapid German victory over the British empire.[53]

The view of foreign policy indicated here, which may be considered as the consequence of Ribbentrop's concept, also explains his 'generous' declaration of renunciation to Japan. In the main he was eager to put together a world-wide anti-British alliance which was also intended to neutralise the USA. Because of this, he needed Japan as an important cornerstone in the new world order at which he was aiming. With the help of his European-Asiatic continental bloc, he wanted to keep the traditional sea power of Great Britain within bounds – an aim similar to that of German foreign policy before the First World War – and at the same time release the German Reich from its continental European straitjacket. Only in this way, in Ribbentrop's opinion, could Germany grow to be a world power on an equal footing with the British empire and the USA. With this concept of a continental bloc Ribbentrop was identifying closely with the ideas of the geo-politicians Friedrich Ratzel, Erich Obst, Otto Maul and above all Karl Haushofer, who in the tradition of Halford J. Mackinder, Alfred T. Mahan and James Fairgrive, based their theories on the premise that a German-Russian union would create a European-Asiatic bloc which, at least from the geo-political viewpoint, would be predestined for world dominance.[54] 'The new bloc which would result would be able to span the whole of Europe and Asia with its power, then, with the basic resources of the two continents, build a powerful fleet, and the *Weltreich* would be in sight.'[55] In contrast, however, to Ribbentrop, whose idea of the crowning glory to his foreign policy lay in 'permanent' cooperation with the Soviet Union and Japan, incorporated in a powerful continental bloc which would rule the world, Hitler's relations with Tokyo and Moscow were involved mainly in the transformation of the fronts. Was it not Hitler who wanted close cooperation with Great Britain on a 'basic of a sharing-out of the world' and, by means of an ideological war of extermination against 'Jewish-Bolshevist' Russia, with them to become conquerors of a gigantic eastern empire, in order to enable Germany to emerge as a new world power alongside Great Britain, the USA and Japan? After the successful Scandinavian campaign and the rapid capitulation of France in June 1940, Hitler had achieved virtually everything that was set out in his 'programme'[56] devised as early as the 1920s. Only Great Britain, 'the key in the lock of German foreign policy from Bismarck through William II, and Tirpitz down as far as Hitler, was not behaving "according to programme"'.[57] All 'generous' offers to the English side were rejected.[58] Hitler was only able to explain the decision of the British government to continue the war despite its hopeless position and not to act upon his suggestions of an alliance, by thinking that London was still counting on two allies, the United States and the Soviet Union, so that in time an enormous anti-Hitler coalition could be formed, aimed at gradually starving out and finally conquering the German Reich, in much the same way as in the last phase of the First World War.[59] [That this view of Hitler's emerged only gradually during the summer and autumn months of 1940 is shown in the next contribution below. *Ed.*]

Accordingly, after the summer of 1940, the following alternatives arose for Hitler: *either* he could (as his foreign minister, especially, never tired of requesting) form a powerful anti-British alliance in which, alongside Italy, France, Spain and countless satellite states in south-east Europe, as well as Japan in the Far East, the Soviet Union would ultimately have to play a major part in order to deal the final, decisive and eliminating blow to the British by means of a global pincer operation through the Mediterranean, the Indian Ocean and the Atlantic; *or* he could (because the USA could not be seen as opponents for a reasonable period of time) overrun the Soviet Union by way of a *Blitzkrieg* on a large scale, thereby, as well as achieving more of his planned *Lebensraum* conquests, also banishing the 'continental sword' from the hands of Great Britain, and forcing London to be more reasonable. In addition, as Ribbentrop also hoped, Japan could concentrate its entire military strength against the United States and thus keep

Roosevelt from entering the war on the side of England. The neutralising of the USA and the isolating of Great Britain would therefore be attained as a side issue.

'The inclusion of the Soviet Union in the new continental bloc represented in itself a significant alternative to a German offensive against that country.'[60] While Hitler would be making adjustments to his 'programmed' march to the East and against the North, the German Reich could negotiate the partition of the British empire with the help of the Soviets and Japanese. A new partition of the world at Great Britain's expense would be the logical procedure to adopt. These external political alternatives governed all German foreign policy in the second half of 1940, until finally Hitler's 'programmed' war of extermination against the Soviet Union was set in motion.[61]

Hitler's conversion to opportunism in power politics, the key to Ribbentrop's foreign policy, was accordingly only of short duration and in its final analysis was a result of the 'unprogrammed' behaviour of Great Britain. The *Führer's* monomania kept him firmly on the path of his policy of racial ideology, which had as its objective the destruction of the Soviet Union. In this respect, Hitler's 'most remarkable utterance' made to the Swiss League of Nations Commissioner in Danzig, Carl J. Burckhardt, contained also his ultimate intent: 'Everything that I undertake is directed against Russia; if the West is too stupid and too blind to understand this, I shall be compelled to come to an agreement with the Russians, conquer the West and then, after its defeat, turn my attention again with my entire forces against the Soviet Union.'[62] [How far this utterance is authentic and reflects Hitler's thinking is subject to debate among historians. Burckhardt published it only in 1961. *Ed.*]

10. Hitler's 'Programme' and the Genesis of Operation 'Barbarossa'

H. W. KOCH

I

Hitler's foreign policy is still an area of widespread interest – particularly the question of its inner coherence. The present consensus goes back to the early 1950s and 1960s, when the German attack upon Russia was viewed as one stage in Hitler's quest for European hegemony or even world domination. While Alan Bullock viewed Hitler as an opportunist, Hugh Trevor-Roper in his essay on Hitler's war aims interpreted Hitler's invasion of Russia as a systematic step in Hitler's programme.[1] Since then this model has been highly refined and systematised, notably by Andreas Hillgruber,[2] who argues that Hitler's foreign policy programme had already been formulated long before he came to power, particularly in *Mein Kampf* and Hitler's *Second Book*. On this model National Socialist foreign policy was programmatically fixed and Hillgruber goes as far as to say that Hitler's programme 'alone determined the great

From *Historical Journal*, 26, No. 4 (1983), 891–919.

line of German policy in general' and that he devoted all
the energies available to him to realising it.[3] Yet even before
Hillgruber had formulated his model, case studies were
available which appeared to contradict its inner coherence
and logic.[4] Serious objections have also been raised by
Martin Broszat, who describes Hitler's idea of an eastern
empire as a 'metaphor and utopian figure of speech'.[5]

Certainly, from an early stage Hitler had based the
content of his foreign policy pronouncements upon racial,
biological and geopolitical principles. In Hillgruber's view,
Hitler's 'programme, his *Stufenplan*, envisaged first of all the
consolidation of the NSDAP within the Reich, then re-
establishment of military sovereignty in the demilitarised
zone of Germany, followed by an aggressive foreign policy
which in stages would ultimately achieve for Germany world
hegemony'. However, one major problem is presented by
the available sources, or rather the way sources have been
used. Hillgruber, who in 1964 had published a brilliant
essay on sources and source criticism in the history leading
up to the Second World War, in his own work ignores the
very warnings which he had given.[6] The most recent
challenge to Hillgruber's thesis of Hitler's long-term aim of
carrying out the 'Final Solution' of the Jewish problem by
way of genocide has come from none other than Martin
Broszat.[7]

It cannot be the task of this essay to dismantle Hillgruber's
thesis piece by piece. However, the analysis of the genesis of
operation 'Barbarossa' serves as a test and an example
demonstrating how questionable apparently closed and
logical models of explanation are. Within the scheme of the
Stufenplan, the conclusion of the Russo-German Non-
Aggression Pact represented the necessary precondition
which enabled Hitler to conduct his war against an isolated
Poland, which he is alleged to have deliberately engineered.
It is conveniently forgotten that the initiative for a bilateral
German–Polish settlement over the Danzig and the Corridor
question had come at the height of the Munich crisis from
the Poles and not from the Germans. The solution then
outlined by Hitler was the same as that put forward by
Ribbentrop from November 1938 onwards; he picked up the

threads which the Polish ambassador in Berlin, Lipski, had begun to spin the previous September.[8]

Also other important motives for Germany's rapprochement with Russia are ignored. Firstly, in view of the Anglo-French–Soviet military talks Hitler could hardly afford to remain passive, since he could not exclude the possibility of a coalition between the three powers. Secondly, and more important, the conclusion of the Russo-German Pact on 23 August 1939 was the motive not to provoke war, *so oder so*, but by means of the agreement to exert such pressure upon the Poles that they would accept the compromise proposals put forward by Hitler and Ribbentrop for the solution of the Danzig and the Corridor problem. Immediately, though unsuccessfully, from the time of the conclusion of the pact until 3 September, Germany sent request upon request to Moscow, firstly to send a Soviet military mission to Berlin and, secondly, to move strong Russian troop concentrations along Poland's eastern frontier.[9] In other words through pressure from the east and west the Poles were to be coerced into realising the hopelessness of their position and accepting the German proposals. A man determined to erase Poland from the political map was hardly likely to have recourse to this wide range of political pressure in order to prevent a war which allegedly he was set upon provoking.[10]

Naturally the Russo-German pact also caused considerable surprise inside Germany. But it is important to distinguish between various important groupings in Germany, since the myth of the German monolith dominated by the Führer has crumbled into dust long ago.[11] Firstly, of course, there was Hitler himself, often erratic and indecisive, difficult in making up his mind, but once made up carrying through a decision relentlessly. Secondly, there was Ribbentrop, foreign minister since 1938 and, contrary to the orthodoxy current in the half century not simply a cypher and his master's voice, but according to the results of recent research a man capable of devising his own concept of a foreign policy, even if this initially did not accord with Hitler's own ideas on the subject.[12] Ribbentrop after his return from his London embassy was convinced that Great Britain would oppose any German expansionist course in Europe. His summing-up report about his ambassadorial activities in London, which the Nuremberg prosecution team, despite repeated requests, withheld from the defence, while it rested peacefully in the archive of the Foreign Office, provides a very realistic assessment of official British attitudes towards the Third Reich.[13] From the moment of becoming foreign minister Ribbentrop consistently worked at achieving one objective: the creation of a continental, even Eurasian bloc against Great Britain, which was to keep her in check on a global scale and allow Germany to reach what had eluded her in 1914: the status of a world power. Such a continental bloc included Italy, but it was also to include Japan and Soviet Russia. The Russo-German pact was not something that for the Germans just luckily dropped out of the blue, but was part of Ribbentrop's scheme of forging a continental bloc directed against Great Britain. It was to be defensive in the sense of preventing Great Britain from pursuing her traditional balance-of-power policy in Europe, but offensive in the sense that it aimed at establishing German hegemony in central and eastern central Europe with sufficient weight to exercise pressure upon Great Britain and France to make concessions to Germany's colonial ambitions.[14]

Thirdly, there was the army, which in spite of Hitler achieving supremacy over it as a result of the Blomberg/Fritsch crisis of 1938, had for some years come to enjoy relative autonomy and some of whose leaders belonged to the circle of opposition to Hitler.[15] Until the winter crisis of 1941–2 they, especially the chief of the general staff, General Halder, exerted decisive influence in military policy making and on occasions showed no hesitation in ignoring or even forgetting about Hitler's orders.[16]

II

The Russo-German pact came as an utter surprise to the members of the German opposition, especially to Col. General Beck, who as chief of the general staff had resigned during the Czech crisis in 1938, not on moral grounds, but because he was sure it would lead to another world war for which Germany was not armed. Out of his retirement Beck continued to pour out a flood of memoranda in which he criticised Hitler's policy and strategy, so much so that General von Tippelskirch asked 'Does this memorandum originate from an Englishman or a German? In the latter case he is over-ripe for a concentration camp'.[17] Halder was a close disciple of Beck's and so were his closest associates.[18] He was a staunch anti-Bolshevik and shared Beck's anxiety that the Russo-German pact would open the door to the Soviets for expansion into the Baltic and Black Sea areas, an anxiety shared by members of the German Foreign Office.[19]

One other important factor was the way in which Hitler set about dealing with problems, which Halder aptly summarised as: 'when it appeared to him [Hitler] unavoidable to deal with an emerging problem, he used, as far as possible, to enter simultaneously upon all the avenues which would lead to the solution of the problem, in order to have some practicable solution at hand in case of a final decision'.[20]

This does not mean that between September 1939 and July 1940 Hitler considered the Soviet Union as a problem in the short term. There is no evidence that Hitler occupied himself with this problem. Indeed until the late summer of 1940 no offensive plan against the Soviet Union existed in the German general staff. All we have is a record of a discussion with the chief of the OKW, General Keitel, of 17 October 1939 concerning the situation in Poland: 'Our interests consist in the following. Preparations are to be made, since the territory has military significance for us as a forward *glacis* which can be used for military assembly. For this reason railways, roads and communications must for our purposes be kept in order and used.' In the General Government the preconditions for military movements were to be maintained, but the Soviet Union was not mentioned directly or indirectly, let alone that a war should be prepared from Polish soil against the Soviet Union.[21]

From Hitler's point of view the campaign in the west had as its objective to deprive Great Britain of its 'continental sword'; for the protagonists of Hitler's 'programme' it was the necessary precondition before smashing Russia. The compromise peace expected with Great Britain would consolidate Germany's position in the west and allow the German armies to turn east. Halder in his diary noted a remark made by the liaison officer between the OKH and the foreign office, Hasso von Etzdort: 'We are looking for feelers with England on the basis of the division of the world.'[22] This comment does not reveal from whom the idea originated and lacks any concrete indication as to what the 'division' was to look like. To this quotation another is frequently added, reported by General Sodenstern, chief of staff of army group A, according to whom Hitler had said on 2 June 1940: 'If England, as I expect, now gives up and is prepared to make a reasonable peace, then finally I will have my hands free for my really great task: the conflict with Bolshevism.' This evidence is complicated by the fact that Sodenstern withheld it 'for political reasons' until 1954 and that it was not published until 1958.[23] However, when Hitler was alleged to have made this remark, at the headquarters of army group A at Charleville, others were present, including General Blumentritt, who maintains that Hitler had mentioned in passing Russia's build-up of forces in her western border areas and that therefore it would be desirable to conclude a sensible peace with England.[24]

Interestingly enough, it was not Hitler but Halder and the foreign office, notably its secretary of state von Weizsäcker, who recognised a threat to Germany's position through Russian troop assemblies in the Baltic states and to the south, opposite Bessarabia. On 23 May reports of strong Russian troop movements reached the German foreign office and Weizsäcker forwarded them to Ribbentrop, noting in his diary, 'in the east there will be probably a further reckoning',[25] while General Jodl, chief of the Wehrmacht's leadership staff in the OKW, noted in his own diary a day later: 'Because of Russian troop assembly position in the east is threatening.'[26] When the news was reported to Hitler he replied saying that Russia in response to his request would limit herself to Bessarabia. But from 25 May onwards Russia created a series of crises with Lithuania, Estonia and

Latvia, all three of which were occupied by Russia and incorporated in the USSR by 17 June 1940. Precisely during that period Hitler planned a drastic reduction of the German army. 'A precondition for this directive is the assumption that with the immediate final collapse of the enemy the task of the army has been fulfilled and that we can carry out in peace this reconstruction in enemy country, as the basis for future peace time organization',[27] noted Halder on 15 June 1940. Russia's moves were felt as an inconvenience by Hitler, since they threatened Germany's supplies of raw materials. On 23 June Russia had demanded the concession for the nickel ores at Petsamo from Finland and four days later participation in the defence of the Aaland Islands or their demilitarisation. This was followed by Russia's invasion of the northern Bukovina on 28 June 1940. There is nothing to indicate that Hitler envisaged at that stage a campaign against Russia; instead he gave priority of armaments to the Luftwaffe and the Navy.[28] On 25 June Hitler had still sounded optimistic:

> The war in the west has ended. France has been conquered, and I shall come, in the shortest possible time, to an understanding with England. There still remains the conflict with the east. That, however, is a task which throws up world-wide problems, like the relationship with Japan and the distribution of power in the Pacific, one might perhaps tackle it in ten years' time, perhaps I shall have to leave it to my successor. Now we have our hands full for years to come to digest and to consolidate what we have obtained in Europe.[19]

Nothing was mentioned of an eastern campaign to be launched in 1940 or 1941. The directives just issued concerning army manpower and equipment for the armed forces would have been contrary to such a plan. It is quite incorrect to assert; 'as soon as it was clear that France was defeated, Hitler's eyes turned eastwards'.[30] It was not Hitler's eyes that turned eastwards, but those of Halder.[31] While on 26 June Halder expressed his opinion that the Bessarabian question could be solved without any warlike complications (an opinion confirmed a day later by Russia's unopposed occupation of that territory),[32] by 3 July 1940 Halder saw two problems, first how to deal with England and secondly the question of the east: 'The latter will have to be considered from the point of view of how a military stroke can be executed against Russia to force it to recognize the predominating role of Germany in Europe. Besides, special considerations like the Baltic and the Balkan countries may cause variations.'[33] This was to counter Russia's moves to extend its power and influence in areas vital for Germany's war economy. Already on 30 June without instructions from Hitler Halder had ordered his staff to examine the possibilities of a campaign against Russia.[30a] It was not until 21 July 1940 that Hitler himself became active in the planning of such a campaign. The reason is not difficult to discern: the British peace offer did not come.[34] Why did England hold out? The answer to Hitler was simple, American support and 'Stalin courts England to keep her in the struggle to tie us down and to gain time to take what he wants to take and which cannot be taken anymore once peace ensues. He will be concerned that Germany does not become too strong. But there are no signs of Russian activity against us.'[35] Hence his directive, 'Russian problem is to be tackled. Mental preparations to be made.'[36]

III

The question which arises is what caused Hitler to change his mind and, following his chief of the general staff, to turn his eyes to the east? The Russo-German pact contained a consultative clause which compelled both partners to consult on issues touching mutual interests. When Germany had occupied Denmark and Norway, she had failed to consult the Soviet Union first. But Ribbentrop managed to explain it away by saying that Scandinavia would have become a theatre of war and, more important, that by allied action the Finnish question would have been resurrected. The Kremlin's fear that Sweden might be drawn into the conflict proved unfounded. Russia, which had stopped its deliveries of grain and oil, resumed its supplies to Germany.[37] But the lesson was not lost in Germany where the ugly words 'Soviet blackmail' made the rounds. Russia's conflict with Finland, settled in March 1940, had also threatened the nickel supplies from Petsamo, essential to the German war economy. It was therefore of paramount interest for the German leadership to contain the conflict in Norway, and bring it to an end as quickly as possible. What applied to Finland applied in equal measure to south-eastern Europe, to Romania in particular, whose oil supplies represented the mainstay of Germany's oil imports until August 1944. Consequently most of the Balkans became for the Germans a security zone within which the allies would have to be prevented from establishing bases which could be used in the launching of air raids against the Ploesti oilfields, or to gain a foothold in the Balkans to mount a land operation in this direction. On the question of oil supplies the Soviet Union occupied a crucial position both as a supplier of oil itself and as the power nearest to Romania's oil. Molotov's proclamation in December 1939 to the effect that Russia's great aims lay in south-eastern Europe and the Black Sea, whose attainment required a quick end to the Russo-Finnish conflict,[38] was bound to have been received with unease by the German leadership whose paramount interest in the Balkans as well as north-eastern Europe was to maintain calm and peace. Another power with traditional Balkan interests was Italy, and Hitler urged upon Mussolini the necessity to keep still in the region, which Mussolini promised to do.[39] However, as a result of the Paris peace treaties of 1919, Romania was surrounded by three 'revisionist' powers, Soviet Russia, Bulgaria and Hungary, each anxious to regain territories lost to Romania. This of course was realised in Germany, but for the moment the launching of the western campaign dominated the thinking of Germany's political and military leaders. Once Germany had launched its offensive, Stalin was not slow in following it up with his own demands, namely Bessarabia. On 22 May 1940 Germany received the news of the Russian demands on Romania but, as we have seen already, Hitler believed they would be satisfied with Bessarabia.[40] King Carol of Romania, who had expected this, had already addressed a letter to Hitler a week before, asking for his support and help in building fortifications on Romania's eastern frontier. Hitler did not bother to reply.[41] But the German army leaders recognised the danger, so did the *Seekriegsleitung*.[42] On 25 May the German foreign office drew Russia's attention to the fact that her moves against Romania at this point were highly inconvenient to Germany and Italy.[43] Great Britain, aware of the difficulties in the Balkans, announced the dispatch of Sir Stafford Cripps as envoy extraordinary to Moscow, a move whose effect the German ambassador in Moscow, Count von der Schulenburg, did his utmost to minimise with a success confirmed by a *Tass* communiqué of 30 May stating that the Soviet government could not receive Cripps or anyone else in the capacity of special or extraordinary plenipotentiary.[44] However, King Carol, when confronted by the Russian pressure, opted for Germany and on 27 May signed the oil pact which Germany had pursued for more than two years.[45]

In the meantime Russia liquidated the Baltic states, a process completed before the campaign in the west had ended and watched with disquiet by the Germans, especially as the Russians occupied a small territorial strip around Mariampul in Lithuania which had originally been consigned to the German sphere of influence in 1939. With that the Russians bolted the door to German access to the Baltic countries. Russia's annexations also had economic consequences. Seventy per cent of the exports of these three countries had been absorbed by Germany, mainly wheat, butter, pork, dairy produce, flax, wood and oil. A German foreign office assessment of the situation recorded that 'the stabilization of the Russian influence in these territories signifies a serious danger for us in so far as these essential supplies are concerned'.[46]

Rumours of Russian troop movements circulated in Berlin, which were immediately denounced by *Tass* as lies.[47] The Russian action in north-eastern Europe was also correctly interpreted as an overture to the solution of the Bessarabian question.[48] Hitler, and Ribbentrop for that matter, had interpreted 'spheres of interest' rather literally, neither of them expecting the total destruction of the sovereignty of the states concerned. Hitler therefore emphasised Germany's economic interest in Romania.[49] On 23 June Molotov informed the German ambassador that the question of Bessarabia would no longer brook any delay, furthermore Soviet demands extended also to the Bukovina whose population he alleged to be Ukrainian.[50] Schulenburg was surprised at the speed of Russia's action. He was also surprised that Russia had successfully sought Italian backing. Relations between Russia and Italy had considerably improved during May 1940, and Italy, which in 1939 had still promised aid to Romania in case of a Russian attack, stepped into accord with Russia, ostensibly to solve the Bessarabian problem with Germany.[51] Ribbentrop tried to counter this development, especially Italy's involvement in the Balkans, because the status quo there was not to be disturbed. He informed the Soviets that Germany had no objection to Russian claims for Bessarabia provided the claims could be realised in a way which would not result in war-like complications. Nevertheless the Italians could not be kept out of the game altogether. Ambassadors were exchanged between Moscow and Rome. This step was welcomed by Ribbentrop because it was in line with the foreign policy aims he had had since 1938.

In principle, harmony with the Soviet Union and Italy was one of Ribbentrop's desiderata, as long as this harmony was not at the expense of the tranquillity of south-eastern Europe. Yet when the Italian ambassador Rosso visited Molotov in the Kremlin on 17 and 20 June, Molotov picked up precisely those issues which were likely to produce conflict. Molotov declared his support for the territorial demands of Bulgaria and Hungary, namely the Dobrudsja and access to the Aegean Sea; Hungary's demands on Romania he felt justified, and in the background of Molotov's elaborations was the unspoken aim of Russian expansion via Bulgaria to the Straits.[52] This, as Molotov pointed out, produced tensions with Turkey, the sources of which needed to be removed, but with due regard for German and Italian interests there. He furthermore acknowledged Italy's predominance in the Mediterranean, provided Italy would do the same as regards Soviet Russia and her claims in the Black Sea.[53]

The country which was expected to pay the highest price for these arrangements was Romania. The German foreign office felt ill at ease in face of Moscow's call to Bulgaria and Hungary to state their claims against Romania. Molotov was obviously a man in a hurry, and he made his demands at a time when a total of a hundred Soviet divisions on Russia's western frontier confronted a weak German covering force. As a result Halder on 25 June increased the German forces in the east to twenty-four divisions, including six armoured and three motorised divisions, a force still small compared with that of Russia.[54] Also Stalin's demand for the Bukovina had made Hitler angry, since it was of strategic importance.[55] Flanking the Moldavian territory, it controls the river Pruth from its source to its mouth, quite apart from the closer proximity of the Russians to the Ploesti oilfields. Hitler was bound to feel that his dependence on Russia was increasing.

Ribbentrop tried to counter the Russian demand for the Bukovina and Molotov ostensibly gave way on 26 June, restricting his claim to the northern Bukovina with the city of Czernowicz which provided the Soviet Union with the important rail link from Bessarabia via Czernowicz to Lvov. The following day Russia issued her ultimatum demanding the cession of Bessarabia and the northern Bukovina.[56] The effects of the ultimatum were profound. Romania, which so far had tried to steer a neutral course between the warring groups in Europe, had to take sides and chose Germany in the hope of German intervention. King Carol was prepared to fight, but Ribbentrop advised Romania to accept the Russian demands in order to avoid war. Only one power could benefit from a war in Balkans: Great Britain. More important, Romania's oil production was bound to suffer. Therefore Ribbentrop and Hitler could do no other than to hold back the Romanians. Romania, on the other hand, asked for a German guarantee of its frontiers and for a German military mission. Hitler failed to reply immediately but ordered that security measures for the oilfields be reinforced.[57] Nevertheless on 1 July Romania renounced all the guarantees previously given by the western powers and on 11 July 1940 left the League of Nations.

IV

The OKH, especially the general staff under Halder, had watched the developments in Romania with apprehension, even with some alarm. Thus Halder recorded on 26 June that Russia wanted Bessarabia, in which Germany was not interested. But 'the question of the Bukovina thrown in by the Russians is new and exceeds the agreements arrived at between Russia and ourselves. But we have the greatest interest that there should be no war in the Balkan countries.'[58] And 'in foreign policy Russia's attitude stands in the foreground. The opinion predominates that the Bessarabia question can be solved without war.'[59] This was followed a day later with a sigh of relief when it became known that Russia had moved into Bessarabia without a struggle.[60] But a new note of alarm was raised, because, while the Russians now seemed to keep quiet, the Hungarians raised their territorial claims on Romania resulting in the massing of troops on both sides of the Hungarian–Romanian border, while at the same time news was received of increasing Russian activity in Estonia.[61] As early as 9 July Halder had noted the increasingly unstable situation in Romania, while Russia's attitude remained unclear and its aims to take control over the mouth of the Danube became more and more suspect. That the Russian moves would also have their impact upon the designs of Bulgaria and Hungary towards Romania was noted, as well as Romania's attempt to move closer to Germany, pretending that it enjoyed German protection. Russia's seizure of Bessarabia and also rumours that Romania was evacuating the southern Dobrudsja elicited strong reactions within Romania, especially among the Fascist Iron Guard under Horia Sima.[62]

The policy of russification of the Baltic states was viewed by the German general staff with dismay. More alarming, however, were rumours of rapprochement between Great Britain and Russia: 'England and Russia look for closer relations with one another. An agreement over Iran cannot be excluded and could provide the basis on which "bear and whale" find an understanding as in 1908.'[63] In the Balkans it was noted that the Dobrudsja had been evacuated for Bulgaria while Hungary had been advised by the Germans to hold back. But how long this could be maintained was a matter of speculation: 'The danger that Romania and thus the whole of the Balkans is exposed to an internal crisis cannot be dismissed. With this England's interests would be served.'[64] On 13 July Halder noted Hitler's observations on the general situation. Hitler intended to bring Spain into line against Great Britain, to build up a front from the North Cape of Morocco. Hitler recognised that it was in Russia's interest for Germany not to become too powerful, but still unaware of the Russo-Italian conversations, he thought that Russia's drive for the Bosphorus would provide discomfort to the Italians. As far as the Balkans were concerned Hitler was sure that Romania would have to foot the bill since Hungary would want its spoils while Bulgaria was taking the Dobrudsja, at the same time seeking access to the eastern Mediterranean at the expense of Greece. Hitler also made reference to the letter written to him by King Carol in which the latter put himself under Germany's protection. He considered that Romania could easily sacrifice something to Hungary and Bulgaria, but

the Führer is most preoccupied with the question of why England does not want to step on to the path of peace. Like us he sees the answer to the question in the hopes which England puts upon Russia. He therefore reckons to have to force England to make peace. But he does not like it very much. Reason: if we smash England militarily, the British Empire will collapse. Germany will not benefit from this. With German blood we would obtain something whose beneficiaries would only be Japan, America and others.[65]

On 21 July the supreme commander of the German Army Field Marshal von Brauchitsch, had a conference with Hitler in Berlin the contents of which he reported to Halder the following day. The main theme was how to tackle Great Britain. A military operation against Great Britain might become necessary; Hitler was very unsure of its nature and expected the chiefs of the three services to put forward adequate proposals, but regarded an amphibious operation as a very serious risk:

> England sees perhaps the following possibilities: to cause unrest in the Balkans, via Russia to deprive us of our fuel supplies and thus ground our air fleet. The same purpose could be achieved by turning Russia against us. Aerial attacks upon our hydrogenation plants. Romania: King Carol II has paved the way for a peaceful solution. Letter to the Führer. If England wants to continue the war, then politically every-thing will have to be harnessed against England: Spain, Italy, Russia.[66]

In other words Hitler slowly began to move towards the idea of the Eurasian bloc as advocated by Ribbentrop. Nevertheless, since Stalin appeared to be courting England, military preparations against Russia were to be taken in hand,[67] a decision which, as we have seen, Halder had already anticipated.[68]

In point of fact, Hitler was in a corner. He did not know how to put an end to the war. Without realising it yet, he had lost the *political* initiative. Obviously the most direct way of dealing with the problem was to attack Great Britain, but in spite of laborious staff and logistics work carried out, Operation 'Sea-Lion' was stillborn. On 13 July the army had submitted its first operational study for a cross-Channel invasion,[69] in response to Hitler's Directive no. 16 of 16 July 1940 concerning a German landing on British soil. During his conference with Brauchitsch he pointed out that it was 'not just a river crossing, but the crossing of a sea dominated by the enemy'.[70] He also added that if preparations could not be completed with certainty by the beginning of September it would be necessary to consider alternative plans.[71] By 31 July the requirements of the army and the inability of the navy to meet them had become so apparent that Raeder proposed that 'Sea-Lion' be postponed to the spring of 1941. Hitler gave no clear-cut assent to this proposal, but instead stated that the Luftwaffe should subject the south of England to eight days intensive bombardment: 'If the effect of the Luftwaffe is such that the enemy air-force, harbour, naval forces and so on are smashed then "Sea-Lion" should be carried out in September. Otherwise postponement to May 1941.' At the same time Hitler emphasised that England's hopes rested with Russia and the USA. Hence Russia would have to be smashed, the quicker the better. Consequently military preparations for a campaign against Russia should be continued.[72]

In effect Hitler's decision envisaged the postponement of 'Sea-Lion' and ultimately its abandonment. However, the continuation of military planning against Russia as such did not settle the final *political* decision that it should be attacked. Indeed, a day prior to the *Führerbesprechung* the alternatives to 'Sea-Lion' were considered by the OKH, which included the containment of Russia by diverting its attention towards expansion to the Persian Gulf. Other alternative steps were considered.[73]

In case a decision against England cannot be enforced, the danger arises that England will ally herself with Russia, the question then arises of whether one should conduct a two-front war resulting from such an alliance, first against Russia; this is answered in that it would be better to keep friendship with Russia. To visit Stalin would be desirable. Russia's aims in the Straits and in the direction of the Persian Gulf do not disturb us. In the Balkans, which economically comes into our sphere, we can avoid one another. The Italians and Russians won't hurt one another in the Mediterranean.[74]

Thus German military planning went in all directions, while the number of political alternatives in Hitler's mind were gradually reduced to two. On the one hand there was a political solution in close collaboration with Russia and its participation in a continental bloc, a solution emphatically endorsed by Ribbentrop; on the other hand, in case of the failure of the continental bloc, plans for a quick decisive campaign against Russia in order to deprive Britain of her last 'continental sword'. This is not to say that Hitler cherished the first alternative, especially since Russia's actions continuously increased his suspicions. North-eastern Europe had been divided into spheres of interest, not so the Balkans. From June 1940 onwards it had become what Hitler attempted to avoid: a source of unrest. While the German military presence in northern Europe was strong, this was not so in south-eastern Europe. Any upset of the status quo there would benefit Great Britain, and it could be triggered off only by two persons: Stalin and Mussolini. The latter he believed would follow his advice. But how far could Hitler afford to give way to Stalin's pressure without becoming more dependent upon him? If Hitler attempted to stop him, he was likely to drive him into the arms of Great Britain. Hence to integrate the USSR into the continental bloc seemed one way out of the dilemma, short of actually fighting her.

From 25 June Sir Stafford Cripps was British ambassador in Moscow. Stalin received him in early July and the German ambassador was informed of the conversations, which Schulenburg reported to Berlin. Cripps had put his finger on the crucial point, namely that His Majesty's Government was of the opinion that it was up to the Soviet Union to rally and lead the Balkan states for the purpose of maintaining the *status quo* there. Under the present circumstances this serious mission could only be undertaken by the Soviet Union.[75] Stalin was careful in his reply to this point, saying that the Soviet Union could not claim an exclusive role in the Balkans, but that nevertheless it was very interested in Balkan affairs.[76] This conversation was received with some alarm in Berlin and no doubt was at the root of Hitler's exposition of 21 July 1940. On the same day the Baltic states were formally annexed and incorporated into the Soviet Union.[77] Also Russia had resumed exerting pressure on Finland. In response Finland ostentatiously granted Germany 60 per cent of the annual output of nickel, which caused serious protest by the Russians.[78] Inevitably the German leadership interpreted the Russian move as one designed to increase Germany's dependence on Russia.

Throughout July, however, the main problem remained Romania. Only on 15 July did Hitler reply to King Carol's letter of 2 July. He offered a German guarantee of Romania's frontiers, dependent on Romanian concessions to Hungary and Bulgaria.[79] This was tantamount to Hitler taking the initiative of reordering the Balkans, it was his response to Russia's moves – a response further nourished by the despatches sent by the Yugoslav ambassador in Moscow, Gavrilovich, to Belgrade which were intercepted by the Germans. They pointed to a closer rapprochement between Russia and Yugoslavia, while the German ambassador to Belgrade summarised the views current there, 'after the present war is terminated a Russo-German conflict, sooner or later, is inevitable. If Germany triumphs, she will attack Russia, if Germany succumbs she will be attacked by Russia.'[80]

Upon Ribbentrop's initiative, Hitler in the conference held on 31 July proposed to breathe new life into German–Japanese relations, essentially for two reasons: firstly in the case of a Russo-German conflict, to divert Great Britain's attention to south-east Asia; secondly, if that conflict could be averted, to recruit Japan to the Eurasian continental bloc against Great Britain.[81] But before any final decision regarding an attack against Russia was made, relationships between the two countries should first be clarified *politically*. As far as Hitler's attitude to the Soviet Union at this point of time is concerned, no evidence whatsoever exists that it was motivated by his postulates about *Lebensraum*. Instead it was determined exclusively by political factors, predominantly those operating in north-eastern and south-eastern Europe.

On 1 August Molotov addressed the Supreme Soviet in Moscow and drew up a balance sheet. He praised the improvement of Anglo-Russian relations as well as those with Finland, but with regard to the latter indicated the possibility of their deteriorating again. He demanded the full mobilisation of Russia's resources so that no surprise of its enemies would meet it unprepared. But, most significantly, he described the successes achieved so far as being of limited value only and that new and greater ones would have to be achieved.[82] But where could the new achievements be attained? Mainly in the Balkans, the Straits and Finland. There is no record of a German reaction to this speech, but if there was one it can hardly have been favourable.

Still, in spite of continuing military planning against Russia, the Luftwaffe and the Navy retained priority in raw materials allocations and production programmes. On the diplomatic front Ribbentrop was convinced of the need for a speedy settlement of Hungary's and Bulgaria's territorial claims on Romania, the need to fan the glowing embers of the conflict between Russia and Turkey to prevent an Anglo-Russian rapprochement under Turkey's mediation and to prevent bilateral agreements between Italy and Russia – aims the achievement of which should be crowned by an overall political settlement with Russia within the framework of a Berlin–Rome–Moscow–Tokyo agreement.[83] But under any circumstances peace would have to be maintained in the Balkans! Mussolini and his foreign minister Count Ciano had let it be known that they planned an attack on Greece and Yugoslavia, a plan which Hitler vociferously opposed.[84] On 24 August in a letter to Hitler, Mussolini promised not to venture anything in the Balkans, but instead to take the offensive in North Africa and, furthermore, that he could help to improve Russo-Japanese relations in the interest of the Axis policy.[85]

But Germany's policy of keeping the peace in the Balkans at almost any price was being threatened by the rapid deterioration of the relationships between Romania and Hungary. King Carol had requested Germany on several occasions to dispatch a German military mission. Upon Hitler's initiative Romanian–Hungarian negotiations had begun on 16 August but collapsed on the 24th. War threatened.[86] Germany was further alarmed by news of Russian troop movements in Bessarabia and in the northern Bukovina.[87] It quickly became clear that the Russians aimed at the occupation of the southern Bukovina, which Stalin had only given up under Hitler's pressure on 26 June.[88] The OKW on 25 August immediately decided to transfer demonstratively ten divisions to the east, including two armoured divisions which should ensure the possibility of 'quick intervention for the protection of the Romanian oilfields'.[89] An exasperated Halder noted on 27 August

> Conference with ObdH ... one intends to take Spain into harness, without realizing the economic consequences, one counts North Africa as a theatre of war against England ... one wants to secure Romania without trying as yet to provoke the Russians too much. One wants to be prepared in the north Petsamo in case Russia attacks Finland. The army should be prepared for everything without receiving any clear-cut orders.[90]

However, by 29 August preparations for the occupation of the Romanian oilfields were running at full speed,[91] and Jodl declared that the Führer had now decided that after the determination of the new frontiers between Hungary and Romania he would dispatch a German military mission to Bucharest.[92] Ribbentrop invited the Hungarian, Romanian and Italian foreign ministers to Vienna for 29 August and a day later the Vienna Arbitration Treaty was signed as a result of which Romania ceded the northern part of Transylvania to Hungary. Germany and Italy now guaranteed the territorial integrity of Romania.[93] Thus Germany for the first time countered Russian moves in south-eastern Europe by the overt threat of force of arms. Russo-German relations were clearly deteriorating. The treaty had serious consequences inside Romania. King Carol abdicated, handing over his crown to his son Michael, and the government to Marshal Antonescu.[94]

At the same time the crisis continued to develop in north-eastern Europe. In the secret protocol of the Russo-German pact Finland had been assigned to the Russian sphere of influence. When new tensions between Russia and Finland began to develop from the end of July 1940 onwards, Hitler changed his mind, not least because of a memorandum from the war economy and armaments office which pointed out that Petsamo's nickel was as important to Germany's war effort as was the oil from Ploesti.[95] War was threatening between Russia and Finland, which inevitably would result in Russia's capture of Petsamo. Germany concluded a transit agreement with Finland which allowed the transport of German forces through Finland to the extreme northern point of Norway, Kirkenes. The German military delegation which had negotiated this agreement in Helsinki had been received with full military honours and great public enthusiasm. The agreement itself was signed on 22 September. This does not mean that German forces were actually stationed in Finland. Until May 1941 only German forces in transit entered Finland. But in northern Norway mountaineering forces were placed in a state of readiness, so as to occupy Petsamo immediately, if the situation should require this.[97] A period of lull seemed to intervene but was disrupted by news received by the OKW that Russia had made new demands on Finland.[98] General von Falkenhorst was personally entrusted with guaranteeing the security of Petsamo.[99] Hitler also sanctioned the supply of weapons of all kinds to Finland, a step he had previously blocked.[100] Furthermore, he decided upon a public demonstration directed against Russia by assembling 88 mm flak batteries and their crews, fully uniformed and the guns for all to see to be transported through Finland to Norway.[101] The Vienna Arbitration Treaty, the 'public' transport of fully armed German forces through Finland as well as the transit agreement were a clear signal to Russia: *So far and no further!* Neither over the arbitration treaty nor the transit agreement had Ribbentrop consulted the Russians; it was his reply to Russia's proceedings in the Baltic countries, Bessarabia and the Bukovina. On the question of the transit agreement he left it to the Finnish government to inform the Russians. He subsequently informed Molotov about the contents of the arbitration treaty, justifying the speed with which it had been concluded by the imminent danger of war.[102] He did not hide his anger about Russia's Balkan policy, pointing out that the year before Russia had expressed merely her interest in Bessarabia. Although Germany had declared her lack of political interest, her economic interests were of vital importance in view of the connection with oil and grain supplies. Apart from that Germany had not been consulted over the annexation of the Baltic states, nor the occupation of the strip of Lithuania which should have fallen to Germany.[103] Molotov accepted the note, promising a written reply, but cryptically assuring the German ambassador that nothing had changed the Russian attitude.[104] Molotov gave his written reply on 21 September 1940. In it he rejected the German arguments point for point and thus put an end to common Russo-German policy as it had been inaugurated on 23 August 1939.[105] Germany did not realise this immediately, though Hitler was more sceptical than Ribbentrop. Whilst the latter still worked for a joint Russo-German policy, Hitler doubted that it could be realised, though he did not exclude a political arrangement between the two countries until two months later. Hitler's scepticism was fully justified in view of the Kremlin's continuation with its previous policy. It supported Bulgaria's claim for the southern Dobrudsja, and what was all the more alarming to Hitler was that Bulgaria had appealed to Russia directly.[106] On 14 September Hitler had convened a conference whose major topic was 'Sea-Lion'. Hitler stated that a landing was not fixed for a specific time and was not constrained by any special set of circumstances. But one could not deny that the longer the war lasted, the greater would become the political tensions. Russia had expected Germany to bleed herself white in the west. The result had been a disappointment for Moscow. Hence Russia's speedy pressure upon Finland and the Balkans, whereas Germany was interested in maintaining a stable situation in northeastern and southeastern Europe: 'A long duration of the war is not desired. All that which is of practical value to us we have already obtained. Politically and economically the bases gained are sufficient.'[107] As far as 'Sea-Lion' was concerned he admitted that the pre-conditions for it had not been achieved, but it should not yet be cancelled. The Luftwaffe's chief of staff, Jeschonnek, demanded the bombardment of British residential areas, a demand which Hitler rejected, emphasising that decisive targets would be railways, water and gas supplies. The bombing of the population must be a threat, a final resort.[108] It was a confession that Hitler did want to end the war, but did not see any way of how to do so. Instead of decreasing, complications increased. Early in October the Russians raised new demands for concessions in the Petsamo nickel mines. Ribbentrop advised the Finnish government to use delaying tactics.[109] He was playing for time in the course of which he hoped to come to a general settlement with the Soviet Union, by way of Molotov's visit to Berlin.

Romania provided further cause for friction in the form of a German military mission consisting of army and Luftwaffe officers, to which were attached training units of both services. Germany did so on the explicit request of Marshal Antonescu.[110] While the Germans wanted only a force strong enough to protect the oilfields, Antonescu really desired a sizeable German contingent in order to train the Romanian army for what he considered to be the inevitable conflict with Russia.[111] At this stage Hitler turned down the request, making only one division available for Romania. The function which the German troop transit through Finland was to achieve *vis-à-vis* Russia, one German division, plus Luftwaffe detachments were to achieve in the Balkans.[112] But Russia was not the only power German military presence was aimed at. It was aimed equally at Great Britain, from whom Hitler feared a direct intervention in Greece and Crete.

V

Although the east was beginning to dominate Hitler's attention, the forging of a continental bloc against Great Britain also required that he turn his attention to the west. Vichy-French forces on 23 September had successfully repulsed a British attempt to land at Dakar. France seemed a likely recruit for the continental bloc. So was Spain, where a successful attack by the Germans of Spanish–German forces upon Gibraltar could block the western entry into the Mediterranean. The Hitler–Franco meeting on 23 October at Hendaye proved a fiasco. Franco was not

prepared directly to commit himself.[113] Hitler then went on
to Montoire to meet Marshal Pétain. The results were
equally inconclusive.[114] It is quite probable that in principle
neither Franco nor Pétain would have had any objection to
joining Germany provided Great Britain had been forced to
her knees. By October 1940 this was obviously less likely
than it had seemed during the previous early summer months.
Moreover America's economic weight came increasingly to
play in support of Great Britain and exerted pressure on
Spain and Vichy. Still, Hitler retained the impression that
at the right time under the right circumstances these two
countries could be welded into the projected continental
bloc. The surprise he received came from Mussolini, whom
he met on 28 October and who informed him that Italy had
just commenced its attack upon Greece. The OKW had
anticipated this move: German forces in Romania and later
Bulgaria were reinforced.[115] Still, it was an unpleasant
surprise to Hitler who had warned Mussolini against taking
this step. Its results were disastrous and brought to nought
Hitler's intention to preserve the peace in the Balkans. The
OKW's prophecy came true; Italy's forces were contained
by the Greeks and ultimately German forces had to come to
their rescue.[114] The most immediate consequence was that
Italy's action provided the British with the opportunity to
establish bases in Greece and Crete.

In the meantime military preparations in the east went
ahead, as did Ribbentrop's endeavours to forge his bloc.
Once Hitler had become convinced that peace with Great
Britain could not be obtained, he abandoned his notion of
restoring the General Government of Poland into a German
satellite state.[117] Instead came the order *Aufbau Ost*, frequently
considered as a preparatory measure for 'Barbarossa'.[118] This
interpretation has been strongly contradicted by Keitel,
Raeder, von Brauchitsch, Jodl and Halder.[119] It served two
ends, first the securing of sufficient training bases for the
German army as storage areas for equipment to be removed
from areas accessible to the RAF, and secondly as a blunt
indicator to Russia that Germany could defend her interests
in the Balkans.

Quite apart from that, the OKW's work and that of the OKH was not dominated by preparations for an eastern campaign. A host of other projects were worked on.[120] What did take place was a transfer of substantial forces into the southern corner of the General Government, so as to have a strong force in reserve to intervene in Romania to protect the oilfields. There were now only 8 divisions in East Prussia compared with 16 divisions in the Cracow area.[121] Moreover, these troop movements were not carried out in any concealed fashion but *openly* to ensure that the Russians would take due notice of them.[122] On the contrary, the transfer of German forces from the west to the east

> must not create in Russia the impression that we are preparing an offensive in the east. On the other hand, Russia will recognize that strong, high-quality German troops are in the [General] Government, in the western provinces as well as in the Protectorate and they will draw the conclusion that we can protect our interests – notably in the Balkans – at any time with strong forces.[123]

The size of the German forces was nevertheless inferior to those of the Russians. Between 1 September 1939 and 31 December 1940 Russia had doubled her forces from two to four millions on her western frontier.[124]

The diplomatic sphere was now dominated by the consequences of Mussolini's action in the Balkans, by the increasing activity of the USA and its deliveries of war material and foodstuffs to Great Britain. However, upon Hitler's orders German U-boats were prohibited from attacking American shipping, even if it sailed for British harbours.[125] For in 1940 there was no fear of any direct intervention of the USA in Europe, as it was election year and the promise of non-intervention a major plank in the election platforms of both Democrats and Republicans.[126]

Therefore the attempt had to be undertaken either to keep the USA out of the war or divert its attention to the Pacific. Once again Ribbentrop's concept of a Eurasian bloc came into play, at first in the form of the German–Italian–Japanese Tripartite Pact.[127] Ribbentrop's estimate of the

American military potential and the speed with which it could be mobilised was somewhat more realistic than that of his Führer.[128] Russia could interpret the tripartite pact as another version of the Anti-Comintern pact, despite Ribbentrop's endeavours to mediate between Russia and Japan. The result could well be driving Stalin into the arms of Germany's enemies. Therefore, from Ribbentrop's point of view, the new alliance would make sense only if Russia were included. Early in August 1940 the prospect of such a pact seemed rather remote because of Hitler's still prevailing scepticism towards it. But when on 17 August Roosevelt and the Canadian prime minister Mackenzie King met in Canada and agreed on joint staff talks and Canada made bases available along Nova Scotia for the US navy and air forces,[129] following the conclusion of the Lend-Lease agreement between the USA and Great Britain,[130] Hitler drastically changed his mind. He sent his special envoy Stahmer to Tokyo, where he arrived on 7 September.[131] The Japanese prime minister Konoye shared Ribbentrop's view that Germany, Japan, Italy and Soviet Russia should join in one common front in spite of unresolved differences between Japan and Russia going back to the treaty of Portsmouth of 1905.[132] Mussolini, who during the initial sounding had been ignored, was informed personally by Ribbentrop who brought a personal letter from Hitler to Rome. Ribbentrop, in the course of his conversations with the Duce, admitted that the tripartite pact ran the risk of driving Russia towards Great Britain and the USA, but Germany intended to divert Russia towards the Persian Gulf and to India. He welcomed the Italo-Russian rapprochement, though he shared Hitler's view that in any dealings with the Russians the spheres of interest would have to be defined very clearly and precisely. The only alternative to Russia's present Balkan policy would be to tie Russia even closer to the Axis powers, by which he meant having Russia join the alliance.[133]

In September 1940 Hitler had hoped that the Vienna arbitration treaty and the conclusion of the tripartite pact would act as a deterrent to Russia's Balkan ambitions (as well as to America's further involvement in the war).[134] This was the primary reason why he urged the speedy conclusion of the pact rather than waiting until negotiations aimed at bringing Russia into the bloc (negotiations which, as Hitler knew, were bound to be lengthy) were completed. The pact was signed on 27 September 1940; from Hitler's point of view the foundation had been laid for a structure which, as we have already seen, he intended to extend to the west in the following months. Ribbentrop informed Russia two days before the pact was signed. According to Ribbentrop's instructions it was to be emphasised that the treaties concluded by the three powers with Russia, especially the Russo-German pact, would remain fully in force. Furthermore Ribbentrop would address a personal letter to *Herr* Stalin in which he would in detail and confidence put down the German opinion about the present political situation. The letter would also contain an invitation for Molotov to visit Berlin in order to discuss important questions concerning common political aims for the future.[135] The secretary of state von Weizsäcker also informed the Russian ambassador in Berlin accordingly.[136] Ribbentrop, and the somewhat more sceptical Hitler, aimed at a 'once-and-for-all' settlement of the open questions between Germany and Russia not outside the tripartite pact but within it – supplementing it with an alliance with Russia and with other European countries and thus creating a consolidated front against Great Britain and for that matter against the USA. The German chargé d'affaires von Tippelskirch was kept waiting because Sir Stafford Cripps had a rather lengthy interview with Molotov. When he was finally received, Molotov received the news without great surprise and appeared pleased about the news of the impending letter to Stalin. But he did ask for the text of the agreement and for information about any secret agreements.[137] Ribbentrop let it be known that no secret agreement existed and that according to article 4 of the pact none of the existing agreements of the signatory powers affected the political status which existed between them and the Soviet Union.[138] It soon became evident that Molotov in reality was more concerned than he showed.[139]

Both Hitler and Ribbentrop were now set upon bringing about a general clarification of the relations between

Germany and Russia. That this would not be an easy task was obvious in the light of the existing tensions. But both the German foreign office and the OKW were of the opinion that these tensions were of a transient nature only, that relaxation in Russo-Finnish relationships could be observed and that Moscow was stopping its forward policy in the Balkans.[140] On 24 October Halder noted that Brauchitsch, as a result of a conversation with Hitler, expected Russia to join the Tripartite pact and again on 1 November that Hitler hoped 'to build in' Russia to the front against England.[141]

Yet in this period of high hopes new difficulties arose, this time over the Danube. The International and the European Danube commissions had ceased to exist and Ribbentrop convened a new European one, however omitting Russia, which in the meantime had gained a foothold on the mouth of the Danube. On balance it seems that he had overlooked Russia, because when the Soviet Union on 12 September submitted its protest. Ribbentrop immediately extended his invitation to her. Molotov demanded the reconstitution of the European commission but only by states along the Danube. This would have meant the exclusion of Italy. Now Ribbentrop protested and Molotov gave in. A preparatory conference was to meet on 29 October in Bucharest.[142] But three days before, the Russians unexpectedly occupied those islands in the Danube delta which controlled the entire navigable mouth of the Danube and its traffic.[143] While the OKW took due notice of this step as well as the arrival of four Russian officers in Bucharest to observe the German forces there,[144] Hitler ignored this step, which amounted to a consequent continuation of Russia's Balkan policy, in the hope that this would be one of the many issues to be dealt with by the Russians during Molotov's visit. The conference in Bucharest prorogued itself on 21 December, never to meet again.

VI

Molotov's visit was not necessarily ill starred, but it did take place at a time when Russo-German relations were burdened with heavy liabilities. This is reflected in Hitler's Directive No. 18, worked out by the *Wehrmachtsführungsstab* under Jodl. The OKW and the OKH had observed the gradual massing of Russian forces on her western frontier, and in response the 30 German divisions in the east were increased up to 100. 'Russia would bite on granite; but not probable that Russia puts herself in opposition to us, "in Russia rule men with reason"'.[145] Also the fact that Romania and Bulgaria wished to join the tripartite pact was registered with satisfaction with the aim of a 'continental front against England',[146] and then a little later, 'Molotov on 10 November in Berlin. Reply by Stalin to letter by the Führer. He agrees with him. Molotov is coming to Berlin. Then one expects Russia's entry into the Tripartite pact.'[147] Also Hitler's attempts were registered to have Russia exert pressure on Turkey in order that the latter maintain her neutrality.[148] But the precondition for that was the continuation, indeed the intensification of Russo-German collaboration. This in turn caused Brauchitsch and Halder to enquire what the real intentions of Germany's political leadership were. But Russia 'remains the great problem of Europe. Everything must be done for great reckoning'.[149] Against this background Directive No. 18 was drafted.[150] It stands out from all other directives in listing operations the premises for which were as yet questionable or incomplete. In the form of a military directive it was the concept of a European coalition against Great Britain, in which Russia was expected to take part after Molotov's visit. To combine Germany, Italy, France, Spain and Japan was part of a scheme from which the attempt to draw Russia into it cannot be separated. Directive No. 18 reflected these endeavours.[151] After France, the Iberian peninsula, Italy and the Balkans Russia was mentioned in the fifth point. 'Political talks with the aim of clarifying Russia's attitude in the near future have been introduced. Irrespective what the results of these talks may be, all orally ordered preparations against the east are to be continued. Directives about this follow as soon as the basic lines of the operational plan of the army have been submitted and approved by me.' But then follows point six: 'Due to *changes* in the *general situation* (author's italics) the possibility or the necessity may arise that in the spring of 1941 we still come back to Operation "Sea-Lion", consequently all three branches of the Wehrmacht must seriously endeavour to improve the foundations of such an enterprise in every respect.'[152] Halder in his entry from 4 November had already noted that one had to be prepared for 'Sea-Lion', but parallel to it preparations for the east would have to be continued. In other words Hitler was making provisions for both contingencies, as Directive No. 18 clearly shows, especially when one does not take point 5 in isolation but reads it with point 6; 'Sea-Lion' without Russian cooperation would have been impossible.

Ribbentrop's letter to Stalin had been handed over to Molotov on 17 October. It was a lengthy document, based on the premise that the war against Great Britain was already won. Molotov received it with reserve. He could not reply to the invitation yet, he would withhold his answer until Stalin had studied the letter.[153] But already on 19 October Molotov indicated a favourable response.[154] On 21 October the reply was given.[155] While Ribbentrop had suggested a joint meeting between the foreign ministers of Germany, Russia, Italy and Japan, Stalin expressed his preference, at least initially, for a joint Russo-German meeting between 10 and 12 November.[156] Molotov also refused publication of the date of his visit until the moment of his departure. As Hungary, Romania, Bulgaria and Slovakia were about to join the tripartite pact, the German ambassador pressed for publication of this news to be withheld until after Molotov's visit.

Molotov arrived in Berlin on 12 November. Already at midday on the day of his arrival, Molotov and the deputy people's commissar for foreign affairs, Dekanosov, shortly to be ambassador in Berlin, met Ribbentrop, who wanted to brief him about what Hitler intended to talk about in the afternoon.[157] According to Ribbentrop England was beaten; even the entry of the USA would not change this fact. Germany was about to unite the European states into an anti-British coalition. The tripartite pact was the suitable instrument which otherwise served peaceful purposes.

Ribbentrop's personal aim was to bring about a rapprochement between Russia and Japan. In the same way in which spheres of influence between Germany and Russia had been defined, this should be possible between Russia and Japan. It was the Führer's aim to specify the spheres of influence between Germany, the USSR, Japan and Italy. This should present no great difficulty since the main interest of all countries concerned lay in a southern direction. The German Reich tended towards Central Africa, Italy to North and East Africa and Japan into the southern Pacific. The real question was whether or not Russia could see that its true interests lay in a southern expansion. Germany was interested in Russia's expansion towards India and the Persian Gulf, this would take pressure from the Baltic and the Straits.[158] Ribbentrop's exposition, painted with broad strokes on a wide canvas, shows that the wish was father to the thought. Molotov was quick to detect the weaknesses in Ribbentrop's argument. But to remain conciliatory Ribbentrop pointed to the possibilities in the Dardanelles such as the revision of the Montreux Convention, but ruled out any suggestion of Russian naval bases at the Bosphorus. Molotov's reply was concise. With the exception of the Finnish question to which he would come shortly, the laying down of spheres of interest in 1939 had only been a partial solution which had been overtaken by the events of 1940. Much to Ribbentrop's discomfort he continued in this vein for some time.[159]

In the afternoon Molotov was received by Hitler, who went out of his way to charm him and make him comfortable.[160] Hitler talked quietly, making no attempt at intimidation. He pointed out that Germany was not seeking direct military help from the Soviet Union; the war and its development had forced Germany into areas in which it had primarily no political or economic interest. But as long as the war lasted, the Reich was dependent upon certain raw materials which it could not do without. Then he turned to the question of how in the future the collaboration between Germany and Russia could be more clearly defined and strengthened. Germany's most important problem had been that of living space, but in the course of the war it made conquests which it would take a century to digest, also Germany was interested in Central Africa because of the raw materials there. In addition there were certain areas in which Germany could not allow any rival to have air or naval bases. On none of these points existed any reason for conflict between Germany and Russia. Although the USSR and Germany could never be one world, there were good preconditions for co-existence. Hitler admitted that there were a number of points which touched the interests of both countries. Germany desired to break out of the North Sea, Italy out of the Mediterranean and Russia, too, was striving for access to the open seas. The question was whether or not there was the possibility of achieving this without these countries coming into conflict with one another. With France he had settled everything in a manner to put an end to the age-old historical conflict. Germany had no interest in the Balkans, although there were important raw materials there and consequently the Reich would do everything to prevent the British from gaining a foothold in that region. For this reason the presence of German forces would be temporarily necessary. He, Hitler, wished for peace because war was a bad business. The long-term threat originated from the USA. For that reason he was in touch with France to formulate a European Monroe Doctrine. In other areas in which Russia was primarily interested she should be a privileged power and her interests would dominate. Out of this situation emerged a power grouping, whose cohesion might well be difficult, but which should not represent an unsurmountable obstacle. Naturally Germany would assist Russia in the revision of the Dardanelles question.[161]

Hitler's exposition had been rather more specific than that of Ribbentrop. But there remained points over which Hitler was vague and imprecise, as for example over the time when German forces would be withdrawn from the Balkans.

Molotov's answer was relatively short, but to the point. At the outset he declared that Stalin and he were of the same opinion. He agreed with the Reich chancellor that the Russo-German treaties had brought advantages to both

sides. And he underlined the fact that Germany's advantages
were in no small measure due to the loyalty of Russia. He
ignored Hitler's reference to the Dardanelles question.
Instead he immediately raised the Finnish problem. The
Finns had fulfilled the Moscow Treaty but for one point.
Molotov asked Hitler whether the Russo-German agreement
of 1939 still applied to Finland. Apart from that these
agreements were only partial solutions. Other problems had
moved to the fore and demanded solution. What did the
German Reich understand by the establishment of a new
order in Europe and Asia? To what extent were Russian
interests, especially in Bulgaria, Romania and Turkey
touched by it? What was one to make of the Greater Asia
Co-Prosperity Sphere? Certainly these were details he could
discuss with Ribbentrop in Moscow, but he was anxious to
hear the Führer's own opinions.

Hitler was slightly annoyed by the directness of Molotov's
questions since they touched upon problems he would rather
have deferred dealing with, or ignored altogether, especially
those concerning the Balkans and Finland. At this point he
became vague. Not Russo-German relations but Franco-
German relations had been his most difficult problem. Now
that he had resolved the latter, he would return to the
former. The first stage of cooperation of the nations of
western Europe had been achieved. It was a policy which
also envisaged cooperation with the east, with Russia and
Japan. The main problem was to keep the USA from
Europe, Africa and Asia. Molotov noted well that Hitler
was avoiding a direct answer, but expressed his general
agreement and readiness for Russia to cooperate with the
tripartite pact, as long as she would partner and not
object.[162]

The second meeting between Hitler and Molotov was, as
far as Hitler was concerned, determined by the conviction
he had gained that the position of the Soviets could not be
shifted. Russia concentrated on two aims: Finland and
Romania. This meant, sooner or later, the annexation of
Finland and the extension of Russian influence over the
Balkans. Hitler in his talk with Molotov emphasised that on
the question of respective spheres of interest Germany had

strictly adhered to the Russo-German agreements, something which Russia in some cases had not done, especially in Lithuania and the Bukovina. Hitler then touched on the Finnish problem. In principle Germany had no interest there, but as long as the war lasted it was dependent on Finnish supplies of timber and nickel. Therefore Germany did not desire a new conflict in the Baltic region. With regard to Russo-Finnish relations he pointed to the widespread sympathies of the German public for the Finns in the Russo-Finnish conflict and the difficult stand he had had then. He did not wish in the foreseeable future to be put in a similar position again. As long as the war lasted Finland was as important to Germany as was Romania, although these areas belonged to the Russian sphere of influences. Molotov interjected that the Russo-German agreement had concerned a first stage, the second stage had come to an end with Germany's victory over France, and now the third stage was being confronted. Germany must show sympathies for Russia's claim for the southern Bukovina. Hitler blocked this demand and underlined his wish to avoid war in the Baltic and Balkan regions. Otherwise previously unforeseen complications could arise. To avoid war there did not by any means imply a breach of the Russo-German agreement. Nor was it a breach when Germany guaranteed the territorial integrity of Romania.[163]

Molotov remained unimpressed. He returned to the Finnish problem, which led to a short but sharp exchange between him and Hitler. Hitler put an end to it by asking Molotov how he envisaged the solution of the Finnish problem. Molotov blandly replied that he saw it in much the same way as in the Baltic countries and Bessarabia. Thus Molotov had put his cards on the table. Hitler replied that there must be no war in the Baltic region. Molotov demanded that Germany adopt the same attitude which it had adopted during the winter of 1939–40. Thus both positions had been clearly defined, especially Russia's expansionist aims in south-eastern and north-eastern Europe. But both Hitler and Ribbentrop returned for the last time to the attempt to divert Russian expansionism to the south, a solution which Hitler by that time seems to have lost faith in, though not Ribbentrop, who also submitted a draft treaty for Russia to join the tripartite pact which he handed to Molotov.[164] Molotov produced one last shock, namely the question of Russia's free access from the Baltic. Ribbentrop, at first at a loss for an answer, replied that for the duration of the war the status quo in the Baltic would have to be preserved. Molotov then remarked that he would submit the draft treaty to Stalin and discuss it with him.[165] For Hitler the conversations with Molotov had been a 'test', whether Germany and Russia 'stood back to back, or chest to chest'.[166]

Even after Molotov's departure some weak hopes remained; Hitler and Ribbentrop waited for Stalin's answer. But Hitler's scepticism was justified when on 18 November Molotov warned the Bulgarian envoy against accepting a German guarantee without the participation of Russia.[165] Shortly thereafter news reached Berlin that Hungary's, Romania's, Bulgaria's and Slovakia's accession to the tripartite pact had not met with Russian approval.[168] Finally on 25 November Molotov handed Russia's official reply to the German ambassador. Russia made her joining the tripartite pact conditional on the withdrawal of all German forces from Finnish soil. All economic obligations towards Germany by Finland would be assumed by Russia. Furthermore, Russia insisted on bases for land and naval forces at the Bosphorus and the Dardanelles. Thirdly the Kremlin demanded Germany's recognition of Russian claims to the territory south of Baku and Batum in the direction of the Persian Gulf. Lastly Japan would have to cede to Russia its concessions for the exploitation of oil and coal resources in North Sakhalin. And last but not least, Moscow demanded the abrogation of the Russo-German secret treaties in its favour.[169] Hitler read the note, put it on his desk and did not bother to reply. The dice had been cast.

Was 1941 meant to be a preventive stroke, or was it simply an act of aggression? It was both. Hitler could under no circumstances risk Soviet intervention in Finland. He could not afford to expose himself further to the Russian threat of blackmail, irrespective of whether it was Finland, Romania or any other Balkan country. Against the background of the Soviet attitude and actions adopted since June 1940 he was convinced that Stalin would not keep to the letter of any agreement, but would from time to time, according to the prevailing situation, tighten the thumbscrews in order to gain further concessions from Germany, territorial or political. Russia's entire policy in 1940 had aimed at predominance in south-eastern and north-eastern Europe, a policy consistently pursued until 22 June 1941. Hitler was not prepared to accept the risk of conducting war in which he was dependent on the goodwill of Stalin, whose ambitions he assessed rather more realistically than either Churchill or Roosevelt. Without doubt, in August 1939 Hitler, as was so often the case, had fixed his eyes upon one aim only, this time Poland, without taking into consideration the ultimate consequences of a German dependence upon Russia. He calculated that the end of this dependence would come at the latest after the defeat of France and Great Britain, or at the earliest as a result of these two powers failing to enter into a European war in the light of the power constellation as it existed on 23 August 1939. Only stage by stage did he recognise the Soviet aims and their effect upon Germany's position in Europe. It was only as a last resort that he found himself forced in the interest of Germany and Europe, as he interpreted it, to point to the Soviets the limits of their power. Thus 25 November 1940 becomes the key date in Russo-German relations as well as in German military planning aimed at attacking the Soviet Union. On 5 December Brauchitsch and Halder submitted the first operational plan of the German attack against Russia. Hitler baptised it 'Barbarossa'.[170] Operation 'Sea-Lion' 'can remain outside our consideration'.[171] Seven days later in Directive No. 21. 'Case Barbarossa', Hitler stipulated that decisive importance was to be placed upon the German preparations for the attack in the east not being recognised.[172] Whereas before, Hitler, in order to contain Russian ambitions, had carried out German troop movements in north-eastern and south-eastern Europe demonstratively, this was now no longer the case.

The war against Poland, as Ernst Nolte has argued, was in its inception a war of national restitution, that in the west one of the revision of Versailles.[173] The war against Russia, however, was an attempt also to impose Germany's 'Manifest Destiny' under the slogan 'Eastwards the course of Empire': the attempt to transpose upon Germany the process of territorial expansion analogous to that experienced by the USA and Russia in the preceding century. Only Germany did not face fragmented Indian tribes, Tartars or Mongolians whose subjugation and even extermination was relatively easy to accomplish, about whose disappearance hardly anyone cared. To transpose the American and Russian experience by Germany upon eastern Europe meant the subjugation of over 200 million people. Hitler's own ideology, largely left in limbo since 1933, came to full fruition. Theory and practice coincided. Both preventive war and ruthless territorial aggrandisement, accompanied by mass enslavement and extermination on a scale which Stalin apart, no one in Europe had practised in modern times, merged into an orgy of destruction.

VII

This study of Russo-German relations in 1940, however, demonstrates how mistaken it is to see in Hitler's aims a detailed 'programme', conceived long before 1933, executed with remorseless logic and consistency. Hitler, like any other statesman, could only act and react within the context of the changing political constellation. Until the late summer of 1940 a compromise with, or a defeat of, Great Britain stood at the centre of Hitler's aims. However, these were subject to gradual change in the face of Soviet actions in north-eastern and south-eastern Europe. But even at a time when he had begun to recognise the cloud on the horizon, he still believed he could leave it to 'a successor' to deal with. And, even more important, at the moment when there could be no longer any doubt about Soviet intentions in Europe, he and Ribbentrop tried to contain or absorb them within the framework of the tripartite pact, or to divert them into other regions as well as harness Russia into a common front against Great Britain. All the alternatives available to the Third Reich were put into play, but Stalin and Molotov rejected them. Germany's arsenal of traditional diplomacy was exhausted. Not fate, but old ambitions, German and Russian alike, rekindled and refashioned, took their course.

PART III

Introduction

The German economy during the Third Reich has been the subject of intensive research and highly differing conclusions and to deal with them adequately would require a volume by itself. A general consensus exists only on the point that the National Socialist regime managed to achieve economic recovery by large deficit spending in most sectors of the economy. Early, somewhat premature opinions, before, during and shortly after the Second World War maintained that this was mainly due to Germany's rearmament programme. However, within the first twelve months of its existence, when large-scale arms programmes were still on paper, the number of unemployed was reduced by half. By the end of 1935 the first signs of a shortage of skilled labour became noticeable, and increased further until the outbreak of war, when in fact full employment had been operating for nearly three years and the German government found itself in the position of issuing decrees to make labour compulsory and assuming the right to deploy labour where it thought it was needed. There is no evidence to show that Germany's economists were applying Keynesian economies, the 'pump-priming system' according to which increased investment by the state would give the private sector of the economy the necessary confidence for investments of its own, thus creating jobs, thereby increasing the purchasing power of the individual in the consumer sector, and increasing the demand for consumer goods which would stimulate their production. Economic policy in Germany in the 1930s probably operated in ignorance of Keynesian theories, as for that matter did F. D. Roosevelt in his 'New Deal' in the USA. Unlike Hitler, Roosevelt actually met Keynes on one occasion, but the meeting proved a disappointment to both: neither appeared to have much to say to the other.

Deficit financing has been held by some historians such as K. D. Bracher to be the prime motivating factor in Germany's foreign policy. This rather determinist thesis maintains that by 1936 the German economy had arrived at the crossroads at which Schacht's policy of fiscal and monetary expedients had to be abandoned, the alternative facing Hitler being a return to the ordered channels of the international economy. Since the basic premise of Hitler's policy is seen in the extension of *Lebensraum*, such a return would tend to frustrate the rapid mobilisation of Germany's economic and military resources necessary for such a course. Consequently, Hitler had not only to continue the course of expedients but indeed to try to extend it on a scale far wider than hitherto practised, with the result that, faced with an alleged economic crisis (for which to this date no reliable statistical figures have been produced) cheques were drawn, metaphorically speaking, on non-existent capital, or more correctly the proceeds of conquered lands were used before these territories had actually been obtained. To take an example: was predominantly agrarian Austria in fact an industrial asset after the *Anschluss*? Certainly it provided some help in the agrarian sector, but industrially it had to be opened up first, and that required large sums for investment to build an industrial infrastructure. If attention is concentrated on the industrial sphere then one conclusion is clear, namely that Austria emerged after 1945 with an industrial base which had hardly existed before 1938. In an overall German context investment in the Austrian provinces between 1938 and 1945 was many times larger than the value of industrial output of that region over the same period.

Austria also facilitated Germany's access to the economies of the countries of south-eastern Europe from which she derived great economic benefits in terms of agricultural produce and scarce minerals such as crude oil. It has been argued by the German economic historian Bernd-Jürgen Wendt, that Germany's economic policy in this area of Europe must be viewed in the context of the long-term strategy of National Socialist foreign policy. Although he does not go as far as others have done in asserting that German policy was one of exploitation, in his view it reduced these countries to a state of dependence on Germany. South-eastern Europe, organised in economic terms as the 'Reichsmark bloc' was to become a self-contained economic hinterland, over which Germany exercised a kind of 'informal empire' which would absorb German industrial goods in exchange for agrarian produce and raw materials. Based on bilateral trading and bartering agreements, the system excluded recourse to the international market, thus eliminating any drain on the foreign currency reserves of which Germany suffered an acute shortage.

Alan Milward's essay soundly contradicts this view by a detailed examination of the 'Reichsmark bloc'. For reasons of space the statistical data and tables have been omitted and the reader interested in them is advised to consult the volume in which this essay originally appeared. Milward demonstrates that the economic policy of the Third Reich in this area of Europe, or for that matter in other parts of the world such as the major countries of South America with which the same sort of bartering arrangement existed, was not a novelty but had already been introduced during the days of the Weimar Republic. As far as South America is concerned, these agreements did not establish a German 'informal empire'. Nor can this be said about south-eastern Europe. Here it was a question of gradually pushing out French and British influence and replacing it as far as possible by that of Germany. As far as the degree of dependency, or the lack of it, is concerned, Bulgaria provides a telling example. Although it was one of the major members of the 'Reichsmark bloc', and in 1940 joined with other countries in the tripartite pact, it still conducted its foreign policy independently of the Third Reich and in the Russo-German conflict from late June 1941 onwards actually remained a neutral power, a status which the Soviet Union in the summer of 1944 failed to respect. Milward also convincingly demonstrates that what the *Anschluss* with Austria did for her in the industiral sphere, the 'Reichsmark bloc' did for many south-eastern European countries: it provided a major impetus for the industrialisation of south-eastern Europe.

The next major problem is that of German rearmament, or more precisely its actual extent. Immediate post-war literature accepted uncritically the highly inflated sums given by Hitler in his public speeches. These we find reproduced almost verbatim in Churchill's memoirs. Yet Göring's hypothetical choice of *Kanonen oder Butter* was in reality scarcely posed. German policy was one of guns as well as butter, and continued well into the Second World War. One of the reasons for the lack of a drastic arms policy before the war and the lack of a total mobilisation of Germany's manpower reserves during it, was the experience of the First World War, notably the collapse of the home front which in turn gave birth to the 'stab-in-the-back-legend'. Hence for years total mobilisation, especially of women, was out of the question, as was the cessation of the production of consumer goods in favour of arms. Rearmament and even war should be carried on with as little impact on the German domestic scene as possible. There was to be no repeat of '1918'! This policy was only gradually given up once the tide of war had turned against Germany, and even then not as fully as had been the case in Britain since 1940. Thus Speer in 1944 managed to triple Germany's output of arms with the productive capacity of 1941.

It cannot be said either that following Hitler's coming to power a coherent plan of German rearmament was pursued. In this sphere the polycratic structure of the regime was as much a handicap as in other spheres. The individual branches of the armed services proposed and pursued their programmes with little or no coordination. Rivalry for scarce raw materials was endemic, at times even vicious. The announcement of the 'Four-Year Plan' under Göring in 1936 produced no alleviation in inter-service rivalries. Hitler approved armaments programmes with little perception of actual reality. Assuming that all the armaments programmes proposed and approved by Hitler in 1938–9 could have been realised by the three services, including a vast expansion of the *Luftwaffe* and the 'big-ship' building by the navy, the so-called 'Z-plan', Germany would have needed crude oil reserves of an amount in excess of the then total annual world production. When the German army attacked Russia in 1941 only 46 divisions out of roughly 150 were fully equipped with German arms, the remainder were either deficient in equipment, mainly armour and anti-tank guns, or equipped with captured arms of both Czech and French origin.

The first economist to expose the myth and depict the economic reality of German rearmament and arms production was the Harvard economist Burton H. Klein. A fierce debate among economic historians immediately centred on his findings, but on the whole, with a few amendments here and qualifications there, consensus appears to rest on his findings and conclusions. As impediments to the policy of rearmament Klein identifies four major factors. First, the fear of inflation caused by further deficit spending, secondly the unwillingness of Germans to restrain or stop consumption, thirdly the inefficiency of German planning, and fourthly the opposition among the various interest groups. All but the second point can be accepted without qualification. The second point, however, raises the virtually unanswerable question whether it was the German public that was really unready and unwilling to surrender part of their new-found relative prosperity *or* whether that was just the assumption of the NS leadership concerned to prevent '1918' occurring again, a consideration operative also in other sectors such as the judiciary, where the 'NS People's Court' in particular used a very wide interpretation of 'treason' to combat any sign of 'defeatism' with draconian punishments.

Perhaps Klein's conclusion that it was the resources of the USA which finally decided the war also requires some qualification. Considering the war in Europe as a whole, it emerges that it was the Soviet Union's Red Army which for years had borne the brunt of the fighting and turned the tables on their opponents, much more than the western Allies. When the Allies landed in Normandy they faced, apart from a few elite divisions which were in France for refitting, only what by then was already the burnt-out hulk of the *Wehrmacht*, whose biggest graveyard had been Russia.

One conclusion which Klein shares with other economic historians such as Alan Milward, Bernice Carroll and Dieter Petzina is that in the final analysis it was Hitler's intention to arm not in depth but in breadth so as to have a striking force suitable for small and localised wars, an army for the *Blitzkrieg*, a type of war in which the German army proved its worth. Any intention to develop such an army for that type of war is contradicted by Hitler's own frequent dissatisfaction with the progress of German rearmament and his endorsement of an armaments programme of the fantastic proportions already mentioned. Also, to look at German rearmament policy from the vantage point of the *Blitzkrieg* distorts the perspective, because originally there was no such concept in German military planning. As Martin Cooper has rightly pointed out, the concept of the *Blitzkrieg* evolved from a convenient way of explaining the unknown into a strict definition of a new form of warfare believed to be the basis for the impressive early German victories. Though a German word combination, the term was actually coined by *Time* magazine in 1939. The outbreak of a general war caught the German army leadership unawares. They viewed dealing with Poland with optimism, but as soon as the western campaign was envisaged most of them foretold a repetition of 1914–18. In their view, which was also the view of Hitler, four more years were needed to transform the armed forces 'from a purely numerical factor into a qualitative basis for military endeavour'. If the French and the British were surprised at the defeats they sustained, so were the German generals at the extent of their success. The German army of 1940 was not the exclusively motorised, mechanised and armoured force which the *Blitzkrieg* historians and countless illustrated volumes and magazines would have us believe. Horses and carts and infantry predominated over motorised transport and armoured troop carriers. What was new was the cooperation between armour and a tactical air force. Quantitatively in 1940 the armoured forces of both sides were about the same, qualitatively as far as armour and firepower were concerned the Germans were inferior. And the western campaign was marked by frequent scares about overexposed flanks, alarm at the wear-and-tear on German armour and halts to allow infantry to catch up. The only campaign conceived by the German general staff from its inception as anything resembling a *Blitzkrieg* was the invasion of Russia and the results of that need no repetition here.

11. The Reichsmark Bloc and the International Economy

ALAN S. MILWARD

I

German international economic policy in the 1930s has almost invariably been interpreted as an integral aspect of an aggressive foreign policy designed to satisfy the major international political ambitions of the National Socialist government. The changes which occurred after 1933 in Germany's economic relationships with other countries are always presented as deliberate, positive, choices of policy. There has been considerably more doubt expressed about the precise purpose of these policies but the overwhelming majority of opinion has ascribed to them a nefarious purpose. Historical and economic discussion has focused mainly on the pattern of bilateral trading agreements with central and south-eastern European countries and the creation of a central clearing system in Berlin to support the ever-increasing trade which these agreements produced. In effect six European countries forming a contiguous block of territory in central and south-eastern Europe, all of them relatively low per capita income economies and primary exporters, saw their trade with Germany under these

From G. Hirschfeld and L. Kettenacker (eds), The 'Führer State': Myth and Reality conditions grow steadily as a proportion of their total foreign trade after 1933. They were Bulgaria, Greece, Hungary, Romania, Turkey and Yugoslavia. This phenomenon has already been much analysed. . . . This trading area was often thought of in the 1930s as forming a small German counterpart to the nascent sterling area and for convenience I shall refer to it as the Reichsmark bloc.

This growing commerce has been most frequently discussed as the 'exploitation' by National Socialist Germany of the less-developed European economies, an 'exploitation' which was allied to the NS government's territorial and diplomatic ambitions, an economic domination which served in some sense as a preliminary to subsequent political or military domination. The Reichsmark bloc thus appears as an economic *Drang nach Osten*, a sinister foreshadowing of things to come.[1] The tone was set by the first scholarly analysis of European payments patterns in the 1930s, that of Howard Ellis, whose work has had a great influence on most subsequent scholars in the area.[2] Ellis's argument was that the National Socialist government, although it may have suffered initial losses from bilateral trade in the Reichsmark bloc, was deliberately using its monopsonistic powers against the less-developed economies to turn the terms of trade in its own favour. In this case the monopsony arose from the great disproportion between the high relative importance of the German market to the total foreign trade of each of the less-developed economies and the low relative importance as a proportion of total German imports of the imports which they despatched to Germany. The total share of the Reichsmark bloc in German imports rose from 5·6 per cent in 1933 to 18·5 per cent in 1939, its share in German exports from 3·8 per cent to 18·3 per cent. However, even from Greece, the Reichsmark bloc country with the lowest share of its total trade with Germany, exports to Germany represented 27·5 per cent of all exports in 1939, while 67·8 per cent of Bulgarian exports in the same year went to Germany. Germany's share in the total imports of each Reichsmark bloc country was in the same proportion, from which other scholars deduced that Germany could equally well turn the terms of trade in its own favour by

overpricing its exports.[3] Accepting overpriced exports under
the terms of annual bilateral trading treaties with a much
stronger power was, it was argued, the only way to clear
the accumulation of blocked mark (*Sperrmark*) balances. The
idea that the clearing accounts were used in Berlin as a
weapon to manipulate foreign trade prices and the corollary
idea that the much greater overall size of the German
economy compared to those of the other trading partners
necessarily gave the opportunity for monopsonistic exploitation still deeply imbue most general accounts of the
German and the international economies in this period.[4]

Another strand is added to this argument by historians
who explain the economic 'exploitation' of the 1930s as the
first steps in attaining the foreign policy objectives of the
NS regime. The increasing trade with central and south-
eastern Europe is presented as the first stage in the creation
of an autarkic *Grossraumwirtschaft*, relatively isolated from
exogenous economic forces, to be eventually realised in its
entirety by invasion and occupation. Thus Volkmann,
arguing that 'In the Third Reich foreign trade was the
expression of the political and economic struggle for power',
has presented the formation of the Reichsmark bloc as an
attempt to further Germany's rearmament, a device to
permit greater strategic safety in the event of a further war
and the formation of a *Grossraumwirtschaft*, three policies
which were economically and politically interdependent.[5]
Using the Marxian concepts of 'unequal exchange' and
Galtung's theories of the 'core' and the 'periphery' Doering
explained the Reichsmark bloc within a general theory of
imperialism. The National Socialist government has frequently been portrayed as an example of an especially
vicious stage of late imperialism, in which the role of the
National Socialist party was to preserve an archaic capitalist
structure in Germany by economic and political imperialism
outside Germany. In a Galtungian framework the less-
developed European economies become a periphery 'penetrated' by the core country, Germany, to its own benefit,
the mechanism of 'penetration' being the theory of 'unequal
exchange' of which bilateral trading treaties and exchange
controls manipulated by the imperialist power are merely

one expression. The interest in Doering's work is that she dates this deliberate policy on Germany's part from the depression itself, 1930, rather than from the NS take-over. The failed attempt at a customs union with Austria in fact presaged the Reichsmark bloc and was intended to serve the same exploitative purposes.[6] This is an interpretation, of course, which in a more traditional analytical framework is habitual in the German Democratic Republic and Berndt has sought to show that in this respect there was no inherent difference between the NS regime and the Weimar Republic.[7] An aggressive external economic policy thus becomes a test for classifying the stage and nature of the capitalist system.

Recently the problem has come to be seen rather more from the standpoint of the less-developed economies themselves as empirical research has shown more accurately the central importance of the fall in foodstuff prices after 1928 for their development.[8] Seen from their standpoint the main objective of external economic policy became to secure markets which had some guarantee of continuity, at least in the medium term. This policy objective opened considerable political possibilities to the greater European powers who could expect important advantages in return for the extension of trade preferences or guarantees. The failure of the German-Austrian customs union plans and the growing political and economic interest of the Weimar Republic in central and south-eastern Europe during the depression have to be seen against a complex background of political manoeuvring tied to the possibility that France or, more remotely, Britain might offer better guarantees of markets to underdeveloped Europe.[9] After the *Machtübernahme* one foreign policy choice for Britain, a choice on occasions deliberately adopted, was to withdraw from this competition and in doing so to hope to 'satisfy' in a safe direction the aspirations of the Reich to a more influential status in Europe.[10] It might have been thought that empirical research in these directions would have examined the question whether for the less-developed European economies it did not in some ways prove fortunate to have found such firm markets in a major European economy where, although the distribution of power and income was shifted drastically away from lower income groups, disposable incomes were nonetheless rising throughout the 1930s. Indeed, it was surely implicit in the British policy of 'economic appeasement' that the Reich could only satisfy its ambitions in an easterly direction by sustaining the development and perhaps guaranteeing the 'stability' of the large tract of underdeveloped Europe lying between itself and the Soviet Union. Both in Germany and south-eastern Europe, however, the Reichsmark bloc, although it may be seen in these empirical studies as having a more complicated motivation, is still depicted as the result of a German economic offensive in which the weaker parties had to give ground.

How far is this view correct? Were the international economic relations between Germany and the Reichsmark bloc those between the strong and the weak, between exploiter and exploited? Did they presage the attempt to achieve *Lebensraum* in the east by military methods? Were they but the first step in this more drastic 'solution'? It is necessary at this stage to enter three warnings. Firstly, were the economic relations within the Reichsmark bloc not of this kind this, of course, would not mean that no such drastic military 'solution' was ultimately intended. If less-developed Europe benefited from its close attachment to the German market after the depression this would in no way weaken the fearful threat to the whole area which the economic revival of National Socialist Germany implied nor diminish the very strong likelihood that Hitler would indeed seek to reshape the countries, with little regard for governments or peoples, as part of an intended war against the Soviet Union. Secondly, it was of great importance to NS propaganda to suggest that Germany drew great benefits from the Reichsmark bloc and that those benefits were consonant with the general economic *Weltanschauung* of National Socialism. Thus increased trade with the countries of the Reichsmark bloc had to be portrayed as a step towards independence from the 'plutocratic' international capitalist framework which was itself exploiting Germany. It had also to be portrayed as a triumph of consciously-planned, thrustful, self-confident economic and diplomatic action. There is therefore no shortage of statements at all levels of the NS power structure which could easily lead us to accept the propaganda picture and the economic ideology at face value and accept the Reichsmark bloc for what NS ideologists and propagandists wanted it to be, a device to further the economic policies of the new Germany by fashioning a new Europe. What it was really like is therefore much more accurately judged from the economic facts than from the written word. Thirdly, if the Reichsmark bloc was not, on the evidence of those facts, the exploitation of the less-developed economies by a stronger Germany, that would not necessarily mean that it was not intended to be so. That the aspirations and intentions of policy can be very different from reality is illustrated so frequently in the history of National Socialist Germany that the point need hardly be emphasised. All that said, what do the economic facts indicate about the economic relations between Germany and less-developed Europe?

If an economic argument is to be made in favour of Germany's 'exploitation' of the Reichsmark bloc the precise element of 'exploitation' has to be identified. Two scholars have recently challenged the almost universally-held assumption that such an element did exist. Neal has convincingly shown the lack of empirical proof of the argument that Germany could use monopoly power to turn the terms of trade in her own favour and Marguérat has rejected the idea that Germany's economic relationship with Romania between 1933 and 1938 showed a growing subjection of Romanian to German economic interests over the period.[11] Both rely almost entirely on statistical and economic evidence. The wider and vaguer political arguments may therefore be set for the moment on one side for in general, until their work, the discussion has greatly suffered through arguing from political assumptions rather than from the data. However, to these political questions we shall return for they are fundamental and unavoidable.

Neal's evidence can be joined to the other empirical studies of terms of trade in the 1930s which indicate that they may not have moved in Germany's favour and indeed were more likely to have moved against her. Benham's calculations of the terms of trade of Hungary, Bulgaria, Romania and Turkey with Germany in this period show that in the case of Hungary, Bulgaria and Turkey export prices either rose more than or fell less steeply than import prices.[12] Neal in his recent article examines the unit values of the import and export trade of Romania and Hungary with the Reich and concludes that,

> In general, unit values increased for the exports of both Hungary and Romania to Germany after 1932, although they never reached the 1928 level. Unit values of imports of the two countries from Germany dropped considerably after 1928 and showed no tendency to rise after 1934.[13]

It might be impossible ever to offer by such methods a definitive proof that Germany did not succeed in turning the terms of trade within the Reichsmark bloc in her own favour. The structure of German trade was very complex. She exported raw materials in large quantities as well as the expected high proportion of manufactured goods. In such circumstances the variety of weightings which might be attributed to the various commodities in any such calculation is large. What is more the movement of prices, itself very erratic over the period, is further disguised by the utter artificiality of Reichsmark prices. Neal's calculations are all in the same currency, blocked marks (*Sperrmark*). But the denominated price in *Sperrmark* of any commodity in a bilateral trade agreement was only one aspect of a complicated bargain and to that extent it might not be possible to get nearer to the heart of the argument other than by a painstaking and minute examination of the economic realities of each separate bilateral agreement and perhaps not even then. That caution entered, it must be firmly stated that both Benham and Neal tested the conventional historical and economic hypotheses about German 'exploitation' in a much more searching way than other historians and, to say the least, have found them wanting.[14]

It was never a legitimate critique of German policy in the Reichsmark bloc to argue that *Sperrmark* prices were exploitative because they were in *Sperrmark*. As Neal shows, *Sperrmark* balances could function as reserves in the sense that they could be used as backing by the central bank for an increase in currency and credit. Where a country chose to pursue this policy, as Hungary, in contrast to Romania, did, it was accepting one way, possibly the only way, out of the severe deflation provoked by the drying up of capital inflows after 1928. Certainly payment in blocked marks through the mechanism of the central clearing in Berlin could enable Germany to postpone the date on which a Reichsmark credit would be transformed into actual commodities or services.[15] But that, after all, was one useful advantage of bilateral trade which was in theory equally available to any other member of the bloc, for their currencies were no less strictly controlled than that of Germany. In general the large balances were in marks and Germany the debtor. This, however, was by no means always so and no one has yet produced evidence to show that before 1939 countries in the Reichsmark bloc were forced to accumulate such debts. The movement of the German-Turkish clearing balances is instructive in this respect. When German debts accumulated beyond what the Turkish government considered desirable the strict application of import and export controls in Turkey reversed the situation in little longer than a year. Only with the increase in military imports from Germany in 1938 did the *Sperrmark* balance again build up.[16] Since it can be generally observed in the trade negotiations of that decade that Germany was always reluctant to commit a significant proportion of her armaments output to the export market it must be assumed that this swing back to Germany as the overall debtor was a deliberate act of choice on the part of the Turkish government.

This particular part of the argument badly needs to be seen in the common sense perspective of economic relations between less-developed and developed economies in the inter-war period and away from the lurid light thrown on it by the eventual outcome of German foreign policy. The six less-developed members of the Reichsmark bloc were, together with Denmark, the only European countries whose share of international trade increased in the 1930s, an experience shared by only a small number of extra-European less-developed countries. When foodstuffs were at times destroyed elsewhere in the world because no worthwhile market could be found, there is a lack of proportion in

suggesting that the European less-developed economies were
particularly penalised through having to accumulate blocked
balances in return for rising exports.[17] The balances were in
any case far smaller than those which other less-developed
economies were to accumulate in London in the immediate
ensuing period. Their first cause was the collapse of
international food markets and prices in the depression and
the priority which thenceforward had to be attributed to
continuity of markets over prices. In fact the disjointed
information on prices suggests that the price of food imports
into Germany was higher than the 'international' prices in
Britain and the Netherlands, thus giving the European less-
developed economies the best of both worlds.

This does not meet the criticism that trade under such
conditions imposed severe restrictions on the freedom of
choice of the less-developed importer. That their choice of
capital goods imports was limited by the need to clear the
mark balances is obvious. Whether the contrast with the
'free' choice of imports supposedly permitted in previous
decades by capital imports is as strong as many authors
seem to suggest may, however, be doubted. Ellis argued
that German exports were initially priced low in order to
acquire markets which the importer was subsequently forced
to provide by the need to clear the balances even when
import prices had become high. But as we have seen the
evidence suggests that the relative price of German imports
compared to exports from the less-developed economies did
not increase, so the penalties on the less-developed economies
were no more than a restriction on the choice of supplier.
Given the urgent priority which they had to attribute to
their exports this penalty was not so severe.

There remains the classical criticism that trade under
conditions of bilateralism, although it might initially benefit
the less-developed economy if GNP was growing rapidly in
the more developed partner (as in this case it was), would
nevertheless ultimately result in costly misallocations of
resources from which the weaker economy was more likely
to suffer harm. Suppose that German import policy kept
food prices so high in central and south-eastern Europe as
to prevent exports from that area finding any alternative

outlet. Those inefficiencies might then create political pressure groups and vested interests in the less-developed economies which would seek to perpetuate the established export trade to Germany and to prevent development beyond the stage of primary exporting.[18] The historian might well regard the theory of international trade under perfect competition as having so little to do with the realities of the 1930s as to be no use even as an intellectual yardstick. What alternative markets did exist for the foodstuff exports within the Reichsmark bloc? . . . Britain was the only other major food-importing country to show in the 1930s a comparable rise in food consumption to that in Germany. In these circumstances alternative markets for the less-developed economies, if they wanted them, could only have been obtained through a deliberate act of political choice by the British government and, as Wendt has shown, the choice was usually being strongly influenced in the opposite direction.[19] Even had Britain chosen to provide alternative markets it would have been at much lower prices.

It would be impossible here to deal satisfactorily with the suggestion that the primary export trades within the Reichsmark bloc introduced a damaging bias into the political structures of the less-developed economies. It can be readily agreed that political developments in those countries after 1933 offered no comfort to those of a progressive cast of mind. To attribute the gradual abolition of democratic forms of policies to the influence of the vested interests of primary exporters is, none the less, somewhat far-fetched when there were so many other political and economic forces making in the same direction. And in any case the political and economic bases of authoritarian rule in these countries in the 1930s showed great differences from country to country, as did the choice of economic policy. Where Romanian governments pursued the same determined policies of industrialisation as their liberal precursors the Bulgarian royal dictatorship was, for example, more consciously 'agrarian' and conservative in its choice of development policy. There is certainly no apparent correspondence between the various unpleasant groups which exercised power in any of these countries and any vested interests created by the strength and persistence of the German export market. Nor, of course, did these governments have much in common with the government in Berlin apart from their authoritarian nature. If the Hungarian government was perfectly willing, as Neal shows, to use its *Spermark* balances as a basis for reflation, that was not out of political sympathy with the NSDAP but simply because Hungary had nothing to lose and probably very much to gain from tying herself more closely to German economic and political expansion. Romania could only lose from any revision of the Versailles settlement and that must have greatly influenced the decision in Bucharest to maintain a strict differentiation between reserves and blocked balances and in no way to regard the latter as backing for the money supply. In that way the internal economic shock of clearing the balances, which it was necessary to consider might have to be done at any time, would be less.

It must be acknowledged that where a country had 52 per cent of her import trade and 59 per cent of her export trade with Germany, as was the case with Bulgaria in 1938, the German bargaining position in bilateral negotiations was a strong one, especially as imports from Bulgaria accounted for only one and a half per cent of all German imports in the same year. It would be absurd to suppose that Germany did not seek to obtain every advantage she could from this disproportion. This also, however, has to be seen in context. No other Reichsmark bloc country had the same high proportion of its foreign trade with Germany and there were other economies outside the Reichsmark bloc in an equivalent degree of trade-dependence on one developed economy to Bulgaria. The dependence of Ireland and New Zealand on Britain was greater, but even larger and more complex economies could find themselves approaching the same state in the 1930s. Of South Africa's exports 33 per cent went to Britain and 43·4 per cent of her imports came from the same source in 1938. For Australia the equivalent proportions were 55·7 per cent and 41·4 per cent and for India 33·7 and 31·4 per cent.[20] It should also, however, be pointed out that although the sterling area would provide most such examples of trade-dependence in the 1930s, its internal trade and payments arrangements were effectively multilateral whereas mark balances in the Reichsmark bloc were not transferable.

Marguérat's work brings another strand into the argument by illustrating the difficulties for Germany which arose from the entrenched positions which British and French capital had previously acquired in underdeveloped Europe.[21] It has most frequently been assumed that there was a close harmony between German foreign policy and the pattern of German foreign investment. Proportionately to the quantity of British and French investment in the underdeveloped Reichsmark bloc countries German investment was still very low in 1938 although it showed a marked upward trend. Marguérat traces German interest in Romanian oil supplies and the attempt to secure a greater proportion of them. Although it might have been thought that Romanian oil would have been of particular interest to Germany's rearmament plans from 1934 it was not so until summer 1938. Before that date German mobilisation plans envisaged an increase of oil consumption over peace-time levels of no more than about 20 per cent and much of this increase was intended to be met out of synthetic production. It was only Hitler's realisation that he might, after all, be at war with France and Britain simultaneously and at an earlier date than originally foreseen, together with the forced downward revision of synthetic fuel production targets in July 1938, the so-called *Wehrwirtschaftlicher Neuer Erzeugungsplan*, that caused Germany for the first time to bring severe economic pressure to bear on Romania. A comparison of the statistical evidence does, indeed, show that to classify Romania before that date with the other Reichsmark bloc countries is to a certain extent misleading. The increase in her trade with Germany as compared to the period 1925–8 is much less marked after 1933 than in the case of the other countries although the increase as compared to the depression years is very high. It would be reasonable to argue from the evidence that the increase in German-Romanian trade in the 1930s represented no more than a recovery from the disastrous years 1928–32. However after 1938 when Germany sought to change this situation Marguérat argues that it proved very difficult for her to bring any effective economic pressure to bear on Romania because of the dominating position of British and French capital there. In 1939 Anglo-Dutch capital accounted for 39·8 per cent of all capital participation in the Romanian oil industry, by that time Germany's chief interest, French capital 16·6 per cent and American capital 12·5 per cent.[22] The international oil companies not only withstood German pressures but actually reduced the flow of Romanian oil to Germany until the annexation of Bohemia and the sponsorship of the annexation by Hungary of the Carpatho-Ukraine in March 1939. After that Germany enforced the new trade agreement of 23 March 1939.[23] . . .

Outside the sphere of international trade, therefore, at least in the case of Romania, evidence of 'exploitation' is lacking until the final collapse of Czechoslovakia. That this collapse was of major importance to the countries of the Reichsmark bloc can scarcely be doubted. Czechoslovakia was an important market for them and there were extensive Czech capital investments there. Basch berated the British and French for having made an economic surrender at Munich and for having thrown away an economic position in central and south-eastern Europe acquired over many decades.[24] Until the Munich agreements it would be impossible to claim that, setting aside foreign trade, German economic 'penetration' was a matter of any significance. History indeed records no greater disproportion between foreign trade and investment than that shown in the economic relationship between National Socialist Germany and central and south-eastern Europe in the 1930s. It might be just as logical to ask the question, 'Why, when the proportion of foreign trade with Germany was so very high for these countries, was the level of German investment there so low?' Part of the answer would obviously be the loss of German investments there in the aftermath of the First World War. The recovery of German investment after 1933 appears nevertheless on the scant evidence available to have been remarkably feeble compared to the recovery of German trade. In Bulgaria the proportion of German capital in total foreign capital in the one estimate that is usually cited is put at 16 per cent in 1939.[25] Since the proportion of German foreign investment to total foreign investment was smaller in the other economies and the increase in foreign trade with them less, it seems unlikely that the increase in German foreign investment there would have been more striking. Lamer's calculations suggest that total German foreign investment in Yugoslavia in 1936 was statistically insignificant by the side of that of west European countries.[26] Even after the *Anschluss* German capital in Romania was probably no higher than 8 per cent of total foreign capital.[27]

The proportions of capital investment may be less revealing than the actions and plans of German companies. By 1940 at least some major German companies had far-reaching plans for central and south-eastern Europe, which could not unfairly be labelled as economic 'penetration'.[28] The military defeat of France offered large possibilities to a multinational like I. G. Farben. What is not known is how far German firms were able to pursue such policies before 1938 nor how far firms with much less intimate connections with the government than I. G. Farben harboured similar ambitions to control important sections of manufacturing in the less-developed economies. Teichova's study of foreign investment in Czechoslovakia argues that there was a close association between the political aims of the NS government to expand their power into central and south-eastern Europe and the investment policy of German firms. The mechanism by which these aims were to be realised was not, she argues, investment *per se* but the integration of firms in the smaller economies into German-controlled cartels.[29] Although Teichova's work contains an immense quantity of data on the intricate patterns of international ownership and agreements affecting Czech (and therefore in many cases Reichsmark bloc) firms the precise data which would establish her argument seems lacking.[30] To establish them it would be necessary, no doubt, to trace the relationships of a large selection of firms with the National Socialist regime and to try to establish how far their economic interests coincided, or were made to coincide with, the external ambitions of the NS regime. Even were it to be shown that in a large number of cases they did do so it would still be necessary to show that in the period before Munich government and firm were able to implement their ambitions. It may not, indeed, as several studies including that of Teichova herself imply, have been all that easy even after

Munich. And, lastly, the intimate embrace of German companies may not have been necessarily a bad thing on all occasions. That, too, might depend, even if it is accepted that the intentions of the National Socialist government towards the Reichsmark bloc countries were ultimately aggressive, on the extent of the agreement between the National Socialist government and German companies on the desired nature of political and economic society inside and outside Germany. That this is a richly-complicated subject on which scholars are far from agreement no student of the period nor reader of this volume will need reminding. As things stand, therefore, there is no more evidence of German economic exploitation of the Reichsmark bloc countries outside the field of foreign trade than there is inside it.

II

Those who argue that German trading policy was exploitative would surely be unhappy with any refutation of their argument which did not consider the longer run aims of German foreign policy. Most, like Ellis, appear to consider Germany's external policy as a set of predetermined goals wherein the political objectives were reinforced by the economic. The Reichsmark bloc thus becomes a stage in National Socialist foreign policy and there is little point in demonstrating that in its early stages the less-developed economies benefited from it and may even have done so more than Germany since the ultimate disadvantages to them, seen from a political standpoint, were frightening. This view simplifies beyond acceptability the problem of NS foreign policy. The furious debate among diplomatic historians about Hitler's ultimate objectives and about the consistency with which they were pursued is far from a satisfactory conclusion. Even those scholars most committed to the argument that the firmly consistent intentions of the German government were to create by armed force a 'Greater Germany' beyond the eastern frontiers of the Weimar Republic[31] would now accept, however, that this goal involved many important, albeit temporary, shifts of policy along the way. Few would be so bold now as to maintain that the area of any future 'Greater Germany' did not depend on shifting diplomatic and economic eventualities in the 1930s. Among these eventualities the shifting positions of the smaller central and south-eastern countries played an important role. It is wrong to attribute a consistent economic motive to Germany's relations with them on the grounds that it was part and parcel of a consistent political motive, for even if, which is not certain, in the long run the political motive was consistent, in the short and medium run the fate which the NS government had in store for these smaller countries certainly varied as Germany's relationships with the greater powers changed.

One argument which seems to have been generally accepted throughout, although Marguérat's work refutes it in the case of Romania, is that one purpose of the Reichsmark bloc was to promote rearmament and permit a 'war economy' in Germany in pursuit of these political aims. Faced with the virtual certainty in any future war of another blockade of her overseas trade and this time with a much smaller domestic raw material base to fall back on Germany is claimed to have used the device of bilateral trading treaties to force exports of strategic materials from the Reichsmark bloc which were, so the argument normally runs, equipping the German armed forces for a future attack on her trading partners. For this it might well be worth paying over the odds for foodstuff imports.

This argument exaggerates the strategic economic importance of the Reichsmark bloc to German economy. Setting aside for a moment the question of food supply there were only three strategic raw materials which the area could provide in such quantities that they were statistically significant as a part of total German supply, chromite, bauxite and oil. Although chromite was traded in only small quantities it was an almost irreplaceable component of armaments steel. Turkey was the world's second largest producer and chromite represented 3 per cent of the annual value of her exports.[32] Both Greece and Yugoslavia were also each larger producers than the United States and the combined output of the region amounted to over a quarter of average annual world output. Similarly, Hungary, Yugoslavia and Greece produced between them about one quarter of the world's output of bauxite, effectively the sole ore from which aluminium could be manufactured on a large scale. The importance of aluminium was that it was the basic constructional material for most aircraft. Germany was devoid of significant reserves of either raw material. Chromite, of course, can be stockpiled much more effectively than bauxite which is consumed in far greater quantities and accumulation of a sufficient stockpile to meet the demands of the war of only limited duration and output at which German strategy aimed would mean that the level of demand from Germany, once this aim had been met, might be less high and less sustained than for bauxite. At the end of 1939 stockpiles of chromite were sufficient to meet presumed future demand for two years without further imports.[33] Nevertheless, it can also be presumed that Germany would not import chromite from hard currency areas if it could be obtained through bilateral agreements with the Reichsmark bloc countries. The strategic importance of oil needs no elaboration and Romania was the second largest European producer.

The exact figures for output and exports of bauxite and chromite remain in some doubt, a doubt which may well linger given their sensitive nature. Yet there is a clear difference in the two cases in the response of the Reichsmark bloc countries to German demand. Over the period 1935–8 Germany probably obtained no more than 30 per cent of the total output of Greek, Turkish and Yugoslav chromite. . . . The imprecision arises not so much from the lack of any Yugoslav export figures for 1935 as from the possibility that some of the relatively high exports to Austria could have found their way as ore or in semi-manufactures to Germany. Until 1938, however, the main market for Turkish chromite exports was the United States. The aftermath of the Turkish rearmament loan in 1938 was that the proportion of Turkish chromite exports going to Germany increased steeply but it was still only 49·6 per cent. Conversely the proportion of Yugoslav exports going to Germany (including Austria) fell to 12·6 per cent from its previous year's level of 30·1 per cent and of Greek exports the proportion dropped over the same two years from 42·8 per cent to 40·5 per cent. Italy was throughout the period a more important market than Germany for Greek chromite and Britain of almost

equal importance. Chromite was one primary product which
could still be sold for hard currency at competitive prices on
world markets and with the growth of rearmament outside
Germany this became still more the case. The Reichsmark
bloc countries could in fact resist German pressure to
include greater quantities of chromite in the bilateral
agreements and did so successfully until the outbreak of
war. German supply from South Africa purchased in sterling
between 1933 and 1938 was almost as large as from Turkey.

With bauxite the opposite applied because Allied demand
was lower for a long time and could easily be satisfied
elsewhere. Bauxite, unlike chromite, is a common raw material.
British, American and Canadian aluminium companies
obtained their raw material from the Caribbean and France.
France was a major world producer with a large export
surplus after meeting the demand from her own industry.
Production of bauxite tended to be in exact measure to
demand from predetermined markets and it was seldom
offered freely for hard currency on open markets. The growth
of bauxite mining in the Reichsmark bloc was thus a direct
response to the surge of demand emanating from Germany,
the world's biggest aluminium producer throughout the period.
The rapidly rising output of bauxite in Hungary and
Yugoslavia was almost entirely for the German market and
only relatively small quantities of Greek output went elsewhere.
These combined resources were supplying about three-quarters
of total German consumption. Even though the main final
consumer of these exports was the German aircraft industry,
their immediate value to the exporting country must also of
course be taken into account. In Hungary they were the
origin of an important new industry.

The relative lack of importance of Romanian oil in
Germany's total oil imports is explained by German strategy
and mobilisation plans before 1938. Before 1939 exports of
Romanian oil products to Germany never exceeded 15·7 per
cent of total annual exports of these products. Imports of oil
products from the Soviet Union were in fact marginally
more important in the pre-war period than those from
Romania. The largest part of imports remained vulnerable
to blockade. The Anglo-Dutch refineries on Curaçao were
the chief suppliers and in addition there was a high level of

imports from the United States and Iran which, on the eve of war, was supplemented by increasing imports from Mexico. About 60 per cent of oil product imports still came from outside Europe. Oil, like chromite, could be sold on hard currency markets and there was every reason why the Romanian government and the oil companies alike should not allow any more than a small proportion to be sold for blocked marks and probably no way in which Germany could have acquired more of it through bilateral clearing other than by, as in 1939, extreme menaces.

There remains the question of food supply, for in the context of German military strategy in Europe and the intended Allied response of blockade, food was also a strategic good of the highest importance. It might well be worth paying more than the depressed world prices in order to establish direct links between producers and the German market, which governments would be reluctant to disrupt even when Germany was involved in hostilities and which Allied powers could not interrupt by naval blockade. In fact the biggest single component of the increase of Reichsmark bloc exports to Germany is exports of foodstuffs. The proportion of total German foodstuff imports coming from the area rose from 11·1 per cent in 1930 to 28·2 per cent in 1939. . . . The actual volume and value of foodstuff imports as a proportion of total foodstuff consumption fell under the National Socialist government's import-saving policies so that in real constant prices foodstuff imports from the Reichsmark bloc did not surpass their level of the previous period of rising German incomes, 1925–8. Nonetheless Germany was breaching its high trade barriers to let in increasing quantities of foodstuffs at prices well above prevailing averages. It was the shift in the origins of German foodstuff imports in the 1930s which constituted the biggest part of the altered pattern of European trade in that decade and it was the exchange of food against manufactured goods which held together the Reichsmark bloc as a trading area.

Yet even the statistical evidence on the development of these various foodstuff trades does not provide a convincing picture of trade-dependence. Here it is necessary to tread carefully. The statistical information is by no means all available, most usually because the particular commodities in question were not satisfactorily disaggregated in trade statistics. [The author presents detailed statistical tables on the various types of foodstuffs and the countries of origin and destination respectively. *Ed.*] Nonetheless these tables are strongly suggestive of certain interpretations. No calculations have been made for Bulgaria on the grounds that if half its exports were to Germany and its exports largely consisted of foodstuffs it would be axiomatic that something like that proportion of its main foodstuff exports (those making the biggest contribution to the total value of all food exports) would also have gone to Germany throughout the period. For the other Reichsmark bloc countries the distribution of the most prominent foodstuff exports has been calculated, although the data for Yugoslavia are not such as to enable any satisfactory conclusions to be drawn. The conclusions which could be drawn from these tables are the following.

Firstly, where a staple export of the underdeveloped economy became more heavily concentrated on the German market than it had been in 1928 that shift often took place most decisively before 1933. There are noticeable exceptions to this in the case of livestock exports from Romania and grain exports from Turkey. Secondly, the only non-German market which diminished in importance for these staple export trades in the 1930s was Italy. That perhaps is explained by the movement towards import-substitution in the Italian economy. As that movement weakened after 1936 it is noticeable that Italy again re-enters these trades as an active purchaser. British purchasing in these trades in particular did not decline (the average level of food consumption was also increasing in Britain in the 1930s) and there are certain striking examples of great increases of British purchases in Romania and Turkey after Munich, presumably as a political response. Lastly, and most importantly, the differences between the separate economies and also between separate trades in one economy dominate the picture. This might well suggest that the pattern of the foodstuffs trade in the Reichsmark bloc was dominated by the particular commodity structure of each underdeveloped country's trade. Few of these trades were so dependent on the sole German market as to leave no hope at all of adjustment should there be a threat to withdraw that market.[34] In fact the increase in the proportion of these staple trades going to Germany does not seem adequately to account for the increase in the proportion of all foodstuff exports from the bloc to Germany and it may be that some part of that increase is accounted for by new foodstuff exports developed especially for the German market rather than by these staples. A certain amount of German capital did go into projects for cultivating oil seeds and other crops for export to Germany. The quantity was probably small and the schemes, still unstudied, do not seem on present evidence to have been very impressive. They would, nevertheless, have been beneficial to the underdeveloped economy rather than exploitative.

The increase in the proportion of any staple trade going to Germany seems on present evidence to be no more than a rational response to the higher prices prevailing on the German market. There is no attempt here to make a comprehensive comparison of the relative prices obtaining on different markets in these trades for, again, the evidence is not sufficiently comprehensive to justify such an effort. But such evidence as there is strongly bears out the conclusions of both Neal and Benham on the relative terms of trade. There is an especially striking example in 1939 of the price differentials that existed. In that year Germany and Britain took an exactly equal proportion by weight of Turkish nut exports. Their sale price to Germany was 2·2 million Turkish pounds; to Britain 0·9 million Turkish pounds. France took a much larger share than Germany but at a price considerably lower, 1·4 million Turkish pounds, than the price paid by Germany for her smaller quantity.[35]

'The exchange of grain for manufactured products', wrote Herbert Backe, Minister of Food in the National Socialist government, 'is the sound and natural basis of trade with the east and south-east.'[36] From the perspective of the less-developed economies the advantage of the Reichsmark bloc was that with the decline in capital inflows exports had come to have a greater importance for development. For them exportable food surpluses were but a stage towards another goal, industrialisation. Whether this goal would be acceptable in Berlin or whether it would overturn the 'sound and natural basis' of trade are questions which, once again, can only be answered by reference to Germany's political aims in Europe. If the interest in trade with the Reichsmark bloc stemmed from a static analysis of the European economy in which south-eastern Europe remained perpetually underdeveloped it may also have stemmed from a similarly static analysis of Germany's economic future. Measured over the period 1926–74 the proportion of German exports, including after 1953 the trade of the German Democratic Republic, going to the higher per capita income countries of Europe, has shown a slow but persistent increase with the striking exception of the period 1934–9 when this trend was sharply reversed.[37] Exports to low per capita income European economies[38] showed a decisive upward trend from 1934 to 1939 which is also clearly distinguished from the long-term pattern of German trade, although the fluctuations of this trade between 1925 and 1933, it might reasonably be argued, are fluctuations around a much more slowly rising trend. Obviously this striking deviation from the long-run pattern of German trade was not reflected in lower rates of growth of GNP, they were higher in the National Socialist period than at any time other than the boom of the 1950s. Nevertheless, foreign trade was not in the long run a force for growth in the German economy after 1933 for the constant increase in the proportion of German exports directed towards underdeveloped Europe between 1933 and 1939 was also a constant increase in the constraints which external economic policy imposed on growth and a constant increase in the pressures to sustain the growth of incomes through internal economic policy.

It would be foolish to assert that strategic considerations were not involved in this deviation from trend and impossible to extricate them from its foreign exchange saving component. Yet the origin of the growth of this trade, and indeed the origins of the Reichsmark bloc itself, date from before the National Socialist take-over and were a response to the loss of foreign exchange in 1930, the difficulties created for Germany by the rapid burgeoning of exchange controls from Hungary to Greece and the British devaluation against gold in 1931. All the main principles of bilateral trading agreements with underdeveloped Europe were worked out in the Republic before 1933. Schacht's *Neuer Plan* in 1934 merely systematised into deliberate policy a set of trading devices which were already widespread and also extended into deliberate policy a geographical pattern of trade which had in any case begun to emerge as a response to Germany's alarming external situation in the depression. The main difference in 1934 was that as a result of National Socialist domestic economic policy the predicted foreign exchange deficit threatened briefly to acquire the proportions of 1928. In effect 1934 was the first year since 1928 when Germany recorded a deficit on the balance of commodity trade. It became necessary to classify as plans and policy what had over the last four years been only desperate expedients.

There is, lastly, little geographical congruence between the Reichsmark trading bloc and any future *Grossraumwirtschaft* or *Lebensraum* which Hitler or the National Socialist party may have intended. Two countries in particular stood immediately in the way of German expansion and the overwhelming weight of the historical evidence is that both, Czechoslovakia and Poland, were destined for 'reconstruction'. Those who maintain that Hitler's foreign policy was consistently aimed at obtaining *Lebensraum* in the east all accept that it was to be obtained at the expense of the Soviet Union also. These were the three countries most likely to be the victims of German territorial aggression. Czechoslovakia remained firmly outside the Reichsmark bloc and German trade with both Poland and the Soviet Union diminished to insignificance after 1933. In the period 1925–34 Poland provided an annual average of 2·15 per cent of all German imports and took 2·12 per cent of all German exports. In the period 1934–8 she provided only 1·4 per cent of German imports and took only 1·25 per cent of German exports. The example of the Soviet Union is even more striking. The Soviet Union had been a major trading partner of the Weimar Republic, so important indeed in 1932 as to have been responsible, by one of history's great ironies, for sustaining even the low level of German manufactured exports of that year and providing an invaluable prop to the international capitalist economy. Over the period 1925–33 the USSR took an annual average of 4·71 per cent of German exports and provided 3·68 per cent of imports. Over the period 1934–8 the comparable figures were only

1·54 per cent of exports and 2·84 per cent of imports.[39] It remains only to add that once the *Grossraumwirschaft* of NS propaganda became a reality in 1940 the statistical contribution of the Reichsmark bloc countries to German supply dwindled into relative insignificance, not just when compared to the great increase of manufactured imports from western Europe, but even when the comparison is restricted to foodstuff imports. From 1940 onwards foodstuff imports from occupied western Europe far eclipsed imports from central and south-eastern Europe.[40]

III

The grounds, therefore, for arguing that the Reichsmark bloc was a positive step in German foreign economic policy seem as unsure as those for continuing to argue that it was an instrument of 'exploitation' of the less-developed European economies. There is very little evidence for either and a certain amount of evidence to the contrary. Both arguments in fact are based on the assumption that the National Socialist government was able to choose a positive and aggressive external economic policy. But was it? Was not the economic reality more one in which in deeply discouraging economic circumstances the NS government gave overwhelming priority to its own domestic economic and social policies and in so doing made Germany's already weak external economic situation even weaker, untenable, indeed, without assuming permanent trade and exchange controls and a very wide and possibly permanent discrepancy between German prices and those of the other major traders? From the moment Hitler became Chancellor any chances of reintegrating Germany into an internationally-agreed payments system disappeared. The Reichsmark bloc, far from being a positive policy, was a desperately unsatisfactory attempt to maintain, at high international costs to the German economy, the absolute primacy of domestic economic policy.

The evidence that the terms of trade in the 1930s may have moved against Germany is in fact exactly what we should expect to find. It was part of the price paid for defending other priorities. As Romanian prices increased Germany was unable to maintain the Reichsmark/leu exchange rate at the level she would have wished. To put up the price of German exports would have made competition on the Romanian market in textiles and metal products against Britain and France impossible. Nor was Germany able to raise the Reichsmark's value in the annual bilateral trade negotiations, partly because Romania was still able to sell oil against sterling and hard currency and, later, because British imports of Romanian cereals showed a steep increase. Romanian *Sperrmark* balances in Berlin represented not a cunning exploitation by Germany, but genuine difficulties in footing the bill for cereal and oil imports, difficulties which threatened repeatedly to disrupt German-Romanian trade.[41]

Exchange control began under the Brüning government in order to staunch the outflow of reserves. Germany had in fact only been able to meet her international obligations in 1930 because the collapse of primary product prices drastically reduced the cost of her imports. The fall in exports and the run on the reserves in 1931 left little choice but a system of exchange controls which was thought of as temporary, introduced by a series of administrative decrees in July and August. Immediately afterwards the Wiggin Committee sat to find a basis on which German trade could continue so that creditors (including recipients of reparations) could continue to be paid in spite of the cessation of capital inflows. Its deliberations took place against the background of a restless search by a powerful, if disunited, political opposition for a new basis of economic policy. In this search the National Socialist Party emerged triumphant, not least by combining all the various recipes of the other opposition groups. Like the parties of the left it espoused the cause of employment-creation programmes, like those of the right it demanded the removal of all international restrictions on German tariffs. It cut the ground from under the agrarian parties in rural areas by proclaiming the necessity of self-sufficiency in food production and high levels of agricultural protection. Even if this were ill-understood at the time by the leaders of the NSDAP it was still true that even half this programme would have meant perseverance with trade and exchange controls for a much longer time. Because the NSDAP started from the assumption that the existing state of affairs was intolerable and *must* be changed in order to offer any hope of a reasonable national existence it was not likely to be deterred by these international obstacles. As the Party approached electoral victory Germany's international situation became even more precarious by virtue of the relative fall in the price of British finished export goods compared to those of Germany.

In November 1931 a set of principles for foreign exchange allocation was determined whose intention was expressly non-discriminatory. There were, however, finite limits over which any foreign exchange allocation scheme which was based, as this one was, on an average need for exchange in the pre-control period, could last while still making economic sense. In any case it was unthinkable that a party like the NSDAP would not manipulate such a scheme, if in power, for its own political purposes. The use of blocked mark balances began in February 1932 when German creditors were allowed to use up to 50 per cent of their loans to purchase German securities at the low prevailing prices providing the securities remained 'blocked' for five years. In the next two months the first bilateral trading agreements were signed and the agreement between the Reemstma cigarette company and the Greek government linked bilateral trade to the clearing of blocked balances in each currency.[42] In summer 1932 the Reichsbank allowed exporters, who were able to demonstrate that their trade would otherwise have been impossible, to buy German bonds at their low foreign values and resell them at the higher prices on the German market to subsidise losses sustained in exporting goods to markets where the price level was now below that in Germany. Every principle of trade and exchange control and export subsidisation used during the NS regime was already in place before the seizure of power. The von Papen government's very restricted expenditures on public works in September 1932 were left well behind by von Schleicher and the Gereke Plan, which created the same methods of financing job creation which the National Socialist government would also employ under the Reinhardt plan, far outdistanced any previous or other contemporary programme of public works expenditure. Between 1932 and the seizure of power about 500 to 600 million marks were spent on purely 'civil' public works. The National Socialist government was to spend 2,450 million Reichsmark for the same purpose in 1934 alone and 4,000 million in the years 1933 and 1934 together.[43] Expenditure on armaments reached roughly the same amount.[44] To this was added expenditure on the subsidisation of the agricultural sector. The foreign exchange deficit in autumn 1934 reached 700 million Reichsmarks. The purpose of the *Neuer Plan* was no more than to permit domestic economic policy to continue in spite of this deficit and the effect it would otherwise have had in any attempt to bring exchange rates and prices back into line with those of western Europe. It used all the earlier methods and in addition gave power to the exchange control boards, whose number was increased, to discriminate against a wide range of finished and semi-finished imports. In effect trade controls now had the positive purpose of backing up the job-creation schemes rather then the merely negative one of restricting the outflow of reserves.

Rearmament was still at low levels. The difficulties of distinguishing between public expenditure on civil and on military purposes are insuperable and the distinction does not in any case make much sense in the case of the National Socialist government. Schweitzer estimates that expenditure on the second category had already added 243 million Reichsmarks to the import bill in 1934 as compared to 1933.[45] Be that as it may the lowest set of calculations of rearmament expenditure (Klein) show expenditure for this purpose at 4,000 million Reichsmarks in 1935 and 6,000 million in 1936, increases of more than 50 per cent a year.[46] A substantial part of these increases came, however, out of the decrease in expenditure on public works. In fact the deficit of government expenditure over receipts fell slightly in 1935 but in spite of the great increase in revenue which came with full employment and fuller utilisation of resources in 1936 the budget deficit doubled in that year. If there had ever been a chance that full employment and recovery would provide the occasion for re-establishing an equilibrium rate for the mark it ended in 1936. The Four Year Plan with its massive commitment of investment to synthetic production and import substitution pushed expenditure to new heights and led initially to a further demand for imports for which there was no means of payment. Total gold and foreign exchange reserves were about two and a half per cent their level of 1930 and in the second half of 1936 there was a foreign exchange deficit of 637·7 million Reichsmarks.[47] Yet this was the moment at which rearmament expenditure was to show a marked upward movement and also the starting point of the 5,300 million Reichsmarks extra expenditure between summer 1936 and the end of 1939 on the Four Year Plan itself.[48]

In relation to the size of GNP the volume of German imports fell throughout the 1930s. Foreign exchange shortages and the desire for strategic safety from blockade alike combined to push economic policy towards import substitution and towards a shift in the source of imports. The high price of German goods reduced the choice of export markets. From this forced shift in German trade the Reichsmark bloc countries were the major beneficiaries supplying 18·5 per cent of all German imports in 1939 compared to the 3·9 per cent they had supplied in 1928. By contrast German trade with the gold bloc countries inevitably encountered severe difficulties. Imports from France, which had accounted for 5·3 per cent of all imports in 1928 were but 2·6 per cent of a lower total in 1938 even when Austrian imports from France in that year are included. The decline in German-United States trade is the most dramatic. The United States had been by a long way Germany's most important supplier in the 1920s. The drying-up of capital flows from America led to a fall in importance of United States imports from 14·4 per cent of all imports in 1928 to 7·4 per cent in 1938. This last figure was in fact exceptionally high because of the increase in wheat imports from America in that year; for 1937 the proportion was only 5·2 per cent. The increase in imports from America in 1938 was further testimony to the inadequacy of the Reichsmark bloc to sustain Germany's strategic needs.[49] Its inadequacy to cater for her longer-term economic needs has already been noted.

Even within the bloc the position of the Reichsmark was often a weak one. Turkey was not the only member to put Germany in difficulties by altering the balance of trade in order to mop up its accumulated *Sperrmark*. Romania similarly forced a reduction of the *Sperrmark* balances from September 1935 by allowing the Reichsmark effectively to float against the leu and from September 1936 by placing stricter limitations on the permissible percentage of oil products in total exports to Germany. The flow of interest payments and profits on British investments in Romania was met by increased oil exports to Britain. Because the pound rose against the leu as the Reichsmark fell, Romanian exporters marked up prices to Germany to try to reach the equivalent rate of return on exports to Britain so that in bilateral negotiations the sterling/leu exchange rate was often dictating the negotiated Reichsmark/leu rate.[50]

The long- and short-run weaknesses of Germany's position are unmistakable. That the formation of the Reichsmark bloc should be seen as National Socialist 'exploitation' or 'penetration' of south-eastern Europe is a remarkable tribute to the ability of National Socialism to explain all events, however, unwelcome, as being in accord with the new *Weltanschauung*. It is true that the Reichsmark bloc did save gold and foreign exchange and that it was an essential part of the trade and exchange controls which preserved the absolute primacy of domestic economic priorities. It may well be that had it not been for the determined attention paid to the mechanisms of Reichsmark bloc trade Germany's terms of trade would have been less favourable and in that sense, which is by no means the sense in which the word has so far been used, there would be a certain element of 'exploitation' of the less-developed economies. Otherwise, on present evidence, the word is entirely unjustified. National Socialist domestic economic policy meant that Germany's international economic bargaining power was distinctly weak before 1939. From this weakness the less-developed European economies were able to extract great advantage for themselves in what would otherwise have been a desperate situation. They, almost alone amongst the world's primary exporters in the 1930s, were able to show an increase in export earnings and an increase in the growth of national income. The concentration of economic policy on achieving the immediate internal aims of the NS regime opened up possibilities of development to underdeveloped Europe when the depression seemed otherwise to have foreclosed all such possibilities. Historians should turn their attention to the successful exploitation of Germany's economic weakness before 1939 by the small economies of central and south-eastern Europe.

12. Germany's Economic Preparations for War

BURTON H. KLEIN

[Extracts]

CONCLUSIONS ON THE ECONOMIC REARMAMENT OF GERMANY

In the pre-war period, the German economy produced both 'butter' and 'guns' – much more of the former and much less of the latter than has been commonly assumed. By 1937, civilian consumption, investment in consumer goods industries, and government non-war expenditures equalled or exceeded previous peak levels. There is no question, therefore, of a rearmament programme so large that it prevented a substantial recovery of civilian production.

The volume of expenditures for rearmament was actually quite modest. In the period 1933 through 1938 rearmament expenditures absorbed less than 10 per cent of Germany's gross national product, and even as late as 1938, only 15 per cent. The volume of munitions production and the

Extracts from Burton H. Klein, *Germany's Economic Preparations for War*, Harvard Economic Studies (Harvard University Press, Cambridge, Mass., 1959), pp. 76–82, 235–8.

number of divisions which Germany mobilised was, by comparison with published appraisal, small. Investment in those industries comprising the war potential was not much larger than the volume reached in the prosperous years of the previous decade and was small in relation to total investment.

The review of Germany's raw material preparations for war shows that at the time the National Socialists came into power Germany was not self-sufficient in such important materials as iron ore, ferroalloys, oil, copper, rubber, aluminium, bauxite, and foodstuffs. Of these, only in foodstuffs and rubber did the Germans attain a substantial degree of self-sufficiency prior to the war. They found it impossible to become independent of foreign sources for such important materials as copper ores, bauxite, and ferroalloys because Germany lacked the basic resources. For other important raw materials, notably iron ore and synthetic oil, the self-sufficiency programmes were largely unsuccessful because they were begun too late and were inadequately implemented.

Raw material distribution controls were largely unsuccessful in increasing the flow of raw materials into the war sector of the economy. Priorities and allocation schemes were applied to only a few commodities and in those cases where they were used they were largely ineffective.

The stockpiling programme also did little to improve Germany's raw material position. At the beginning of the war such important materials as gasoline, rubber, iron ore, copper ore, and bauxite were in sufficient supply for less than six months of estimated needs. After this period Germany's current output of these materials could cover only a fraction of stated requirements. The weakness of Germany's raw material position at the beginning of the war was recognised both by Hitler and by the German General Staff.

Concerning Germany's mobilisation of manpower, the National Socialists increased their total labour supply only in so far as they eliminated unemployment. A larger percentage of the population was not taken into the labour force, working hours were increased only slightly, and labour efficiency in industry was not, in general, improved. Second, it was shown that the National Socialists did not shift a large proportion of the labour force into war activities. The only two major changes in the distribution of the labour force between 1925 and 1939 were a decline in agricultural employment and an increase in public employment. The shrinkage in the agricultural labour force was contradictory to NS policy. A large increase in the army from the 100,000 limit set by the Treaty of Versailles is hardly surprising. What is surprising, however, is the fact that the relative size of the industrial labour force was no greater in 1939 than in 1925, and that the relative numbers engaged in civilian production hardly declined.

On the basis of these observations it was concluded that there was no real mobilisation of manpower prior to the outbreak of war.

Thus, whether we examine the general nature of the German economic recovery, or the raw material self-sufficiency programme, or the mobilisation of manpower, the same general conclusion is evident: the scale of Germany's economic mobilisation for war was quite modest.

A number of reasons have been given why the rearmament was not, in general or in special aspects, on a larger scale.

A basic reason why the Germans did not have a rearmament on the scale popularly assumed is simply that their war plans did not require such a large effort. As we have emphasised, Hitler hoped to satisfy his territorial ambitions in a piecemeal fashion; he hoped to conquer each enemy so speedily that the democracies would not have time to intervene, and to have a breathing space after each conquest during which preparations could be made for the next. There is no doubt that this type of strategy called for less massive preparations than one involving a prolonged struggle against a coalition of major powers.

While this blitzkrieg strategy explains why Germany did not undertake preparations on an enormous scale, it cannot explain why they were not at least moderately larger. In the first place, while Hitler hoped not to get involved in a major war, he did not dismiss that possibility. Moreover, there is ample evidence that both he and the General Staff wanted a larger economic effort.

This was prevented by a variety of factors, consideration of which yields four principal reasons why the German rearmament was not, in fact, larger. The first and probably the most important reason is that the government was unwilling to increase public expenditures and incur larger deficits. A larger deficit, it was thought, would destroy confidence in the currency and lead to inflation. This fear of inflation was a major factor in explaining economic policy of the pre-NS governments. It played an important role in determining National Socialist policy for economic recovery, and it was a restraining influence on both total military expenditures and the development of Germany's raw material industries. There is no doubt that without this concern about inflation, and without such an effective exponent of financial conservatism as Schacht, Germany would have had a larger rearmament.

The second reason was the unwillingness of the Germans to surrender a part of their prosperity level of consumption. The government's disinclination to ask for civilian sacrifices was demonstrated in a number of instances. One of these was its refusal to consider higher taxes as an alternative to deficit spending; another was its unwillingness in 1937 to cut food imports in favour of increased raw material imports; still another was its failure to transfer workers out of unessential occupations.

Until 1936, rearmament and increased civilian consumption could be achieved simultaneously by drawing on unemployed resources. Indeed, the rearmament deficits had a stimulating effect on consumption. There was no conflict, therefore, in having both more 'butter' and more 'guns'. In the years 1937 and 1938, however, the German economy was operating at near full employment, and a sizable increase in armament expenditures could have been achieved only at the expense of some decline in civilian consumption. It would have required at least a sharp curtailment of some types of civilian goods production, notably consumer durables and residential construction. It appears, however, that the German government was unwilling to ask for such sacrifices.

It must be admitted that even if the above factors limited the amount of resources available for war preparations, the size of these preparations to some extent was dependent on the efficiency with which the programme was directed. National Socialist inefficiency in planning and carrying out their war production programme is the third reason why war preparations were not larger. Note, for example, the manner in which the various branches of the armed forces procured their material. It is a first principle of war economy that competition between the branches of the armed forces for supplies is not the most efficient method of procurement; this was learned in World War I. Yet, as we have seen, before the outbreak of war there was no central agency which examined and coordinated the material demands of the German army, navy, and air force.

The review of Germany's raw material preparations for war showed a lack of efficiency in both the planning and execution of the programme. In drawing up the plans the idea of attaining a balanced programme seems to have been given little consideration. As a result the planned production of some commodities was ample, if not excessive, for wartime requirements, while for others it was not nearly sufficient. Once drawn up, the adequacy of the measures taken to implement the various plans was not solely a matter of their importance. The iron ore and synthetic oil programmes were designated by Hitler as top priority projects; yet it was in these fields that Germany's preparations were most deficient. The National Socialist pre-war experience with raw material distribution controls is another example of inefficient economic administration. A steel priority system was instituted in 1937, yet by 1941 an effective method still had not been found.

Something else which makes us suspicious of NS economic organisational ability is the composition of their governmental expenditures. Given the difficulty of increasing public outlays, and assuming that preparations for war had priority over other governmental activities, it follows that the latter should have been cut to an absolute minimum. But, as we have seen, public non-war expenditures in 1937 and 1938 were much above any previous peak. Especially prominent in the German budget were expenditures on highway construction, municipal improvements, and party buildings.

In the light of such evidence, it would be difficult to deny that a more rational and better executed programme would have given the National Socialists larger rearmament.

The fourth reason why war preparations were not larger was that Hitler was unable to subordinate various vested and emerging interests to his central task of preparing for war. One of these interests was the National Socialist party itself. The opposition of this group made it difficult to cut public non-war expenditures. When Schacht attempted to cut expenditures for municipal improvements, he was invariably opposed by some prominent party members. When, on numerous occasions, he tried to reduce the budget of the German Labour Front, the issue was taken to Hitler, who invariably decided in favour of the latter. Because it was contradictory to its ideology, the party also opposed measures to force a larger number of women into the labour force.

The German industrialists were another group whose interests could not be disregarded. In our account of Germany's iron and steel expansion programme, we showed that the interests of the steel cartel conflicted with those of the state; that the industrialists refused to carry out the programme themselves; that they strongly voiced their opposition to the government's undertaking of the project; and that eventually the government had to drop its elaborate plans for expansion of iron ore and steel capacity.

Part of the government's reluctance for incurring large deficits may have been the concern that they would destroy the confidence of the industrialists in the regime and hence their cooperation in rearmament. Certainly there was little ground for fearing that moderately larger deficits would have led to a runaway price inflation. For by 1936 Germany had adequate machinery for controlling wages and prices; this was demonstrated during the war when, in spite of enormous government outlays and deficits by pre-war standards, prices increased very little.

An adequate account of the importance of pressure groups in NS Germany will have to wait the studies of political scientists who were close to the situation. When such studies are made, it is likely that it will be found that the resistance of particular groups to Hitler's aims, for one reason or another, was as effective in circumscribing the German war potential as a lack of iron ore or oil.

The contrast between the conclusions reached in this summary of Germany's economic preparations for war and those of earlier studies should be re-emphasised.

That the National Socialists were undertaking massive preparations for war was the central assumption of practically all political and economic writings on NS Germany. In achieving this end, it was supposed that only money and not resources mattered to the Germans, that the civilian population as well as various private interests were compelled to make large sacrifices, and that the government was superefficient in directing the programme.

Actually, Germany's rearmament was on a much smaller scale than was generally assumed and it did not involve a large drain of resources from the civilian economy. The factors which prevented the National Socialists from having a larger rearmament were, first, the fear of larger deficits; second, the government's unwillingness to ask for civilian sacrifices; third, Hitler's inability to subordinate various private interests to his aims; and, finally, a lack of efficiency in the direction of the programme. Even without these restraining influences, however, it is unlikely that Germany would have made the tremendous preparations with which she was credited. Such an economic effort was not required by Hitler's strategy.

THE GERMAN WAR ECONOMY 1939–44: SUMMARY AND CONCLUSIONS

The general picture of the German war economy emerging from this study is not that of a nation geared to total war. It is rather that of an economy initially mobilised for fighting relatively small and localised wars, and subsequently responding to the pressure of military events only after they had become harsh facts. Thus, in the autumn of 1939 Germany's preparations in steel, oil, and other important materials were far from adequate for a sustained effort against the major powers. Her levels of civilian output were still very comfortable. Her total output of munitions was not impressively larger than Britain's.

The weakness of Germany's position in terms of a long war was fully understood by the German war leaders. The decision to undertake a lightning attack through the Lowlands was not made on the basis of a high confidence in its success; it was undertaken as the only possible way that Germany might avoid a major military defeat.

For the war against Russia, fuller preparations were made, but preparations which hardly strained the capacity of the economy. Indeed, one of the reasons for temporarily giving up the idea of an invasion of Britain in favour of a blitzkrieg attack on Russia was that the latter would not require a massive economic effort. Soon after the attack began some important types of munitions output were allowed to decline on the premise that the war would soon be over. And even the first winter's defeats did not result in a major revision of Germany's military or economic strategy; in Berlin they were regarded as only a temporary setback.

It was only after the Battle of Stalingrad and the initiation of large-scale air raids on her cities that Germany began to mobilise in earnest. The peak of her war effort was not reached until mid-1944, and was reached only after her defeat was a foregone conclusion.

Contrary to the impression that most of us have had, the Germans did a far from distinguished job in managing their wartime economy. Both Britain and the United States moved much faster in developing efficient techniques for determining military production objectives and for assuring that the objectives were reasonably met. It was not until the third year of the war that the Germans finally managed to work out a realistic picture of materials requirements, and not until then that a partially effective materials rationing system was substituted for an unworkable priorities scheme.

The improvements in the economy brought about by Speer and his associates during the last two years of the war were very impressive (the gain in military output far outweighed the loss through the use of additional resources) but mainly by comparison with the previous state of affairs. Many of Speer's 'revolutionary' measures were revolutionary only to Germany. For example, his great drive to rationalise fighter aircraft production in 1944 consisted essentially of adopting practices that were common in the United States and Britain.

Like the democracies, Germany relied almost exclusively on direct controls. Fiscal policy played an insignificant role in restraining inflationary pressures and in facilitating a transfer of resources to war purposes. But what is particularly paradoxical about German fiscal policy is that, whereas during the depression years any deficit financing was regarded as a dangerous threat to the future stability of the country, in wartime, when the inflationary pressures became acute, there was very considerable resistance to increases in tax rates and little apparent concern over the incurrence of huge deficits.

What the Germans really excelled in was in improvising. The measures taken to get around the shortage of ferroalloys were truly ingenious. The kinds of measures taken to restore production after bombing attacks and the speed with which production was restored were remarkable.

Behind the inability of those responsible for war production to increase the total effort as rapidly as they would have wanted, or to introduce various kinds of effective controls much earlier than they were able to, was the reluctance of the National Socialist party and of the German industrialists to give up various peacetime objectives until events made it plainly clear they had to. There was a good deal of opposition to restrictions on the production of civilian goods. Speer's efforts to get more people into war production were seriously impeded by that part of NS ideology that claimed that women's place was in the home. The industrialists, remembering the inflation after World War I, were able to put up a very stout resistance to measures designed to prevent them from hoarding hard goods.

Thus it can be seen that the classic image of the ruthless efficiency of dictatorships – of their ability to subordinate a variety of competing objectives to such a central purpose, as winning the war – is not borne out in the case of Germany.

How then was Germany able to do so well militarily? Her conquest of France was certainly one of the greatest military victories of all times. And considering especially that she elected to attack on a front stretching from the Baltic to the Black Sea, it seems remarkable that Germany was able to come as close as she did to conquering all of western Russia.

Not being a military expert, I am not hesitant about giving my opinions. The French were completely defeated, it now seems, because they staked everything on a single strategy – the Maginot Line. When the attack did not come as expected, the French and British armies were unable to do anything except to attempt to retreat with a minimum of losses.

Though it is easy to blame the French for their single-mindedness and the British for their acquiescence, even now it may be wondered if the main lessson of this terrible defeat has really been learned. For example, when one hears of the apparent willingness of the British to put everything into building a powerful H-bomb capability, one cannot help wondering if they aren't simply building for themselves a new kind of Maginot Line.

As for Russia, doesn't the fact of the huge German victories – despite Hitler's decision to attack on a front running thousands of miles and despite Germany's limited preparations for the war – suggest simply that the Russians were not as formidable a military power as they were generally pictured to be? If we overestimated Germany – and we certainly did – by the same token we overestimated Russia. Russia did not withstand a maximum German effort. There is little doubt, to be sure, that on the basis of Russia's poor showing against Finland, Hitler underestimated the Russians. But considering how close Germany actually came to conquering all of Russia west of the Urals, it hardly can be said that he grossly underestimated them. And apparently the Russians have drawn the same conclusion, for what appears to concern them even more than the H-bomb is the rearmament of Western Germany. However, if Russia was a second-rate military power in World War II, we can take little comfort in that fact now. Today, unfortunately, her military strength appears to be enormously greater than it was then.

The main lesson that comes out of Germany's experience is simply that a nation's economic war potential may be a very poor measure of her actual military strength. It is hardly surprising that Germany eventually lost the war to a combination of powers whose economic war potential vastly exceeded hers. What is much more surprising is how well she did, despite the economic odds against her.

Conversely, from our own point of view we can take little comfort in the fact that it was America's resources that ultimately resulted in Germany's defeat. On the contrary, we ought to be telling ourselves that it was a matter of good luck that events turned out as they did. Suppose that Hitler had decided that conquering the whole of western Russia was too much of a gamble. Suppose he had taken Göring's advice and contented himself with Western Europe, North Africa, and the Middle East. Suppose that the Germans had managed to get jet fighters into production two years earlier than they did – something they could easily have done. In brief, if a few things had happened differently, Germany's ultimate defeat would have demanded an enormously greater sacrifice on our part – perhaps ten times the casualties we actually incurred.

The lesson that we ought to draw from this experience is that whether future wars be nuclear wars or conventional wars, we should count much less on our potential military strength than on our actual military strength.

PART IV

PART IV

Introduction

It was left to a British historian, David Irving, to act as apologist for Hitler by asserting that he knew nothing about the mass murder of the Jews until 1943 and that this was perpetrated by Himmler behind Hitler's back, though the very document Irving produces to support his argument provides evidence to the contrary.

What is surprising is the calm with which Irving's book was received by reviewers in this country and abroad. When one recalls the public furore which A. J. P. Taylor's *Origins of the Second World War* caused when first published, Irving has certainly received mild treatment from reviewers such as Hugh Trevor-Roper and even in Martin Broszat's essay in this volume; yet the murder of millions of Jews ranks second only to the murders carried out by Stalin's regime, while in spite of the Nuremberg trials 'wars of aggression' have continued up to the present.

The sources of Hitler's radical anti-semitism have been much discussed without producing conclusive results. One reason for this is that many writers rely too heavily on Hitler's own autobiographical account in *Mein Kampf* which is completely misleading both for a biography of Hitler and for the establishment of the origins of his anti-semitism. No one who knew Hitler as an adolescent or a young man noted any anti-semitism in him. Jewish art dealers gave him support in his years in Vienna, which he appreciated at the time. It has been alleged that Hitler read the anti-semitic pamphlets of Lanz von Liebenfels during his Vienna years, but this is pure conjecture. As Hans Deuerlein remarked more than twenty years ago it is inadmissible to describe Lanz as the man who provided Hitler with his ideas.

More recently American 'psycho-historical' interpretations like that of John Binion, and at a more popular level that of John Toland, have construed a causal connection between the death of Hitler's mother and his own anti-semitism. Hitler's mother suffered from breast cancer and the family doctor, Dr Bloch, a Jew, treated her in an extremely painful manner. This, together with an allegedly exorbitant bill, subconsciously laid the foundations for Hitler's anti-semitism. When Binion's and Toland's works were reviewed in the German magazine *Der Spiegel* a reply was soon forthcoming from none other than Dr Bloch's daughter in New York. In her reply she dismisses the notion that her father had poisoned Hitler's mother, the use of iodine for treating open cancer sores being customary at that time. Nor did Hitler complain about the bill; on the contrary, he was full of effusive gratitude to Dr Bloch, to whom he sent several of his postcard size watercolours from Vienna as well as a large painting as tokens of his gratitude. At the time of the *Anschluss* with Austria Hitler put Dr Bloch and his family under his personal protection and that of the Gestapo. Immediately upon entering Linz, Hitler asked the assembled city administrators: 'Say, is my good old Dr Bloch still alive? Well, if all Jews were like him. . . .' Bloch and his wife were given permission if they so wished to reside in their beautiful house in Linz for the rest of their lives, while all other Jews had to leave the city within eight days. Bloch's daughter and her husband were allowed to stay unmolested until emigration was possible. When Dr Bloch and his family opted for emigration, all foreign currency restrictions were lifted in his case and he was able to leave German soil with his entire property. Finally Hitler ordered that Dr Bloch should be photographed in his surgery for the benefit of the *Reichsarchiv*. So much for that 'psycho-historical' interpretation of Hitler's anti-semitism.

The first documentary evidence of Hitler's anti-semitism turns up in September 1919, when, upon the instruction of his commander, Captain Mayr, Hitler wrote his own exposition of the 'Jewish problem' in the form of a letter. In this he argued strongly that pogrom methods should be avoided in dealing with the problem, it should be dealt with 'scientifically' and dispassionately. This immediately raises the question why in 1919 and not before? The tentative answer of the editor is that it was in the revolutionary

upheaval in Germany in 1918–19, and in Bavaria, in
particular, that Jews played a very prominent part in the
Bavarian Soviet Republic. It was not only German
nationalists who attributed the blame to the Jews. Some
Jews themselves expressed feelings like those of the Austro-
German writer Stefan Zweig, who in a letter of 8 December
1918 to the Jewish philosopher Martin Buber mentioned
that he was thinking of a very necessary action, a call to all
Jews in Germany and Austria 'not to push themselves
forward now, not to pull the reins of politics into their
hands. A call for moderation. It is disgusting to see how
Jews are taking everything by storm – revolution, Red
Guards, ministries, what impure greed for power by impure
people is now being gratified. Should it not be the
responsibility of us all – I believe Schnitzler, Wassermann,
Heimann and many others would participate – to anticipate
the justified anti-semitic indignation and call them back to
their senses.' Otherwise, Zweig feared, Germany would
experience anti-semitic pogroms similar to those which were
taking place in the newly founded Polish national state.
Buber's reply is not contained in his published correspondence, but it must have been negative, because in a further
letter Zweig says 'I am sorry that we are not of one opinion:
but I repeat that whatever is attained or lost henceforward,
guilt for the collapse will for centuries to come be
attributed in Germany to Jewish leaders (and indeed their
disorganisational actions, their impatience, is reponsible for
much).'
   Even for Ludendorff's successor, General Wilhelm Groener, later to become one of the staunch defenders of the
Weimar Republic against the extremes of left and right, the
Jews were 'the wirepullers of international revolution'. For a
relatively politically simple-minded front-line soldier like
Hitler and for many like him, for whom the issue was not
Germany's defeat so much as *how* she was defeated, who
were forever looking for an explanation of the seemingly
inexplicable, the 'Jewish conspiracy' provided a seemingly
logical explanation – and the Jews provided the scapegoat.
It is more than a coincidence that at the time of the largely
Jewish Soviet Republic in Bavaria the hard-core of the

radical anti-semites of the future NSDAP should be in Munich or in Bavaria.

If in the course of his career Hitler had made his specific brand of racial anti-semitism a major plank of his platform, it is doubtful whether his movement would ever have moved out of the confines of the lunatic fringe. Other factors, other arguments were put to the fore, as any analysis of Hitler's speeches demonstrates. With anti-semitism alone no mass power base could be gained. Once in power, it has often been argued, Hitler's propagandist intention to destroy Jewry root and branch was one of the long-term aims which he ultimately implemented. But this argument, based on highly selective quotations, often taken out of their context in *Mein Kampf* or Hitler's speeches, ignores what the American historian K. A. Schleuners has called *The Twisted Road to Auschwitz*, the complexity of National Socialist Germany's Jewish policy between 1933 and 1939.

It seems to have been completely forgotten that the boycott of Jewish businesses in Germany on 1 April 1933 was in retaliation to a boycott against German goods and businesses in the USA and, to a lesser extent, in Great Britain. The NS radicals called for an unlimited boycott and it was limited to one day only on Hitler's personal insistence. For the period 1933–5 there are ample letters in the archives in which prominent German Jews appeal to their co-religionists in Great Britain to stop the 'atrocity propaganda' since, apart from not corresponding with the facts, it inevitably rebounded on the Jews in Germany. The 'Aryan Paragraph' in the Law for the Restoration of the Professional Civil Service of 1933 still contained exemptions for those Jews who had fought in the First World War and for those who had lost their husbands, fathers or brothers in it. The infamous 'Nuremberg Laws' were in part the product of the power struggle within the NS polycracy. In order to take the 'Jewish Question' out of the hands of the NS radicals, Dr Wilhelm Frick, the minister for the interior, consented to these discriminatory measures on the grounds that they would end arbitrary individual action. Even these laws, however, contained exemptions; for example, civil servants who were to be retired by 31 December 1935 and who had fought in the First World War would receive their full retirement pension. However discriminatory the provisions were, Jews in Germany believed that they did at least have the firm foundation of the law under their feet again.

The objective was to force them to leave Germany, to emigrate, an objective mainly pursued by Heydrich's SS Security Main Office where from 1935 SS officials tried with the active collaboration of the Zionist Haganah to recruit emigrants to Palestine. Special camps were set up in Germany where under Zionist leadership potential emigrants were not only trained in the agricultural sciences but also received military training. This is what the SS called the rationalist solution of the 'Jewish Problem'. As late as May 1938 Adolf Eichmann endeavoured to persuade Julius Streicher to abandon his radical and obscene anti-semitic line in his paper *Des Stürmer*. Eichmann failed: Himmler and Heydrich were not as yet all-powerful. Both of them regarded the pogrom of 9/10 November 1938 as 'a shot against the rationalist policy of the SS, an attack against the predominance of the SS in all matters concerning Jewish emigration'. Nevertheless this 'rationalist policy' continued, with the collaboration of Zionist representatives, until the outbreak of the Second World War and beyond. The last train of Jewish emigrants left German soil from Vienna in the spring of 1941, making its way via the Soviet Union to China, where the emigrants ended up in internment camps in Shanghai. But major difficulties had already arisen before the outbreak of war, notably through militant Arab opposition to further Jewish immigration into Palestine which caused the British mandatory power severely to curtail it. Furthermore, the country which raised the greatest public protest against National Socialist Jewish policy, the USA, was not prepared to waive or extend its immigration quotas for the benefit of those persecuted. Prominent Jewish intellectuals and scientists had little difficulty in gaining access, but the bulk of German and later European Jewry wishing to emigrate knocked in vain on closed doors.

One cannot but agree with Hans Mommsen that the question of ideological long-term aims such as the destruction of the Jewish race in Europe, which emerged in propaganda at an early stage but without any real political strategy for their realisation, represents the central problem in throwing light on the twisted road to Auschwitz. Even after the outbreak of war neither Himmler nor Heydrich thought in terms of a systematic physical annihilation of Europe's Jewry, and nor did Hitler, as is demonstrated by the project to settle the Jews in the eastern part of German-occupied Poland, the Nisko Project, which had to be abandoned in the face of the fierce opposition of the Governor General Hans Frank and by the Madagascar Plan. Nor was the public affirmation of a radical anti-semitism sufficient to set into motion the 'Final Solution'. Other factors and other institutions have to be considered to explain this catastrophic development.

Jews in safe havens abroad did not do very much to help their brethren in Germany. Ernst Nolte in his essay refers to the declaration of war by the head of the Jewish Agency, Dr Chaim Weizmann, contained in an open letter to Chamberlain, published in *The Times* on 5 September 1939 and in the *Jewish Chronicle* on the 8th of the same month:

'In this hour of supreme crisis, the consciousness that the Jews have a contribution to make to the defence of sacred values impels me to write this letter. I wish to confirm in the most explicit manner, the declaration which I and my colleagues made during the last months, and especially in the last week: that the Jews 'stand by Great Britain and will fight on the side of the democracies.' Our urgent desire is to give effect to these declarations. We wish to do so in a way consonant with the general scheme of British action, and therefore place ourselves, in matters big and small, under the co-ordinating direction of His Majesty's Government. The Jewish Agency is ready to enter into immediate arrangements for utilising Jewish manpower, technical ability, resources etc. The Jewish Agency has recently had differences in the political field with the Mandatory Power [in Palestine]. We would like these differences to give way before the greater and more pressing necessities of the time. We ask you to accept this declaration in the spirit in which it is made.

This letter did little to ameliorate the fate of the Jews in territories under German control. The Jewish historian H. G. Adler states that it was hardly a diplomatic masterpiece and 'provided the National Socialist state with a welcome weapon for propagandistic and much more tragic ends, when hundreds of thousands and four weeks later millions of Jews were under its power'. The importance of documents such as this as factors making for further radicalisation of NS Jewish policy should not be underestimated. A little later Theodore N. Kaufmann's book published in the United States, *Germany Must Perish*, which advocated the forcible sterilisation of all male Germans, was another such factor. Finally, Sebastian Haffner, an *Observer* correspondent until 1960, could not envisage a solution of the German problem without mass liquidations of *Waffen-SS* soldiers.

All this was not simply grist to the mill of German propaganda, but was also readily believed in the NS hierarchy. Yet even when Auschwitz was already in operation, the future of the Jewish problem was not settled within the SS leadership, because from mid-1942 onwards two divergent strands of policy began to appear, the precise details of which are still unclear. One strand, represented in the SS Economy Main Office (*Wirtschaftshauptamt*), set out slowly to make its bid for overall control of the German economy, already possessing its own economic complex in the form of SS-owned economic enterprises, and more important, in the form of the labour force contained in the concentration camps. To representatives of that group the wholesale physical destruction of their inmates, including the Jews, was counter-productive for Germany's war effort; they should be deployed for its aims and be treated in a manner which would maintain their productive capacity. The other opposing strand was made up of SS racial fanatics, centred after Heydrich's death in 1942 within the Reich Security Office (*Reichssicherheitshauptamt*), some of whom, even after Himmler had issued orders to stop the extermination of Jews in September 1944, continued the gassings of Hungarian Jews. The tug-of-war was never decided. The course of the war put an end to this grim process, which Martin Broszat analyses in great detail from a functionalist angle which seems to make more sense than the concentration on mainly propagandistic long-term aims of a highly speculative nature.

Bernd Wegner, author of the pioneering monograph, *Hitlers Politische Soldaten: Die Waffen-SS 1933–1945* [English translation about to be published by Blackwell, Oxford. *Ed.*] considers the armed field formations of the *SS*, since 1940 known as the *Waffen-SS*. One of the early studies of this formation was written by Gerald Reitlinger with the apt title *SS – Alibi of a Nation* because the post-1945 historiography is marked by a drastic distinction between the German army on the one hand and the *SS* on the other. Former *Wehrmacht* generals wrote their memoirs with the explicit thesis that the *Wehrmacht* fought an impeccably clean war while all the dirty work was done by the *SS*, notably the *Waffen-SS*. Even today's *Bundeswehr* rests on this myth, a myth which anyone who knows the evidence should discard, quite apart from the more general question whether any army during the Second World War fought entirely by the book.

To describe the *Waffen-SS* as 'political soldiers' really raises the question whether the entire *Wehrmacht* had not become 'political soldiers' by virtue of the personal oath sworn to Hitler on 2 August 1934. No doubt at their inception the armed *SS* were intended to be at the *Führer*'s personal disposal, which explains their original name of *SS-Verfügungstruppe*. It is argued that they were to be used for policing functions in case of internal unrest or revolution. However, some of their more prominent survivors have pointed out, and the evidence confirms, that their military training was in principle the same as that of the army. They were led, however, by men like Paul Hausser, former general staff officer of the Imperial Army and the *Reichswehr*, and Felix Steiner who had also served in the Imperial Army in the First World War, who looked at the *Reichswehr* leadership as a body of fossilised old men, and who wanted to employ new tactics in land warfare, applying the lessons learned between 1914 and 1918. That opportunity was given to them. They were beholden to Hitler and Himmler, though the relationship between *Waffen-SS* commanders and Himmler in the course of the Second World War became so strained as to become irrelevant. Himmler's lamentation was great, as his correspondence shows, but to no effect.

Between 1933 and 1939, however, they were part of that complex *SS* empire which Himmler and Heydrich slowly built up. With the ultimate aim of taking over German counter-espionage, Heydrich and his Security Main Office tried to make inroads into the *Abwehr* under Admiral Canaris and his deputy General Oster. Oster was one of the driving forces of the military opposition to Hitler, but there was one feature which Oster and Heydrich shared: both had been forced to leave the *Reichswehr* for 'dishonourable behaviour': Heydrich because of an affair he had had as a naval lieutenant; Oster, a married man, because of an affair with the wife of a fellow officer. Only Hitler's advent to power restored them to positions from which they could ultimately exercise great power and influence. Heydrich's bid for the *Abwehr* did not succeed until a year after his assassination in 1943, but by that time Himmler had made many serious inroads in other sectors. By 1937 he had secured the right of the Gestapo to have all files of persons tried before the NS People's Court handed over to them; an acquittal by the court did not necessarily mean liberty for the accused, for in most cases he or she was rearrested and transferred to a concentration camp. By the outbreak of war Himmler had already achieved what the governments of the Weimar Republic always aimed for, but failed to achieve because of the federal structure of the state: a unified police force. Had it existed before 1933 the combat against the extremes of left and right would have been more successful than it was. In the hands of Himmler it became a highly effective force, by no means overstaffed; indeed there were fewer policemen per 1000 of population than in the present Federal Republic, though the computerised data banks and all the technological and electronic paraphernalia at the disposal of today's police forces were something Himmler could not even have dreamt of.

In short, Himmler's influence in most sectors of German life was already far-reaching even before the war and was to increase further during it. Beside Göring, Himmler held the largest number of offices but unlike Göring, Himmler also proved to be a painstaking adminstrator. Wegner makes the point that Himmler's pre-1939 inroads signalled the end of federalism, and that the measures introduced were not warranted by the constitution. This, it would appear, ignores the simple fact that the Weimar Constitution by virtue of the Enabling Law had not been abolished but suspended. Up to 1943, there were, as already mentioned, endeavours by Frick and Hans Frank to introduce a specifically National Socialist Constitution which in view of Hitler's opposition came to nothing.

Of this vast *SS* empire the *Waffen-SS* was only one branch, led and trained by former *Reichswehr* officers, or officers seconded from the army. It is also important to note that it actually came under the command of the *Wehrmacht* in the event of war. Throughout the Second World War the *Waffen-SS* fought under army command. It never had its own general staff, *Waffen-SS* general staff officers were trained with those of the army. Charismatic *Waffen-SS* leaders, such as Sepp Dietrich, commander of Hitler's body guard, ultimately the *Leibstandarte-SS Adolf Hitler*, who in the First World War was no more than a sergeant, realised his limitations, and made sure that he had capable staff officers whose advice he would follow to the letter.

Service within the *Waffen-SS* counted as national service, but service in the Death's Head units which guarded the concentration camps did not, nor did service in any other branch of the *SS*. Thus, to take one prominent example, Reinhard Heydrich, *SS-Obergruppenführer* (general) and Head of the Reich Security Main Office, was in his military capacity a major of the *Luftwaffe* Reserve, and flew missions as a fighter pilot over Poland and France. Once war broke out the dilemma arose that a substantial part of the manpower of Himmler's empire would have been subject to conscription by the army. It was provisionally overcome by an Army Order, marked 'Secret', of 8 March 1940 in which the Death's Head units were put under the command of the

Waffen-SS and definitely decided by another secret order of 16 July 1941 under which the composition of the *Waffen-SS* came to embrace virtually all sectors of *SS* activity including the Death's Head units and the concentration camps they operated and guarded. The field commanders of the *Waffen-SS* and their men were never informed of this order and only discovered it after the war. Shortly after the outbreak of war the 3rd *SS-Totenkopf* Division was raised from a nucleus of concentration camp guards, some 6,500 men, but the large bulk of the division came from other *Waffen-SS* volunteers who had never had anything to do with concentration camps, the total numbering over 18,000 men. The *SD-Einsatzgruppen*, the liquidation squads, were primarily composed of members of the Security Service and regular police formations, to which on occasions both *Waffen-SS* and army units were added; immediately behind the front line, on occasions even in it, they carried on their grisly business of anti-partisan warfare and wholesale liquidation of Jews. There was no great competition to command these *Einsatzgruppen*; Otto Ohlendorf refused such a command twice, accepting only when refusal was no longer possible, and in the end was hanged for the atrocities committed by his unit. The only volunteer was Arthur Nebe, a member of the resistance to Hitler, who nevertheless liquidated some 40,000 Jews, and was also hanged, but for his resistance to Hitler. As the reports of such generals as Hoepner, Karl-Heinrich von Stülpnagel, von Reichenau, von Manstein and others show, they did not dissent from the activities of the *Einsatzgruppen* but expressed their warmest appreciation, while it was NS functionaries, the *Gauleiter* Heinrich Lohse and Wilhelm Kube, both administrators of occupied eastern territories, who raised open protests against the practice of mass liquidation 'besmirching the German name'.

Initially service in the *Waffen-SS* was voluntary and volunteers had to meet rigorous physical and 'racial' requirements. With its vast expansion in 1942–3, volunteers were no longer coming forward in sufficient numbers, so many young Germans who had volunteered for the air force or the navy found themselves after their call-up in *SS* barracks, initially much to their dismay. This was true of almost all the members of the 12th *SS* Division, the 'Hitler Youth' division. It says much for the talents as instructors of the officers and NCOs, mainly transferred from the *Leibstandarte*, that they succeeded in transforming these 16- and 17-year-old youths into one of the most efficient and toughest divisions which the British army met on the Normandy beachhead. The losses of this division speak for themselves. On D-Day it numbered over 13,000 men; two months later a mere 600 were left. Conversely, late in 1944, 10,000 men of the army and *Luftwaffe* who were no longer fit for service in the field were transferred to guard the concentration camps inside Germany, the previous guards being thrown into the front line. It was these men who in the main met the Allies when the concentration camps were liberated, and they had to bear the immediate consequences.

Books on the *Waffen-SS* are full of assertions that it received preferential treatment in arms and equipment, at the expense of the army. Again this is nonsense. It may be true of the elite divisions which comprised less than a third of a total of 38 divisions by the end of 1944, but it is equally true of elite army divisions, such as the *Grossdeutschland* division or the *Panzer-Lehr* division, to mention but two.

What gave the *Waffen-SS* its unique feature was its international composition. Himmler, restricted by army regulations in the numbers of Germans he could recruit, was already before the war beginning to take northern and western Europeans of 'Germanic' stock. With the invasion of Russia, the 'Crusade against Bolshevism', the army tried to recruit foreigners but met with a poor response. When the *Waffen-SS* began recruiting the response was rather different. It did not carry the Prusso-German image but projected that of a European warrior caste. Though conclusive figures of total membership in the *Waffen-SS* have never been produced and it is doubtful whether they ever will be (estimates range from just under 600,000 to 910,000), by the end of 1943 half of them were non-Germans, and of these half again northern and western Europeans, approximately 150,000–200,000 men. The strongest individual foreign contingent was supplied by the Dutch with 25,000–30,000 men, a fact many Dutch today choose to forget; they prefer to live with the memory of Anne Frank, though even she was betrayed by a Dutch policeman. The Belgian contingent would have been equally as strong but for its division into Walloon and Flemish divisions. Next in strength was what ultimately came to be named the French 'Charlemagne, division, and this was followed by Scandinavians, notably Norwegians and Danes, the latter with the express approval of their king. These northern and western European contingents together with their German comrades remained the elite. *Waffen-SS* divisions recruited in eastern and south-eastern Europe were rather low grade, and they were correspondingly badly equipped. They sufficed to keep Tito at bay until the autumn of 1944, but not for much longer.

What Wegner's essay hardly touches upon is the war crimes committed by the *Waffen-SS* in action. The example of Poland is often invoked, though again the records show that regular army units were as much involved as those of the *SS*. And what is conveniently forgotten is that in 1939 crimes in Poland took place against the background of mass murder by Poles of the German minority immediately after the outbreak of war. The massacre of British prisoners at Le Paradis during the Western Campaign is often mentioned. The *SS* Lieutenant Fritz Knöchlein was held responsible for this and after the war was tried and hanged. His defence that British troops had used dumdum bullets and a few days earlier several hundred *Waffen-SS* prisoners had been killed by the British was not allowed – a feature of all war crimes trials after the war was that the *tu quoque* argument was ruled out of order. Nicholas Harmann, in his book *Dunkirk: The Necessary Myth*, established beyond doubt first that British combat units had orders to take no prisoners, except when specifically ordered to take Germans captive for interrogation; secondly that 'soft-nosed' (dumdum) ammunition was used; and thirdly that, a few days prior to the killing of British prisoners, men of the Durham Light Infantry 'did murder an unknown number of Germans who had surrendered, and were legitimate prisoners of war'. The number is unknown because on the surviving copy of the document in the Public Records Office the digit preceding the two zeros has been cut out of the paper, apparently in the process of clipping it into a file.

The Russian campaign was probably the most merciless of all; the casualties on both sides tell their grim tale. The greatest crime there was committed by the German Army Command in their treatment of Russian prisoners of war. Of a total of 5·7 million Russian prisoners 3·3 million were allowed to perish. Lack of a logistical apparatus to cope with such large numbers played its part, but the greatest number perished in 1941–2 as part of a deliberate policy sanctioned by the German Army High Command. Beside this, frequent spasms of taking no prisoners as an act of reprisal (a practice used by both sides) pale into insignificance. And in the partisan warfare in eastern and south-eastern Europe neither side asked for or gave any quarter.

The situation is different if we turn to the west again. France had been defeated and its head of state, Marshal Pétain, had been appointed by the French National Assembly and given virtually dictatorial powers. The armistice agreement contained an entire section under which the French were to refrain from taking up arms again and any opposition to the occupying power carried draconian penalties. In this respect Churchill's policy to 'set Europe ablaze' was bound to have repercussions which would in the main be borne by the innocent. Two incidents shortly after D-Day to this day remain symbols of remorseless *Waffen-SS* brutality: those at Tulle and Oradour-sur-Glane. On 8 June 1944 Field Marshal von Rundstedt forwarded an OKW directive according to which active members of the French Resistance were to be treated as guerrillas. At the same time all army and *SS* units were ordered to apply relentless rigour 'to remove the danger to the rear of our fighting troops'. The 2nd *Waffen-SS* Division *Das Reich* was ordered to come by road from southern France to Normandy. The vanguard of the division had already been under fire en route in the town of Tulle, which for a short time was in the hands of the French Resistance, where they found 62 mutilated bodies of German soldiers who had surrendered to the Resistance. In accordance with their orders no hostages were taken, but with the aid of the local prefect and the mayor all male strangers in the town were identified and segregated, of whom 21 were released because of their youth and the remaining 99 were hanged. The dead bodies were not, as has often been maintained, thrown into the river but were handed over to the bishop of Tulle for burial. For this act of retribution the divisional commander Lammerding and the officer carrying out the execution were in 1951 sentenced to death *in absentia*. On the same day, 9 June 1944, Lammerding was informed from the *SD*-office in Limoges that the *Maquisards* had a strong point in Oradour, further to the north. This was confirmed a few hours later by First Lieutenant Gerlach, who arrived tattered and torn at the divisional headquarters. He had been a member of the vanguard, was captured by armed civilians and taken through Oradour, which was full of *Maquisards*. He and his driver were going to be shot but the driver's resistance caused a temporary commotion in which he was killed but which allowed Gerlach to escape and make his way back. A few hours later news was received that the highly decorated and popular Lt Colonel Kämpfe had also fallen into the hands of the Resistance. His car was found, and his military identification card. During the course of the morning of 10 June Major Dickmann, a close friend of Kämpfe's, reported that two French civilians had announced that a high German officer had been taken prisoner and was to be publicly burned in Oradour. It could only have been Kämpfe since no other officer was missing. Two decisions were taken by the divisional headquarters. Firstly a captured *Maquisard* was released on condition that he got in touch with the headquarters of the *Maquisards*, offering 30 French Resistance fighters held captive in Limoges plus 40,000 francs in exchange for Kämpfe. However, the freed Resistance fighter reported back only once by telephone saying that as yet he had not established contact with the *Maquisards*. The second decision was to accede to the request made by Dickmann, that he might take a company to Oradour to free Kämpfe. He was given strict orders that if he could not find Kämpfe he was to take as many *Maquisards* as possible prisoner in order that an exchange could be arranged. Dickmann took one company of the regiment *Der Führer* to Oradour, a company consisting largely of Alsatian conscripts. On entering Oradour the company found by the roadside a smouldering German army ambulance in which the driver and co-driver had been chained to the steering wheel and burnt alive together with their wounded passengers. Due to the geographic configuration Dickmann was out of radio contact with the division and made his own decisions. All male inhabitants were rounded up, and all women and children arrested and held in the church. Thereupon Dickmann ordered a house-to-house search for Kämpfe and for any weapons or ammunition. Houses in which arms were found were to be burnt down. As this was going on Dickmann was told to come to a local bakery, where the remnants of a corpse were still smouldering; upon closer examination of the remnants, a Knight's Cross was found which Dickmann identified as belonging to his friend Kämpfe. What happened then is still shrouded in mystery but Dickmann appears to have lost his nerve. All male prisoners were shot, except for a few who managed to escape. Houses in which weapons were found were burnt and explosions occurred. According to one version the *SS* set fire to the church and the women and children were burned to death, except for two women and one child who managed to escape the inferno, assisted by two *SS* men. However, according to the testimony of these survivors the church burned down because fires raging in its immediate vicinity caused an explosion in the belfry, which had served as an arms and ammunition dump for the *Maquisards*. In any event, Dickmann had exceeded his orders; he submitted his report and court martial proceedings were initiated against him, but before it came to a hearing Dickmann was killed in Normandy. The Oradour trial took place in Bordeaux in the early months of 1953. Lammerding, in spite of the death sentence pronounced against him in 1951, offered to go to France to give evidence. Both the German authorities in Bonn and the French authorities turned down the offer. The sentences given at the Oradour trial were extremely light, because most of the accused were Alsatians and there was considerable unrest in Alsace over the case.

Furthermore many of the accused had in the meantime served with distinction in Indo-China. By the end of 1958 all those convicted over Tulle and Oradour had been freed. General de Gaulle put a 100-year embargo on all files relating to these cases, an embargo which is still in force. When in 1960 Lammerding tried to have the case reviewed, he was again turned down by Germans and French alike. In the days of the Franco-German rapprochement between de Gaulle and Adenauer it was apparently an embarrassing topic to both sides.

Not much attention need be given to the so-called 'Malmedy massacre' during the Ardennes offensive in December 1944. Suffice it to say that the irregularities of the investigation and the trial proceedings were such that both the American defence and prosecuting attorneys later became the advocates of those convicted. The trial held at Dachau in 1946 resulted in 43 death sentences and numerous prison sentences. None of the death sentences was carried out and by 1955 every one of the accused was free again. The trial caused a furore in the United States and a Congressional Committee was set up which while trying to whitewash the US army authorities as best it could, also ensured that none of the accused would come to further harm.

In a purely German context the *Waffen-SS* committed its share of war crimes, but so did the German army. The role of the *Waffen-SS* as the Alibi of the Nation appears unjustified. In a more general context all those convicted for 'war crimes' seem to have died in vain, if the aim was to return to a more humane conduct of war. Indonesia, Malaya, Indo-China, Kenya, Tunisia, Algeria, Vietnam, Palestine, Lebanon, Afghanistan and Central America, let alone Africa, demonstrate that not even conventional warfare has become more humane. The age of the 'body count', the age of barbarism will see this century out, if indeed this century does not see the end of almost 2000 years of western civilisation.

13. Hitler and the Genesis of the 'Final Solution': An Assessment of David Irving's Theses

MARTIN BROSZAT

The English edition of David Irving's Hitler book,[1] published in the spring of 1977, two years after the expurgated German edition,[2] has created a furore both in England and elsewhere. The British author, who gained a reputation as an *enfant terrible* with earlier publications on contemporary history,[3] has propounded a thesis which is embarrassing even to some of his friends and admirers.[4]

Hitler, according to Irving, had pursued the aim of making Germany and Europe *judenfrei*, that is, clear of Jews; he had not, however, desired the mass murder of the Jews and had not ordered it; this had been instigated by Himmler, Heydrich and individual chiefs of the civilian and security police in the East.

This essay endeavours to re-examine the subject beyond shedding light on David Irving's contentious arguments, an

From *Vierteljahrshefte für Zeitgeschichte*, No. 4 (October 1977), 739–75. English translation published in *Yad Vashem Studies* (Jerusalem, 1979).

issue already treated unequivocally by internationally recognised historians and Hitler researchers.[5] In view of the confusion which may be sensed by those readers of this well-written book, particularly teachers of history who are insufficiently versed in the details, it seems pertinent to combine a critical analysis of Irving's arguments and text with a documentation of the significant sources which, although known to the author and copiously cited in his work, are nonetheless frequently obscured by him.

Despite their faulty reasoning Irving's theses do, however, afford the challenge of tracing the arguments relating to the origins of the National Socialist extermination of the Jews, which remain controversial to this day; these arguments also touch on an explicit annihilation order issued by Hitler, if such ever existed.

What is important, after all, is the context. The author of this treatise is not concerned solely or directly with a review of the history of National Socialist Jewish policy; Irving is primarily engaged in a re-evaluation of Hitler himself, claiming a solid foundation on known and hitherto unknown sources.

I THE CONTEXT: THE 'NORMALISATION' OF HITLER

Perhaps one day after he was dead and buried, an Englishman would come and write about him in an objective manner. Hitler is said to have made this remark some time in 1944. Irving grasps at it eagerly in his Hitler book.[6] He seems determined in his own way to make this apocryphal remark come true. His book would finally bring about a de-demonisation of Hitler, so he asserts in his introduction with a sideswipe to Joachim Fest (p. xvii) who anticipated him, without – according to Irving – finding it necessary to comb the archives for new sources. Irving claims, on the basis of newly discovered documents, to draw Hitler as he really was, the real human being: 'An ordinary, walking, talking human, weighing some 155 pounds, with graying hair, largely false teeth and chronic digestive ailments' (p.

xviii). He emphatically promises the reader to purge Hitler's image of the accumulated contamination of the legends of Allied war propaganda and post-war accusations. The tone is set by compensatory overpressure on the part of the author who makes it his business to point out their omissions to his colleagues, and to overturn current concepts about Hitler. For years, according to Irving, historians had only copied from one another: 'For thirty years, our knowledge of Hitler's part in the atrocities has been based on interhistorian incest' (p. xiii).

The author's mastery of his sources, at least regarding the limited scope of his presentation, is incontrovertible; he has also managed to produce a number of remarkable and hitherto unknown contemporary notebooks, diaries and letters of the National Socialist period.[7] These stem mainly from Hitler's inner circle at the *Führer's* headquarters, and from liaison officers of the *Wehrmacht* as well as from individual Reich ministers, adjutants, secretaries, valets and stenographers. These documents are not of equal significance; although they contribute to a clearer understanding of the events at the *Führer's* headquarters (primarily the 'Wolf's Lair' at Rastenburg in East Prussia) and illustrate the atmosphere in Hitler's immediate vicinity, they add hardly anything at all to our understanding of major military or political decisions and actions on Hitler's part, and hardly justify the author's exaggerated claims of innovation. The discovery and utilisation of contemporary primary sources has long been a sort of adventuresome passion of Irving the historian.[8] However, the unprejudiced historian and researcher is obstructed by the passionately partisan author whose insistence on primary sources lacks the control and discipline essential in the selective interpretation and evaluation of material.

He is too eager to accept authenticity for objectivity, is overly hasty in interpreting superficial diagnoses and often seems insufficiently interested in complex historical interconnections and in structural problems that transcend the mere recording of historical facts but are essential for their evaluation. Spurred by the ambition of matching himself against professional historians in his precise knowledge of documents, he adopts the role of the *terrible simplificateur* as he intends to wrest fresh interpretations from historical facts and events and spring these on the public in sensational new books.

Earlier theses of Irving's[9] revealed the obstinacy of which he is so proud; his Hitler book proves it anew. The perspective of the presentation, however effective it may be from a publicity point of view, shows *a priori* a narrowing of scope in favour of Hitler. In an attempt to illustrate as far as possible the flux of political and military events from Hitler's point of view, from 'behind his desk' (p. xvi), Irving attaches exaggerated importance to the antechamber aspect of the *Führer's* headquarters and to the testimonies of employees, in many cases subordinate officials, his new sources there. This 'intimacy with Hitler' and his claims to objectivity are proved mutually contradictory from the beginning.

The manner of their presentation lends them a particular character. Irving positions and hides himself behind Hitler; he conveys a military and political evaluation of the situation as well as the cynical utterances of the *Führer* concerning his opponents (Churchill and Roosevelt) and the alleged failure of his own generals and allies, mostly with no comment. Beside Hitler all other characters remain merely pale shadows. This subjective likeness of Hitler (as documented by the author) forms the skeleton of a biography and war account.

A great part of the apologetic tendencies of the work stems from this conceptual arrangement, in spite of its reliance on documentation. The terse chronological description of the ever-shifting military and political problems which were brought before Hitler (others are not noted) causes the spotlight to fall mainly on Hitler. As a result, military and political developments appear incomplete since they are not presented in their true perspective.

This lack of critical comment on the part of the author, who pretends merely to describe events in chronological order, reveals his bias. Quite two-thirds of the book, which numbers over 800 pages, deals with Hitler's conduct of the war, with military events and problems. This is not the author's first description of World War II from the German point of view, others are yet to come.[10] The struggle of the German *Wehrmacht* under the command of Adolf Hitler holds a spell for the author. What emerges 'between the lines' of this detailed and well-documented chronicle is the fascinating story of the superior leader and general and the superior army, who could but yield, after an heroic struggle, to the overwhelming masses of men and *matériel* of an inferior enemy. This is a later version of Ernst Jünger's interpretation of World War I. David Irving, according to an English critic's pointed remark,[11] has remained the schoolboy who during the war stared fascinated at the wreckage of a Heinkel bomber. As an historian he turns his 'childhood war' upside down and fixes his attention on the techniques of armament and strategy and the great and heroic battles of destiny. Above all, his talents as a writer are engaged; on occasion he totally disregards reliable documents. The author is writing a war novel. . . . [Irving's] 'strategy' of de-demonisation is based simply on the attempt to shunt ideological and political considerations onto the broad periphery of purely military events. For instance, actions like Hitler's secret euthanasia order just after the outbreak of the war[12] are frequently (and wrongly) connected with, or justified by military exigencies. In some cases Irving dispenses entirely with reference to documentary evidence.

To this class belongs the newly revived theory (against all well-founded judgements) that Hitler's campaign in Russia forestalled a Soviet attack. Mysterious versions of aggressive speeches secretly made by Stalin to officers of the Red Army at the Kremlin on 5 May 1941, extensively quoted without any proof by Irving (pp. 238ff.) are mustered in support of Irving's thesis of a preventive war. [The author does not seem to be aware that Irving, without acknowledging his source, has taken the quotations from Alexander Werth's book *Russia at War 1941–1945* (London, 1964) pp. 122ff. The book has been translated into German. Stalin in his speech envisaged the possibility of Russia initiating offensive action. *Ed.*] It is on such pseudo-documentation that he bases his rationale for Hitler's orders concerning the liquidation of

Soviet commissars: 'Now the Soviet Union began to reap the harvest she had sown' (p. 262). The shooting of the commissars, according to Irving, was Hitler's answer to the projected 'eradication of the ruling classes' (p. 263) in the western countries which the communists intended to attack – an interpretation which would have been truly congenial to Hitler.

Irving does not conceal isolated acts of killing or annihilation which can be traced to Hitler, but he describes them apologetically and sometimes distortedly and obscures their basic differences. The fanatical, destructive will to annihilate, he defines as mere brutality and he encompasses Hitler in the common brutality of warfare in which the total partisan warfare in the East and the bombing raids of the Allies in the West played equal parts. War itself, the main character in this book, becomes the great equaliser of violence. In this respect Hitler is no longer an exceptional phenomenon.

The predominance of war in Irving's presentation also furnishes him with an explanation concerning the structure and the distribution of power within the National Socialist regime during the war: the 'powerful military *Führer*' played but a small part in the country's domestic policy during the war. While Hitler was conducting his war, it was Bormann, Himmler, Goebbels and others who ruled the Reich (p. 251): 'Hitler was a less than omnipotent leader, and his grip on his immediate subordinates weakened as the war progressed' (p. xv). Irving himself designates this as his central theme. However, while it might not be entirely mistaken in this generalised form, it is completely erroneous when one applies it, as does the author, to Hitler's part in the annihilation of the Jews during the war. It becomes evident that the policy of the mass murder of the Jews does not fit into the picture of generalised brutality of war as drawn by Irving. Without the unreserved acquittal of Hitler on this, the greatest crime in German history, no 'normalisation' of Hitler could be possible.

Somewhat more is involved than just Hitler and his responsibility, for otherwise we could disregard Irving's thesis or even welcome it as a necessary contribution to the controversial interpretations of German contemporary history, where Hitler's sole responsibility, if not explicitly assumed, is at least occasionally implied. Irving's thesis touches the nerve of the credibility of the recorded history of the National Socialist period. It was not with Himmler, Bormann and Heydrich, not even with the National Socialist party, that the majority of the German people so whole-heartedly identified themselves, but rather with Hitler. This poses a particular problem for German historians in their review of the National Socialist period. To bear the burden of such a disastrous mistake and to explore the meanings without minimising them, will remain a difficult task for German historical scholarship, but without doing so, the inherent truth would be lost. The distorted picture of Hitler as a mere madman, which Irving pretends to destroy, has long ceased to exist for serious contemporary historical research, if indeed it ever existed. Hitler's place in history does not admit of any such caricature. But the catastrophic influences which he set in motion and which he bequeathed to posterity also preclude any 'normalisation' towards which there seem to be some tendencies, mainly in the Federal Republic, using Irving as a reference.[13] Hitler's power, based above all on his capacity to personify and mobilise the fears, aggressions and utopias of his time and society as no other could – and to make this faculty appear as solid statesmanship – cannot be separated from the mediocre falsehoods, the disgusting monstrosity of the mental and spiritual makeup of this 'non-person', his totally irresponsible, self-deceiving, destructive and evilly misanthropic egocentricity and his lunatic fanaticism which confront the unbiased historian on all sides. All of this cannot be made to disappear through an appreciation of the 'greatness' of his historical influence or through later 'over-Machiavellisation' or rationalisation of Hitler and even less through 'ante-chamber' humanisation of the subject.

Irving himself, near the end of his book (p. 773) cites an utterance that testifies significantly against his Hitler image. In his last address before *Gauleiters* of the NSDAP, on 24 February 1945, in the face of the ruins of his policy and conduct of the war, this *Führer* who had so long been worshipped by such a great part of his people and who was no longer prepared to make a public speech to them,[14] declared that if the German people now defected to the enemy, they deserved to be annihilated. The monstrosity (not the monster of the caricature) revealed by such utterances can in no way be transformed into the image of a normal war leader.

II THE GENESIS OF THE NATIONAL SOCIALIST ANNIHILATION OF THE JEWS

Comprehensive descriptions of the 'final solution of the Jewish problem' which have existed for years, may mask the fact that many aspects of the genesis of this programme are still obscure. Careful examination has been checked to a degree by the tendency to regard the extermination of the Jews as a sort of metahistoric event which could have been 'logically' predicted long before 1933 on the basis of Hitler's radically dogmatic anti-semitism and from his preformed psychological motive of destruction.[15] As crucial as this point – Hitler's pathological philosophy – may be for the explanation of the whole, this does not release us from the responsibility of clarifying the historical question of how this ideology came into being and under what conditions, and by what institutional and personal levers it was 'transmitted' and possibly 'distorted'.

Definite as our knowledge seems to be of the various phases, arenas and modes of the execution and of the act of annihilation, based on contemporary documents and later statements of the perpetrators and victims, we know but little of the murderous final step towards the radicalisation of NS policy *vis-à-vis* the Jews, of those who had shared in the decision-making and of the precise content of these decisions; we know equally little of the form and the manner of their transmission to the special commandos and official agencies who were charged with their execution. In spite of the destruction of the pertinent files, mainly those of the *Sicherheitspolizei* (Security Police) who were primarily responsible, and the methodical removal of all traces after the actions, as well as the misleading phrasing of the documents themselves, the acts as such could not be hidden. Given the centralisation of all decision-making, however, the attempts to obscure evidence were to a large extent successful.

It is doubtful whether the files of the *SD* chief, who on 31 July 1941 was charged with the organisation of the 'final solution', the files of the *Führer*'s Chancellery, which supplied the gassing specialists (formally employed in the euthanasia programme), or Bormann's personal files at the *Führer*'s headquarters could have provided unequivocal answers to these questions even if this material had not been largely destroyed before the end of the war. It is remarkable that prominent National Socialist figures who had had frequent dealings with Hitler during the war and who were connected at least partially with the Jewish question and who after the war were still available as witnesses (for instance Göring, Ribbentrop, Hans Frank) or who left extensive notes (like the diaries of Goebbels), while obviously informed about the annihilation of the Jews could make no statement about a specific secret order on the part of Hitler. This not only indicates that all agreements about the ultimate aim of the 'final solution' were adopted and transmitted verbally[16] but also shows that the physical liquidation of the Jews was set in motion not through a one-time decision but rather bit by bit.

The first extensive liquidation act, the mass execution in the summer and fall of 1941, of hundreds of thousands of Jews in the occupied Soviet territories by the *Einsatzkommandos* of the security police and the SD was no doubt carried out on the personal directive of Hitler. This, like the order to shoot all Soviet commissars, was obviously based on the fanatical determination of the National Socialist leadership to eradicate 'Jewish Bolshevism' root and stem. This does not yet necessarily signify that physical liquidation, including the Jews of Germany, was the overall aim of NS Jewish policy, and had already been adopted at that time, nor that Göring's order to Heydrich for the preparation of a comprehensive programme for the deportation of Jews dated 31 July 1941, should be interpreted in this sense. Uwe

Dietrich Adam in his study of the National Socialist Jewish policy had rejected this theory some years before, and with good cause.[17]

While the mass murder of Jews (including women and children) as first perpetrated in the occupied Soviet territories necessarily contributed to the adopting of this means of liquidation as the 'simplest' form of the final solution, plans then being formulated for the deportation of the German Jews remained to a great extent undetermined, as was the question of their destination and treatment. All emphasis and decisions were aimed at one target: to get rid of the Jews, and above all to make the territory of the Reich *judenfrei*, i.e. clear of Jews, since earlier plans to deport the Jews from Germany in the winter of 1939–40 had to be postponed.

When in the summer and fall of 1941 in their discussions and written communications the participants spoke only in vague terms of deportation 'to the East', this was not merely semantic obfuscation – it was typical of the manner in which Hitler, Himmler and Heydrich approached the problem of a 'radical solution' to major racial, social and völkisch-political questions. Extensive actions for the transport of masses of people were begun without any clear conception of the consequences. Regarding the deportation of Jews to the East, conceived and planned ever since the summer of 1941 and begun, in fact, in the middle of October 1941, in all probability there existed only a vague idea: to employ the Jews in the East, in ghettos and in camps, at forced hard labour. Many of them would perish; as for those incapable of work, one could always 'help along' their demise, as had been done in German concentration camps and in the labour camps of Poland. They were governed by the concept that the enormous spaces to be occupied in the Soviet Union would in any case offer a possibility for getting rid of the Jews of Germany and of the Allied and occupied countries, and above all, of the multitudes of Jews in the ghettos of the General Government, which since 1940 was visualised as a settlement area for the Germanisation of the East.

In the summer and autumn of 1941, it was clearly Hitler himself who voiced the imminent possibility of deporting Jews to the East to some of the Reich *Gauleiters*, to the Reich Protector of Bohemia and Moravia and to the Governor General of the occupied Polish territories, as well as to the Axis satellite governments; he himself urged its realisation and thereby in a way set off a lively competition to make their respective territories *judenrein* as quickly as possible.

Some relevant testimonies of this phase show that in spite of the determination of the National Socialist leadership to handle the Jewish question radically, no clear aims existed with respect to the subsequent fate of the deportees. Alongside the Russian East, the old Madagascar plan still figured with Hitler and the competent officials of the SD as an alternative scheme.

The diary of the Governor General (Hans Frank) notes on 17 July 1941:[18]

The Governor General wishes to stop the creation of further ghettos, since according to an express declaration of the Führer of June 19, the Jews will be removed in due course from the General Government, and the General Government is to be, so to speak, only a transit area.

In conference with the Croatian Marshal Kvaternik on 17 July 1941 Hitler remarked, according to the minutes:[19]

The Jews were the scourge of humanity, the Lithuanians as well as the Estonians are now taking bloody revenge on them. . . . When even one state, for any reason whatsoever, tolerated one single Jewish family in its midst, this would constitute a source of bacilli[20] touching off new infection. Once there were no more Jews in Europe there would be nothing to interfere with the unification of the European nations. It makes no difference whether Jews are sent to Siberia or to Madagascar. He would approach every state with this demand. . . .

A certain light is also shed on the planning and thinking of this phase by some parts of Goebbels' diaries[21] which surfaced a few years ago and which have not yet been published; they contain the following remarks under the date 8 August 1941, concerning the spread of spotted typhus in the Warsaw ghetto:

> The Jews have always been the carriers of infectious diseases. They should either be concentrated in a ghetto and left to themselves or be liquidated, for otherwise they will infect the populations of the civilized nations.

On 19 August 1941, after a visit to the *Führer*'s headquarters, Goebbels notes:

> The *Führer* is convinced his prophecy in the *Reichstag* is becoming a fact: that should Jewry succeed in again provoking a new war, this would end with their annihilation.[22] It is coming true in these weeks and months with a certainty that appears almost sinister. In the East the Jews are paying the price, in Germany they have already paid in part and they will have to pay more in the future. Their last refuge is North America but even there they will have to pay sooner or later . . .

The next day, 20 August 1941, Goebbels supplements the impressions he brought back with him from the *Führer*'s headquarters:

> . . . even if it is not yet possible to make Berlin a city entirely free of Jews, the Jews should no longer be seen in public; the *Führer* has promised me, moreover, that immediately after the conclusion of the campaign in the East, I can deport the Jews of Berlin to the East. Berlin must be cleared of Jews. It is revolting and scandalous to think that seventy thousand Jews, most of them parasites, can still loiter in the capital of the German Reich. They not only spoil the general appearance of the streets, but also the atmosphere. This is going to change once they carry a badge but it can only be stopped once they are removed. We must approach this problem without any sentimentality.

Other testimonies of this time also confirm that Hitler set the targets of this, by now accelerated, activity. On 18 September 1941 Himmler wrote to the *Gauleiter* and Reich Governor of the Warthegau, *SS-Obergruppenführer* Greiser:[23]

> The *Führer* wishes that the Old Reich and the Protectorate should be emptied and freed of Jews from the West to the East as soon as possible. I shall therefore endeavour to transport the Jews of the Old Reich and the Protectorate as far as possible this year; as a first step, into the newly acquired eastern regions that were annexed by the Reich two years ago, in order to deport them further to the East in the spring. Over the winter I intend to send about sixty thousand Jews of the Old Reich and the Protectorate into the ghetto of Litzmannstadt, which, as I hear, is barely able to accommodate them. I ask you not to misunderstand this measure which will no doubt entail difficulties and troubles for your district, but to support it wholeheartedly in the interests of the whole Reich.

It is possible that Himmler's communication, according to which the placing of the Jews in Litzmannstadt was intended as a temporary solution until they could be transported further to the East the following spring, was a feint while their murder in the occupied Polish areas was already planned at this point.[24]

At the beginning of October 1941, serious controversies broke out over the possible absorption of 20,000 Jews from the territory of the Reich between the governor of Litzmannstadt, *SS-Brigadeführer* Übelhör, and Himmler, and, after deportation had started (in the middle of October), between Übelhör and the security police, because the governor categorically refused to concede any absorptive capacity for the ghettos.[25] This would be hard to explain if the plan for the extermination of the Jews had already been decided upon. Goebbels, too, was informed by Heydrich at the *Führer*'s headquarters on 23 September 1941 that (possibly because the transport trains were required by the army and because of the limited capacity of the available camps and ghettos in the East) there were still temporary difficulties in the smooth deportation of the Jews of Berlin. In his notes of a discussion with Heydrich on 23 September 1941 (entry in diary 24.9.1941 – partly or totally indecipherable). Goebbels states (pp. 18f):[26]

This could occur as soon as we arrive at a clarification of the military situation in the East. They [the Jews] shall finally be transported into the camps which have been erected by the Bolsheviks . . . these [were erected by the Jews themselves] . . . [what could be more fitting than] . . . that they should now also be populated by Jews. . . .

Elsewhere (24 September 1941) in the diary (pp. 35ff.), concerning his visit at the *Führer*'s headquarters, Goebbels writes:

The *Führer* is of the opinion that the Jews are to be removed from Germany step by step. The first cities that have to be cleared of Jews are Berlin, Vienna and Prague. Berlin will be the first of these and I hope that we shall manage to deport a considerable portion of the Jews of Berlin in the course of the current year.

A month later Goebbels was to learn that a rapid and wholesale deportation of the Jews of Berlin into occupied Soviet territory was not feasible. He notes in his diary on 24 October 1941:

Gradually we are also beginning with the deportation of the Jews to the East. Some thousands have already been sent on their way. They will first be brought to Litzmannstadt.

On 28 October 1941 Goebbels again complained in his diary about the opposition that prevented the evacuation of Jews from Berlin in the 'shortest possible time'. Steps such as the evacuation had a more negative propaganda influence in the capital than in other cities since 'we have here all the diplomats and the foreign press'. He noted on 18 November 1941:

Heydrich advised me of his plans concerning deportations from the area of the Reich. The problem is more difficult than we had originally envisaged: 15,000 Jews must remain in Berlin as they are employed in the war effort and in dangerous jobs. Also a number of elderly Jews can no longer be deported to the East. A Jewish ghetto could be set up for them in a small town in the Protectorate. . . .

On 21 November 1941, Hitler, who had also come to Berlin, obviously had to damp the hopes of the Minister of Propaganda and *Gauleiter* of Berlin regarding the pace of the deportations. Goebbels noted the following day: 'He [the *Führer*] desires an aggressive policy towards the Jews which, however, should not create unnecessary difficulties for us.'

Considerable difficulties indeed arose, mainly through the unexpectedly arduous progress and, finally, the standstill of military operations in the East and the extra burdening of the already overloaded transportation system.

The situation into which the National Socialist leadership had manoeuvred itself in the planning of large-scale deportations of Jews becomes sufficiently clear through the documents already cited. As is clear from Hitler's declarations, Hitler, Himmler and Heydrich launched preparations for the wholesale deportation of Jews as a matter of ideology to be pursued with fanatical eagerness. They made this principle clear in their contacts with the *Gauleiters* of the cities with overwhelmingly large Jewish populations (Goebbels in Berlin, Schirach in Vienna) or the Governor General of Poland. The Chief of the Security Police (Heydrich) and his expert on Jews (Eichmann) had prepared plans for the deportation and had sent their 'advisers' on Jewish questions to the southeastern satellite governments with large Jewish communities. These 'experts' had been sent to Bratislava, Bucharest and Agram (Zagreb) with the objective of including Jews of these areas in the deportations to the East. Hitler obviously had no intention of halting the plan for the massive evacuation of the Jews even when the military situation in the East proved more difficult than had been assumed in the summer of 1941. It was for this reason that the original plans for deportation were curtailed on the one hand, while on the other decisions were made aimed at eventually removing at least part of the evacuated Jews 'by other means', i.e. planned killing operations.

It thus seems that the liquidation of the Jews began not solely as the result of an ostensible will for extermination but also as a 'way out' of a blind alley into which the National Socialists had manoeuvred themselves. The practice of liquidation, once initiated and established, gained predominance and evolved in the end into a comprehensive 'programme'.

This interpretation cannot be verified with absolute certainty but in the light of circumstances, which cannot be discussed here in detail, it seems more plausible than the assumption that there was a general secret order for the extermination of the Jews in the summer of 1941.[27]

The first massacre of Jews deported from the Reich took place in November of 1941. The Jews of some transports that had been diverted to the *Reichskommissariat* Ostland, mainly to Riga, Minsk and Kovno, were not assigned to the local ghettos or camps, as were the majority of the later transports; these Jews were shot upon arrival together with the local Jews in the executions already started by the *Einsatzkommandos* of the Security Police and the SD, as for instance in Riga on the so-called Bloody Sunday of 30 November 1941. At about the same time (November 1941), in the *Reichsgau* of Wartheland the 'Lange Special Commando' arrived in Chelmno (Kulmhof) and proceeded to construct temporary extermination facilities, such as the gas vans of the type used by this commando during the euthanasia killings in the transit camp of Soldau, and as of December 1941 for the killing of Jews, mostly from the ghetto of Litzmannstadt. The action in Chelmno was obviously closely connected with the disputes that had arisen concerning the transport of German Jews to Litzmannstadt. The idea that was initiated the previous summer in Posen,[28] according to which the situation in the ghetto could be relieved through the killing of Jews unable to work 'by means of a quick-acting medium', had apparently fallen on fertile ground. The erection of Chelmno was intended mainly for this limited purpose – to create room for the second and third waves of Jewish transports from the Reich which would be 'temporarily' lodged in Litzmannstadt during the winter of 1941–2. The ghetto should be cleared of those unable to work (above all women and children), who would be brought to Chelmno for gassing. This action was mainly completed by the summer of 1942 (with the annihilation of about 100,000 Jews). Its *ad hoc* character becomes clear from a letter by *Reichstatthalter* Greiser addressed to Himmler and dated 1 May 1942. With a frankness unusual in a written communication, he reports:

> The action for the special treatment of about 100,000 Jews in my province that has been approved by you in agreement with the chief of the RSHA, *SS-Obergruppenführer* Heydrich, will be concluded in the next two or three months.[29]

Only relatively few transports reached Chelmno after the summer of 1942: the installations were dismantled in March 1943 and all traces of the killings were removed. (Only in the spring of 1944 were the buildings again required for further killings.)[30] This process illustrates that the initiative for this partial action originated from the local Security Police staff and the office of the *Reichsstatthalter*. It was however in all probability initiated within the general context of decisions on the increased use of liquidation measures adopted after October-November 1941. An additional document shows that at that time there existed no general order for the annihilation of Jews but rather sporadic liquidation measures prompted by an inability to carry out the programme of deportations as planned. This is the draft of a letter by the expert on Jewish questions of the Reich Minister for the Occupied Eastern Territories to the *Reichskommissar* for Ostland, dated 25 October 1941, concerning the use of a gassing van[31] for the killing of Jews; the chief of the *Führer*'s Chancellery Viktor Brack (who was responsible for gassing methods after the euthanasia action), had promised to manufacture and deliver it. He writes among other things:

May I point out that *Sturmbannführer* Eichmann, the expert on Jewish questions at the RSHA, agrees to this process. According to reports by *Sturmbannführer* Eichmann, camps will be erected for the Jews at Riga and Minsk which may also be used for the accommodation of Jews from the Old Reich. Jews evacuated from the area of the Old Reich will be brought to Litzmannstadt and also to other camps to be later assigned to forced labour in the East (to the extent that they are able to work). With the present state of affairs, there should be no hesitation about doing away with those Jews who are unable to work, with the aid of Brack's expedient. In this manner occurrences like those at the time of the execution of Jews at W[ilna], as described in a report I have before me, prompted by the fact that the executions were carried out in public in a way that can hardly be tolerated, will no longer be possible. . . .

The practice of annihilation became even more widespread and at this stage was discussed with cynical frankness at the German agencies of administration in the East. Hans Frank declared on 16 December 1941 at a government session in the office of the Governor of Cracow in connection with the imminent Wannsee Conference:[32]

Regarding the Jews, to start with, principally, there is one concern – that they disappear. They have to go. I have started negotiations with the aim of deporting them [the Polish Jews in the General Government] to the East. A major conference on this question will convene in Berlin in January to which I shall appoint Assistant Secretary Dr. Bühler as a delegate. The meeting will take place at the RSHA office of *SS-Obergruppenführer* Heydrich. This will mark the beginning of a great Jewish migration. What however shall happen to the Jews? Do you believe that they will be accommodated in settlement villages in the East? In Berlin they say, why all this bother. We have no use for them either in Ostland or in the *Reichskommissariat*, liquidate them yourselves. . . .[33] In the General government we have an estimated two and a half and, with half-Jews and their families, three and a half million Jews. These three and a half million Jews we cannot shoot, we cannot poison, yet we must take measures that will somehow result in extermination so that this will be in concert with the major campaign launched by the Reich. The General Government must be as *judenfrei* as the Reich. . .

This additional evidence confirms the impression gained from other documents of this period: the various authorities of the National Socialist regime were ready in late autumn of 1941 for the extermination process aimed at reducing the number of Jews; there existed no real capacity to absorb the mass deportations which everybody urged and, further, the campaign in the East, which had reached a stalemate in the winter, offered no prospect for sending the Jews 'behind the Urals'. There were other reasons as well: the ghettos which had been created in order to isolate and select the Jews for deportation (in occupied Poland as early as 1939–40) spread destitution and disease, which were now regarded by those responsible as typically Jewish 'sources of pestilence' that were to be wiped out.[34] Epidemics and a high mortality rate suggested the possibility of 'helping nature along' in a systematic fashion.

The Jews had to be 'exterminated somehow'. This fatal expression recurs again and again in documents of various origins at this stage (autumn 1941), revealing evidence of the 'improvisation' of extermination as the 'simplest' solution – one that would, with additional extermination camps in occupied Poland,[35] finally generate the accumulated experience and the institutional potential for the mass murders. It could also be exploited in the course of later deportations from Germany and from occupied or Allied countries in Europe.

If we base our interpretation on the concept that the annihilation of the Jews was thus 'improvised' rather than set off by a one-time secret order, it follows that the responsibility and the initiative for the killing were not Hitler's, Himmler's or Heydrich's alone. This does not however free Hitler of responsibility.

We know almost nothing about the way in which Hitler spoke about these matters with Himmler and Heydrich, who bore institutional responsibility for the acts of liquidation performed by the SD- and SS-Commandos, and who at this time frequently visited the Führer's headquarters. We shall discuss the reasons that prompted him to hide the full truth even from high-ranking associates; we shall also examine the fact that these strictly unlawful measures could be ordered only by verbal instructions on the part of Hitler and not by way of legally binding formal directives (written communications). Hitler's responsibility for the murder of the Jews can in any case be established only indirectly: the idea that it would be possible to 'prove' this by means of some document signed by Hitler as yet undiscovered or destroyed before 1945 is derived from false suppositions: Hitler, as is well known, rarely processed files himself, and his signature or handwriting on documents of the Third Reich, except in the case of laws and ordinances, is hardly ever found.

Indications pointing at his responsibility are nevertheless overwhelming. A great number of documents concerning anti-Jewish legislation during the National Socialist period, as for instance the official definition of the concept 'Jew' (in this case Hitler had no need to hide his participation), prove that Hitler concerned himself with numerous details of the planned anti-Jewish measures and that these were contingent on his decisions. It could not be hidden from any prominent functionary of the National Socialist regime that Hitler had the greatest interest possible in the solution of the Jewish question. To assume that such important decisions as the measures for the destruction of Jewry could be usurped by an individual in 1941–2 without Hitler's approval is tantamount to ignoring the power-structure and hierarchic framework of the *Führerstaat*. It is especially baseless with respect to Himmler, whose loyalty to the Führer, especially in questions of basic ideology, was at this stage absolute. Such a concept is also untenable as the preparations for the extermination of the Jews (e.g. the question of transportation and the release of Jews from work essential to the war effort) interfered directly with the interests of the *Wehrmacht* (and frequently collided with it) and could not at any rate be implemented by Himmler or Heydrich, in view of their limited competence, without the backing Hitler alone could impose. Goebbels reveals in his diaries that every important stage of the deportation of the Jews from the capital of the Reich required the approval of Hitler: at the Wannsee Conference (20 January 1942), which convened to discuss the 'final solution of the Jewish question', Heydrich makes pointed reference to the necessary 'previous authorization by the *Führer*'.[36] All this leads of necessity to the conclusion that the Führer specifically vested authority in the *Reichsführer*-SS and the Chief of the Security Police with regard to the massive actions of liquidation, regardless of who might have proposed these measures. (It is indeed possible that it was only with Himmler and Heydrich that the matter was discussed openly.) That Hitler knew of this already in 1941–2 – even while trying to hide it from any wider circle of listeners – becomes clear from the notes of participants in confidential conversations with him at this time (winter 1941–2).

At a 'table talk' at the *Führer*'s headquarters on 25 October 1941, in the presence of Himmler and Heydrich, Hitler remarked:[37]

From the rostrum of the *Reichstag* I prophesied to Jewry that, in the event of war's proving inevitable [here the translation is faulty: '. . . wenn der Krieg nicht vermieden bleibt . . .' if the war is not being avoided. See W. Jochmann (ed.), *Monologe im Führerhauptquartier 1941–1944* (Hamburg, 1980), p. 106 *Ed.*] the Jew would disappear from Europe. That race of criminals has on its conscience the two million dead of the First World War, and now already hundreds of thousands more. Let nobody tell me that all the same we can't park them in the marshy parts of Russia! Who's worrying about our troops? It's not a bad idea, by the way, that public rumour attributes to us a plan to exterminate the Jews. Terror is a salutary thing. . . . [Heim's original notes record: 'It's a good thing that terror precedes us, that we are exterminating

Jewry. The attempt to create a Jewish state will prove a failure.' *Ed.*]

On 23 January 1942, three days after the Wannsee Conference, during a 'table talk' at the *Führer*'s headquarters in the presence of Himmler and Lammers, Hitler again referred to the Jewish question:[38] 'One must act radically. When one pulls out a tooth, one does it with a single tug, and the pain quickly goes away. The Jew must clear out of Europe. Otherwise no understanding will be possible between Europeans.'

Further on in the same 'table talk', after Hitler had cited the discrimination that the Roman Church State had levelled in former centuries against the Jews, he referred with a mixture of obvious cynicism and hypocritical obscurity to the current deportations and occasional acts of annihilation:

For my part, I restrict myself to telling them they must go away. If they break their pipes on the journey, I can't do anything about it. But if they refuse to go voluntarily, I see no other solution but extermination.[39] Why should I look at a Jew through other eyes than if he were a Russian prisoner-of-war?

In the p.o.w. camps, many are dying. It's not my fault, I didn't want either the war or the p.o.w. camps. Why did the Jew provoke this war? [The notes of those taking down the 'Table Talk', Heinrich Heims, and Dr H. Picker, do not contain this passage. It is to be found only in the English translation of *Hitler's Table Talk*, introd. by H. R. Trevor-Roper. *Ed.*]

Four days later (27 January 1942) Hitler again said on the occasion of a 'table talk' at the *Führer*'s headquarters:[40]

The Jews must pack up, disappear from Europe. Let them go to Russia. Where the Jews are concerned, I'm devoid of all sense of pity. They'll always be the ferment that moves peoples one against the other. They sow discord everywhere, as much between individuals as between peoples.

It's entirely natural that we should concern ourselves with the question on the European level. It's clearly not enough to expel them from Germany. We cannot allow them to retain bases of withdrawal at our doors. . . . [These lines are also not contained in the original notes. *Ed.*]

On 24 February 1942 Goebbels notes in his diary after a visit of Hitler's to Berlin:[41]

The *Führer* again voices his determination to remorselessly cleanse Europe of its Jews. There can be no sentimental feelings here. The Jews have deserved the catastrophe that they are now experiencing. They shall experience their own annihilation together with the destruction of our enemies. We must accelerate this process with cold brutality; by doing so we are doing an inestimable service to humanity that has been tormented for thousands of years. . . .

The accumulation of Hitler's aggressive statements and destructive will regarding the Jewish question, at this stage, as well as the allusions inherent therein to concrete measures for the Jews' expulsion and decimation, are sufficiently conclusive when interpreted within their historical context. They clearly reveal Hitler's fixation concerning the Jewish question and show his passionate interest in it. These facts preclude any possibility of his indifference to the continuing progress of the solution of the Jewish question.

At a much later period, in a secret speech of Hitler's to generals and officers of the *Wehrmacht*[42] on 26 May 1944, in which he expounded on the liquidation of the Jews which had meanwhile been largely completed, he let drop a remark which seems to confirm that the annihilation of the Jews, as it 'developed' in the winter of 1941–2, was a radical 'expedient' adopted as an escape from the difficulties into which the National Socialists had led themselves. 'If I remove the Jews', according to Hitler's justification at a later stage of the war, 'I have removed any possibility of the development of revolutionary cells or sources of infection.

Someone might ask me: could this not have been achieved in a simpler manner – or, rather, not simpler, *because anything else would have been more complicated*[43] – but solved more humanely . . .?'

David Irving has correctly deduced that (p. xiv) the annihilation of the Jews was partly a solution of expedience, 'the way out of an awkward dilemma'. However, he finds himself on an apologetic sidepath if he concludes, contrary to all evidence, that some of the subordinate *SS* and party leaders had instituted the murders in cynical extrapolation of Hitler's remarks and against his will.

III DAVID IRVING'S 'PROOFS'

In his book about Hitler, David Irving has not presented in any systematic way either the factual events of the 'final solution' or Hitler's manifold utterances about the treatment of the Jews during the war. His revisionist theory is not derived from any incontrovertible historical conclusion; rather the arguments mustered in its support to which he constantly refers, often arbitrarily scattered in the text and footnotes, are in the main controversial, drawn from a dozen different sources, citing only specific aspects and documents relating to 'Hitler and the extermination of the Jews'. He marshals inconclusive arguments to which he authoritatively appends irrelevant and erroneous inferences, presenting them as foregone conclusions or to be assumed as such. Once the author had committed himself to this theory, no shred of seeming evidence was too shabby to support it.

The other Irving appears again and again behind the laboriously spliced argument of his revisionist theory, with ambition and great acrimony vaguely citing all pertinent documents even when these barely relate to the main argument. And within the categorical vindication of Hitler one suddenly encounters thoughtful and cautious reflections and formulations: Hitler's role in the context of the 'final solution' was a 'controversial issue' and 'the negative is always difficult to prove' (p. xiii). In another place (p. 391):

'Hitler's was unquestionably the authority behind the *expulsion* operations; on whose initiative the grim procedures at the terminal stations of this miserable exodus were adopted, is arguable.'

Irving poses the justified question (pp. 270ff.): what exactly did Hitler mean when he promised the Governor General (of Poland) in June 1941 to expel the Jews 'further to the East': '. . . did Hitler now use "East" just as a generic term, whose precise definition would be perdition, oblivion, extermination? The documents at our disposal do not help us.'

Unfortunately the author did not confine himself to such cautious questions. He blocked the path for new insights for himself and others by presenting false stereotypes and artifical argumentation clearing Hitler.

In his introduction the author already reveals what he regards as his principal discovery (p. xiv): Hitler ordered on 30 November 1941, that there was to be 'no liquidation of the Jews'. In a facsimile of the original documents (p. 505) which Irving appends to his book, the reader can see for himself: a page from Himmler's hand-written telephone notes dating from the years 1941 to 1943.[44] Although nothing is found there concerning Hitler or any general prohibition of the liquidations, Irving, in his senseless yet literal interpretation of this note, would like to make us believe so in various parts of his book. This document reveals one fact only: Himmler held a telephone conversation from the *Führer*'s bunker at the Wolf's Lair with Heydrich in Prague at 13:30 hours on 30 November 1941, and as one of the subjects of the conversation he noted: 'Jew transport from Berlin, no liquidation.' Whether Himmler had spoken to Hitler before this conversation and if its contents derived from Hitler is questionable.[45] In any case, this contention cannot be substantiated, nor can it be conclusively stated that Himmler relayed an order of Hitler's to Heydrich. The contents of the note prove one thing: the words 'no liquidation' are connected with 'Jew Transport from Berlin'. This was a directive or an agreement concerning a *particular* situation, and not a *general* order. It is not possible to determine precisely the occasion and the subject of the conversation from these few words; however, what can be determined with certainty, is that they were connected with the execution of Jews from the Reich that had taken place some days before in Kovno (Kaunas).[46] The purpose of the telephone conversation between Himmler and Heydrich was evidently to forestall the liquidation of another Jewish transport from Berlin that had left for Riga on 27 November 1941, which obviously could not have been prevented. On precisely that day (30 November 1941) an extensive mass execution took place near Riga and this was the reason that Himmler telephoned Heydrich once again on 12 December 1941.[47] These semi-public executions as well as the treatment of the German Jews who had been deported to the East, had been attracting considerable attention among the German military authorities, as well as among some members of the civil administration in the Ostland. *Gauleiter* Kube, the *Kommissar* General of White Ruthenia who the day before had visited the German Jews who had newly arrived in Minsk, to the surprise of the local *SS* and Security Police, had remarked angrily that in his view a number of persons whose close relatives served at the front had been unjustly deported. Heydrich was forced to contend with these reproaches for months to come.[48]

It might have been this intervention or the particularly sensitive situation in Berlin, where American journalists had begun to evince interest in the fate of the deported Jews – until the entry of the USA into the war even Hitler had to take this mood into consideration – that made the liquidation in Kovno or Riga of the Jews of Berlin, which could not be kept secret, seem undesirable either to Hitler or to Himmler. This and no more can be inferred from the telephone note. This is additional evidence pointing to the improvisatory character of the annihilation, still typical for this phase, with all its contradictions and occasional misunderstandings between those who had been charged with the execution of the 'final solution' and those who issued the orders. Even assuming that the telephone conversation between Himmler and Heydrich was based on Hitler's directive (with the aim of preventing the transport of Berlin Jews on their way to Riga from being executed upon arrival) as had been done once before in Kovno), one cannot conclude, as Irving does, that Hitler was not aware of the murder of the Jews. On the contrary: the exceptional directive (in *this* case) would indicate that Hitler knew in principle about the practice of annihilation.

Irving's interpretation, that Hitler had on 30 November 1941 issued a general prohibition against the liquidation of the Jews which would also be binding for the years to come is, however, totally mistaken. In fact it was at this point that the more institutionalised and better 'regulated' way of carrying out the 'final solution' began. On 20 January 1942 the Wannsee Conference in Berlin took place, which made it clear, even in vaguely worded minutes, that those in charge intended to make sure that a great part of the deported Jews would not long survive deportation.[50]

The first extensive mass execution of Polish, German and Slovak Jews began in the spring of 1942 at Auschwitz and in the newly erected extermination camp of Belźec in the eastern part of the General Government (the first of four extermination camps under the supervision of *SS* and Police *Führer* Globocnik at Lublin). Goebbels notes this in his diary[51] on 27 March 1942:

Beginning with Lublin, the Jews under the General Government are now being evacuated eastward. The procedure is pretty barbaric and is not to be described here more definitely. Not much will remain of the Jews. About 60 per cent of them will have to be liquidated; only about 40 per cent can be used for forced labour.

The former *Gauleiter* of Vienna, who is to carry out this measure, is doing it with considerable circumspection and in a way that does not attract too much attention. Though the judgment now being visited upon the Jews is barbaric, they fully deserve it. The prophecy which the Führer made about them for having brought on a new world war is beginning to come true in a most terrible manner. One must not be sentimental in these matters. If we did not fight the Jews, they would destroy us. It's a life-death struggle between the Aryan race and the Jewish bacillus. No other government and no other regime would have the strength for such a global solution as this. Here, once again, the Führer is the undismayed champion of a radical solution, which is made necessary by existing conditions and is therefore inexorable. Fortunately a whole series of possibilities presents itself to us in wartime which would be denied us in peace. We shall have to profit by this. The ghettos that will be emptied in the cities of the General Government will now be refilled with Jews thrown out of the Reich. This process is to be repeated from time to time. Jewry has nothing to laugh at.

One feels, on reading this document, that Goebbels, who apparently had just heard of the new practice of murder through gassing, was talking himself out of his feeling of horror and clinging desperately to the bacillus theory of his *Führer* whom he calls 'the champion of a radical solution'.

Irving's interpretation of this well-known diary entry is revealing. He mentions it without citing it in detail (p. 392) and above all, conceals the explicit reference to 'the *Führer*'. He even manages to indicate the reverse by his accompanying remark. Basing himself on his theory of Hitler's prohibition of the liquidation, he submits that the Minister of Propaganda as well as Himmler and Heydrich were one with the plotters whose purpose was to hide from Hitler the fact that new acts of murder had begun on the largest possible scale. Goebbels, so he writes, entrusted his diary with a frank description of the horrible events in the death camps 'but he obviously kept silent when he met Hitler two days later'. Further, so the author doggedly insists when writing about this conference, Goebbels had noted in his diary only the following expressions of Hitler concerning the Jewish question: 'The Jews must pack up, disappear from Europe; if necessary we have to apply the most brutal means.' Since there is no record of Hitler using the word gassing, he knew nothing about it; this is the manner in which Irving arrives at his 'faithfully documented' deductions to prove his point, here as well as in other parts of his book. When examining Irving's thesis the historian, who is obliged to be sceptical as well as critical, might wonder why

Hitler's statements concerning the Jewish problem during the war contain – contrary to Irving's statement – words like extermination and annihilation which are by no means scarce,[52] and generally reveal Hitler's murderous intentions but make hardly any direct references to various phases or specific aspects of the extermination of the Jews.

The fact that no written order signed by Hitler concerning the exterminations has come down to us cannot be recognised as a decisive factor. We have already indicated that it is quite possible that such a one-time general order to wipe out the Jews never existed. It might be added that the act of mass execution according to legislation still in force at that time made a *a priori* a written confirmation of the order by the head of the German Reich quite unthinkable, unless Hitler was prepared to risk causing extreme embarrassment to the orderly administration and the judicial authorities of the Reich which were still fundamentally based on law and justice. This was the advantage of strict adherence to rules of semantics: the various branches of the civil administration, without whose organisational cooperation it would not have been possible to carry out the mass actions of the 'final solution', were informed 'officially' only about those aspects or portions of the general action which were still just permissible from a legal point of view: about 'evacuations', 'Jew transports', etc. Those parts of the action which were totally criminal and unlawful – the liquidations – occurred under the formal responsibility of special bodies in the Security Police and the *SD* who were above the law. More or less open mention of these matters was therefore acceptable on occasion, as can be seen on inspecting written communications between the *SS* and police authorities or between them and the heads of civil administration in the occupied areas of the East, who were outside the scope of the ordinary administration of the Reich.

Hitler as Head of State had to be far more formal and punctilious than, for instance, Himmler, about the process of law and order in the regular administration of the country. He had ample reason to refrain from any explicit verbal or written reference that a third party could have interpreted as an official directive on the unlawful annihilation of the Jews. It is also known that at the time of the euthanasia programme Hitler was patently unwilling to furnish even a minimum of formal confirmation in the form of an obscure handwritten 'authorization' (by no means 'order'). However, confirmation was unavoidable in 1939, for with the killing of the mentally deficient being carried out within the boundaries of the German Reich, i.e. within the sphere of competence of regular civil administration and judicial authority, the euthanasia doctors and specialists had to be in a position, if necessary, to cite a formal authorisation on the part of Hitler. But as far as the killing operations in the occupied territories were concerned, within the framework of the prevailing emergency situation, the manifold restrictions within the jurisdiction of the civil administration obviated this necessity. Here Hitler could content himself with verbal authorisations that were kept strictly secret.

Thus, when Himmler, at a later date, for instance in his secret speeches at Posen before *SS* commanders and district governors on 4 and 6 October 1943, spoke openly about the annihilation of the Jews, he called this 'the heaviest task' of his life;[53] the reason probably was not that 'faithful Heinrich' had acted behind the *Führer*'s back in the extermination of the Jews, or had voluntarily 'relieved' him of this burden – as Irving claims contrary to all evidence – but obviously that Himmler could not cite any official mandate because Hitler entrusted him not only with the massacre of the Jews but, in addition, expected him to keep the order strictly secret. The extent to which Hitler took pains to keep that 'last' truth about the fate of the Jews from the German public is also revealed in Bormann's confidential circular addressed to Reich and district governors of the NSDAP, dated 11 July 1943.[54] He prohibits 'by order of the *Führer*' any mention of a 'future overall solution' in public dealings on the Jewish question and advises only mentioning 'that the Jews are being employed in gangs as a labour force'.

It was very likely that not only formal considerations led Hitler to refrain from referring explicitly to the extermination of the Jews. With the sure instinct of the demagogue, and such he remained at his table conversations, he knew just what demands he could make on his listeners. In his official speeches during the war any declaration of his virulent anti-semitism – his desperate determination to take 'revenge' on the Jews – was received with applause (as for instance in his speech of 30 January 1942); any description of an actual massacre of the Jews however would have (as in the case of Goebbels) aroused quite different emotions. Since our knowledge of Hitler's attitude towards the Jewish question during the war is based almost exclusively on records of his conversations and speeches, our interpretation is confined by the limits of his demagogic point of view.

There is, however, some indirect evidence about Hitler's intervention in measures connected with the annihilation of the Jews. We may take as an indication the stepping-up of the killings that became operative in the summer of 1942 with the 'running in' of Sobibor and Treblinka in the General Government. Himmler as well as SS and Police Commander Globocnik were, for reasons of secrecy, anxious to carry out the action 'as quickly as possible'.[55] There was some resistance on the part of the *Wehrmacht*, because of the need for Jewish labour (for instance regarding the *c.* 400,000 Warsaw Ghetto Jews) and further, due to the still chronic shortage of transport trains, for which the *Wehrmacht* had other priorities. For that reason Himmler required Hitler's full support. It was obviously on this subject that he conferred with Hitler at the *Führer*'s headquarters on 16 July 1942 and it was from there, on the same day, that his liaison officer to Hitler, *SS-Obergruppenführer* Wolff, made an urgent telephone call to the Assistant Secretary in the Ministry of Transport, concerning the availability of additional transport trains. It was three days later, only after these conditions had been met, that Himmler could, on 19 July 1942, issue the directive to the senior SS and Police Commanders that the accelerated resettlement of the entire Jewish population of the General Government was to be carried out and terminated by 31 December 1942. Exempted should be solely the Jews in some of the labour camps.[56] On 28 July 1942, Assistant Secretary Ganzenmüller issued Wolff this comforting communication: 'Since July 22, one train per day with five thousand Jews was leaving

Warsaw for Treblinka, and that twice a week a train was leaving Przemysl with five thousand Jews for Belzek [!] . . .'

Wolff expressed his gratitude on 13 August 1942 for the efforts in this matter and declared that it gave him 'special pleasure' to learn that 'daily trainloads of five thousand members of the Chosen People are going to Treblinka and that we are thus being enabled to accelerate this migration'.[57] Wolff's intervention on the day of Himmler's conference with Hitler is only one of the indications that deportation and extermination activities were repeatedly granted special priority by the *Führer*'s headquarters.[58]

It is all the more fantastic when Irving claims (p. 327) that not only Hitler's secretaries and stenographers, but Wolff who accompanied Himmler while inspecting Auschwitz, as well as Globocnik at Lublin, in the summer of 1942 still knew nothing about the killings. It was in this vein that Wolff pleaded against charges of complicity in the killings at his trial in the Munich District Court in 1964. The court could not, as recorded in its judgement 'accept the claim of the defendant since it is not in accordance with the truth'.[39] Nevertheless, Irving treats Wolff's version as if it were a proven fact and makes no mention of the dissenting opinion of the court although he was aware of this.

On the whole it seems that the author owes a great debt to Wolff.[60] It was the latter who in the early 1950s was the first to propound the theory that Himmler, in his bizarre zeal for the *Führer* and the *Führer*'s ideology, saw it as his task personally to relieve the Commander-in-Chief, engaged in an external war with the world, and to take upon himself the anti-semitic objectives without burdening Hitler himself. This theory of Irving's was obviously supported by the evidence of the author's witnesses of preference, Hitler's junior staff, who knew Hitler from a servant's perspective only as a more or less charming 'boss'. They could well imagine that 'A.H.' (as they were still calling him) was once again kept in the dark, as Hitler had claimed often enough, and deceived on account of his good nature and naïvety.[61] Even Hitler's valet, Krause, whose memoirs lend wholehearted support to the popular refrain 'if only the *Führer* knew about this', has not been shunned by David

Irving as a source of information.[62] On the other hand Irving often failed to take into consideration, or treated with impatience, the post-war statements of witnesses who were personally involved in the killings or who had had access to secret information. He refers to the statements by Walter Blume and Otto Ohlendorf, the former commander of one of the *Einsatzgruppen*, confirming the 1941 verbal instructions to commanders about the killings, expressly issued under Hitler's instructions; although these are cited by the author they are distorted in the reproduction.[63] He completely ignores the remarkable statement of the former *SD* officer Wilhelm Höttl[64] and those of the commander of Auschwitz, Rudolf Höss.[65] The testimony of Adolf Eichmann, too, is passed over and declared misleading (p. 858).

Irving claims that the only evidence of the fact that Hitler had ordered the annihilation of the Jews came from the former *SD* officer and expert on Jewish questions in Bratislava, Dieter Wisliceny, but is of no value.[66] Irving attempts to refute this testimony by citing a particularly weak parallel – 'Given the powerful written evidence that Hitler again and again ordered the "Jewish problem" set aside until the war was won' (p. 858/fn). He refers to the conversations with Bormann, Goebbels and others in the summer of 1941 concerning oppositional stirrings within the Catholic Church (Count Galen), in which Hitler opposes the tendency to apply radical measures against the opposition spokesmen of the Catholic clergy suggested by the NSDAP and particularly by Bormann in order to forestall opposition of the Church-going public. Just as in the case of the Church, Irving claims (p. 331) that Hitler sought to postpone the Jewish problem until after the war. That Irving does not hesitate to manipulate his documentary evidence in order to add conviction to a thesis that is misleading *ab initio*, reveals the obstinacy of his reasoning.[67]

This argument is obviously intended to support Irving's main thesis that Hitler was too busy with the conduct of the war to attend to the Jewish question himself and left Heydrich and others to deal with it. Irving's want of historical understanding and his lack of textual cohesion become especially obvious in this thesis. Even a cursory inspection of Hitler's wartime declarations concerning the Jews makes it clear that there was a widely motivated and powerful link in Hitler's thinking and will between military operations, particularly the war against the Soviet Union, and his ideological war against the Jews. It is precisely this very obvious connection that robs Irving's revisionist theses of all conviction, especially since without this ideological-pathological linkage between the war and the annihilation of the Jews (in Hitler's world-view) the latter could hardly be explained.

If one seeks to grasp the full significance of this philosophy as a motivating force, it does not suffice to trace it back to a paradigm of rational ideological interactions.[66] Hitler's philosophy, and especially the anti-Jewish components, had always been a non-wavering dogma, combined with sudden outbursts of paranoic aggressiveness. Anyone considering only the first portions necessarily concludes that there had been neither evolution nor radicalisation. The final solution of the Jewish problem appears as a realisation of a long-established programme methodically and 'logically' carried out step by step. Closer inspection of the National Socialist Jewish policy shows that such a hypothesis is incorrect and does not adequately explain some important facts. The violent *Reichskristallnacht* which opened the door for the lawless persecution of the Jews is a particularly telling example. Ever since, Hitler's fixation and impatience for a solution of the Jewish question were reinforced – evident from the frequency and intensity of his official utterances and the diplomatic activities with which he approached the Jewish question at the beginning of 1939 – and cannot be explained on the basis of Hitler's ideology alone. Whichever explanation – with its inevitable concomitant psychological undertones – one prefers, be it the overwhelming euphoria of success to which Hitler was then subject and which drove him to exceed his still rational, political aims, means and calculations; or the later (post-winter 1941) and by no means insignificant motive of revenge and retribution for the unsuccessful conduct of the war, it is certain that Hitler's dogmatic ideological anti-semitism was not independent of factors of time and events. Its development was not merely programmatic but rather pathological and was weakened or intensified by current events; these fluctuations were at least as important a motive for decision and action as was a fixation on a specific dogma. This is mirrored in the alternately spontaneous or constrained nature of actions relating to the Jewish policy and the killings, which did not proceed smoothly and according to plan but rather in an improvised and jerky fashion.

From this angle the interdependence between the war and the Jewish question gains even greater importance. The war did not only offer – as noted cynically by Goebbels in his diary on 27 March 1942 – opportunities for violent procedures that did not exist in peacetime, but was *welcomed* (and not only *risked* for political imperialist reasons). Hitler's prophesied destruction of Jewry, made on 30 January 1939, in the event of a new world war which has subsequently been cited so frequently, was from a psychological point of view not only a 'warning' but in itself part of the motivation.

The war, however, in its further course, offered ideal fuel for the constant 'recharging' of a manic-aggressive anti-semitism, and not to Hitler alone. The confrontation with the masses of *Ostjuden* in occupied Poland, in the Baltic states and in Russia, provided emotional nourishment and confirmation for an imperialist racial ideology that had until then been propagated only in the abstract; there now existed a concrete picture of an inferior race which had to be eradicated. The psychologically cheapest and most primitive form of self-confirmation and self-fulfilling prophecy could now be set in motion: the discriminated against, crowded, tormented and frightened Jews in the East finally looked the way they were caricatured in the anti-semitic periodicals. Epidemics in the ghettos made them a threat to the health of the general population; their terrified flight into the forest created the danger of 'Jewish gangs' that one pretended to remove prophylactically just as one had to eradicate their expected propagation of defeatist ideas and plots in the occupied or Allied neighbouring countries. All this and other motives were exploited not only by Hitler and Himmler but also by Goebbels and Ribbentrop and by the district military and civil administration chiefs. They were also employed by diplomats charged with the pressuring of the Allies into further intensification of the final solution in Europe, and were used and produced especially in the last stages of the deportations and exterminations in 1943–4. These motives can be understood not only as semantic rules for the accomplishment of real ideological objectives, but rather as a conglomeration of various factors stemming from ideology, propaganda and, first and foremost, unexpected reactions of the individual which exceeded objectives set forth by racist ideology and brought into play so many 'accomplices' and 'assistants'.

With Hitler, too, the assessment of the motives mirrored in his remarks on the Jewish question during the second half of the war is of major significance. As the military struggle appeared to become hopeless, the 'war of fate' against Jewry was promoted as the real war (which would be won).[69] The death of hundreds of thousands of German soldiers had to be expiated and biologically revenged through the liquidation of an even greater number of Jews. Also with Hitler the 'security' problem came to the fore; Jews had to be eliminated, otherwise he feared that there could be internal unrest[70] due to increased partisan warfare in the rear, defeatism and defection of Axis countries. It was for that reason the final intensification of radicalism took place in Hitler after Stalingrad, and seems to be one of the motives for the intensified measures that aimed to encompass, if possible, all the Jews within the German sphere of influence into the extermination programme.[71]

Hitler's numerous references to the interrelation of the war and the Jewish question show with sufficient clarity how untenable Irving's argument is. One example of Hitler's increased intervention in the final solution after Stalingrad is his discussions with the Romanian head of state, Marshal Antonescu, and with the Hungarian Regent Admiral Horthy in April 1943.[72] We shall examine these records in more detail at the close of this discussion, since not only do they once more document Hitler's intransigence and his way of thinking, but also give us an opportunity to demonstrate how the author of the Hitler book manipulates such documents. By describing the anti-Jewish measures in

Germany (in the area of the Reich there remained only a few thousand Jews), Hitler attempted to persuade both heads of state to adopt a similar radical line towards the Jews of their respective countries. He bluntly expressed himself to Horthy on 16–17 April 1943. It had aroused his particular dissatisfaction that Hungary's 800,000 Jews could, in spite of some anti-Jewish laws that were promulgated in 1938, still move about with relative freedom. On 16 April 1943[73] Horthy answered the reproaches levelled against him on this matter by enumerating the manifold measures that had been taken by his government to restrict the Jewish influence; he closed his remarks with a clear allusion to the reports known to him about the German measures for the liquidation of the Jews: 'He had done everything that could decently be done against the Jews, but it was after all impossible to murder them or otherwise eliminate them'. Hitler, who was obviously embarrassed by this hint, declared, according to the records: '. . . there is no need for that; Hungary could put the Jews into concentration camps just as had been done in Slovakia. . . .' He continued by counter-attacking while twisting the argument in his typical manner: 'When there was talk of murdering the Jews, he [the *Führer*] had to state that there was only *one* murderer, namely the Jew who had provoked this war . . .' Hitler and Ribbentrop did not give up and on the next day (April 17) brought up the subject again. The most important parts of the record read:

In reply to Horthy's question, what should be done with the Jews after he had deprived them of almost any means of existence – to murder them is not possible – the Foreign Minister answered that the Jews must either be destroyed or put in concentration camps – there is no other way.

Hitler complemented the straightforward speech of his Foreign Minister first by a long-winded dissertation on the decay that the Jews caused wherever they were found and, with a typical mixture of openness and obscurity, arrived at the heart of the matter: the massacre of the Jews in the concentration camps, to which Horthy had alluded.

> They [the Jews] are just parasites. This state of affairs had not been tolerated in Poland; if the Jews there refused to work, they were shot. Those who could not work just wasted away. They had to be treated as tuberculosis bacilli which could infect a healthy organism. This was by no means cruel when one considered that even innocent creatures like hares and deer had to be put down to prevent damage. Why should the beasts that had brought Bolshevism down on us, command more pity.

These documented statements on the part of Hitler could not be ignored even by Irving. He reproduces some passages (p. 509) but attempts to modify their significance methodically by a number of manoeuvres: Ribbentrop's declaration in the presence of Hitler (that the Jews must either be destroyed or put in concentration camps) is concealed in a footnote to the appendix of the book.[74] Hitler's own remark (in Poland the Jews who refused to work were shot and those who could not work perished) Irving introduces with the reference to the Warsaw Ghetto Revolt which had been suppressed shortly before (and that had not even been mentioned in the conference with Horthy); he thus makes it falsely appear as only referring to an action that was limited in scope and carried out for a specific reason. In order completely to obscure the impression that the *Führer's* utterances, which could hardly be misunderstood, were indeed a confirmation of this policy of annihilation, Irving allows the discussion with Horthy to terminate, contrary to the documented facts, with Hitler's evasive remark of the previous day (16 April 1943) in reply to Horthy's direct question if he should murder the Jews ('there is no need for that'). Irving cites these words at the end of his quotation and they are the only ones he cites *verbatim* and stresses with quotation marks. Irving finally ends the thoroughly manipulated course and content of the conference with some further remarks that are intended to relieve Hitler of responsibility and are typical for Irving's apologetic interpretation (p. 509). As an illustration we shall quote them *verbatim*:

What had prompted the earthier [!] language now employed? It is possible to recognise the association in his mind of certain illogical ideas; half were unconscious or the result of his own muddled beliefs, but half had deliberately been implanted by trusted advisers like Himmler and Goebbels: the Jews had started the war; the enemy was the international Jew; the most deadly of the Bolsheviks, like Stalin's propagandist Ilya Ehrenburg, were Jews: Ehrenburg and the Jews behind Roosevelt were preaching the total extermination of the German race. The saturation bombing of German cities, their blasting and burning, were just the beginning. In his warning to Horthy that the 'Jewish Bolsheviks' would liquidate all Europe's intelligentsia, we can identify the influence of the Katyn episode. . . . But the most poisonous and persuasive argument used to reconcile [!] Hitler to a harsher treatment of the Jews was the bombing war. From documents and target maps recently found in crashed bombers he knew that the British aircrews were instructed to aim only at the residential areas now and to disregard the industrial targets proper. Only one race murdered, he told the quailing Horthy, and that was the Jews, who had provoked this war and given it its present character against civilians, women and children. He returned repeatedly to this theme as 1943 progressed; in 1944 it became more insistent; and in 1945 he embodied it in his Political Testament, as though to appease his own conscience and justify his country's actions.

With these 'explanations' our author has done it again: without the British bombing war that had been initiated by Churchill, Hitler would not have been such a hater of the Jews. The prejudice of the author, transforming his hatred of Churchill into an apology for Hitler, is apparent in this passage, and indeed, characterises the whole book.

It is not possible, and indeed it is quite unnecessary to delve into Irving's distorting interpretation. Over and above our criticism, it is a point in the author's favour that we are provided an opportunity to re-examine the subject. In spite of his mistaken conclusions Irving has drawn our attention to some of the hitherto inadequate information and existing interpretations.

14. The 'Aristocracy of National Socialism': The Role of the *SS* in National Socialist Germany

BERND WEGNER

In 1956 Gerald Reitlinger published a (now outdated) book on the history of the *SS*, *The* SS – *Alibi of a Nation*.[1] The title suggests one of the main difficulties previously complicating the historian's analysis of the *SS*: the impact of the Black Order's monstrous amorality on the post-war generation, since, after 1945, the executors of the holocaust became, so to speak, the 'whipping boys' of German atonement. In countless books, films and magazine articles the *SS* has been presented as the incarnation of all evil. For many people both inside and outside Germany the delicate moral question of their own involvement in the events of the NS period seemed expeditiously answered simply by reference to the terror apparatus of the *SS* and the universal threat it

Original contribution to this volume.

represented. Confronted by an historical issue so entangled in emotional commitments, it is understandably difficult for the scholar to maintain the requisite 'intellectual distance'.

There are two other considerations which complicate an analysis of the *SS*. One of them is that the *SS* – though it left deep traces on the map of Europe – was in historical terms very much an ephemeral phenomenon. Historians concerned with the evolution of political parties, armies, economic or religious institutions, may look back over decades, even centuries, and thereby get to the heart of the matter. But the *SS* lasted hardly 20 years: a ridiculously short time which becomes even shorter when one realises that in its first seven years the organisation led at best a shadow existence. But what a breathtaking development during those two decades: from the bodyguard of an initially rather unsuccessful *völkisch* politician named Hitler to the 'party police' of the NS movement; from the party police to the keystone of German domestic policy; from this domestic springboard to a controlling influence in the German war effort and to a mastery over large parts of German-occupied Europe. The climax of this unique expansion of power was the *SS*'s vain attempt to establish itself as a new elite, and as the chief organising force of a new 'Germanic Europe'. The development of the *SS* was like an historical brush fire: never in its short history was there a period of constancy or stability, or a moment of calm; every objective that was achieved was swallowed up by its ever-expanding appetite.

A third problem for the historian of the *SS* is its enormously varied character. The *SS* was a conglomeration of loosely connected offices and branches, which often had little to do with one another, and which fulfilled radically different duties. The historian's judgement is therefore shaped by whichever aspect or branch of the '*SS* State' he studies: the concentration camp system or the *Waffen-SS*, the organisation's economic enterprises or the *SD* (*Sicherheitsdienst*), the *SS*'s secret service, the so-called 'General *SS*' (*Allgemeine SS*) or the *SS* authorities in German-occupied countries. In addition, as each section of the *SS* had its own distinctive domain and flavour it is difficult to draw any general conclusions on the 'Black Order' as a whole.

I

As the above has made clear the *SS* is far from being a well-defined, easily graspable and homogeneous object of historical research: rather it is an extremely dynamic, protean and heterogeneous phenomenon. What, then, besides the personal role of Heinrich Himmler as *Reichsführer-SS*, held it together?

Perhaps the single most cohesive factor was a common mentality, more a nebulous attitude towards life than a coherent ideology. This attitude, best captured by the term *politisches Soldatentum* [the *SS* as 'political soldiers' *Ed.*] was by no means shared by every member of the *SS*, but was sufficiently popular within all parts of the leadership for it to become the ideological underpinning for the *SS*'s boundless thirst for power. What exactly was this attitude, what does the term *politisches Soldatentum* mean?[2]

In National Socialist ideology the notion of struggle (*Kampf*) focused centrally on both the individual and collective, *völkisch* life. It was not seen as a limited contest according to a set of definite rules laid down in order to achieve an assigned objective – as, for example, in sports or in eighteenth-century warfare – but as a struggle for existence (*Daseinskampf*). This concept of struggle, influenced by traditions of Social Darwinism, we find well expressed in Hitler's own book[3] according to which the National Socialist, if he took his ideology seriously, was a *Kämpfer* (fighter, warrior) by nature, and it was in this sense that he called himself a 'soldier' – or, more precisely, a 'political soldier' (*politischer Soldat*). It is quite obvious that soldiering of this kind had little to do with soldiering as a military profession. Himmler himself stressed this distinction, when he said in a speech in November 1938 with regard to the *SS* Death's Head units:

The *Totenkopfverbände* were established from the guards in the concentration camps. Of course, they have – and I think that is our mission – become a troop; from jailers they developed into soldiers. I am convinced that in all things we do, we'll become soldiers sooner or later. This will be so in administration, it was the case with the guard troops [meaning here Hitler's personal bodyguard, ultimately the *Leibstandarte—SS Adolf Hitler*, commanded by Sepp Dietrich, an *SS* commander who managed to keep his distance from Himmler. *Ed.*] and it is the same with the secret and criminal police. *We always become soldiers, not military, but soldiers.*[4] (Author's italics)

Himmler's statement is typical of the National Socialist understanding of what a *politischer Soldat* was. Accordingly, every NS activist, regardless of his profession, was a 'soldier' and the military was one among others.

The fundamental difference between the military and the political types of soldier becomes still more obvious when we look at the object against which force is used. Concerning the professional military man, there was no doubt: he fought at a clearly defined time, that is in war, with military means against a clearly defined external enemy. The case of the *politischer Soldat* was quite different. His enemy · was everywhere, inside Germany as well as outside the country. In his view Marxism, 'plutocracy', freemasonry and Christianity were nothing other than different faces of one universal threat, the focal point of which became the Jew. So *SS* officer cadets had to learn, for example, that: 'The enemies of Germany are all led by Jewry or are its children in spirit.'[5] From this and many other documents it becomes quite clear that the Jew was simply the common denominator of all possible adversaries of National Socialism. Because of this view, the *SS* man's perception of the world became extremely bi-polar and one-dimensional. As a high-ranking *SS* officer said in 1939, months before the outbreak of war:

[The *SS*] is never tired, it is never satisfied, it never lays down its arms, it is always on duty, always ready to parry the enemy's blows and to fight back. For the *SS*, there is only one [!] enemy, the enemy of Germany, there is only one [!] friend, the German people.[6]

This totalitarian ingroup-outgroup ideology of the *SS* destroyed all differences between internal and external enemies and, as a consequence, those between war and peace, between military and civil life. As the enemy was ever present, it had to be fought at any time and in any place. Thus it is not surprising to find Himmler, for example, in his wartime speeches comparing the current war with the National Socialist struggle for power in the Weimar period. For him, as for many other *SS* leaders, there was no difference in principle between the political and the military struggle. They were the same battle against the same enemy, fought only by different means and on different battlefields. As the *SS* saw itself as the power elite destined by history to fight that battle, it consequently demanded the right to incorporate all forces in state and society which seemed appropriate to its purpose. Thus the *SS* understood itself not so much as an organisation designed to fulfil a limited concrete social task (such as the army or the police did), but rather as an elite of the society as a whole. This is what Himmler meant when he called the *SS* a modern 'knighthood' or Germany's new aristocracy.[7]

II

The totalitarian and autocratic character of the *SS* becomes evident in its development even during the early years of the Third Reich. Himmler tried to gain mastery over as many sectors of politics as possible. So even before the outbreak of the war, the *SS* had succeeded in influencing no fewer than five large and significant areas.

One sphere of influence, where the *SS* began its calculated takeover as early as 1933, was ideology and propaganda. After the *SA*'s loss of power in the summer of 1934, the *SS* was well on its way to being the ideological arbiter and *avant garde* of National Socialism. They claimed to be not only the pioneers of the NS movement, but also a model for, and the educator of, the German nation. Himmler, convinced that Germany had been led astray for the last thousand years by Christianity, saw the restoration of the old pre-Christian, Germanic culture and lifestyle as the main task of the *SS*.[8] To this end, the *SS* sponsored many different cultural and scientific activities. For the sake of ideological education countless articles, books – mainly published by its own publishing house, Nordland-Verlag – and films were produced. Himmler's organisation also controlled the *Nationalpolitische Erziehungsanstalten*, the elitist National Socialist grammar schools[9] [Himmler did not obtain control of these institutions until Hitler's order of 7 December 1944 when under the impact of war they were already in the process of dissolution. *Ed*.] and established a network of homes destined to look after *SS* members studying at the university. The *SS* encouraged research on early Germanic history and archaeology and founded a research society of its own, the *Ahnenerbe*, exclusively for this purpose.[10] The *Lebensborn* was another society formed by the *SS* to further the production of racially pure children without regard to their legitimacy.[11] [That the *Lebensborn* was an institution for the deliberate 'production' of racially 'pure stock' was established as a myth at the Nuremberg trials. It was the one institution of the *SS* which received a 'clean bill of health'. The institution owned homes in which primarily, but not exclusively, unmarried women could bear their children with proper medical and post-natal care. *Ed*.]

Secondly, more important than the ideological activities of the *SS*, from the perspective of power politics, was its role in the field of domestic security, where the *SS* achieved a monopoly within a few years. The monopoly was principally based on three instruments of power at the disposal of the *SS*: the secret service (*Sicherheitsdienst*), the police and the concentration camps (including its armed guard units, the so-called *Totkenkopfverbände*). All of these subgroups expanded rapidly in size and competence. The *Sicherheitsdienst*, for example, founded by Heydrich in 1931, managed to monopolise all intelligence activities within the NS movement until 1934. Furthermore, in 1938, it began to penetrate the state administration.[12] Five and a half years later the *SD* had its finest hour: in February 1944, several months before the officers' *putsch* against Hitler, it took over the *Wehrmacht*'s counter-intelligence agency, the *Abwehr*, which under the command of Admiral Canaris had been the only secret service organisation not controlled by the *SS*.[13]

In the case of the concentration camps the development was even more remarkable. After the so-called 'Röhm Putsch' in the summer of 1934 all camps were put under the command of the *SS* and a special administration was established, the head of which became Theodor Eicke, a former commander of the Dachau concentration camp. Using this camp as a model,[14] Eicke within a few years developed a centralised and strictly regulated repressive machine. He also organised special armed units, the 'Death's Head units' (*SS-Totenkopfverbände*), for guarding the camps. By early 1939 its forçe was almost 9,000 strong.[15] The most important aspect of this development was that by establishing the concentration camp system the *SS* gave itself a freedom of action which was independent of the existing law and administration of justice. This meant in practice that anybody could be arrested at any time and sent to a concentration camp indefinitely without legal procedure or even after being discharged by a court. It was this lack of legal security which, more than the calculable, albeit rigid, and unjust, laws of the Third Reich, helped to intimidate the German people and thus cripple the forces of opposition.

The *SS*'s most significant concentration of power was to be found in its domination, and eventual assimilation, of the police force. Himmler acquired authority over it by several steps: first, he gained control over the secret police (*politische Polizei*) in the German *Länder* (1933–4); then through his appointment as *Reichsführer-SS und Chef der deutschen Polizei* (17 June 1936) he integrated the police forces into the administrative structure of the *SS*.[16] Himmler's aim was to form a complete amalgamation of both organisations, a gigantic 'state protection corps' (*Staatsschutz- korps*).[17] For at least two reasons this meant a complete change of constitutional principles. The police traditionally had formed part of the prerogative of the German *Länder*. Himmler's appointment to chief of the German police, however, constituted a centralisation of the police by the Reich's authorities. Thus here, as in many other fields, National Socialist rule led to an end of federalism. Furthermore, the fusion of police and *SS* meant the amalgamation of a state agency with an organisation of the

NSDAP. Consequently the SS enjoyed many privileges usually reserved by the public administration, and the police force threatened to lose its character as an organisation of public service, changing instead to an instrument of the *Führer*'s will.

Thirdly, the advance of the SS into the fields of the prerogative of the armed forces proved to be less spectacular, though none the less effective. Despite strong opposition, mainly from the army high command, Himmler managed within a few years to organise a 'second army' in the form of the SS Reserve Troops (*SS-Verfügungstruppe*), the core of the later *Waffen-SS*. Even if this amounted only to a few thousand soldiers, such a development was not warranted by any provisions in the constitution, and it challenged the already delicate balance of power between the political and military forces in Germany.

After the National Socialists' accession to power Hitler had defined this balance by referring to the 'two pillars' that would support the new state: the Party and the *Wehrmacht*. The liquidation of the SA leaders, whom the *Wehrmacht* had feared as potential rivals, seemed to underline this policy of an 'equal partnership' between the political and military spheres. The dictator himself stressed at that time the principle that the *Wehrmacht* was to be the only 'Bearer of Arms' in the Nation.[18] The army generals were all the more astonished when a few months later the SS leadership began to build up a small army of its own, namely the *SS-Verfügungstruppe*, which it then trained and equipped in a military fashion. The army leaders accepted this development in the following years only because the SS units were too small to constitute a genuine threat to *Wehrmacht* supremacy, and because their training and equipping could be closely supervised and even controlled by the military. Moreover, both Himmler and Hitler stressed repeatedly that the *SS-Verfügungstruppe* was to have no military, but only domestic police-like functions.[19] By the end of 1938 at the very latest, however, it turned out that Himmler had deceived the Army generals both about the actual size of the SS units and about their real purpose. They had by then expanded to well over 14,000 men, and were on the threshold of an even more explosive expansion. Most alarmingly, their officer corps contained a disproportionally high percentage of *SS* officers who had been educated in special *SS* officer cadet academies (the *SS-Junkerschulen*). The leadership was organised along the lines of a divisional staff. The recruiting of former army officers and NCOs as a training cadre ensured that service in the *SS* would be solidly military in nature, and would therefore fulfil the obligatory standards of the *Wehrmacht*.[20]

As for the army high command, it had largely lost control of the *SS-Verfügungstruppe* by 1938. Even more importantly, the crises concerning the commander-in-chief of the army, General von Fritsch, and his chief of staff, Col.-General Beck [there was no crisis about Beck, who resigned his post in protest at Hitler's policy in the Czech crisis of 1938, because he was sure that Britain and France would intervene, involving Germany in a war for which it was not armed. *Ed.*], cost the army its two most influential opponents of the *SS* during these crucial years, and resulted in a general loss of political influence on the part of the army. The *SS* managed to exploit this situation to its own advantage. A *Führer*-order dated 17 August 1938, which had been drafted by Himmler, established that the *SS-Verfügungstruppe* was to be used for its former, domestic purposes (which were not specified even now) as well as in 'a mobile role as part of the wartime army'.[21] [This provision was already contained in Blomberg's directive of 24 September 1934 – see note 19. *Ed.*] A few months later, with the prospect of war imminent, the *SS-Verfügungstruppe* was allowed to develop into a full-scale division. Moreover, the *Totenkopf* units, which had hitherto served only to guard the concentration camps, were also expanded considerably and were now allowed to be used as a reserve for the front-line units.[22]

All these rulings had shifted the scales decisively in favour of the *SS* in its quarrel with the army. It was no longer a question of whether the *SS* units would be allowed to share in military conquests in the years to come; the disputes now concerned only their assignment, size and organisation.

Himmler had finally succeeded in what he had planned since 1934 – he had secured a foothold on army territory.

Fourthly, apart from cultural life and the spheres of internal and military security, foreign policy was another area in which the *SS* tried to gain an influence. Here, however, its success was less spectacular, and it was never able to help shape Hitler's fundamental decision-making process. Still, it found a wide scope of action when it came to implementing the Führer's general political guidelines. In this context, the so-called *Volksdeutsche Mittelstelle* [the *SS* agency responsible for racial Germans, or German minorities living outside the frontiers of the Reich. *Ed.*] of the *SS* as well as the foreign department of the *SD* both tried to gain influence on the often large German communities in eastern, central and southern Europe, that is in those countries which were soon to become either the allies or the victims of German expansionist policies.[23] Himmler also tried to involve his *SS* in discussions regarding the policing of future German colonies.[24] More importantly, he endeavoured to have the *SS* form the core of a future, supra-national racially hetrogenous 'police defence front against Bolshevism', which would comprise all the potential allies of Germany.[25] We can assume that all these instances formed part of Himmler's policy to gain some share of influence on foreign policy.

When Joachim von Ribbentrop was made foreign secretary in February 1938, the *SS* seemed to have come very close to attaining its goal. Ribbentrop was thought to be closely intimate with Himmler, and he was an 'honorary leader' (*Ehrenführer*) of the *SS*. In his hope of influencing official German foreign policy, Himmler hastened to receive other high-ranking officials of the Foreign Office into the *SS*. However, his hopes in this area were soon dashed: during the two Czech crises in the autumn of 1938 and the spring of 1939, a lively struggle over competence erupted between the Foreign Office and the *SD*. As it turned out, the Foreign Office was not prepared to follow the dictates of the *SS*, although it, too, was increasingly influenced by National Socialism. The conflict then escalated further as Himmler's and Ribbentrop's basic ideas in foreign policy – especially concerning German-Soviet relations – were diametrically opposed.[26]

Finally, there was a fifth section in which the *SS* contrived unobtrusively to gain some measure of power – namely the economy. The economic plans of the *SS* sprang from its desire to use the concentration camps and their large manpower reservoirs more systematically and efficiently. In this endeavour the organisation founded a few of its own enterprises,[27] and after about 1938 it began systematic economic expansion in certain key fields of production. By the end of the war, the *SS* owned more than 40 different enterprises embracing about 150 plants and factories. It was involved in stone and earthworks, in the production of food and drinks, in agriculture and forestry, in timber and iron processing, in leathers and textiles as well as in publishing.[28]

This official entrepreneurial engagement was supplemented by semi-official contacts with influencial circles in the German economy. These contacts were supported mainly by the *Freundeskreis Reichsführer-SS*, a loose group of a few dozen industrialists, bankers and high-ranking civil servants who were interested in having some degree of connection with the *SS* without actually joining. For the *SS*, these contacts payed off in the literal sense: the members of the *Freundeskreis* supported the work of the *SS* with substantial sums of money and were also prepared to help in other ways, for example in granting cheap loans.[29]

III

The substantial early influence the *SS* had achieved in internal, foreign, economic, police and military affairs shows that its ambition was aimed at the reformation of society as a whole. It is within this context that the different activities of the *SS* – however varied they may seem at first sight – take on their proper significance. In fact, this overall aim constituted the foundation of the *SS*'s political influence. The ideological and propaganda apparatus of the 'General *SS*' (*Allgemeine SS*), for example, would probably not have been taken seriously, if it had not been supported by the ever-present threat of the Gestapo and the concentration camps. The establishment of an *SS* military force would not have been possible without Himmler's commanding position in domestic affairs. At the same time, it turned out that the military training increasingly received by *SS* volunteers was very useful for domestic repression as well. [In this context however, it is important to note that the most serious threat to the NS regime, the plot of 20 July 1944, was suppressed by the *Wehrmacht* and not by the *SS*. *Ed*.]

Himmler did all he could to impress the importance of these interlocking relationships upon his confidants. He realised very well that the *SS*'s powerful position within the National Socialist system could be preserved only if it succeeded in maintaining its character as a cohesive community of 'political soldiers' without regard to different branches. Its members had to be more than just concentration camp guards, policemen, soldiers, security agents or propagandists. Himmler feared, above all, that the wide variety of functions within the *SS* might result in a drifting apart of the individual parts. Particularly during the war, there was a real threat that one branch or other of his empire might succeed in gaining its independence. This, Himmler thought, would be 'the first step towards the end' of the *SS*: 'then all would . . . within a generation . . . revert to its former insignificance'.[30] Consequently, he endeavoured to link the individual activities of the *SS* as closely as possible: his organised 'glue' induced a common ethic ideal, the creation of only one channel of education for a wide scope of activities, the constant transfer of young *SS* leaders to new and different posts; the integration of *SS* and police personnel, the standardisation of ranks, and many similar measures.

Thus at the end of the 1930s the influence of the *SS* was extensive and varied, but it did have its limits. As we saw, the old elites had not been pushed aside everywhere as easily as they had been in the police force. In general, it can be said that the *SS* reached the limits of its power when it had to compete with old or new leadership groups without having Hitler's backing. However, it was also the general consolidation and stabilisation of political structures which helped to retard the *SS*'s evolution towards its goal of becoming the new aristocracy of a National Socialist society. For Himmler had had his successes only as a result of the social and political convulsions which shook Germany following the National Socialist seizure of power. Once these convulsions receded, and once the new regime had firmly established its control, the *SS* could no longer manoeuvre so freely. However, the further evolution of the NS system by no means completely shackled the *SS*. On the contrary, its power expanded even more rapidly than before. The reason was that the early period of domestic upheaval did not lead to stabilisation, but passed over to a new phase of external violence and war. The year 1938 marks this change.[31] Hitler's self-appointment as military commander-in-chief indicated that the National Socialist 'seizure of power' had come to a temporary end. On the other hand, his annexation of Austria and the Sudetenland in the same year inaugurated a new policy of external expansion. In other words: all that the *SS* had accomplished so far had resulted from domestic infighting; all that it would henceforth achieve would come in the wake of Germany's foreign conquests. The outbreak of war and the ensuing revolution in European affairs gave the *SS* a unique opportunity to maintain its momentum and extend its successes beyond the German borders. Thus, the war became a *conditio sine qua non* for the further evolution of the *SS* as envisaged by Himmler.

There are many indications that Himmler had anticipated this development even before the war began. As early as November 1938 he described in a speech to the higher *SS* leaders his vision of Germany as 'the greatest empire ever created by man and ever seen on earth'.[32] He left no doubt that the *SS* would help to build this 'Great Germanic Empire', even if it required him 'to go out and rob and steal Germanic blood throughout the entire world'.[33] Thus it is obvious that the *SS* intended to use the war to become the dominant power in a new 'Germanic Europe'.

In fact, the course of the war after 1942 prevented the *SS* from achieving this aim. [However, it was after Stalingrad that the *Waffen-SS* experienced its most rapid phase of expansion, amounting by 1944 to over 900,000 men. *Ed.*]

On the other hand, the various ways in which this organisation managed to expand were so extensive that they cannot be adequately described here. Therefore I shall limit myself to illustrating the process by focusing upon two characteristic examples: the concentration camp system and the armed formations of the *SS*, the so-called *Waffen-SS*.

IV

As for the concentration camp organisation, the outbreak of war brought decisive changes both in scope and structure. When the war began, the total number of concentration camp inmates was about 25,000. Within the next four years, that is until the autumn of 1943, this number rose to 224,000, almost nine times the 1939 figure. From then on the expansion was even more dramatic: in August 1944 500,000 and in January 1945 more than 700,000 prisoners populated the SS concentration camps; an estimated third of them died within the last months of the war during the evacuation of the camps close to the front line.[34] But however shocking they may be, these figures represent only the 'tip of the iceberg' when seen within the total context of *SS* extermination policy. They refer only to the prisoners actually living in the camps and do not include the hundreds of thousands who died there due to inhumane living and working conditions.[35] Nor do they include the around 5 million Jews who were murdered by the mobile '*SS* Action Groups' (*SS-Einsatzgruppe*) of the *SD* and the *Sicherheitspolizei* or were gassed in the specially designed extermination camps.[36]

Therefore, the *SS* as an instrument of repression served two very different, even conflicting purposes: on the one hand it became the executor of the 'final solution' ordered by Hitler – a policy which was not, as far as we know, proposed by Himmler, but which he loyally carried out as efficiently and as quietly as possible;[37] on the other hand, it amassed large numbers of prisoners in the concentration camps, whose labour became invaluable to the German war effort. How significant – even crucial – this economic aspect eventually became, is reflected in the takeover of the concentration camps in 1942 by the SS-Economy and Administration Board (*SS-Wirtschafts- und Verwaltungshauptamt*). From then on, if not earlier, Himmler was working to create a vast *SS* armaments industry exploiting the labour force in the concentration camps. This, in turn, was part and parcel of his plan to develop the *SS* into an organisation which would ultimately be financially independent of the state budget. For years, however, Himmler's ambitions led to a confrontation with Albert Speer's ministry of armaments – which may in fact have been exactly what Himmler wanted. But in the end it was Speer's continuous resistance as well as the incompetence of the respective *SS* functionaries in economic affairs that foiled the *Reichsführer*'s ambitions.[38]

Nevertheless, the basic role of the concentration camps had changed drastically due to the aims of the higher *SS* echelons. No longer did demands of 'state security' alone decide who would disappear into a concentration camp and how long they would stay; equally important was the increasing demand for cheap labour. To satisfy this demand, two things were necessary: on the one hand a steadily increasing 'supply' of prisoners, as well as longer stay in the camps; on the other, an increase of the inmate's productivity. As for the latter, the efforts of the *SS* leadership met with little success. On the contrary, for several reasons mortality among the concentration camp inmates rose dramatically after the outbreak of war and achieved the tragic climax of nearly 60,000 in the second half of 1942. Due to increasingly hard working conditions, reduced food rations, deficient housing and hygiene, the *SS* leadership was unable to preserve the prisoners' physical fitness. Nor could productivity be improved by threats of punishment or by offering minor advantages to prisoners. According to Speer's figures, the average work done by a concentration camp inmate amounted to only one-sixth of what a free civilian labourer could achieve.[39] In short, it turned out that a system based on repression, dehumanisation and physical extermination could hardly be converted into a high-productivity economic enterprise.

For this reason every conceivable effort had to be made to increase the number of inmates. As early as the beginning of the war the *SS* was empowered to detain in 'protective custody' (*Schutzhaft*) an ever widening circle of political, social or 'racial' offenders. Moreover, it was decided that for the duration of the war there would be no releases except for a few special cases. Since the new powers of the *SS* were not limited to the Reich territory, the conquest of an increasing amount of foreign territory opened up huge new possibilities to the Security Police. Thus, in the autumn of 1941, the monthly *Schutzhaft* figure was about 15,000, about ten times that of 1935–36.[40] Also, increasing numbers of mainly Polish and Russian 'foreign workers' (*Fremdarbeiter*) were sent to the camps during the last war years. This changed the ethnic structure in the camps; only 5 to 10 per cent of the inmates were German by the end of the war.[41]

Summing up, it can be said that the concentration camps were greatly expanded due to the war and that this brought a fundamental change in their role. Before the war, their main purpose was to neutralise the regime's internal enemies. Later they retained this function, but after 1942 it was increasingly superseded by two other tasks: mass extermination and economic exploitation. These were mutually contradictory: economic exploitation required the preservation of the workforce; extermination meant its destruction. The *SS* simply never succeeded in solving this problem.

V

The development of the *Waffen-SS* was basically similar. Here, too, we see a massive increase in size due to the war combined with a fundamental change of structure and purpose. For the *Waffen-SS* this qualitative change could be characterised as the development from an elitist Pretorian Guard to a mass army. Again, a few figures can serve to illustrate this alteration: at the beginning of 1935 the overall strength of the armed *SS* formations was about 7,000. By the beginning of 1939 this figure had about tripled to just under 23,000. By mid-1944 it had grown to nearly 600,000 men, or 85 times its 1935 size.[42] [There is still some confusion on the numbers serving in the *Waffen-SS*. The author's figure is the lowest estimate. The highest figure cited and statistically verified is 910,000 by the end of 1944, though large numbers had been drafted or transferred from the navy and air force. *Ed.*]

What made this explosive increase possible, after every peacetime effort to recruit more volunteers for the armed *SS* had come to nothing through the veto of the *Wehrmacht* high command? There were three methods used by the *SS*: first, it asked to be granted a higher quota of recruits by the *Oberkommando der Wehrmacht* (OKW) responsible for the assignment of conscripts. This proved more or less unsuccessful until 1941; the *Wehrmacht* needed every man for itself and was not prepared to set aside additional personnel for the *SS*.[43]

The second method was to enlist as many volunteers as possible without regard to the quota set by the OKW.[44] This required, however, that it should hide the additional enlistments from the *Wehrmacht* authorities responsible for recruitment. It is obvious that this could only be practised on a restricted scale and over a limited time.

The third, and in the long run most successful, way for the *SS* to meet the increasing demand for personnel was to resort to 'reservoirs' outside the Reich borders and therefore not accessible to the *Wehrmacht*. This meant mainly the millions of people of German origin living in south-east Europe or in the Baltic states, as well as the non-German, but 'Germanic' volunteers from west or north European countries either allied with, or occupied by, Germany. In the spring of 1940 the first two regiments with a few hundred 'Germanic' volunteers each were established. This was the first step in the direction of reorganising the *Waffen-SS* into a multinational force; by the end of the war, only about 40 per cent of the *Waffen-SS* men had been born within the Reich borders.[45]

The development of the *Waffen-SS* into a multinational army was a practical response to the problem of the scarcity of recruits, a problem which increased in urgency as the war went on. But it was also consistent with the ideological and power-political aim of the *SS*, which was to become the elite of a 'Greater Germanic Empire' transcending the borders of the Reich. How outrageously ambitious this was is illustrated by Himmler's plans for a post-war 'pan-Germanic army' to be set up on the basis of conscription, and under the control of the *SS* in the 'Germanic' countries.[46] Even more absurd were the deliberations of the *SS*-leadership in the summer of 1940, when they wondered whether they should eventually recruit the millions of people of German descent living in Australia, Canada, the United States and South America for the resettling of the East.[47]

While the development of the *Waffen-SS* into a multi-national force was still an ideologically justifiable consequence of the demands of war, the same cannot be said of some other tendencies within it. One of these potentially suspect tendencies was the gradual subversion of the principle of voluntary service. It is not that the *Waffen-SS* was ever officially changed into a conscript army; the principle of voluntary enlistment of the *SS* man was far too important a part of the *SS* identity as an ideological order to allow that. However, in the totalitarian 'national community' (*Volksgemeinschaft*) of the Third Reich, there were ample opportunities of coercing massive numbers of young people into 'voluntarily' joining the ranks of the *SS*. The *SS* recruitment authorities were not slow to avail themselves of these opportunities, and by 1942 coerced 'volunteering' was more or less the norm.[48]

Indeed, *SS* recruitment policies were in a dilemma that could hardly be solved: it needed at one and the same time to satisfy Himmler's ambition of having at his disposal a maximum number of new *SS* divisions and army corps, and to try and make good the extremely high losses sustained by the existing *SS* formations. By the end of 1943, about 50,000 *SS* soldiers had fallen; more than twice the overall strength of armed *SS* forces a year before the outbreak of war. These losses hit, above all, the divisions which had been developed from pre-war *SS* formations (i.e. the *Leibstandarte-SS Adolf Hitler*, *Das Reich*, *Totenkopf* and *Wiking* divisions). With the best possible staff and equipment, they were surely among the elite of the German armed forces.[49] Almost exclusively employed as a 'fire-brigade' on critical spots of the eastern, western and southern fronts, they were responsible for the legendary military reputation of the *Waffen-SS*.

Their extremely high losses, especially among their officers, were the price they had to pay for this reputation. In the long run, however, these losses endangered the existence of the whole formation: the feverish creation of even more new divisions resulted in a *Waffen-SS* that bore hardly any resemblance to the pre-war contingency force. By mid-1944, out of all generals and colonels, less than 50 per cent had served in the armed *SS* forces before the war. Consequently, the higher echelons were anything but unanimous in their ideology, and there were vast differences in their social and educational backgrounds.[50] The lack of a unified ideology was even more marked among the ranks, above all among those drafted into the *SS*. This also held true for foreigners who had usually joined for reasons which were anything but specifically National Socialist.[51] In short, its military successes notwithstanding, the *Waffen-SS* was losing its political and ideological profile during this vast expansion. As the *Waffen-SS* now formed by far the largest part of the *SS*, we can make the generalisation that even as the *SS* was increasing its power, its cohesiveness was being eroded. Due to the exigencies of war, the efforts of central *SS* authorities to remedy this through additional political instruction and other means remained without much success.

Even from a military point of view, the efforts of the *SS* leadership to develop the *Waffen-SS* into a mass army without sacrificing its claim as an elite had to lead to a dilemma. In the long run, it was not possible both to expand in size and to maintain very high standards at the same time. Therefore an increasingly varied range of quality developed within the *Waffen-SS*. The elite Panzer divisions which formed the backbone of the defence of the now hard-pressed German front were only the smaller part of the *Waffen-SS* of the later years. More typical for the overall picture were by now divisions whose training and equipment were clearly deficient and whose fighting power was at best limited.[52] In other words, with the wave of new formations created by 1943, the *Waffen-SS* had ceased to be a military elite *per se*. The *SS* leadership accepted this only because, once again, it hoped to use this change of structure towards a mass army for its own long-term political aims. Its military planning for the post-war period involved two aspects: the reorganisation of the *Waffen-SS* as the military spearhead of the *SS* order with the wartime elite divisions as a core, and a Germanic-European army which would not be part of the *SS* but would be controlled by it. This would consist of the other formations with their mainly foreign troops.[53] Its grip on such a European army would certainly have made the *SS* the key power in a National Socialist-dominated Europe.

VI

We were only able to follow the history of the *SS* by drawing on two of its component parts, the concentration camps and the *Waffen-SS*. Our selectivity here should not obscure the fact that we are in reality dealing with a massive wartime augmentation of power – a process which threatened, even more than in pre-war years, to engulf the whole of society. It was particularly during the war that the interdependencies among the various components of the *SS* became clear. We have seen how the development of the concentration camp system helped shape the role the *SS* could play in the armaments sector; this in turn directly affected the *Waffen-SS*'s *materiél* standards. The latter group proved to be not only a powerful military instrument, but also a suitable instrument for the realisation of the foreign and occupational aims of the *Reichsführung-SS*. The drafting of hundreds of thousands of *Volksdeutsche*, racial Germans, can only be understood within the context of the massive resettlement programme which Himmler planned in his capacity as 'Reich's Commissar for the strengthening of the German Race' (*Reichskommissar für die Festigung deutschen Volkstums*).[54] The negative side of this ambition was, however, the deportation, enslavement and partial extermination of the Slav population. Also in the establishment of 'Higher *SS* and Police Leaders' (*Höhere SS- und Polizeiführer*),[55] for example, or in the foundation of a 'General-*SS*' (*Allgemeine SS*) on the German model in the occupied 'Germanic' countries, *SS* interests in the field of home affairs, occupational, military, police and ideological policies closely meshed. This network of interlocking interests tightened as Himmler took over more and more offices or functions within the regime. We should remind ourselves in this context that after October 1939 the *Reichsführer SS* was also 'Reich's Commissar for the Strengthening of German Race' and that, in August 1943, he became minister of the interior as well. After the breakdown of the Army Group Centre [during the Russian summer offensive launched on 22 June 1944 *Ed*.], Himmler was given command of the newly drafted *Volksgrenadier*-divisions, and eventually of the POW camps as well. [However, this did not change the administration and guarding of POW camps which remained in *Wehrmacht* hands. *Ed*.] Finally he became commander-in-chief of the Reserve Army and head of army armaments (*Befehlshaber des Ersatzheeres und Chef der Heeresrüstung*) after the failure of the 20 July 1944 assassination attempt.[56]

In retrospect, we can say that Heinrich Himmler's empire was the result of an exceptional historical situation. More precisely, it was a function of the unusual dynamism of the National Socialist system. The *SS* profited from this socio-political fluidity first during the internal restructuring of Germany after the NS seizure of power in 1933, and then during the military 'reorganisation' of Europe in the war. During the first phase, roughly until 1938, the *SS* succeeded in establishing its power only after strong competition both with older functional elites and with rival NS groups. From this position of strength it became, during the war, the catalytic element behind the radicalisation of the *Führer* regime. In other words, the *SS* helped continue the 'National Socialist Revolution' under the cover of wartime exigencies. It seems that this process accelerated as the regime's chances of survival diminished. It is certainly no coincidence that Himmler reached the zenith of his power at a time when the German defeat was no longer in doubt. By late summer 1944, the *SS* had become, in virtually every respect, the last hope for the 'Thousand Year Reich'.

PART V

PART V

Introduction

When writing a historical biography the modern historian is confronted by the question whether historical events and developments can be best explained by the actions of prominent personalities or in terms of the factors, structures and processes behind them. The materialist school, of which the Marxists are the most extreme, dismisses categories such as 'explanation' and 'understanding' and equates them with 'apology'. As for the regulative idea of 'objectivity', since complete objectivity can never be achieved (as Ranke was one of the first to admit), those attempting to be objective are indicted as being committed to an historical status quo, thus obstructing 'progress' and 'emancipation' (whatever that may mean).

Representatives of the individualising method, in our case historical biographers, will readily admit that the subject of their biography is essentially shaped by the social, economic, and intellectual environment into which that person was born and within which he developed, but they will also insist that a 'great' personality will imprint his own individual stamp upon his time. The question then is how strong is the imprint?

It is, and for decades will remain, difficult to be objective about Hitler. But why? If we look at the treatment of Stalin by historical biographers in the West, his mass murders, which exceed those of Hitler many times over, are deplored, on occasions even only peripherally mentioned, but on the whole he is credited with having pulled Russia firmly into the twentieth century, built up a highly industrialised society and so forth. In other words, whatever else he did, he nevertheless brought about progress. The excesses he committed in the name of a materialistic determination may be deplorable, but in the end they are relativised, so that when the balance sheet of Stalin's rule is studied a plus emerges.

This is not the case where Hitler, and the excesses he committed in the name of a biological determinism, is concerned. It was only in the early 1960s that sociologists, and not historians, began to draw the carefully phrased conclusion that the Third Reich pulled Germany into modernity. Whether it did so intentionally or as a mere by-product of its actions is still a question of heated debate. To mention but a few examples, between 1933 and 1945 a much greater proportion of working-class children gained access to grammar schools and institutions of higher education than was the case in the days of either the empire or the Weimar Republic. If one considers the generals of Germany's armed services and compares late 1936 with late 1944, a profound change in their age structure is revealed, those in 1944 being much younger and of socially much more diverse origins than those in 1936 – a trend which continues into the present in the East and West German forces. The traditional elites disappeared almost completely, so the idea of the *Volksgemeinschaft* seems to have been more than mere rhetoric after all and to have produced some profound changes, leading (albeit under the impact of war, defeat and utter destruction) to a classless society without whose existence the 'economic miracle' could hardly have been attained in West Germany, or in East Germany; certainly the class-ridden, divided society of Wilhelmine Germany or the Weimar Republic would have made these changes impossible. Why do historians find it so difficult to give credit to Hitler which many of them are willing to extend to Stalin? Is it because Soviet Russia is a distant country, never fully in the mainstream of western civilisation, a country in which a degree of barbarism is taken more or less for granted, while Germany, once the centre of European culture, represents a much greater deviation from the established norm, and therefore the excesses committed in its name are far more deplorable? People do make history: history is more than just the consequence of impersonal forces and currents. No doubt after 1918 there was room in Germany for a radical nationalist party, if only as a counter-weight to internationalist Marxism. But the National Socialist movement that emerged carried the imprint of Hitler's personality and will. Like his own life, it began very modestly, often stood at the brink of crisis and was even dissolved, yet in the end Hitler carried it to victory. Of course, National Socialism would have been possible even without Hitler, but in the hands of, say, Göring, it would have had a different complexion, always providing that it had attained power in the first place.

This is precisely what justifies a biography of Hitler. Hitler was a man given, as Hans Mommsen put it, rather more to *idées fixes* than to concrete political calculation. Whether they were entirely his own ideas is irrelevant. What is important is that he shaped them and also partly realised them. Even fixed ideas, once they take on a dogmatic shape, have their own remorseless logic, which can hardly be countered with the aid of formal logic. The social and intellectual environment may explain the origins and specific character of these ideas, but they do not explain their further development or their consequences. Thus a modern biography of Hitler has to emphasise the ambivalence of the historical process in the person of Adolf Hitler. By this criterion any biography of Hitler stands or falls.

In his essay William Carr provides his own assessment of the host of books on Hitler. This assessment, as the reader will notice, differs in some respects from that of the editor. Toland's biography of Hitler has already been mentioned in Part IV. It is, as its author readily admits, a 'no thesis' book, a narrative of Hitler in private. Binion's study *Hitler among the Germans* has also been mentioned already and his attempts at a 'psycho-historical' interpretation.

From the entire range of Hitler biographies only a few appear to have withstood the test of time. First in the field after 1945 was Alan Bullock's *Hitler: a study in tyranny*, first published in 1952. Most reviewers found it a masterpiece, though even then some raised the question whether printed primary sources alone were sufficient basis for a biography and whether actual research in the field would not yield further, hitherto unknown and unfamiliar material. As time has shown, the question was not unjustified.

Bullock's biography is cast in the mould of the traditional political biography, but even so it contains an internal imbalance. Thus Hitler's 'formative years' up to 1918 are covered in just over 30 pages, completely ignoring intellectual currents fashionable in Europe prior to the First World War. The period 1919–33 is covered in about 190 pages, while the bulk – almost 600 pages – is devoted to the years 1933–45. Had Bullock carried out research abroad he would inevitably have come across the sources Werner Maser was to publish in the early 1960s, for they were already accessible by the late 1940s, and this would have saved him from the pitfall of relying on Hitler's completely misleading autobiographical references in *Mein Kampf*. Next to *Mein Kampf* Bullock's single main source on Hitler's early life was Konrad Heiden's biography of 1936, which, as J. P. Stern in his *Hitler: The Führer and the People* quite rightly remarks, deserved fuller acknowledgment than it received. From the editor's own experience, Bullock was wise not to interview the survivors of Hitler's entourage, as later biographers such as Toland and Irving have done. Experience has shown that in many cases where interviews with former high-ranking NS officials could be cross-checked with the actual archival material, the interviews had to be discarded. Bullock's biography provided the first coherent historical portrait. Subsequent editions underwent some changes in the light of new historical findings, but the basic imbalance remained.

Little more than twenty years later Joachim C. Fest's *Hitler* appeared. If the causal interconnection of social, economic, political and ideological processes and their reflection in the thought and action of one man can be considered a decisive criterion of a modern biography, then Fest scores full marks, while in Bullock's work these factors receive only marginal, if any, attention. Fest's reflective chapters which are interspersed with his main text, for example the one on the situation after 1918, which discusses German history prior to 1914 and traces striking contours, providing insights into the development of Hitler and his uniqueness as a typical example of a specific situation. Fest's analysis of the origins of the climate within which the leadership myth and National Socialism could flourish is unique among other Hitler biographers.

It has been said that Fest all too often neglects detail for the benefit of a coherent description and interpretation of the man and the epoch he embodied. This may be true, but he cannot be accused of having departed from his initial statement that description and interpretation of Hitler's life would hardly be worth the effort if his biography were not also a biography of the period. The great merit of Fest's biography – frequently overlooked by British reviewers though much less so by American reviewers – is the well-documented conclusion that Hitler was as much a figure who integrated the many and diverse tendencies of his time as he was the person who provided events with direction and radicalism.

But Fest's work has its shortcomings too. He does nothing to give further precision to the highly ambivalent concept of Fascism, and probably his weakest passages are those in which he takes refuge in psycho-historical interpretations where he, like others, is clearly out of his depth. A more serious criticism, which does not apply to Fest alone, is that though his book is a biography of Hitler, it is, as far as the 'decision-making process' is concerned, too Hitler-centred. All decisions are traced back to Hitler. Things were not as simple as that. However much and with whatever emphasis the *Führerprinzip* may have been propagated, decisions rarely came directly from the top. As has already been shown, the National Socialist ideological indoctrination of the German armed forces did not begin with an order issued by Hitler but was initiated by the *Reichswehr* leadership itself. A number of other similar examples have already been cited.

If we turn to the Second World War, the *Barbarossa* decree, according to which all Russian political commissars were to be liquidated, and the murderous activities of the *SD* execution squads cannot, as for instance Fest does, be traced back directly to Hitler. There is not a scrap of evidence which demonstrates that Hitler exercised any direct influence upon those decisions taken by the German army high command which spelt death for millions of Russian prisoners of war. The discovery that there was no written order by Hitler which instigated the process of genocide, with which Irving makes so much play, is completely irrelevant, as Martin Broszat's contribution to this volume amply demonstrates. As head of state and supreme commander Hitler took responsibility and gave his sanction to all that was done, but this is different from arguing that everything originated in Hitler's mind and was his personal decision. After Hitler's death it was useful and of benefit to argue that every vital decision was that of the almighty *Führer* alone, even though Hitler's power did have certain limits as Edward N. Peterson's study, *The Limits of Hitler's Power*, has shown. Hitler was not simply surrounded by receivers of orders and yes-men, but by men from the civil service, the NSDAP and the armed forces high command, who shared many of his sentiments and acted accordingly, frequently taking initiatives of their own and having them sanctioned by Hitler after the event. This Hitler-centred perspective distorts Hitler as well as the history of the Third Reich as a whole.

In other works there are distortions of another kind. One of them is provided by Klaus Hildebrand in his study *Vom Reich zum Weltreich*. The NSDAP headquarters included a colonial office. Once Hitler was in power, given his preoccupation with central Europe, the colonial office had very little to do except devise ambitious colonial plans for the indefinite future. Apart from acknowledging its existence with an occasional friendly nod, Hitler took little interest in what the colonial office did since there were more urgent matters to attend to. But the endless reams of paper covered with colonial plans have here been turned into a huge volume by an able but speculative scholar. The topic may have merited a short precise monograph, but the molehill has become a mountain of irrelevance, with no practical bearing on actual events.

The same may be said of Jochen Thies's *Architekt der Weltherrschaft*, though it must be conceded that Thies, unlike Hildebrand, maintained a sense of proportion at least as far as the physical dimensions of his book are concerned. Extrapolating from Hitler's architectural plans a consistent policy of territorial expansion aiming at world empire represents an original approach and an interesting though somewhat extravagant hypothesis which finds no direct support in the actual sources. Furthermore, if one retains a critical distance to Speer's own account, which has recently encountered serious modification, and if one also considers the account of Hitler's other major architect Hermann Giesler (Speer was not, as he implicitly suggests, the only one), then one finds that the more the tide of war turned against Hitler, the more extravagant his building plans became – a demonstration of the unreality of it all.

Central to all Hitler biographies, of course, is genocide. William Carr relates Hitler's policy to a quotation in *Mein Kampf*, although something quite different emerges if it is read in context. Another trap into which this editor once stumbled himself is the speech of 30 January 1939 in which Hitler threatened the destruction of European Jewry if it should succeed in throwing the nations into yet another war. Students would be well advised to read the paragraph following that threat, which produces an entirely different connotation from that given by reading the first paragraph in isolation.

If the question is raised again whether a political biography is still a suitable instrument through which to perceive and comprehend historical developments, then even in the case of Hitler the answer must be affirmative, but the biography must not place its main weight exclusively on the significance of the individual within the context of the historical process, but also upon demonstrating the ambivalence of that process as mirrored in the individual. Any biography must show that it is not so much the personal habits and inclinations of an individual which are important but the social, political and ideological structures which shape that individual and are crystallised in his actions.

Thomas Nipperdey, along with Ernst Nolte the most important of present-day German historians, in his essay makes a plea for a return to sanity, addressed in the main, one feels, to many of his German colleagues. Historical debate about the Third Reich in West Germany is much more constricted than in the Anglo-Saxon world. The extent of this constriction is demonstrated by the fact that at the time of writing the Federal German Government is considering, with the support of the Social Democrats, the enactment of a law which would make it a punishable offence to raise public doubts on a number of 'historically established facts'.

Not only a whole school, but a whole generation of historians in West Germany has dissected many aspects of the Third Reich with great meticulousness, often guided by teachers who are anxious to wash away the NS stains on themselves. The new generation has at the same time taken a step backwards and projected the historical experience of the Third Reich on Bismarckian and Wilhelmine Germany and beyond to 1848. They are retracing the steps, though with more sophisticated methods, of propaganda tracts like Lord Vansittart's *The Nature of the Beast* and those of a host of lesser lights.

Nipperdey's plea is an appeal to reason, not an attempt to whitewash the past. He refers to the tragic legacy left by the *Kulturkampf* and the anti-Socialist legislation, but if one applies a comparative yardstick, was anti-Socialist action in France, for instance, not an immensely bloodier business than Bismarck's legislation? Was the struggle between church and state much less divisive in France than in Germany?

It is important to note that the industrialists during the Weimar Republic kept their distance from the state, but that may be said with equal validity of the Weimar's left-wing intelligentsia, and perhaps even more pertinently, because by their incessant attacks on and derision of the republic they eroded its own self-confidence, presupposing that it ever possessed any, and among the public in general undermined any confidence in the new state – the very institution which ensured their liberty of speech. The left-wing intelligentsia did have its one great hero, Benito Mussolini, but nowadays this is conveniently forgotten. In view of the endemic instability of the governments of the Weimar Republic one would not contest that there was a turn towards authority, but the call for a decisive leadership had already been raised in the days of the empire, in the light of the kaiser's vacillating leadership. 'Thank God, at long last we have a *Führerstaat*!' This exclamation by a prominent Weimar politician was not made on 30 January 1933 but in March 1930 when Dr Heinrich Brüning was appointed chancellor!

In conclusion one cannot but agree with Nipperdey that Weimar was not given a chance. Reading some of the more recent accounts about the attitudes of Germany's former opponents in the First World War to the new Republic, which describe the generosity they displayed and so on, one wonders whether it is ignorance or sheer hypocrisy which turns such phrases. Assuming that reparation payments had continued according to the Young Plan, then the last payment would be due in 1986! When they were finally cancelled it was already too late and the German electorate was in despair. Taking the extreme right and left together, 62 per cent voted against the republic in the elections of 1932. Had Weimar been given half the chance by Germany's former opponents which the Federal Republic was given after 1949, it is doubtful whether Hitler would ever have emerged from provincial obscurity. Once in power Hitler simply took what previous German governments had asked for in vain. Now the former enemies acquiesced and called it appeasement. As long as the republic lasted it was scarcely given a helping hand from within or without.

Nipperdey does not reject historical continuities, but he recognises their ambivalence and the existence of alternatives; he defines and differentiates continuities anew but refrains with cogent reasoning from formulating any dogma about 'historical inevitability'. Hitler was not inevitable.

15. The Hitler Image in the Last Half-century

WILLIAM CARR

For half a century Hitler has rarely if ever been out of the mind of my generation. It is nearly forty years since his suicide in the sordid surroundings of the Berlin bunker yet there is no sign of any diminution of interest in the Hitler phenomenon amongst historians. The reason for this lies not in Hitler's repellent personality but in the impact the National Socialist dictatorship made on the structure of the modern world.

The Second World War left Europe weak and defenceless, a shadow of its former self. It brought about a significant shift in the balance of power towards the Soviet Union; it witnessed the collapse of colonial empire first in India and south-east Asia and later in Africa; and it marked the end of a phase in the history of Germany which began with the proclamation of the German Empire in the Hall of Mirrors at Versailles in January 1871. Another reason why Hitler will be long remembered is for his complicity in the Holocaust. Even in a world growing daily more accustomed to violence and sudden death the cold-blooded murder of $6\frac{1}{2}$ million Jews can still numb the conscience of mankind. Although it is inconceivable that this monstrous figure could ever be rehabilitated, nevertheless the 'Hitler image' has

Original contribution to this volume, based on an article published in *German Life and Letters* in January 1981.

undergone significant mutations over the years. This essay will attempt to plot the changes decade by decade.

The rapid expansion of the National Socialist party in the early 1930s, Hitler's accession to power and the consolidation of the regime in the course of that decade was accompanied by a considerable output of literature, much of it fiercely polemical and ephemeral in nature, of interest today only to the antiquarian. This decade also witnessed the publication of the first serious biography of Hitler, a salutary reminder that events can be assessed dispassionately by contemporaries within the limits of the material available at the time. The author, Konrad Heiden, a German socialist and staunch opponent of Hitler, had the considerable advantage of having observed Hitler at close quarters in Munich in the early 1920s before the party hagiographers got to work and created the image of the 'omnipotent Führer'. What is remarkable about Heiden's work, looking back forty-five years later, is his objectivity. At a time when the strident dictator aroused the deepest passions Hitler emerges from Heiden's book as 'neither superman nor puppet but an interesting contemporary figure and ... the greatest disturber of mankind in world history', a measured judgement which has stood the test of time.[1]

With the outbreak of war in 1939 the propaganda machines took in all the belligerent countries and objectivity went out of fashion. Truth is invariably the first casualty of battle. In Allied countries it was usual to depict Hitler either as the ridiculous posturing figure immortalised by Charlie Chaplin in *The Great Dictator*, a film released in 1940, or more often as the incarnation of evil, an inhuman Frankenstein who had run amok and had to be destroyed at all costs to make the world safe for democracy for the second time in a generation. Initially the Allies drew a distinction between the National Socialists and the German people. But as the war progressed Hitler was soon slotted into the mainstream of German history as the natural successor of Frederick the Great, Bismarck and Wilhelm II; he was, so it was suggested, their natural heir, the latest in a line of Prusso-German militarists bent on the plunder of their neigbours and (in the twentieth century) on world domination. In this respect the constant efforts of the National Socialists to emphasise their continuity with the past in the interests of the consolidation of the regime (e.g. Potsdam Day in March 1933) [The day of the formal opening of the Reichstag, which was preceded by a ceremony in the garrison church of Potsdam, which held the remains of King Frederick William I and his son Frederick the Great. At the ceremony the Reich President von Hindenburg gave a speech, followed by one from Hitler, in both of which the 'hallowed traditions' of Prussia were invoked. *Ed.*] played into the hands of Allied propagandists.

The steps taken by the victorious Allied powers to dismantle the Prussian state and to place Germany's military leaders on trial for war crimes reveals just how deep-rooted the belief was that 'Prussian militarism' bore a major share of responsibility for two bouts of German aggression in twenty-five years. It was reflected as well in the popularity of works such as William L. Shirer's massive compilation *The Rise and Fall of the Third Reich. A History of Nazi Germany*, published as late as 1960.

The collapse of Hitler's Reich in 1945 and its division into four zones of occupation (originally intended to be temporary only) signified the end of a united Germany. A generation of German historians brought up on Hegel and Ranke were forced to take a long hard look at the course of their history. In the immediate post-war years scholars such as Friedrich Meinecke and Hans Herzfeld concluded that National Socialism was no aberration but had grown out of Germany's past. Its roots could be traced back, if not to Luther and Frederick the Great at least to the Bismarckian tradition of the *Obrigkeitsstaat* and to the xenophobic nationalism of Wilhelm II's Germany. At the same time they drew attention to similarities between National Socialism and Communism which pointed the way towards a more general and less specifically German explanation of National Socialism.[2]

It was the international situation that finally decided the course German historians were to take. Between 1946 and 1953 relations between the United States and Great Britain on the one side and Soviet Russia on the other steadily deteriorated; the western zones merged together and by 1949 two separate German states glared at each other across the Iron Curtain; Russian Communism replaced National Socialism as the bogeyman threatening the West. With the Cold War at its height in the early 1950s a German military contribution was – incredible though it seemed to many contemporaries – being actively sought to help defend Europe against the foe in the East. And in 1955 the Federal Republic became a member of the North Atlantic Treaty Organisation.

The theory of totalitarianism was a product of the Cold War. It was argued that the many similarities between National Socialism and Communism – the one-party state, the cult of the leader, the propaganda monopoly, the secret police and the disregard for human rights shown by Fascists and Communists – represented the true essence of the two creeds and were infinitely more significant than the differences in their social and economic systems. Some scholars traced totalitarianism back to Rousseau and the Jacobin Reign of Terror; others were content to see its origins in the soul-destroying effects of technology and industrialisation in the twentieth century. Because totalitarianism was seen as a general European phenomenon which had afflicted several states in the inter-war period, Germans began to feel slightly less guilty about their own past. National Socialism had not, after all, been a specifically German phenomenon born out of Germany's authoritarian past but rather a *Betriebsunfall*, an aberration from the normal developmental pattern. Added plausibility was given to the 'accident' theory by the perpetuation of the myth that Hitler was an *unperson*, a demoniacal carpet-biting maniac who in the midst of a great economic crisis had succeeded by guile and deception in seducing the German people from their true allegiance. The deceased *Führer* became a convenient scapegoat on whom sole responsibility for Germany's catastrophe could safely be pinned. In a flood of memoirs appearing in the post-war years a number of ex-generals and ex-civil servants used this alibi to exonerate themselves from all blame for their part in the crimes of the National Socialist regime.

In the 1950s what is still probably the best biography of Hitler appeared: Alan Bullock's *Hitler. A study in tyranny*, first published in 1952. At that time only a foreigner at one remove from the German scene could have declared that it was not his intention 'either to rehabilitate or to indict Adolf Hitler' but simply to let the facts of his life speak for themselves.[3] Basing his account on the mass of material produced by the Nuremberg Trial of Major War Criminals and subsequent war trials, on captured German documents and on the innumerable memoirs (not only German) published after the war, Bullock told the story of Hitler's life superbly well. While the author leaves the reader in no doubt whatsoever that Hitler was the prime mover in the events of the 1930s and 1940s, an all-powerful dictator who imposed his will on those around him, nevertheless Bullock tried to place the banal and repellent *Führer* in his historical context alongside Attila the Hun. As a piece of dispassionate historical writing Bullock's book is still far superior to the biographies written twenty years later.

The 1960s was a period of rapid advance in the study of National Socialism. Scholarly research in this decade has considerably modified the accepted picture of NS Germany with implications for the Hitler image which will be discussed later. The decade began dramatically with the appearance of a book which exerted more influence on German historical writing than any other in the last thirty years: Fritz Fischer's *Griff nach der Weltmacht. Die Kriegszielpolitik des kaiserlichen Deutschland 1914–18* (Düsseldorf, 1961). In his analysis of German aims during the First World War Fischer argued that Imperial Germany bore prime responsibility for the tragic plunge into war in 1914. This thesis (already advanced by the Italian Luigi Albertini in *The Origins of the War of 1914*, published in 1952–7) sparked off a bitter controversy in Germany before his views were fairly generally accepted by historians.[4] The particular relevance of the book for the study of National Socialism lay, however, in the clear implication that the goals of Imperial Germany had been indistinguishable from those of NS Germany. Far from being a *Betriebsunfall*, an aberration from the normal pattern, National Socialism would have to be seen in a much broader historical context. Therefore Fischer's book was instrumental in reawakening interest in the theme of continuity and discontinuity in which interest had declined in the 1950s (except in the field of Bismarckian studies) as long as totalitarianism was the fashionable creed. In the more relaxed international climate of the 1960s (after the Cuban Missile Crisis) German historians turned to this theme once again.[5]

Secondly, Fischer laid great emphasis on social and economic factors as a major cause of Germany's decision to risk war in 1914. In so doing he broke sharply with the Rankean tradition of historical writing which elevated the study of foreign policy, equated it with diplomatic history and relegated economic and social history to the periphery as a study unworthy of serious historians. Fischer's book gave an impetus to the writing of structural history, that is to the examination of those broad social, economic and cultural trends which establish the parameters within which all political decisions (including foreign policy decisions) are made. For the time being the Rankean primacy of foreign policy was dethroned in favour of an equally unbalanced primacy of domestic policy. When serious research into contemporary history began in the 1960s with the return to Germany of archival material held in the United States, pupils of Fritz Fischer were in the forefront with important studies of the structure of the Third Reich.

The popular belief that NS Germany had been a monolithic state run on rigid centralised lines by an all-powerful dictator was discredited in three important pieces of research: Hans Mommsen's study of the civil service, Richard Bollmus's investigation of Rosenberg's *Aussenpolitisches Amt* and Martin Broszat's general analysis of the NS state.[6] These studies suggested that NS Germany might be more aptly compared with a feudal empire where powerful tenants-in-chief struggled with each other to control the person of a *Führer* who showed little interest in domestic affairs and much preferred to stay aloof from power struggles until such time as he could side with the victor, that is with the faction which, in accordance with Social Darwinist principles, had emerged as the strongest. A complex of overlapping and competing authorities at all levels of the state apparatus, each striving for independence, added to the confusion and semi-anarchy of the polycratic state. It was much the same in foreign affairs, as Hans Jacobsen demonstrated in a study of the structure of foreign policy between 1933 and 1938; many organisations such as the *Aussenpolitisches Amt*, the *Auslandsorganisation* and the *Dienststelle Ribbentrop* competed with the Foreign Office and with each other to exert some (though admittedly limited) influence on the formation of foreign policy.[7]

The Hitler image presented by the 'revisionist' school differed sharply from the orthodox picture of the omnipotent dictator with his finger on the pulse of events. Mommsen saw Hitler as essentially 'a man of improvisation, experimentation and of sudden impulses', a weak dictator uncertain of the next step, reluctant to arrive at decisions if these could be postponed, and a man amenable to the influence of his immediate entourage.[8] Broszat described him as 'an indispensable integrating figure', not a prime mover but a man whose function it was to hold together antagonistic and centrifugal forces threatening to tear society apart.[9] It is only fair to point out that a majority of historians working on NS Germany – the intentionalists led by Andreas Hillgruber and Klaus Hildebrand – do not accept the arguments of the functionalists. The former point out that while an element of built-in 'authoritarian anarchy' in the Third Reich was identified over thirty years ago by writers such as Fraenkel and Petwaidic, this does not alter the fact that the will of the *Führer* remained the linch-pin of NS Germany;[10] or as Norman Rich put it even more bluntly: 'in all essential respects it was Hitler who determined German policy during the Nazi era'.[11]

Another important development in the 1960s which tended to strengthen the arguments of the intentionalists was a reappraisal of Hitler's basic philosophy of life. Just after the war it was fashionable to dismiss Hitler's ideas as a smokescreen put up by a man who ruthlessly exploited men and ideas alike in pursuit of power-political goals. This view rested in part on a misunderstanding of the testimony of Hermann Rauschning and Konrad Heiden. The former, an ex-National Socialist and one time *Gauleiter* of Danzig, in 1939 published his reminiscences of what Hitler allegedly told private meetings of party officials in the mid-1930s about his ultimate objectives.[12] Both Rauschning and Heiden did, however, make it quite clear that Hitler was an ideological fanatic as well as an unscrupulous opportunist. Bullock and other writers heeded only the second part of the message possibly because the Non-Aggression Pact Hitler signed with the Soviet Union in August 1939 had not been forgotten or forgiven by contemporaries who denounced it at the time as a cynical betrayal of western values leading directly, as it did, to a great extension of Russian control over eastern Europe.

In 1960 Hugh Trevor-Roper expressed the first doubts about this interpretation. He argued forcibly that one has only to compare Hitler's outpourings in *Mein Kampf* and in the *Second Book* (written in 1928 but only discovered in 1961) with Rauschning's account, with the *Table Talk* of 1941–2 and with the so-called *Testament* of February 1945, based on Bormann's notes, to be instantly aware of a remarkable degree of consistency throughout.[13] From this Trevor-Roper inferred that Hitler was no opportunist on the make but a genuine *Ideologe* who pursued one goal from 1923 to 1945 with fanatical determination: the acquisition of *Lebensraum* in the east to form the core of a German-dominated empire. In the course of the 1960s Eberhard Jäckel undertook the first scholarly analysis of Hitler's speeches and writings.[14] Like Trevor-Roper he came to the conclusion that the crude mixture of Social Darwinism, anti-semitism and *Lebensraumpolitik* fermenting in Hitler's head justified the status of a *Weltanschauung* and one which had, in fact, exerted decisive influence on his actions.

At the other end of the spectrum Broszat, writing from an extreme functionalist standpoint, rejects totally any explanation of National Socialism which equates it with Hitler's odd ideas. *Lebensraum*, in his opinion, was simply an 'ideological metaphor', a mechanism helping the restless National Socialists overcome internal tensions by mobilising support for an expansionist policy which had no specific goal.

It is difficult not to feel that there is an air of unreality about this whole controversy. For, as Rauschning [see pp. 13–14 above. *Ed.*] and Heiden realised long ago, to hold a set of beliefs, loosely formulated but fanatically adhered to, is not incompatible with a high degree of flexibility in manipulating situations and in determining interim objectives. Such was the case with Hitler. In the world of politics there are no examples of pure opportunism or pure fanaticism. The real problem for the historian is to plot the changing relationship between Hitler's dogmatic rigidity in matters of principle and his extreme flexibility in tactical matters.

Out of this controversy another developed in the course of the 1960s, this time concerning Hitler's alleged 'world ambitions'. [See Aigner's contribution in this volume, pp. 251ff. *Ed.*] Historians writing in the 1950s assumed that Hitler was essentially Eurocentric in his attitude with little understanding of or interest in the wider world. Günter Moltmann expressed the first doubts in 1961.[15] In 1963 Andreas Hillgruber, in a study of Hitler's strategy in 1940–1, advanced the novel *Stufentheorie*.[16] He argued that, although flexible in his tactics, Hitler operated in accordance with a clear programme. The conquest of Europe from the Atlantic coast to the Ural mountains represented only the first stage. This would be followed, long after Hitler's day, by a second phase: the struggle for world mastery between a German-dominated Europe (possibly with Great Britain as a junior partner) and the United States. The outbreak of war brought forward the timing of this operation. Hitler's demands in 1940 for colonial possessions in Africa and strategic points in the Atlantic coupled with the reactivation of the Z-Plan to build a huge navy are cited by Hillgruber as evidence of preparatory measures before the struggle for world domination. Not until the winter of 1941–2 did the exigencies of the military situation persuade Hitler that his world ambitions could not be realised.

This thesis has been elaborated by Klaus Hildebrand in a study of NS Germany's attitude to the acquisition of colonial possessions, and by Jochen Thies in a study relating Hitler's architectural plans to his world ambitions.[17]

This is not the place to enter into a discussion of the arguments advanced in support of the thesis. The present writer remains sceptical, feeling that the evidence is, on the whole, insufficient to sustain it. It seems doubtful whether Hitler, a notoriously garrulous character, had more than a general desire – like Wilhelm II – to make Germany a world power one day, not necessarily the dominant world power. The relevance of the controversy in the context of the Hitler image is that it keeps the discussion about Hitler's ideas alive and strengthens the intentionalist view that his *Weltanschauung* was a decisive factor in the total situation. What is sorely needed to correct this perspective is a broader study of the intellectual climate around Hitler. This might well show that there was no programme for world conquest but that Hitler's 'world ambitions' waxed and waned in response to the influence of individuals or groups upon him.

Finally, a feature of note in the 1960s was the beginning of a significant renaissance in Marxist studies. The official Communist pronouncement on Fascism was made in 1935 by the Comintern, when it was defined as 'the openly terroristic dictatorship of the most reactionary and most chauvinistic elements of finance capitalism'.[18] Hitler was little more than an absurd puppet with no will of his own, an agent manipulated by a small coterie of industrialists, bankers and great landowners who had financed the National Socialists from the earliest days and manoeuvred them into power at the height of the 'general crisis of capitalism'. This was the final stage in the development of monopoly capitalism when free institutions would be destroyed, the working class enslaved (more than before) and Germany would be prepared for wars of aggression to maintain the capitalist system intact.

In the German Democratic Republic (DDR), the 'agent theory' of Fascism enjoys the seal of official approval to which historians pay lip service, though this has not prevented first-class work being produced on the role of the giant industrial combines in NS Germany.[19] In the West Marxist historians had become increasingly impatient with what, it might be cogently argued, was a distortion of Marxism grossly oversimplifying complex historical phenomena. Going back to the half-forgotten 'unorthodox' works of August Thalheimer and Otto Bauer written in the 1930s and beyond them back to the writings of Karl Marx on Napoleonic France (especially 'The eighteenth Brumaire of Louis Napoleon' and 'The class struggles in France 1848 to 1850') a younger generation of Marxist historians developed a more subtle and historically valid interpretation of the events of the 1930s.[20]

These historians insist, rightly, on the structural identity of capitalism and Fascism while wisely leaving the door open to speculation (and research) into the precise nature of this relationship. Their resurrection of the 'Bonapartist theory' enables them to make an important distinction between political and socio-economic power. The argument is that in Germany (as in mid-nineteenth-century France) the bourgeoisie, fearful of the growing power of the proletariat but unable to destroy parliamentary institutions on their own, handed over political power to the National Socialists in order to retain social power in bourgeois hands. Naturally opinions differ widely about the extent to which the 'partnership' between Fascism and industry was ruptured with the passage of time. Some argue that it ended in 1936 when the NS party succeeded in establishing absolute ascendancy over the economy with the introduction of the second Four-Year Plan.[21] Others favour the view that the partnership lasted much longer for although the National Socialists controlled investment, industry was still free to run itself without party interference and to amass huge profits. But because the NS political machine was autonomous it could and did in the end force on industry the economic madness of the Holocaust and the continuation of hopeless military resistance and eventual material destruction, neither of which can by any reckoning have been in the interests of monopoly capitalism but which can be explained in terms of the doctrinal intransigence of Hitler and his followers. Such an interpretation can accommodate the plain fact that Hitler did not have, nor did he wish to have, close contact with the captains of industry; there was no equivalent of Albert Ballin (the confidant of Wilhelm II) in Hitler's petty bourgeois entourage.

Similarly in respect of foreign policy there is no evidence that industrial magnates exerted direct influence over National Socialist policy. Timothy Mason, in a recent analysis of the origins of the Second World War, rejects the proposition that a direct causal relationship existed between the mounting economic crisis in Germany in 1938–9 and Hitler's decision to attack Poland.[22] Wars have long-term causes and these Mason rightly locates in the rabid racialism and anti-Communism of the NS leadership as well as in the economic imperialism of the great industrial combines. There is no doubt that it makes more sense historically to think of the economic imperialism of the great industrial combines, whose object was the domination of markets in central and south-eastern Europe [see Alan Milward's contribution to this volume, p. 331. *Ed.*] as running in 'series parallel' with the territorial ambitions of the National Socialists. Nurtured in the same soil, they affected each other's growth but – and this is the crucial point – they were still able to act independently of each other.

One might have expected this shift away from an intentionalist to a functionalist and social-science oriented approach to be reflected, to some extent at least, in the Hitler biographies which were a feature of the 1970s. That was not the case. The reason lies only partially in the strength and influence of the intentionalist school. A powerful contributory factor was the growth of 'psycho-history', a new discipline which infused fresh life into the traditional personality-oriented biography and which has without doubt retarded the development of history into a critical social science.

What has psycho-history to offer the student of National Socialism? In theory an alluring blend of historical insight and psycho-analytical experience; in practice, however, works classed as psycho-historical turn out all too often to be written either by psychiatrists without any historical training or by historians primed with psycho-analytical jargon.

A classic example of the first category and a book which attracted wide attention was Walter Langer's *The mind of Adolf Hitler* (London, 1972). This work originated during the Second World War when Colonel William Donovan, head of the *Office of Strategic Services* in Washington (the forerunner of the CIA), asked Langer, a practising psychiatrist, to prepare a report on Hitler's mental condition. It was thought important by the OSS to try and determine whether Hitler was likely to take his own life now that the war had turned decisively against Germany. Langer gathered a team of fellow-psychiatrists together and they studied the (frequently sensational and highly unreliable) accounts of Hitler's private life and interrogated exiled Germans who claimed to have an intimate knowledge of Hitler. The report did, in fact, predict Hitler's suicide. Long after the war it was declassified and published by Langer in an amended form in 1972.

The book met with a hostile reception. Historians were critical of Langer's methodology. Having decided, after a preliminary review of the material, that Hitler was a 'neurotic psychopath', Langer and his team proceeded to evaluate the data 'in terms of probability' or, as he put it: 'Those fragments that could most easily be fitted into this general clinical category were tentatively regarded as possessing a higher degree of probability ... than those which seemed alien to the clinical picture'.[23] This methodology, while perfectly proper in psychiatry, is unacceptable to historians. Furthermore, Langer attached far too much weight to the testimony of hostile witnesses such as Otto Strasser and 'Putzi' Hanfstaengl whose dubious recollections of Hitler's allegedly bizarre sex life happened to fit the chosen clinical diagnosis.

Of the many attempts to understand the psychopathology of Hitler the most convincing to appear in the 1970s was probably Helm Stierlin's *Adolf Hitler. Familienperspektiven* (Frankfurt, 1975). An expert on family psychiatry, with much experience of American clinical practice, Stierlin argued that the hierarchical structure of the old order, where everyone knew his or her place in the scheme of things, had been destroyed by the spread of industrialisation.

As a consequence rapid social advancement was now a possibility for the young who could in this way realise their parents' frustrated social ambitions. Hitler fitted neatly into this theory as a disturbed adolescent to whom his mother had 'delegated' certain tasks. He was expected to remain dependent on her and to show her affection to relieve her of the great guilt she felt about the death of her first three children within a few months of each other. But he was also expected to make a name for himself in history and by so doing rescue her from provincial obscurity, and, finally, he was to avenge her on her husband who had tyrannised her for so many years. The tensions created in young Adolf by the contradictory demands of the 'delegacy' – to prove his affection for her he must remain at home, yet to realise other objectives he must leave her – turned him into an irascible and deeply insecure individual always seeking to project his guilt on to anyone who happened to oppose him in the slightest degree. What saved Hitler from complete emotional shipwreck was his quite fortuitous entry into politics after the war; for in this way he could at last realise the ambitions of his deceased mother. Stierlin admits freely that his explanation of the 'Hitler riddle' is highly speculative in nature. All the same it seems to this writer that the 'disturbed adolescent' theory, either in this or a modified form, is a more plausible explanation of Hitler's behaviour than those offered by Binion and Waite.[24]

Rudolf Binion's *Hitler Among the Germans* probably represents the most ingenious contribution to psycho-historical literature in the decade. Binion set out to explain the origins of Hitler's violent anti-semitism and also his belief in the necessity of eastward expansion. Contrary to the general belief that Hitler's virulent hatred of Jewry was born in Vienna before 1914, Binion argues that Hitler came from Vienna to Munich a repressed anti-semite. Only during his hospitalisation in Pasewalk in 1918, where he was recovering from the effects of a mustard gas attack which temporarily blinded him, was his anti-semitism activated. In hospital (so Binion claims) he was hypnotised by a consultant psychiatrist who wrongly diagnosed his condition as a case of hysteria. This treatment set up in

Hitler's subconscious a 'psychic continuum' between two events: the death of his mother from cancer in 1907 and the recent gas attack. Although outwardly on good terms with the Jewish doctor, Bloch, who treated his mother (unsuccessfully), like all bereaved people Hitler subconsciously hated the medical practitioner 'responsible' for her death. Furthermore, so Hitler claimed later, he received from on high a call to save Germany from the 'Jewish traitors' who had (so it was widely believed in right-wing circles) stabbed her in the back. This hallucination was, in Binion's opinion, a direct result of the hypnotic treatment. The murder of the Jews thirteen years later was the logical extension of Hitler's desire for revenge on a people who had 'murdered' his mother when Dr Bloch treated her with iodoform, a substance used at that time for the treatment of cancer and which gave off an odour not unlike the mustard gas to which he was subjected in the trenches. Binion concludes that Pasewalk was the real turning point in Hitler's life; it transformed 'a marginal loner and underling into a dynamic demonic mass leader'.[25] [On Hitler's relationship with Dr Bloch and his family, see p. 374 above. Ed.]

More ingenious still – and even less persuasive – is Binion's explanation of Hitler's fixation on eastward expansion. The starting point was the death of Klara Pölzl's [the maiden name of Hitler's mother. Ed.] three children from diphtheria; certainly a traumatic experience which, one can safely assume, would generate excessive anxiety in any mother about her next born, young Adolf. Thus maternal anxiety was transmitted to the infant through excessive feeding. Thirty years later Hitler's pre-oedipal dependence on his mother for food was translated into a political programme for the conquest of Lebensraum (i.e. feeding-ground) in the East. His mother's traumatic experience, relived by her as she nursed Adolf, coincided after the war with the attempt of the German people to relive the trauma of defeat by repeating the experience as soon as possible. Finally, Hitler's anti-semitism and his desire for eastward expansion became inextricably intertwined through the 'discovery' that 'Bolshevism' was the instrument for 'Jewish world domination'. Here for once we are on safer ground for it can be demonstrated that Rosenberg supplied Hitler with the missing link between 'Bolshevism' and 'World Jewry'. Binion's thesis has been astonishingly well received by many historians when one considers its inherent implausibility.[26] [That Hitler's anti-semitism pre-dates his meeting with Rosenberg see p. 374 above. However, there can be no doubt about the influence of Baltic Germans, among them Rosenberg and the politically much more experienced Erwin von Scheubner-Richter during Hitler's early phase, late 1919 to November 1923. *Ed.*]

Robert Waite's *Adolf Hitler. The Psychopathic God*, which appeared in 1977, is much less sensational in character. Waite, like Langer and the French psychiatrist Jacques Brosse, attaches crucial importance to the oedipal situation in explaining Hitler's psychological hang-ups. The essentials of this familiarly Freudian argument are that Hitler – so far as one can judge from the scanty evidence about his early childhood – was the victim of an arrested oedipal development; he hated his father and was overdependent on his mother. His mother fixation allied with the absence of one testicle – if we can rely on the Russian autopsy report on Hitler's charred remains – produced a deeply insecure individual who projected his aggressive drives and sense of sexual inadequacy on to convenient scapegoats in the shape of Jews. Waite adds to this analysis one further speculation: in adult life Hitler believed (erroneously) that he might have had a Jewish grandfather and this despite extensive Gestapo inquiries into his genealogical tree. This fear must have made his anti-semitism more virulent still in Waite's opinion. So he concludes that 'the German motherland became a substitute through displacement for his own mother; and the Jews, also through displacement, became a father substitute – a substitute made more real in his mind by his suspicion that his father's father might actually have been a Jew'.[27]

All explanations of the Hitler phenomenon which rest for their validity on psycho-historical insights raise two serious problems for historians. The conjectural element in all analyses of this kind must, of necessity, be extremely high simply because the diagnosis of the patient is at best second-hand. Secondly, interesting though an analysis of the psychopathology of an individual can be for a proper understanding of his actions, it cannot explain how the psychic tensions in that individual – even when properly diagnosed – are translated into political action. To suggest that the trauma of an individual coincides with the collective trauma of a whole people does not get one much further.

Furthermore the tendency of psycho-historians to concentrate on the psychopathology of the 'great men' of history (whether it be Luther, Bismarck or Hitler) deflects attention from the collective phenomena which are of prime importance in explaining the rise of National Socialism. For as one distinguished historian has remarked, 'the real problem is not Hitler's personal psychopathology but the condition of a society which allowed him to rise to power and to rule until April 1945'.[28] Long before the war that point was perceived by Wilhelm Reich when he attempted to marry Freudian psychology with Marxist insights, much to the discomfiture of fellow-Communists. In *Massenpsychologie des Faschismus* (Copenhagen, 1933) he pointed the way ahead with his well-known thesis that the lower middle class was the real mainstay of German Fascism not only for historical and economic reasons but also because of repressed sexuality in the home. A combination of economic, historical and psychic factors attracted these young men to the mumbo-jumbo of the National Socialist pseudo-religion.

As it stands, that thesis too is highly speculative. In recent years, however, much promising research has been carried out along these lines by social psychologists.[29] What emerges from their findings is ample confirmation of the coincidence between many of the prominent features of Hitler's personality – his aggressiveness, hatred of all opposition and total commitment to a cluster of paranoid beliefs – and the behavioural pattern of rank-and-file National Socialists. More studies of this kind will go some way towards turning the generalisations about collective pathology encountered in the works of psycho-historians into concrete terms capable of satisfying the more exacting criteria of professional historians.

The biographies of the 1970s, although more up-to-date on points of detail were, generally speaking, inferior to Bullock's masterpiece. The first to appear was Werner Maser's *Adolf Hitler. Legende Mythos und Wirklichkeit* (Munich-Esslingen, 1971). Maser, a somewhat controversial figure in Germany, has a very well-deserved reputation as an indefatigable researcher into obscure areas of Hitler's life. His book was not, in fact, arranged chronologically but in topics; Maser examined aspects of Hitler's career such as family antecedents, medical history, artistic ambitions, intellectual interest and military capabilities. He unearthed much fascinating material about the young Hitler especially; he dispelled several myths surrounding the man; and he corrected factual errors in previous biographies. Of particular interest was the attempt to trace the effects Hitler's illnesses had upon his conduct of military operations especially after 1942. But unfortunately Maser made not the slightest attempt to place Hitler in any kind of historical perspective, leaving the reader to infer what he or she pleased from a towering mass of detailed information. The book was essentially a source book, valuable to any student of the period but not biography in the accepted sense of the word.

In 1973 Joachim Fest's *Hitler* appeared. This was not by any means the first biography written by a German but it was instantly acclaimed as the best.[30] While it cannot in my opinion supersede Bullock's masterpiece, nevertheless as a synthesis of the secondary literature it is superior to rival biographies published in the 1970s and a tolerable runner-up to Bullock.

Fest, a former editor-in-chief for North German television, was already well known for perceptive vignettes of the leading Nazis in *Das Gesicht des Dritten Reiches. Profile einer totalitären Gesellschaft* (Munich, 1963). He realised at the outset that 'Hitler's life would hardly deserve the telling if it were not that extrapersonal tendencies or conditions come to light in it; his (Hitler's) biography is essentially part of the biography of the age'.[31] There is no doubt that Fest was much more successful than Maser and Toland in placing Hitler in a meaningful historical context. Many of Fest's comments were incisive and stimulating, although the discussion in the three 'interpolations' is often pretentious and the generalisations rather unhelpful. On the other hand, compared with Bullock, Fest's book was constructed in inverse proportion to Hitler's growing stature on the international stage; 150 pages were devoted to the war years compared with 600 on the period before 1939 and well over half of this on the years before 1933. [By comparison Bullock spent only 37 pages on Hitler up to 1919, and another 196 up to 1933 and over 550 on the years 1933–45. In terms of both a political and a personal biography it seems that Hitler's early years, as well as the development of the early NSDAP, receive rather short shrift. To some extent this was unavoidable when, as Bullock does, one relies exclusively on the scant and deliberately misleading biographical information supplied in Hitler's *Mein Kampf*. Ed.]

This was not accidental. Fest disagreed with Bullock's description of Hitler as a man driven on basically by a simple lust for power, and spent much time analysing Hitler's early career in terms of classic Freudian psychology to show that he was really a neurotic personality driven on by deep anxieties about his identity and status. From his Vienna days onward these fears found expression in hatred of one group after another in society: the bourgeoisie, the Slavs and the Jews. And once a fear-ridden German people had put him in a position of power these psychic tensions erupted into aggression. Not surprisingly in view of Fest's fixation with the personality of one man, there was no serious analysis of the socio-economic correlation between leader and led to which he constantly drew attention in the text and which is indeed one of the fundamental problems posed by the subject.

John Toland's voluminous *Adolf Hitler* was both superior and inferior to Fest. Superior in as much as it was based on some years of research: Toland, a professional biographer, interviewed over 250 survivors of the regime – generals, diplomats and close associates of the *Führer* – and extracted from them interesting nuggets of information about Hitler's private life. But whereas Fest did at least grapple with the broader issues posed by the subject, settling uneasily for 'negative greatness' as a description of Hitler, Toland offered the reader no conceptual framework whatsoever. He stated candidly at the outset that 'any conclusions to be found in it were reached only during the writing; perhaps the most meaningful being that Hitler was far more complex and contradictory than I had imagined.'[32] While it would be churlish not to concede that Toland wrote an absorbing book, it is also true to say that it was basically a narrative account short on analysis. Sources are often accepted uncritically; social and economic factors treated summarily – the notion, for example, that Hitler was a 'social leveller' must be qualified in the light of David Schoenbaum's researches into this area; and, finally, Toland refused to attempt any historical evaluation of the man in the context of his times. Like Fest Toland dabbled in psycho-history and came down in favour of Binion's rather dubious theses.

Last of all in point of time David Irving's *Hitler's War* (London, 1977). Strictly speaking, this was not biography in the accepted sense any more than Maser's. But without doubt Irving has written the best account of Hitler during the war years. Like Maser, Irving is also an indefatigable researcher who drew in his book on interviews with several survivors of the regime who were close to Hitler at his headquarters. [For the actual value of these sources see M. Broszat's evaluation of them in his contribution to this volume, pp. 390ff. *Ed.*] The English edition of the book was marred by a few pages in which the author argued, wrongheadedly, that Hitler knew nothing of the extermination of the Jews until 1943. That apart, though well-written, the book was very firmly *Führer*-centred and no attempt was made to relate Hitler convincingly to his background.

Where does this leave the Hitler image at the beginning of the 1980s? Pointing in two directions. The dichotomy is mirrored in two books: the first by Norman Stone published in 1980, the other by myself, first published in 1978 but (hopefully) different in kind from the biographies of the 1970s.

Stone's *Adolf Hitler* makes no claim to be based on in-depth research. It is, in effect, a brief biography aimed at a mass market. Within the compass of 200 pages Stone offers a highly readable outline of Hitler's career. On the other hand, while correcting some misconceptions about Hitler (notably on the Holocaust) Stone's rather flippant style leads him into other misconceptions of complex historical phenomena. Take, for example, his description of German foreign policy in the 1930s. Stone inclines to the view, advanced by A. J. P. Taylor in his *The Origins of the Second World War*, that Hitler was bluffing over Czechoslovakia and was not ready for war. This is to ignore much evidence that up to the last minute Hitler was deeply involved in the minutiae of the military preparations for the attack. And while it is true that Germany was not ready for war with the western powers, Hitler assumed that they would not intervene. Given that, his generals agreed with him that the Czechs could be defeated quickly. That he expressed strong dissatisfaction with the Munich agreement is also indisputable. In any case if Hitler was indeed bluffing over Czechoslovakia, why did he then go to war over Poland? Stone offers no explanation but merely asserts that 'Hitler determined to challenge the British (who had just guaranteed Polish independence) and to risk the war that they loudly and often threatened'.[33]

Stone's book belongs very firmly in the mainstream of the biographies of the 1970s. Stone, like Fest, Maser, Toland and Irving, assumes that the history of the Third Reich can be equated with the career of Hitler. In recent years a number of historians have begun to question the usefulness of traditional biography as a vehicle for encompassing the complexities of historical phenomena in advanced industrial societies where structural pressures force ruler and people into a position of interdependence not encountered in pre-industrial societies. To point the way to a rather different approach which takes account of the research carried out by functionalist as well as intentionalist historians, in my study of Hitler I avoided a cradle-to-grave biography, and – like Maser – concentrated on aspects of Hitler's career: the politician struggling for power, the dictator and his role in policy-making, his career as a military commander, his illnesses, and his ideological prejudices.[34] This was not in the hope of rivalling Maser's extremely thorough investigations into the fringes of Hitler's life but rather to try and come to grips with a problem of fundamental importance to historians; the fluctuating relationship between Hitler's personal psychopathology and the structural determinants of the period.

How successful this book was is for the critic, not the author, to say. Nor does he suggest that all biographers of Hitler have failed to anchor him firmly in his proper historical context. What he would claim is that once due emphasis is laid on the structural determinants of a period one is more likely to become aware of the historical parameters within which the 'great men of history' actually influence events. This is not to retreat into a facile determinism turning Hitler into little more than a figurehead. On the contrary, all the research which has been done into the Third Reich confirms the abiding importance of his role. What structural history does is to 'direct attention more to the conditions, to the limits of and the possibilities inherent in human behaviour as recorded in history rather than to the motives of individuals, and to decisions and actions in themselves; it throws light more on collective phenomena than on the individuality of phenomena'.[35]

The advantages of adopting this approach can most easily be illustrated by considering a specific issue: the question of Hitler's responsibility for the Holocaust on which research by functionalist historians has shed new light. Hitler's biographers (with two exceptions) take the view that he was solely responsible for the extermination policy. To Bullock that policy was the 'logical realization of views he had held since his twenties'. Bullock never doubted that 'the man in whose mind so grotesque a plan had been conceived was Hitler'.[36] Fest agreed that the murder of European Jewry could not be explained as a primitive act of revenge to even up the score now that the war was going badly for Germany; on the contrary, it was 'fully consistent with Hitler's thinking and was, given his premises, absolutely inevitable'.[37] The use of gas by the extermination squads was, in Fest's view, related to Hitler's experiences during the First World War; he quoted the well-known passage in *Mein Kampf* where

Hitler declared that 'twelve or fifteen thousand of these Hebrew corrupters of the people' should have been exposed to poison gas like soldiers in the trenches: 'Twelve thousand scoundrels eliminated in time might have saved the lives of a million real Germans.'[38] Maser is equally adamant, on the basis of passages in *Mein Kampf* and on Hitler's comments in the 1920s, that Hitler believed from the very beginning that the conquest of *Lebensraum* would be fruitless unless accompanied by the extermination of the Jews. Finally, Toland states bluntly that 'He [Hitler] alone conceived the Final Solution. . . . Without him there would have been no Final Solution.'[39]

The exceptions are Stone and Irving. Although Stone is an intentionalist, he inclines in his all-too-brief excursion into the Holocaust towards functionalist arguments without advancing any clear reason for this preference. Irving, another intentionalist, approaches the matter very differently. His thesis is that Himmler was responsible for the decision to murder the Jews of Europe, and that in order to relieve the pressure on the *Führer*, now totally absorbed in the conduct of the war, he deliberately kept him in the dark about the operation until 1943. It is frankly inconceivable that Himmler, an underling utterly subservient to Hitler, would have been capable of such an undertaking without express approval from his master. [In the light of what Himmler already knew in 1943 about the anti-Hitler conspiracy, that utter subservience is open to doubt, quite apart from his actions between February and late April 1945. *Ed.*] Nor could knowledge of an operation of this magnitude have been concealed from a man who, though he did not concern himself overmuch with domestic policy, nevertheless always had his finger on the pulse of great events and had always shown a keen interest in the persecution of the Jews. The absence of a written order authorising the extermination campaign, a point to which Irving attaches much importance, is not proof of Hitler's innocence. It is true that in respect of the German doctors engaged in the euthanasia campaign between 1939 and 1941 Hitler did sign a written order to allay their consciences. But Himmler, *Reichsführer* of the *SS*, needed no more than a verbal order from his *Führer* to carry out his grisly task. Nor does Irving's use of documentation inspire confidence in the thesis. Far too much importance is attached to witnesses such as *SS* General Karl Wolff, Himmler's chief-of-staff and liaison man at Hitler's headquarters, who was the first to suggest in the 1950s that Himmler was to blame for the Holocaust, while the testimony of a witness such as Otto Ohlendorf, a man deeply implicated in the murders, is dealt with cursorily.

There are obvious methodological dangers in stringing together quotations from Hitler's speeches and writings, as intentionalists tend to do, in an attempt to prove that Hitler was committed to the physical extermination of the Jews from the beginning to the end of his career. This is to make no allowance for changing circumstances which may have moderated (or intensified) the virulence of his anti-semitism. For example, after his release from Landsberg prison in 1924 the vulgar anti-semitic rabble rouser worked hard to transform himself into the philosopher-statesman waiting in the wings for disaster to overtake the republic. In those years Marxism and republicanism became the main targets for his invective, and his anti-semitism was muted in tone. Certainly by 1938 the virulent strain was again in the ascendancy, and with the outbreak of war his hatred of the Jews, whom he held responsible for the hostilities, clearly intensified. Even so, recent research suggests that there are at least some grounds for thinking that the decision to murder European Jewry was *ad hoc* in nature and that it is not explicable simply and solely in terms of one man's ideological hang-ups.[40]

The same is generally true of NS policy towards the Jews between 1933 and 1941. The pressure of external events, the shifting power structure in the Third Reich and the influence of individuals close to the *Führer* seem to have been just as important in determining policy as Hitler's personal inclinations and the inherent radicalism of the party. This is illustrated, to take one example from the pre-war period, by *Reichskristallnacht*, the pogrom on 9/10 November 1938 which heralded the beginning of a more radical period in the persecution of the Jews. The pogrom cannot really be attributed entirely to Hitler's desire for blood-letting as a substitute for the war the western powers had just cheated him of at Munich. Other factors were involved. The dismissal of Blomberg, Fritsch and Neurath, the decline of Schacht and the rise of Göring and Ribbentrop altered the internal balance of power in favour of the radicals. Schacht with his international financial connections sharply opposed radical measures against the Jews; but Göring was contemptuous of foreign opinion and anxious to make a clean sweep of the Jews. Important, too, was the influence of Goebbels, seeking to ingratiate himself with the *Führer*; his intervention was probably decisive in persuading Hitler to agree to the pogrom. Nor can one entirely discount the possibility that the great industrial combines who were able to absorb the small but lucrative Jewish firms when the economy was 'Aryanised' after the pogrom may have been a factor of importance. [However, legislation pointing in this direction had already been enacted on 6 July 1938. *Ed.*]

Nor does the evidence on the whole suggest that Hitler ever had a clear idea of what should happen to the Jews beyond turning them into pariahs. For that reason he fell in readily with whatever 'solution' of the 'Jewish problem' was in vogue in the corridors of power. Before the war Hitler seems to have gone along with the emigration policy favoured by Himmler, a rising star in the Nazi firmament. The outbreak of war put a stop to that policy but opened the door to other 'solutions'. [In practice a stop had been put to emigration prior to the outbreak of war. The USA were not prepared to relax their immigration quota in favour of a large influx of German and European Jews. Emigration to Palestine was cut by the British mandatory power, in response to an Arab wave of protest and violence against the 'undesired' immigrants. *Ed.*] At first Hitler favoured the concentration of all Polish Jews and subsequently western Jews in ghettos in eastern Poland as a prelude to the creation of a huge Jewish reserve between the rivers Vistula and Bug. Then in the summer of 1940 he toyed with the Madagascar plan for shipping western Jews to that island. British naval superiority ended any hope of implementing that plan. Possibly in the summer of 1941, when the Russian collapse seemed imminent, he entertained briefly the idea of establishing a Jewish reserve east of the Urals. Stiffening Russian resistance ruled out that 'solution'. Only then did the 'final solution' – the physical annihilation of the Jews – take shape.

The circumstances surrounding the decision to murder the Jews are not likely to be clarified definitively. While intentionalists insist that Hitler was the originator of the Holocaust, functionalists such as Mommsen argue – more realistically in my opinion – that the Holocaust was 'in no way attributable to Hitler alone but to the Third Reich's complex structure of decision-making which led to a progressive and cumulative radicalisation'.[41]

A number of factors combined to make mass murder a feasible proposition. Of course, Hitler's decision in the spring of 1941 to wage a savage racial war in the Soviet Union was of prime importance. To murder the 'Jewish-Bolshevik' ruling elite *Einsatzgruppen* (special squads first used in Poland to murder the Polish ruling class) were set up. [Originally *Einsatzgruppen* were already set up in 1938 when in the course of the *Anschluss* they moved into Austria. They operated also in the Sudetenland and Czechoslovakia, and after the outbreak of war with full force in Poland. *Ed.*] Between June and December 1941, with the connivance of the German army, these squads murdered half a million people including many Jews who were not *apparatchiki*. Meanwhile in eastern Poland, in the overcrowded ghettos, living conditions, never good, steadily deteriorated as Jews from western Europe started to arrive in large numbers. As already indicated Russian resistance made their transportation eastwards impossible. Radical action was already being taken at local level to relieve these pressures; in October hundreds of newly arrived Jews were summarily shot at Riga, Minsk and Kowno; and in November at Chelmno, under the jurisdiction of the rabid anti-semite *Gauleiter* Greiser, a mobile gas chamber was installed to murder the Jews in a neighbouring ghetto. Against this background, so the functionalists argue, Hitler and Himmler must have reviewed the situation. Whether Hitler or Himmler proposed the extension of local murders into genocide at some specific point in time, or whether they merely noted the gradual escalation of local murders up to the Wannsee Conference in January 1942 we do not know.

This explanation does not in any way exonerate Hitler from his heavy responsibility for the Holocaust. Indeed, without his constant support for and fanatical encouragement of the dreadful work between 1942 and 1944 it is not inconceivable that, as the military situation deteriorated still further, mass extermination, which made heavy demands on badly needed transport, might have been suspended. What the functionalists succeed in doing in respect of the origins of the Holocaust, is to place the horrific event in a more credible historical perspective where the general radicalisation of Nazi attitudes towards the Jew, the changing military situation in the east and the existence of organisational structures geared to mass murder are seen to play a significant role alongside the brutal anti-semitism of the head of state.

16. 1933 and the Continuity of German History

THOMAS NIPPERDEY

I

In treating this subject we can only hope to go beyond mere trivialities and gain in knowledge if we approach it as a problem. Continuity becomes a problem particularly when we regard the element of discontinuity as well as the contradiction in that which we call continuity; and when we ask ourselves what meaning the category continuity has for history and historians. To what extent does the continuity of German history explain what happened in 1933, and to what extent can that which came before be explained from the perspective of 1933?

No one would expect the complete history of Germany to be presented in a nutshell, in relation to 1933, in a short paper. Nor will specific periods or major problems in German history be discussed. The intention is rather first to consider the importance of some aspects of continuity and discontinuity, and then the sense of the category of continuity in general. In doing so, I shall try to remain concrete and repeatedly call to mind what is generally known about German history. In the first part I shall distinguish my position from, on the one hand, interpretations in which the element of continuity hardly plays a part, and, on the other

Lecture held at the University of York, spring term 1977, and made available for this volume.

hand, from interpretations in which the importance of
continuity is so enlarged that precise questions can no
longer be raised. In the second part I shall deal with the
subject matter itself, that is the content of the continuity
that binds 1933 with the main strand of German history.
And thirdly I shall raise the question: what meaning can
the category of continuity have for historical investigation?

One more preliminary remark. An approach that handles
continuity as a problem rather than as a foregone conclusion
arouses the suspicion of being an apologia. One is
uncomfortably reminded of the strange mixture of self-pity
and self-justification that characterised a part of post-war
German historical literature. In view of this is not the so-
called 'critical perspective' the only legitimate approach to
German history? In the last part I shall show why I hold
the alternative 'criticism' vs 'apology' to be theoretically
useless or why any meaningful approach must go beyond
these alternatives. From the outset I must make it clear
that our situation in 1977 is completely different from the
situation after 1945. Unlike the historians Meinecke, Ritter
or Dehio who wrote on this subject after 1945, no historian
of my generation would say that *we* (i.e. we Germans)
would have done this or that in 1870 or 1890. This
identification is a thing of the past. We regard German
history from a detached point of view; above all the
imperialist phase of German history between 1871 and 1945
is no longer a nostalgic memory, but rather something
foreign, if not lurid or hostile. Differing opinions regarding
history are no longer able to arouse political emotions. For
this reason it seems to me that the basis for an apologia of
German history has disappeared, and this in turn gives the
discipline another kind of freedom.

First of all, I want to discuss a few aspects that speak
against (an overemphasis on) continuity; obvious apologetic
opinions such as those viewing 1933 as an unintentional
accidental breakdown in German history need not concern
us, they have no explanatory value and for scientific
purposes they simply do not exist. Similar and yet essentially
different are those interpretations which explain 1933 either
by the singular (demoniac) character of Hitler, or by a

singular string of events of the Weimar Republic – the economic crisis preceded by a period of inflation, the aftermath of defeat – or by both. Such interpretations do not answer the question why an exceptional individual, which Hitler surely was, should have been successful in Germany; why the economic crisis which affected all industrial countries should have had these consequences and why a defeat like that of 1918 should have produced precisely these results 14 years later. That is why these interpretations are of no use. Nevertheless, it is not superfluous to mention them. They remind us that the historical process is not entirely determined; that there is on the one hand an element of contingency, or of coincidence in history. It is obviously nonsense to maintain that Hitler was a historical necessity: he was not. On the other hand these interpretations remind us that the immediate or proximate causes have considerable weight in a series of determining factors; that the process itself is not completely determined before the event in question has actually taken place; that, for example, without the Great Depression 1933 is hardly imaginable. When considering the question of continuity one can only look for preconditions which explain why in singular, non-predictable constellations precisely these consequences occurred.

A different and much more plausible explanation, beyond the question of German continuity, is the concept of Fascism. Fascism is on the one hand a European phenomenon, and even more so 'the crisis of democracy' – of the 25 European democracies from 1919, for example, only 10 were left in 1938. And on the other hand Fascism is a phenomenon belonging to a particular period of the epoch set off by the drastic events of the First World War, the Russian Revolution, and the precarious victory of liberal democracy – Fascism was an answer to this particular situation. Therefore it is a phenomenon *sui generis*, not to be reduced to prior events, or to be derived from prior events. It is something new. Consequently what becomes important is not the uniqueness of German history, but rather what it has in common with other national histories, such as the history of Italy. Without doubt the revival of the concept of Fascism by scholars can no longer be excluded from our explanations of 1933. The year 1933 therefore can be explained in terms of its period and the parallel nature of the European movements of this time. To this extent the concept of Fascism modifies the explanatory value of all interpretations that base their arguments on the continuity of German history alone. But this by no means solves our problem. The question of continuity remains, even in connection with the concept of Fascism. First of all, even though Fascism was not just successful in Germany alone, why was it precisely in Germany that it prevailed, whereas in the industrial nations of the West or the democracies of the North, and even in the authoritarian non-democracies of east, central and southern Europe it was not successful? And secondly, why was it that German National Socialism became the most radical and violent form of Fascism? Both of these questions call for a specific explanation based on particularly German conditions. The importance of continuity may be modified by the epochal and new elements in Fascism, but the importance, nevertheless, remains.

One must of course guard against stretching the concept of continuity too far. 1933 stands in a continuum with all prior events in German history, but when one says that, one equates continuity with causality, and discontinuity, the prerequisite of all talk about continuity, is eliminated as a category. Such an all-encompassing use of continuity becomes trivial. But this is not what we mean when we speak of continuity. The fact that there was a strong Marxist labour movement in Germany is certainly one of the causes for the use of anti-Marxist National Socialism; without socialism, no National Socialism. But it would be sheer nonsense to speak of continuity here. Continuity presupposes a similarity of parts among which continuity is said to exist; it presupposes a partial identification.

If one talks about continuity in this sense, it seems to me to be necessary to disassociate my position from three currently held models of continuity. The first views 1933 as a part of European continuity – an uneasiness with regard to modernity, the phenomenon of alienation, the crisis of liberalism, the revolutionary mobilisation of the masses, the totalitarian and anti-institutional tendency of radical democracy – Social Darwinism, imperialism and finally secularisation. These are European phenomena and elements of European continuity that cannot be overlooked. But they do not explain why it was in Germany that Fascism was successful. The same holds true, paradoxically, for the orthodox-Marxist interpretation which traces Fascism back to monopolistic capitalism. The fact that the majority of capitalist systems did not become Fascist and that Italy was not yet a capitalist system in the true sense of the word shows the weakness of this approach, and shows in particular that in order to explain 1933 additional assumptions must be made which do not follow from the structure of capitalism, but rather from the continuity of German history.

Beside these general aspects of continuity there is a kind of thesis regarding German continuity that Dahrendorf has called 'Tacitus-hypotheses' because they go back so far. Edmond Vermeil went back to the Middle Ages. He tried to see a development from the politics of the German emperors to the idea of national mission. From the parallelism of the Hanseatic League and mysticism he attempted to derive the explosive mixture of expansion and national inwardness. Another author goes back to the Battle of the Teutoburg Forest since thereby the Romanisation of Germany was prevented and thus the way opened to 1933. And A. J. P. Taylor after all reckons the last 450 years of German history to this continuity. It has often been maintained that there is a straight development from Luther, who is said to have fostered the obedience of the subject and the specifically German non-political inwardness, to Frederick the Great, the protagonist of Prussian militarism and aspiration for power, to Bismarck, Nietzsche and Hitler.

No one would deny that there are long-term connections, but to assume continuity here is unhistorical. Such constructions are contradicted by the Lutheranism in democratic Sweden and by the absolutist power politics in non-Prussian Europe in the eighteenth century. Of course it is difficult to say how far back one should go. It is undeniable that Bismarck's empire stands in continuity with the Third Reich. But if one goes back further, should one also include the failure of the Liberals in the Revolution of 1848, the cessation of the reforms after 1815, the, in the final analysis, negative German reaction to the French Revolution, the idealising of the State and trust in an evolutionary development, the early fixation on national goals? And is it not then necessary to include the fact that enlightened absolutism itself prevented a revolutionary situation through its reforms? In this way of thinking it seems difficult to set up criteria for differentiating the meaningful from the absurd. I shall return to this later. For the moment I want to concentrate on the continuity from the Bismarck era up to 1933. How the Reich was founded and how the industrial revolution developed – these are the basic facts in the pre-history of 1933.

Finally, the last qualification. There is of course that which we could call a counter-continuity – the continuity of the democratic, the liberal movement – even the Weimar Republic was an alternative within the course of German history. The Resistance to Hitler had its continuity as well, just as the Federal Republic has its own. But these are not the dominant continuities of German history. Nevertheless, a counter-continuity reminds us again that the strands of German history that go further back into the past are not so uniform or determined as one might think; that continuity only produces a certain degree of probability in an attempt at a causal explanation. Having made these qualifications, I shall now turn to certain aspects of German history from the 1860s onwards.

II

The Prusso-German national state, the German Reich, existed from 1866–71 up to 1945. This Reich was a major power. Seen in terms of power politics, its foreign policy shows a high degree of continuity. This is particularly obvious for any foreign observer. Dehio described this as a policy of hegemony. Hillgruber has provided a more modern and detailed study of this continuity: how the claim to sovereignty in foreign policy necessarily drove the Reich, in connection with European imperialism, out of its middle position in Europe to world politics and to an increase in power; how this assertion of power continued in a somewhat modified form in the revisionist foreign policy of the Weimar Republic with the goal of regaining the position of a great power, and how it culminated in Hitler's *Weltmacht* policy, and how the consensus among the ruling classes regarding Germany's position as a great power extended from the *Kaiserreich*, through the republic up to Hitler. Even Hitler's radical *Lebensraum* policy stood in continuity to the concepts not only of the Pan-Germany, but also the General Headquarters in the First World War, the conception of the block-free, self-sufficient extended area. This was the bridge from the classical continuity of the great power to the revolutionary change given to it by Hitler. Hitler's voters and allies in 1933 could not help but see him in the continuity of German great-power policy.

It is obvious that a proportion of the old power elites worked for the downfall of the republic and enabled Hitler's seizure of power, being convinced that Hitler belonged to their camp or could be used as their tool. The *Junkers*, the military, the higher bureaucracy, the leaders of the German National People's Party, a good part of traditional Germany that can be symbolised by the name Hindenburg – these old elites may have lost their position as political leaders under the republic, but they still maintained considerable, institutionally protected influence. Keeping in mind these limitations, one can speak of a continuity of their position of power. It is somewhat more difficult in the case of the leading representatives of capitalism, whose position of power extends back uninterruptedly to the *Kaiserreich*. They kept their distance to the republic, they did nothing to stabilise democracy, they tended to admire authoritarian models of the government. All this is clear. On the other hand they did not play the decisive part in the rise of National Socialism or in Hitler's assumption of power. Their relation to National Socialism was altogether ambivalent. The continuity that is readily seen here is an ideological construction, which merely speaks of the essence of capitalism and Fascism without taking the facts into consideration.

Setting up a continuity between the system of capitalism which prevailed in Germany, the system of organised capitalism characterised by concentration, cartels, powerful interest groups and state intervention and the year 1933 seems to me to be extremely unlikely. This is not a problem peculiar to Germany. One need only think of the USA; and it cannot be demonstrated that organised capitalism stood in a closer relationship to National Socialism than unorganised capitalism. Looking at the statistical-economic side, the German social structure, and finally the class structure produces no novel striking insights. It is much more similar to that of the western industrial states than to that of Italy – a continuity that could explain 1933 cannot be found here, or at least not at the moment.

The types of continuity at which I shall now look could be grouped together under terms such as political culture, political behaviour or mentality. We are concerned with collective values and dispositions to which National Socialism could appeal. First of all there was German nationalism which had separated itself from its liberal-universalist roots and which had become something hot-tempered, aggressive and chauvinistic; a nationalism which was unsure of its own identity, which allegedly had come too late and got less than its share, the nationalism of a nation belated and unfinished; a nationalism that took on a more radical form after 1918, and that Hitler (this must be seen perfectly clearly), joined together with another kind of nationalism, the anti-*étatist*, irredentist greater German *völkisch* nationalism of the conquered of 1866. Then there is the militarism, which goes back to the older Prussian tradition, the special position of the military and the prestige of military values and ways of life: command, obedience, discipline, determination, struggle, and the intensification of military values in the Wilhelminian period; ideologising, making light of warfare or glorifying it, turning politics in a machiavellian and militaristic direction, reducing it to the element of power struggle. National Socialism stood in this tradition and could appeal to it all the more; the mass of its supporters could not recognise the inherent, absolute resolve to warfare, but the obvious playing with war met with no resistance.

Then there is of course the continuity associated with the authoritarian state, the *étatist* confidence in *Doktor von Staat*; confidence in the state's expertise, in the impartiality and non-partisanship of bureaucracy, in its strict organisation, efficiency and welfare services, the desire for authority and leadership and since Bismarck, the priority that authority had had over freedom, since the dangers of freedom, anarchy and inefficiency seemed more threatening than the danger of order. Even more crucial was the corresponding reserve or aversion towards democracy, parliamentarianism and political parties, towards liberal individualism and a pluralistic-antagonistic society. To this also belongs the much described *Sonderweg* of German political thinking.

The move was away from enlightenment, natural law, rationalism, common sense, away from universalism and individualism to the polemical setting up of opposites: culture as opposed to civilisation, community as opposed to society, elites as opposed to the masses, organic variety as opposed to the levelling effects of equality. In other words the turn was away from 1789 and away from the western tradition, as expressed in the misconceived ideas of 1914 or much more enticingly in Thomas Mann's *Reflections of a Non-political Man*. In addition we could mention the harmonistic model of society where competition, conflict and pluralism have no place. We could also mention what has polemically been called 'the inwardness protected by power', ascribing a higher value to an unpolitical attitude and a negative value to a political one. The anti-parliamentarianism and anti-liberalism of National Socialism attached itself to these values and norms. I want to emphasise a particular continuity which grew out of this political mentality and practice, since it was especially important for 1933. This was the expectation of certain classes and groups that the state would protect their status, an expectation particularly promoted by the Wilhelminian state. This applies to the so-called middle classes, peasants, craftsmen, and small shopkeepers, and particularly to the white-collar workers. As the National Socialists developed their slogans aimed at the middle classes they could refer to such protective expectations, which were increased by the disappointment over the failure of democracy in the economic crisis.

One can speak of a socio-psychological continuity, which can help explain not only National Socialism itself but also the response that it found. I am thinking of the simultaneity of the unsimultaneous, the complex mixture of pre-modern and modern social strata as well as attitudes. In socio-psychological terms we are concerned with the uncertainty caused by the pace of modernisation, the uneasiness and resistance towards modernisation, of which one was at one and the same time a part and also wanted to be part. National Socialism, with its mixture of modern and pre-modern or anti-modern tendencies, belongs, together with its answer to the crisis of modernity, within this continuity. There are two basic elements of National Socialism besides anti-liberalism and warfare which I have not yet mentioned: anti-semitism and anti-Marxism. Anti-semitism, of course, the most hideous aspect of National Socialism, stands in a German and Austrian continuity. However, although restraints against anti-semitism were broken down during this process, anti-semitism does not belong to the dominant trends of German continuity. Hitler did not come to power in 1933 because he was an anti-semite, that fact was simply accepted, evil though it may have been. Anti-Marxism, however, is a different story. National Socialism can be defined as nothing less than a new, militant-extremist form of anti-Marxism. Its opposition to parliamentary democracy stemmed from the fact that the parliamentary system and liberalism were in the view of the National Socialists the basis for the success of the Marxists. Anti-Marxism was part of a vital, political tradition in Germany. The anti-Socialist effect necessarily increased in the republic as the Socialists demanded their share of power, and as the Communists – who were at the same time creatures, brothers and deadly enemies of the socialists – threatened the bourgeois world with destruction. This contributes a great deal to an explanation of 1933. I do not, however, view this anti-Socialism as a specific kind of German continuity. The prevailing opinion that the class struggle in Germany was intensified by the overlaying of capitalist and feudal privileges, by the non-integration of the workers, gives me cause to doubt when I observe the European class struggles and anti-Socialism of the European bourgeoisie. This anti-Marxism is, unlike anti-liberalism, not something specifically German. Two consequences can be drawn so far from this summary.

Much as these types of continuity contribute to an explanation of 1933 – in particular to the attitude of traditional Germany and the conduct of the voters – the essential thing for Hitler and National Socialism is that he latched on them and in the end disrupted them. It is essential to observe this qualitative break. There is a proximity to National Socialism, characteristic of traditional Germany, but this proximity is by no means identity, it changes into enmity. It was no coincidence when Hitler towards the end of the war remarked that his arrangement in 1933 with the conservatives, the established powers, was his greatest mistake. It was no coincidence that his struggle against a bastion of tradition, against Christianity, was planned to assume radical form after the final victory. It was no coincidence that resistance came out of the same continuity of traditional Germany. Hitler's conception of a world power on a racial basis constitutes a break with the classical, great-power continuity. The difference between Bismarck, Bethmann-Hollweg and Stresemann on the one hand and Hitler on the other cannot be seen in relative terms. The difference here is not quantitative, but rather qualitative. The same applies to Hitler's total subordination of domestic policy to fit his goals of foreign policy – or the elimination of this distinction. The 'Greater Germanic Empire' based on race was precisely the negation of the idea of the nation: it was precisely the special position of the military that was annulled; the military was put in the hands of political commissars and the ideologues of the SS. The totalitarian state, even in its anarchic shape, was not the traditional authoritarian state, which was founded on institutions, bureaucracy and not least also on law. The totalitarian society with its political religion was not the authoritarian society with its separation of the political and non-political. The capitalist private enterprise system was not the centralised 'command-economy' of ten years of the Third Reich. The expectations of the middle classes were no more fulfilled than those of the old elites. These elites made Hitler's seizure of power possible – what they did not do was to create National Socialism or enable its rise. One may use terms like bridge, dialectical conversion or *Aufhebung*, but a perspective on continuity that draws abstractions from these opposites explains nothing, just as the counter-term discontinuity would explain nothing.

Continuity is actually a number of different continuities. Not only are National Socialist continuity and anti-democratic continuity to be distinguished from each other, but the latter consists in turn of a number of varying, even opposing continuities. The Prussian *étatist* idea of the state, and the *volkisch* anti-*étatist* nationalism, the authoritarianism of the old elites, the protective desires of the middle classes, capitalistic and middle-class anti-Socialism, the criticism of democracy stemming from the Youth Movement and the ideas of the corporate state, the tradition of the non-political and the definitely political enmity towards democracy: these are all different continuities. The same difference can be seen in the fact that the national revisionism and *Anschluss* of Austria formed parts of the Weimar coalition consensus in foreign policy. These continuities do not constitute a unified nexus or syndrome. The success of National Socialism can be explained precisely by its omnibus structure which joined together several continuities, having made the appropriate promises to each. It would, of course, be foolish to overlook the fact that there were forerunners for these connections, for these anti-democratic, right-wing constellations and combinations, that the proximity of the factors mentioned varied. But it is an abstraction to construct a unity of several kinds of continuities using an either/or classification (revolution or counter-revolution, democracy or anti-democracy, progress or reaction) and have all this culminate in 1933. Nothing is explained by it. For Hitler's seizure of power occurred in 1933 and not earlier, the history of the years prior to 1933 is characterised by the very fact that these continuities come together. 1933 does not just mean an intensification and radicalisation, but a new combination of continuities. Having made this distinction we can say on the one hand that 1933 did *not* develop from *the continuity* of German history, but that, on the other hand, 1933 is closely connected with several *dominant continuities* in German history, and that without reverting to these continuities no historical explanation is possible. This is to be borne in mind when I return in the final part to making certain critical reservations on the applicability of the category of continuity to German history.

III

It would be naïve to think that continuity lies simply in the subject matter itself. Continuity is a category of historical consciousness by which we select and organise historical material. Reality can always put up resistance to such attempts at organisation, but continuity remains a category of the retrospective observer. Up to now we have looked back to the continuities of 1933 in order to explain 1933; our direction went from later events to earlier ones and our story would have to have been one that began in 1933 and proceeded backwards, going in the opposite direction to the actual course of time. I now want to turn the direction of my inquiry around: I will try to explain, let us say, 1871, and the question is if and how we can make use of the continuity and real course of time that led to 1933. In other words, not what 1871 – the earlier event – has to contribute to an explanation of 1933 – the later event – but rather what 1933 has to contribute to an explanation of 1871; not the question of the history that came before, but rather the question of the effects these historical events have had upon a certain kind of historiography. There is today a widespread tendency to proceed this way. This school places an explanation derived by a functional, quasi-teleological approach beside a causal explanation and an explanation of the intentions of historical persons. We could call the representatives of this approach the continuity-historians.

For them the logical distinctions we have made so far do not apply. To them 1933 becomes the central question, the tendencies that led to 1933 become the central, dominating ones. These continuity-historians are in many ways connected with the so-called 'critical approach', that is the approach that measures and criticises the past on the basis of our own values and assumes for German historiography for example the task of converting Germany to a peaceful, progressive emancipated democracy. Whoever does not approach the past in this way, assumes, as they believe, an affirmative and thereby apologetic stance. The 'critical' historians proceed, as it were, by putting the past on trial. The historian assumes the part of the prosecuting counsel and in the end, of course, the part of the judge. In this trial guilt is then assigned, if need be, under extenuating circumstances. The popular guilty parties of today are no longer the *Junkers* and the military alone, but the conformist bourgeoisie and the social democratic leadership.

My thesis is that the critical, continuity-approach is not adequate. I shall substantiate this first with a number of examples. Ernst Fraenkel remarked that German parliamentarianism lacked a period of patronage and corruption that would have made it able to govern. Dahrendorf is of the opinion that Bismarck's social insurance policy weakened the chances of freedom to the advantage of the state, and therefore he puts this policy in a continuity with 1933. Sell saw nationalism as the tragedy of liberalism, and considered the anti-national Metternich to be a quasi-liberal. Stadelmann saw the weaknesses of German democracy grounded in the reforms of enlightened absolutism, reforms which prevented a democratic revolution. The fateful decisions of the founding period of the Reich, the annexation of Alsace and the *Kulturkampf* would not have been made any differently by a liberal-democratic Germany than they were by Prusso-authoritarian Germany. It was precisely the early introduction of universal suffrage that decisively weakened German liberalism. The authoritarian government in Bavaria before 1914 was more progressive than its democratically elected parliament. The vertical social mobility of the students in Germany was higher than in any of the western European democracies. The egalitarian effect brought about by the modernising of German society after 1933 was one of the most important results of the 'Brown Revolution'.

It is obvious that what we judge to be positive or negative, good or bad, is in many ways intertwined: on the one hand intertwined under the aspect of simultaneity – universal suffrage and weakening of the liberals; and on the other hand under the aspect of sequence – National Socialism and the modernising of society. Our value conceptions, in life as in history, are not to be found together on one side; the good do evil and the evil good and usually there is a mixture of both. That which we do not particularly like emerges among those in whose tradition we would gladly stand and vice versa. The democrats are frequently nationalists, non-pacifist, even anti-semitic. If one looks at the Anglo-Saxon democracies they do not rest, as our values would like to have it, on rationality, but partially on non-rational foundations. The famous authoritarian family existed happily alongside radical-democratic France, liberal England, and authoritarianism in Germany: the corrupt cities existed alongside American democracy, free academic research alongside the German authoritarian state. The liberal state was no jot less a class state than the authoritarian state. Bismarck was not a nationalist, his opponents – *Grossdeutsche* and Socialists, Catholics and Democrats – by no means of the same opinion, and so on. Reality is not unambiguous, it is not particularly homogenous as the 'continuity-historians' demand; instead it is contradictory and ambiguous. It is, to use an old-fashioned word, tragic, that is, full of insoluble contradictions. It is not a system in which everything is uniformly ordered, as science would like to have it. It does not yield to our 'either/or', it is moved by other conflicts than the 'continuity-historians' allow to be seen. We cannot comprehend social insurance and universal suffrage under the perspective of 1933.

No one would underestimate the importance of the Prussian military-*Junker* complex, or the bureaucratic-authoritarian complex, or of the so-called conformity of the bourgeoisie to the ruling order. No one would exclude the analysis of unintended results or structural functions from the business of the historian.

No one would deny that the ambiguous and ambivalent character of reality is to be ordered under certain main categories, such as the antagonisms democracy/authoritarian state. But we cannot maintain that there is only one main antagonism in a period without violating reality. We are not interested in excluding a look at 1933, but rather maintain that this viewpoint is *not sufficient* for 1871, 1890, 1914 or 1928.

Some German historians believe that one can operate with the concept of cost, the social costs, and thus be able to draw an overall balance, which of course divides into positive and negative. I do not believe that one gets around the problem this way. Between 1871 and 1945 there was a long discussion about the costs of the Reformation for German history, often in the form of the outmoded question, whether it was fortunate or unfortunate for Germany. That is certainly not unreasonable. However, the results show with certainty that a concluding, overall balance is not possible. This also applies to later periods. The clear-cut polarisation of reality practised by the 'continuity-historians' is in the end unjust. They proceed anachronistically by applying our standards to the past, taking advantage of the benefit of hindsight. They lose touch with reality by examining only injustice, imperfection, contradiction and crisis, as if there were a perfect society. They deny their own legitimacy to those groups that do not accept their patent democratic Utopia: Catholics who do not want to democratise their church; fathers who do not want to democratise their families; white-collar workers who do not want to democratise their insurance.

It is a rather petty endeavour to stretch Wagner or Nietzsche or Max Weber on the Procrustean bed of our concept of democracy and to examine them for 'pre-Fascist' tendencies or results. That is the tyranny of suspicion. Such an approach often becomes trivial – that the *Junkers* were *Junkers*, the liberals liberals, the peasants, peasants and that they defended their own interests and not our own, is not a new idea and is rather tedious.

My second point is that the ambivalence or the multivalence of reality and its resistance to our one-sided value judgements comprises the openness of reality, its potential for development. The 'continuity-historians' tend to overestimate the degree of necessity of a development and to underestimate the chances of a different development. The Weimar Republic still had its chances – the National Socialists were only a splinter group in 1928, the integration of the conservatives into the democracy was possible, as shown by the Westarp-Wing. [That wing of the German National People's Party (DNVP) which separated from the more radical right wing under Hugenberg. *Ed.*] 'The ideas of 1914' were not so powerful that Thomas Mann or Ernst Troeltsch could not have found a new orientation; the republic had its pre-history in the *Kaiserreich*, in the decline of the monarchy and in the rise of the Reichstag. Germany was somewhat behind the West, but yet on the right track, as many Englishmen thought.

There are many, though not unlimited, continuities, depending on which cross-section I choose, or on my starting point in the present. The questions raised today are different from those raised in (and after) 1933. French history appears different in the light of 'Gaullism' from in the light of resistance to Fascism. English history differs depending on whether we choose the susceptibility to Fascism or the crisis of the present state of society as our theme. The history of the Wilhelmine period can be written as the pre-history of the [1969–82] social-liberal coalition; one can write history from many points of view: the ungovernability problem, the losses caused by modernisation, the deficit of meaning or legitimacy, the pollution of the environment or who knows what next. The continuities intertwine and overlap, the past becomes a network of pre-histories that are certainly meaningful and legitimate but the number of continuities makes the importance of each individual continuity relative. No one continuity can exhaust the past, instead it distorts or makes the past one-sided. If we want to obtain a clear picture of the past, we cannot place our confidence in this or that problem of continuity alone.

The 'continuity-historians' make value judgements, they are partisan, even when they view the present in one way or another. How can such value judgements be legitimate when the present, as has always been the case, is full of conflicts about value judgements? Should science be partisan? There is a basic consensus inherent to a scientific approach (an ethic as the pre-condition of science itself). And there is a democratic consensus, from which we can attain intersubjective agreement regarding value judgements and the structuring of certain continuities. We can also attempt to formulate the survival conditions of a modern politico-social system that respects individual freedom, in the sense of democracy. But these consensuses are very general and do not solve the urgent value conflicts of the present. They cannot prevent evaluating criticism or an evaluating construction of continuity from becoming partisan. Such value judgements are relative, as a look at history and the variety of the continuities of history shows. Should we – having burned our fingers on the excesses of nationalism – look back in anger on nationalism and its so-called perversion? Is not a completely different perspective provided by the renaissance of nationalism from de Gaulle, Quebec and Scotland to the rediscovery of ethnic identity, and especially by the force with which nationalism forms and integrates the societies of the Third World (all this independent of what we like and what we do not like)? The 'continuity-historians' themselves show how they are swayed by values of natural law, by liberal-conservative, emancipatory or Socialist values; for many Friedrich Ebert is no longer the representative of the republic but has become its traitor, for others he has become the person who held back the truly democratic, Socialist, and in 1919, possible revolution. We are not concerned here with which political values are held to be true, but rather with the fact that political values cannot be introduced into science without destroying the claim of science to general validity. The 'continuity-historians', however, exemplify this tendency.

IV

On the basis of these critical remarks, I would like to draw two basic conclusions. First, I am a proponent of the rehabilitation of the idea of objectivity – objectivity as universal validity among contemporaries and objectivity as justice with regard to the past. The trivial objection that there is no such objectivity says nothing, since we are concerned here not with an empirical assertion, but rather with a regulative idea or a norm. Value judgements are important in the formation of scientific statements, they are, however, irrelevant for the validity of these statements. The sociology of science is not its logic. Historical 'science' cannot – beyond its basic consensus – decide the value-conflict question: this has been shown by Max Weber and Popper; it is obligated to the idea of *Wertfreiheit*, the freedom of values, and to the idea of objectivity. Seen in this way the alternative criticism or apologia is a pseudo-alternative.

Secondly, the inquiry into continuity by which the later event is explained by the earlier event is, as we have seen, both necessary and legitimate. The direction of the inquiry is not, however, reversible. I cannot explain the earlier event from the later alone as if there were a quasi-teleology. Otherwise I would shorten or distort the past or make it one-sided. Even the plurality of meaningful continuities ought to prevent such violence to the past, such distortion of historical judgement. In opposition to the constructions of the 'continuity-historians' we are concerned with saving the past and to do this not only the variety of continuities is necessary, but first of all, methodically, their suspension (their suspension, not their exclusion). In this way we free ourselves from distorting the past. The past is more than it appears to be in every 'continuity-perspective' and it is different.

The past is more than pre-history. Every epoch stands in a mediate relationship with Hitler, but the immediate relationships are different, here the past is itself. That is the non-mythological meaning of Ranke's statement, every epoch stands in immediate relationship with God. We must give back to the past that which it once possessed, and which the present always possesses: the fullness of the possible future, the uncertainty, the freedom, the finitude, the contrariety. In this way history performs a valuable service to society – it holds the future open against all technological or ideological claims to the absolute. It stabilises the consciousness of our plurality, our finitude, our freedom.

Notes and References

2 1933: THE LEGALITY OF HITLER'S ASSUMPTION OF POWER

1. Purely Marxist interpretations apart see K. D. Bracher, *Die Auflösung der Weimarer Republik* (Villingen, 1960), Chapter XI; K. D. Bracher, W. Sauer and G. Schulz, *Die nationalsozialistische Machtergreifung* (Cologne, 1960), Chapter 1; A. Bullock, *Hitler: a study in tyranny* (London, 1962), p. 253 and, though devoid of scholarly value but still widely read, W. L. Shirer, *The Rise and Fall of the Third Reich* (London, 1960), pp. 181ff.

2. See for example the 1928 SPD election film *Was wählst Du?* or *Der Deutschen Volke* held by Bundesarchiv Koblenz.

3. *Protokoll. Sozialdemokratischer Parteitag Magdeburg 1929* (Berlin, 1929), p. 67.

4. Ibid., p. 170.

5. See the call by *Schulrat* Runkel (DVP) and his call to put the nation before party political interests in *Kölnische Zeitung*, 11 March 1930.

6. See Heinrich Brüning, *Memoiren* (Munich, 1972), p. 170; E. Forsthoff, *Deutsche Verfassungsgeschichte der Neuzeit* (Stuttgart, 1961), p. 189; *Reichstagsprotokolle*, 16 July 1930, p. 6407; H. Heiber, *Die Republik von Weimar* (Munich, 1966), p. 225; W. Hubatsch, *Hindenburg und der Staat* (Göttingen, 1966), *passim.*, see also *Times Literary Supplement* review of this work, 12 May 1966.

7. H. W. Koch, *A Constitutional History of Germany in the 19th and 20th Centuries* (London, 1984), p. 269.

8. Bundesarchiv Koblenz (BAKO) R43/I No. 1870 *Verfassungsrechtliches Gutachten von Prof. Dr. Carl Schmitt über die Frage, ob der Reichspräsident befugt ist, auf Grund von Art. 48, Abs. 2, RV finanzgesetzvertretende Verordnungen zu erlassen*, July 1930; Carl Schmitt, *Die Diktatur des Reichspräsidenten nach Art. 48 der Reichsverfassung.* Veröffentlichung der Vereinigung Deutscher Staatsrechtslehrer, (Berlin, 1924), pp. 72f.; ibid., 'Legalität und Legitimität', first published in 1932 and now contained in *Verfassungsrechtliche Aufsätze aus den Jahren 1924–1954. Materalien zu einer Verfassungslehre* (Berlin, 1958), pp. 263f. See also p. 345 and his warnings about the potential misuse of Article 76 of the Weimar Constitution.

9. Brüning, *Memoiren*, p. 192.

10. See E. Eyck, *Geschichte der Weimarer Republik* (Zürich, 1956), vol. II, p. 350; see also the leading article of the liberal *Frankfurter Zeitung*, 15 September 1930.

11. See G. Stoltenberg, *Politische Strömungen im schleswig-holsteinischem Landvolk 1918–1933* (Düsseldorf, 1962), *passim.*

12. D. Orlow, *The History of the Nazi Party 1919–1933* (Newton Abott, 1969), pp. 177ff.

13. Ibid., Chapters 4 and 5.

14. P. H. Merkl, *Political Violence under the Swastika* (Princeton, 1975), pp. 33, 469.

15. H. H. Hofmann, *Der Hitlerputsch. Krisenjahre deutscher Geschichte 1920–1924* (Munich, 1961), *passim*; Bullock, *Hitler*, pp. 130, 166ff., 222ff.

16. P. Bucher, *Der Reichswehrprozess. Der Hochverrat der Ulmer Reichswehroffiziere 1929/30* (Boppard/Rgein, 1967', pp. 24ff.

17. Ibid., pp. 237ff.

18. *Völkischer Beobachter*, Munich, 11 September 1930.

19. BAKO Film Archive, *Reichskanzler Adolf Hitler spricht!*

20. That is to say, Carl Schmitt clearly recognised this danger: '*As soon as the presupposition of a mutually accepted legal basis is no longer accepted, there is no longer any way out*: . . . The opposition party, once it gains power by legal means, will use everything in its power to entrench itself within this power, to close the door behind it in order to remove the principle of legality by legal means.' (Schmitt's italics) in *Legalität und Legitimität*, cited in n. 8 above.

21. See W. J. Helbich, *Die Reparationen in der Ära Brüning. Zur Bedeuting des Young-Planes für die deutsche Politik 1930–1932* (Berlin, 1962), *passim*.

22. Brüning in *Vossische Zeitung*, Berlin, 8 December 1931.

23. In *Zentrum*, April 1931, pp. 64ff.; see also *Konjunkturstatistisches Handbuch 1933* (Berlin, 1933), p. 116.

24. *Konjunkturstatistisches Handbuch*, op. cit., pp. 76–9; BAKO R43 I/1446 *Drucksache des vorläufigen Reichswirtschaftsrates*, 12 August 1930.

25. *Schulthess' Europäischer Geschtskalender*, ed. U. Thuerauf (Munich, 1932), p. 10; *Richtlinien der Reichszentrale für Heimatdienst*, No. 217, 'Das Weltwirtschaftsmoratorium und seine Bedeutung', Berlin, July 1931, also No. 219, 'Wirtschaftskrise und öffentliche Finanzen', Berlin, Sept. 1931; No. 220, 'Die dritte Notverordnung vom 6. Oktober 1931', Berlin, Oct. 1931; 'Die öffentlichen Ausgaben und ihre Sekung', Berlin, Nov. 1931; C. Goerdeler, 'Preisüberwachung' in *Heimatdienst*, 1 Jan. 1932.

26. See n. 24 above, pp. 497f.

27. See Jacques Doriot on 13 Nov. 1930 in the Chamber of Deputies in *Journal de la République Française, Débates Parlementaires, Chambre des Députés*, (Paris, 1930), p. 3362; *Documents on British Foreign Policy 1919–1939*, 2nd Series, vol. II, Wiggin Report, Appendix II, pp. 492f.

28. In winter 1930/31 reaching almost 5 million: *Wirtschaft und Statistik* (Berlin, 1933), p. 19.

29. That Hindenburg, true to his military ethos, tried to stand above parties and politics is confirmed by such different historians as J. Wheeler-Bennet, *The Wooden Titan* (London, 1936), W. Hubatsch, *Hindenburg und der Staat*, and H. Heiber, *Die Republik von Weimar*. It is also the message he conveys clearly in the re-election film made in 1932 for the presidential elections (held in BAKO Film Archive). He was all the more bitter when as a result of his victory he was drawn in to the cauldron of centre-to-moderate left party politics, for which he blamed Brüning, in addition to which came the fact that even after two years Brüning was unable to govern constitutionally.

30. For new background on Brüning's resignation see F.-K. v. Plehwe, *Reichskanzler Kurt von Schleicher* (Esslingen, 1983), pp. 184ff.

31. Ibid.; also F. v. Papen, *Memoirs* (London, 1952), pp. 153, 161.

32. Letter by *Legationsrat* Kurt v. Lersner, 20 May 1932 to Schleicher, cited in Ch. Barber, *Wehrmachtsabteilung and Ministeramt*, PhD thesis, University of Wisconsin, 1971, p. 372.

33. On Papen's constitutional schemes see his *Memoirs*, pp. 152, 163, 166–9, 253.

34. O. Meissner, *Staatssekretär unter Ebert, Hindenburg und Hitler* (Hamburg, 1950), pp. 245ff.; Th. Vogelsang, 'Zur Politik Schleichers gegenüber der NSDAP 1932' in *Vierteljahrshefte für Zeitgeschichte 'VfZg'* (Munich, 1958), pp. 105f.

35. See Bracher, *Auflösung*, pp. 647f.; more recently V. Hentschel, *Weimars letzte Monate* (Düsseldorf, 1978), p. 17.

36. So Bracher in *Auflösung*, also his *Die nationalsozialistische Machtergreifung* and *Die Deutsche Diktatur* (Cologne, 1969), *passim*.

37. See C. L. Mowatt, *Britain between the Wars* (London, 1961), *passim*, and W. E. Leuchtenburg, *F.D.R. and the New Deal* (New York, 1963), *passim*.

38. Plehwe, *Reichskanzler Kurt von Schleicher*, p. 258; E. Matthias and E. Morseu (eds), *Das Ende der Parteien* (Düsseldorf, 1960), p. 176.

39. A. Werner, *SA und NSDAP. Studien zur Geschichte der SA und der NSDAP 1920–1933*, PhD Dissertation, University Belangen-Nürnberg 1954, pp. 548f.

40. Apart from Bracher, *Auflösung, see Orlow, History of the Nazi Party*, pp. 286ff. and W. Horn, *Führerideologic und Parteiorganisation in der NSDAP* (Düsseldorf, 1972), pp. 369f.

41. On the Tat-Kreis see K. V. Klemperer, *Germany's New Conservatism* (Princeton, 1957), pp. 117ff.; J. Petzold, *Wegbereiter des deutschen Faschismus: Die Jungkonservativen in der Weimarer Republik* (Berlin, 1978), pp. 273ff.

42. A. Mohler, *Von Rechts gesehen* (Stuttgart, 1975), p. 25.

43. Already, during the last phase of Brüning's government, the Centre Party had issued a communiqué rejecting 'the temporary solution provided by the present cabinet, and demands that the situation should be clarified by placing the responsibility for forming a government into the hands of the National Socialist Party', quoted by Papen, *Memoirs*, p. 161. As late as 26 January 1933 Prelate Kaas addressed a letter to Hindenburg demanding a return to a constitutionally legal majority government, which, of course, could only be formed with but not against the National Socialists, quoted in Forsthoff, *Deutsche Verfassungsgeschichte*, p. 192.

44. For this conversation see F. L. Carsten, *The Reichswehr and Politics 1918–1933* (Oxford, 1966), pp. 391f.

45. Bracher, *Auflösung*, p. 713.

46. Institut für Zeitgeschichte, Munich, ZS No. 279, p. 18, Aufzeichnungen von E. Ott.; Plehwe, *Reichskanzler Kurt von Schleicher*, p. 282; Dr H. Picker, *Hitler's Tischgespräche im Füherhauptquartier* (Stuttgart, 1976), entry 21 May 1942, p. 326.

47. Hugenberg to the leader of the ex-servicemen's organisation *Stahlhelm* in Th. Duesterberg, *Der Stahlhelm und Hitler* (Wolfbüttel, 1949), p. 38; to the conservative Ewald v. Kleist-Schmenzim (later to be executed because of his participation in the 1944 July bomb plot against Hitler) Papen said, 'I have got Hindenburg's confidence. In two months' time we will have squeezed Hitler into a corner till he squeaks', cited in E. v. Kleist Schmenzin, 'Die letzte Möglichkeit', *Politische Studien* (1959), 89f.

48. See H. Bennecke, *Hitler und die SA* (Munich, 1963), p. 211; see also n. 39 above.

49. J. Goebbels, *Vom Kaiserhof zur Reichskanzlei* (Munich, 1938), pp. 190ff.

50. See the following by Henry Ashby Turner, Jr, 'Big Business and the Rise of Hitler', *American Historical Review* (1969), 56f., 'Hitler's Secret Pamphlet for Industrialists', *Journal of Modern History* (1968), 348ff., 'Emil Kirdorf and the Nazi Party', *Central European History* (1968), 324f., 'The Ruhrlande. Secret Cabinet of Heavy Industry in the Weimar Republic', *Central European History* (1970), 195f., 'Fritz Thussen und das Buch 'I paid Hitler', *VfZg* (1971), 275f., 'Grossunternehmertum und Nationalsozialismus 1930–1933', *Historische Zeitschrift* (1975), 19f. For a restatement of the Marxist 'agent theory' see E. Czichon, *Wer verhalf Hitler zur Macht? Zum Anteil der Industrie an der Zerstörung der Weimarer Republik* (Cologne, 1967).

51. See H. Mommsen's contribution to this volume. F. Tobias, *Der Reichstagsbrand* (Rastatt, 1962).

52. Apart from being periodically prohibited from speaking in various parts of Germany, Hitler and the NSDAP had no access to the new medium of

broadcasting, as had the other established Weimar parties. This in turn led to a massive schedule of addressing public meetings, and the availability of chartering a Lufthansa aircraft proved a way out of this serious dilemma. 'Modernity' was discovered as it were by accident and with it the slogan 'Der Führer über Deutschland'.

53. See H. Schulze, *Otto Braun – oder Preussens demokratische Mission* (Berlin, 1981) in which Schulze unwittingly admits that in spite of Brüning's drastic legislation against transferring capital assets from Germany to countries abroad, Braun must have violated this legislation massively because after Hitler had come to power his (Braun's) assets allowed him to live comfortably in Switzerland until his death after 1945. See also G. Kotowski, 'Preussen und die Weimarer Republik' in *Preussen: Epochen und Probleme seiner Geschichte* (Berlin, 1964), pp. 145f.

54. Estimates range between 380 and 400 fatal casualties including the 16 killed in the November *putsch* of 1923. Bayerisches Hauptstaatsarchive, Abt. I., NS Hauptarchiv 71 999 Zusammenstellung der Blutopfer der NSDAP 1919 bis 1933.

55. Tobias, *Der Reichstagsbrand*, who also reprints the protocols of the cabinet sessions from 30 January until the end of March 1933.

56. R. Morsey, 'Hitler's Verhandlungen mit der Zentrumsführung am 31. Januar 1931', *VfZg* (1961), 182f.; and J. Becker, 'Zentrum und Ermächtigungsgesetz 1933', *VfZg* (1961), 195f.

57. M. Domarus (ed.), *Hitler: Reden und Proklamationen 1932–1945* (Wiesbaden, 1973), vol. I, p. 237.

58. See Bracher, Sauer and Schulz, *Machtergreifung*, p. 136. *Gleichschaltung* was achieved within a few days after the Enabling Act, i.e. 'Vorläufiges Gesetz zur Gleichschaltung der Länder mit dem Reich', 31 March 1933, *Reichsgesetzblatt* (*RGBl.*) I, 1933, p. 153; 'Zweites Gesetz zur Gleichschaltung der Länder mit dem Reich', 7 April 1933, *RGBl.* I, 1933, p. 173; 'Gesetz über die Aufhebung des Reichsrats', 14 February 1934, *RGBl.* I, 1934, p. 89; 'Reichsstatthaltergesetz', 30 January 1935, *RGBl.* I, 1935, p.65; since March 1933 most German *Lands* were headed by a new Reich Commissioner or *Reichsstatthalter* under whom the *Land* governments, staffed in part by NS personnel, continued to operate, but in a purely administrative capacity and subject to the Reich Ministry of the Interior. Thus Bavaria continued to have its prime minister, as did Prussia, whose prime minister was to be Göring.

59. 'Gesetz über das Staatsoberhaupt des Deutschen Reiches', 1 August 1934, *RGBl.* I, 1934.

60. Domarus, *Hitler*, p. 279.

3   THE REICHSTAG FIRE AND ITS POLITICAL CONSEQUENCES

1. Ernst Hanfstaengl, *Unheard Witness* (Philadelphia, 1957). pp. 210f.; corroborated by Goebbels, *Vom Kaiserhof zur Reichskanzlei* (Munich, 1934), pp. 269f.; cf. H. Fraenkel, below, p. 14, who supports Hanfstaengl's version.

2. Göring's reaction was later attested by F. W. Jacoby, who was then his aide-de-camp (F. W. Jacoby, 'Mitteilung vom 16.2.1961', Archiv Tobias): 'On the day of the Reichstag fire, I who was then his only aide-de-camp, reported the incident to Göring. I was then convinced and still am convinced that his surprise was authentic.' Similarly the statement of Undersecretary [Staatssekretär] Grauert of 3 October 1957 (Archiv Tobias): he was in conference with Göring when an official (Grauert had Daluege in mind, but it was Jacoby) rushed in and announced that the Reichstag was on fire. 'Göring's reaction was so unmistakable and convincing that Grauert did not have the slightest doubt either then or later that Göring was

truly surprised.' Cf. Fritz Tobias, *Der Reichstagsbrand, Legende und Wirklichkeit* (Rastatt, 1962), p. 108.

3. Martin Sommerfeldt, *Ich war dabei* (Darmstadt, 1949), p. 25; 'Aussage Gempp', Tobias, *Der Reichstagsbrand*, p. 668. See also n. 8 below.

4. 'Aussage Grauert', corroborated by Göring's statement before the Reich Court, see Stenographischer Bericht der Reichsgerichtsverhandlung gegen van der Lubbe u.a., 2 Sitzungstag (henceforth referred to as ST), 31, pp. 104f.

5. Ibid., p. 94: 'When (after being stopped by the police guard) I heard the word "arson" . . . it was as if the curtain had risen at one stroke and I saw the play clearly before me. The moment the word "arson" fell, I knew that the Communist Party was guilty and had set the Reichstag on fire.' If this was true, it provides one more indication that 'Reichstag fire myths' beclouded men's minds from the start.

6. Rudolf Diels, *Lucifer ante portars* (Stuttgart, 1950), p. 192, who mistakenly places the hearing in the Reichstag building (guardroom at Brandenburg Gate) but characteristically cites Lateit's impression that van der Lubbe was a madman (cf. Tobias, *Der Reichstagsbrand*, pp. 66f).

7. Ibid., p. 111. In 1960 Weber expressly confirmed to Tobias the statement he then made.

8. Goebbels, *Vom Kaiserhof zur Reichskanzlei*, p. 170.

9. Sommerfeldt, *Ich wer dabei*, p. 25.

10. Tobias, *Der Reichstagsbrand*, App. 14, p. 635.

11. Sefton Delmer, *Die Deutschen und ich* (Hamburg, 1962), p. 188. English original, *Trial Sinister* (London, 1961).

12. Franz von Papen, *Der Wahrheit eine Gasse* (Munich, 1952), p. 303.

13. DBFP, No. 245; Rumbold managed to enter the cordoned-off Reichstag on the night of the fire.

14. Delmer, *Die Deutschen und ich*, pp. 191f.; Letter to *Der Spiegel*, No. 52, 1959; earlier in *Daily Express*, 21 July 1939.

15. Delmer, *Die Deutschen und ich*, p. 190.

16. Diels, *Lucifer*, p. 193.

17. Ibid., pp. 140–1.

18. We are aware that Diels's statements must be treated critically. However, in matters connected with the Reichstag fire, they are largely corroborated by Sommerfeldt and by the testimony of the witnesses. Above all, Schnitzler corroborates his crucial account of the events in the burning Reichstag building. Diels had no cognisance of Schnitzler's article until it was in proof (Diels, *Lucifer*, p. 200), and Diels's account, as a comparison of their texts shows, was not influenced by Schnitzler; from 1934 on, the relations between the two men were strained. Schnitzler checked his information chiefly by consulting Heisig, who had no reason for taking an apologetic attitude (cf. Schnitzler's letter to Heisig, Archiv Tobias, and correspondence with Tobias), and also questioned Zirpins. Cf. also Schnitzler's letter in IfZ Zeugenschrifttum, which Wolff rather surprisingly failed to take into consideration. The parallel accounts of Diels and Schnitzler preclude our original supposition that the arrests were first decided upon in the session at the Prussian Ministry of the Interior (Goebbels speaks of a cabinet meeting).

19. Heinrich Schnitzler, anonymous article, 'Der Reichstagsbrand in anderer Sicht', in *Neue Politik, Organ für Freiheit und Recht* (Zürich, 1949), Vol. 10, No. 2 (quoted from photocopy in IfZ-Zeugenschrifttum A-7), p. 2.

20. Goebbels, *Vom Kaiserhof zur Reichskanzlei*, p. 270.

21. Diels, *Lucifer*, p. 194; Schnitzler, 'Der Reichstagsbrand in anderer Sicht', p. 2; before the Reich Court Helldorf denied having been at Göring's on the night

of the fire, whereas Göring – truthfully in all likelihood – declared expressly that Helldorf had come in response to his summons (31 ST, p. 105). One of these two witnesses was guilty of perjury. Sahm's presence is indirectly confirmed; [former German Nationalist Party leader Gottfried] Treviranus, who had been invited to Sahm's that evening, has stated verbally that Sahm came home at about 11.15. Cf. Tobias, *Der Reichstagsbrand*, p. 112.

22. Delmer, *Die Deutschen und ich*, p. 192; Delmer's interpretation of the conversation reported to him between Hitler and Papen is dubious, particularly because Papen was present at the later conference at the Prussian Ministry of the Interior.

23. *Völkischer Beobachter*, 1 March 1933, 'Der Fanal des Bolschewismus'.

24. Diels, *Lucifer*, pp. 194f. When one has read Diels's account of these events, it seems impossible to dispose of Hitler's speech as 'play-acting', even if one takes account of Henderson's remark (in Alan Bullock, *Hitler. Ein Studie über Tyrannei* (Düsseldorf, 1961), p. 375) that Hitler's capacity for deluding himself was a part of his technique.

25. Schnitzler, 'Die Reichstagsbrand in anderer Sicht', p. 11.

26. Even earlier, by order of the Prussian Ministry of the Interior, a police radio call (No. 171) had gone out to 'all police headquarters and top police officers of the West sectors', invoking the Reichstag fire and 'increased activity of the KPD' and ordering confiscation of all leaflets and periodicals of the KPD and SPD, alerting the local riot police, calling up the auxiliary police, and ordering 'a thorough surprise search action at the homes of all Communist functionaries' (St. A. Oldenburg. Best. 205, Staatspolizei [Schutz-Ordnunspolizei, Aktenband Geheim und 'Persönliches' vom 1.1.29.3.1933]; I owe this and other documents to the careful researches of State Archivist Doctor Schieckel).

27. 2 ST, pp. 71ff.

28. Goebbels, *Vom Kaiserhof zur Reichskanzlei*, p. 254.

29. Ibid., p. 270.

30. WTB, 2nd early ed., 28 February 1933, in Tobias, App. 14, p. 633. When van der Lubbe was questioned by Heisig, it was not clear at first whether he was a Communist or a Social Democrat. Cf. 'Aussage Heisig', 2 ST, p. 61. That night it was inferred from van der Lubbe's working-class contacts that he was connected with the KPD, and it was mistakenly concluded that he had confessed to Social Democratic connections (cf. 'Aussage Goering', 31 ST, p. 104). Denials in *Völkischer Beobachter*, 23 March 1933, and elsewhere. Cf. Tobias, p. 112. The suspicion cast on the SPD was immediately doubted by the non-National Socialist press. Cf. *Frankfurter Zeitung*, 1 March 1933, leading editorial: 'It is only too understandable that in view of an election campaign which consists essentially in upholding the fiction of a common "Marxist front", which in the National Socialist formulation brands the Social Democrats and the Communists indiscriminately as "Communist rabble", defensive alliances may spring up spontaneously in the working class.' But, the article concludes, it is absurd to accuse the Social Democrats of originating the fire. (WTB, Wolffs Telegraphen Bureau.)

31. *Reichsgesetzblatt (RGBl)*I, 1933, p. 86. Cf. also Tobias, p. 113.

32. Cf. *Braunschweigische Landeszeitung*, 28 February, telegram.

33. 31 ST, p. 106.

34. 46 ST, pp. 60ff.; as the order for the arrest of Torgler (Archiv Tobias) indicates, the arrest orders were mimeographed in the first hours of 28 February. They invoked Sec. 22 of the emergency decree of 4 February.

35. 'Aussage Grauert vom 3.10.51', Archiv Tobias. According to this statement, Hitler himself took no part in drafting the law.

36. IfZ-Zeugenschrifttum ED 1 – Liebmann, p. 44. General Liebmann's manuscript notes.

37. There is no other evidence of Hitler's initiative. The records of the Reich Chancellory (BA Koblenz) contain none, those of the Reich Ministry of the Interior are missing; hence it is not possible for the present to go beyond hypotheses in respect to the genesis of the Reichstag fire decree. Papen, who might have been expected to know what happened, obviously confuses this decree with the Decree to Combat Treason Against the German Nation, of 28 February (*Der Wahrheit eine Gasse*, p. 304).

38. Goebbels, *Vom Kaiserhof zur Reichskanzlei*, pp. 270f.; Henry Picker, *Hitlers Tischgespräche im Führerhauptquartier, 1941–1942*, ed. P. E. Schramm (Stuttgart, 1963), p. 325; the account of Wilfried von Oven (*Mit Goebbels bis zum Ende* (Buenos Aires, 1949–50), pp. 115ff.) is not credible.

39. Joseph Goebbels, *Wetterleuchten* (Berlin, 1943), pp. 373ff.; cf. Diels, *Lucifer*, p. 195.

40. In Tobias, App. 14, p. 633.

41. Cf. ibid., pp. 262ff.

42. VB, 1 March 1933. The lists of persons to be assassinated were alleged to include names from every section of the bourgeoisie. On 2 March the paper reported that van der Lubbe had regularly attended meetings of the Communist action committee, which he had persuaded to enlist his services for the incendiary action. Most of the other news stories about the fire consisted of false reports issued by the police, for example, the rumour that the Communist leaders had given advance notice of the Reichstag fire (VB, 4/5 March 1933). Dertinger's report (Sammlung Brammer, BA Koblenz) of 2 March 1933, speaks of a 'news muddle'. The countless conflicting rumours bear witness to the agitation of the public.

43. VB, 1 and 2 March 1933.

44. Sommerfeldt, *Ich war dabei*, p. 26.

45. Cf., for example, Delmer, *Die Deutschen und ich*, p. 190.

46. Cf. Siegfried Bahne, 'Die Kommunistische Partei Deutschlands', in *Das Ende der Parteien*, E. Mattias and R. Morsey (eds) (Düsseldorf, 1960), pp. 685ff., 710ff. However, there is no reliable material on the basis of which to appraise Communist activity after the seizure of power (cf. Schulz, in Bracher, Sauer and Schulz, *Die nationalsozialistische Machtergreifung*, 2nd edn (Cologne, Opladen, 1962), p. 527, n. 48). In her memoirs Maria Reese (BA Koblenz, Kl Erw. 379–4) criticises the KPD severely for putting out irresponsible propaganda while remaining passive in practice. Some informative material, though for the most part confined to Communist propaganda, is to be found in the records of the *Reichssicherheitshauptamt* (R 58) in BA Koblenz. The latent civil war situation with numerous bloody clashes continued (cf. Diels, *Lucifer*, pp. 186ff., 402ff.); also the account of the atmosphere in Hamburg in Jan Valtin, *Tagebuch der Hölle*, German edn (Berlin, 1957).

47. Cf. the intention of the National Socialists, described by Bracher, to change the order of the agenda if necessary in order to obtain a majority for the Enabling Act (Karl Dietrich Bracher, 'Stufen der nationalsozialistischen Machtergreifung', in *Vierteljahrshefte für Zeitgeschichte*, No. 4 (1956), pp. 158f.).

48. As late as the cabinet meeting of 24 March 1933, Hitler doubted the expediency of suppressing the Communist Party. Such a measure, he held, would serve a purpose only 'if it were possible to deport the Communists'; there was no point in sending them to concentration camps. Tobias, p. 628.

49. Cf. the material presented at the trial (45 and 46 ST), and the memoirs of Maria Reese (n. 46, above).

50. For example on 24 January 1933, the news bureau of the Reich Ministry of the Interior distributed to the news bureaux of the *Länder* an educational pamphlet [RFB-Schulungsmaterial] entitled 'Der bewaffnete Aufstand in Reval' (R 58/1, 672). This material is used tendentiously in Martin H. Sommerfeldt, *Die Kommune* (Berlin, 1934).

51. Diels, *Lucifer*, pp. 189f. Adolf Ehrt's propagandist work *Bewaffneter Aufstand* (Berlin/Leipzig, 1933), is based on this material. Göring took up most of the 2 March cabinet meeting with it.

52. St. A. Oldenburg, cf. n. 26, above.

53. Sent out by the news bureau on 19 April 1933 (BA R 58/1-78).

54. 46 ST, p. 61, 'Aussage Heller'; 'The evidence presented leaves no room for doubt that the KPD intended very seriously . . . to stage a general strike, followed by an armed uprising.' But on p. 64 he declared that the KPD had organised the Reichstag fire in order to put the blame on the National Socialists and so 'create an unbridgeable gulf between them and the supporters of the SPD, the members of the unions and the members of the Reichsbanner.' This was the true and intended significance of the Reichstag fire. Thus it was intended less as a signal for action, as it was partly taken to be in the provinces, than as the central action that would draw the hesitant masses over to the Communists.' To which Torgler replied: 'I can only say with Herr Goebbels: that is completely absurd.' Typical for the state of the evidence is a communication of 7 April 1933, from Nuremberg police headquarters to the effect that there had indeed been prospects of a violent seizure of power by the KPD, 'but that positive evidence pointing to a direct connection between the Reichstag fire and such revolutionary intentions is not available' ('Handakten Sack', Tobias, vol. i, pp. 343ff.).

55. Cf. Diels, *Lucifer*, pp. 170f.

56. 31 ST, pp. 34–40, 43ff., 52.

57. Cf. Schulz, *Die nationalsozialistische Machtergreifung*, pp. 430ff., 438ff.; also Sauer, ibid., pp. 866ff.; Schnitzler, 'Die Reichsbrandstrand in anderer Sicht', p. 5.

58. 31 ST, pp. 81f.; IMT ix, pp. 481f.; Diels, *Lucifer*, pp. 194f.; and Grauert's statement of 3 October 1957 (Archiv Tobias).

59. DBPF Second Series, Vol. iv, No. 253, p. 438.

60. Cf. Bahne, 'Die KPD,' p. 692.

61. 31 XXX ST, pp. 86ff.

62. Cf. Bracher, cited in n. 47 above, pp. 158ff. The change in the agenda seems to have been a mere stopgap, for in fact the mandates of the Communist Reichstag members were not annulled formally as originally intended, but rendered inoperative by their arrest.

63. 31 ST, p. 84.

64. Cf. above; on it is based the interpretation of M. Broszat ('Zum Streit um den Reichstagsbrand', *Der Spiegel*, 8 (1960), pp. 176f.) among others. Broszat says the National Socialists 'quickly and shrewdly exploited a political revolution; they did not bring it about.'

65. 31 ST, pp. 72f.

66. DBPF Second Series, Vol. iv, No. 246, p. 431; cf. Tobias, p. 133.

67. Reprinted in Tobias, App. 11, p. 623; also numerous press reports to the effect that the elections would take place 'in any case' (cf. *Generalanzeiger* [Wuppertal], 28 February 1933, *Braunschweiger Neueste Nachrichten*, 2 March 1933, *Nazionalzeitung* [Berlin], 28 February 1933, etc.).

68. Tobias, App. 11, p. 623.

69. In any case it was unclear whether Communist Reichstag members were to be included in the arrest action (cf. 47 ST, p. 94).

70. Drafted on 28 February, proclaimed on 1 March 1933 (*RGBl* i, 1933, pp. 84ff.); Bracher (*Die nationalsozialistische Machtergreitung*, p. 87) speaks somewhat misleadingly of 'Reichstag fire decrees'.

71. Helmut Krausnick, 'Stationen der Gleichschaltung', in *Der Weg in die Diktatur 1918 bis 1933* (Munich, 1962), p. 183.

72. Bracher, *Die nationalsozialistische Machtergreitung*, p. 83.

73. 'Reichskabinettsitzung vom 28.2 vormittags', in Tobias, App. 8, p. 619.

74. *RGBl* i, 1933, pp. 35ff.

75. Tobias, p. 617.

76. 'Reichskabinettsitzung vom 27.2' (ibid., p. 617).

77. Cf. Schulz, *Die nationalsozialistische Machtergriefung*, p. 434.

78. Cf. Gotthard Jasper, 'Der Schutz der Republik', *Studien zur staatlichen Sicherung der Demokratie in der Weimarer Republik, 1922–1930* (Tübingen, 1963), p. 162, the example of the suppression of the Red War Veterans' Association; Hans Buchheim, 'Die organisatorische Entwicklung der Politischen Polizei in Deutschland in den Jahren 1933 und 1934', in *Gutachten des Instituts für Zeitgeschichte* (Munich, 1958), pp. 197ff.

79. Cf. Telegr. pol. Funkdienst Leitstelle Braunschweig (Records of the Braunschweig Staatsministerium, copy in Archiv Tobias). In Hamburg the arrests seem to have begun only after the appointment of the police senator (testimony of Kriminalkommissar Will, 47 ST, pp. 94ff.; testimony of Kriminalsekretär Staeglich, ibid., pp. 110ff.). Braunschweig, Oldenburg and Mecklenburg applied the police measures immediately (cf. *Völkischer Beobachter*, 3 March 1933, and the Oldenburg State Police records mentioned in n. 24 above). It would be worthwhile to investigate the behaviour of the South German *Länder*. Neither Besson nor Schwend (cf. n. 80 below) mentions a corresponding request on the part of the Reich Ministry of the Interior. With the exception of the Rhine Province and Westphalia, where according to the *Völkischer Beobachter* of 3 March 1933, respectively 1200 and 850 persons had been arrested the previous day, the arrests were slow in getting under way in the Prussian provinces, as can be seen from the statements of the police officials before the Reich Court.

80. Cf. Waldemar Besson, *Württemberg und die deutsche Staatskrise 1928–1933* (Stuttgart, 1959), pp. 336f.; Karl Schwend, *Bayern zwischen Monarchie und Diktatur* (Munich, 1954), p. 510.

81. Besson, *Württemberg*, p. 338.

82. They were concerned with the question of jurisdiction, which, their authors claimed, was not with the Reich Ministry of the Interior but with the Reich government as a whole. They also introduced a substantive restriction by adding the words 'insofar as'. Cf. Schulz, *Die nationalsozialistische Machtergreifung*, p. 432, n. 225. The commentary of Ministerialdirektor Kurt Häntzschel of the Reich Ministry of the Interior (*Die Politischen Notverordnungen* . . . , 4th ed. (Berlin, 1933), Stilkes Rechtsvibliothek, No. 115) has the following to say on Article 2: 'By Reich government is here meant the competent minister, i.e., the Reich Minister of the Interior!'

83. Besson, *Württemberg*, p. 538.

84. Unfortunately it has not been possible to establish who was entrusted with the drafting of the decree. Possibilities are Doctor Werner Hoche, Ministerialrat at the Reich Ministry of the Interior and author of the emergency decree of 4 February (cf. *Juristische Wochenschrift* 8 [1933], p. 506), Dammers, or Doctor Kaisenberg.

85. *Frankfurter Zeitung*, 1 March 1933, 1st ed., telegraphic dispatch of 28 March.

86. Bracher, 'Stufender nationalsocialistischen Machtergreifung', p. 86; he rightly stresses that even before this time the police authorities had for all practical purposes been free to act as they saw fit.

87. 'Reichskabinettsitzung vom 28.2 nachmittags' (Tobias, p. 619). Broszat correctly points out that the cabinet approved the decree in 'all essential points' ('Zum streit um den Reichstagbrand', p. 276). Thus his contention that Göring, Hitler, and Frick had played 'adroitly, each taking his allotted role' (p. 275) is groundless, especially as at this time Papen neither could nor wished to raise any further objection, and Gürtner obviously supported the decree.

88. Cf. *Völkischer Beobachter*, 28 February 1933: Report on the suppression of numerous publications (*Die Rote Fahne* until 15 April) including newspapers of the Centre Party in Bavaria.

89. Tobias, App. 10, p. 622.

90. DZA Potsdam, Rep. 77 (Microfilm IfZ MA 198/2).

91. *Frankfurter Zeitung*, 1 March 1933, 1st ed., leading editorial.

92. Cf. DAZ, 28 February 1933; *Niedersächsische Zeitung*, 1 March 1933; *Frankfurter Zeitung*, 1 March 1933; *Nazionalzeitung*, 28 February 1933.

93. IfZ Zeugenschrifttum ED 1 – Liebmann, p. 40.

94. Letter from Liebmann, 8 August 1955 (ibid., pp. 361f.), who dates the meeting of the High Command (which earlier writers assumed to have taken place before the Reichstag fire) on 1 March. This is confirmed by the transparent allusion to the 'emergency decree' in Liebmann's notes. Liebmann rejects Ott's contention (IfZ Zeugenschrifttum 279/I – Ott, p. 9) that not Blomberg but Reichenau presided over the conference. Blomberg was present at the Reich cabinet meeting on 28 February. The content of his speech presupposes previous negotiations with the National Socialist leadership and shows that the Reichstag fire must have played a role of considerable importance in regularising the relations between the Reichswehr and the National Socialist movement, chiefly by paralysing the opposition within the Reichswehr.

95. Liebmann's notes on the questions raised by Blomberg's speech (ibid., p. 43).

96. Ibid., pp. 46f.

97. Tobias, p. 623.

98. The Reichswehr should 'not be involved in this question of domestic politics' (telegraphic report of 28 February in 1st ed. of 1 March 1933); cf. the remarks of Sauer, *Die nationalsozialistische Machtergreifung*, pp. 720ff.

99. BA Koblenz, Sammlung Brammer, Zsg. 101/26, pp. 167, 175; Cf. the report of 11 March, p. 181, which reiterates that Papen and Blomberg had demanded martial law, but that the president had urged a compromise with Hitler.

100. Liebmann-Notizen, cited n. 93 above, pp. 40ff. The tactical arguments suggest Hitler's influence, although there is no proof that he made any such statements, and these matters were not mentioned at the cabinet meeting of 28 February; on Blomberg's attitude, cf. H. Krausnick, 'Vorgeschichte und Beginn des militärischen Widerstandes gegen Hitler', in *Vollmacht des Gewissens* (Munich, 1956), pp. 210f.; on the other hand the version of the High Command meeting now available shows that on 1 March Blomberg deviated from the suprapartisan attitude of the Reichswehr: '*One* party on the march. In such a situation "suprapartisanship" loses its meaning and there remains only one answer: unreserved support.'

101. DBFP Second Series, Vol. IV, No. 253, p. 438. Göring denied this in his radio speech and spoke of forged SA and Stahlhelm orders (in Tobias, p. 640).

102. DBFP Second Series, Vol. IV, No. 255, 3 March 1933, p. 439, according to which Neurath spoke up at the cabinet meeting and in a conversation with

Rumbold expressed the hope that the decree would be annulled immediately after the elections. 'In his opinion it was not possible to maintain such a state of exception for any length of time.'

103. Tobias, pp. 113, 115f.

104. Goebbels, *Wetterleuchten*, p. 271.

105. 'Reichskabinettssitzung vom 28.2 vormittags', op. cit., p. 618.

106. Ibid., App. 17, pp. 641f.

107. 'Reichskabinettssitzung vom 2.3. 1933' in Tobias, p. 623. Cf. Schulz, *Die nationalsozialistische Machtergreifung*, p. 527: 'No further proof is needed that the material with which Göring duped the Reich ministers on the day after the Reichstag fire existed only in his imagination.' At the cabinet meetings Göring argued on the strength of material that had been put at his disposal by the Political Police. Later as well Göring made use of the thoroughly dubious conjectures brought forward in the preliminary investigation, which were not even very suitable for propaganda purposes. The questioning of the police inspectors before the Reich Court (45, 46, and 47 ST) throws light on the genesis of the material incriminating the KPD, yet the participants, including so outstanding an expert as Heller, held this material to be reliable. For example, the charge of 'poisoning public kitchens' (cf. 'Aussage Kriminalkommissars Will,' 47 St, pp. 24f.) goes back to an episode in Düsseldorf when the police believed they had arrested a 'Communist poisoning team'. Experts calculated that the confiscated poison would have sufficed to poison 18,000 persons. Although the investigation had not even begun, the report was passed on to higher authority. This impelled Gürtner to introduce into the emergency decree a provision for increased penalties in cases of murder by poisoning. The assertion that van der Lubbe had had close ties with Moscow ('Kabinettssitzung vom 2.3', WTB, 28 February) derived from van der Lubbe's statement that he had wished to visit the Soviet Union in 1932. It is characteristic of the uncritical mentality of all the participants that the German Embassy in Moscow was subsequently asked to track down the alleged instigators of the Communist uprising in Germany. The embassy wired back on 14 September 1933: 'It would be desirable that the State's Attorney's sources should provide more detailed information if we are to arrive even at indirect conclusions that may be of any use' (telegrams to ORA, AA/Rechtsabt.: 'Korrespondenz und Zeitungs-Ausschnitte zum Reichstagsbrandprozess', Microfilm IfZ MA–194, I, p. 125).

108. Cf. the telegrams of 28 February and 3 March 1933, to the foreign missions, reprinted in Tobias, App. 15, pp. 636f.

109. Mentioned in Schulz, *Die nationalsozialistische Machtergreifung*, p. 527. This shows the utter helplessness of the government in the face of Münzenberg's offensive; cf. also BA Koblenz, R 58/718: 'Denkschrift über die kommunistische Wühlarbeit im Winter 1932/33 betr. die Vorbereitung der gewaltsamen Verfassungsänderung durch die KPD vom 14.3. 1933.'

110. This has never been investigated in detail. For the Political Police's dubious appraisal of Communist tactics, cf. confidential report of 7 April 1933 (Nachrichtensammlung, R 58/626): Up to 5 March, it was believed, the Communists had considered themselves to be in the stage of preparation for an armed uprising, but Neumann's more radical view set forth in his book *Der bewaffnete Aufstand* was making headway.

111. Cf. Rudolf Hess's letter of 16 September 1933, to the Supreme SA Command, requesting it to send immediately all available material proving that the Communists were planning an uprising, and to find out 'whether there are in the SA any former Communists who are able and willing to testify if necessary that arson etc. are among the methods forseen by the KPD within the framework

of such actions' (BA Koblenz, Sammlung Schumacher, *Röhm, Röhmputsch und Reichstagsbrand*, p. 402).

112. Sammlung Brammer, BA ZSg. 101/26, Anweisungen Nos. 55, 62, 77, Mitteilung No. 107.

113. A. François-Poncet, *Als Botschafter in Berlin 1931–1938* (Mainz, 1949), p. 94; but cf. *Hitlers Tischgespräche*, p. 325.

114. Cf. for example the report of the *Münchern Neueste Nachrichten*, 14 December 1933.

115. Cf. Diels, *Lucifer*, pp. 269f.

116. Cf. Schulz, *Die nationalsozialistische Machtergreifung*, p. 523, 'Urteil', p. 94ff., also Schlegelberger's affidavits and opinions, BA Koblenz, RK 43/II/294.

117. Tobias (p. 470) correctly points out that the *in dubio pro re* principle was crassly transgressed in the verdict, which started from the assumption that van der Lubbe had acted 'in conscious and deliberate collusion with unknown accomplices'. Seuffert moved that van der Lubbe's action be qualified only as 'an act of preparation for high treason', which would have avoided the death penalty (cf. 55 ST, pp. 133ff. and Sack, BA,Ll.Erw. 396/1, reprinted in Tobias, pp. 269ff.). The attempt to rehabilitate van der Lubbe in 1955 is irrelevant to the present context (Aufh. 473/55, Gen. St. A., Berlin). On 6 August 1963, the Oberlandgericht in Düsseldorf took the position that there was no reason to presume 'that the judgment of the Reich Court was a deliberate miscarriage of justice, or that the judges of the Reich Court stretched the law', but admitted that the verdict had been strongly influenced by National Socialist thinking.

118. Cf. Tobias, p. 628. The harsh criticism of the Leipzig verdict in the National Socialist press and the attitude of the Reich Ministry of Justice are dealt with in Schulz, *Die nationalsozialistische Machtergreifung*, p. 563, and in Hubert Schorn, *Der Richter im Dritten Reich* (Frankfurt, 1959), pp. 67ff.

119. The position taken by Bormann in a letter of 2 March 1933, to Elfriede Conti strikes me as characteristic: 'It seems almost unbelievable that Communists should have been so exceptionally idiotic as to stage the fire in the Reichstag building a few days before the elections, because from a pure party standpoint nothing better could have happened to us' (Sammlung Schumacher, see n. 111 above).

120. Goebbels, *Wetterleuchlen*, p. 271.

121. This expression is recorded by Delmer, *Die Deutschen und ich*, p. 195.

122. Cf. the analysis of Rudolf Vierhaus, 'Faschistisches Führertum. Ein Beitrag zur Phänomenologie des europaischen Faschismus,' in HZ 189 (1964), p. 631: 'The leadership cult prevented almost everyone from seeing to what extent the leaders were the playthings of their wishful thinking. . . .'

123. Op. cit., p. 593. For all our criticism of this exaggerated interpretation, Tobias' guiding idea should not be overlooked, to wit, the fundamental importance 'of the incorrigible blindness to reality [that prevails] in an authoritarian Führer-state'. It is only with this in mind that we can gain a full historical understanding of the actions of the National Socialists.

4 SOCIAL AND PSYCHOLOGICAL ASPECTS OF THE FÜHRERS RULE

1. Alexander and Margarete Mitscherlich, *Die Unfähigkeit zu trauern* (Munich, 1968), pp. 27ff., 71ff.

2. Recent review of literature in Klaus Hildebrand, *Das Dritte Reich* (Munich and Vienna, 1979), p. 202f.; see also Wolfgang Wippermann, *Faschismustheorien* (Darmstadt, 1976); Richard Saage, *Faschismustheorien* (Munich, 1976); Manfred Clemenz, *Gesellschaftliche Ursprünge des Faschismus* (Frankfurt, 1976); Renzo de Felice, *Interpretations of Fascism*, trans. from the Italian (Harvard UP, 1977); Reinhard Kühnl (ed.), *Texte zur Faschismusdiskussion* (Hamburg, 1974); Helga Grebing, *Aktuelle Theorien über Faschismus und Konservatismus. Eine Kritik* (Stuttgart, 1974). No end can be seen to this debate, which is far too abstract, for instance, in its handling of historical truth.

3. See the chapter 'Das System plebiszitärer Akklamation' in Karl Dietrich Bracher (ed.), *Stufen der Machtergreifung* (Frankfurt, 1974), pp. 472–98, which for the most part deals with coercion, terrorism and manipulation, to convey a somewhat distorted picture of the events after the seizure of power.

4. From a contribution by T. Mason at the conference of the German Historical Institute, London.

5. This is true especially of the biography, so successful in my opinion, by Joachim Fest, *Hitler* (Frankfurt, 1973) and the discerning observations of Sebastian Haffner, *Anmerkungen zu Hitler* (Cologne, 1978).

6. Review of the existing social-psychological research in Wippermann, *Faschismustheorien*, pp. 56–63 and also De Felice, *Interpretations*, pp. 78–87. Also the most recent 'psycho-historical' examination by Rudolph Binion, *Das ihr mich gefunden habt. Hitler und die Deutschen* (Stuttgart, 1978) does not contain what the book jacket promises. It deals with psycho-analytical impressions and speculation, which scarcely do justice to the complex historical reality and especially the political culture of Germany.

7. Wilhelm Reich, *Die Massenpsychologie des Faschismus* (Frankfurt, 1979), p. 58.

8. It was this concept, 'the horrible word "re-education" ', which was, moreover, repudiated by the experts of the military government (Education Branch), and not the culture of the occupied land. In addition, see Robert Birley, 'British Policy in Retrospect', in Arthur Hearnden (ed.), *The British in Germany. Educational Reconstruction after 1945* (London, 1978), p. 46.

9. Cf. the two volumes by Annedore Leber, edited in co-operation with Willy Brand and Karl Dietrich Bracher, *Das Gewissen entscheidet* and *Das Gewissen steht auf* (Berlin, 1959 and 1960).

10. For early, contemporary indications, see Hildebrand, *Das Dritte Reich*, pp. 123ff. and also Wippermann, *Faschismustheorien*, pp. 11—55. For arguments dealing with present theories see Grebing, *Aktuelle Theorien* and also Heinrich August Winkler, *Revolution, Staat, Faschismus* (Göttingen, 1978), pp. 65–117.

11. In the last, partly free elections on 5 March 1933, the NSDAP obtained 17,277,180 votes (43·9%). See *Statistisches Jahrbuch für das Deutsche Reich, Year 52* (Berlin, 1933), p. 540. For a current interpretation then see Hildebrand, *Das Dritte Reich*, p. 5: 'They, [the NSDAP] have never, therefore, ever been elected by a majority of the German people'.

12. On taking over the office of *Reichspräsident* after the death of Hindenburg, the concept of the *Führer* gained official validity through the law of 1 August 1934, a decisive step in the process of ensuring the autonomy of the executive. See Martin Broszat, *Der Staat Hitlers* (Munich, 1969). For 'Hitler's emancipation from the State', see also Peter Diehl-Thiele, *Partei und Staat im Dritten Reich* (Munich, 1971), pp. 21ff.

13. In addition see the two prefaces by Heinz Boberach (ed.), *Meldungen aus dem Reich*, a selection from the secret situational reports of the security service of the SS, 1939–1944 (Neuwied and Berlin, 1965), and also reports of the SD and the Gestapo on churches and church people in Germany, 1934–1944 (Mainz, 1971).

522 ASPECTS OF THE THIRD REICH

14. See in addition Ian Kershaw, *Der Hitler-Mythos Volksmeinung und Propaganda im Dritten Reich* (Stuttgart, 1980).

15. This historical concept, which has been afforded academic recognition for the early part of modern times by Peter Blickle *Die Revolution von 1525* (Munich and Vienna, 1975), pp. 177ff., is also applicable in my opinion to research into the attitudes of mind of later centuries.

16. Martin Broszat, 'Soziale Motivation und Führer-Bindung des NS', in Wolfgang Michalka (ed.), *NS-Aussenpolitik* (Darmstadt, 1978), pp. 92–116. In addition see also J. P. Stern, *Hitler. The Führer and the People* (London, 1975).

17. Heinrich August Winkler, '*Der entbehrliche Stand*. On the politics of the middle classes in the Third Reich', *AfS*, 17 (1977), 1–40. In another place Winkler emphasises quite rightly the 'deferment of concrete, economic interests in favour of rather vague class interests', most noticeable among the white-collar worker class. ('Extremism of the centre? Social-historical aspects of the NS seizure of power', now in: *Liberalismus und Antiliberalismus* (Göttingen, 1979), p. 212.)

18. Cf. also Albrecht Tyrell (ed.), *Führer befiehl. Selbstzeugnisse aus der Kampfzeit* (Düsseldorf, 1969), pp. 307ff.

19. To my knowledge this concept was first used by J. P. Stern, *Hitler* (pp. 9–22): 'One is struck by the representativeness of the public and private figures alike, by his grasp of most aspects (other than literature) of the "culture" of his day' (p. 20).

20. Ralf Dahrendorf, *Gesellschaft und Demokratie in Deutschland* (Munich, 1966), pp. 431–47 (*Democracy and Society in Germany*, London, 1968); David Schoenbaum, *Hitler's Social Revolution. Class and Status in Nazi Germany 1933–1939* (London, 1967).

21. Karl Griewank, *Der neuzeitliche Revolutionsbegriff* (Frankfurt, 1973), pp. 21f.

22. Theodor Schieder, '*Stichwort "Revolution"*', *Sowjetsystem und Demokratische Gesellschaft*, Vol. 5 (Freiburg, 1972), p. 697.

23. In addition see, more recently, Wolfgang J. Mommsen, 'Die deutsche Revolution 1918–1920. Politische Revolution und soziale Protestbewegung', in *Geschicte und Gesellschaft* (1978), 372–91.

24. Dahrendorf, *Gesellschaft und Demokratie*, p. 432.

25. Thus in the *Statistisches Jahrbuch des Deutschen Reiches*, Year 52 (Berlin, 1933), p. 539.

26. Cf. also Hans Mommsen, 'On the limiting of traditional and fascist leading groups in Germany during the transition from the movement- to the system-phase', in Wolfgang Schieder (ed.), *Faschismus als soziale Bewegung. Deutschland und Italien im Vergleich* (Hamburg, 1976), pp. 157–81; Fritz Fischer, *Bündnis der Eliten*, on the continuity of the power structures in Germany 1871–1945 (Düsseldorf, 1979) and also the contributions of Wolfgang Wette and Wilhelm Deist, in *Ursachen und Voraussetzungen der deutschen Kriegspolitik*, edited by the Militärgeschichtliches Forschungsamt Freiburg (Stuttgart, 1979).

27. See Renzo de Felice, *Der Faschismus. Ein Interview mit Michael A. Ledeen*, with an epilogue by Jens Petersen (Stuttgart, 1977), p. 54: 'The real problem which must be solved if one wishes to understand the seizure of power of fascism, does not lie in the attitude which the economy adopted towards it, but in the behaviour of the masses who supported fascism in the years 1921–22, both the committed supporters and also the broader reaches of public opinion.'

28. See in addition, Paul Kluke, 'Der Fall Potempa. Eine Dokumentation', *Vierteljahrshefte für Zeitgeschicte* (1957), 279–97.

29. Fest, *Hitler*, p. 976.

30. According to Adolf Heusinger, *Befehl im Widerstreit* (Tübingen, 1950), p. 367.

31. The reaction of the German people to the seizure of power does not exactly fall among the popular topics of research. The reports in the not yet fully

integrated press cannot all be due to manipulation. See the documentation of, among others, Joachim Kuropka (ed.) on *Die Machtergreifung der Nationalsozialisten*, dealing with the example of the town of Münster (Münster, 1979), which was a completely bourgeois town, loyal to the Centre.

32. Quotation from Philipp W. Fabry, *Mutmassungen über Hitler. Urteile von Zeitgenossen* (Düsseldorf, 1969), p. 153.

33. See also the pitiful end of the only combative group within the Weimar coalition: Karl Rohe, *Das Reichsbanner Schwarz-Rot-Gold* (Düsseldorf, 1966), pp. 110ff.; also Karl Dietrich Bracher, *Die Deutsche Diktatur* (Cologne, 1969), pp. 235ff.

34. Barbara Marshall, 'German Attitudes to British Military Government 1945–1947', in *Journal of Contemporary History* (1980/81). In most of the prisoner-of-war camps a militant Nazi spirit existed right up to the end of the war, as Barry Sullivan found out, see his *Threshold of Peace. Four Hundred Thousand German Prisoners and the People of Britain* (London, 1979), pp. 86–112. The British Camp Guard teams could not prevent political dissidents from being 'executed' by fanatical Nazis. The interrogating officers had to prove that the POWs supported National Socialism mainly because of its apparent social and economic achievements, but especially also because of the policy of removal of class barriers which it pursued (p. 95).

35. Ibid.

36. Party Statistics (in the *IfZ*), edited by the *Reichsorganisations Chief of the NSDAP* (Robert Ley), Vol. 1 (Munich, 1935), p. 70.

37. *Statistical Yearbook of the German Reich, Year 52* (Berlin, 1933), p. 19 and also *Party Statistics*, Vol. 2, p. 164.

38. Michael H. Kater, 'Sozialer Wandel in der NSDAP im Zuge der nationalsozialistischen Machtergreifung', in Schieder (ed.) *Faschismus als soziale Bewegung*, p. 53.

39. See also especially Seymour Martin Lipset, 'Fascism, Left, Right and Center', in *Political Man. The Social Bases of Politics* (Garden City, 1960), pp. 217–79. The theories of Seymour M. Lipset and Reinhard Bendix on the body of electors of the NSDAP in the light of more recent results of research, are found in Peter Steinbach (ed.), *Partizipation als Mittel der politischen Modernisierung* (Stuttgart, 1980).

40. See also especially the work of Jürgen Kocka, *Klassengesellschaft im Krieg 1914–1918* (Göttingen, 1973), Heinrich August Winkler, *Mittelstand, Demokratie und Nationalsozialismus* (Cologne, 1972) and Arthur Schweitzer, *Die Nazifizierung des Mittelstands* (Stuttgart, 1970) on the development of the old and the new middle classes from the First to the Second World War, the composition of which is, without exception, governed most strongly by socio-economic questions and thereby suggests that the economic situation was the all-important factor.

41. Theodor Geiger, *Die soziale Schichtung des deutschen Volkes. Soziographischer Versuch auf statistischer Grundlage* (Stuttgart, 1932).

42. Hans Speier, *Die Angestellten vor dem Nationalsozialismus* (Göttingen, 1977). Speier is looking for answers to the question: 'The class theory explains the middle-class alignment of the bourgeois white-collar groups as "false awareness". How, though, does it explain this false awareness?' (p. 87).

43. Rainer Lepsius, *Extremer Nationalismus. Strukturbedingungen vor der nationalsozialistischen Machtergreifung* (Stuttgart, 1966).

44. Geiger, *Die soziale Schichtung*, p. 77.

45. Cf. to a certain extent Reich, *Die Massenpsychologie des Faschismus*, pp. 40ff.

46. Geiger, *Die soziale Schichtung*, p. 78.

47. Speier, *Die Angestellten*, p. 120.

48. Lepsius, *Extremer Nationalismus*, pp. 13ff.

49. The highest number of votes for the NSDAP were in the rural areas of the Eastern provinces, mainly in East Prussia (56·5%) and Pomerania (56·3%). But also in the constituencies of Chemnitz-Zwickau (50·0%) and Breslau (50·2%) half of all valid votes fell to the Hitler movement. *Statistisches Jahrbuch des Deutschen Reiches* (Berlin, 1933), p. 540.

50. *Party Statistics*, Vol. 1, p. 56.

51. Hermann Rauschning, *Gespräche mit Hitler* (Zürich, 1940), p. 181. Cf. also Hitler's speeches on May Day, especially on 1 May 1933, shortly before he dissolved the trade unions (Max Domarus (ed.), *Hitler. Reden und Proklamationen*, Vol. 1 (Munich, 1962), pp. 259ff.).

52. Haffner, *Ammerkungen zu Hitler*, pp. 50f.

53. In the sphere of law the connection between Hitler and the 'purity of national sentiment' was most clearly to be seen. This was mentioned in an *SD* report on the mood of the populace after Hitler had become indignant on 26 April 1942 about the 'formal concepts in the law', and it was stated that 'with his words on justice and officialdom the Führer had expressed the opinion of a large proportion of the people', Boberach, *Meldungen*, p. 259. For Hitler's criticism of the administration of justice in the courts see also Henry Picker, *Hitlers Tischgespräche im Führerhauptquartier* (Stuttgart, 1976), pp. 103f. and also Martin Broszat, 'Zur Perversion der Strafjustiz im Dritten Reich' (Dokumentation) in *VjhZG* (1958), 390–443.

54. It was even on cigarette cards, for which there was an album, that Hitler's closest colleagues reported about their wonderful boss. See for example, *Adolf Hitler. Bilder aus dem Leben des Führers*, edited by Cigaretten-Bilderdienst (Hamburg-Bahrenfeld, 1936), especially the chapter by his driver Julius Schreck, 'Der Führer auf Reisen', pp. 9ff.

55. See in addition the catchword *Vorsehung* (Providence) in the index in Domarus (ed.), *Hitler*, Vol. 11, p. 2290.

56. Cf. also the speech at the conference of the NS Women's Movement of 5 September 1934 in Domarus (ed.), *Hitler*, Vol. 1, pp. 449ff. On the NS Women's policy generally, Dörte Winkler, *Frauenarbeit im 'Dritten Reich'* (Hamburg, 1977).

57. Speech before the Hitler Youth on 14 September 1935, in which were uttered the words so often quoted later, 'German boys were as fleet as greyhounds, as tough as leather and as hard as Krupp steel'; Domarus (ed.), *Hitler*, Vol. 1, pp. 532f.

58. The embodiment of the intellectual in politics was, for Hitler, Reichskanzler von Bethmann-Hollweg. According to his opinion it was 'a disaster that our people had to fight out its very battle for existence under the Reichschancellorship of a philosophising weakling', instead of having 'a more robust man of the people as their leader/Führer' (*Mein Kampf*, 241/245, Munich 1937 edn, p. 481). See also the countless references to the catchword 'Intellektuelle' in Domarus (ed.), *Hitler*, Vol. 11, p. 2283 ('root out', 'inferior types', 'rabble of the nation').

59. Domarus (ed.), *Hitler*, Vol. 1, p. 116.

60. More information about radio as a political medium in Heinz Pohle, *Der Rundfunk als Instrument der Politik* (Hamburg, 1955), pp. 252–72, where there are also some reviews of topics and statistics of numbers of listeners (p. 328ff.). See also Willi A. Boelcke, *Die Macht des Radios. Weltpolitik und Auslandsfunk, 1924–1976* (Frankfurt, 1977), on the power struggles in Berlin about foreign broadcast propaganda which was mainly directed at German minorities abroad.

61. Cf. Hans-Joachim Giese, *Die Film-Wochenschau im Dienste der Politik* (Dresden, 1940), pp. 49ff.; on the film in general: Erwin Leiser, *Deutschland Erwache. Propaganda im Film des Dritten Reiches* (Hamburg (rororo), 1968); Gerd Albrecht,

NOTES TO CHAPTER 4

Nationalsozialistische Filmpolitik, a sociological examination of feature films of the Third Reich (Stuttgart, 1969) and also from the Marxist point of view Wolfgang Becker, *Film und Herrschaft* (Berlin, 1973) and, not least, Walter Hagemann, *Publizistik im Dritten Reich. Ein Beitrag zur Methodik der Massenführung* (Hamburg, 1948), pp. 61ff.

62. See now, in addition, the filmstrips available from the Bundesarchiv (Filmarchiv: Findbuch, Vol. 8, Koblenz 1977) on the Nürnberg Party Rallies before 1933. In addition see also the commentary by Haffner, *Ammerkungen zu Hitler* (pp. 35f.) on the NS election machine compared to the more commonplace functions of other parties.

63. John W. Wheeler-Bennett, *Hindenburg. The Wooden Titan* (London, 1936).

64. On the very distinct nature of court ceremonial of the German princely houses right up to the turn of the century, see Helmut Reichold, *Bismarcks Zaunkönige. Duodez im 20. Jahrhundert* (Paderborn, 1977), pp. 130–57.

65. Cf. Elizabeth Fehrenbach, *Wandlungen des Kaisergedankens, 1871–1918* (Munich, 1969), pp. 216f.

66. Lepsius, *Extremer Nationalismus*, p. 4.

67. Cf. in addition Marlis G. Steinert, *Hitlers Krieg und die Deutschen. Stimmung und Haltung der deutschen Bevölkerung im Zweiten Weltkrieg* (Düsseldorf, 1970), pp. 91f.

68. Broszat, 'Soziale Motivation', pp. 103f.

69. T. W. Mason, *Arbeiterklasse und Volksgemeinschaft* (Opladen, 1977). Even Mason concedes that the DAF were concerned with improving the economic and social position of the workers.

70. Jürgen W. Falter, 'Wer verhalf der NSDAP zum Sieg?', in *Aus Politik und Zeitgeschichte*, supplement to the weekly *Das Parlament* (1979), B 28/29, p. 19.

71. See in addition Henry A. Turner, 'Hitlers Einstellung zu Wirtschaft und Gesellschaft', in *GG* (1976), 1, 89–117.

72. For statistics on legal wrangles (which did not return to zero, but nevertheless were reduced by half between 1932 and 1935 (from 371,000 to 188,900), see Willy Müller, *Das soziale Leben im neuen Deutschland unter besonderer Berücksichtigung der DAF* (Berlin, 1938), p. 153.

73. Domarus (ed.), *Hitler*, Vol. 1, pp. 350f. (27 January 1943).

74. Schoenbaum, *Hitler's Social Revolution*, p. 107.

75. Wolfgang Buchholz, *Die nationalsozialistische Gemeinschaft 'Kraft durch Freude'. Freizeitgestaltung und Arbeiterschaft im Dritten Reich*, Dissertation (Munich, 1976), p. 398.

76. Dahrendorf, *Gesellschaft und Demokratie*, pp. 447f.

77. *Party Statistics*, Vol. 1, p. 53. Of all workers 5·1% belonged to the NSDAP, as against 12·0% of all white-collar workers, 15·2% of all self-employed persons and no less than 20·7% of all civil servants. Within the party the three last-named groups, with 53·8%, held the absolute majority.

78. The farmers made up 20·7% of the working population (workers/artisans: 46·3%), and accounted for 10·7% (workers/artisans: 32·1%) of party members and 14·7% (workers/artisans: 23·0%) of political activists. See *Party Statistics*, Vol. 2, p. 157.

79. See ibid. Even if middle-class socialism, as it had seemed to promise before 1933, did not succeed (cf. Winkler, Mittelstand, *Demokratie und Nationalsozialismus*, note 17 and Schweitzer, *Die Nazifizierung des Mittelstands*, pp. 100–36), nevertheless, white-collar workers, the self-employed and civil servants (including teachers) were noticeably dominant within the party. Although their proportion of the working population was only 26·8%, they formed 53·8% of all party members and no less than 59·7% of all political activists.

80. For the social-democratic club-life and its effect, see George L. Mosse, *Die Nationalisierung der Massen* (Frankfurt, 1976), pp. 190–212. In addition, see also Reich, *Die Massenpsychologie des Faschismus*, p. 80: 'The lower middle-class bedroom which the "prole" procured for himself as soon as he had the means and, even if he was otherwise revolutionary minded, the closely associated suppression of the wife, even if he was a communist, the "proper" clothing on Sundays, the stiff-backed dances he liked and a thousand other trifling details, when taken to extremes of effect, had incomparably more reactionary influence than thousands of revolutionary rally speeches and hand-outs could ever have achieved'.

81. Max Weber, *Wirtschaft und Gesellschaft*, edited by Johannes Winkelmann, vol. 1 (Tübingen, 1976), p. 141.

82. See note 19 above.

83. Broszat, 'Soziale Motivation', pp. 106f.

84. Eberhard Jäckel, *Hitlers Weltanschauung. Entwurf einer Herrschaft* (Tübingen, 1969).

85. Strassburger Neueste Nachrichten, 10 February 1941. Further examples in Binion, *Das ihr mich gefunden habt*, pp. 166f. Fest quotes the first devotional address of the young Goebbels to Hitler imprisoned at Landsberg: 'God gave us you to tell of our suffering. You transformed our torment into words of salvation' (p. 288).

86. Fritz Stern, *Kulturpessimismus als politische Gefahr* (Stuttgart and Vienna, 1963), pp. 190ff. (*The Politics of Cultural Despair*, New York, 1959).

87. Cf. the cultural speeches, especially those given in Munich and Nürnberg; references in Domarus (ed.), *Hitler*, Vol. II, p. 2284. See also Arne Fryksen, 'Hitlers Reden zur Kultur. Kunstpolitische Taktik oder Ideologie', in *Probleme deutscher Zeitgeschichte* (Läromedelsförlagen, 1970), pp. 235–66; further Hildegard Brenner, *Die Kunstpolitik des Nationalsozialismus* (Hamburg, (rororo) 1963), pp. 82ff.

88. One exception were the commanders of the Reichswehr to whom Hitler outlined his far-reaching plans as early as 1 February 1933. Cf. Wolfram Wettes' contribution in: 'Ursachen und Voraussetzungen der deutschen Kriegspolitik', Vol. 1 of the series *Das Deutsche Reich und der Zweite Weltkrieg*, edited by the Militärgeschichtliches Forschungsamt (Stuttgart, 1979), pp. 121f.

89. Karl Dietrich Bracher, *Zeitgeschichtliche Kontroversen um Faschismus, Totalitarismus, Demokratie* (Munich, 1976), p. 81.

90. See note 32 above.

91. Thus Picker, *Hitlers Tischgespräche*, p. 122. For Hitler and his philosophy of will-power, cf. Stern, *Kulturpessimismus*, pp. 56ff.

92. On Hitler's rhetoric see the splendid description of atmosphere in Fest, *Hitler*, pp. 448ff.

93. Hitler, *Mein Kampf*, pp. 369ff.

94. Rauschning, *Gespräche mit Hitler*, p. 189.

95. Hitler, *Mein Kampf*, p. 22.

96. Cf. Picker, *Hitlers Tischgespräche*, p. 61 (1 August 1941). These were Hitler's words directed against any uniformity of Reich legislation. Frequently he meant the civil servants whenever he cut loose against the lawyers.

97. See note 49 above.

98. Rauschning, *Gespräche mit Hitler*, p. 58.

99. Cf. Fest, *Hitler*, p. 615, who reports that, even as Reichskanzler, Hitler had found the time to immerse himself again in most volumes of this youthful literature.

100. In addition, Picker, *Hitlers Tischgespräche*, pp. 168f. His sister and half-sister were to receive sufficient from his legacy to maintain a lower-middle-class living.

101. Mosse, *Die Nationalisierung der Massen*, pp. 213–39.

102. Jochen Thies, *Architekt der Weltherrschaft. Die Endziele Hitlers* (Düsseldorf, 1976), pp. 70ff.

103. Domarus (ed.) *Hitler*, Vol. 1, p. 613 (27 March 1936).

104. See in addition Klaus Schwabe, *Wissenschaft und Kriegsmoral. Die deutschen Hochschullehrer und die Grundfragen des Ersten Weltkriegs* (Göttingen, 1969), pp. 21ff. Cf. also Thomas Mann, 'Gedanken im Kriege', in *Politische Schriften und Reden*, Vol. 2 (Frankfurt, 1968), pp. 7–20.

105. For the *Vaterlandspartei* which is indicated here, see Dirk Stegmann, *Die Erben Bismarcks. Parteien und Verbände in der Spätphase des Wilhelminischen Reiches* (Cologne, 1970), pp. 497–519.

106. For the connection between experience of war and social criticism, see Rudolf Vierhaus, 'Faschistisches Führertum', *Historische Zeitschrift* (1964), 614–39.

107. Rauschning, *Gespräche mit Hitler*, p. 44.

108. See in addition, Rohe, *Reichsbanner*, pp. 110ff. as well as Peter H. Merkl, *Political Violence under the Swastika* (Princeton, 1975), pp. 138ff.; also Kurt Sontheimer, *Anti-demokratisches Denken in der Weimarer Republik* (Munich, 1962), pp. 115–39.

109. Hitler, *Mein Kampf*, p. 270.

110. See Lothar Kettenacker, *Nationalsozialistische Volkstumspolitik im Elsass* (Stuttgart, 1973), p. 34.

111. Rauschning, *Gespräche mit Hitler*, p. 79.

112. See also the comments on the theme 'Justiz im Krieg' in Picker, *Hitlers Tischgespräche*, p. 103 (8 February 1942); also Stern, *Kulturpessimismus*, pp. 116–29, who reports on the introduction of the death penalty for motorway robbery which found great acclaim among the ordinary people and which was introduced, in fact, by Hitler himself in one set of summary proceedings.

113. Cf. Rauschning, *Gespräche mit Hitler*, p. 25.

114. Title of a book which appeared anonymously before 1914 by Heinrich Class (Daniel Frymann), the director of the *Alldeutsche Verband*.

115. Robert Koehl, 'Feudal Aspects of National Socialism', in *American Political Science Review* (1962), 921ff.

116. Robert Coulborn (ed.), *Feudalism in History* (Princeton, 1956).

117. Robert L. Koehl, *RKFDV. German Resettlement and Population Policy 1939–1945* (Harvard, 1957).

118. In addition, see Horst Gies, *R. Walther Darré und die nationalsozialistische Bauernpolitik 1930–1933*, Dissertation (Frankfurt, 1965).

119. Cf. Josef Ackermann, *Heinrich Himmler als Ideologe* (Göttingen, 1970).

120. Koehl, 'Feudal Aspects', p. 921.

121. Cf. Picker, *Hitlers Tischgespräche*, p. 463 (26 July 1942).

122. This aspect has been emphasised especially by Hans Mommsen, as in the article: 'Ausnahmezustand als Herrschaftstechnik des NS-Regimes', in Manfred Funke (ed.), *Hitler, Deutschland und die Mächte* (Düsseldorf, 1978), pp. 30–45.

123. Picker, *Hitlers Tischgespräche*, p. 285 (12 May 1942).

124. Ibid., p. 62 (1 August 1941).

125. Ibid., p. 381 (23 June 1942).

126. Ibid., pp. 247 (27 April 1942) and 440 (18 July 1942).

127. See Wippermann, *Faschismus theorien*, p. 147.

5 THE STRUCTURE AND NATURE OF THE NATIONAL CONSERVATIVE OPPOSITION IN GERMANY UP TO 1940

1. General on the literature and development of research, see the specialist biographies of U. Hochmuth, *Faschismus und Widerstand: 1933–1945, ein Verzeichnis*

deutschsprachiger Literatur (Frankfurt, 1973) and R. Büchel, *Der deutsche Widerstand im Spiegel von Fachliteratur und Publizistik seit 1945* (Munich, 1975), also the literary reviews of K. Frhr. v. Aretin in *Geschichte in Wissenschaft und Unterricht*, 25 (1974), 507–12, and 565–70; R. Mann, 'Widerstand gegen den Nationalsozialismus,' in *Neue politische Literatur*, 22 (1977), 425–42, and G. Plum, 'Das "Gelände" des Widerstandes,' marginal notes on literature about the resistance to National Socialism, in W. Benz (ed.), *Miscellanea, Festschrift für Helmut Krausnick zum 75. Geburtstag* (Stuttgart, 1980), pp. 93–102. For the GDR (Eastern Germany) the latest state of interpretations is given by K. Mammach, *Die deutsche anti-faschistische Widerstandsbewegung 1933–1939* (Berlin 1976).

2. On this and the following, see in more detail K.-J. Müller 'Die deutsche Militäropposition gegen Hitler', on the problem of its interpretation and analysis, in *Armee, Politik und Gesellschaft in Deutschland 1933–1945*, studies on the relationship between the army and the NS system, 3rd edn. (Paderborn, 1981), pp. 101–23; also the relevant literature cited there.

3. See Hans-Josef Steinberg, 'Thesen zum Widerstand aus der Arbeiterbewegung', in Ch. Klessmann and F. Pingel (eds), *Gegner des Nationalsozialismus* (Frankfurt/ New York, 1980), pp. 67–72 and D. Peuckert, Zur Rolle des Arbeiterwiderstandes im "Dritten Reich", ibid. pp. 73–90, on the rôle of workers' resistance in the Third Reich.

4. See Günther van Norden, 'Widerstand im deutschen Protestantismus 1933– 1945', in ibid., pp. 103–25 and L. Volk SJ. 'der Widerstand der katholischen Kirche, in ibid., pp. 126–39.

5. See A. Klönne, *Gegen den Strom*, report on youth resistance in the Third Reich (Hanover and Frankfurt, 1957) and K.-H. Jahnke, *Entscheidungen. Jugend im Widerstand 1933–1945* (Frankfurt, 1970). Also H. W. Koch, *The Hitler Youth: Origins and Development 1922–1945* (London, 1975), Chapter 10.

6. P. Hüttenberger, 'Vorüberlegungen zum "Widerstandsbegriff"', in *Theorien in der Praxis des Historikers*, ed. Jürgen Kocka (*Geschichte und Gesellschaft*, Sonderheft, 1977).

7. See also in detail K.-J. Müller, *Armee und Drittes Reich. Versuch einer historischen Interpretation* (Stuttgart, 1969).

8. See Manfred Messerschmidt, 'Werden und Prägung des deutschen Offizierkorps', in *Offiziere im Bild von Dokumenten aus drei Jahrhunderten* (Stuttgart, 1964), as well as Karl Demeter, *Das deutsche Offizierkorps in Gesellschaft und Staat 1650–1945* (Frankfurt, 1964, revised and extended ed. 1965), available also in an English translation, *The German Officer Corps.*

9. On this interpretational assessment of the structure of the Prussian-German Empire see Hans-Ulrich Wehler, *Das Deutsche Kaiserreich 1871–1918* (Göttingen 1973, 1975), and the important reviews on it by Thomas Nipperdey, 'Wehler's "Kaiserreich". Eine kritische Auseinandersetzung', in *Geschichte und Gesellschaft*, 1 (1975), 539–60, as well as by Hans-Günter Zmarzlik, 'Das Kaiserreich in neuer Sicht?', in *Historische Zeitschrift*, 222 (1976), 105–26. See also the counter-critique in H. W. Koch, *A Constitutional History of Germany in the Nineteenth and Twentieth Centuries* (London, 1984) pp. 236ff and D. Calleo, *The German Problem Reconsidered* (Cambridge, 1980).

10. On this and on the following, see Theodor Schieder, *Das deutsche Kaiserreich von 1871 als Nationalstaat* (Cologne and Opladen, 1961).

11. In general, on this see the omnibus volumes: *Reichsgründung 1870/71. Tatsachen, Kontoversen, Interpretationen*, ed. by Th. Schieder and Ernst Deuerlein (Stuttgart, 1970), and *Das kaiserliche Deutschland. Politik und Gesellschaft 1870–1918*, ed. by Michael Stürmer (Düsseldorf, 1970). Also R. Dahrendorf, *Democracy and Society in Germany* (London, 1969) and H. W. Koch, *A History of Prussia* (London, 1978).

12. Apart from the literature mentioned in note 8 above, see M. Messerschmidt, *Militär und Politik in der Bismarckzeit und im wilhelminischen Deutschland* (Darmstadt, 1975) as well as Martin Kitchen, *The German Officer Corps, 1890–1914* (Oxford, 1973).

13. See 'Die politsche Geschichte der preussisch-deutschen Armee,' in *Handbuch zur deutschen Militärgeschichte*, ed. for the Militärgeschichtliches Forschungsamt by O. Hackl and M. Messerschmidt, Vol. 2 (Munich, 1975).

14. On this point see the fundamental works of M. Geyer, especially: *Aufrüstung oder Sicherheit. Reichswehr und die Krise der Machtpolitik 1924–1936* (Wiesbaden, 1980), and his, 'Der zur Organisation erhobene Burgfrieden', in K.-J. Müller and Eckhardt Opitz (eds), *Militär und Militarismus in der Weimarer Republik* (Düsseldorf, 1978), pp. 15–100. In these works Geyer develops a comprehensive interpretative and inter-related framework, the basic essence of which is the idea of the 'industrialisation of war', the 'delimitising of the use of (military) force' and the 'socialisation of war' together with the more general 'socialisation of danger'. This central idea of Geyer's, of the 'industrialisation of war', in my opinion, puts too little emphasis on the importance of the ever-constant socio-politically structured traditions of the Prussio-German state and of its officer corps. In addition, it appears to me, on the subject of the industrialisation phenomenon, that too little consideration has been paid to the immense importance of the new technology for the military. I would therefore prefer the term 'technical-industrial war'. Excellent on the historical dimension is Michael Howard, *War in European History* (London, Oxford, New York, 1976).

15. The objective of the restoration of Germany as a great power had already been clearly expressed during the well-known meeting of leading officers of the general staff on 20 December 1918 in Berlin, at which both Seeckt and Schleicher appeared as main speakers: see the description in Francis L. Carsten, *Reichswehr and Politics 1918–1933* (Oxford, 1966).

16. See Müller, *Armee und Drittes Reich* cited in note 7 above.

17. Hans Meier-Welcker, *Seeckt* (Frankfurt, 1967), particularly chapters x–xii and xvii; in addition see Carl Guske, *Das politische Denken des General v. Seeckt. Ein Beitrag zur Diskussion des Verhältnisses Seeckt-Reichswehr-Republik*, Lübeck (Hamburg, 1971), H. J. Gordon Jr, *The Reichswehr and the German Republic 1919–1926* (Princeton, 1957); H. W. Koch, *Der Deutsche Bürgerkrieg 1918–1924* (Berlin, 1978).

18. See A. Schildt, *Militärdiktatur mit Massenbasis? Die Querfrontkonzeption der Reichswehrführung um General von Schleicher am Ende der Weimarer Republik* (Frankfurt/New York, 1981); D. Groener-Geyer, *General Groener, Soldat und Staatsmann* (Frankfurt, 1955); F.-K. v. Plehwe Reichskanzler Kurt v. Schleidner (Esslingen, 1983).

19. See M. Messerschmidt, *Die Wehrmacht im NS-Staat. Zeit der Indoktrination* (Hamburg, 1969), *passim*.

20. Quoted from R. A. Blasius, *Für Grossdeutschland – gegen den grossen Krieg. Ernst v. Weizsäcker in den Krisen über die Tschechoslowakei und Polen* (Cologne/Vienna, 1981), p. 24 (also the relevant literature cited there on E. v. Weizsäcker).

21. Ernst v. Weizsäcker, *Die Weizsäcker-Papiere*, ed. by L. E. Hill (Berlin, 1974).

22. Hüttenberger, 'Vorüberlegungen zum "Widerstandsbegriff"', p. 133.

23. On the Röhm affair see K.-J. Müller, *Das Heer und Hitler. Armee und nationalsozialistisches Régime 1933–1940* (Stuttgart, 1969), Chapter iii, as well as his, 'Reichswehr und "Röhm-Affäre"', in *Militärgeschichtliche Mitteilungen* (in future referred to as *MGM*) 3 (1968), 107–44 and Ch. Bloch, *Die SA und die Krise des NS-Regimes 1934* (Frankfurt, 1970).

24. On this point see Blasius, *Für Grossdeutschland*, *passim* and the literature mentioned there.

25. Ibid., pp. 120, 121, 125. See special emissary Henderson's letter to Lord Halifax of 21 August 1939, about Weizsäcker's suggestion that General Ironside should send a warning letter from the British prime minister to Hitler: 'His visit might at least help to discredit Ribbentrop', *Documents on British Foreign Policy 1919–1939*, ed., by E. L. Woodward and R. Butler (London, 1946) (in future abbreviated to *DBFP*), 3rd series, vol. vii, No. 117, p. 109.

26. See K.-J. Müller, *Das Heer und Hitler* (Stuttgart, 1969), Chapter iv, 'Blomberg-Skandal und Fritsch-Krise', as well as H. C. Deutsch, *Das Komplott oder die Entmachtung der Generale. Blomber- und Fritsch-Krise. Hitlers Weg zum Krieg* (Zürich, 1974).

27. B. Scheurig, *Henning von Tresckow. Eine Biographie* (Hamburg, 1973, 1980). H. Graml, 'Der Fall Oster,' in *Vierteljahrshefte für Zeitgeschichte* (Munich, 1966), pp. 26–39. General Beck noted at the time his impression that the Fritsch case 'had opened a chasm between Hitler and the officer corps, especially in respect of mutual trust, which could never again be bridged', *Bundesarchiv-Militärarchiv* (in future abbreviated to *BA-MA*) no. 28/3, sheet 43–5, note of 29 July 1938; cf. H. Höhne, *Canaris, Patriot im Zwielicht* (Munich, 1976).

28. See G. Ritter, *Carl Goerdeler und die deutsche Widerstandsbewegung* (Stuttgart, 1956).

29. B. Scheurig, *Henning von Tresckow. Eine Biographie* (Hamburg, 1973).

30. See on this point, Müller, *Heer und Hitler*, Chapter vii and viii, as well as P. Hoffmann, *Widerstand, Staatsstreich, Attentat. Der Kampf der Opposition gegen Hitler* (Munich, 1979), Chapter iv.

31. On this, see especially Höhne, *Canaris*, Chapter 8. along with the most recent literature.

32. With reference to the inter-connections of personnel, especially informative is: Hoffmann, *Widerstand*, Chapter ii; the quotation is from there, p. 52.

33. See Müller, *Heer und Hitler*, pp. 232ff.

34. See G. Ritter, *Carl Goerdeler und die deutsche Widerstandsbewegung* (Stuttgart, 1956), pp. 154ff., 167f. Goerdeler sent his tour reports among other things to Göring and Schacht as well as to the *Reichskanzlei* (Wiedemann).

35. British reactions to Goerdeler's information and the assessment of his reports are described in detail by S. Aster, *1939: The Making of the Second World War* (London, 1973), especially pp. 43ff., 45–9, 57, 230ff., 345, 362.

36. See on this and on the following, Deutsch, *Das Komplott*, as well as the relevant chapters in Hoffmann, *Widerstand* (Chapter iii) and Müller, *Heer und Hitler* (Chapter vi). For Canaris see Höhne, *Canaris*, pp. 244ff.

37. The background to which these developments took place was the increasingly critical attitude which prevailed in sections of the national-conservative milieu, who were disappointed with the development of the regime. The rapidly spreading dissatisfaction in these circles, which had helped in 1933 to carry the 'national rebirth' as far as possible, is however, in no way to be labelled 'opposition'. At best it was the root-base for a possible formation of such opposition, but nothing more, even if many of these disappointed national-conservatives were inclined to profess themselves to be an 'opposition', especially when describing to counterparts abroad the whole mood of their circles, even though completely misunderstanding the true nature of the existing power relationships, (see as example, the comments of Koerber to Mason MacFarlane, *DBFP*, 3rd series, vol. ii, no. 595, p. 65.). Beck, Canaris and Hossbach, on the other hand, were completely free of such illusions at this time.

38. On Canaris see Höhne, Chapter 8; on Hossbach see Deutsch, *Das Komplott*, and on Beck see Müller, *Heer und Hitler*, pp. 262, 267ff., 281–98, as well as Müller,

Ludwig Beck, Studien und Dokumente zur politisch-militärischen Vorstellungswelt und Tätigkeit des Generalstabschefs des deutschen Heeres 1933–1938 (Boppard, 1980), Chapter III.

39. Printed in Müller, *Heer und Hitler*, document no. 34. Especially informative on the nature of the power struggle, there is the formula, 'the setting-free of the Wehrmacht' (therefore not primarily the nation!).

40. On this and on the following see H. K. G. Roennefarth, *Die Sudetenkrise in der internationalen Politik, Entstehung, Verlauf, Auswirkung*, vol. 2 (Wiesbaden, 1961); as well as Müller, *Ludwig Beck*, Chapter v and vi, and R. A. Blasius, *Grossdeutschland, passim* (along with the most recent literature). Also K. G. Robbins, *Munich* (London, 1978) and E. H. Carr, *The Twenty Years' Crisis* (London, 1939), *first edition only.*

41. This suggests mainly the work by Hoffmann, *Widerstand.*

42. For this and for the following, in detail, see Müller, *Ludwig Beck*; a synopsis of the findings in this book in Müller, *Armee, Politik und Gesellschaft* (cited in n. 2 above), the paragraph headed 'Generaloberst Ludwig Beck. Generalstabchef des deutschen Heeres 1933–1938. Einige Reflektionen und neuere Forschungsergebnisse', pp. 51–100.

43. See G. R. Ueberschär, 'Generaloberst Halder im militärischen Widerstand 1938–1940', in *Wehrforschung*, I (1973), H. I, 20–31.

44. See, in addition, Höhne, *Canaris, passim.*

45. See Blasius, *Grossdeutschland.*

46. See, on this point, Weizsäcker's similar thoughts in a note of February 1939 (*Die Weizsäcker-Papiere*).

47. Printed as documents 31 and 43 in Müller, *Ludwig Beck.*

48. Ibid., document no. 46, notes of 29 May 1938.

49. Official documents – *Akten zur Deutschen Auswärtigen Politik 1918–1945* (in future abbreviated as *ADAP*), D, vol. I, no. 21 and *Weizsäcker-Papiere*, p. 126: entry of 19 April 1938.

50. Müller, *Ludwig Beck*, document no. 55.

51. Blasius, *Grossdeutschland*, Chapter 2, paragraph I, especially pp. 41ff.

52. Ibid., p. 49.

53. Weizsäcker-Papiere, p. 168: 'Ribbentrop took complete charge, therefore, of the Czech issue'. See also ibid., p. 145 (note of 9 October 1938), where Weizsäcker, thinking back to the Godesberg talks with Chamberlain, writes: 'The group which wanted war, namely Ribbentrop and the SS, would nearly have been successful after all in causing the Führer to hit out'.

54. Thus, in contrast to the majority of relevant investigations, Hoffmann, *Widerstand*, pp. 104ff. and 685f. (See there, also, the relevant literature.)

55. Thus, the great majority of literature assimilated in formulae used by W. Foerster, *Generaloberst Ludwig Beck. Sein Kampf gegen den Krieg* (Munich, 1953).

56. See Höhne, *Canaris*, pp. 284ff.

57. See Blasius, *Grossdeutschland*, pp. 51ff.

58. The memoranda and notes, often quoted in this connection, of high-ranking naval officers (Guse, Heye) from July 1938, in which warnings of the risk of war appeared, have been overrated, as more recent investigations have shown, thus H. Krausnick, 'Vorgeschichte und Beginn des militärischen Widerstandes gegen Hitler', in *Vollmacht des Gewissens*, ed. by the Europäische Publikation e.V., vol. I (Frankfurt, Berlin, 1960), pp. 177–384, here pp. 315ff. – 'zu unrecht als Widerstandshandlung' (thus also, M. Salewski, *Die deutsche Seekriegsleitung, 1935–1945*, vol. I: *1935–1941* (Frankfurt, 1970), p. 45).

59. See Beck's memorandum of 16 July 1938 (printed in Müller, *Ludwig Beck*, doc. no. 49/50), where it says: 'the intention of delaying a solution by force of the

Czech problem for so long until the military prerequisites for it have been fundamentally changed. At present I consider it hopeless.'

60. E. v. Weizsäcker, *Erinnerungen. Mein Leben*, ed. by R. v. Weizsäcker (Munich, Leipzig, Freiburg, 1950) recorded a very carefully worded passage in which he indicated that he was in fact never a member of a subversionary group in the foreign office, intent only on the removal/extermination of Hitler, but that he had always acted like a 'supporter' and, since summer 1938, had always advocated the removal of Hitler. This statement finds no corroboration whatever in the *Weizsäcker-Papiere*, the cause of which may, nevertheless, have been the peculiarity of conspiratorial behaviour patterns. At any rate, the most recent thorough investigation also comes to the conclusion (Blasius, *Grossdeutschland*, Chapter 3), that no participation by Weizsäcker in the subversion plans was evident.

61. See on this point, G. Schreiber, *Revisionismus und Weltmachtstreben. Marineführung und deutsch-italienische Beziehungen 1919 bis 1944* (Stuttgart, 1978), Chapter III, as well as his, 'Zur Kontinuität des Grossund Weltmachtstrebens der deutschen Marineführung,' in *MGM*, 2 (1979), 101–72.

62. Verification for this in Müller, *Ludwig Beck*, Chapter IV; on the assessment of enemy disposition with special reference to France see also the situation appraisal in H. Speidel, *Aus unserer Zeit, Erinnerungen* (Frankfurt, Berlin, Vienna, 1977), pp. 431–53: 'Französischer Sicherheitsbegriff und französische Führung'; the particulars of the manoeuvres undertaken by the General Staff for the most part in BA–MA Wi/IF 5.1502.

63. See note 53 above.

64. Thus in *Weizsäcker-Papiere*, p. 128 (22 May 1938: 'Wir bluffen') and pp. 131f. (Dangers of a bluff-policy) as well as in the Rückblick – in retrospect (9 October 1938), p. 145 ('The supposition is therefore incorrect that the Führer had been intent on a huge bluff taken to extreme degrees.')

65. On these diplomatic steps and activities see B. Scheurig, *Ewald v. Kleist-Schmenzin. Ein Konservativer gegen Hitler* (Oldenburg and Hamburg, 1968), pp. 155ff.; Krausnick, *Vorgeschichte*, pp. 307, 330f., 340f: Roennefarth, *Sudetenkrise*, vol. I, Chapter 8; H. Groscurth, *Tagebücher eines Abwehroffiziers 1938–1940*, with further documents on the military opposition to Hitler, ed. by H. Krausnick, H. Deutsch and H. v. Kotze (Stuttgart, 1970), p. 102; E. Kordt, *Nicht aus den Akten* . . . (Not from the official documents . . .) *Die Wilhelmstrasse in Frieden und Krieg, Erlebnisse, Begegnungen und Eindrücke 1928–1945* (Stuttgart, 1950), pp. 228ff.; Höhne, *Canaris*, pp. 287ff.; *Weizsäcker-Papiere*, pp. 142f.

66. See Blasius, *Grossdeutschland*, pp. 60f.

67. See *Weizsäcker-Papiere* p. 169: 'A committed opponent of the war was the Chief of the General Staff Beck. He told me at the beginning of August that he was leaving, because he did not wish to bear any part of the responsibility for the evil to come. To my attempts to change his mind, he answered by saying that, at the moment of crisis a soldier could not leave and, therefore, he should do it beforehand. As for myself, he felt I could stay, since the politician, as opposed to the soldier, had various possibilities to turn away, right up to the end (note of mid-October 1939).

68. On the role of the brothers Theo and Erich Kordt in the foreign office, about the circle around these two and their contacts with other oppositionists see Blasius, *Grossdeutschland*, pp. 55f., 141ff. (with corresponding sources and literature).

69. On this point, see S. Aster, *Second World War, 1939* (London, 1973), as well as B.-J. Wendt, *München 1938. England zwischen Hitler und Preussen* (Frankfurt, 1965).

70. On this, see the works of Aster, *Second World War*; J. Henke, *England in Hitlers politischem Kalkül 1935–1939* (Boppard, 1973); W. Michalka, *Ribbentrop und die*

deutsche Weltpolitik, 1939–1940. Aussenpolitische Konzeptionen und Entscheidungsprozesse im Dritten reich (Munich, 1980) as well as *Weizsäcker-Papiere.* In the relevant literature there is still too little distinction between official, semi-official and conspiratorial contacts abroad. See also the recent essay by Oswald Hauser, 'England und der deutsche Widerstand im Spiegel britischer Akten', in *Weltpolitik, Europagedanke, Regionalismus. Festschrift für Heinz Gollwitzer zum 65. Geburtstag,* ed. by Heinz Dollinger, Horst Gründer and Alwin Hanschmidt (Münster, 1982).

71. Blasius, *Grossdeutschland,* pp. 51ff. attempts an analytical distinction in 'Einflussnahme auf dem Dienstweg', 'Einwirkung von innen' und 'Beeinflussung von aussen'; then, however, he adopts (p. 57) Weizsäcker's own post-war formulations to describe the Henderson–Weizsäcker talks: 'Conspiracy with the potential opponent for the purpose of securing peace' (Weizsäcker, *Erinnerungen,* p. 178). Here, the expression 'conspiracy' is certainly inappropriate as one could sooner express it as 'personal diplomacy' or, at most, 'counter-diplomacy' on the part of the state secretary, or as 'opposition by means of departmental opportunity'.

72. There is a detailed description of the development in Hoffmann, *Widerstand,* Chapter iv/4 as well as a thorough analysis in Müller, *Heer und Hitler,* Chapter viii ('Die September-Verschwörung').

73. Politically important in this was the feeling between Halder and Schacht, as well as the somewhat looser contacts with Goerdeler, which functioned via Gisevius; technically valuable were the relations with Police-President Helldorff and his deputy Schulenburg; the group around F. W. Heinz had some loose contacts with a few former trade unionists (Leuschner).

74. Details about Oster's plans in Hoffmann, *Widerstand,* pp. 118ff and Müller, *Heer und Hitler,* p. 369. Attention is drawn, in addition, to the fact that the main source on which the relevant investigations are based is exceptionally narrow and qualitatively very bad. It is a question, exclusively, of statements after the event.

75. Brauchitsch was apparently brought into the anti-war activities by Halder and Witzleben during the crisis of the German-British talks of 26–29 September; it remains uncertain whether he was informed about the planned course of action. Weizsäcker, on the other hand, refused to support the overthrow of Hitler as being too risky at the time, though he, nevertheless, was in touch with the conspirators; see Blasius, *Grossdeutschland,* p. 160.

76. See the wording in Goerdeler's letter of 11 October 1938 in Ritter, *Goerdeler,* p. 198 and the diary notes in U. v. Hassell, *Vom anderen Deutschland. Aus den nachgelassenen Tagebüchern 1938–1944* (Zürich–Freiburg, 1946), p.18; cf. also Weizsäcker's remark to Canaris: 'An internal action would be impossible if there were no Führer present and the people had got used to living in a Napoleonic age' (Groscurth, *Tagebücher,* p. 159, entry of 14 December 1938).

77. Not until 24 September were the conspirators successful in obtaining a groundplan of the *Reichskanzlei* which was necessary for the assault troops (Kordt, *Niche aus den Akten,* p. 263); Halder complained that Witzleben had not taken enough trouble with details of the planning (Ritter, *Goerdeler,* p. 479, n. 75). Cf. also Müller, *Heer und Hitler,* pp. 360, 375.

78. There is a synopsis of all relevant research in Hoffmann, *Widerstand,* Chapter iv, paras 1 and 2, as well as in, with a different evaluation, Müller, *Heer und Hitler,* Chapter ix.

79. See, for example, the entry by Hassell (*Vom anderen Deutschland,* p. 59) in his diary, 7 August 1939, on information from a confidant in the foreign office: 'Ribbentrop is behaving like a madman . . . Göring still appears to be the most sensible one there, but does not want . . . to be accused of being a coward again. There can be no hope among the Generals. Of Keitel there can be no doubt, but Brauchitsch also now completely in the hands of the Party. Few kept a cool head: Halder, Canaris, Thomas.'

80. On this point see Müller, *Heer und Hitler*, Chapter IX, specifically pp. 399–405.

81. See the critical appraisal of one of those involved: H. B. Gisevius, *Bis zum bitteren Ende. Vom Reichstagsbrand bis zum 20. Juli 1944* (Sonderausgabe) (Hamburg, 1964), pp. 403f. Even the occupation of the rest of Czechoslovakia – as Beck maintained – was no great rousing event (ibid., p. 389).

82. After great difficulties a meeting was arranged between Beck and Halder which ended in discord. It is true that both men agreed absolutely on the appraisal of the situation, but Halder considered a state coup in the present situation to be hopeless, since the right moment had not yet been reached. Beck departed deeply disappointed from his successor (see Müller, *Heer und Hitler*, pp. 395f. and Ueberschär, *Halder*, pp. 24f.).

83. The only diplomatic steps which were not initiated by Weizsäcker and which were not checked over with him as to their central issues, were those undertaken by the Kordt brothers in London in June 1939; along with other approaches to the British government, to persuade it to issue a clear warning to Hitler in order to prevent him from declaring war, these were meant to initiate a public British declaration against Hitler's war policy, which in turn would be the key factor in the overthrow of the regime (see on this point, the supporting evidence and critical analysis in Blasius, *Grossdeutschland*, pp. 141ff.). There could be here a tentative point of contact between the anti-war policy and certain aspects of the plans for a coup at that time; at any rate, in view of the existing disparity of the radical opposition, one fails to see how and by whom, as a result of a public British declaration, a coup of this kind was supposed to have been carried out in Germany. As recognisably as the diplomatic steps taken by the Kordts in London are supported with evidence, so equally unrecognisable is any concrete proof of a planned coup or even any relevant preparations.

84. See Müller, *Heer und Hitler*, Chapter IX, as well as Höhne, *Canaris*, pp. 318f., 329f. Moreover, Keitel seems, for a time, really to have tried to persuade Hitler to avoid war: W. Görlitz (ed.), *Generalfeldmarschall Keitel, Verbrecher oder Offizier? Erinnerungen, Briefe, Dokumente des Chefs OKW* (Göttingen, Berlin, Frankfurt, 1961), p. 208.

85. On this point, see Weizsäcker's retrospective report of October 1939, *Weizsäcker-Papiere*, p. 172, as well as Michalka, *Ribbentrop*, Chapter IV and Blasius, *Grossdeutschland*, pp. 92ff., 117ff., as well as Henke, *England*, Chapter III.

86. Thus Blasius, *Grossdeutschland*, p. 91.

87. For the British side see S. Aster, *Second World War*. Further, see Hoffmann, *Widerstand*, pp. 138ff.

88. See Höhne, *Canaris*, Chapter 9.

89. The best known example is the text of Hitler's speech of 22 August 1939, doctored up for the purpose, which was then played to the British: see Müller, *Heer und Hitler*, pp. 409–13; H. W. Koch, 'The Origins of the Second World War: Second Thoughts on the Status of some Documents', in *Historical Journal*, (1968).

90. Blasius, *Grossdeutschland*, p. 162.

91. *Ibid.*, pp. 98ff.

92. See the résumé of the analysis by Blasius, *Grossdeutschland*, p. 162: Weizsäcker, 'it is true, despised the Nazi regime, but, because of his attitude during the crises concerning Czechoslovakia and Poland is not to be considered as a "man of resistance" against Hitler. Weizsäcker was counting on the common sense of the *Führer*; and, in order to influence the *Führer*'s decisions, he thought it necessary to wrestle with the "war-monger" Ribbentrop.'

93. Quotation from Aster, *Second World War*, pp. 230f.

94. Gisevius, *Bis zum bitteren Ende*, pp. 403f.

95. This is shown most impressively by the findings evaluated in Aster, *Second World War*. In addition, the British also had dealings to attend to with Hitler's official emissaries, who came to London outside the normal diplomatic channels, such as Wiedemann, Reichenau, etc.

96. For example, Schwerin suggested to the British that they should send a part of the fleet into the Baltic as a demonstration, while, at the same time, Weizsäcker was busy persuading Hitler, by reason of détente, not to send a German fleet to Danzig. (On the Schwerin mission: Aster, *Second World War*, pp. 235, 237f.)

97. *Weizsäcker-Papiere*, p. 163 (31 August 1939).

98. On Canaris see Höhne, *Canaris*, pp. 302f., 320ff., as well as Groscurth, *Tagebücher*, pp. 171, 173 ('The great Reichstag speech of the Führer now sets in motion our work against Poland. That is good and is about time, too.') and pp. 178ff.; on Weizsäcker see *Weizsäcker-Papiere*, pp. 150ff., 175f. (quotation p. 157, entry of 30 July 1939); on Halder: see in Müller, *Heer und Hitler*, pp. 545f., 567 the supporting proof of Halder's innate anglophobia and his essential agreement on the need for a settlement of the question of the eastern borders; on 15 October 1965 Halder wrote to the author: 'That England was, in fact, the key protagonist in the struggle between the western powers and Germany, I have never doubted.'

6 HITLER'S PLANNING FOR WAR AND THE RESPONSE OF THE GREAT POWERS

1. E. M. Robertson, *Hitler's Pre-War Policy and Military Plans* (Longmans, 1963), especially p. 113 and p. 173. References to documents held officially in the United Kingdom, when I was engaged on the original text, will be given below.

2. R. G. L. Waite, *The Psychopathic God Adolf Hitler* (New York, 1977), p. xi. For an admirable discussion on the problems of writing a biography of Hitler, see H. Graml, 'Probleme einer Hitler-Biographie: Kritische Bemerkungen zu Joachim C. Fest's', in *Vierteljahrshefte für Zeitgeschichte*, 1 (1974).

3. E. M. Robertson (ed), *Origins of World War II* (London, 1971), 'World War II: The Historians and their materials', pp. 1–35, discusses some of the controversies and the work includes a valuable article by A. Bullock, 'Hitler and the Origins of World War II', pp. 189–224, but the introduction does not take into account many works then being published in Germany.

4. *Hitler's Zweites Buch: Ein Dokument aus dem Jahre 1928* (ed.) G. L. Weinberg (Stuttgart, 1969).

5. K. Hildebrand, *Vom Reich zum Weltreich: Hitler, NSDAP und Kolonialfrage 1919–1945* (Munich, 1969); his *The Foreign Policy of the Third Reich* (London, 1972) and 'Hitlers 'Programm' und seine Realisierung 1938–1942', in G. Niedhart (ed.), *Kriegsbeginn 1939* (Darmstadt, 1976). See also A. Hillgruber, *Hitler's Strategie, Politik und Kriegsführung 1940–1941* (Frankfurt, 1956); W. J. Mommsen and L. Kettenacker, *The Fascist Challenge and the Policy of Appeasement* (London 1983). Many valuable articles can be found in K. Bracher, M. Funke and H.-A. Jacobsen (eds), *Nationalsozialistische Diktatur 1933–1945: Eine Bilanz* (Bonn, 1983) and in K. Rohe (ed.), *Die Westmächte und das Dritte Reich 1933–1941* (Paderborn, 1982).

6. J. Dülffer, *Weimar, Hitler und die Marine: Reichspolitik und Flottenbau 1920 bis 1939* (Düsseldorf, 1973).

7. Ibid., p. 547, n.27a.

8. 'Dokumentation, Hitler's Brief an Reichenau vom 4. Dezember 1932' in *Vierteljahrshefte für Zeitgeschichte*, 7 (1959), 428–37, T. Vogelsang (ed.). There is an English translation in A. Adamthaite (ed.), *The Lost Peace: International Relations in Europe 1918–1939* (London, 1980) pp. 130–6. The importance of this document needs to be more fully appreciated.

9. See M. Hauner, 'Did Hitler want a World Dominion?', *Journal of Contemporary History*, 13, no. 1 (January 1978).

10. T. V. Compton, *The Swastika and the Eagle. Hitler, the United States and the Origins of the Second World War* (London, 1968), p. 27 and J. Thies, *Architekt der Weltherrschaft: Die 'Endziele' Hitler's* (Düsseldorf, 1976) pp. 147–8.

11. Dülffer, *Weimar, Hitler und die Marine*, p. 547.

12. Thies, *Architekt der Weltherrscheft*, p. 119.

13. Ibid., p. 119, M. Domarus, *Hitler, Reden und Proklamationen 1932–1945* (Hamburg, 1963), vol II, pp. 1058, 1061–2.

14. Thies, *Architekt der Weltherrschaft*, pp. 112–18 and H. Groscurth, *Tagebücher eines Abwehroffiziers, 1938–1940* ed. H. Krausnick (Stuttgart, 1970), 10 February 1938, pp. 166–8. Hitler also declared that he alone could lead Germany in a way for *Lebensraum*, at a talk to generals and senior officials on 28 May 1938, see. W. Förster, *Ein General kämpft gegen den Krieg: Aus den nachgelassenen Papieren des Generalstabschefs Ludwig Beck* (Munich, 1949), pp. 88–90.

15. Ibid.

16. For a general discussion of Hitler's foreign policy, see W. Carr, 'National Socialism: Foreign Policy', in *Fascism, a Readers' Guide*, ed. W. Laqueur (Harmondsworth, 1976). See also A. Hillgruber, 'Forschungsstand und Literatur zum Ausbruch des Zweiten Weltkrieges', in W. Benz and H. Graml (eds), *Sommer 1939. Die Grossmächte und der Europäische Krieg* (Stuttgart, 1979), and A. Hillgruber 'Tendenzen, Ergebnisse und Perspektiren der gegenwärtigen Hitler-Forschung', in *Historische Zeitschrift* 226 (1978), 600–21.

17. H. Mommsen, 'Nationalsozialismus oder Hitlerismus', in *Sowjetsystem und demokratische Gesellschaft*, ed. D. Kernig, vol. IV (Freiburg, 1971) column 702, maintains that Hitler was often incapable of taking decisions and was in many respects a weak dictator but N. Rich in *Hitler's War Aims*, vol. I, *Ideology, the Nazi State and Course of Expansion* (New York, 1973), p. 11 convincingly maintains that Hitler was master of his Reich.

18. David Irving, *Hitler's War* (Longmans, 1977).

19. S. Newman, *March 1939: The British Guarantee to Poland* (Oxford, 1976), pp. 136, 152–3, 219.

20. According to the translation by N. Baynes, Hitler is alleged to have said that if war were to break out 'it will be the end of the Jews in Europe', not 'the annihilation of the Jewish race in Europe', which is the correct wording; *The Speeches of Adolf Hitler*, vol. 11, pp. 1567–78, cf. Domarus, *Hitler, Reden und Proklamationen*, vol. II, p. 1058.

21. Waite, *Psychopathic God*, and R. Binion, *Hitler among the Germans* (Elsevier/New York, 1976).

22. J. Petersen, *Hitler – Mussolini: Die Entstehung der Achse Berlin-Rom 1933–1936* (Tübingen, 1973), pp. 336–8 and E. M. Robertson, *Mussolini as Empire-builder: Europe and Africa* (London, 1977), pp. 74, 78–9.

23. E. Hill (ed.), *Die Weizsäcker-Papiere 1933–1950* (Frankfurt, 1974), *Weizsäcker-Papiere* used below, 16 March 39, p. 152.

24. Robertson, *Hitler's Pre-War Policy*, introduction and p. 194.

25. *Weizsäcker-Papiere*, 9 October 38, p. 145. G. L. Weinberg, in *The Foreign Policy of Hitler's Germany: Starting World War II 1937–1939* (Chicago and London,

1980), pp. 336–40 takes the view that Hitler had decided on an attack on Czechoslovakia before the May crisis. See also D. C. Watt, 'Hitler's Visit to Rome and the May Weekend Crisis: A Study in Hitler's Response to External Stimuli', in *Journal of Contemporary History*, 9, no. 1 (January 1974), 23–32 and K. Robbins, *Munich 1938* (London, 1968), Chapter 6.

26. *Weizsäcker-Papiere*, p. 195.

27. J. Henke, *England in Hitlers politischem Kalkül 1935–1939* (Boppard, 1974) Chapters II and III and A. Hillgruber, 'England's Place in Hitler's Calculations', in *Journal of Contemporary History*, 9, No 1 (1974). *The Documents of British Foreign Policy* (second series) (*DBFP*), vols XIV–XIX ed. W. N. Medlicott, are absolutely indispensable for an analysis of Hitler's reactions to British policy in the years 1935–7. See also K. Robbins, *Munich*, pp. 181–3 and R. Douglas, *In the Year of Munich* (London, 1977), *passim*.

28. Weinberg, *Starting World War II*, pp. 61–2 discusses attitudes to appeasement within the Foreign Office as well as Hitler's apprehensions, pp. 335–6; for the changes which occurred in London after Munich, ibid., p. 544.

29. W. Treue (ed.), 'Hitlers Rede vor der deutschen Presse' (10 November 1938), *Vierteljahrshefte für Zeitgeschichte*, vi (1958), 175–91. Hitler boasted that only the top 10,000 were against him. See also U. von Hassell, *Vom andern Deutschland* (Zürich, 1946), 15 October 19 38, p. 24.

30. Domarus, *Hitler, Reden und Proklamationen*, vol. I, pp. 954–6 and Weinberg, *Starting World War II*, p. 515.

31. *Treue*, 'Hitlers Rede', pp. 182–6, 188. See also H. Mommsen, 'Gesellschaftsbild und Verfassungspläne des deutschen Widerstandes', in *Der deutsche Widerstand gegen Hitler*, W. Schmitthanner and H. Buchheim (eds) (Cologne and Berlin, 1966), pp. 73–161. For Hitler's later attack on the intellectuals, see Domarus, *Hitler, Reden und Proklamation* vol. II, p. 1051.

32. H. Krausnick, 'Judenverfolgung', in H. Buchheim *et al.* (eds), *Anatomie des SS-Staates* (Breisgau, 1965) vol II, pp. 283–448.

33. *Weizsäcker-Papiere*, p. 145.

34. *Treue*, 'Hitlers Rede', pp. 183–4.

35. For details of telephone lines being tapped by the Germans, see D. Irving, *Breach of Security: The German Intelligence File on Events Leading to the Second World War*, with an introduction by D. C. Watt (London, 1968). For the effects of Czech acceptance of the Anglo-French Plan, see Robertson, *Hitler's Pre-War Policy*, pp. 141–2. In the original manuscript of this work an intelligence report of 22 September 38, *Lagebericht* 41 and Jodl's *Diary* are quoted.

36. *Weizsäcker-Papiere*, 13 February 1939, p. 150 and *Documents on German Foreign Policy* series (*DGFP*) (D), vol. IV, letters exhanged between Weizsäcker and Dirksen, German ambassador in London, 14 October 1938, Nos 251, 253, 254, 255 and 256.

37. *Weizsäcker-Papiere*, 10 October 1938, p. 143.

38. *DGFP* (D), vol. IV, nos. 81 and 152, military directives for an invasion of rump Czechoslovakia of 21 October and 17 December 1938. Newman, *March 1939*, p. 88 refers only to the former directive.

39. This is evident from Blomberg's directive to the Armed Forces of 26 June 1937, *Nuremberg Documents*, 139-C.

40. *DGFP* (D), vol. IV, nos. 476 and 477 and vol. 11, nos. 261, 267, 838 and 897. See also J. Erickson, *The Soviet High Command* (London, 1962), pp. 466–7, 494, 503. See Ribbentrop's talk with Chvalkovsky, the Czech foreign minister, of 13 October, *DGFP* (D) vol. IV, no. 54 and A. Adamthwaite, *France and the Coming of the Second World War* (London, 1977), p. 273.

41. I am most obliged to Miss Noelle Jordan who is working on a PhD thesis, 'The Popular Front and the Dilemmas of French Impotence in Central Europe 1936–1937', for providing me with this information. See also, J. Haslam, 'The Soviet Union and the Czech Crisis of 1938', *Journal of Contemporary History*, 14, No. 3 (July 1979), 441–61.

42. Adamthwaite, *France and the Coming of the Second World War*, pp. 273–6.

43. For the unpreparedness of the German army in 1938, see A. Seaton, *The German Army* (London, 1982) pp. 93, 129–30 and W. Deist, *The Wehrmacht and German Rearmament* (London, 1982), pp. 88–9, 93–4, 129–30.

44. See the discussions between Hitler and his generals of 3 September 1938 in *DGFP* (D), vol. VII, Appendix III, pp. 640–3. Hitler was so obsessed by fortifications that in July 1938 he wrote a memorandum on the subject: see 'Denkschrift zur Frage unserer Festungsanlagen', in O.-W. Förster, *Das Befestigungswesen: Rückblick und Ausschau* (Neckargmund: Vorwinkel, 1960), pp. 123–48.

45. Hassell, *Vom andern Deutschland*, p. 25 and 16 December 1938, p. 32. See also Seaton, *The German Army*, pp. 94–5.

46. E. L. Homze, *Arming the Luftwaffe: The Reich Air Ministry and the German Aircraft Industry* (Nebraska, 1976), pp. 222–27 and R. G. Overy, 'Hitler's War and the German Economy: A Reinterpretation', in *Economic History Review* (second series) XXXV, no. 2 (May 1982). See also W. Deist, *Wehrmacht*, pp. 94–5 and Dülffer, *Weimar, Hitler und die Marine, passim*.

47. Deist, *Wehrmacht*, Chapter 5; Dülffer, *Weimar, Hitler und die Marine*, pp. 471ff; M. Salewski, *Die Deutsche Seekriegsleitung 1935–1945*, vol. 1 (Frankfurt, 1970), pp. 44–5. Hauner, 'Did Hitler want a World Dominion?' also deals with naval expansion.

48. Dülffer, *Weimar, Hitler und die Marine*, 546–7, 553. For the Hossbach conference of 5 November 1938, *DGFP* (D), vol. I, no. 19.

49. Ibid., and Weinberg, *Starting World War II*, pp. 34, 37; Dülffer, *Weimar, Hitler und die Marine*, pp. 444–7, 536–7. For Hitler and the construction of heavy battleships see Dülffer, pp. 537–8, 546–7 and also Salewski, *Die Deutsche Seekriegsleitung*, pp. 33ff.

50. Report of the conference of 20 May *Admiralty* PG 33272, p. 160, OKL, 1 Abt 44/38, 144/38, p. 160; for the Chief of Naval Operations views ibid., PS 33306 C, pp. 141–74 especially p. 154. Two *Luftwaffe* appreciations of 2 June and 23 August 1938 can be found in *Nuremberg Docs* R:150 and PS:375. See also Dülffer, *Weimar, Hitler und die Marine*, pp. 462–3.

51. Salewski, *Die Deutsche Seekriegsleitung*, pp. 39–45; Dülffer, *Weimar, Hitler und die Marine*, pp. 468–70, 547–9. See also Henke, *England in Hitlers politischem Kalkül*, Chapter 3 and Salewski, *Die Deutsche Seekriegsleitung*, pp. 50–1. I am thankful to Professor Dülffer for having clarified certain points mentioned above.

52. Förster, *Das Befestigungswesen*, pp. 88–90 and Henke, *England in Hitler's politischem Kalkül*, pp. 153–6.

53. Dülffer, *Weimar, Hitler und die Marine*, p. 489 and Robertson, *Hitler's Pre-War Policy*, pp. 131–2.

54. See Keitel's memorandum of 30 November 1938 in M. Toscano, *The Origins of the Pact of Steel* (Baltimore, 1964), pp. 80–3.

55. Deist, *Wehrmacht*, pp. 90–1. See also Overy, 'Hitler's War', p. 277.

56. Dülffer, *Weimar, Hitler und die Marine*, pp. 477, 484–6, 497–8, 502 and Salewski, *Die Deutsche Seekriegsleitung*, p. 44.

57. Dülffer, *Weimar, Hitler und die Marine*, pp. 470, 490–503, 535–6. Dülffer has developed his ideas in Bracher, *Nationalsozialistische Diktatur*, cited in n. 5 above.

58. Salewski, *Die Deutsche Seekriegsleitung*, pp. 60–1, 65; Dülffer, 499–502, 512; Henke, *England in Hitlers politischen Kalkül*, pp. 212–17; and Deist, *Wehrmacht*, pp. 77–85, 90–1.

59. S. Aster, *1939. The Making of the Second World War* (London, 1973), p. 58. See also, Henke, *England in Hitlers politischem Kalkül*, pp. 226, 250–1.

60. A. Milward, *The German Economy at War* (London, 1965).

61. Overy, 'Hitler's War', pp. 273, 278–9, 287.

62. Dülffer, *Weimar, Hitler und die Marine*, pp. 550–5 and Overy, 'Hitler's War', p. 547 n. 27a.

63. Förster, *Das Befestigungswesen*, pp. 88–90. For the embargo on war material and the recall of the German military to China see J. P. Fox, *Germany and the Far Eastern Crisis 1931–1938* (Oxford, 1982), Soviet High Command, pp. 328–331. For the Soviet military mission in China, see Erickson, *Soviet High Command*, pp. 490, 491, 494–9.

64. Erickson, *Soviet High Command*, p. 499.

65. The British military attaché in Tokyo told his German colleagues in 1937, 'Thank God for the Japanese army', see W. M. Chapman, *The Price of the Admiralty* (Sussex, 1982), vol. 1: *1939–1940*, p. xix. For recent Japanese accounts, see B. Bridges, 'Mongolia in Soviet Japanese Relations 1933–1936', in *Some Aspects of Soviet-Japanese Relations* (International Studies 1982, No. 11, London School of Economics), pp. 15–31 and J. Haslam, 'Soviet Aid to China and Japan's Place in Moscow's Foreign Policy 1937–1939', ibid, pp. 35–58.

66. Fox, *Germany and the Far Eastern Crisis*, p. 325.

67. Thies, *Architekt der Weltherrscheft*, p. 108.

68. Fox, *Germany and the Far Eastern Crisis*, pp. 303–4.

69. *DBFP* (third series), vol. VIII, nos. 338 and 342 and Appendix 1. See also B. A. Lee, *Britain and the Sino-Japanese War 1937–1939* (Oxford, 1973), pp. 149, 156–7.

70. Toscano, *Origins of Pact of Steel*, 114–15, 131ff.; also T. Sommer, *Deutschland und Japan zwischen den Mächten 1935–1940* (Tübingen, 1963), *passim*.

71. Ciano, *Diaries*, 28 October and 31 December 1938, translated with notes by A. Mayor, introduction by M. Muggeridge (London, 1952). See also C. J. Lowe and F. Moarzari, *Italian Foreign Policy 1870–1940*, Chapter XIV, 'Munich and After' (London, 1975).

72. See R. Pankhurst, in 'Fascist Racial Policies in Ethiopia 1922–1941', in *Ethiopian Observer*, XII, no. 4 (1969) for the passage of racial laws in metropolitan Italy; see also M. Michaelis, *Mussolini and the Jews: German–Italian Relations and the Jewish Question in Italy 1922–1945* (Oxford, 1978), pp. 125–6, 151–9 and G. Bernadini, 'The Origins and Development of Racial Anti-Semitism in Fascist Italy', *Journal of Modern History* 49, no. 3 (September 1977). The author does not share Weinberg's view in *Starting World War II*, p. 311, n. 228 that the laws against the Jews in Italy were passed by Mussolini to ape Hitler.

73. *DGFP* (D), vol. VI, Appendix I, especially pp. 1124–5.

74. M. Knox, *Mussolini Unleashed 1939–1941. Politics and Strategy in Fascist Italy's Last War* (Cambridge, 1982), pp. 38–40. See also R. Quartararo, *Roma tra Londra e Berlino* (Rome, 1980), pp. 407–25.

75. Toscano, *Origins of Pact of Steel*, pp. 80–5.

76. The German naval high command expressed this view on 26 April 1938, *Admiralty* P G 33272, 148–59 A 1 a 17/138.

77. Groscurth, *Tagebücher eines Abwehroffiziers*, 9 December 1938, p. 156 and *Weizsäcker-Papiere*, 5 January and 25 February 1939, pp. 149, 150.

78. *DGFP* (D), vol. I, no 19.

79. See H. Booms, 'Der Ursprung des Zweiten Weltkriegs-Revision oder Expansion', in *Kriegbeginn 1939* (see n. 5 above), p. 96n, and Groscurth, *Tagebücher eines Abwehroffiziers*, 31 March 1938, p. 176.

80. C. Burckhardt, *Meine Danzinger Mission 1937–1939* (Danzig, 1960), p. 348.

81. *Treue*, 'Hitlers Rede', pp. 190–1.

82. Groscurth, *Tagebücher einer Abwehroffiziers*, p. 176.

83. Domarus, *Hitler, Reden und Proklamationen*, vol. 11, p. 1067.

84. See F. Blaich, 'Wirtschaft und Rüstung in Deutschland 1933–1939', in *Sommer 1939* (cited in n. 16 above), pp. 33–61 and L. Herbst, 'Die Mobilmachung der Wirtschaft 1933–1939 als Problem des nationsozialistischen Herrschaftssystem', ibid., pp. 62–106.

85. Hildebrand, *Vom Reich zum Weltreich* (cited in n. 5 above), pp. 214, 231.

86. Himmler discussed changes within the *SS* in a speech to its senior officers on 8 November 1938, see B. F. Smith and A. P. Peterson (eds), *Heinrich Himmler: Geheimreden 1933 bis 1945* (Frankfurt, 1974), with an introduction by J. Fest, pp. 32, 39. For the growth of the *Volksdeutsche Mittelstelle*, see H.-A. Jacobsen, *Nationalsozialistische Aussenpolitik 1933–1939* (Frankfurt, 1968) pp. 234–46 and J. Ackermann, *Himmler als Ideologe* (Göttingen, 1970), *passim*.

87. Smith and Peterson, *Heinrich Himmler*, p. 36 and Herbst, 'Die Mobilmachung', p. 82.

88. Smith and Peterson, *Heinrich Himmler*, pp. 36–7.

89. Herbst, Die Mobilmachung', p. 73ff. and Smith Peterson, *Heinrich Himmler*, p. 18.

90. Smith and Peterson, *Heinrich Himmler*, pp. 26, 37–8, 49.

91. Ibid., pp. 16, 38, 198.

92. Booms, 'Der Ursprung', p. 65.

93. For the Polonisation of Germans, see *DGFP* (D) vol. v, no 18 and vol. vi, no 125; Jacobsen, *Nationalsozialistische Aussenpolitik*, p. 593 and D. Wynot, 'The Polish Germans 1919–1939: National Minority in a multi-national State', in *Polish Review*, 17, no 1 (Winter 1972), 23–64.

94. For the extradition of Jews to Germany, see *DBFP* (3), vol. iii, nos 260 and 289; also Weinberg, *Starting World War II*, p. 486 and P. V. Cannistraro, E. D. Wynot Jr and T. P. Kovaloff (eds), *Poland and the Coming of the Second World War: The Diplomatic Papers of AJD Biddle, Jr, United States Ambassador to Poland 1937–1939* (Ohio, 1976) p. 253, n. 6, henceforth described as *The Biddle Papers*.

95. *DGFP* (D) vol. v, nos 99, 123, 131, 134 and Booms, 'Der Ursprung', p. 86. See also, Weinberg, *Starting World War II*, p. 502, n. 149. For the reactions of the South Tyrol Germans to the idea of resettlement in the East, see Hassell, *Vom andern* 21 June 1939, pp. 53–4. See also Himmler's speech of 29 February 1940 in Smith and Peterson, *Heinrich Himmler*, pp. 123–4.

96. Smith and Peterson, *Heinrich Himmler*, pp. 47–8.

97. Hassell, *Vom andern Deutschland*, 27 November 1938, p. 27.

98. *Das politische Tagebüch Alfred Rosenbergs*, ed. H. G. Seraphim (Munich, 1956), pp. 80–1; also Groscurth, *Tagebücher eines Abwehroffiziers* 21 December 1938, p. 161 and H.-A. Jacobsen, *Nationalsozialistische Aussenpolitik*, pp. 87–9, 330, 449–52. See also W. Michalka 'Conflicts within the German Leadership on the Objectives and Tactics of German Foreign Policy, in Mommsen and Kettenacker, *The Fascist Challenge* (cited in n. 5).

99. Dr R. Overy kindly informed me that the documents concerning the economic integration of parts of Poland into the Reich are among *The Christie Papers*, Churchill College, Cambridge.

100. H. Graml *et al.*, *Der Deutsche Widerstand gegen Hitler* (Cologne, 1966), p. 19ff. For Goerdeler's memorandum of 4 December 1938 see A. P. Young, *The X Documents*, ed. S. Aster (London, 1974), pp. 154–6. Hitler told the Polish foreign minister Beck on 5 January 1939 that Germany was in vital need of colonies, see *The Biddle Papers*, p. 305. See also Weinberg, *Starting World War II*, p. 512.

101. Booms, 'Der Ursprung', pp. 55–6, n. 10, also, pp. 73–4, 78.

102. For Germany and Poland, see *DGFP* (D), vol. v, nos 54, 55 61 and 62; for Germany and Hungary, ibid., vol. iv, nos 28, 48, 62, 167 and vol. v, no 252.

103. Ibid., vol. iv, nos 45–6, 50, 55 and 82.

104. See Ribbentrop's conversation with F. Chvalkovsky of 13 October 1938, *DGFP* (D), vol. iv, nos 46, 50, 55.

105. *DGFP* (D), vol. iv 22 October, no 83 and an OKW memorandum of 6 October and a Foreign Ministry memorandum of 7 October, no 45.

106. Booms, 'Der Ursprung', pp. 74–6, Hassell, *Vom andern Deutschland*, p. 32 and *DGFP* (D), vol. iv, nos 28, 132, 133 and 167.

107. Weinberg, *Starting World War II*, pp. 435–6, 479ff., 481ff.

108. Adamthwaite, *France and the Coming of the Second World War*, Chapter xv.

109. *DGFP* (D), vol. iv, nos 286, 287 and Aster, *1939*, pp. 41–2.

110. Weinberg, *Starting World War II*, p. 490ff. and *The Biddle Papers*, pp. 302–3.

111. *The Biddle Papers*, pp. 24–5, 43–6, 261. See also *Polnische Dokumente über die Ursachen des Krieges* (Berlin, 1940).

112. *The Foreign Relations of the United States* no 1, J. Szembek, *Journal* (Paris, 1952), p. 498, Weinberg, *Starting World War II*, p. 489, and C. A. MacDonald, *The United States, Britain and Appeasement* London, 1981), pp. 8, 95, 113.

113. See *DGFP* (D), vol. vi, no 64.

114. Weinberg, *Starting World War II*, p. 497ff. and Hitler's conversation with General Brauchitsch of 25 March 1939, *DGFP* (D), vol. vi, no 99.

115. *DGFP* (D), vol. iv, nos 479, 487 and Weinberg, *Starting World War II*, pp. 531–2.

116. Groscurth, *Tagebücher einer Abwehroffiziers*, pp. 165, 168, 32. See also Domarus, *Hitler, Reden und Proklamationen*, vol. ii, p. 1040, Hassell, *Vom andern Deutschland*, 26 January 1939, pp. 43–4, and *Weizsäcker-Papiere*, 5 and 13 February 1939, p. 149.

117. *DGFP* (D), vol. v, nos 100, 252 and vol. iv, no 167. See also *Weizsäcker-Papiere*, 27 March 1939, pp. 152–3 and Weinberg, *Starting World War II*, p. 477.

118. Aster, *1939*, pp. 21–3, 28–9.

119. A. J. P. Taylor, *English History 1914–1945* (Oxford, 1966), pp. 419–20. See also L. Kettenacker, 'Die Diplomatie der Ohnmacht. Die gescheiterte Friedenstrategie der britischen Regierung vor Ausbruch des Zweiten Weltkrieges', in Benz and Graml, *Sommer 1939* (cited in n. 16 above), pp. 223–51.

120. See *DBFP* (Third Series), vol. iii, nos 302, 305 and 313. See also Krausnick, 'Judenverfolgung' (n. 32 above), pp. 331–47.

121. *Weizsäcker-Papiere*, 9 October 1938, pp. 17, 22 and Hassell, *Vom andern Deutschland*, 17 September 1938 p. 17.

122. Krausnick, 'Judenverfolgung', pp. 337–8.

123. Ibid., pp. 338–40.

124. Ibid., pp. 342–3 and *The Biddle Papers*, p. 305.

125. Domarus, *Hitler, Redun und Proklamationen*, vol. ii, p. 1058. For Hitler as the liar who spoke the truth, see D. Bonhoeffer, *Ethik*, ed. E. Bethge (Munich, 1953) p. 11ff. The significance of this remarkable work for an understanding of Hitler has not been recognised.

126. N. Gibbs, *Grand Strategy*, vol. i, *Rearmament Policy* (London, 1976), pp. 690–1; Aster, *1939*, pp. 52–6; Newman, *March 1939*, pp. 79–80.

127. MacDonald, *US, Britain and Appeasement*, pp. 112–15; Aster, *1939*, pp. 52–3. See also Newman, *March 1939*, pp. 79–80, D. C. Watt, *Too Serious a Business* (London, 1975), pp. 117–22 and N. Gibbs, *Grand Strategy*, vol. 1, *Rearmament* (London, 1976), pp. 460ff.

128. *The Biddle Papers*, pp. 300–14 and MacDonald, *US, Britain and Appeasement*, p. 129.

129. Domarus, *Hitler, Roden und Proklamationen*, vol. II, pp. 1052–3 and MacDonald, *US, Britain and Appeasement*, pp. 108ff., 128–30; see also MacDonald's 'Die USA und die Appeasement Politik 1936–1939', in *Die Westmächte und das Dritte Reich* (cited in n. 5 above) and D. Reynolds, *The Creation of the Anglo-American Alliance 1937–41* (Europa, 1981) especially pp. 40–4. See also Hillgruber, 'Forschungsstrand und Literatur. . . .', cited in n. 16 above, pp. 355–7, and his 'Der Faktor Amerika in Hitlers Strategie 1938–1941', in *Deutsche Grossmacht and Weltmacht* (Düsseldorf, 1977) and M. M. Löwenthal, 'Roosevelt and the Coming of the War', *Journal of Contemporary History*, 16, no 3 (July 1981), 413–40 and *DBFP* (3), vol. VIII, Appendix 1.

130. Löwenthal, 'Roosevelt', and MacDonald, *US, Britain and Appeasement*, pp. 84–5.

131. *The Secret Diary of Harold L. Ickes*, vol. II, *Inside Struggle* (London, 1955), 29 January 1939, p. 571 and MacDonald, *US, Britain and Appeasement*, pp. 126–7.

132. Aster, *1939*, pp. 39–40, and Watt, *Too Serious*, pp. 117ff.

133. Hassell, *Vom andern Deutschland*, 25 November 1938, pp. 26–7. Goerdeler discussed Niemoeller's plight with the Archbishop of York, W. Temple and other churchmen, see Young, *The X Documents*, pp. 59–62, 146–7. See also Groscurth, *Tagebücher eines Abwehroffiziers*, pp. 161, n. 293, pp. 177–8 and Domarus, *Hitler, Reden und Proklmationen*, vol. II, pp. 1058–62.

134. Weinberg, *Starting World War II*, pp. 515–16, 203, p. 524, n. 249, and Aster, *1939*, pp. 235–6.

135. Aster *1939*, pp. 42ff.

136. Letter from Colonel Arthur Murray to Roosevelt of 15 December 1938, 'The Murray Papers', National Library of Scotland, Edinburgh.

137. Aster, *1939*, pp. 45–8, 49. Also Young *The X Documents*, p. 153 and Adamthwaite, *France and the Coming of the Second World War*, pp. 252–3. Cf. Hassell, *Vom andern Deutschland*, 14 January 1938, p. 43.

138. Watt, *Too Serious*, pp. 126–9. See also Young, *The X Documents*, p. 545 and Newman, *March 1939*, p. 76, n. 6, p. 183 n. 6. For British military preparations, taken as a result of the rumour see, Newman, ibid., p. 78 and Gibbs, *Grand Strategy*, Chapter 13.

139. *DBFP* (Series 3) vol. IV, nos 5, 26. Also MacDonald, *US, British and Appeasement*, pp. 125ff. The incident was all the more embarrassing since the crash involved a prototype of the B–17, the Flying Fortress.

140. Weinberg, *Starting World War II*, pp. 525–7, 543–4. See also Gibbs, *Grand Strategy*, pp. 498–502, 654–7 and Adamthwaite, *France and the Coming of the Second World War*, pp. 252–3.

141. Adamthwaite, *France and the Coming of the Second World War*, pp. 256, 262–3. See also Weinberg, *Starting World War II*, p. 545.

142. Domarus, *Hitler, Reden und Proklamationen*, vol. II, p. 1062 and Toscano, *Origins of Pact of Steel*, pp. 122–3.

143. Knox, *Mussolini Unleashed*, pp. 38–40.

144. Adamthwaite, *France and the Coming of the Second World War*, p. 254.

145. Ibid., Chapter VII, and Newman, *March 1939, passim*.

146. *DGFP* (D), vol. V, nos 105, 108 and vol. VI, 125, Rosenberg, cited in n. 98 above, 21 May 1939, pp. 85–6, 19 July, p. 93 and a letter intended for Hitler of 15 June 1939, pp. 172–6. See also Groscurth, *Tagebücher eines Abwehroffiziers*, 21 December 1938, p. 161, 15 March 1939, p. 171, and J. A. Armstrong, *Ukrainian Nationalism* (Columbia, 1963), pp. 27ff.

147. Aster, *1939*, pp. 41–2 and Toscano, *Origins of Pact of Steel*, pp. 136–8.

148. For the text see, Royal Institute Affairs, 'Documents 1939', pp. 361–70. Also, E. H. Carr, *German-Soviet Relations between the Wars* (Oxford, 1952), pp. 126–7 and Erickson, *Soviet High Command*, pp. 510–13.

149. *DGFP* (D), vol. IV, nos 198, 199, 215, 218; vol, VI, no 125 and Weinberg, *Starting World War II*, pp. 476–9, 535. For anti-German feeling in Hungary, see Domarus, *Hitler, Reden und Proklamationen*, vol. II, p. 1038.

150. *DGFP* (D), vol. VI, no 64. According to Weinberg, *Starting World War II*, pp. 533–6, Peter Kleist, a member of Ribbentrop's staff, told a Soviet agent on 13 March that Hitler intended allowing the Carpatho-Ukraine to go to Hungary. Hitler's aims were first, war with Poland, then the West and finally the Soviet Union. H. W. Koch has given cogent reasons for thinking that Hitler did not act as systematically as assumed by Weinberg. See his article below.

151. Rosenberg, cited in n. 98 above, pp. 85–6 and Groscurth, *Tagebücher eines Abwehroffiziers*, 15 March 1938, p. 171.

152. Booms, 'Der Ursprung', p. 84.

153. C. A. MacDonald, 'Britain, France and the April Crisis of 1939', in *European Studies Review*, no 2 (1972), 151–69.

154. Henke, *England in Hitlers politischen Kalkül*, p. 243, and A. M. Cienciala, *Poland and the Western Powers* (London 1976), Newman, *March 1939*, p. 219. For a contrary view of the guarantee, see Gibbs, *Grand Strategy*, pp. 804–5.

155. *DGFP* (D), vol. VI, no. 211. For a brief account of Russo-German relations in 1939, see D. C. Watt, 'The Initiation of the Negotiations leading to the Nazi-Soviet Pact: A Historical Problem' in C. Abramsky (ed.), *Essays in Honour of E. H. Carr* (London, 1974), pp. 157–70 and Weinberg, *Starting World War II*, pp. 657–8.

8 HITLER'S ULTIMATE AIMS – A PROGRAMME OF WORLD DOMINION?

1. One glaring example of terminological juggling is the German title of Fritz Fischer's spectacular book *Griff nach der Weltmacht*. *Weltmacht* (World Power) signifying the *status* of a 'nation having influence in world politics', 'reaching for it' is a malapropism; what the author obviously wished to convey was *Weltherrschaft* (World Dominion). For reasons of space it was necessary to restrict references in this paper to the barest essentials.

2. A. Hitler. *Mein Kampf* (Munich, 1941), pp. 741–2. Cf. D. Aigner, *Das Ringen um England* (Munich, 1969), pp. 84, 244, ibid., *Anmerkungsband*, pp. 68, 139; see also n. 34 below. One of the chief champions of this controversy, H. W. Steed, former editor of *The Times*, had already written in 1924, when referring to Wilhelminian Germany: 'The German watchword "*World Mastery* [sic!] or Downfall" ["*Weltmacht* oder Untergang", D.A.] tersely stated the alternatives. . . . The rest of the world had to choose between submission and resistance to it.' (H. W. Steed; *Through 30 Years*, vol. 2 (London, 1924), p. 389.

3. Norman Cohn, *Die Protokolle der Weisen von Zion. Der Mythos von der 'judischen Weltverschwörung'* (Cologne, 1969) (English version, *Warrant for Genocide*) ('One of the most fervent and trusting readers of [the "Protocols of the Elders of Zion"] was Adolf Hitler'); cf. also Albert Speer, *Spandauer Tagebücher* (Berlin, 1975), p. 45. Jochen Thies, *Architekt der Weltherrschaft* (Düsseldorf, 1976), p. 188 is of the opinion that it is this belief which inspired Hitler with ideas of world dominion of his own.

4. *Annual Register 1939* (London, 1940), pp. 27–8. Chamberlain used the same language when addressing the Foreign Policy Committee of the British Cabinet; see S. Newman, *March 1939 – The British Guarantee to Poland* (Oxford, 1976), p. 152.

544 ASPECTS OF THE THIRD REICH

5. A vivid and thoroughly representative cross-section of 'world opinion' regarding Hitler's Germany is provided by a two-volume NS documentation called *Hitler in der Karikatur der Welt*, ed. by Ernst Hanfstaengl (Berlin, 1933/1934).

6. See, among others, S. Erckner, *Hitler's Conspiracy Against Peace* (London, 1937), pp. 149–94 (chapters 'Germany – lord of the Earth' and 'A Deal with England') where the term 'conquest by stages' (p. 184) is used for the first time, and 'James Turner' [i.e. the Communist scholar Jürgen Kuczynski], *Hitler and the Empire* (London, 1936), pp. 14, 39.

7. Erckner, *Hitler's Conspiracy*, p. 152 and *passim* (Delbrück, Max Weber and Johannes Haller as chief witnesses for Pangermanism with a direct reference to the London *Morning Post*).

8. See, among others, H. Wanderscheck, *Weltkrieg und Propaganda* (Berlin, 1936), pp. 100–13. 'Deutschland über alles' was superseded during the 1930s and 1940s by what seemed to some authors another call for world domination: 'Today Germany is ours, tomorrow the whole world'. The author of these lines, Hans Baumann, wrote them in 1932 for a Catholic youth group, of which he was a member. The song was later adopted – with some variations – by the Hitler Youth. However, the words have been falsified. The original, as sung by the Hitler Youth, runs as follows: 'Today Germany listens to us – tomorrow the whole world'.

9. See, among others, *The British Way and Purpose*, published by the Directorate of Army Education, B.W.P. 1 (November 1942) pp. 13–14. (The fighting spirit of the German soldier is seen to derive from his 'unshakable faith' in Hitler's power 'to lead the German people to victory and the world dominion by the "master race". . . . To take part in the conquest of the world may be a villainous thing, but it can stir the blood and inspire self-sacrifice'.)

10. Stephen L. Vaughn, *Holding Fast the Inner Lines – Democracy, Nationalism and the Committee of Public Information* (Chapel Hill, 1980), pp. 83—97.

11. See, among others, *The Public Papers and Addresses of Franklin D. Roosevelt*, 1938 volume, pp. 491–3; also the 1941 volume, pp. 387–9, 529–30, 532 ('the Government of Germany, pursuing its course of world conquest . . .'). For the role of NS activists in the United States see G. H. W. Grässner, *Deutschland und die Nationalsozialisten in den Vereinigten Staaten von Amerika 1933–1939* (PhD thesis, Bonn, 1973) and S. A. Diamond, *The Nazi Movement in the United States 1924–1941* (Ithaca, 1974).

12. PRO 1939 C18260/1645/18, C1323/53/18, W9815/72/49, C620/620/18, L1649/1649/407; Beatrix Bouvier, *Die Deutsche Freiheitspartei* (PhD thesis, Frankfurt, 1972) pp. 87—91, 95, 99–100. In the US Rauschning was the author of a number of purely propagandist publications, including 'Hitler Told Me This', in *The American Mercury*, December 1939, pp. 385–93; 'Hitler Could Not Stop', in *Foreign Affairs*, October 1939, pp. 1–12; *Hitler Wants the World* (London, 1941), also in Spanish under the title *Hitler codicia el mundo*. Rauschning's 'revelations' of Hitler's alleged intentions in Latin America have been unanimously discounted by specialists working in this field: Arnold Ebel (1971), Klaus Volland (1976), and Reiner Pommerin (1977). Recent American research dispenses with Rauschning altogether.

13. Even during the course of the Second World War the US State Department was forced to concede that it did not possess any hard evidence: 'It is impossible to adduce from the writings of Hitler or other Nazi leaders direct statements indicating that they aspire to the domination of the entire world'. See *National Socialism. Prepared by the Special Unit of the Division of European Affairs*, Dept. of State, by Raymond E. Murphy (Washington, DC, 1943), p. 56. See also G. Moltmann, 'Weltherrschaftsideen Hitlers', in *Europa und Übersee: Festschrift für*

Egmont Zechlin (Hamburg, 1961), p. 221; B. M. Russett, *No Clear and Present Danger – A skeptical view of the U.S. entry into World War II* (New York, 1972).

14. *The Nuremberg Verdict*. German edition, *Das Urteil von Nürnberg, 1946* (Munich, 1961), pp. 42–6.

15. See, for example, M. Michael's review of Klaus Hildebrand's 'Vom Reich zum Weltreich', *International Affairs*, 64 (1970), 749, and Newman, *March 1939*, p. 222.

16. See, for example, 'Erklärung der Kommission der Historiker der DDR und der UdSSR' of 1 September 1969, *Zeitschrift für Geschichtswissenschaft*, 17, (1969), 1448.

17. See the relevant publications by Hans Mommsen and Martin Broszat, notably also T. W. Mason, *Arbeiterklasse und Volksgemeinschaft* (Opladen, 1975). For the controversy between 'functionalists' and 'intentionalists' among German historians see, among others, *Der 'Führerstaat' – Mythos und Realität* (Stuttgart, 1981) (publications of the German Historical Institute, London, Vol. 8).

18. This stance was first taken by A. J. P. Taylor and has been adopted by a number of younger British historians such as R. Skidelsky, E. M. Robertson, M. Cowling, S. Newman, and N. Stone; in Germany notably by Oswald Hauser, Josef Henke, and the author of this paper.

19. *Mein Kampf*, pp. 728–43; see also A. V. N. van Woerden, 'Hitler Faces England', *Acta Nederlandica*, 3 (1968), 150–1, note.

20. See in particular Andreas Hillgruber, *Hitlers Stragie* (Frankfurt/Main, 1965); also his 'Der Faktor Amerika in Hitlers Strategie 1938–1941', *Aus Politik und Zeitgeschichte*, 19 (1966), 3–21; his 'England's Place in Hitler's Plan for World Dominion', *Journal of Contemporary History*, 9 (1974), 5–21. Klaus Hildebrand, *Vom Reich zum Weltreich* (Munich, 1969); also his *Deutsche Aussenpolitik 1933–1945*, 4th edn (Stuttgart, 1980). Milan Hauner, 'Did Hitler Want a [sic] World Dominion?', *Journal of Contemporary History*, 13 (1978), 15–32. Hauner's Cambridge doctoral dissertation *India in Axis Strategy* (Stuttgart, 1981), fails to substantiate his contention that Hitler followed 'a preconceived plan of world conquest'.

21. Hillgruber, *Hitlers Strategie, passim*, notably p. 592.

22. Bernd Martin, *Friedensinitiativen und Machtpolitik im Zweiten Weltkrieg 1939–1942* (Düsseldorf, 1974), pp. 300–1, assumes from Hitler's peace initiative in July 1940 that Britain was not to be accepted as a partner on equal footing. This may be true for 1940, but would this also apply for the years before the war had started?

23. See ibid., especially pp. 132–53 and 207–33. Hitler's attitude towards the US is made plain in his speeches of 28 April 1939 and 11 December 1941. The 1938/39 Washington reports of Polish ambassador Count Potocki, published by the German Foreign Office in March 1940, have now generally been accepted as authentic: *Roosevelts Weg in den Krieg. Geheimdokumente zur Kriegspolitik des Präsidenten der Vereinigten Staaten von Amerika*, herausgegeben von der Archivkommission des Auswärtigen Amtes (Berlin, 1943). There is little doubt that they largely contributed to Hitler's view of the US as a potential enemy.

24. Hillgruber, *Hitlers Strategie*, pp. 90–102, 310–34; also his 'Der Faktor Amerika', pp. 9–15; and in *Weltpolitik II* (Göttingen, 1975), p. 270.

25. For the basic world-wide antagonism towards NS Germany see, among others, Erhard Forndran *et al.* (eds), *Innen- und Aussenpolitik unter nationalsozialistischer Bedrohung* (Opladen, 1977); G. Wollstein, *Vom Weimarer Revisionismus zu Hitler* (Bonn, 1973); H. Hörling, 'L'opinion française face à l'avènement d'Hitler au pouvoir', *Francia*, 3 (1975), 584–641; G. L. Weinberg, *The Foreign Policy of Hitler's Germany* (Chicago, 1970), pp. 39, 144–5, 150. The former tendency among German historians to stress British readiness for concessions towards Hitler has found little

sympathy with those who had worked through the British documents released under the thirty years rule. See especially W. N. Medlicott's Preface to vol. XIX (2nd series) of *Documents on British Foreign Policy 1919–1939* (London, 1982); Oswald Hauser, *England und das Dritte Reich*, vol. 2, *1936–1938* (Göttingen, 1982); and Newman, *March 1939*. 'Containment' appears to have been the dominant motive in British foreign policy towards Hitler.

26. Josef Henke, *England in Hitlers politischem Kalkül 1935–1939* (Boppard, 1973); Hauser, *England und das Dritte Reich*.

27. Hitler in conversation with Count Ciano after receipt of the so-called 'Eden dossier', October 1936: 'If they [i.e. the British] leave me another five years, so much the better' (Ciano's *Diplomatic Papers*, London, 1948, pp. 56–7). When haranguing National Socialist party functionaries on 29 April 1937, Hitler said: '. . . we must only hope that this conflict [deemed inevitable, D.A.] will not happen today, but only in several years time, the later the better'. It might be useful to remember that Hitler was, and remained, convinced, as shown in *Mein Kampf*, that Britain had obeyed its long-term national interest in 'causing' the 1914–18 war.

28. There are a number of revealing observations on Hitler's attitude towards an invasion of Britain (*Operation Seelöwe*) in Walter Ansel, *Hitler Confronts England* (Durham NC, 1960).

29. A. Tyrell, *Vom 'Trommler' zum 'Führer'* (Munich, 1975). If it is true that Hitler conceived his 'ultimate foreign policy aims' with their 'global setting' during the years 1919 and 1920 (Thies, *Architekt*, p. 188), then it becomes imperative to re-evaluate their programmatical relevance in the light of Hitler's self-conceived role of a 'drummer' rather than a 'leader' at this stage.

30. See, among others, the verbatim transcript of Hitler's conversation with David Lloyd George, in M. Gilbert, *The Roots of Appeasement* (London, 1966), pp. 197–211.

31. See n. 12 above.

32. *Hitlers Zweites Buch* (Stuttgart, 1961), pp. 123–32. Among the numerous publications of the 1920s dealing with 'the American Menace' and the prospect of an impending war between Britain and the US mention will only be made here of the German editions of J. M. Kenworthy's *Will Civilisation Crash?* (1928) and Ludwell Denny's *American Conquers Britain* (1930). The idea of American 'racial superiority' was promulgated by American anthropologists such as L. Stoddard and M. Grant whose writings were promptly translated into German. There is, moreover, a striking similarity between some relevant paragraphs in Hitler's *Second Book* and an article first published in the *North American Review* (March/May 1926) and republished in German (*Archiv für Politik und Geschichte*, 4 (1926), 488–9). Cf. also H. F. K. Günther, *Rassenkunde Europas* (Munich, 1926), pp. 212–14, and – as an assessment of the Johnson Act with its racialist restriction on US immigration – Wilhelm Frick, *Wir bauen das Dritte Reich* (Oldenburg, 1934), p. 63.

33. Otto Strasser, *Ministersessel oder Revolution?* (Berlin, 1930), pp. 13–15. 24–5.

34. *Mein Kampf*, pp. 741–2. Hitler's famous dictum 'Germany will be a World Power or it will recede to naught' (ibid.), often quoted in support of the 'globalist' view, should be read in conjunction with the generally overlooked sentence immediately following it: 'For attaining World Power [Germany] needs a size commensurate with its importance and adequate for providing sustenance to its citizens' (*Mein Kampf*, p. 742). This should remove any doubt that for Hitler 'world power' was not tantamount to 'world dominion'. As for the dangers of a blockade, see C. J. Burckhardt, *Meine Danziger Mission* (Munich, 1960), p. 342.

35. 'The German national interest requires an alliance with Britain because this is indispensable for a Nordic-Germanic hegemony over Europe and – in conjunction

with a Nordic-Germanic America – over the world.' (Strasser, *Ministersessel oder Revolution?*, p. 15).

36. See, in particular, H. Fischelmayer, *Sandungsideologische Konzeptionen in Grossbritannien im Zeitalter des Imperialismus 1880–1914*, PhD thesis (Erlangen, 1975), pp. 126–53, and H. W. Koch, *Der Sozialdarwinismus* (Munich, 1973); Koch, 'Die Rolle des Sozialdarwinismus als Faktor im Zeitalter des neuen Imperialismus um die Jahrhundertwende', *Zeitschrift für Politik*, 17 (1970), 51–70.

37. A. Speer, *Spandauer Tagebücher* (Berlin, 1975), pp. 221–2; *A. Hitler: Monologe im Führerhauptquartier 1941–1944. Die Aufzeichnungen Heinrich Heims*, ed. by Werner Jochmann (Hamburg, 1980), p. 58 ('It would be beneficial for the German people to have to fight a war every 15 or 20 years') *et passim*. Even Hillgruber makes the point that 'Hitler clung to his Social-Darwinist basic idea of the *eternal struggle* [italics are mine, D.A.] even at the height of his power'. (Preface to *Staatsmänner und Diplomaten bei Hitler*, vol. 1 (Frankfurt/Main, 1967), p. 19.)

38. Thies, *Architekt*, pp. 55–6.

39. ADAP D, I Nr 19, p. 25. For Hitler's premonitions of death in 1937 see W. Maser, *Adolf Hitler – Legende, Mythos, Wirklichkeit* (Munich, 1975), pp. 374–5.

40. Under the impact of the German people's 'failure of nerve' during the crisis of September 1938 and immediately following British propaganda initiatives Hitler ordered the German media to launch a large-scale campaign 'for reinforcing German self-reliance' (*Zur Stärkung des deutschen Selbstbewusstseins*). See Jutta Sywottek, *Mobilmachung für den totalen Krieg* (Opladen, 1976), pp. 162–80, and Aigner, *Ringen*, p. 333. It is in this context that Hitler's statements and architectural projects of 1939 as quoted by Thies (*Architekt*, p. 95) should be evaluated.

41. See, for example, *Weltmacht Deutschland* (Schulungsdienst der Hitler-Jugend, Folge 1/1940 of September 1940).

42. See also L. de Jong, *Die Deutsche Fünfte Kolonne im Zweiten Weltkrieg* (Stuttgart, 1959).

43. No one has provided a more penetrating and more perceptive analysis of Hitler's quandary in a war he could start but could not bring to an end short of total victory than Andreas Hillgruber (see n. 20 above). It is, for this reason, rather difficult to understand what useful purpose could be served by the concept of a *Stufenplan* as an explanatory model for Hitler's moves in this war. There is an additional reason for being on guard against all rationalisations *e eventu* when viewing recent research on Hitler's Jewish policy: U. D. Adams, *Judenpolitik im Dritten Reich* (Düsseldorf, 1974); K. A. Schleunes, *The Twisted Road to Auschwitz* (Urbana, Ill., 1970); E. Ben Elissar, *La diplomatie du IIIe Reich et les Juifs 1933–1939* (Paris, 1969).

9 FROM THE ANTI-COMINTERN PACT TO THE EURO-ASIATIC BLOC: RIBBENTROP'S ALTERNATIVE CONCEPT TO HITLER'S FOREIGN POLICY PROGRAMME

N.B. *ADAP*   *Akten zur Deutschen Auswärtigen Politik* (Documents on German Foreign Policy)
     FRUS   Foreign Relations of the United States

1. See Galeazzo Ciano, *L'Europa verso la catastrofe* (Verona, 1948), p. 217.
2. Galeazzo Ciano, *Tagebücher 1937/38* (Hamburg, 1949), p. 32.
3. Grew to Hull, in (FRUS) 1937, Japan, pp. 159ff.

4. Ribbentrop's Main Report, 'London A 5522', of 28 December 1937, was first published in Annelies von Ribbentrop, *Die Kriegsschuld des Widerstandes. Aus britischen Geheimdokumenten 1938/39. Aus dem Nachlass*, ed. by Rudolf von Ribbentrop (Leoni, 1975). The final conclusions to it in *ADAP*, D, I, No. 93. See, in addition, the interpretation of Wolfgang Michalka, *Joachim von Ribbentrop und die deutsche Englandpolitik 1933–1940. Studien zur aussenpolitischen Konzeption-Diskussion im Dritten Reich* (Munich, 1980), pp. 196ff. For the subsequent comments see ibid., pp. 352ff.

5. Ciano, *Tagebücher*, p. 36; entry of 1 November 1937.

6. Ibid., p. 37, entry of 2 November 1937.

7. Ibid., pp. 38ff., entry of 6 November 1937.

8. Ibid.

9. For Ribbentrop's alternative concept see Michalka, *Joachim von Ribbentrop, passim*.

10. For the policy and personality of ambassador Ulrich von Hassell see the analysis by Jens Petersen, *Hitler–Mussolini. Die Entstehung der Achse Berlin–Rome 1933–1936* (Tübingen, 1973), pp. 74ff.

11. Ulrich von Hassell, *Vom andern Deutschland* (Frankfurt Main, Hamburg, 1964), p. 13. From his posthumous diaries 1938–44, with a preface by H. Rothfels.

12. See also, in a wider context, Michalka, *Joachim von Ribbentrop*, pp. 138ff.

13. See ibid., pp. 236ff.

14. See ibid., pp. 227ff.

15. *ADAP 1918–45*, D, vol. I, No. 93. Series, volume and Document Nos correspond with *Documents on German Foreign Policy*.

16. Ibid., No. 19.

17. Theo Sommer, *Deutschland und Japan zwischen den Mächten 1935 to 1940. Vom Antikominternpakt zum Dreimächtepakt. Eine Studie zur diplomatischen Vorgeschichte des Zweiten Weltkrieges* (Tübingen, 1962), p. 100.

18. *ADAP*, D, II, No. 133.

19. See also D. C. Watt, 'Hitler's visit to Rome and the May Week-End Crisis', *Journal of Contemporary History*, 1 (1974), 23–32.

20. See Michalka, *Joachim von Ribbentrop*, pp. 324ff.

21. Cf. also Sommer, *Deutschland und Japan*, p. 122.

22. *Die Weizsäcker-Papiere 1933–1950*, ed. by Leonidas E. Hill (Frankfurt, Berlin, Vienna, 1974), p. 126.

23. Cf. ibid.

24. *ADAP*, D, I, Nr 93.

25. See Sommer, *Deutschland und Japan*, pp. 124f.

26. Wording taken from ibid., p. 151.

27. Ciano, *Diaries 1939–1943* (Bern, 1946), p. 17; entries of 1 January 1939.

28. Quoted from Sommer, *Deutschland und Japan*, p. 166.

29. Cf. ibid., p. 168.

30. Ciano, *Diaries*, p. 20; entry of 7 January 1939.

31. Max Domarus, *Hitler: Reden und Proklamationen 1932–1945. Kommentiert von einem deutschen Zeitgenossen* (Hamburg, 1963), Vol. II, 1, p. 1063.

32. Sommer, *Deutschland und Japan*, p. 169.

33. For Hitler's policy during the Abyssinian War see Manfred Funke, *Sanktionen und Kanonen. Hitler, Mussolini und der internationale Abessinienkonflikt 1934–36* (Düsseldorf, 1970).

34. See also Bernd Martin, *Deutschland und Japan im Zweiten Weltkrieg* (Göttingen, Zürich, Frankfurt, 1969), pp. 17ff., and also, 'Die deutsch-japanischen Beziehungen während des Dritten Reiches', in Funke, M. (ed.), *Hitler, Deutschland und die Mächte. Materialien zur Aussenpolitik des Dritten Reiches* (Düsseldorf, 1976), pp. 454–70.

35. See also Gottfried Niedhart, 'Die britisch-französische Garantieerklärung für Polen vom 31. März 1939: Aussenpolitischer Kurswechsel der Westmächte?, *Francia*, 2 (1974), 597–618; more recently also S. Newman, *March 1939 – The British Guarantee to Poland. A Study in the Continuity of British Foreign Policy* (Oxford, 1976).

36. Sommer, *Deutschland und Japan*, p. 201.

37. Ciano, *Diaries*, p. 89; entry of 13 May 1939. For the 'Steel Pact' see D. C. Watt, 'The Rome-Berlin Axis, 1936–1940. Myth and Reality', *Review of Politics*, 22 (1960), 519–43; F. Siebert, *Italiens Weg in den Zweiten Weltkrieg* (Bonn, 1962).

38. Sommer, *Deutschland und Japan*, pp. 228ff.

39. For the German-Soviet relations which led to their Non-Aggression Pact of 23 August 1939, see the documentation of J. W. Brügel, *Stalin und Hitler. Pakt gegen Europa* (Vienna, 1973); also G. L. Weinberg, 'Deutsch-sowjetischer Nichtangriffspakt', in *Marxismus im Systemvergleich*, ed. by C. D. Kernig; cf. also D. C. Watt, 'The Initiation of the Negotiations Leading to the Nazi-Soviet Pact: A Historical Problem', in *Essays in Honour of E. H. Carr* (London, 1975), pp. 152–68.

40. *ADAP*, D, vi, Nr 264.

41. See Sommer, *Deutschland und Japan*, p. 246.

42. *ADAP*, D, vi, Nr 618.

43. Ibid., Nr 617.

44. For Ribbentrop's Russian policy see Michalka, *Joachim von Ribbentrop*, pp. 399ff.

45. Sommer, *Deutschland und Japan*, pp. 295f.

46. Ibid., p. 300.

47. See Attolico to Ciano of 16 September 1939, in *DDI*, 9, i, No. 308.

48. Sommer, *Deutschland und Japan*, p. 305.

49. Ciano on 1 October 1939, in *L'Europe verso la catastrofe*, p. 476; cf. also a similar comment by Ribbentrop on 10 March 1940 in Rome, in *ADAP*, D, viii, No. 665.

50. See also R. Wall, 'Japans Politik in den Vorkriegsjahren', in O. Hauser, (ed.), *Weltpolitik* ii, *1939–1945* (Göttingen–Frankfurt–Zürich, 1975), pp. 253f.

51. See Sommer, *Deutschland und Japan*, p. 335.

52. Quoted from ibid., p. 352.

53. For the relations of the Third Reich with South America see Reiner Pommerin, *Das Dritte Reich und Latein-Amerika. Die deutsche Politik gegenüber Süd- und Mittelamerika 1939–1942* (Düsseldorf, 1977).

54. See G. Bakker, *Duitse Geopolitik 1919–1945. Een imperialistische Ideologie* (Assen, 1967). For Haushofer see U. Laack-Michel, *Albrecht Haushofer und der Nationalsozialismus* (Stuttgart, 1974); H.-A. Jacobsen, *Karl Haushofer. Leben und Werk*, 2 vols (in preparation); further see G. Heyden, 'Kritik der geopolitischen Expansionstheorien des deutschen Imperialismus', in *Beiträge zur Kritik der gegenwärtigen Geschichtsphilosophie*, ed. by R. Schulz (Berlin, 1964).

55. Bakker, *Duitse Geopolitik*, p. 171.

56. For the genesis of Hitler's foreign policy 'programme' see Azel Kuhn, *Hitlers aussenpolitisches Programm. Entstehung und Entwicklung 1919–1939* (Stuttgart, 1970). For 'Programme' discussion cf. the contributions printed here, especially those by H. R. Trevor-Roper, D. Aigner and H. W. Koch.

57. K. Hildebrand, *Deutsche Aussenpolitik 1933–1945. Kalkül oder Dogma?*, 3rd edn (Stuttgart–Berlin–Cologne–Mainz, 1976), p. 28.

58. For Hitler's 'generous' offers to London see especially A. Hillgruber, *Hitlers Strategie. Politik und Kriegführung 1940–1941* (Frankfurt, 1965), *passim*; also B. Martin, *Friedensinitiativen und Machtpolitik im Zweiten Weltkrieg 1939–1942* (Düsseldorf, 1974).

59. See H. Greiner, *Die Oberste Wehrmachtführung 1939–1941* (Wiesbaden, 1951), p. 322; cf. also *ADAP*, D, xi, pp. 60, 123; also Hillgruber, *Hitlers Strategie*, p. 196.

60. Sven Allard, *Stalin und Hitler. Die sowjetrussische Aussenpolitik 1930–1941* (Bern–München, 1974), p. 232.

61. See especially Hillgruber, *Hitlers Strategie*, *passim*; Michalka, *Joachim von Ribbentrop*, pp. 412ff.

62. Carl J. Burckhardt, *Meine Danziger Mission 1937–1939* (Munich, 1962), p. 272.

10 HITLER'S 'PROGRAMME' AND THE GENESIS OF OPERATION 'BARBAROSSA'

I wish to express my gratitude for the suggestions made by my former colleague, the present Master of St Peter's College, Professor G. E. Aylmer, as well as to my son R. W. J. Koch and to my colleague J. W. D. Trythal for their assistance as far as stylistic improvements are concerned.

1. A. Bullock, *Hitler: a study in tyranny* (London, 1952), H. R. Trevor-Roper, 'Hitler's Kriegsziele', in *Vierteljahrhefte für Zeitgeschichte (VfZg)* (1960).

2. A. Hillgruber, *Hitlers Strategie und Kriegsführung 1940–41* (Frankfurt, 1965); ibid., *Deutsche Grossmacht und Weltpolitik im 19. und 20. Jahrhundert* (Düsseldorf, 1977); K. D. Bracher, *Die deutsche Diktatur* (Cologne, 1969); H.-A. Jacobsen, *1939–1945, Der Zweite Weltarteg in Chronik und Dokumenten* (Darmstadt, 1965); E. Jackel, *Hitlers Weltanschauung Entwurf einer Herrschaft* (Tübingen, 1969); A. Kuhn, *Hitlers aussenpolitisches Programm und Entwicklung 1919–1939* (Stuttgart, 1977); K. Hildebrand, *Deutsche Aussenpolitik 1939–1945. Kalkul oder Dogma* (Stuttgart, 1970); J. Thiess, *Architekt der Weltherrschaft. Die Endziele Hitlers* (Düsseldorf, 1976).

3. Hillgruber, *Hitlers Strategie*, pp. 564ff.

4. J. Gehl, *Austria, Germany and the Anschluss 1931–1938* (Oxford, 1963); W. Rosar, *Deutsche Gemeinschaft. Seyss-Inquart und der Anschluss* (Vienna, 1971); W. Schieder, 'Spanischer Bürgerkrieg und Vierjahresplan', in U. Engeihardt, V. Sellin, H. Sruke (eds), *Soziale Bewegung und politische Verfassung. Beitrage zur Geschichte der modernen Welt* (Stuttgart, 1976), pp. 162–90; W. Conze, *Die deutsche Nation. Ergebnis der Geschichte* (Göttingen, 1963), p. 144.

5. M. Broszart, 'Soziale Motivation und Führerbindung' in *VfZg* (1970); for a perceptive discussion of the ambivalent terms 'world power', 'world dominion' and 'world domination' see D. Algner's essay above.

6. A. Hillgruber, 'Quellen und Quellenkritik zur Vorgeschichte des Zweiten Weltkrieges' in *Wehrwissenschaftliche Rundschau*, 14 (1964).

7. A. Hillgruber, 'Die Endlösung und das deutsche Ostimperium als Kernstück des rassenbiologischen Programms des Nationalsozialismus', in Hillgruber, *Deutsche Grossmacht*, pp. 252–75; M. Broszat, 'Hitler und die Genesis der Englösung' in *VfZg* (1977); Broszat, while rejecting D. Irving's nonsense on the subject, convincingly argues and demonstrates that the 'Final Solution' was not the product of a programme but based on a number of *ad hoc* decisions by local SD and NSDAP officials on the spot which in course of time became institutionalised. Broszat's arguments receive confirmation from a surprising quarter, none other than Adolf Eichmann in his posthumous memoirs, *Ich, Adolf Eichmann* (Leoni, 1980) in the introduction of which he explicitly declares himself guilty as an accessory to murder.

8. T. Desmond Williams, 'Negotiations leading to the Anglo-Polish Agreement of 31 March 1939', in *Irish Historical Studies*, x, 59–93 and 156–92; *Documents and materials relating to the eve of the Second World War* (Moscow, 1948, pp. 176–83).

9. *Documents on German Foreign Policy* (DGFP), Series D, VII, docs. nos. 360, 383, 387, 388, 413, 414, 424, and 446. See also *Generaloberst Halder Kriegstagebuch* (*Halder-KTB*) (Stuttgart, 1962), I, entry 29 Aug. 1939.

10. H. W. Koch, 'Hitler and the origins of the Second World War; second thoughts on the status of some documents', in *Historical Journal* (1968); some additional material has since come to light which shows that Hitler's speech to his generals on 23 May 1939 was put on paper only in early November 1939 of that year and D. Kluge's study, *Das Hossbachprotokoll: Die Zerstörung einer Legende* (Leoni, 1980) conclusively proves, at least to this author, that the document submitted at Nuremberg under that name is a falsification. W. Bussmann's contribution on the origins of the Hossbach Memorandum (*VfZg*, 1968) adds nothing to the debate, while W. Baumgart's analysis of Hitler's speech to his generals on 22 August 1939 rests on the hypothesis tentatively put forward by the late Gerhard Ritter, that in fact there may have been two speeches, a hypothesis firmly contradicted by such participants in the conference as Admiral Böhm and General Halder in his diary. See *VfZg* (1971). For the most recent source criticism see B. Stegmann, 'Hitler Ziele im ersten Kriegsjahr 1939/40. Ein Beitrag zur Quellenkritik', in *Militärgeschichtliche Mitteilungen*, I (1980), and for a summary criticism of Hitler's 'programme' N. Stone, *Adolf Hitler* (London, 1980) *passim*.

11. See for instance M. Broszat, *Der Staat Hitlers* (Munich, 1969); A. Speer, *Erinnerungen* (Berlin, 1969); ibid. *Der Sklavenstaat* (Berlin, 1980); H. Höhne, *Der Orden unter dem Totenkoof* (Gütersloh, 1969); P. Hüttenberger, 'Nationalsozialistiche Polykratie', in *Geschichte und Gesellschaft. Zeitschrift für historische Sozialwissenschaft* (Göttingen, 1976).

12. W. Michalka, *Ribbentrop und die deutsche Weitpolitik 1933–1940* (Munich, 1980); also his 'Von Antikominternpakt zum Euroasiatischen Kontinentalblock: Ribbentrops Alternativkonzeption zu Hitlers aussenpolitischen Programm' in Michalka, *Nationalsozialistische Aussenpolitik* (Dormstadt, 1981) pp. 474–92.

13. Ribbentrop's 'Hauptbericht London A 5522, 28 Dezember 1937' reprinted in full in Annelies von Ribbentrop, *Die Kriegsschuld des Widerstandes* (Leoni, 1974) pp. 64ff., also his *Schlussfolgerungen*, 2 Jan. 1938, ibid., pp. 75ff. Michalka, *Ribbentrop*, pp. 224ff.

14. Michalka, 'Von Antikominternpakt', pp. 477ff.

15. See G. Ritter, *Carl Goerdeler und die deutsche Widerstandsbewegung* (Munich, 1964); P. Hoffmann, *Widerstand, Staatsstreich und Attentat* (Munich, 1969). For a more critical and differentiated assessment of the army opposition see K. J. Müller, *Armee, Politik und Gesellschaft in Deutschland 1933–1945* (Paderborn, 1979), especially his essay 'Die deutsche Militäropposition gegen Hitler. Zum Problem ihrer Interpretation und Analyse' and, by the same author, *Generaloberst Ludwin Beck* (Boppard/Rhein, 1980).

16. Hitler in the summer of 1942 realised the sectors vulnerable to a Soviet breakthrough. He issued orders to reinforce them by anti-tank defences in depth and the transfer of one Panzer Division from France. Halder did nothing. The Russian breakthrough in November 1942 occurred at precisely the point predicted by Hitler. See W. Warlimont, *Im Hauptquartier der Wehrmacht 1939–1945* (Frankfurt, 1962), p. 266; M. Kehrig, *Stalingrad: Analyse und Dokumentation einer Schlacht* (Stuttgart, 1974), *passim*.

17. Quote from H. Groscurth, *Tagebücher eines Abwehroffiziers 1938–1940* (Stuttgart, 1970), p. 478. But see also B. A. Leach, *German strategy against Russia 1939–1941* (Oxford, 1973), pp. 53ff. and Ritter, *Goerdeler*, pp. 209ff.

18. Such as General Karl-Heinrich von Stülpnagel, the deputy chief of the general staff, General Wagner, the quartermaster-general, General Fellgiebel, inspector-general of signals, and Colonel (later General) von Treskow, staff officer

Ia of the operations department of the general staff, as well as members of the OKW, like the chief of the *Abwehr* Admiral Canaris, General Oster, one of his departmental heads, and General Thomas, head of the war economy and armaments office.

19. Groscurth, *Tagebücher*, pp. 490–9.

20. F. Halder, *Hitler als Feldherr* (Munich, 1950), p. 47.

21. *Halder-KTB*, I, 18 Oct. 1939.

22. Ibid., 21 May 1940.

23. K. Klee, *Das Unternehmen 'Seelöwe'* (Göttingen, 1958), p. 189.

24. W. Ansel, *Hitler confronts England* (Durham, N. C., 1960), p. 108.

25. L. E. Hill (ed.), *Die Weizsäcker Papiere 1933–1950* (Berlin, 1974), p. 204.

26. *Jodl-Diary* quoted by Jacobsen, *1939–1945*, p. 145.

27. *Halder-KTB*, I, 15 June 1940.

28. Ibid., 28 May; 7 June; 12 June; 16 June and 19 June 1940; also G. Wagner (ed.), *Lagevortrage des Oberbefehlshabers der Kriegsmarine vor Hitler 1939–1945* (Munich, 1972), 14 June 1940.

29. H. Böhme, *Der deutsch-französische Waffenstillstand im Zweiten Weltkrieg. T.t. Entstehung und Grundlagen des Waffenstill standes von 1940* (Stuttgart, 1966), p. 79.

30. Leach, *German strategy*, p. 55.

30a. *Halder-KTB*, 30 June, 3 and 9 July.

31. *Trial of the major German war criminals before the International Military Court* (Nuremberg, 1947), XX, 576–7 (*IMT*).

32. *Halder-KTB*, 26 and 27 June 1940.

33. Ibid., II, entry for 3 July 1940.

34. Public Records Office (P.R.O.) London, War Cabinet minutes, May–June 1940, CAB 65/7; July–August 65/8; Premier: miscellaneous correspondence on peace negotiations, I, 1940. PREM 1/443, private papers of Lord Halifax (1938–40), FO 800/317, 322, 326; correspondence, Germany 1940, confidential, printed for use of the Foreign Office, FO 408/70; *Foreign relations of the United States (FRUS)* I, *General* (Washington, 1959); II, *General relations of the United States* (Washington, 1957); III, *The British Commonwealth*, and IV, *The Far East* (Washington, 1955). E. L. Woodward, *British foreign policy in the Second World War* (London, 1962), and subsequent multi-volume versions of the same work maintain a discreet silence over the tensions and divisions within the British Cabinet and government at the time over the issue of a negotiated peace, although there is ample evidence in the P.R.O. and the relevant volumes of the *FRUS* as well as in the Swedish archives. The latter have closed access since the embarrassing revelations of the Swedish ambassador in London at the time, Björn Prytz. The best and only volume dealing with this complex matter is Bernd Martin's *Friedensinitiativen und Machtpolitik im Zweiten Weltkrieg* (Düsseldorf, 1974), parts IV and V, pp. 234–370.

35. *Halder-KTB*, II, Brauchitsch's report of the Führer's conference of 21 July 1940 in Berlin, p. 32.

36. Ibid.

37. A. Seidl (ed.), *Die Beziehungen zwischen Deutschland und der Sowjetunion 1939–1941* (Tübingen, 1949), doc. nos. 127, 128. This collection of official documents comes mainly from the Nuremburg Trials. Part of it has been reprinted in *DGFP*, though the bulk of the material is now in the *Politisches Archiv* of the Bonn Foreign Office. Information supplied to the author by the *Politisches Archiv*, July 1974.

38. *IMT*, XXXIV, Assmann diary, entry 22 May 1940, p. 682.

39. *Jodl-Diary*, *IMT*, XXXVIII, 414.

40. *Halder-KTB*, I, entry 22 May 1940.

41. A. Hillgruber, *Hitler, König Carol und Marschall Antonescu: die deutsch-rumäntischen Beziehungen 1938–1944* (Wiesbaden, 1954), p. 71.

42. Assmann in *IMT*, XXIV, 685 and also Hillgruber, *Hitler, König Carol.*
43. Seidl, *Die Beziehungen*, doc. no. 149.
44. J. Degras (ed.), *Soviet documents on foreign policy*, III, 1933–41 (London, 1953), p. 450; Seidl, *Die Beziehungen*, doc. no. 134; *Soviet Documents*, p. 452.
45. *DGFP*, series D, IX, p. 459.
46. Seidl, *Die Beziehungen*, doc. no. 134.
47. Ibid., doc. no. 138.
48. Ibid., doc. no. 139.
49. Ibid., doc. no. 149.
50. Ibid., doc. no. 137.
51. *DGFP*, series D, IX, doc. nos. 344, 349, 359.
52. Seidl, *Die Beziehungen*, doc. no. 142; *Soviet documents*, p. 457.
53. *Soviet documents*, cited above.
54. *Halder-KTB*, I, 25 June 1940.
55. *IMT*, x, Ribbentrop evidence, p. 331.
56. Seidl, *Die Beziehungen*, doc. no. 141.
57. Ibid., doc. no. 145.
58. *Halder-KTB*, I, 25 June 1940.
59. Ibid., 26 June 1940.
60. Ibid., 27 June 1940.
61. Ibid., 5 July 1940.
62. For the Iron Guard and Horia Dima see E. Nolte, *Die faschistischen Bewegungen* (Munich, 1968), pp. 168ff., also Hillgruber, *Hitler, König Carol, passim.*
63. *Halder-KTB*, II, 9 July and 11 July 1940.
64. Ibid., 11 July 1940.
65. Ibid., 13 July 1940; see also Raeder notes on this conference in Klee, *Das Unternehmen*, p. 240; Jacobsen, *1939–1945*, p. 157 and *IMT*, XXXIV, 713.
66. *Halder-KTB*, II, 22 July 1940.
67. Ibid.
68. See note 31 above.
69. R. Wheatley, *Operation Sea Lion: German plans for the invasion of England 1939–1942* (Oxford, 1958), pp. 32–5.
70. See note 60; also Wagner, *Lagevorträge*, 21 July 1940.
71. *Lagevorträge*, cited above.
72. Ibid. Besprechung beim Führer am 31 Juli auf dem Berghof, pp. 125–8; *Halder-KTB*, II, 31 July 1940.
73. Such as an attack on Gibraltar via Spain, the support of the Italians by German armoured units in North Africa to capture Egypt and the Suez Canal striking as far north as Haifa.
74. *Halder-KTB*, II, 31 July 1940.
75. Seidl, *Die Beziehungen*, doc. no. 148.
76. Ibid.
77. B. Meissner, 'Die kommunistische Machtübernahme in den Baltischen Staaten' in *VfZg* (1954).
78. *DGFP*, Series D, x, doc. no. 221.
79. Ibid., doc. no. 171.
80. Ibid., doc. nos. 215 and 238.
81. See note 72.
82. *Soviet Documents*, III, 461ff.
83. *DGFP*, series D, x, doc. nos. 348, 349, 353.
84. Ibid., doc. no. 129.
85. Ibid., doc. no. 388.
86. Ibid., doc. nos. 154, 384.

87. See note 55.

88. *Bundesarchiv-Militärarchiv* (BA-MA), Freiburg, Nachlass Greiner, fo. 17, *DGFP*, series D, x, 541, note 1; also doc. no. 389.

89. H. A. Jacobsen (ed.), *Kriegstagebuch des Oberkommandos der Wehrmacht* (*KTB-OKW*), 1 (Frankfurt, 1965), 25 and 29 Aug. 1940.

90. *Halder-KTB*, 11, 29 Aug. 1940.

91. *Soviet documents*, 111, 462.

92. *KTB-OKW*, 1, 29 Aug. 1940.

93. *DGFP*, series D, x, doc. no. 413.

94. For detailed discussion see Hillgruber, *Hitler, King Carol*.

95. Nuremberg document no. PS-2353, copy in *Institut für Zeitgeschichte*, Munich.

96. G. Mannerheim, *Erinnerungen* (Zürich, 1952), p. 425; *Halder-KTB*, 11, 22 Aug. 1940; *DGFP*, series D, xi, doc. no. 86.

97. *Halder-KTB*, 11, 22 Aug. 1940; Klee, *Das Unternehmen*, p. 184.

98. *BA-MA*, Nachlass Greiner, fo. 11. Surprisingly, this and several other entries have not been included in the *KTB-OKW*.

99. *KTB-OKW*, 1, 14 Aug. 1940 and 29 Aug. 1940.

100. Ibid., 30 Aug. 1940.

101. Ibid., 10 Sept. 1940.

102. Seidl, *Die Beziehungen*, doc. no. 154.

103. Ibid., doc. nos. 157, 158, 159.

104. Ibid., doc. no. 160.

105. Ibid., doc. no. 162.

106. *Soviet Documents*, 111, 468.

107. *Halder-KTB*, 11, 14 Sept. 1940.

108. Ibid.

109. Seidl, *Die Beziehungen*, doc. no. 168.

110. *KTB-OKW*, 1, 19 Sept. 1940.

111. Ibid., 19 Sept. 1940; *Halder-KTB*, 11, 9 Sept. and 19 Sept. 1940.

112. Hillgruber, *Hitler, König Carol*, pp. 101ff.

113. *DGFP*, series D, xi, doc. no. 227.

114. Ibid., doc. no. 246.

115. *KTB-OKW*, 1, 22 Oct. 1940.

116. Ibid., 9 Nov. 1940.

117. Ibid., 2 Aug. 1940.

118. G. L. Weinberg, 'Der deutsche Entschluss zum Amgriff auf die Sowjetunion' in *VfZg* (1953).

119. *IMT*, x, 589ff.; xiv, 117ff.; xx, 629ff.; xv, 428ff. For the sheer dilettantism, the haphazard and improvised nature of *Aufbau-Ost* see the details provided by E. Helmdach, former group commander of the Wehrmacht's 'Fremde Heere Ost' (he was personally responsible for the Soviet Union) in *Überfall: Der deutsch-sowjetische Aufmarsch* (Neckargemünd, 1975), and also his *Täuschungen und Versäumnisse* (Berg am See, 1979).

120. Operation 'Felix' (the capture of Gibraltar, the Azores, the Canary and Cape Verde Islands); Operation 'Marita' (the support of the Italians in Greece); Operation 'Attila' (the occupation of Vichy-France if the need should arise); the defence of the Romanian oilfields are but a few of the projects.

121. *BA-MA*, Schematische Gliederung der Kommandobehörden und Truppen 1940 vom 9 June 1940 bis zum 21 Dec. 1940, no. H 10-3/33 1–51.

122. *KTB-OKW*, 1, 29 Aug. 1940; Hitler made the point that German military measures had already had a 'braking effect' upon the Russians in Finland and the Balkans.

123. *KTB-Greiner*, 5 Sept. 1940 in *IMT*, xxvii, 72 doc. no.1229-PS. Again this entry has been omitted in the published version of the *KTB-OKW*.

124. *KTB-OKW*, i, 30 Jan. 1941.

125. *Kriegstagebuch der Seekriegsleitung* (KTB-SKL), 2 Jan. 1940 in *IMT*, xxxii, 178.

126. S. Adler, *The isolationist impulse: its twentieth-century reaction* (New York, 1957), pp. 250ff.

127. For this aspect see Adler, *Isolationist impulse* and W. L. Langer and S. E. Gleason, *The undeclared war 1940/41* (New York, 1953); S. Friedländer, *Hitler et les Etats-Unis (1933–1941)* (Geneva, 1963); E. L. Presseisen, *Germany and Japan, a study in totalitarian diplomacy 1933–1941* (The Hague, 1958); P. W. Schroeder, *The Axis-Alliance and Japanese–American relations 1941* (New York, 1958).

128. Joachim von Ribbentrop, *Zwischen London und Moskau* (Leoni, 1953), p. 218.

129. *DGFP*, series D, x, doc. nos. 333, 362; Presseisen, *Germany and Japan*, p. 255.

130. Langer–Gleason, *Undeclared war*, p. 702.

131. *DGFP*, series D, xi, doc. no. 44; Presseisen, *Germany and Japan*, pp. 256ff.

132. *IMT*, xxviii, doc. no. 2842-PS, p. 570.

133. Ibid. See also Adler, *Isolationist impulse, passim*.

134. *Halder-KTB*, ii, 23 Sept. 1940.

135. Seidl, *Die Beziehungen*, doc. no. 167.

136. *DGFP*, series D, xi, doc. no. 129.

137. Seidl, *Die Beziehungen*, doc. no. 167.

138. *DGFP*, series D, xi, doc. no. 118; see also J. M. Menzel, 'Der geheime deutsch-japanische Notenaustausch zum Dreimächtepakt' in *VfZg* (1957).

139. *IMT*, xxxiv, Assmann evidence, p. 691; Wagner, *Lagevorträge*, p. 143, contains a detailed report of the views put by Raeder to Hitler on 26 Sept. 1940. Russian concern was not mentioned; Russia in fact was mentioned in passing only, the main issues being the Mediterranean, the prospective talks with Franco and Pétain and colonial problems. The report contradicts Assmann's evidence. As to the reception of the tripartite pact within the diplomatic circles in Moscow see G. Grafencu, *Europas letzte Tage* (Zürich, 1946), pp. 133ff.

140. *IMT*, xxiv, Assmann evidence, pp. 690, 692.

141. *Halder-KTB*, ii, 24 Oct. 1940, also 1 Nov. 1940.

142. *DGFP*, series D, xi, doc. nos. 50, 53, 56, 174, 188, 201, 230, 236, 280, 281 and 299; also Grafencu, *Europas letzte Tage*, p. 92; Hillgruber, *Hitler, König Carol*, p. 104.

143. *DGFP*, series D, xi, doc. no. 236.

144. *KTB-OKW*, 28 Oct. 1940.

145. *Halder-KTB*, ii, 15 Oct. 1940.

146. Ibid.

147. Ibid., 24 Oct. 1940.

148. Ibid., 4 Nov. 1940.

149. Ibid.

150. *DGFP*, series D, xi, doc. no. 172.

151. W. Hubatsch (ed.), *Hitlers Weisungen für die Kriegsführung 1939–1945* (Munich, 1965), pp. 81ff.

152. Ibid.

153. Seidl, *Die Beziehungen*, doc. no. 172.

154. Ibid., doc. no. 175.

155. Ibid., doc. no. 178.

156. Ibid., doc. nos. 178–179.

157. *DGFP*, series D, xi, doc. no. 325.

556 ASPECTS OF THE THIRD REICH

158. Ibid. See also G. Hilger, *Wir und der Kreml* (Frankfurt, 1955), pp. 297ff., P. Schmidt, *Statist auf diplomatischer Bühne* (Bonn, 1954), pp. 525ff.
159. See note 157.
160. Hilger, *Wird und der Kreml*, p. 302.
161. *DGFP*, series D, xi, doc. nos. 326, 328.
162. Ibid.
163. Ibid., doc. nos. 329, 348.
164. Ibid., doc. no. 309.
165. See note 163.
166. Thus Hitler to his army adjutant Major Engel, quoted by Hillgruber, *Hitlers Strategie*, p. 356.
167. *DGFP*, series D, xi, doc. no. 379.
168. Ibid., doc. no. 405.
169. Ibid.
170. *KTB-OKW*, i, 5 Dec. 1940; *Halder-KTB*, ii, 15 Dec. 1940.
171. *Halder-KTB*, cited above.
172. Hubatsch, *Hitlers Weisungen*, Weisung Nr. 21: Fall 'Barbarossa', pp. 97ff.
173. E. Nolte, *Der Faschismus in seiner Epoche* (Munich, 1963), p. 433.

11 THE REICHSMARK BLOC AND THE INTERNATIONAL ECONOMY

1. Probably the most-read work on the inter-war international economy, William A. Lewis, *Economic Survey 1919–1939* (London, 1949), is a rare exception. Lewis was saved from this interpretation by the general bias of his work which was to exaggerate the extent to which the stagnation of the inter-war period was a consequence of the inadequacy of markets and prices for exports from the less-developed economies. He was thus as much influenced, rightly, by the benefits accruing to the lower income countries in the Reichsmark bloc as by the natural desire to condemn all policies of Nazi Germany.
2. Howard S. Ellis, *Exchange Control in Central Europe* (Cambridge/Mass., 1941).
3. Claude W. Guillebaud, *The Economic Recovery of Germany* (London, 1958), p. 158.
4. Gustav Stolper, Karl Hauser and Knut Borchardt, *The German Economy 1870 to the Present* (New York, 1967), p. 143; A. G. Kenwood and A. L. Loughheed, *The Growth of the International Economy* (London, 1971), p. 213.
5. Hans-Erich Volkmann, 'Aussenhandel und Aufrüstung in Deutschland 1933 bis 1939', in Friedrich Forstmeier and Hans-Erich Volkmann (eds), *Wirtschaft und Rüstung am Vorabend des Zweiten Weltkriegs* (Düsseldorf, 1975), p. 110; also his 'NS-Aussenhandel im geschlossenen Kriegswirtschaftsraum (1939–1941)', in Friedrich Forstmeier and Hans-Erich Volkmann, *Kriegswirtschaft und Rüstung 1939–1945* (Düsseldorf, 1977).
6. Dörte Doering, 'Deutsch-österreichische Aussenhandelsverflechtung während der Weltwirtschaftskrise', in Hans Mommsen, Dietmar Petzina and Bernd Weisbrod (eds), *Industrielles System und politische Entwicklung in der Weimarer Republik* (Düsseldorf, 1974); also his *Deutsche Aussenwirtschaftspolitik 1933–1935, Die Gleichschaltung der Aussenwirtschaft in der Frühphase des nationalsozialistischen Regimes*, Thesis, F. U. Berlin 1969.
7. Roswitha Berndt, 'Wirtschaftliche Mitteleuropapläne des deutschen Imperialismus 1926–1931', *Wissenschaftliche Zeitschrift der Universität Halle*, 14 (1965), 4.
8. See, for example, V. Bozga, *Criza agrară în România dintre cele două războaie mondiale* (Bucharest, 1975) and R. Schönfeld, 'Die Balkanländer in der Weltwirtschaftskrise', *VSWG*, 62 (1975).

9. H. Sundhausen, 'Politisches und wirtschaftliches Kalkül in den Auseinandersetzungen über die deutsch-rumanischen Präferenzvereinbarungen von 1931', *Revue des Etudes Sud-Est Européenes*, 14 (1976), 3; Bernd-Jürgen Wendt, 'England und der deutsche "Drang nach Südosten". Kapitalverflechtungen und Warenverkehr in Südost-europa zwischen den Weltkriegen', in Imanuel Geiss and Bernd-Jürgen Wendt (eds), *Deutschland in der Weltpolitik des 19. und 20. Jahrhunderts* (Hamburg, 1973).

10. The diplomatic aspects of the question are discussed in Bernd-Jürgen Wendt, *Economic Appeasement* (Hamburg, 1971).

11. Larry Neal, 'The Economics and Finance of Bilateral Clearing Agreements: Germany, 1934–1938', *Economic History Review*, 32 (1979) 3; Philippe Marguérat, *Le III*ᵉ *Reich et le pétrole roumain 1938–1940* (Leiden, 1977).

12. Royal Institute of International Affairs, *Southeastern Europe, a Political and Economic Survey* (London, 1939), p. 197.

13. Neal, *Economics and Finance*, p. 403.

14. As Neal points out Benham's conclusions were in part suppressed. They appeared in 1939 and he was publicly attacked for giving comfort to the enemy. Both sets of calculations are in accord with the more long-term calculations of Kindleberger who found that over the period 1870–1952 the terms of trade of the United Kingdom and Belgium with 'non-industrial Europe' improved more than those of Germany (Charles P. Kindleberger, *The Terms of Trade. A European Case Study*, New York, 1956).

15. There is really no more to Einzig's criticisms of Benham's work than this, one more example of how the argument was always conducted in terms of the differences between the National Socialist and other capitalist economies rather than those between developed and less-developed economies. See Paul Einzig, *Hitler's 'New Order' in Europe* (London, 1941) and his 'Why Defend Nazi Trade Methods?', *The Banker*, 58 (1941).

16. Osman Torgay, *Der deutsch-türkische Handel. Organisation und Technik* (Hamburg 1939).

17. There are certain inherent aspects of the international trade in foodstuffs which predispose the exporter towards the idea of accumulating credit balances, especially the fact that certain foodstuffs come on the market in very variable quantities over the year, which is not so with manufactures.

18. This argument is briefly touched on by Nikola Momtchiloff, 'Ten Years of Controlled Trade in South-East Europe', in *N.I.E.S.R. Occasional Papers VI* (Cambridge, 1941).

19. Wendt, *Economic Appeasement.*

20. Calculated from national trade statistics.

21. Marguérat, *Le IIIe Reich et le pétrole roumain.*

22. There are different estimates. These are the estimates of the British government given in William N. Medlicott, *The Eonomic Blockade*, vol. 1 (London, 1952).

23. The oil companies were still frequently forced to act directly contrary to the wishes of the Antonescu government by the British and French governments.

24. Antonin Basch, *The Danube Basin and the German Economic Sphere* (London, 1944).

25. L. Berov, 'The Withdrawing of Foreign Capital from Bulgaria on the Eve of the Second World War', *Studia Balcanica*, 4 (1971).

26. Mirko Lamer, 'Die Wandlungen der ausländischen Kapitalanlagen auf dem Balkan', *Weltwirtschaftliches Archiv 1938*.

27. Marguérat, *Le III*ᵉ *Reich et le pétroles roumain*, pp. 34ff.

28. Their plans are published in Dietrich Eichholtz, *Geschichte der deutschen Kriegswirtschaft 1939–1945*, vol. 1: *1939–1941* (Berlin, 1969), pp. 248ff.; Dietrich Eichholtz and Wolfgang Schumann (eds), *Anatomie des Kriegs. Neue Documente über die Rolle des deutschen Monopolkapitals bei der Vorbereitung und Durchführung des Zweiten Weltkrieges* (Berlin, 1969); Wolfgang Schumann, 'Das Kriegsprogramm des Zeiss-Conzerns', *Zeitschrift für Geschichtswissenschaft*, 11 (1963/4).

29. 'After Hitler came to power the well-known conscious long-term objective of German heavy industry, to penetrate into Czechoslovak industrial and banking combines in order to attain a basis for further advances into southeast Europe, was openly and aggressively pursued by German political and economic representatives' (Alice Teichova, *An Economic Background to Munich*, Cambridge, 1971, p. 91).

30. The large number of German-Czech cartel agreements is well-established by Teichova's work. But their rate of increase declined under the Nazi government while that of British-Czech cartels increased. Ibid., table 1, p. 56, for example, gives a total of 243 German-Czech agreements over the period 1926–32 and only 170 over the period 1933–8. The comparable figures for British-Czech agreements are 21 and, in the Nazi period, 47. Given the very much greater volume of British and French direct and portfolio investment in Czechoslovakia compared to that of Germany their need for cartel agreements might well have been correspondingly less. German direct capital investment there at the end of 1937 was slightly more than one quarter of that of Britain (ibid., p. 48).

31. Lest there be misunderstanding I should point out that my intention here is in no way to support Taylor's 'revisionist' view of Hitler's foreign policy. Indeed there is nothing in this article that could logically do so.

32. National trade statistics.

33. United States Strategic Bombing Survey, *The Effects of Strategic Bombing on the German War Economy*, Appendix Table 83.

34. One that clearly was was the export of hazel nuts from Turkey. But it was almost matched by the Greek export trade of currants, etc. to Britain.

35. Turkey, Ministère des Finances, *Statistiques Annuelles du Commerce Extérieur de la Turquie*.

36. Herbert Backe, *Um die Nahrungsfreiheit Europas. Weltwirtschaft oder Grossraum* (Leipzig, 1942), p. 225.

37. The calculations to 1955 are represented in Alan S. Milward, 'Der deutsche Handel und der Welthandel 1925–1939', in Mommsen, Petzina and Weisbrod (eds), p. 477. No one is likely to require evidence of the extrapolation beyond that date in view of the more systematic and generalised evidence in Alfred Maizels, *Industrial Growth and World Trade* (Cambridge, 1963).

38. Bulgaria, Esthonia, Finland, Greece, Hungary, Latvia, Lithuania, Poland, Romania, Spain, Turkey and Yugoslavia.

39. *Statistische Jahrbücher.*

40. See the calculations in Alan S. Milward, *The New Order and the French Economy* (Oxford, 1970), pp. 257–8.

41. Pierre Marguérat, 'Le protectionisme financier allemand et le bassin danubien à la veille de la seconde guerre mondiale. L'exemple de la Roumanie', *Relations internationales*, 16 (1978).

42. Basch, *Danube Basin*, p. 167.

43. Kenyon E. Poole, *German Financial Policies 1932–1939* (New York, 1939), p. 94.

44. Burton A. Klein, *Germany's Economic Preparations for War* (Cambridge/Mass., 1959), p. 16.

45. Arthur Schweitzer, *Big Business in the Third Reich* (Bloomington, 1964), p. 428.

46. Klein, *Germany's Economic Preparations*, Statistical Appendix: Table 60. p. 254.

47. Dietmar Petzina, *Autarkiepolitik im Dritten Reich* (Stuttgart, 1968), p. 30.

48. Ibid., p. 183. Rearmament expenditures were about 8,000 million Reichmarks in 1937.

49. Imports of wheat from the United States rose from 17,000 tons in 1937 to 243,900 tons in 1938, the highest annual quantity since 1928 (*Sondernachweis des Aussenhandels Deutschlands*).

50. Marguérat, 'Le protectionnisme'.

13 HITLER AND THE GENESIS OF THE 'FINAL SOLUTION': AN ASSESSMENT OF DAVID IRVING'S THESES

1. David Irving, *Hitler's War* (London, 1977).

2. David Irving, *Hitler und seine Feldherren* (Frankfurt, 1975). The German publisher (Ullstein Verlag) insisted on the omission of those theses of Irving's that were, in his opinion, untenable and irresponsible: relieving Hitler of the responsibility for the extermination of the Jews. The publishing of the German edition caused a breach between author and publisher.

3. *Accident, The Death of General Sikorski* (London, 1967) German edition: *Mord aus Staatsräson, Churchill und Sikorski, eine tragische Allianz* (Berne, Munich, Vienna, 1969) and *The Destruction of Convoy PQ 17* (London, 1968), which had sensational repercussions in court (see note 9 below). 'PQ 17' is the story of the sinking of the British convoy, which was withheld from the public, the blame for which Irving placed on the commander of the Navy's escort flotilla.

4. See the discussion by Heinz Höhne in *Der Spiegel* of 4 July 1977, pp. 71–4. One of Irving's German friends Rolf Hochhuth, who adopted Irving's thesis about Churchill's alleged assassination of Sikorski and used it as the theme of his play *Soldaten*, found it necessary to dissociate himself decidedly from Irving's theory, in his introduction to Goebbels' diaries of 1945, published by Hoffmann and Campe, Hamburg (Introduction, p. 40).

5. Cited here primarily are the detailed discussions by Alan Bullock in the *New York Times Book Review* of 26 May 1977, of Hugh Trevor-Roper in the *Sunday Times Weekly Review* of 12 June 1977 and of Eberhard Jäckel in the *Frankfurter Allgemeine Zeitung* of 25 August 1977.

6. Irving, *Hitler's War*, p. 424. The abridged German edition does not carry this passage. According to Irving, this remark was made in the course of a discussion between Hitler and one of his doctors on the Englishman J. Daniel Chamier's book about Emperor Wilhelm II. Hitler had remarked on this occasion, so Irving cites (p. 424) significantly: 'that a foreigner probably finds it easier to pass judgement on a statesman, provided that he is familiar with the country, its people, language and archives'. Irving does not refer to the source of his quote in the notes.

7. To be noted here among others is a not very extensive notebook of the former ambassador Walter Hewel, Foreign Minister Ribbentrop's liaison at the Führer's headquarters (it had to be partly translated from the Indonesian and was therefore particularly attractive to Irving) and the probably more significant notes of Dr Werner Koeppens, liaison officer to Alfred Rosenberg, the *Reichsminister* for the Occupied Eastern Territories, recording conversations at the Führer's headquarters. See the introductory part of Irving's book. A great part of this material has been put at the disposal of the Institut für Zeitgeschichte (IfZ) by Irving. It is to be commended that he has not, as a rule, withheld his sources

from other historians and has also made them accessible to his critics. This has allowed the author of this paper access to Irving's material and helped him to grasp how Irving made use of it.

8. Characteristic is the description of his – in this case futile – search of several weeks' duration (with a supersensitive mine-detector) in a forest in East Germany for a waterproof container with a microfilm copy of Goebbels' diaries allegedly buried there in 1945. See Introduction, p. xxi.

9. Best known is Irving's alleged proof that the fatal 1942 airplane crash involving the Polish prime minister in exile, General Sikorski, was caused by sabotage on Churchill's order. Irving reverts to this thesis in his Hitler book (Introduction, p. xiii) although a British court of law established its untenability. Trevor-Roper deals with it in his discussion in the *Sunday Times Weekly Review* on 12 June 1977 and writes: 'It is well known that some years ago Mr. Irving convinced himself that General Sikorski, who died in an air crash at Gibraltar, was "assassinated" by Winston Churchill, to whom in fact his death was a political calamity. Not a shred of evidence or probability has ever been produced in support of this theory and when it was tested in the courts, Mr. Irving's only "evidence" was shown to be a clumsy misreading of a manuscript diary (I have myself seen the diary and feel justified in using the word "clumsy").'

10. Cf. David Irving, *The Destruction of Dresden* (London, 1963) (German edition Gütersloh, 1964) and by the same author. *Die Tragödie der deutschen Luftwaffe, Aus den Akten und Erinnerungen von Feld-marschall Milch* (Frankfurt, Vienna, 1970); *The Trail of the Fox*, The Life of Field Marshal Erwin Rommel (London, 1977), *The War Path* (London, 1978).

11. Michael Radclife in *The Times*, 16 June 1977, p. 14.

12. Irving introduces the paragraph about this event (p. 20) with the remark: 'The ostensible occasion for this formal decision was related to war needs. About a quarter of a million hospital beds were required for German mental institutions. . . They occupied bed space and the attention of skilled medical personnel which Hitler now urgently needed for the treatment of the casualties of his coming campaigns.' None of the relevant documents contains this particular justification of the euthanasia programme.

13. The *National-Zeitung* published in Munich dedicated its front page on 2 September 1977 to 'New Ideas about the Führer', and exulted over Irving's book and the illustrated pocketbook of the Hitler film by Joachim Fest: 'the demonization of Hitler is approaching its end' and a 'normalization' of Hitler in contemporary history is slowly taking place. [Irving, sponsored and paid for by the editor of the *National-Zeitung*, has and still is addressing private and public gatherings in West Germany. These are held under the auspices of the *Deutsche Volks Union* (DVU), a body close to Irving's 'Focus' group in the UK. *Ed.*]

14. See Joseph Goebbels, *Tagebücher 1945*, Die letzten Aufzeichnungen, (Hamburg, 1977); English edition, Joseph Goebbels, *The Final Entries 1945*, The Diaries of Joseph Goebbels (London, 1978). The entries of 27 and 28 March 1945 show that at that time Goebbels urged Hitler in vain to broadcast to the German people.

15. Characteristic of these is one of the most recent comprehensive commentaries on the NS Jewish policy, Lucy Dawidowicz, *The War Against the Jews 1933–1945* (London, 1975).

16. The post-war statements of persons who had been entrusted with individual acts of extermination of Jews refer to verbal instructions: see below, notes 62–65.

17. Uwe Dietrich Adam, *Judenpolitik im Dritten Reich* (Düsseldorf, 1972), esp. pp. 305ff.

18. *Das Diensttagebuch des deutschen Generalgouverneurs in Polen 1939–45*, published by Werner Präg and Wolfgang Jacobmeyer (Stuttgart, 1975), p. 386 (hereafter –

Diensttagebuch). That at that time (summer 1941) the authorities of the SD who were dealing with the Jewish problem were still unaware of the general extermination order (which would have been surprising if it had already existed) is illustrated by the draft of a letter by the chief of the SD unit in Posen who was in charge of the Warthegau and was addressed to the expert on Jewish questions, Adolf Eichmann, at the RSHA on 17 July 1941, precisely because this draft deals with an independent decision on the part of the security police and the SD in Posen to kill a part of the Jews of the ghetto of Litzmannstadt. It was to be considered, so the document says, referring to a conference about 'the solution of the Jewish question' which took place at the office of the district governor in Posen, that in view of the overcrowding of the Litzmannstadt ghetto it might be the most humane solution to finish off those Jews who were unable to work by some quick-acting medium. In any case this would be more pleasant than to let them starve. 'These things sound partly fantastic,' writes the SD chief of Posen, 'but are, in my opinion, absolutely feasible.' Copy of this draft was discovered in Posen and was presented in evidence at the trial against *Reichsstatthalter* Greiser in *Biuletyn Głównej Kómisji Badania Zbrodni Hitlerowskich w Polsce*, vol. XIII (Cracow, 1960), doc. 27f/28.

19. See Andreas Hillgruber, *Staatsmänner und Diplomaten bei Hitler*, vol. II, (Munich, 1970), p. 556.

20. According to a note by Werner Koeppens, for which we are indebted to David Irving, Hitler remarked on the evening of 10 July 1941 at the Führer's headquarters: 'I feel like Robert Koch in politics. He discovered the bacilli and pointed many things in a new direction. I discovered the Jews and the bacillus and their fermenting agent of social decomposition. . . .' IfZ Archives, Irving Collection.

21. These are in the possession of the Hoffmann and Campe publishing house, Hamburg (hereafter quoted as Goebbels' Diary, Hoffmann and Campe). For permission to inspect these closely I am indebted mainly to the former business manager of the firm, Dr Knaus.

22. Hitler stated at the Reichstag on 30 January 1939: 'If the international finance-Jewry inside and outside Europe manages just once more to precipitate the world into war, the outcome will be, not the Bolshevization of the earth and the consequent triumph of Jewry, but the annihilation of the Jewish race in Europe.' During the war Hitler again and again referred to this speech in public addresses as well as in private conversation, for instance in his speeches at the *Reichstag* on 30 January 1941 and on 30 January 1942. However, he dated them incorrectly (intentionally or subconsciously) to 1 September 1939. That it was an intentional change of date, in order to stress the connection of the military struggle against the Jews, is indicated by its regular appearance and the fact that it was retained in the official publications of Hitler's speeches, for instance in the *Völkischer Beobachter*.

23. Personal Staff RFSS, IfZ Archives, MA 3/9, folder 94.

24. According to Koeppens' notes on 7 October 1941, Hitler stated on 6 October 1941 concerning the Protectorate: 'All Jews have to be removed from the Protectorate, not only to the General Government but straight on to the East. Only the great shortage of transport prevents this being done at once. Together with the Jews of the Protectorate all the Jews of Vienna and Berlin must disappear.' IfZ Archives, Irving Collection.

25. See a letter from Übelhör to Himmler dated 4 October 1941, from Himmler to Übelhör on 10 October 1941 (containing the sentence: 'I demand that they [the Jews] be placed in the houses that, due to the considerable decrease in the number of Jews in the last one and a half years [throug.. mortality and

deportations to the General Government] have become vacant.'), Personal Staff
RFSS, IfZ Archives, MA 3/9, folder 94.

26. The following quotations according to Goebbels' diaries, Hoffmann and
Campe (see note 21).

27. Also Adam, *Judenpolitik*, (especially p. 312) assumes such a secret order but
prefers to date it later ('between September and November 1941'). It appears to
me however that no comprehensive order for the extermination existed and that
the 'programme' for the extermination of the Jews developed through individual
actions and gradually attained its institutional and factual character by spring of
1942 after the construction of the extermination camps in Poland (between
December 1941 and July 1942).

28. See above, note 18.

29. Nuremberg document NO–365.

30. Details about Chelmno are contained in documents published by Adalbert
Rückerl, *Nationalsozialistische Vernichtungslager im Spiegel deutscher Strafprozesse – Belzec,
Sobibór, Treblinka, Chelmno* (Stuttgart, 1977), see also Ino Arndt-Wolfgang Scheffler,
'Organisierter Massenmord an Juden in nationalsozialistischen Vernichtungslagern',
in *Vierteljahrshefte für Zeitgeschichte*, No. 4 (Stuttgart, 1976), 116ff, (hereafter –
Vierteljahrshefte).

31. Nuremberg document NO–246/247.

32. See *Diensttagebuch* of the Governor General . . . ibid., p. 457.

33. Omitted in the original diary.

34. An illustration of this is the 'report' that Goebbels wrote in his diary on 2
November 1941 about his visit to the Vilna ghetto the day before. Goebbels'
Diary, Hoffman and Campe pp. 15ff.: 'The picture becomes terrifying on a short
tour of the ghetto. The Jews are squeezed together here, horrible creatures not to
be looked at even less to be touched.... Horrible shapes loiter in the streets whom
I would not care to meet at night. The Jews are the lice of civilized humanity.
They have to be exterminated somehow; otherwise they will continue to play their
tormenting and troublesome role.'

35. The Belzec extermination camp in the Lublin district was opened as early
as March 1942: the gassings at Auschwitz-Birkenau began at about the same time,
the extermination camps of Sobibór and Treblinka in the Eastern part of the
General Government were erected in the following month, July, where already in
1942 a great part of the Jews of the General Government perished. See Arndt-
Scheffler, 'Organisierter Massenmord. . . .' pp. 105–35.

36. See the exact quotation below, note 50.

37. The following (retranslation) of *Hitler's Table Talk 1941–44* (London, 1953),
p. 87.

38. *Hitler's Table Talk*, p. 235.

39. Ibid., pp. 235–6.

40. Ibid., p. 260.

41. *Goebbels – Tagebücher*, published by L. P. Lochner (Zurich, 1948), p. 87. In
the English edition, *The Goebbels Diaries*, translated and edited by Louis P. Lochner
(London, 1948), this entry was omitted.

42. Personal Staff RFSS, IfZ Archives, MA 316, BL 4994ff.

43. Italics are the author's.

44. Collection of copies in IfZ Archives, F 37/2.

45. As can be seen from the note, Himmler had already telephoned to Berlin
two hours before (11:30 hrs) from his own special train ('Sonderzug Heinrich').
He had been, as can be seen from Hitler's table talk (p. 135), among others, a
guest at Hitler's table in the evening. Accordingly any long conversation with

Hitler on 30 November 1941, could only have taken place on the afternoon of this day.

46. See 'Gesamtaufstellung der im Bereich der Einsatzkommandos [*Einsatzgruppe* A of the Security Police and the SD] bis zum 1.12.1941 durchgeführten Exekutionen' (IfZ Archives, Fb 101/20). The documents show than on 25 November 1941, at Fort IX in Kovno, which had been used as an execution place by the *Einsatzkommandos*, 2,934 Jews from Munich. Berlin and Frankfurt had been shot. A further shooting on 29 November 1941 ended the lives of 2,000 Jews from Breslau and Vienna.

47. See note No. 43. A telephone note of Himmler's on 1 December 1941 states: '13:15 hrs, SS *Ogr.* Heydrich, execution at Riga.'

48. See fragment of action report by SS *Obersturmführer* and Criminal Commissar Kurt Burkhardt, concerning this affair, dated January-February 1942, IfZ Archives, Fb 104. Also Helmut Heiber, 'Aus den Akten des Gauleiters Kube', *Vierteljahrshefte*, No. 4, (1956) 67–92.

49. Goebbels had already pointed out those sensibilities in his diaries (see above, p. 91). From his entries (they are missing for the month of December 1941) we can derive no clues for the interpretation of Himmler's telephone notice on 30 November 1941.

50. Heydrich referred at this conference particularly to 'further possibilities of a solution after previous authorization by the Führer' which was the ultimate purpose of the 'evacuation of the Jews to the East'. He explained further:

Under appropriate direction, in the course of the final solution, the Jews are now to be suitably assigned to labour in the East. In big labour gangs, with the sexes separated, Jews capable of work will be brought to these areas, employed in roadbuilding, in which task a large part will undoubtedly disappear through natural diminution.

The remnant that may eventually remain, being undoubtedly the part most capable of resistance, will have to be appropriately dealt with, since it represents a natural selection and in the event of release is to be regarded as the germ cell of a new Jewish renewal.

Minutes of the conference, pp. 7ff., made public at the Eichmann Trial, Document of evidence No. 74.

51. This entry became known through *The Goebbels Diaries*, published by L. P. Lochner, that were accessible to him at the time (see above note 41). The last sentence is missing in the English edition.

52. See e.g. the above-mentioned table talk of Hitler's on 23 January 1942. Accordingly it is simply not correct when Irving states on p. 327 of his book: 'All the surviving adjutants, female secretaries and staff stenographers' had 'testified unanimously' that the extermination had never been mentioned at the Führer's headquarters. This thesis, whose confirmation Irving had obviously obtained from Bormann's assistant at the time, Heinrich Heim, is all the more misleading since Heim has recorded the above-mentioned table talk as well as other brutal utterances on the part of the Führer and the records of the table talks are based mainly on Heim's notes. To what extent Irving's still living 'star witnesses' contribute to this thesis was discovered by the English writer Gitta Sereny who took the trouble to interview five of those questioned by Irving. They all declared, as was to be expected, that Hitler never spoke about the extermination of the Jews in their presence; they could not however imagine that he had known nothing about them. A report about this is in the *Sunday Times Weekly* dated 10 July 1977. [As indicated above Heim's notes do not contain this passage. They record Hitler's words only during the night 22/23 January 1942 and resume on 24 January 1942 in the evening of that day. *Ed.*]

53. In Himmler's address at Posen before SS commanders [This is in need of qualification: 'Higher SS- and Police Leaders' were present but not a single commander of the Waffen-SS. *Ed.*] (4 October 1943) he revealed in a remarkable twist the meaning of the formula that had long been used by saying: 'I am referring now to the evacuation of the Jews, the extermination of the Jewish people.' This 'the heaviest' task as he declared in the address of 6 October 1943 had been undertaken by the SS 'as an obligation towards our people, our race . . . our Führer'. See text in IfZ Archives, F37/3.

54. Part of the collection of printed matter 'Vertrauliche Informationen der Parteikanzlei', IfZ Archives, Db 15.06.

55. Illuminating for this is a letter by *SS-Oberführer* Brack (Chancellery of the Führer) to Himmler on 23 June 1942 (Nuremberg document NO–205) in which the former reports that he had supplied further specialists upon Globocnik's request (for the gassing installations). 'On this occasion Globocnik advocated finishing the whole Jewish action as quickly as possible so as not to remain stuck midway. . . . You yourself, *Reichsführer*, have stated to me that one had, if only for reasons of camouflage, to work as quickly as possible.' If one wanted to achieve this and on the other hand wished to employ the Jews who were able to work for the production of armaments, Brack continued, he recommended the sterilisation of all the Jews who were still employed by means of 'X-ray castration' which could be accomplished 'in the shortest time'.

56. Since it also evolved that in the district of Lublin a number of Jewish workers could not yet be spared, e.g. those employed at Beskiden Oil Co. on behalf of the *Wehrmacht* and thus the planned Germanisation of the district with ethnic Germans (*Volksdeutsche*) – requiring total evacuation of the Jews – could not yet be achieved, Himmler turned to Hitler with this problem once more in the middle of September 1942. The outline of Himmler's talk with Hitler on 17 September 1942 contains, under the heading 'Folkdom and Resettlement' the note '1) Deportation of Jews, how to proceed further, 2) Resettlement Lublin: Lothringians, Germans from Bosnia, Bessarabia . . .' IfZ Archives, F37/3.

57. Nuremberg document NO–2207.

58. Additional evidence is Himmler's draft for an address before Hitler on 10 December 1942. In that draft he noted among other things: 'In France there are still 600,000–700,000 Jews and other enemies of the Reich.' After the discussion Himmler noted: 'To get rid of them.' On the same day Himmler noted: 'The Führer has issued the directive that the Jews and other enemies in France are to be arrested and deported. However this is to be done only after he has discussed the matter with Laval.' (Microfilm IfZ, Archives, MA 316, Bl. 615330 and Nuremberg document PS–1994.) The above testimonies are all contained in the file which Irving assembled in preparation for his book, but their contents have hardly been used in his presentation. When a year later, in June 1943, Himmler was concerned with getting rid of the remaining Jews in the General Government in view of the increased danger of partisan warfare, he turned again to Hitler in an address on 19 June 1943. In a note on this address to the Führer we read: 'The Führer in response to my address, expressed the opinion that the evacuation of the Jews had to be carried out radically in spite of the disturbances that might break out in the next 3–4 months.'

59. Sentence of the Jury at the District Court in Munich II in the criminal action against Karl Wolff, p. 236 (Copy IfZ, Qm 07.29/2).

60. He adopts for example the opinion (certainly misleading and advocated by Wolff for obvious reasons) that only about 70 persons in Germany had known about the extermination of the Jews.

61. Notes by Karl Wolff, 11 May 1952, IfZ Archives, ZS 317.

62. Karl Wilhelm Krause, *Zehn Jahre Kammerdiener bei Hitler* (Hamburg [1949]). On page 71 we find among others the following conclusion on the part of Krause: 'Hitler had no perception of people ... the greatest part of the responsibility for the crimes that were perpetrated in Hitler's name should rest with the *Reichsleiter* Martin Bormann and Himmler. ... Hitler had been informed about many things ... either nothing at all or very little or vaguely through these two evil spirits. About the horrors in the concentration camps nothing was known in the circle surrounding Hitler. These matters were never discussed. ... I wish to state again that these matters and also the fight against the Church have their origin with Bormann and Himmler.'

63. Ohlendorf, chief of the *Einsatzgruppe* D in 1941–2, had stated on 3 January 1946 at the Nuremberg Trials: 'In the late summer of 1941, Himmler was in Nikolaiev. He assembled the officers and men of the *Einsatzkommando* and reiterated the extermination order that had been issued to them ... the responsibility was his and the Führer's.' Irving (p. 326) quotes the last sentence in this manner: 'That he [Himmler] alone, in association with Hitler was responsible.' The 'alone' is Irving's invention. In continuation he mitigates the blame further: 'Himmler's formulation was perhaps purposefully vague.'

64. Höttl stated during the Eichmann Trial in Jerusalem in June 1961: The leader of *Einzatzgruppe* A, Dr Stahlecker, had explained to him during the war that the orders to the *Einsatzgruppen* concerning the annihilation of the Jews 'came from Hitler personally and were communicated to the *Einsatzgruppen* by Heydrich'. Höttl further stated that as witness in Nuremberg in the years 1945–7 he spoke with former leading functionaries: 'the unanimous understanding of these people' had been 'that the physical annihilation of the Jewish people should definitely be traced back to Hitler personally'. Eichmann Trial, interrogation of Wilhelm Höttl by the District Court Bad Aussee, 19–21.6.1961, proceedings, p. 22.

65. *Kommandant in Auschwitz*, Autobiographische Aufzeichnungen von Rudolf Höss (Munich, 1963), p. 157; English edition, *Commandant of Auschwitz*, The Autobiography of Rudolf Hoess, translated by Constantine FitzGibbon (London, 1959), p. 153.

66. Wisliceny claimed after 1945 that Eichmann had shown him a written order concerning the extermination of the Jews. Eichmann denied this in his statements in Jerusalem; he confirmed however, that Heydrich had summoned him (Eichmann) to inform him that the Führer had ordered the physical annihilation of the Jews. Irving seizes upon this contradiction between the statements of Wisliceny and Eichmann, that does not however touch upon the essence of the matter, which is their unanimous statement that the extermination programme, as they had been told, derived from Hitler, as the occasion for an arrogant remark with which he tries to play down the significance of these testimonies: 'This kind of evidence, of course, would not suffice in an English Magistrate's court to convict a vagabond of bicycle stealing.' (p. 858fn.).

67. Irving refers to the note of Hitler's table talk on 25 October 1941 (this appears only in the English version, p. 91) where Hitler remarked in the presence of Himmler and Heydrich in the course of a discussion of Christianity, the Church and other subjects: 'I have numerous accounts to settle, about which I cannot think today. But that does not mean I forget them. I write them down. The time will come to bring out the big book. Even with regard to the Jews, I've found myself remaining inactive. There's no sense in adding uselessly to the difficulties of the moment. ... When I read of the speeches of a man like Galen, I tell myself that ... for the moment it is preferable to be silent. ...' The formulation 'even with the Jews' makes it clear that Hitler viewed this question differently from the question of the Church. Irving falsifies this by omitting the word 'even' in his

566   ASPECTS OF THE THIRD REICH

quote of this sentence (p. 331) and inserts instead 'too' which does not appear in the original version. In place of the recorded sentence ('Even with the Jews I found myself remaining inactive') Irving writes: 'with the Jews too I have found myself remaining inactive'. It may be that Hitler referred in this remark to the earlier enforced 'inactivity' concerning the aim to make Germany *judenfrei* that had meanwhile been replaced by a purposeful activity. It is however possible that he was referring to the difficulties that had been set in the path of a rapid deportation of the Jews by the unexpected course of the eastern campaign; see the above remark by Hitler to Goebbels on 21 November 1941 (p. 752).

68. This is also the weakness of Eberhard Jäckel's study, *Hitlers Weltanschauung* (Tübingen, 1969); English edition, *Hitler's Weltanschauung*, A Blueprint for Power, translated by Herbert Arnold (Middletown, Connecticut, 1972).

69. Indicative of this are Hitler's detailed utterances regarding the Jewish question, recorded in Goebbels' diary on 13 May 1943: 'Therefore the modern nations have no other choice than to exterminate the Jews. They will resist this gradual extermination campaign with all the means at their disposal. One of these means is war. We have to realize that in this confrontation between Aryan humanity and the Jewish race, we shall have to endure many hard battles, because Jewry has managed to bring great population groups of the Aryan race, knowingly or unknowingly, into its service.... It is the firm conviction of the Führer that world Jewry is facing a great fall ... the nations which have first recognized and resisted the Jew for what he is shall rule the world in his place.'

70. In his secret address to officers and generals at Obersalzberg on 26 May 1944 (see above, note 42) Hitler declared among other things: 'I have squeezed Jewry out of its positions, without consideration ... with this I have removed the last catalyst from the masses. By removing the Jews, I have removed any possibility for the formation of a revolutionary infection....'

71. The intensification of the deportations from France beginning in the spring of 1943, the simultaneously increased pressure on Hungary *vis-à-vis* the Jews, the annihilation of the Jews in the Ukraine (spring 1943) and other evidence point to the fact that the war of extermination against the Jews was again waged with the greatest intensity, after the military struggle was already, more or less, lost. Eichmann too, during his trial in Jerusalem, testified on 21 June 1961 that after 'Stalingrad' a 'considerable effort on the part of the Reich leadership' could be noted 'in order to intensify the deportations [of the Jews].' The first 'high point' of the intensification had been in the spring of 1942, the second after the death of Heydrich, the third fell in the phase after Stalingrad.

72. See the minutes of Hitler's conference with Antonescu and Horthy according to the German records in Hillgruber, *Staatsmänner und Diplomaten bei Hitler*, Vol. II (1970). On Hitler's utterances concerning the Jewish policy (p. 233) e.g. the following sentences: 'For this reason, it was the Führer's opinion, in contrast to Marshal Antonescu, that the more radically the Jews were dealt with, the better ... he [the Führer] ... would rather burn all bridges behind him, since the Jewish hatred was in any case enormous. In Germany one had, due to the solving of the Jewish question, a unified nation without opposition at one's disposal. However, there was no turning back once this path had been taken.' Although Irving mentions the conference (p. 508) he omits Hitler's remark about the Jewish question.

73. Minutes see Hillgruber, *Staatsmänner*, Vol. II, pp. 245ff., 256ff.

74. P. 872 (note on p. 509). Horthy had correctly interpreted Hitler's remark as a request for the annihilation of the Jews. This is confirmed by the draft of a letter from Horthy to Hitler regarding the conference at Klessheim, which was prepared by the Hungarian Foreign Ministry and which reads: 'Your Excellency further

reproached me that my government does not proceed with stamping out Jewry with the same radicalism as is practiced in Germany.' (In Horthy's actual letter to Hitler, dated 7 May 1943 this passage had been omitted; see *The Confidential Papers of Admiral Horthy* (Budapest, 1965). However, in his footnote Irving 'coyly' cites the term *Ausrottung* as 'extirpation'; whereas in the text of the book he uses the vague 'stamping out' (not as he did originally in the handwritten translation in the margin of the copy of the Horthy letter used by him, IfZ, Irving Collection).

14 THE 'ARISTOCRACY OF NATIONAL SOCIALISM', THE ROLE OF THE *SS* IN NATIONAL SOCIALIST GERMANY

1. G. Reitlinger, *The SS: Alibi of a Nation, 1922–1945* (London, 1956). The most authoritative analysis of the SS as a whole is now as before the collaborative work by H. Buchheim *et al.*, Anatomie des SS-Staates, 2 vols (Freiburg–Olten, 1965). (English abridged edition, *Anatomy of the SS-state*, New York, 1968).

2. For a broader analysis of the ideological impact of the idea of *politisches Soldatentum* see H. Buchheim, 'Befehl und Gehorsam', in *Anatomie des SS-Staates*, vol. 1; and B. Wegner, *Hitlers Politische Soldaten: die Waffen-SS 1933–1945. Studien zu Leitbild, Struktur und Funktion einer nationalsozialistischen Elite* (Paderborn, 1982), Part I.

3. A. Hitler, *Mein Kampf* (Munich, 1933), p. 386.

4. Speech by Himmler on 8 November 1938, as quoted in B. F. Smith and A. Petersen (eds), *Heinrich Himmler – Geheimreden 1933 bis 1945* (Frankfurt, Berlin, Vienna, 1974), pp. 31f.

5. *Reichssicherheitshauptamt/ Amt I/ Arbeitsgemeinschaft für SS-Führeranwärter: Grundriss Nr. 9, Judentum* (Bundesarchiv Koblenz: R 58/844, Bl. 72).

6. *SS-Gruppenführer* Pancke as quoted in J. Ackermann, *Heinrich Himmler als Ideologe* (Göttingen, 1970), p. 156.

7. As he did, for example, in a speech on 8 November 1937: 'we want to create an upper class for Germany, selected constantly over centuries, a new aristocracy, recruited always from the best sons and daughters of our nation, an aristocracy that never becomes old' (National Archives: microfilm T-175/ roll 90/ . . . 2447).

8. 'Erschliessung des germanischen Erbes', undated memorandum of the *Reichsführung-SS* (1937), published in Ackermann, *Heinrich Himmler*, pp. 253f.

9. For details see H. Ueberhorst, *Elite für die Diktatur. Die Nationalpolitischen Erziehungsanstalten 1933 bis 1945. Ein Dokumentarbericht* (Dusseldorf, 1969); H. Scholtz, *NS-Ausleseschulen. Internatsschulen als Herrschaftsmittel des Führerstaates* (Göttingen, 1973). H. W. Koch, *The Hitler Youth: Origins and Development* (London, 1975).

10. See M. Kater, *Das 'Ahnenerbe' der SS 1935–1945. Ein Beitrag zur Kulturpolitik des Dritten Reiches* (Stuttgart, 1974).

11. See L. V. Thompson, *Lebensborn* and the Eugenics Policy of the *Reichsführer-SS*, *Central European History*, IV (1971), 54–77.

12. A decree of the *Reichsminister des Innern* of 11 November 1938 allowed the SD to work for the state administration as well; see also *Anatomie des SS-Staates*, vol. I, p. 74.

13. G. Buchheit, *Der deutsche Geheimdienst. Geschichte der militärischen Abwehr* (Munich, 1967), pp. 428ff.

14. For the 'Dachau model' see M. Broszat, 'Nationalsozialistische Konzentrationslager 1933–1945', in *Anatomie des SS-Staates*, vol. II, pp. 46ff., and F. Pingel, *Häftlinge unter SS-Herrschaft. Widerstand, Selbstbehauptung und Vernichtung im Konzentrationslager* (Hamburg, 1978), pp. 35ff.

15. Details of the numerical development are given in *Hitlers Politische Soldaten* Wegner, p. 104 (Table 2).

16. With the establishment of the *Hauptamt Ornungspolizei* and the *Reichssicherheit-shauptamt* the top police administration became correspondingly organised to the central *SS* administration. For details see H.-J. Neufeldt *et al.*, *Zur Geschichte der Ordnungspolizei 1936–1945* (Koblenz, 1957) and G. Browder, *SIPO and SD, 1931–1940. Formation of an Instrument of Power*, unpublished PhD thesis (University of Wisconsin, 1977).

17. The most lucid contemporary comment on the *Staatsschutzkorps* concept was given by W. Best, 'Die Schutzstaffel der NSDAP und die deutsche Polizei', *Deutsches Recht*, 9 (1939), edition A, 44ff. For further consideration see Wegner, *Hitlers Politische Soldaten*, pp. 110ff.

18. For the general background see K. J. Müller, *Das Heer und Hitler. Armee und nationalsozialistisches Regime 1933–1940* (Stuttgart, 1969), p. 147.

19. This is well expressed, for example, in the regulations from the minister of defence on 24 September 1934, concerning the organisation of the *SS-Verfügungstruppe* (published in P. Hausser, *Soldaten wie andere auch. Der Weg der Waffen-SS*, Osnabrück, 1966, pp. 232ff., doc. no. 1).

20. This referred only to service in the *SS-Verfügungstruppe*, whereas service in the *SS* war academies or the *SS* Death's Head units was not accepted as military service in pre-war years.

21. *Führer* decree of 17 August 1938, published in Hausser, *Soldaten wie andere auch*, pp. 252ff., doc. no. 6.

22. *Führer* decree of 18 May 1939 (Bundesarchiv Koblenz: R 2/ 12 172a); a detailed analysis may be found in Wegner, *Hitlers Politische Soldaten*, Chapter 8.

23. See R. M. Smelser, *The Sudeten Problem 1933–1938. Volkstumspolitik and the Formulation of Nazi Foreign Policy* (Folkestone, 1975), pp. 166ff. and A. Ramme, *Der Sicherheitsdienst der SS. Zu seiner Funktion im faschistischen Machtapparat und im Besatzungsregime des sog. General-gouvernements Polen* (Berlin, 1969), pp. 87ff.

24. O. Groehler, 'Kolonialforderungen als Teil der faschistischen Kriegsziel-planung', *Zeitschrift für Militärgeschichte*, 4 (1965), 552.

25. H. A. Jacobsen, *Nationalsozialistische Aussenpolitik 1933–1938* (Frankfurt–Berlin, 1968), pp. 461ff.

26. Ribbentrop's relationship to the *SS* is sketched by R. M. Smelser, *The Sudeten Problem*, pp. 179f.

27. In pre-war years the two most important *SS* enterprises were the 'Deutsche Erd- und Steinwerke GmbH, founded in 1938, and the 'Deutsche Ausrüstungswerke GmbH', founded in 1939. An account of their development is given by E. Georg, *Die wirtschaftlichen Unternehmungen der SS* (Stuttgart, 1963), pp. 42ff., 58ff.

28. Ibid., p. 10.

29. For further details see R. Vogelsang, *Der Freundeskreis Himmler* (Göttingen, 1972).

30. Speech of 4 October 1943, as quoted in H. Buchheim, 'Die Höheren SS-und Polizeiführer', *Vierteljahreshefte für Zeitgeschichte* 11 (Munich, 1963) 379f. In a speech on 8 November 1938 Himmler had already expressed himself in the same sense: 'We must . . . take care, that all the branches established always feel as part of the whole. . . . For every single one of these branches this should hold true: everybody is an *SS* man before everything else, then he belongs to the General *SS*, the Reserve Troops, the Death's Head units or the secret service.' (As quoted in *Heinrich Himmler – Geheimreden* op. cit., p. 29.)

31. The relevance of 1938 for the development of National Socialist Germany will be reflected in a forthcoming book, edited by F. Knipping and K. J. Müller.

32. Speech by Himmler of 8 November 1938, as quoted in *Heinrich Himmler – Geheimreden*, p. 49.

33. Ibid., p. 38.

34. This is estimated as the minimum by Broszat in *Anatomie des SS-Staates*, vol. II, p. 132.

35. For details on the deathrate in concentration camps see Pingel, *Häftlinge unter SS-Herrschaft*, pp. 80ff., 181ff.

36. The classic work on the holocaust is still R. Hilberg, *The Destruction of the European Jews* (Chicago, 1961). For the role of the Action Groups (*Einsatzgruppen*) see the exhaustive study by H. Krausnick and H. H. Wilhelm, *Die Truppe des Weltanschauungskrieges. Die Einsatzgruppen der Sicherheitspolizei und des SD 1938–1942* (Stuttgart, 1981).

37. The latest result of the newly revived debate on the genesis of the 'final solution' is a detailed analysis of Hitler's personal involvement: G. Fleming, *Hitler und die Endlösung. 'Es ist des Führers Wunsch . . .'* (Wiesbaden–Munich, 1982).

38. Pingel, *Häftlinge unter SS-Herrschaft*, pp. 123ff., A. Speer, *Der Sklavenstaat. Meine Auseinandersetzungen mit der SS* (Stuttgart, 1981), and, more recently, L. Herbst, *Der totale Krieg und die Ordnung der Wirtschaft. Die Kriegswirtschaft im Spannungsfeld von Politik, Ideologie und Propaganda* (Stuttgart, 1982). Herbst (pp. 253ff.) deals with a rather neglected aspect, which is the SS's interest in the ministry of economy.

39. Speer, *Der Sklavenstaat*, p. 61.

40. M. Broszat, 'Nationalsozialistische Konzentrationslager', in *Anatomie des SS-Staates*, vol. II, pp. 94f.

41. Pingel, *Häftlinge unter SS-Herrschaft*, p. 129.

42. Wegner, *Hitlers Politische Soldaten*, p. 210 (Table 8).

43. For the negotiations between the SS-Hauptamt and the armed forces' high command in the early years of the war see G. H. Stein, *The Waffen-SS: Hitler's Elite Guard at War, 1939–1945* (Oxford and Ithaca, New York, 1966).

44. Ibid., pp. 31ff., 87ff.; see also G. Rempel, 'Gottlob Berger and Waffen-SS Recruitment, 1939–1945', *Militärgeschichtliche Mitteilungen*, 27 (1/1980), 107–122.

45. To date, we lack an authoritative analysis of the SS as a multinational army. First approaches are Ph. H. Buss and A. Mollo, *Hitler's Germanic Legions. An illustrated history of the Western European Legions with the SS, 1941–1943* (London, 1978); H. W. Neulen, *Eurofaschismus und der Zweite Weltkrieg. Europas verratene Söhne* (Munich, 1980).

46. For supporting documents see B. Wegner, 'Auf dem Wege zur pangermanischen Armee. Dokumente zur Entstehungsgeschichte des III. (*germanischen*) SS-Panzerkorps', *Militärgeschichtliche Mitteilungen*, 28 (2 Freiburg 1980), 101–36, especially pp. 112f.

47. Ibid., p. 102.

48. Wegner, *Hitlers Politische Soldaten*, pp. 273ff.

49. There are critical accounts of the history of two of those divisions: J. J. Weingartner, *Hitler's Guard. The story of the Leibstandarte SS Adolf Hitler, 1933–1945* (London–Amsterdam, 1974); Ch. W. Sydnor, Jr, *Soldiers of Destruction. The SS Death's Head Division 1933–1945* (Princeton, 1977). For additional bibliographical information see B. Wegner, 'Die Garde des "Führers" und die "Feuerwehr" der Ostfront. Zur neueren Literatur über die Waffen-SS,' *Militärgeschichtliche Mitteilungen*, 23 (1/1978), 210–36.

50. For a detailed sociographic analysis of the higher echelons of the Waffen-SS officer corps see Wegner, *Hitlers Politische Soldaten*, Part IV (pp. 217ff.) and, by the same author, 'Das Führerkorps der Waffen-SS im Kriege,' in H. H. Hofmann (ed.), *Das deutsche Offizierkorps 1860–1960* (Boppard a.Rh., 1980), pp. 327–50.

51. This holds particularly true for the period after the German attack on the Soviet Union.

52. See also Stein's critical judgement, *The Waffen-SS*, pp. 172ff.

53. See note 46 above.

54. One of the most impressive documents of this policy is the so-called *Generalplan Ost* from summer 1941; see G. Eisenblätter, *Grundlagen der Politik des Reichs gegenüber dem Generalgouvernement, 1939–1945*, Diss. phil. (Frankfurt, 1969), pp. 205ff.; for the general background see R. Koehl, *RKFDV: German resettlement and population policy 1939–1945. A history of the Reich commission for the strengthening of Germandom* (Cambridge, 1957).

55. For the role of the *Höhere SS- und Polizeiführer* within the SS administrative structure see H. Buchheim, 'Die Höheren SS- und Polizeiführer', *Vierteljahreshefte für Zeitgeschichte* 11 (Munich 1963), 362–91.

56. Himmler's self-assessment at the culminating point of his career is well reflected in his speech to the *Gauleiter* of 3 August 1944, in *Vierteljahreshefte für Zeitgeschichte* (Munich, 1953), 357–94.

15 THE HITLER IMAGE IN THE LAST HALF-CENTURY

1. K. Heiden, *Adolf Hitler. Das Zeitalter der Verantwortungslosigkeit. Eine Biographie* (Zürich, 1936), p. 6. Other works from this decade which still have much to offer include: T. Heuss, *Hitlers Weg. Eine Schrift aus dem Jahre 1932*, a perceptive analysis of the theory and practice of National Socialism deservedly republished in 1968; and T. Geiger, *Die soziale Schichtung des deutschen Volkes. Sozialgraphischer Versuch auf statistischer Grundlage* (Stuttgart, 1932), an excellent analysis of the social basis of NS support.

2. F. Meinecke, *Die deutsche Katastrophe. Betrachtungen und Erinnerungen* (Wiesbaden, 1946).

3. A. Bullock, *Hitler. A study in tyranny* (London, 1952), p. 14.

4. This is much less true of his second major work, *Krieg der Illusionen. Die deutsche Politik von 1911 bis 1914* (Düsseldorf, 1969), in which he argues that Imperial Germany deliberately sought war from 1911 onwards.

5. For example, A. Hillgruber, *Deutschlands Rolle in der Vorgeschichte der beiden Weltkriege* (Göttingen, 1967); and the same author's *Kontinuität und Diskontinuität in der deutschen Aussenpolitik von Bismarck bis Hitler* (Düsseldorf, 1971).

6. H. Mommsen, *Beamtentum im Dritten Reich. Mit ausgewählten Quellen zur nationalsozialistischer Beamtenpolitik* (Stuttgart, 1961); M. Broszat, *Der Staat Hitlers. Grundlegung und Entwicklung seiner inneren Verfassung* (Munich, 1969) (English edn, *The Hitler State*, London, 1982); R. Bollmus, *Das Amt Rosenberg und seine Gegner. Zum Machtkampf im nationalsozialistischen Herrschaftssystem* (Stuttgart, 1970).

7. H. A. Jacobsen, *Nationalsozialistische Aussenpolitik 1933–1938* (Frankfurt, 1968).

8. H. Mommsen in a review of H. A. Jacobsen's book in *Militärgeschichtliche Mitteilungen*, 7 (1970) 183; contemporary pamphleteers such as Weigand von Miltenberg, *Adolf Hitler. Wilhelm III* (Berlin, 1931) and F. Plümer, *Die Wahrheit über Hitler und seinen Kreis* (Munich, 1925), make much the same point.

9. M. Broszat, 'Soziale Motivation und Führer-Bindung des Nationalsozialismus', *VfZG*, 18 (1970).

10. E. Fraenkel, *The Dual State. A contribution to the theory of dictatorship* (London, 1941); W. Petwaidic, *Die autoritäre Anarchie* (Hamburg, 1946).

11. N. Rich, *Hitler's War Aims*. vol. 1: *Ideology, the Nazi State and the Course of Expansion* (New York, 1973) p. 11.

12. H. Rauschning, *Gespräche mit Hitler* (Zürich, 1940).

13. H. Trevor-Roper, 'Hitlers Kriegsziele', *VfZG*, 8 (1960) 121–33.

14. E. Jäckel, *Hitlers Weltanschauung. Entwurf einer Herrschaft* (Tübingen, 1969).

15. G. Moltmann, 'Weltherrschaftsideen Hitlers' in O. Bruner and D. Gerhard (eds), *Europa und Übersee. Festschrift für Egmont Zechlin* (Hamburg, 1961).

16. A. Hillgruber, *Hitlers Strategie. Politik und Kriegführung 1940–1941* (Frankfurt, 1963).

17. K. Hildebrand, *Vom Reich zum Weltreich. NSDAP und koloniale Frage 1919–1945* (Munich, 1969); J. Thies, *Architekt der Weltherrschaft. Die 'Endziele' Hitlers* (Düsseldorf, 1976).

18. W. Pieck, G. Dimitroff and P. Togliatti, *Die Offensive des Faschismus und die Aufgaben der Kommunisten im Kampf für die Volksfront gegen Krieg und Faschismus. Referate auf dem VII Kongress der Kommunistischen Internationale 1935* (Berlin, 1957), p. 87.

19. For example, D. Eichholtz, *Geschichte der deutschen Kriegswirtschaft 1939–1945*, vol. I, *1939–41* (Berlin, 1971); K. Gossweiler, 'Der Übergang von der Weltwirtschaftskrise zur Rüstungskonjunktur in Deutschland 1928 bis 1934', in *Jahrbuch für Wirtschaftsgeschichte 1968*, Part II (Berlin, 1968).

20. For example W. Abendroth (ed.), *Faschismus und Kapitalismus. Theorien über die sozialen Ursprünge und die Funktion des Faschismus* (Frankfurt, 1972); N. Kadritzke, *Faschismus und Krise. Zum Verhältnis von Politik und Ökonomie im Nationalsozialismus* (Frankfurt–New York, 1976).

21. For example, A. Schweitzer, *Big Business in the Third Reich* (London, 1964); T. Mason, 'Der Primat der Politik – Politik und Wirtschaft im Nationalsozialismus', *Das Argument*, 41 (1968).

22. T. Mason, 'Innere Krise und Angriffskrieg 1938/9', in F. Forstmeier und H.-S. Volkmann (eds), *Wirtschaft und Rüstung am Vorabend des Zweiten Weltkrieges* (Düsseldorf, 1975).

23. W. Langer, *The Mind of Adolf Hitler* (London, 1973), p. 17.

24. Cf. E. H. Erikson, 'Hitler's imagery and German youth', *Psychiatry*, 5 (1942); and his *Childhood and Society* (New York, 1950).

25. R. Binion, *Hitler Among the Germans* (New York, 1976), p. 22.

26. For a critical evaluation of the Binion thesis cf. *History of Childhood Quarterly* (autumn 1973) 218–58.

27. R. Waite, *Adolf Hitler. The Psychopathic God* (New York, 1977), p. xiv.

28. H.-U. Wehler, 'Zum Verhältnis von Geschichtswissenschaft und Psychologie', in *Geschichte und Psychoanalyse* (Cologne, 1971) p. 25.

29. For example, P. Merkl, *Political Violence under the Swastika.581 Early Nazis* (Princeton, 1975); H. V. Dicks, *Licensed Mass Murder: a socio-psychological study of some SS killers* (London, 1972); P. Loewenberg, 'The psychological origins of the Nazi Youth cohort', *American Historical Review*, 76 (1971); K. Theweleit, *Männerphantasien*, vol. I: *Frauen, Fluten, Körper, Geschichte*; vol. II: *Männerkörper – zur Psychoanalyse des weissen Terrors* (Frankfurt, 1977–8).

30. Other biographies include: H. Heiber, *Adolf Hitler.Eine Biographie* (Stuttgart, 1952); H. B. Gisevius, *Adolf Hitler.Eine Biographie* (Munich, 1963); worthy of special note is the all-too-brief but excellent *Hitler.Eine politische Biographie* (Munich, 1963) by the late Ernst Deuerlein.

31. J. Fest, *Hitler* (Frankfurt, 1973) p. 6.

32. J. Toland, *Adolf Hitler* (New York, 1976), p. xi.

33. N. Stone, *Adolf Hitler* (London, 1980), p. 113.

34. W. Carr, *Hitler. A study in personality and politics* (London, 1978).

35. J. Kocka, 'Struktur und Persönlichkeit als methodologisches Problem der Geschichtswissenschaft', in M. Bosch, *Persönlichkeit und Struktur in der Geschichte* (Düsseldorf, 1977) pp. 162–3.

36. Bullock, *Hitler*, pp. 702–3.

37. Fest, *Hitler*, p. 680.

38. A. Hitler, *Mein Kampf*, trans. R Manheim (Boston, 1943) p. 679.

39. Toland, *Adolf Hitler*, p. 1039.

40. U. Adam, *Judenpolitik im Dritten Reich* (Düsseldorf, 1972); M. Broszat 'Hitler und die Genesis der Endlösung', *VfZG* (1977); H. Mommsen, 'Nationalsozialismus oder Hitlerismus' in Bosch, *Persönlichkeit und Struktur*.

41. H. Mommsen, 'Nationalsozialismus', p. 66.

Bibliography

NB: Although the bibliography is arranged by topics, naturally a great many books are related to more than the one topic under which they are listed.

Part I

Commentary

Abellio, R. *et al.*, *Omagi a Brassillach* (Rome, 1967)

Abetz, O., *Das offene Problem. Ein Rückblick auf zwei Jahrzehnte deutscher Frankreichpolitik* (Cologne, 1951)

Ambri, M., *Il falsi fascismi* (Rome, 1980)

Amouroux, H., *La grande histoire des Français sous l'occupation*, 5 vols (Paris, 1976–1981)

Armstrong, J. A., 'Collaborationism in World War II. The integral nationalist variant in Eastern Europe', *Journal of Modern History* (1968)

Aron, R., *Historie de Vichy 1940–1944* (Paris, 1954)

Aster, S. (ed.), *The X-Documents* (London, 1974)

Backhaus, H. G. *et al* (eds), *Gesellschaft: Beiträge zur Marxschen Theorie* (Frankfurt, 1977)

Bardèche, M. (ed.), *Il fascismi scenosciuti* (Milan, 1970)

Bardèche, M. *et al.*, *Etudes sur le fascisme* (Paris, 1974)

Benewick, R., *The Fascist Movement in Britain* (London, 1969)

Boveri, M., *Der Verrat im XX. Jahhundert. Für und gegen die Nation*, vol. I (Hamburg, 1961)

Bracher, K. D., *Zeitgeschichtliche Kontroversen. Um Faschismus, Totalitarismus und Demokratie* (Munich, 1976)

Brasillach, R., *Lettere ad un soldato delle classe 40, a cura di Adriano Romualdi* (Rome, 1975)

——, *Notre avant-guerre. Une generation dans l'orage. Mémoires* (Paris, 1973)

Brissaud, A., *Hitler et l'ordre noir. Histoire secrète du national-socialisme* (Paris, 1977)

Brochi, D. (ed.), *'L'Universale'* (Milan, 1971)

Buchheim, H., *Aktuelle Krisenpunkte des deutschen Nationalbewusstseins* (Mainz, 1967)

Carli, C. F., *Architettura e fascismo* (Rome, 1980)

Carlucci, G. (ed.), *Repubblica Sociale Italiana. Storia* (Rome, 1959)

Davey, O. A., 'The Origins of the Légion des Volontaires Français contre le Bolshevisme', *Journal of Contemporary History* (1971)

Degrelle, L. *Hitler per mille anni* (Molfacone, 1970)

Dioudonnat, P.-M., *Je suis partout 1930–1944. Les maurassiens devant la tentation fasciste* (Paris, 1973)

Drieu la Rochelle, P., *Mesure de la France, suivi des Ecrits 1939–1940*, Paris 1964

——, *Le jeune européen, suivi de Geneve ou Moscou* (Paris, 1978)

——, *Socialismo fascista* (Rome, 1973)

——, *Socialismo, fascismo, Europa. Scritti politici scelti e presentati de Jean Mabire* (Rome, 1964)

Duprat, F., *Les campagnes de la Waffen-SS*, 2 vols (Paris, 1972–73)

——, 'La croisade antibolchevique', parts i–ii in *Defense de l'Occident* (Paris, 1973–4)

Evola, J. (ed.), *Diorama. Problemi dello spirito nell'etica fascista. Antologia della pagina speciale di 'Regime Fascista' diretta Julius Evola*, Vol. i (Rome, 1974)

Felice, R. de, *Mussolini il Duce. Gli anni del consenso 1929–1936* (Turin, 1976)

Field, F., *Three French Writers and the Great War: Barbusse, Drieu la Rochelle, Bernanos* (Cambridge, 1975)

Gordon, B. M., *Collaborationism in France during the Second World War* (New York, 1980)

Hamilton, A., *The Appeal of Fascism: A Study of Intellectuals and Fascism 1919–1945* (London, 1971)

Hänel, W., *Hermann Rauschnings 'Gespräche mit Hitler -eine Geschichtsfälschung'* (Ingolstadt, 1984)

Hayes, P. M., *Quisling: Career and Political Ideas of Vidkun Quisling 1887–1945* (Newton Abbot, 1971)

Hewins, R., *Quisling: Prophet without Honour* (London, 1965)

Jäckel, E., *Frankreich in Hitlers Europa. Die deutsche Frankreichpolitik im Zweiten Weltkrieg* (Stuttgart, 1966)

Jünger, E., *Strahlungen* (Munich, 1955)

Hamilton, R. F., *Who voted for Hitler?* (Princeton, 1982)

Kater, M., *The Nazi Party. A Social Profile of Members and Leaders 1919–1945* (Oxford, 1982)

Kele, M., *Nazis and Workers* (Chapel Hill, 1972)

Kirkpatrick, I., *Mussolini* (London, 1963)

Koch, H. W., *The Hitler Youth: Origins and Development 1922–1945* (London, 1976)

La Maziere, Ch. de, *Le Rêveur Casqué* (Paris, 1972)

Laqueur, W. (ed.), *Fascism* (London, 1979)

Launay, J. de, *La Belgique a l'heure allemande. La guerre et l'occupation* (Brussels, 1978)

Lipset, S. M., *Political Man* (London, 1960)

Lukacs, J., *The Last European War* (London, 1976)

Mabire, J., *Less SS Français. La Division Charlemagne* (Paris, 1976)
Mason, T. W., *Arbeiterklasse und Volksgemeinschaft* (Cologne, 1975)
Merkl, P. H., *Political Violence under the Swastika* (Princeton, 1975)
Mosley, O., *My Life* (London, n.d.)
Müller, K.-J., 'French Fascism and Modernisation', *Journal of Contemporary History* (1976)
Nolte, E., *The Three Faces of Fascism* (London, 1965)
——, *Die faschistischen Bewegungen. Die Krise les liberalen Systems und die Entwicklung des Faschismus* (Munich, 1966)
——, *Theorien über den Faschismus* (Cologne, 1967)
Payne, St. G., *Fascism: Comparison and Definition* (Wisconsin, 1980)
Salomon, E. v., *The Answers of Ernst von Salomon* (London, 1954)
Schoenbaum, D., *Hitler's Social Revolution* (London, 1966)
Sérant, P., *Les vaincus de la Liberation* (Paris, 1965)
Skidelsky, R., *Oswald Mosley* (London, 1981)
Turner, H., Ashby (ed.), *Reappraisals of Fascism* (New York, 1975)
Wolf, D., *Die Doriot Bewegung* (Stuttgart, 1967)

Contributions:

Antonow-Ovssejemke, A., *The Time of Stalin: Portrait of Tyranny* (New York, 1981)
Aster, S., *1939: The Making of the Secound World War* (London, 1973)
Balfour, M. and Frisby, J., *Helmuth von Moltke: A Leader against Hitler* (London, 1982)
Bennecke, H., *Hitler und die SA* (Munich, 1983)
Boberach, H. (ed.), *Meldungen aus dem Reich* (Neuwied, 1965)
Berghahn, V. R., *Der Stahlhelm, Bund der Frontsoldaten* (Düsseldorf, 1966)
Bracher, K. D., *Die Auflösung der Weimarer Republik* (Villingen, 1960)
——, *The German Dictatorship* (London, 1975)
Bracher, K. D., Sauer, W. and Schulz, G., *Die nationalsozialistische Machtergreifung* (Cologne, 1960)
Broszat, M., 'Soziale Motivation und Führer-Bindung des Nationalsozialismus', *Vierteljahrhefte für Zeitgeschichte* (1970)
——, *The Hitler State* (London, 1981)
Brüning, H., *Memoiren*, 2 vols (Munich, 1972)
Bucher, P., *Der Reichswehrprozeas. Der Hochverrat der Ulmer Reichswehroffiziere 1929/30* (Boppard/Rhein, 1967)
Carsten, E. L., *The Reichswehr and Politics, 1918 to 1933* (Oxford, 1966)
Colvin, I., *Hitler's Secret Enemy* (London, 1951)
——, *Vansittart in Office* (London, 1965)
Czichon, E., *Wer verhalf Hitler zur Macht? Zum Anteil der Industrie an der Zerstörung der Weimarer Republik* (Cologne, 1967)
Dahrendoff, R., *Democracy and Society in Germany* (London, 1969)
Delmer, S., *Trail Sinister* (London, 1961)
Demeter, K., *German Officer Corps in Society and State 1650–1945* (London, 1965)

Deutsch, H., *The Conspiracy against Hitler in the Twilight War* (Minnesota, 1968)
——, *Hitler and his Generals* (Minnesota, 1974)
Diehl-Thiele, P., *Partei und Staat im Dritten Reich* (Munich, 1969)
Diels, R., *Lucifer ante portas . . . es spricht der erste Chef der Gestapo* (Stuttgart, 1950)
Domarus, M., (ed.), *Hitler: Reden und Proklamationen 1932–1945*, 4 vols (Wiesbaden, 1973)
Duesterberg, Th., *Der Stahlhelm und Hitler* (Wolfbüttel, 1949)
Dunke, H., *Die KPD von 1933 bis 1945* (Cologne, 1972)
Ehrt, A., *Bewaffneter Aufstand* (Berlin, 1933)
Erdmann, K. D. and Schulze, H. (eds), *Weimar: Selbstpreisgabe einer Demokratie* (Düsseldorf, 1980)
Eyck, E., *Geschichte der Weimarer Republik*, 2 vols (Zürich, 1956)
Fabry, Ph. W., *Mutmassungen über Hitler. Urteile von Zeitgenossen* (Düsseldorf, 1969)
Falter, J. W., 'Wer verhalf der NSDAP zum Sieg?', in *Aus Politik und Zeitgeschehen*, supplement to *Das Parlament* (Bonn, 1979)
Feiling, K., *Life of Neville Chamberlain* (London, 1947)
Felice, R de, *Der Faschismus* (Stuttgart, 1977)
François-Poncet, A., *Souvenirs d'une Ambassade à Berlin* (Paris, 1945)
Fränkel, E., *The Dual State* (New York, 1941)
Gisevius, B., *Bis zum bitteren Ende* (Zürich, 1946)
Goebbels, J., *Vom Kaiserhof zur Reichskanzlei* (Munich, 1938)
——, *Wetterleuchten* (Berlin, 1943)
Gordon Jr, H. J., *The Reichswehr and the German Republic 1919–1926* (Princeton, 1957)
Görlitz, W., (ed.), *Generalfeldmarschall Keitel, Verbrecher oder Offizier? Erinnerungen, Briefe, Dokumente des Chefs OKW* (Göttingen, 1961)
Graml, H., 'Der Fall Oster', *Vierteljahrshefte für Zeitgeschichte* (Munich, 1966)
Groener, D., *General Groener. Soldat und Staatsmann* (Frankfurt, 1955)
Groscurth, H., *Tagebuch eines Abwehroffiziers* (Stuttgart, 1970)
Guderian, H., *Panzer Leader* (London, 1952)
Hagen, H. W., *Zwischen Eid und Befehl* (Munich, 1958)
Hanfstaengl, E., *Unheard Witness* (Philadelphia, 1957)
Hassel, U.v., *Vom anderen Deutschland* (Frankfurt, 1964)
Heims, H. and Jochmann, W., *Monologe im Führerhauptquartier 1941–1944* (Hamburg, 1980)
Helbich, W. J., *Die Reparationen in der Ara Brüning. Zue Bedeutung des Young-Planes für die deutsche Politik 1930–1932* (Berlin, 1962)
Henderson, N. *Failure of a Mission* (London, 1940)
Heusinger, A., *Befehl im Widerstreil* (Tübungen, 1950)
Hill, L. E., (ed.), *Die Weizsäcker-Papiere* (Berlin, 1974), vol. II
Hitler, A., *Mein Kampf* (Dünndruckausgabe, Munich, 1936)
Hoffmann, P. *Widerstand, Staatsstreich, Attentat* (Munich, 1969)
Höhne, H., *Canaris* (Gütersloh, 1967)
——, *Die Machtergreifung* (Hamburg, 1983)

Höhne, H., *Mordsache 'Röhm'* (Hamburg, 1984)

Horn, W., *Führerideologie und Parteiorganisation in der NSDAP* (Düsseldorf, 1972)

Hubatsch, W., *Hindenburg und der Staat* (Göttingen, 1966)

Hüttenberger, P., 'Vorüberlegungen zum "Widerstandsbegriff", in Kocka, J. (ed.), *Geschichte und Gesellschaft* (1977)

Irving, D., *The Trail of the Fox* (London, 1980)

Jacobsen, H. A., *Germans against Hitler* (Bonn, 1969)

Kershaw, I., *Der Hitler-Mythos. Volksmeinung und Propaganda im Dritten Reich* (Stuttgart, 1980). Published in English by OUP.

Kettenacker, L., *Nationalsozialistische Volkstumspolitik im Elsass* (Stuttgart, 1973)

——, and Hirschfeld G. (eds), *The 'Führer State': Myth and Reality* (Stuttgart, 1981)

Kitchen, M., *The German Officer Corps 1890–1914* (Oxford, 1973)

Klemperer K. v., *Germany's New Conservatism* (Princeton, 1957)

Koch, H. W., *A History of Prussia* (London, 1978)

——, *Der Deutsche Bürgerkrieg 1918–1924* (Berlin, 1978)

——, *A Constitutional History of Germany in the Nineteenth and Twentieth Centuries* (London, 1984)

——, *'Im Namen des Deutschen Volkes': Roland Freisler und der NS-Volksgerichtshof* (Percha, 1985)

Kocka, J., *Klassengesellschaft im Krieg 1914–1918* (Göttingen, 1973)

Koehl, R., 'Feudal Aspects of National Socialism', *American Political Science Review* (1962)

——, *RKFDV. German Resettlement and Population Policy 1939–1945* (Harvard, 1957)

Kramarz, J., *Stauffenberg* (London, 1967)

Krausnick, H. and Eschenburg, Th. *et al.*, *The Road to Dictatorship: Germany 1918 to 1933* (London, 1964)

Kühnl, R., *Die nationalsozialistische Linke 1925–1930* (Meisenheim/Glan, 1966)

Leber, A., *Das Gewissen entscheidet* (Berlin, 1959)

——, *Das Gewissen steht auf* (Berlin, 1960)

Lepsius, R., *Extremer Nationalismus. Strukturbedingungen vor der nationalsozialistischen Machtergreifung* (Stuttgart, 1966)

Lerner, D. *The Nazi Elite* (Stanford, 1951)

Matthias, E., 'Die Sitzung der Reichtagsfraktion des Zentrums am 23. März 1922', *Vierteljahrhefte für Zeitgeschichte* (1956)

—— and Morsey, R. (eds.), *Das Ende der Parteien* (Düsseldof, 1960)

Meier-Welcker, H., *Seeckt* (Frankfurt, 1967)

Meissner, O., *Staatssekretär unter Ebert, Hindenburg und Hitler* (Hamburg, 1950)

Messerschmidt, M., *Die Wehrmacht im NS-Staat* (Hamburg, 1969)

Mitschlerlich, A. and M., *Die Unfähigkeit zu trauern* (Munich, 1968)

Mohler, A., *Die konservative Revolution* (Darmstadt, 1978)

——, *Von rechts gesehen* (Stuttgart, 1979)

Mommsen, H., *Das Beamtentum im Dritten Reich* (Stuttgart, 1966)

Mommsen, H., 'Hitlers Stellung im nationalsozialistischen Herrschfts-
system' in Kettenacker and Hirschfeld (eds), *'Führer State'*
——, 'National Socialism: Continuity and Change', in Laqueur, *Fascism*
Mosse, G. L., *Nationalisierung der Massen* (Frankfurt, 1976)
Müller, Ch., *Oberst i.G. von Stauffenberg* (Düsseldorf, 1971)
Müller, K.-J., *Das Heer und Hitler* (Stuttgart, 1969)
——, *Armee, Politik und Gesellschaft in Deutschland 1933–1945* (Paderborn,
1979)
——, *Generaloberst Ludwig Beck* (Boppard/Rhein, 1980)
Neumann, F., *Behemoth* (London, 1942)
Nolte, E., *Marxismus und Industrialisierung* (Stuttgart, 1983)
Orlow, D., *The History of the Nazi Party*, 2 vols (Pittsburgh, 1973)
Papen, F. v., *Memoirs* (London, 1952)
Peter, K. H. (ed.), *Spiegelbild einer Verschwörung. Die Kaltenbrunnerberichte*
(Stuttgart, 1961)
Petersen, E. N., *The Limits of Hitler's Power* (Princeton, 1969)
Petzold, J., *Wegbereiter des deutschen Faschismus: Die Jungkonservativen in der
Weimarer Republik* (Berlin, 1978)
Picker, H., *Hitlers Tischgespräche im Führerhauptquartier* (Stuttgart, 1976)
Plehwe, F.-K. v., *Reichskanzler Kurt v. Schleicher* (Esslingen, 1983)
Rauschning, H., *Hitler Speaks* (London, 1939)
Reich, W., *The Mass Psychology of Fascism* (London, 1970)
Remer, E., *Verschwörung und Verrat um Adolf Hitler* (Göttingen, 1982)
Ribbentrop, A. v., *Die Kriegsschuld des Widerstandes* (Leoni, 1974)
Ritter, G., *Carl Goerdeler und die deutsche Widerstandsbewegung* (Stuttgart,
1956)
Robbins, K. G., *Munich* (London, 1978)
Rohe, K., *Das Reichsbanner Schwarz-Rot-Gold* (Düsseldorf, 1966)
Rothfels, H., *The German Opposition against Hitler* (Chicago, 1949)
Salewski, M., *Die deutsche Seekriegsleitung 1935–1945*, 3 vols (Frankfurt,
1970–3)
Scheurig, B., *Ewald v. Kleist-Schmenzin. Ein Konservativer gegen Hitler*
(Oldenburg, 1968)
——, *Henning v. Treskow Eine Biographie* (Hamburg, 1973)
Schieder, W. (ed.), *Faschismus als soziale Bewegung. Deutschland und Italien im
Vergleich* (Hamburg, 1976)
Schildt, A., *Militärdiktatur mit Massenbasis? Die Querfrontkonzeption der
Reichswehrführung um General v., Schleicher am Ende der Weimarer Republik*
(Frankfurt, 1981)
Schmitt, C., *Legalität und Legitimität* (Bonn, 1932)
——, *Verfassungslehre* (Cologne 1957 – revised version of the 1928 edition)
Schüddekopf, E., *Linke Leute von Rechts* (Stuttgart, 1961)
Schulz, G., *Aufstieg des Nationalsozialismus* (Frankfurt, 1975)
Schulze, H., *Otto Braun oder Preussens demokratische Sendung* (Berlin, 1979)
——, *Weimar, Deutschland 1917–1933* (Berlin, 1982)
Schweitzer, A., *Big Business and the Third Reich* (Bloomington, 1964)
Sontheimer, K., *Antidemokratisches Denken in der Weimarer Republik* (Munich,
1962)

Speer, A., *Inside the Third Reich* (London, 1970)

Stern, J. P. *Hitler: The Führer and his People* (London, 1975)

Stoltenberg, G., *Politische Strömungen im schleswig-holsteinischem Landvolk 1918–1933* (Düsseldorf, 1962)

Tobias, F., *Der Reichstagsbrand. Legende und Wirklichkeit* (Rastatt, 1962)

Turner, H. Ashby, 'Big Business and the Rise of Hitler', *American Historical Review* (1969)

——, 'Hitler's Secret Pamphlet for Industrialists', *Journal of Modern History* (1968)

——, 'Emil Kirdorf and the Nazi Party', *Central European History* (1968)

——, 'The *Ruhrlade*. Secret Cabinet of Heavy Industry in the Weimar Republic, *Central European History* (1970)

——, 'Fritz Thyssen und das Buch "I paid Hitler"', *Vierteljahrshefte für Zeitgeschichte* (1971)

——, 'Grossunternehmertum und Nationalsozialismus 1930–1933', *Historische Zeitschrift*, Munich 1975

Tyrell, A. (ed.), *Führer befiehl . . . Selbstzeugnisse aus der Kampfzeit* (Düsseldorf, 1969)

——, *Vom 'Trommler' zum 'Führer'* (Munich, 1975)

Vogelsang, Th., *Reichswehr, Staat und NSDAP* (Stuttgart, 1962)

Weizsäcker, E. v., *Erinnerungen*, 2 vols (Munich, 1951)

Wheeler-Bennet, J. W., *Hindenburg. The Wooden Titan* (London, 1936)

——, *The Nemesis of Power* (London, 1954)

Winkler, H. A., *Mittelstand, Demokratie und Nationalsozialismus* (Cologne, 1972)

Wippermann, W. *Faschismustheorien* (Darmstadt, 1976)

Part II

Commentary

Hauser, O., *England und das Dritte Reich*, 2 vols (Stuttgart 1972; Göttingen, 1982)

Hildebrand, K., *Vom Reich zum Weltreich* (Munich, 1969)

——, *Deutsche Aussenpolitik 1933–1945. Kalkül oder Dogma?* (Stuttgart, 1971)

Hillgruber, A., *Hitlers Strategie 1940–1941* (Frankfurt, 1965)

——, *Deutsche Grossmacht und Weltpolitik im 19. und 20. Jahrhundert* (Düsseldorf, 1977)

Hofer, W., *War Premeditated* (London, 1962)

——, 'Wege und Irrwege der Forschung? Erneute Auseinandersetzung mit "erneuten Betrachtungen" von A. J. P. Taylor', in W. Pöls (ed.), *Staat und Gesellschaft im politischen Wandel* (Stuttgart, 1979)

Hoggan, D. L., *Der erzwungene Krieg* (Tübingen, 1961)

Hüttenberger, P., 'Nationalsozialistische Polykratie', *Geschichte und Gesellschaft* (1976)

Jäckel, E., *Hitlers Weltanschauung. Entwurf einer einer Herrschaft* (Tübingen, 1969)

Jacobsen, H.-A., *1939–1945: Der Zweite Weltkrieg in Chronik und Dokumenten* (Darmstadt, 1965)

——, Nationalsozialistische Aussenpolitik 1933–1938 (Frankfurt, 1968)

Koch, H. W., 'Hitler and the Origins of the Second World War: Second Thoughts on the Status of some of the Documents', *Historical Journal* (1968), reprinted in E. M. Robertson (ed.), *The Origins of the Second World War* (London, 1971)

Niedhart, G. (ed.), *Kriegsbeginn 1939* (Darmstadt, 1976)

Ribbentrop, J. v., *Zwischen London und Moskau* (Leoni, 1953)

Taylor, A. J. P., *The Origins of the Second World War* (London, 1962: 2nd edition)

——, *1939 Revisited*, The 1981 Annual Lecture, German Historical Institute (London, 1981)

Weinberg, G. L. (ed.), *Hitlers Zweites Buch* (Stuttgart, 1961)

——, *The Foreign Policy of Hitler's Germany*, 2 vols (Chicago, 1970, 1980)

Contributions

Adamthwaite, A., *France and the Coming of the Second World War 1936–1939* (London, 1977)

——, (ed.), *The Lost Peace: International Relations in Europe 1918–1939* (London, 1980)

Adler, S. *The Isolationist Impulse, its Twentieth-century Reaction* (New York, 1857)

Aigner, D., *Das Ringen um England* (Munich, 1969)

Benoist-Mechin, J., *La Cuisine au beurre* (Paris, 1983)

Benz, W. and Graml, H. (eds), *Sommer 1939* (Stuttgart, 1979)

Blasius, R. A., *Für Grossdeutschland – gegen den grosen Krieg. Ernst v. Weizsäcker in den Krisen über die Tschechoslowakei und Polen* (Cologne, 1981)

Bonnet, G., *Vor der Katastrophe* (Cologne, 1951)

Booms, H., 'Der Ursprung des Zweiten Weltkrieges – Revision oder Expansion', *Geschichte in Wissenschaft und Unterricht* (1965)

Bracher, K. D., Funke, F. and Jacobsen, H.-A. (eds), *Nationalsozialistische Diktatur. Eine Bilanze* (Düsseldorf, 1983)

Brügel, J. W., *Stalin und Hitler: Pakt gegen Europa* (Vienna, 1973)

Burckhardt, C. J., *Meine Danziger Mission 1937–1939* (Munich, 1960)

Cadogan, A., *The Diaries of Sir Alexander Cadogan 1938–1945* (London, 1971)

Cannistraro, P. V., Wynot Jr, E. D. and Kovaloff, T. P. (eds), *Poland and the Coming of the Second World War: The Diplomatic Papers of A. J. D. Biddle Jr., United States Ambassador to Poland 1937–1939* (Ohio, 1976)

Carr, E. H., *The Twenty Years' Crisis* (London 1939: 1st edition only)

——, German-Soviet Relations between the Wars (Oxford, 1952)

Carr, W., *Arms, Autarky and Aggression* (London, 1972)

Celovsky, B., *Das Münchner Abkommen von 1938* (Stuttgart, 1958)

Ciano, G., *Diario 1937/38* (Bologna, 1948)

Colvin, I., *The Chamberlain Cabinet* (London, 1971)

Compton, T. V., *The Swastika and the Eagle. Hitler, the United States and the Origins of the Second World War* (London, 1968)

Cowling, M., *The Impact of Hitler, British Politics, and British Policy 1933–1940* (London, 1975)

Craig, G. and Gilbert, F. (eds), *The Diplomats* (Princeton, 1953)

Degras, J. (ed.), *Soviet Documents on Foreign Policy*, 3 vols (London, 1953)

Deist, W., *The Wehrmacht and German Rearmament* (London, 1982)

Dülffer, J., *Weimar, Hitler und die Marine: Reichspolitik und Flottenbau 1920 bis 1939* (Düsseldorf, 1973)

Eden, A., *Facing the Dictators* (London, 1962)

Erickson, J., *The Soviet High Command* (London, 1962)

Eubank, K., *Munich* (Oklahoma, 1963)

Forrestal, J., *The Forrestal Diaries*, ed. by M. Millis (London, 1952)

Förster, O.-W., *Das Befestigungswesen: Rückblick und Ausschau* (Neckargmünd, 1960)

Funke, F., *Sanktionen und Kanonen. Hitler, Mussolini und der internationale Abessinienkomflikt 1934–36* (Düsseldorf, 1970)

Funke, M. (ed.), *Hitler. Deutschland und die Mächte* (Düsseldorf, 1978)

Frye, A., *Nazi Germany and the American Hemisphere 1933–1941* (Yale, 1967)

Gannon, F. R., *The British Press and Germany 1936–1939* (Oxford, 1971)

Gehl, J. *Austria, Germany and the Anschluss, 1931–1938* (Oxford, 1963)

Geyer, M., *Aufrüsten oder Sicherheit. Reichswehr und die Krise der Machtpolitik 1924–1936* (Wiesbaden, 1980)

Gibbs, N., *Grand Strategy*, vol. i (London, 1976)

Gilbert, M., *The Roots of Appeasement* (London, 1966)

Gilbert, M. and Gott R., *The Appeasers* (London, 1963)

Grafeneu, G., *Europas letzte Tage* (Zürich, 1946)

Graml, H. *et. al.*, *The German Resistance to Hitler* (Berkeley, 1970)

Greiner, H., *Die oberste Wehrmachtsführung, 1939–1941* (Wiesbaden, 1951)

Hauner, M., 'Did Hitler want a World Dominion', *Journal of Contemporary History* (1978)

Henke, J., *England in Hitlers politischem Kalkül, 1935–1939* (Boppard/Rhein, 1973)

Henrikson, G., 'Das Nürnberger Dokument 386-PS (das "Hossbach-Protokoll")', *Lund Studies in International History* (1970)

Hesse, E., *Das Spiel um Deutschland* (Munich, 1953)

Hiden, J., *Germany and Europe, 1919–1939* (London, 1977)

Hilger, G., *Wir und der Kreml* (Bonn, 1964)

Hillgruber, A., *Hitler, König Carol und Marschall Antonescu; Die deutsch-rumänischen Beziehungen 1938–1944* (Wiesbaden, 1954)

Hillgruber, A., 'Tendenzen, Ergebnisse und Perspektiven der gegenwärtigen Hitler-Forschung', *Historische Zeitschrift* (1978)

Hillgruber, A., 'England's Place in Hitler's Calculations', *Journal of Contemporary History* (1974)

Hubatsch, W. (ed.), *Hitlers Weisungen für die Kriegsführung 1939–1945* (Munich, 1965)

Irving, D., *Breach of Security: The German Intelligence Files on Events Leading to the Second World War* (London, 1968)

Jacobsen, H.-A. (ed.), *Generaloberst Franz Halder. Kriegstagebuch*, 2 vols (Stuttgart, 1962)

Kennan, G. F., *From Prague after Munich: Diplomatic Papers, 1938–1940* (Princeton, 1968)

Kirkpatrick, I., *The Inner Circle: Memoirs* (London, 1959)

Kluge, D., *Das Hossbachprotokoll: Die Zerstörung einer Legende* (Leoni, 1980)

Klüver, M., *War es Hitlers Krieg* (Leoni, 1984).

Knox, M., *Mussolini Unleashed: 1939–1941 Politics and Strategy in Fascist Italy's Last War* (Cambridge, 1982)

Koch, H. W., 'Die Rolle des Sozialdarwinismus als Faktor im Zeitalter des neuen Imperialismus', *Zeitschrift für Politik* (1970)

——, *Der Sozialdarwinismus: Seine Genese und Einfluss auf das imperialistische Denken* (Munich, 1973)

Kordt, E., *Nicht aus den Akten* (Stuttgart, 1950)

——, *Wahn und Wirklichkeit; Die Aussenpolitik des Dritten Reiches* (Stuttgart, 1948)

Kuhn, A., *Hitlers aussenpolitisches Programm und Entwicklung 1919–1939* (Stuttgart, 1977)

Lammers, D. M., 'Fascism, Communism, and the Foreign Office, 1937–39', *Journal of Contemporary History* (1971)

——, 'From Whitehall after Munich: The Foreign Office and the Future Course of British Policy', *Historical Journal* (1973)

Langer, W. L. and Gleason, S. E., *The Challenge to Isolation 1937–1940* (New York, 1952)

Louis, W. R., *British Strategy in the Far East 1919–1939* (Oxford, 1971)

Löwenthal, M. M., 'Roosevelt and the Coming of War', *Journal of Contemporary History* (1981)

MacDonald, C. A., 'Economic Appeasement and the German Moderates 1937–39', *Past and Present* (1972)

——, *The United States, Britain and Appeasement* (London, 1980)

Marguerat, Ph., *Le IIIe Reich et le pétrole roumain 1938–1940* (Geneva, 1977)

Martin, B., *Friedensinitiativen und Machtpolitik im Zweiten Weltkrieg* (Düsseldorf, 1974)

Maure, R., 'The British Decision or Alliance with Russia, May 1939', *Journal of Contemporary History* (1974)

Metzmacher, H., 'Deutsch-englische Ausgleichsbemühungen im Sommer 1939', *Vierteljahrshefte für Zeitgeschichte* (1966)

Michaelis, M., *Mussolini and the Jews: German–Italian Relations and the Jewish Question 1922–1945* (Oxford, 1978)

Michalka, W., *Ribbentrop und die deutsche Weltpolitik 1933–1940* (Munich, 1980)

——, (ed.), *Nationalsozialistische Aussenpolitik* (Darmstadt, 1978)

Mommsen, W. J. and Kettenacker, L. (eds), *The Fascist Challenge and the Policy of Appeasement* (London, 1983)

Mommsen, H., 'Nationalsozialismus oder Hitlerismus', in *Sowjetsystem und demokratische Gesellschaft*, ed. D. Kernig (Freiburg, 1971)

Müller, K.-J. and Opitz, E. (eds), *Militär und Militarismus in der Weimarer Republik*, (Düsseldorf, 1978)

Newman, S., *March 1939: The British Guarantee to Poland* (Oxford, 1976)

Niedhart, G., 'Appeasement: Die britische Antwort auf die Krise des Weltreichs und des internationalen Systems vor dem Zweiten Weltkrief', *Historische Zeitschrift* (Munich, 1978)

——, *Grossbritannien und die Sowjetunion 1934–1939* (Munich, 1972)

Petersen, J., *Hitler-Mussolini: Die Entstehung der Achse Berlin-Rom 1933–1936* (Tübingen, 1973)

Presseisen, E. L., *Germany and Japan: A Study in Totalitarian Diplomacy* (The Hague, 1958)

Preston, A. (ed.), *General Staffs and Diplomacy before the Second World War* (London, 1978)

Rhodes, A., *The Vatican in the Age of Dictators, 1922–1945* (London, 1973)

Rich, N., *Hitler's War Aims*, 2 vols (London 1973, 1975)

Riekhoff, H. v., *German-Polish Relations, 1918–1933* (Baltimore, 1971)

Robertson, E. M., *Hitler's Prewar Policy and Military Plans 1933/9* (London, 1963)

——, (ed.), *The Origins of the Second World War* (London, 1971)

——, *Mussolini as Empire Builder, Europe and Africa 1932–36* (London, 1977)

Rohe, K. (ed.), *Die Westmächte und das Dritte Reich 1933–1939* (Paderborn, 1982)

Rönnefahrt, H. G. K., *Die Sudetenkrise in der internationalen Politik*, 2 vols (Wiesbaden, 1961)

Rosar, W., *Deutsche Gemeinschaft: Seyss-Inquart und der Anschluss* (Vienna, 1971)

Schieder, W. and Dipper, Ch. (eds), *Der Spanische Bürgerkrieg in der internationalen Politik* (Munich, 1976)

Schmidt, P., *Statist auf diplomatischer Bühne* (Bonn, 1954)

Schmitthanner, W. and Buchheim, H. (eds), *Der deutsche Widerstand gegen Hitler* (Berlin, 1966)

Schramm, P. E. et. al. (eds), *Kriegstagebuch des OKW*, 8 vols (dtv-edition Munich, 1980)

Schreiber, G., *Revisionismus und Weltmachtstreben. Marineführung und deutsch-italienische Beziehungen 1919 bis 1944* (Stuttgart, 1978)

Schroeder, P. W., *The Axis Alliance and Japanese-American Relations 1941* (New York, 1958)

Seidl, A. (ed.), *Die Beziehungen zwischen Deutschland und der Sowjetunion 1939–1941* (Tübingen, 1949)

Seraphim, H.-G. (ed.), *Das politische Tagebuch Alfred Rosenbergs* (Munich, 1956)

Smith, B. F. and Peterson, A. P. (eds), *Heinrich Himmler: Geheimreden 1933 bis 1945* (Frankfurt, 1974)

Sommer, Th., *Deutschland und Japan zwischen den Mächten 1935–1940* (Tübingen, 1962)

Speer, A., *Spandau Diaries* (London, 1977)

——, *Der Sklavenstaat* (Berlin, 1980)

Stegmann, B. 'Hitlers Ziele im ersten Kriegsjahr 1939/40; Ein Beitrag zur Quellenkritik', *Militärgeschichtliche Mitteilungen* (1980)

Szembek, J., *Journal* (Paris, 1952)

Tansill, Ch. C., *Backdoor to War* (New York, 1953)

Thies, J., *Architekt der Weltherschaft: Die 'Endziele' Hitlers* (Düsseldorf, 1976)

Thompson, N., *The Anti-Appeasers: Conservative Opposition in the 1930s* (Oxford, 1971)

Thorne, Ch., *The Approach of War, 1938–1939* (London, 1968)

Vital, D., 'Czechoslovakia and the Powers, September 1938', *Journal of Contemporary History* (1966)

Wagner, G. (ed.), *Lagevorträge des Oberbefehlshabers der Kriegsmarine vor Hitler 1939–1945* (Munich, 1972)

Watt, D. C., 'Hitler's Visit to Rome and the May Weekend Crisis; A Study in Hitler's Response to External Stimuli', *Journal of Contemporary History* (1974)

——, 'The Initiation of the Negotiations leading to the Nazi-Soviet Pact: A Historical Problem', in *Essays in Honour of E. H. Carr* (London, 1974)

Weinberg, G. L. 'Der deutsche Entschluss zum Angriff auf die Sowjetunion', *Vierteljahrshfte für Zeitgschichte* (1953)

Wendt, B.-J., *Economic Appeasement: Handel und Finanz in der britischen Deutschland-Politik 1933–1939* (Düsseldorf, 1971)

Part III

Commentary

Air Ministry, *The Rise and Fall of the German Air Force 1933–1945* (London, 1983)

Cooper, M., *The German Army 1939–1945* (London, 1978)

——, *The German Airforce 1933–1945* (London, 1981)

Deist, W., 'Die Aufrüstung der Wehrmacht', in *Das Deutsche Reich im 2. Weltkrieg*, ed. by *Militärgeschichtliches Forschungsamt*, vol. I (Stuttgart, 1979)

Deutschland im Zweiten Weltkrieg, Autorenkollektiv der Akademie der DDR, vol. I (Berlin, 1978)

Guderian, H., *Erinnerungen eines Soldaten* (Neckargemünd, 1960)

Nehring, W. K., *Die Geschichte der deutschen Panzerwaffe 1916–1945* (Stuttgart, 1974)

Salewski, M., *Die deutsche Seekriegsleitung 1935–1945*, 3 vols (Frankfurt, 1970–5)

Seaton, A., *The German Army 1933–1945* (London, 1982)

Volkmann, H.-E., 'Die NS-Wirtschaft in Vorbereitung des Krieges', in *Das Deutsche Reich im 2. Weltkrieg*, ed. by *Militärgeschichtliches Forschungsamt*, vol. I (Stuttgart, 1979)

Wendt, B.-J., 'Südosteuropa in der nationalsozialistischen Grossraumwirtschaft', in *The 'Führer-State': Myth or Reality*, ed. L. Kettenacker and G. Hirschfeld (Stuttgart, 1981)

Contributions

Basch, A., *The Danube Basin and the German Economic Sphere* (London, 1944)

Berndt, R. 'Wirtschaftliche Mitteleuropapläne des deutschen Imperialismus 1926–1931', *Wissenschaftliche Zeitschrift der Universität Halle* (1965)

Berov, L., 'The Withdrawing of Foreign Capital from Bulgaria on the Eve of the Second World War', *Studia Balcanica* (1974)

Carroll, B., *Design for Aggression: Arms and Economics in the Third Reich* (The Hague, 1968)

Doering, D., 'Deutsch-österreichische Aussenhandelsverflechtung während der Weltwirtschaftskrise', in Mommsen, H., Petzina, D. and Weisbrod, B. (eds), *Industrielles System und politische Entwicklung in der Weimarer Republik* (Düsseldorf, 1974)

Eichholtz, D., *Geschichte der deutschen Kriegswirtschaft 1939–1941*, vol. I (Berlin, 1969)

Eichholtz, D. and Schumann, W. (eds), *Anatomie des Krieges. Neue Dokumente über die Rolle des deutschen Monopolkapitals bei der Vorbereitung und Durchführung des Zweiten Weltkrieges* (Berlin, 1969)

Ellis, H. S., *Exchange Controls in Central Europe* (Cambridge/Mass., 1941)

Erbe, R., *Die nationalsozialistische Wirtschaftspolitik im Lichte moderner Theorie* (Zürich, 1958)

Forstmeier, F. and Volkmann H.-E. (eds), *Wirtshaft und Rüstung am Vorabend des Zweiten Weltkrieges* (Düsseldorf, 1975)

Guillebaud, C. W., *The Economic Recovery of Germany* (London, 1958)

Harper, G. T., *German Economic Policy in Spain during the Spanish Civil War 1936–1939* (The Hague, 1967)

Hilton, St. E., *Brazil and the Great Powers, 1930–1939: The Politics of Trade Rivalry* (Austin, 1975)

Homze, E. L., *Arming the Luftwaffe: The Reich Air Ministry and the German Aircraft Industry 1919–1939* (Lincoln/Nebraska, 1976)

Jäger, J.-J., *Die wirtschaftliche Abhängigkeit des Dritten Reiches vom Ausland dargestellt am Beispiel der Stahlindustrie* (Berlin, 1969)

Kindleberger, Ch. P., *The Terms of Trade. A European Case Study* (New York, 1956)

Klein, B. H., *Germany's Economic Preparations for War* (Cambridge/Mass., 1959)

Lamer, M., 'Die Wandlungen der ausländischen Kapitalanlagen auf dem Balkan', in *Weltwirtschaftliches Archiv* (1938)

Lewis, W. A., *Economic Survey 1919–1939* (London, 1949)

Maizels, A., *Industrial Growth and World Trade* (Cambridge, 1963)

Marguerat, Ph., *Le IIIe Reich et le pétroleroumain 1938–1940* (Geneva, 1977)

——, 'Le protectionisme financier allemand et le bassin danubien à la veille de la seconde guerre mondiale. L'exemple de la Roumaine', *Relations Internationales* 16 (1978)

Milward, A. S., *The German Economy at War* (London, 1965)

——, 'Der deutsche Handel und Welthandel', in Mommsen, Petzina and Weisbrod, *Industrielles system*

Milward, A. S., *The New Order and the French Economy* (Oxford, 1972)

Neal, L., 'The Economics and Finance of Bilateral Clearing Agreements: Germany 1934–38', *Economic History Review* (1979)

Overy, R. J., 'Hitler's War and the German Economy: A Reinterpretation', *Economic History Review* (1982)

——, 'Transportation and Rearmament in the Third Reich', *Historical Journal* (1973)

Petzina, D., *Autarkiepolitik im Dritten Reich: Der nationalsozialistische Vierjahresplan* (Stuttgart, 1968)

Poole, K. E., *German Financial Policies 1932–1939* (New York, 1939)

Radant, H., 'Die IG Farbenindustrie AG und Südosteuropa bis 1938', in *Jahrbuch für Wirtschaftsgeschichte* (1966)

Riedel, M., *Eisen und Kohle für das Dritte Reich: Paul Pleigers Stellung in der NS-Wirtschaft* (Göttingen, 1974)

Royal Institute of International Affairs, *Southeastern Europe* (London, 1939)

Schönfeld, R., 'Deutsche Rohstoffsicherungspolitik in Jugoslawien 1934–1944', *Vierteljahrshefte für Zeitgeschichte* (1976)

Schweitzer, A., *Big Business and the Third Reich* (Bloomington, 1964)

Stolper, G., Hauser, K. and Borchardt, K., *The German Economy 1870 to the Present* (New York, 1967)

Sundhausen, H., 'Politisches und wirtschaftliches Kalkül in der Auseinandersetzung über die deutsch-rumänischen Präferenzvereinbarungen', *Revue des Etudes Sud-Est Européenes* (1976)

Teichova, A., *An Economic Background to Munich: International Business and Czechoslovakia, 1918–1938* (London, 1974)

Tihanyi, J., 'Deutsch-ungarische Aussenhandelsbeziehungen im Dienste der faschistischen Aggressionspolitik 1933 bis 1944', in *Jahrbuch für Wirtschaftsgeschichte*, (1972)

Torgay, O., *Der deutsch-türkische Handel. Organisation und Technik* (Hamburg, 1939)

Treue, W., 'Das Dritte Reich und die Westmächte auf dem Balkan', *Vierteljahrsheft für Zeitgeschichte* (1953)

United States Strategic Bombing Survey (Washington, DC, 1945)

Völker, K.-H., *Die Deutsche Luftwaffe 1933–1939: Aufbau, Führung, Rüstung* (Stuttgart, 1967)

Volkmann, H.-E., 'Ökonomie und Machtpolitik: Lettland und Estland im politisch-ökonomischen Kalkül des Dritten Reiches (1933–1940)' *Geschichte und Gesellschaft* (1976)

Part IV

Commentary

Adler, H. G., *Die verheimlichte Wahrheit, Theresienstädter Dokumente* (Tübingen, 1958)

Adler, H. G., 'Ideas towards a Sociology of the Concentration Camp', *American Journal of Sociology* (1958)
——, 'Selbstverwaltung und Widerstand in den Konzentrationslagern der SS', *Vierteljahrshefte für Zeitgeschichte* (1969)
——, *Theresianstadt 1941–45. Geschichte, Soziologie, Psychologie* (Tübingen, 1960)
Angress, W. and Smith, B. F., 'Diaries of Heinrich Himmler's Early Years', *Journal of Modern History* (1959)
Arendt, H., *Eichmann in Jerusalem* (New York, 1962)
Aronson, Sh., *Reinhard Heydrich und die Frühgeschichte von Gestapo und SD* (Stuttgart, 1971)
Binion, R., *Hitler among the Germans* (New York, 1976)
Boberach, H., 'Die Überführung von Soldaten des Heeres und der Luftwaffe in die SS-Totenkopfverbände zur Bewachung von KZs 1944', in *Militärgeschichtliche Mitteilungen* (Freiburg, 1983)
Brenner, L., *Zionism in the Age of the Dictators* (London, 1983)
Buchheim, H. et. al., *Anatomy of the SS-State* (London, 1968)
Burg, J. B., *Schuld und Schicksal. Europas Juden zwischen Heuchlern und Henkern* (Munich, 1962)
Cohn, N., *Warrant for Genocide* (London, 1967)
Crankshaw, E., *Gestapo* (London, 1956)
Der Spiegel, Issue 50, 5 December 1977
Deuerlein, E. (ed.), *Der Hitler-Putsch* (Stuttgart, 1962)
Friedländer, S., *Kurt Gerstein: The Ambiguity of Good* (New York, 1969)
Goebbels, J., *Tagebücher 1945. Die letzten Aufzeichnungen* (Hamburg, 1977)
Greil, L., *Die Wahrheit über Malmedy* (Munich, 1958)
Harmann, N., *Dunkirk: The Necessary Myth* (London, 1980)
Heiber, H. (ed.), *Reichsführer!* (Munich, 1968)
Hilberg, R., *The Destruction of the European Jews* (Chicago, 1967)
Höhne, H., *The Order of the Death's Head* (London, 1969)
Irving, D., *Hitler's War* (London, 1977)
Jäckel, E. (ed.), *Hitler. Sämmtliche Aufzeichnungen 1905–1924* (Stuttgart, 1980) (though care is to be exercised in its use. It contains over 70 fakes)
Kochan, L., *Pogrom: 10 November 1938* (London, 1957)
Koehl, R. L., *RKFVD: German Resettlement and Population Policy 1939–1945* (Cambridge/Mass., 1957)
Kogon, E., *The Theory and Practice of Hell* (London, 1958)
Lammerding, H., private papers in private ownership containing two sworn affidavits of Oradour survivors, as well as the complete reports of the 1953 Oradour trial printed in *Le Monde*
Salomon, E. v., *The Captive* (London, 1963)
Schaeder, G. (ed.), *Martin Buber; Briefwechsel aus sieben Jahrzehnten*, 3 vols (Heidelberg 1972–5)
Taege, H., *Wo ist Kain? Tulle und Oradour* (Lindhorst, 1981)
Toland, H., *Adolf Hitler* (New York, 1976)

United States Senate Committee on Armed Forces, *Malmedy Massacre Investigation Hearing* (Washington, DC, 1949)
Ziemessen, D., *Der Malmedy Prozess* (Munich, 1958)

Contributions

Ackermann, J., *Heinrich Himmler als Ideologe* (Göttingen, 1970)
Dawidowicz, L., *The War against the Jews 1933–1945* (London, 1975)
Eichmann, A., *Ich, Adolf Eichmann* (Leoni, 1980)
Fleming, G., *Hitler und die Endlösung, 'Es ist des Führers Wunsch . . .'* (Wiesbaden, 1982)
Gilbert, M., *Auschwitz and the Allies: The Politics of Rescue* (London, 1981)
Gollanz, V., *The Case of Adolf Eichmann* (London, 1960)
Härtle, H., *Was 'Holocaust' verschweigt* (Leoni, 1979)
Hausser, P., *Soldaten wie andere auch. Der Weg der Waffen-SS* (Osnabrück, 1966)
Herbst, L., *Der totale Krieg und die Ordnung der Wirtschaft. Die Kriegswirtschaft im Spannungsfeld von Politik, Ideologie und Propaganda* (Stuttgart, 1982)
Hofmann, H. H. (ed.), *Das deutsche Offizierkorps 1860–1960* (Boppard/Rhein, 1980)
Höss, R., *Commandant of Auschwitz* (New York, 1960)
Jong, L. de, 'Die Niederlande und Auschwitz', *Vierteljahrshefte für Zeitgeschichte* (1969)
Kennedy, P. and Nicholls, A. (eds), *Nationalist and Racialist Movements in Britain and Germany before 1914* (London, 1981)
Klietmann, K.-G., *Die Waffen-SS* (Osnabrück, 1965)
Krausnick, H. and Wilhelm, H.-W., *Die Truppe des Weltanschauungskrieges* (Stuttgart, 1981)
Le Chêne, E., *Mauthausen, The History of a Death Camp* (London, 1971)
Lehmann, R., *Die Leibstandarte*, 4 vols (Osnabrück, 1982)
Littlejohn, D., *Foreign Legions of the Third Reich*, 2 vols (San Jose/Calif., 1981)
Meyer, H., *Kriegsgeschichte der 12. SS-Panzerdivision 'Hitlerjugend'*, 2 vols (Osnabrück, 1983)
Naumann, B., *Auschwitz* (Frankfurt, 1965) (Auschwitz Trial)
Neulen, H. W., *Der Eurofaschismus und der Zweite Weltkrieg* (Munich, 1978)
Präg, W. and Jacobmeyer, W. (eds), *Das Diensttagebuch des deutschen Generalgouverneurs in Polen* (Stuttgart, 1975)
Pulzer, P. G. J., *The Rise of Political Anti-semitism in Germany and Austria* (London, 1964)
Rassinier, P., *Le Mensonge d'Ulysse* (Paris, 1959)
Reitlinger, G., *The Final Solution* (London, 1953)
——, *The SS – Alibi of a Nation* (London, 1956)
Rempel, G., 'Gottlob Berger and Waffen-SS Recruitment 1939–1945', *Militärgeschichtliche Mitteilungen* (1980)
Richardi, H.-G., *Schule der Gewalt: Das Konzentrationslager Dachau 1933–1934* (Munich, 1983)
Rückerl, A., *Nationalsozialistische Vernichtungslager im Spiegel deutscher Strafprozesse* (Stuttgart, 1977)

Schlamm, W. S., *Wer ist Jude? Ein Selbstgespräch* (Stuttgart, 1964)

Schleunes, K. A., *The Twisted Road to Auschwitz: Nazi Policy towards German Jews 1933–1939* (Urbana/Ill., 1970)

Schönhuber, F., *Ich war dabei* (Munich, 1981)

Schulza-Kossens, R., *Militärischer Führernachwuchs der Waffen-SS* (Osnabrück, 1982)

Smelser, R. M., *The Sudeten Problem 1933–1938. Volkstumspolitik and the Formulation of Nazi Foreign Policy* (Folkestone, 1975)

Snydor Jr, C. W., *Soldiers of Destruction* (Princeton, 1977)

Stein, G. H., *The Waffen-SS: Hitler's Elite Guard at War, 1939–1945* (Oxford, 1966)

Steiner, F., *Die Freiwilligen* (Göttingen, 1958)

Streit, Ch., *Keine Kameraden* (Stuttgart, 1978)

Wegner, B., *Hitlers politische Soldaten: Die Waffen-SS 1933–1945* (Paderborn, 1982)

——, 'Auf dem Wege zur pangermanischen Armee. Dokumente zur Entstehungsgeschichte des III. ('germansichen') SS-Panzerkorps', *Militärgeschichtliche Mitteilungen* (1980)

——, 'Die Garde des "Führers" und die "Feuerwehr" der Ostfront. Zur neueren Literatur über die Waffen-SS', in *Militärgeschichtliche Mitteilungen* (1978)

Weidinger, O., *Division Das Reich*, 5 vols (Osnabrück, 1976–80)

Weingarten, J. J., *Hitler's Guard* (Southern Illinois University Press, 1974)

Weissberg, A., *Advocate of the Devil: The Story of Joel Brand* (London, 1960)

Part V
Commentary and Contributions

Bollmus, R., *Das Amt Rosenberg und seine Gegener* (Stuttgart, 1970)

Bullock, A., *Hitler. A study in tyranny* (London, 1962)

Carr, W., *Hitler. A Study in Personality and Politics* (London, 1978)

Churchill, W. S., *Great Contemporaries* (London, 1941)

Deuerlein, E., *Hitler. Eine politische Biographie* (Augsburg, 1969)

Erikson, E. H., 'Hitler's Imagery and the German Youth', *Psychiatry*, 5 (1942)

——, *Childhood and Society* (New York, 1950)

Fabry, P., *Mutmassungen über Hitler, Urteile von Zeitgenossen* (Düsseldorf, 1969)

Fest, J., *Hitler. Eine Biographie* (Frankfurt, 1973) (English trans. by Pelican books)

Giesler, H., *Ein anderer Hitler. Bericht seines Architekten Hermann Giesler* (Leoni, 1978)

Görlitz, W. and Quint, H. A., *Adolf Hitler. Eine Biographie* (Stuttgart, 1952)

Graml, H., 'Probleme einer Hitler-Biographie. Kritische Bemerkungen zu Joachim C. Fest', *Vierteljahrshefte für Zeitgeschichte* (1974)

Heiden, K., *Adolf Hitler* (Zürich, 1936)

Heuss, Th., *Hitlers Weg* (Frankfurt, 1932)

Hildebrand, K., 'Der "Fall Hitler". Bilanz und Wege der Hitler Forschung', in *Neue Politische Literatur* (1969)

Hillgruber, A., 'Tendenzen, Ergebinsse und Perspektiven der gegenwärtigen Hitler-Forschung', *Historische Zeitschrift* (1977)

Jetzinger, F., *Hitler's Youth* (London, 1958)

Krogmann, C. V., *Es ging um Deutschlands Zukunft 1932–1939* (Leoni, 1975)

Kubizek, A., *The Young Hitler I Knew* (Boston, 1955)

Langer, W., *The Mind of Adolf Hitler* (London, 1973)

Maser, W., *Hitlers Briefe und Notizen* (Düsseldorf, 1973)

——, *Adolf Hitler: Legende, Mythos, Wirklichkeit* (Munich, 1971) (English trans. by Alan Lane Publishers)

Nipperdey, Th., *Gesellschaft, Kultur, Theorie* (Göttingen, 1976)

Nitschke, A., *Der Feind: Formen politischen Handelns im 20. Jahrhundert* (Stuttgart, 1964)

Schierach, H. v., *Anekdoten um Hitler* (Leoni, 1980)

Schramm, P. E., *Hitler als militärischer Führer* (Frankfurt, 1965)

Smith, B. F., *Adolf Hitler: his Family, Childhood and Youth* (Palo Alto/Calif., 1967)

Stern, J. P., *The Führer and the People* (London, 1975)

Strawson, J., *Hitler as Military Commander* (London, 1971)

Trevor-Roper, H. R., *The Last Days of Hitler* (London, 1951)

Waite, R. G. L., *Adolf Hitler: the Psychopathic God* (New York, 1976)

Ziegler, H. S., *Wer war Hitler* (Tübingen, 1970)

Notes on Contributors

DIETRICH AIGNER, of the University of Mannheim, is best known for his monograph *Das Ringen um England*, an analysis of Anglo-German relations and public opinion in Germany and Britain between 1933 and 1939.

MARTIN BROSZAT, Director of the Munich *Institut für Zeitgeschichte*, is the author of numerous articles and books on the Third Reich. To English readers he will be best known by his work *The Hitler State*.

WILLIAM CARR, of Sheffield University, is the author of numerous historical monographs of which in this context the most well known are *Arms, Autarky and Aggression* and *Hitler. A Study in Personality and Politics*. He is currently engaged on an analysis of NS foreign policy.

LOTHAR KETTENACKER is Assistant Director of the German Historical Institute, London, and author of numerous monographs and articles on the Third Reich.

BURTON H. KLEIN, a Harvard economist now with the RAND-Corporation, instigated a fundamental reassessment of the NS economy by his study, *Germany's Economic Preparations for War*.

H. W. KOCH is author of *Der Sozialdarwinismus: Seine Genese und Einfluss auf das imperialistische Denken*, *The Hitler Youth: Origins and Development 1922–1945*, *A Constitutional History of Germany in the Nineteenth and Twentieth Centuries* and, most recently, *'Im Namen des Deutschen Volkes' – Roland Freisler und der NS-Volksgerichtshof 1934–1945*, of which an English translation is in preparation. He teaches at the University of York.

WOLFGANG MICHALKA, editor of *Die Neue Politische Literatur*, gained considerable prominence through his monograph *Ribbentrop und die deutsche Weltpolitik 1933–1940* as well as his numerous articles on German foreign policy.

ALAN MILWARD, of the University of Manchester, is probably the leading expert on the NS economy in peace and wartime, who has followed up his *The German Economy at War* with numerous other books and articles, but has now turned his attention to post-war Europe.

HANS MOMMSEN teaches at the University of Bochum and his many publications include *Beamtentum im Dritten Reich*, *Arbeiterbewegung und*

Nationale Frage and 'National Socialism: Continuity and Change', in W. Laqueur (ed.), *Fascism* (London, 1976).

KLAUS-JÜRGEN MÜLLER teaches at the Bundeswehrhochschule, Hamburg, and the University of Hamburg. He is the author of *Das Heer und Hitler* and *Generaloberst Ludwig Beck* as well as many other monographs and articles on Fascism, National Socialism, army/civil relationships and modernisation theories.

THOMAS NIPPERDEY, of the Ludwig-Maximilian-Universität, Munich, specialises primarily in German nineteenth-century history, the history of German political parties and the theory of history. His most recent work, *Deutsche Geschichte 1800–1866*, has received universal acclaim.

ERNST NOLTE, of the Friedrich-Meinecke Institut of the Freie Universität, Berlin, is best known to English readers through his path-breaking work *The Three Faces of Fascism*, a work which is part of a trilogy of which *Deutschland und der kalte Krieg* and, most recently, *Marxismus und die Industrialle Revolution* form the other two *essential* parts.

ESMONDE M. ROBERTSON, the author of *Hitler's Prewar Policy and Military Plans 1933–39* and *Mussolini as Empire Builder: Europe and Africa 1932–36* as well of many articles on the period, teaches at the London School of Economics.

H. R. TREVOR-ROPER, now Lord Dacre and Master of Peterhouse, Cambridge, is the author of the virtually timeless study *Hitler's Last Days*.

BERND WEGNER is a historian at *Militärgeschichtliches Forschungsamt*, Freiburg i. Br. and one of the foremost specialists on the *Waffen-SS*, best known by his recent work *Hitlers Politische Soldaten: Die Waffen-SS 1933–1945*.

Index

Union of Soviet Socialist Republics (USSR): atrocities and repression in, 8, 29–30; and 'liberation movements' abroad, 24, 29, 32, 36; internal deportations, 29–30; annihilation therapy in, 34–5; National Socialist attitude to, 183; expected military collapse, 191; German 1939 pact with, 202, 220, 234, 239, 249–50, 275–8, 286–9, 292, 304, 469; role in Europe, 205–6; Polish non-aggression pact with, 206; in Hitler's war plans, 212, 239–44, 249–50, 257–8, 291–2, 300–1, 309, 320–1; relations with Japan, 213–14, 276–7, 280, 310, 315; Rosenberg and, 221; and German eastward expansion, 221–5, 232–3; German co-operation with over Poland, 224–5, 287; and Hitler's concept of power, 237–8; German invasion of ('Barbarossa'), 240, 248, 289–90, 330, 367; Hitler's plans for subjection of, 246, 284; and National Socialist world domination, 253; Ribbentrop on, 271; and defeat of Britain, 283–4; military talks with France and Britain, 287; German fear of expansion, 289; troop movements, 287, 290, 294, 296, 303, 313; seizes Baltic states, 291, 294, 301, 306; occupies Bessarabia, 292, 297, 303, 305; relations with Finland, 292–3, 304–5, 317–18; oil products and supply, 293, 348; territorial claims, 291–7, 301, 303, 305, 318–19; relations with Italy, 295–6, 300, 303; relations with Britain, 298, 300–1, 303; and Balkans, 301, 305–6, 312, 327; military strength, 309; and 1940 Axis pact, 310–16, 319–20; and Danube, 312; spheres of

Union of Soviet Socialist Republics—*cont.*
influence, 315–16; Hitler's proposals to, 315–19; German trade with, 353; German military successes in, 369–70; war crimes against, 386; Irving's aggression theory, 394; hostility to West, 464–5; and Jewish resettlement, 487

United States of America: constitution, 46; recession in, 50; in Hitler's war plans, 198, 207, 211–12; navy, 211, 234; supports Poland, 224; anti-German indignation, 227–8; 1938 economic treaty with Britain, 228; support for Allies, 228–9, 231; disillusionment with Chamberlain's appeasement, 234; and threat of National Socialist world domination, 253–4, 256, 261, 284; 'Fascist International', 265; Japan and, 280–1, 283–4; economic aid for Britain, 308–9; investment in Romania, 343; and chromite, 346–7; oil exports to Germany, 349; German trade, 358; arms production, 367–8; boycott of German goods, 376; and German Jewish policy, 415, 486; organised capitalism in, 496; *see also* Roosevelt

Unruh, Fritz von, 106

Vansittart, Sir Robert (*later* Baron), 264; *The Nature of the Beast*, 460
Vergangenheitsbewältung, 96
Vermeil, Edmond, 493
Versailles Treaty (1919), 14, 157, 188, 190, 197, 238
Vienna Arbitration Treaty, 304–5, 310
Vietnam War, 23
Völkischer Beobachter (newspaper), 56, 70, 91, 187
Volkmann, Hans-Erich, 333